Encampement of the
Light troops under Major
General Mr. de la Fayette's
Command.
Ogles Farm
Carrols Creek
770 yards
Wind Mill
a. State House.
b. M. Lee. h.
c. Church Cercle
d. M. Carrols h.
Governor Folly
Robert's Cr.
Road to Baltimore
Sprigg County Seat
Scale of 700 paces or about 700 yards
Done by Major Capitaine aid of camp to Major G.l Mr. de la Fayette

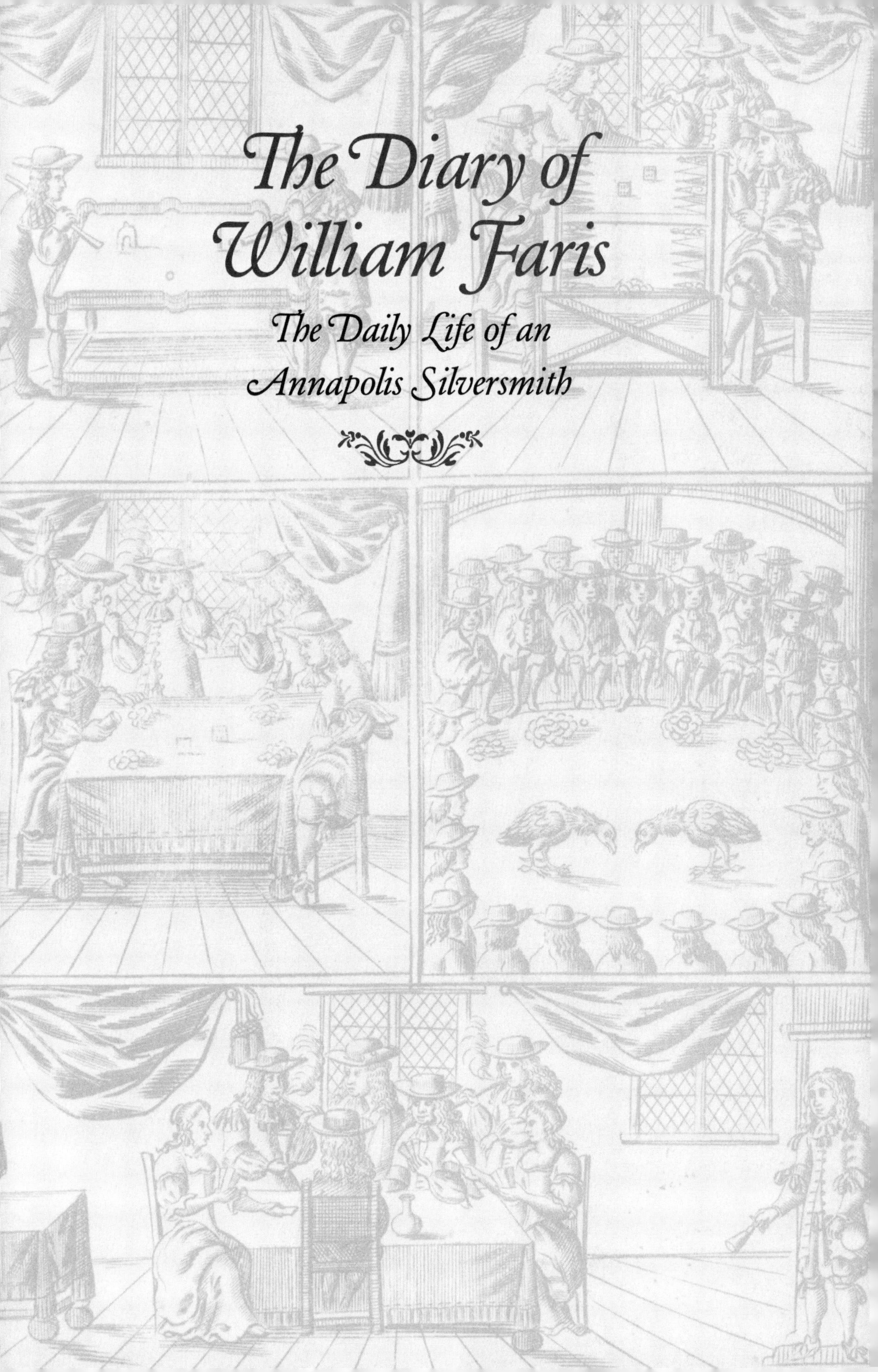

The Diary of William Faris

The Daily Life of an Annapolis Silversmith

Brass Dial of Tall Case Clock, ca. 1770
Photo by James B. Whisker. Private Collection.

The Diary of William Faris

The Daily Life of an Annapolis Silversmith

EDITED BY

MARK B. LETZER
JEAN B. RUSSO

PUBLISHED BY THE PRESS AT THE
MARYLAND HISTORICAL SOCIETY
BALTIMORE MARYLAND
2003

Copyright © 2003 by
The Press at the Maryland Historical Society
201 W. Monument Street
Baltimore, Maryland 21201

DESIGNED BY JAMES F. BRISSON
Printed in the United States of America

Library of Congress cataloging-in-publication data
Faris, William, 1728-1804.
  The diary of William Faris : the daily life of an Annapolis silversmith /
Mark B. Letzer, Jean B. Russo.
    p. cm.
  Includes bibliographical references and index.
  ISBN 0-938420-80-1
  1. Faris, William, 1728-1804—Diaries. 2. Silversmiths—Maryland—Annapolis—
Diaries. 3. Clock and watch makers—Maryland—Annapolis—Diaries. I. Letzer,
Mark B., 1965- II. Russo, Jean Burrell. III. Title.

NK7198.F3 A2 2002
739.2'372—dc21

                                                        2001059328

For

LOIS STRAN JOHNSTON FUNK

my cousin, my mentor, my friend
For all the stories about Ann Faris Pitt, Hannah Pitt Littig,
Ann Maria Littig Shaffer Stran, and Grandmother Jones

— MBL

For

BARBARA WELLS SARUDY

Whose work on Faris's garden brought his diary to light once again
and

SARAH, MATTHEW, LUKE, *and* EMMA

The next generation of historians and gardeners

— JBR

CONTENTS

ACKNOWLEDGMENTS

ASSEMBLING A BOOK of the complexity of William Faris's diary and related activities involved a large number of individuals and organizations whose time and expertise made this work possible.

Among the many contributors to the book, there is one in particular whose work on William Faris should be recognized. Joan Sayers Brown worked as a docent in the 1970s and early 1980s with Historic Annapolis Foundation and during that time assembled a large volume of information on William Faris. She published an article on William Faris in *Antiques* magazine in February 1977, collected material on Faris from different museums and descendants, and made an initial transcription of Faris's diary, that proved useful as a comparison against the photocopy of the original from which the diary transcription was made. We are indebted to her and her extensive notes as well as her photographic slides, which her husband donated to Historic Annapolis at her death in 1983. These comprehensive files made it possible to locate several of the objects pictured in this book; many of these pieces are still in the homes of William Faris's descendants.

Many museums and other institutions contributed to the preparation of this volume. We are especially grateful to the staff of the Maryland Historical Society's Library of Maryland History, particularly Francis O'Neill, Donna Williams, Emily Close, and Robert Bartram. In the manuscript reading room, Jennifer Bryan, Mary Herbert, and Mary Markey were always helpful and ready to assist. Paul Rubenson, associate registrar, was always willing to retrieve objects from the museum's vast collection for examination, and Nancy Davis, Jeannine Disviscour, and Heather Ersts Venters, from the gallery division, always had answers to the many questions regarding these objects. Staff photographer David Prencipe photographed many of the Faris-related pieces in the museum.

The Baltimore Museum of Art kindly provided not only images from their collection of Faris silver, but information on the provenance of these pieces. James Archer Abbott and Catherine Stewart Thomas in the decorative arts department and Nancy Boyle Press in the rights and reproductions office were never more than a phone call away.

Winterthur Museum in Delaware not only houses a ladle attributed to William Faris but an outstanding collection of photographs as well as a decorative arts library of the highest caliber. From the Decorative Arts Photographic Collection, Bert Denker and Margaret Welch were consistently helpful and encouraging and provided numerous images included in this book. In the library, Neville Thompson always seemed to know the call numbers for books without having to look them up. Susan Newton's invaluable assistance with all of the requested images was vital to the completion of this work.

Historic Annapolis Foundation's Alecia Parker was invaluable in providing access to the files of Joan Sayers Brown and for arranging the photography and study of the various Faris pieces in their collection. Alexandra McKee was also instrumental to this project during her tenure as curator.

The staff of the Maryland State Archives responded with their customary grace when called upon to locate a resource or answer an obscure question. We are particularly grateful to Christine Alvey, Elaine Rice Bachmann, Robert Barnes, Kathy Beard, Nancy Bramucci, Mimi Calver, R. J. Rockefeller, Robert W. Schoeberlein, Nadine Shapiro, and Emily Oland Squires for their assistance. Betty DeKeyser, Donna Hole, Elizabeth Hughes, Ann Jensen, Mary McCutcheon, Jane McWilliams, Jason Moser, Emily Peake, the late Joan Scurlock, and Janice Hayes-Williams, of the Annapolis History Consortium, shared their professional expertise with us. Marcia Miller and Mary Louise de Sarran of the Maryland Historical Trust also provided valuable aid.

Other institutions providing help in the way of photographs and related information included the Metropolitan Museum of Art, Yale University Art Gallery, the Frick Art Reference Library, Mount Clare House Museum, Maryland State Archives, the Museum of Early Southern Decorative Arts, Colonial Williamsburg Foundation, National Library of Medicine, the Riversdale Historical Society, and the Hammond-Harwood House, where several portraits of Faris's friends and acquaintances are located. We are grateful to Reverend Edwin Schell, of the Lovely Lane Methodist Museum in Baltimore, for making the records of the Fells Point Methodist Church available to us.

The owners of private collections, Faris descendants and others, graciously gave us access to their objects and to family information that otherwise might not have been revealed. Among these are Richard Adams, Mr. and Mrs. P. McEvoy Cromwell, Mr. and Mrs. William A. Faris, Mr. and Mrs. A. Norwood Funk, Mrs. Arthur H. Hardy Jr., Rear Admiral and Mrs. Charles Herbert Johnston Jr., Mr. and Mrs. George E. Linthicum III, Mrs. Elinor M. Morgan,

Barbara Johnston Ogles, F. Jameson Parker, Judith Armistead Parker, and Mrs. Harriett McCurley Trout. The Reverend R. Douglas Pitt provided great encouragement to MBL during the book's preparation; his friendship and admiration of William Faris are especially appreciated.

Among the curators, historians, specialists, and contributors who gave kindly of their time we are most grateful to Catherine Rogers Arthur, M. Kent Brinkley, Margaret Burri, Sarah Cantor, Dennis Claude, Richard Davis, Philip S. Dubey, William Voss Elder III, Emory Evans, Donald L. Fennimore, Ann Ferguson, Roland E. Fleischer, Ray Fleshman, Heather Foster, Alan Gephardt, Richard Goodbar, Stephen J. Greenberg, Jane W. Hartley, Catherine Hollan, Posey Huppman, William R. Johnston, Kate Van Winkle Keller, Alexandra A. Kirtley, Dean M. Landers, Gordon D. Leary, Bernard and S. Dean Levy, Inc., Mark Mitchell, Matthew Mulcahy, Dennis Myers, Sumpter Priddy III, Mark Stichel, Anne Verplanck, Pat Stroud Walker, Deborah Dependahl Waters, Carolyn Weekley, Beth Carver Wees, James B. Whisker, and Rollin Woolley. Mr. and Mrs. Frederick Duggan and Patrick M. Duggan, scholars of the silver world, afforded invaluable information and encouragement to MBL during this whole process. Their friendship and encouragement are most appreciated.

We are extremely grateful to Kevin Fielding, who frequently accompanied MBL on long trips to photograph Faris-related items. His photographs have greatly enhanced this project.

Several scholars deserve particular recognition for their contributions. We are especially grateful to Jennifer Faulds Goldsborough for taking the time to answer myriad questions and for reviewing the essay on William Faris's silver and clocks and the captions pertaining to Faris's craft work. Her time, comprehensive knowledge, and editorial suggestions were invaluable. We are indebted to colonial music scholar David Hildebrand for his willingness to share his vast knowledge of eighteenth-century musical instruments and compositions. He was particularly helpful in understanding the history of pianofortes in this period and on the significance of the John Wade manuscript, a music book that originated in Faris's tavern in the 1760s. We are grateful to Edward LaFond for his interpretation of William Faris's proficiency as a clock-maker based upon his personal experience with Faris clocks. We are indebted to Gregory Weidman for her assistance in assessing the probability of the two William Farises being in fact separate craftsmen. MBL is grateful to Mount Vernon horticulturist Dean Norton for his willingness to guide him through an unforgettable tour of George Washington's garden. This opportunity was instrumental in furthering our understanding of Faris's approach to gardening in the eighteenth century. JBR would like to thank Jane McWilliams and J. Elliott Russo for their careful reading of several of the Faris essays.

We owe special thanks to Barbara Wells Sarudy, whose research and writing preceded ours and breathed new life and interest into the subject of William

Faris and his diary in the 1990s. Barbara proposed a dozen years ago, after completing her master's thesis on Faris's garden, a joint editorship with JBR of the complete diary, before competing professional obligations consumed the time that each might have devoted to the enterprise. When we decided to take on the project, Barbara generously shared her research with us and was always willing to answer a question or discuss a problem as we grappled with understanding Faris's world.

MBL would like to extend special thanks to his family, to his parents, Jack D. and Eva A. Letzer, to Allison and Jack Jr., and to all the other Faris descendants who gave of themselves, continually encouraged this book, and provided moral support. He is especially indebted to his father, who was his faithful companion on all the Faris-related explorations.

No manuscript can ever be considered finished until it has been carefully polished by astute editors. Donna Blair Shear has painstakingly pored over the manuscript and made countless improvements. We are grateful to the Press at the Maryland Historical Society for recognizing the importance of bringing the annotated diary to print.

EDITOR'S NOTE

Transcription:

The diary transcription reproduces Faris's handwritten diary as closely as his penmanship allows. When the written words were ambiguous in their spelling, the form more consistently used by Faris appears in the text. Similarly, capitalization generally follows Faris's choices, but only for those letters that he used in both upper and lower case. Certain letters, such as S, V, and E, he always capitalized when they began a word; those letters have usually been left as lower case. Faris provided little punctuation for his entries; he used periods and commas only rarely but did employ the dash more frequently. The dashes in the text are Faris's own, but periods (and occasionally commas) have been silently added to provide greater clarity.

Biographical Footnotes:

Every effort has been made to provide accurate information in the biographical footnotes, but the reader should be aware that the large number of individuals mentioned made it impossible to rely solely on primary sources and impractical to provide citations for each footnote. Sources listed in boldface in the bibliography supplied biographical information (as well, often, as other information). Most are either original documents or transcriptions of original records.

PREFACE

D IARIES are personal reflections, where the writer records details of life that are generally of a significance peculiar to his own experience. To be afforded the opportunity to read such renderings fascinates most people. We have an insatiable curiosity when it comes to these private recordings, desiring to cross over into the private world of the writer and to discover something perhaps about ourselves. Diaries are generally written with unlimited candor and few inhibitions because of the expectation that they will never be read by others. William Faris's diary is richer than many, covering *many* aspects of his life. In his diary you will read about Faris's gardening practices, his experiments with electrical machines and use of hydrogen, his fascination with the weather, the activities of his friends and acquaintances, along with the news and events of an Annapolis that disappeared long ago.

William Faris began writing his diary on 1 January 1792. America was a fledgling republic and Annapolis was still feeling the effects of the Revolution, never having fully recovered from the post-war depression. The diary walks us through the town and its inhabitants from the perspective of a clockmaker and innkeeper, unlike other published diaries, such as those of luminaries like George Washington and Thomas Jefferson recording the details of their luxurious lifestyles and management of their plantations. Faris leads us through the icy streets where people are skating, enables us to smell the wood smoke from the burning fires, and allows us to sense and envision his beautiful garden with its aromatic lilies and blooming tulips. His diary affords the reader a view of late eighteenth-century Annapolis not available from any other source. In his daily recordings over a thirteen-year period, Faris brings to life his entire community from the 1790s until the early 1800s. You will discover who these people were and follow the course of events of the lives of many Annapolitans; learn of their births and marriages, deaths and burials, as well as the hot days and heavy rains of summer and the cold, snowy days of winter.

1 ✒ Mrs. Thomas
Parramore Stran (Hannah
Kate Abrahams)
(1846–1923)

2 ✒ Ann Faris Pitt
(1773–1860) and her
daughter Hannah
Williams Pitt
(1800–1837)

The history of the diary is almost as compelling as its author. Upon William Faris's death in 1804, his muslin-covered journal remained at his home on West Street with his widow, and upon her death it stayed in that house, never coming into the hands of his children or grandchildren. William McParlin, who had been Faris's apprentice, purchased the West Street home in 1818 from Faris's heirs. The diary remained with the McParlin family in Annapolis for over one hundred years. In the early years of the twentieth century, William McParlin's grand-daughters gave the diary to Kate Abrahams Stran (Figure 1), a great-great-granddaughter of William Faris. Mrs. Stran preserved the diary, always treasuring its value and further enlightening other family members about William Faris and his importance in Annapolis history. She paid her nieces and nephews handsomely for naming their children either Faris or Stran and collected Faris heirlooms assiduously, owning some of his silver, a case clock, and the portrait of William Faris's daughter, Ann Faris Pitt, and her daughter Hannah (Mrs. Stran's great-grand-mother and grandmother respectively (see Figure 2). At her death, Mrs. Stran bequeathed the diary to her nephew Sumner A. Parker; at his passing his son Jameson Parker inherited the diary. Mrs. Jameson Parker gave the diary to the Maryland Historical Society in 1974 as a memorial to her husband. William Faris's diary ended its journey in a secure and stable environment, where it remains accessible to all students of Maryland history. J. Hall Pleasants edited and published excerpts of the diary in 1933 in the *Maryland Historical Magazine*. It is exciting and indeed momentous to present Faris's diary in its entirety for the first time.

You will find in his diary not only the current events of Annapolis and its environs but also the relationships Faris had with his fellow townspeople from all levels of society. William Faris was a complex yet approachable man. He was complex in his relation-ships with people, his high expectations of his children, and his committed friendships, yet accessible through the frank and candid recordings in his journal. Perhaps we can all find some similarities with Faris. The richness of his diary comes through in reading it repeatedly. The famil-iarity with its inhabitants will become more meaningful the more times it is read. We welcome you to the diary and life of a man who had much to share and we hope you will find him as riveting and charismatic as we have.

— Mark Beatson Letzer

The Essays

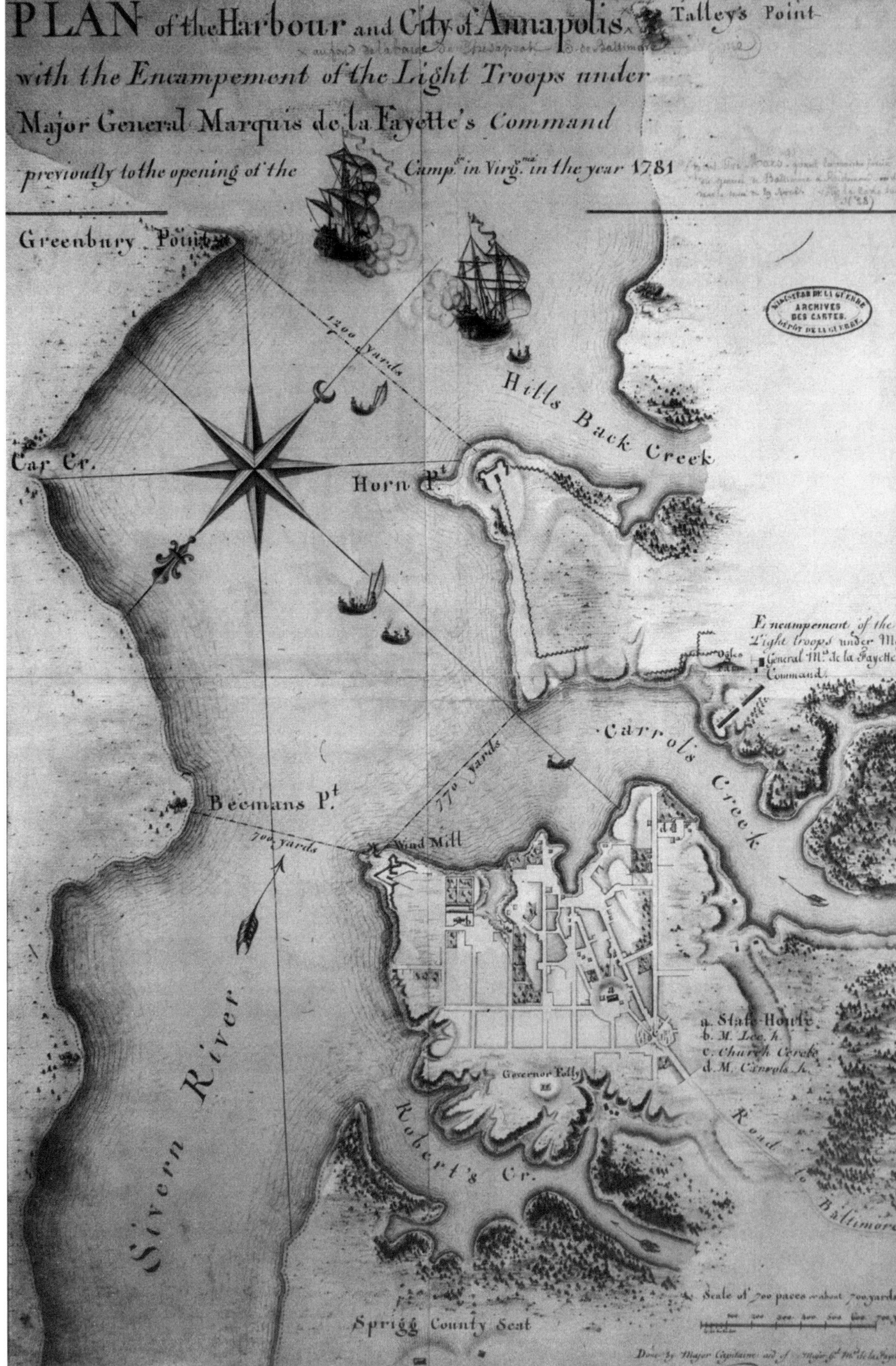

PLAN of the Harbour and City of Annapolis,
with the Encampement of the Light Troops under
Major General Marquis de la Fayette's Command
previously to the opening of the Camp in Virg. in the year 1781
Talley's Point
Greenbury Point
Car Cr.
Horn Pt
Hills Back Creek
1200 yards
Encampement of the Light troops under Maj General Mr de la Fayette's Command
Carrols Creek
Beemans Pt
770 yards
700 yards
Wind Mill
Severn River
a. State House
b. M. Lee h.
c. Church Ccreek
d. M. Carrols h.
Governor Folly
Robert's Cr.
Road to Baltimore
Scale of 700 paces or about 700 yards
Sprigg County Seat
Done By Major Capitaine aid of Major Gl Mis de la Fayette

William Faris's Annapolis

WILLIAM FARIS arrived in Annapolis from Philadelphia in 1756 or 1757, just before the beginning of the period characterized as the city's "golden age," the dozen or so years before the Revolution when Annapolis was not only the political capital of the colony but also its social and economic center. The wealth generated by several decades of prosperity in the tobacco trade as well as the growing market for Maryland wheat began to be spent in the city in the form of elegant brick mansions, fine furniture, lavish wardrobes of silk and velvet, tall case clocks, and silver tableware.

At the time that Faris moved to Annapolis, it was a small town of about one thousand residents occupying an area of about a third of a square mile on a point of land between the Severn River and Spa Creek. The street plan laid out by Governor Francis Nicholson in 1695 had been modified somewhat by the addition of several new streets, particularly in the neighborhood of the dock. The shops of merchants and artisans tended to cluster around the dock and along Church and West Streets but, with no distinction between home and workplace, stores and businesses were scattered about the town. Nor did economic, social, or racial distinctions exist among neighborhoods. There were perhaps several dozen brick homes of some substance, but they were interspersed among many more, generally much smaller, frame houses.

In its earliest years the town had relied on its maritime role (reinforced by its designation as a port of entry) and the presence of a government bureaucracy to sustain its existence. The maritime trades added an important economic element, but the workings of government played the stronger, long-term role in stimulating growth in Annapolis. With the reestablishment of the proprietary government in 1715, Lord Baltimore and his agents began

(FACING PAGE)
3 ↞ *This 1781 plan of the harbor and city of Annapolis includes outline depictions of formal gardens that would have been present during Faris's time.*
See also Figure 15 in color insert.

1

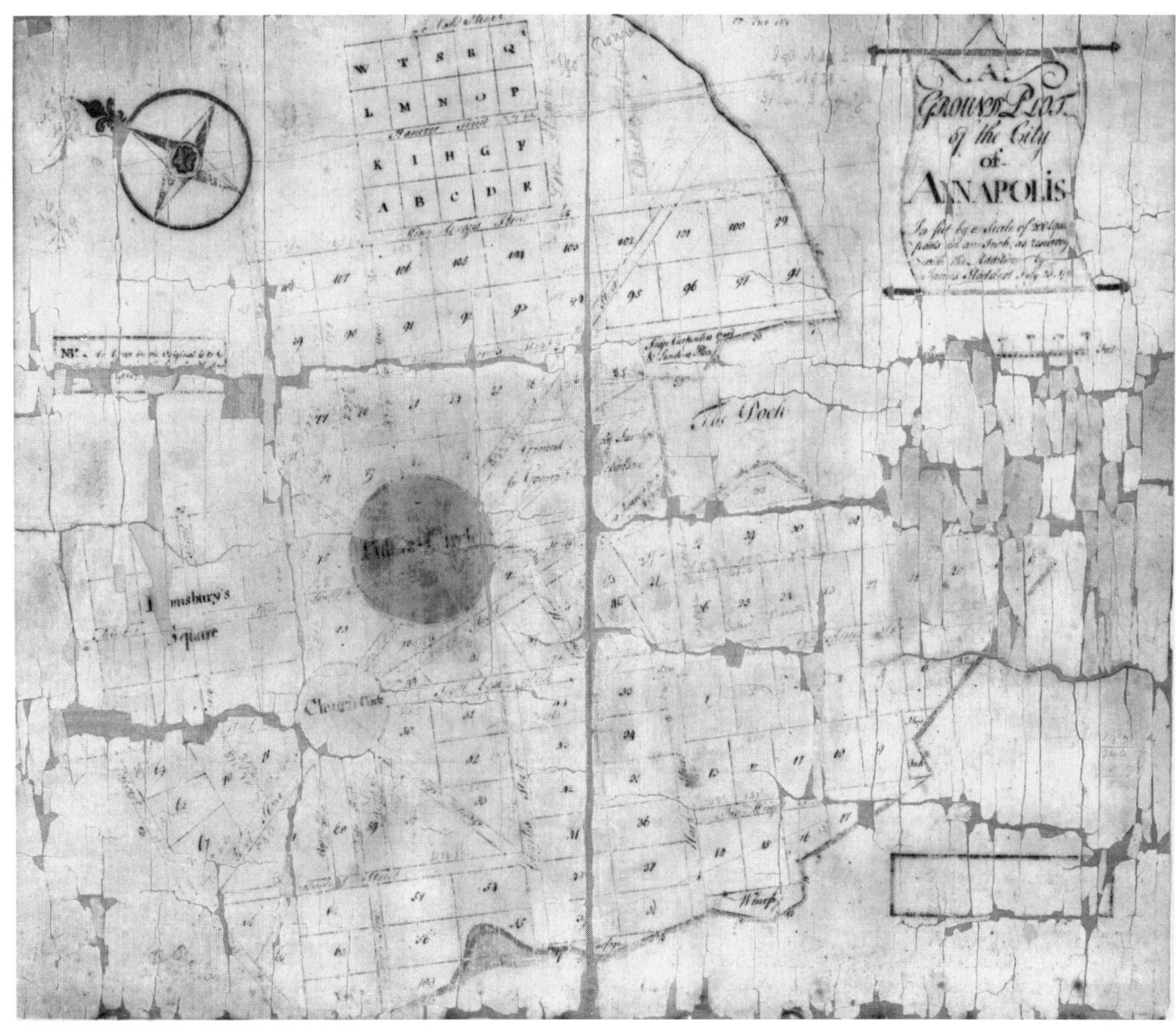

4 ☞ *The plan of Annapolis as laid out when it became the capital of Maryland in the 1690s; with minor changes the survey shows the town that Faris knew.*
See also enlarged view in Figure 8B of the color insert.

a concerted program of extracting revenue from the colony.[1] The colonial bureaucracy gradually expanded to handle the collection of hogshead duties and (eventually) quit rents, to grant land patents, and to oversee other administrative chores for Lord Baltimore. The need to transact business with the proprietor's agents, to appear in the provincial or county court, or to attend a session of the general assembly brought visitors from all parts of the colony to Annapolis. So too did the arrivals of ships from abroad or those engaged in coastal trade. These individuals needed lodging, food, and drink while in town and also used their visit as an opportunity to purchase imported goods that

---

[1] The Lords Baltimore lost administrative control of the colony with the overthrow of proprietary government in 1689, but retained ownership of the land and the right to collect quit rents or their equivalent. After the 5th Lord Baltimore converted to the Anglican faith, he regained control of the political and judicial systems. See Papenfuse, *In Pursuit of Profit*, especially 10–12, for an analysis of the sources of growth.

might not be carried to the landings along the rivers and creeks on which they lived. By 1730, Ebenezer Cook, when writing the *Sotweed Redivivus*, could say that he was

> Bound up to Port Annapolis,
> The famous Beau Metropolis
> Of Maryland, of small Renown
> When Anna first wore England's Crown
> Is now Grown Rich and Opulent
> The awful Seat of Government.[2]

Visitors to Annapolis who did not have family or friends with whom to stay found lodgings at one of the city's many taverns, such as the one that William Faris opened in 1764. Eighteenth-century taverns not only served travelers but also operated as social centers for town residents. Social clubs, beginning with the Tuesday Club in the 1740s, gathered there. Faris, for example, hosted the Homony Club at his tavern in June 1771. Townsmen and visitors alike could gamble at cards, billiards, and backgammon. Merchants and ship captains made taverns their business headquarters as did itinerant painters, barbers, dentists, dancing masters, and other transients who had services to offer.[3] People collected at taverns to bid at auctions of debtors' property or ship cargoes captured by privateers. Letters could be left or picked up and patrons could read copies of newspapers from other colonies and abroad. Traveling exhibitions and entertainments of various kinds put on performances at taverns; eighteenth-century Annapolitans could view a camel, an exhibit of prints of famous European public buildings, or a collection of waxworks. Taverns generally operated in the tavernkeeper's home, and thus could be found in most areas of the city, lending an air of bustle and conviviality to many neigh-borhoods.

By the 1750s, Annapolis had developed a lively social life, with theatrical performances, horse racing for stakes, and balls featuring the latest European dances and fashions during the winter social season when delegates to the assembly were in town, joined by their fellow gentry from around the colony. A dozen or more of these men began to build the town houses that epitomize the "golden age," part of a self-reinforcing process of development, as each new home made the capital city a more desirable place to be. At the same time, the increasing building activity drew more workers in the building trades to

---

[2] As quoted in Land, *Colonial Maryland*, 136.

[3] No one ever advertised those services at Faris's tavern, however.

5 ↝ Frontispiece of *"The Compleat Gamester"* Charles Cotton, London, 1680.

This image, although portraying a period one hundred years before Faris's time, comes from a manual for tavern games, most of which were played at Faris's West Street tavern. Faris also made spurs for cock-fights (shown here) and owned a backgammon table when he died. (See an enlarged view on page 102.)

Annapolis and stimulated markets for the wares of craftsmen who could make the furniture to fill the houses or for merchants whose cargoes included European furniture and decorative arts for those who wanted the highest quality and latest fashion.

The 1760s and early 1770s thus witnessed the expansion of the city's economic life and physical development in several directions. An increasing population; growing demand for the services of woodworkers, metalworkers, and other crafts associated with building and maritime activities; the arrival of silversmiths, tailors, dancing masters, hairdressers and barbers, cabinet-makers, booksellers, watchmakers, painters, and others catering to the needs of the wealthy planting and office-holding clientele, all contributed to economic growth in the town, reflected in changes in the landscape. Significant alterations occurred in the area between the Dock and the Public Circle. In 1769, staymaker Charles Wallace purchased title to the land between Francis and East Streets, originally reserved for Governor Nicholson, from the Bordley family who had owned the property since 1718. Wallace laid out two streets running from the circle to the waterfront, which he named Fleet and Cornhill after two busy London thoroughfares. Along the streets he placed a series of small lots for rental on long-term leases to small tradesmen who built houses and shops. The area developed as a neighborhood inhabited by the middling sort, including several tavernkeepers, a silversmith, and a carpenter. Facing the waterfront, Wallace built a row of four identical and adjoining three-story offices, one of which housed his mercantile partnership of Wallace, Davidson and Johnson. By this time, the character of the area around the Dock had been defined. Merchants' stores occupied the sites along Market Space, warehouses and wharves ran along the south side of the basin, and inns along the north side provided accommodations for sailors and travelers.

Elsewhere in town, the small homes of the middling and lower sorts shared neighborhood streets with the grander homes of the elite. The Carrolls enlarged the family home on Spa Creek, originally built to survey trade along the creek to the early settlement at Acton's Cove. Nearby on Duke of Gloucester and Shipwright Streets, John Ridout and Dr. Upton Scott, both of whom came to Maryland in the 1750s as part of the official entourage of Gov. Horatio Sharpe and then married well, built their homes. Lawyer Stephen Bordley created the city's first five-part Georgian house in the center of a large lot adjacent to the public circle. William Paca's home on Prince George Street overlooked Governor's Pond, an inlet that ran from Spa Creek nearly to the back wall of his elegant garden. King George Street at that time did not extend beyond Paca's property, giving him an uninterrupted view of the Severn. Nearby the homes of Edward Lloyd and Mathias Hammond rose along Northeast Street, the even higher promontory to their west having been claimed by an early governor, Thomas Bladen, for his residence. The unwillingness of the assembly to fund completion of the home to Bladen's tastes meant, however, that it remained unfinished for nearly half a century. Anne Arundel County planter Thomas Rutland's home on Hanover Street also overlooked the Severn, while James Brice's house at the corner of East and Prince George Streets dominated the northeastern end of town as its imposing bulk overlooked the slope to Spa Creek. Both the Frenchman's map, drawn in 1781 by a member of Lafayette's forces, and the 1797 drawing by another French

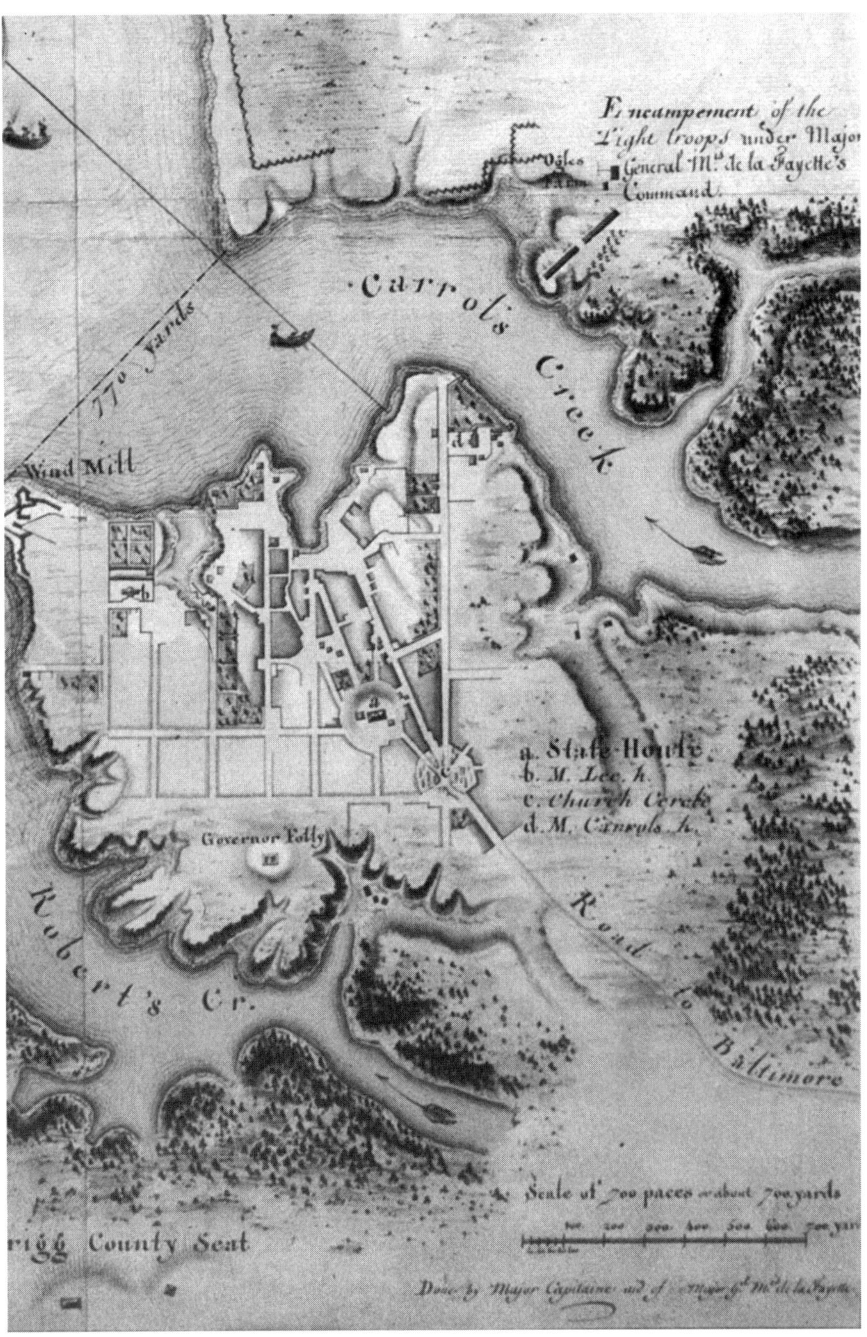

6 ☞ (Detail—see *Figure 3 facing page 1 and Figure 15 in color insert*) Annapolis city and harbor.

visitor showing a view of Annapolis from Strawberry Hill across College Creek depict the sense of openness that still existed and the extent to which the Georgian mansions and public buildings dominated the landscape.

Most Annapolitans must have regarded the new homes—particularly the four distinctive five-part houses of Bordley, Paca, Brice, and Hammond—with

7 ☛ *This watercolor, painted in 1797 by Comte de Maulevier Colbert from the vantage point of Richard Sprigg's plantation, Strawberry Hill, shows Windmill Point, the State House dome, and the spire of St. Anne's Church. See also Figure 8A in color insert.*

a mixture of awe, envy, and pride in the progress and refinement of their town. For craftsmen like William Faris the new wealth also carried the possibility of increased business for their shops. The wealthiest Annapolitans might turn to local watchmakers or silversmiths mostly for repair work, but the money they spent in town put cash in the pockets of local shopkeepers, tavern owners, artisans, and others that could in turn be spent in one another's businesses.[4]

The Reverend Jonathan Boucher, rector of St. Anne's in the early 1770s, described Annapolis as "the genteelest town in North America, . . . I hardly know a town in England so desirable to live in as Annapolis then was."[5]

---

4 Not surprisingly, then, one local middling family could afford over a twenty-year period to buy sets of six silver tablespoons from three different Annapolis silversmiths—including a set from Faris.

5 Jonathan Boucher, ed., *Reminiscences of an American Loyalist, 1738–1789: Being the Autobiography of the Reverend Jonathan Boucher* (Boston: Houghton Mifflin, 1925), 65.

William Eddis, who arrived in Annapolis in 1769, wrote in a letter home that "in a few years [Annapolis] will probably be one of the best built cities in America, as a spirit of improvement is predominant." He later observed that "the quick importation of fashions from the mother country is really astonishing. I am almost inclined to believe that a new fashion is adopted earlier by the polished and affluent American than by many opulent persons in the great metropolis [London]."[6]

8 ✒ *St. Anne's Church, just a short distance down West Street from Faris's home, and Church Circle, around which he walked on his trips to the market. See also Figure 3C in color insert.*

For a different perspective, though, it is useful to study a watercolor depiction of St. Anne's Church and the surrounding area, believed to date from the 1790s, which shows that the reality of life in an eighteenth-century town may have contained less grandeur and more congestion and disorder than suggested by the appellation "golden age." The watercolor shows a jumble of small buildings, most in the vernacular style with the gambrel roofs typical of the town's earliest buildings. Many of the buildings have a disheveled appearance; one appears ready to fall down. The streets are not paved nor are there the sidewalks and paving stones at crossings that eventually made journeys on foot less dirty and troublesome for nineteenth-century pedestrians. The circle around St. Anne's falls sharply to the roadway, leaving bare banks to wash down Church Street and into the basin during heavy rains. Grass and weeds grow in the street and in open spaces around the buildings; elsewhere piles of dirt are scattered randomly about. Not until 1803, the year before Faris

____

6 William Eddis, *Letters from America*, Aubrey C. Land, ed. (Cambridge, Mass.: Harvard University Press, 1969), 13, 57. Faris made a ferule for Eddis's walking stick in March 1776, charging him 7/6 according to the daybook.

died, did the Corporation begin to take notice of the state of the city's streets, passing a by-law appointing commissioners whose duties included care of the streets.7 But even then the required oversight was of a limited nature: to grade and straighten where necessary, to remove any obstacles, and to establish footways for pedestrians on each side of the streets. There is little likelihood, though, of any substantial progress toward the latter goal while Faris was alive. When he observed that snow or sleet had resulted in "slippery bad walking," he did not refer to icy sidewalks but to street surfaces that were a mixture of mud, ice, and slush.

Even when the streets were not covered with snow and ice, pedestrians still needed to be watchful of their footing. Efforts by the Mayor's Court and the Corporation to regulate dumping of refuse and disposal of liquids into the streets suggest the extent to which the thoroughfares were used as a convenient garbage dump. Fifty years after Faris died, the Corporation passed a by-law authorizing a fine for "emptying of soapsuds, fish brine, or other offensive refuse into any gutter provided for draining and cleansing streets."8 Such materials were to be "emptied and scattered" in the unpaved *middle* of the street, where offensive-smelling liquids would be absorbed into the soil. In Faris's day, the entire street, from house front to house front, would have served this purpose.

Nor was garbage the only obstacle. The Milburne watercolor shows chickens in Church Circle. Homeowners also kept cows, pigs, and horses, any of which might be loose in the streets. Fifty years later, in a more densely settled town, residents living around the courthouse—less than a block from where Faris had lived on West Street—asked the Corporation to install a lamp post and lamp because they suffered "greatly dark nights for the want of a little light in our street for it is very dangerous for us in traveling such nights there is always more or less cattle laying on the side walks of the street . . . and we really cannot see them such nights."9 There were few street lights10 in the city when William Faris lived in Annapolis and an equal likelihood of finding cattle "laying on the . . . street."

The drawing provides a healthy antidote to the glorified pictures of genteel life in the Golden Age—it is a reminder that the Georgian mansions represent the world of less than 5 percent of the population. The other 95 percent lived in the Annapolis depicted here. This Annapolis conforms more to the description left of it by visitor Benjamin Mifflin in 1760—laid out on "a very

---

7 The Corporation, composed of mayor, aldermen, common councilmen, and recorder (or lawyer), governed the city, passing by-laws and ordinances to regulate local affairs. Annapolis By-Laws and Ordinances 2, 1792–1816, 194.

8 Annapolis Corporation Proceedings, Box 20, 1852–1854, folder 45.

9 Annapolis Corporation Proceedings, Box 24, 1859, folder 14.

10 Only oil lamps, providing little useful illumination.

irregular plan" with buildings "mostly old and ill-built"—than does the distant view of spires and cupolas observed from Strawberry Hill.

The contrasting watercolors preserve the appearance of Annapolis after the Revolution. While war with England brought independence to the colonies, it signaled the eclipse of Annapolis by Baltimore. The latter city, with its far superior harbor, larger and more prosperous hinterland, and source of water-power in its location on the fall line, had already begun to surpass Annapolis prior to the Revolution as overseas demand for flour brought more and more cargoes of wheat to its mills. With a population in 1776 of 6,700 residents, it was home to over five times as many people as then lived in Annapolis (1,300). During the Revolution, Baltimore assumed a major role in provisioning colonial troops and an even more important role in outfitting privateers to prey on British shipping. By 1790, the population had more than doubled and by 1800 doubled again to over 31,000. Annapolis was left far behind.[11] "Soon after the Revolution, first commerce, then wealth and social influence, deserted Annapolis for Baltimore, the state's rapidly growing center of trade."[12] Annapolis declined to the status of a market town, with its residents acting as middlemen selling goods, originally imported through Baltimore, to farmers in the surrounding countryside. The packet boats and stage services that Faris records in his diary reflect this shift in the balance between the two towns.

Although no longer experiencing the dynamic growth of the pre-war years and no longer setting the pace of fashion, the town did not wither away. Residents built, bought, and sold houses; businesses opened and closed; children went to school and adults to the theatre or the races, but all at a slower pace—and the town continued to be the seat of government. By the decade of the 1790s, several major changes in the landscape had taken place. Shortly before the Revolution the General Assembly decided to replace the dilapidated state house and St. Anne's vestry agreed to build a new church on the site of the run-down structure completed in 1704. War delayed both projects; the unfinished state house was put into use c.1779 but work did not end until the 1790s. The old church was torn down in 1775, but construction of the new St. Anne's did not begin until after the war and stopped only in 1792. The city built a new market house near the dock between 1785 and 1790; here Faris would do the daily marketing for the family. The unfinished structure known as "Bladen's Folly" was completed in 1793 as McDowell Hall, the first building of St. John's College which had been chartered by the legislature in 1784. Local homeowners responded with advertisements in the *Gazette* offering rooms for the expected influx of students, while the college faculty added a cosmopolitan element to the town's population.

---

[11] Papenfuse, *New Guide*, 355–56.

[12] Ibid., 325.

9 ✒ *Although pre-pared fifty years after Faris's death, this view of Annapolis shows the State House, second St. Anne's Church, McDowell Hall at St. John's College, commercial buildings around the dock, and many of the eighteenth-century mansions, all of which Faris knew.*

By 1800, Faris's Annapolis held just over two thousand residents. White Annapolitans accounted for somewhat more than half of the citizens (58 percent). The black population, which comprised the remaining 42 percent of the city's residents, was divided between 273 free blacks (30 percent) and 646 slaves (70 percent). Annapolitans lived in nearly three hundred households, headed by males and females, whites and blacks, free persons and slaves. Two slaves, one male and one female, each headed a household of four people. These families, who lived apart from their masters, may have been given the right to hire out their own time with the eventual hope of earning enough to buy their freedom. The census also listed twenty free black men and twenty free black women as the heads of their own households. Ten of the free black households included slaves; these may have been family members—most likely wives and children—purchased by the husband or parent to remove them from bondage to a white master.[13] A deed of manumission would eventually free them. Of the white households, men headed nearly 90 percent.

---

[13] They may also have been family members whose owners allowed them to live with their free relatives.

10

Of those households headed by whites, one-quarter included only whites, half held whites and slaves, one-tenth encompassed whites and free blacks, and the balance held whites, slaves, and free blacks. Three-quarters, therefore, of white families lived in households that also included black Annapolitans; conversely, almost all black Annapolitans—free or enslaved—lived with white families. The average family owned four slaves, but more families—like the Farises[14]—owned just one than held any number higher than that. The largest slaveholding belonged to Faris's neighbor, Allen Quynn, with nineteen slaves (not all of whom lived in town), as well as having one free black in his household and five whites. In most households the women worked as domestic servants—cooks, laundresses, and housemaids—while the men might be valets ("waiting men"), grooms, coachmen, gardeners, sailors, or craftsmen, depending upon the status and occupation of their owners.

Free Annapolitans—white and black—made their living in ways just as varied as they had been before the Revolution. Notices about tan yards and rope walks appeared in the *Gazette*. Makers of luxury goods included other watchmakers, silversmiths, cabinetmakers, and coachmakers. Astute marketers tried to compete with the new metropolis of Baltimore in the same terms as had been used regarding England before the war: George Smith, for example, advised in 1790 that customers for his service of carving and gilding in oil and burnished gold would enjoy "the great saving of risk and expence in not having to send goods to Baltimore." Shoemakers, hatters, staymakers, saddlers, and tailors supplied the more mundane needs of daily life. As many as a dozen dry goods stores offered wares imported through Baltimore or manufactured along the Eastern seaboard. At the same time, government employment continued to play a prominent role. Many of the individuals we meet in Faris's journal entries spent their working lives as elected officials or government bureaucrats. As the diary also makes clear, Annapolitans continued to enjoy a rich social life, with militia parades, musical and dramatic performances, religious lectures, touring exhibitions, and numerous balls, as well as private gatherings for tea and dancing, offering diversion and entertainment. More serious pursuits could be satisfied by the numerous tutors and teachers interested in the education of adults in music, languages, needlework, and other skills.

The Stoddert plan supplies the stage upon which the diary unfolds; the Frenchman's map, view from Strawberry Hill, and watercolor of St. Anne's provide the sets; the diary sets the actors in motion. The curtain rises on the morning of 1 January 1792.

---

[14] When Faris died, he owned only Sylve, but the diary suggests the presence of other slaves who were part of the household. They might have been hired by Faris from their owners for longer periods than the slaves who occasionally worked in the garden.

10 🖙 William Faris's Diary, Muslin cover, with "January 1th, 1792" inscription
We can imagine Faris opening his diary on a daily basis to record the day's events.
This is the only cover of the diary to survive.

Profile of William Faris

WILLIAM FARIS'S life history, as handed down by his daughter Ann to her children and entered in the family Bible by her son Charles Faris Pitt, states that he was born in London on 16 August 1728, the son of William and Abigail Faris.[1] His father, a clockmaker and a Quaker, reportedly died in prison, put there for refusal to take oaths, to serve in the military, or to pay the mandatory tithes designated for support of the Anglican Church. According to the family history, the widowed Abigail, with William and a nurse, emigrated to America early in 1729, also taking with her five or six clocks made by her husband. The family arrived at the port of Philadelphia, where they settled. We do not know why Abigail Faris (Figure 11) chose to go to Philadelphia, but it is very possible that she had friends or even relatives among the Quaker community there who could be of assistance to her and her son.[2]

Very little is known of the years that William and his mother spent in Philadelphia.[3] Church records document that Abigail married twice, first to John Powell on 11 January 1735 (First Presbyterian Church) and second to Philip Petre (Petro/Pedro/Pederow) on 27 November 1738 (Old Christ Church). These marriages, taking place as they did in Presbyterian and

11 ✒ Abigail Faris

This portrait of William Faris's mother has historically been attributed to his hand, beginning with a memorandum written by his grandson Charles Faris Pitt in the Pitt family Bible: "I obtained from Mr. McParlin (at Annapolis) in a dilapidated state, my great Grand Mother, Abigail Faris' likeness & had it renovated by a Baltimore artist (Vockmar). This likeness was painted by my Grand Father Faris and now adorns my Parlour — March 27, 1864. CF Pitt." The portrait is more likely by the hand of Gustavus Hesselius (1682–1755), who was painting in Philadelphia at this time. The painting of Abigail Faris appears to be an almost identical rendition of Hesselius's portrait of his wife Lydia.

---

[1] There is no doubt about the date of Faris's birth, as he noted his birthday and age almost every year that he kept his diary.

[2] There was a Samuel Faris in Bucks County, Pennsylvania, who died in 1749, with a son named William. He might have been Faris's uncle, but there is no mention of him in the family records and Faris does not name any of his children Samuel.

[3] Information about the Philadelphia period of Faris's life derives, in part, from Lockwood Barr, "William Faris, 1728–1804," *Maryland Historical Magazine*, 36 (1941): 420–39.

Anglican churches, surely resulted in Abigail's expulsion from the Quaker meeting, assuming that she had continued to be a member of the Society of Friends after her arrival in Philadelphia. Abigail's third husband was a shopkeeper, and she appears to have continued the business as a widow. For at least a decade, from December 1745 to April 1755, Abigail maintained an account with the Philadelphia mercantile firm Alex. Hamilton, from whom she bought items for resale. Her purchases of dry goods such as cloth, needles, pins, and ribbons as well as tea amounted to £80 over the ten years, not a large sum if the Hamilton firm were her only supplier.

A short announcement that Abigail placed in the 15 January 1751 issue of the *Pennsylvania Gazette,* suggests a more substantial and fashionable business. The announcement reported a theft that had taken place the previous day and offered a £10 reward for information leading to the arrest of the culprits. The stolen goods consisted of a variety of fabrics, including lawns, silk damasks, and black velvet; silk handkerchiefs, gloves, stockings, and caps; a pair of gold buttons and a gold ring; about fifteen pounds of tea; and about £50 in cash.4

A notice that appeared in the *Pennsylvania Gazette* on 14 July 1757 indicates that Abigail still operated her shop at that time. According to the announcement:

> LOST about a Month ago in Philadelphia, a worked Pocket Book. . . . it contained a good many Notes of Hand, payable to Abigail Pederow, and several Papers of no Use to any Body but the Owner. Whoever brings it and the Papers to Abigail Pederow, shall have a Dollar reward, and any small Bills that were in it.

The "lost Notes of Hand" suggest debts owed by Abigail's customers. The notes would be her means of collecting the debts and so worth the reward offered. This notice is the last reference we have for Abigail Faris; there is no evidence as to the date of her death.

The family home at Market and Water, which Abigail Faris probably rented, put William in the same neighborhood as Philadelphia's established clockmakers, watchmakers, silversmiths, and other craftsmen, whose shops were located on the two blocks south of Market along Front, Second, and Third streets. Four members of the Stretch family, Henry Flower, two Richardsons, and other clock and watchmakers lived and worked in the neighborhood. Both Henry Flower and Isaac Stretch witnessed legal documents for Faris, but there are no surviving records that document a craft association for Faris with any of the city's established master artisans.5 Two mortgages and

---

4 Four individuals (three men and one woman) received death sentences for the crime, and a fifth was branded on the hand. *Pennsylvania Gazette,* 5 February 1751.

5 Any apprenticeship arrangement that Abigail Faris made for her son would have been a private agreement, not having to be legally recorded.

three deeds all identified Faris as a clockmaker or watchmaker, but he may
have been working as a journeyman, for he never advertised his skills during
the time he lived in Philadelphia.

On 31 October 1749 the twenty-one-year-old Faris bought the lease of a lot
in Philadelphia at Spring Garden in the Northern Liberties (now in the area
of Third and Vine streets) for £3. The deed identified Faris as "of Philadelphia,
clockmaker," the "son of Abigail Petro, shopkeeper," who witnessed the deed.
On 16 May 1751 Faris offered the property, now improved by a house, for sale,
with inquiries directed to Abigail Pedro at the corner of Market and Water.
No sale took place, however; instead on 23 January 1752 Faris purchased the
lease of a second lot for £103. The Spring Garden lots remained Faris's property until he sold them on 17 April 1763 for £280; most likely he rented out
the lots during the time that he owned them.[6]

We do not know why Faris decided to leave Philadelphia, nor why he
decided to relocate in Annapolis. The twenty-eight-year-old bachelor had no
known ties to Annapolis that would help establish him in a strange city, nor
does Annapolis, just on the brink of its period of greatest prosperity, appear
to have been a more promising location than Philadelphia. Whatever his
motivation, on 17 March 1757 William Faris's first advertisement appeared
in the *Maryland Gazette*, announcing that he had opened a shop on Church
Street, near St. Anne's Church and next door to Mr. [Charles] Wallace.[7] Faris
described himself as a "WATCH-MAKER, *from PHILADELPHIA.*" To have
arrived from London would have been better, but Philadelphia was an accept-
able alternative — much larger, more cosmopolitan, and more sophisticated
than Annapolis, and a city that many Annapolitans knew well. He offered
work "as well and neat as can be done in any Part of *America*," at the same
prices charged in Philadelphia, as well as several types of clocks that he could
make "as good as can be made in *London*."

Two years later Faris moved from his Church Street shop to the house "late
in the Occupation of Andrew Buchanan, the Sign of the CROWN and DIAL,"
on Prince George Street near the waterfront, as he announced in the 8
November 1759 *Gazette*. Moreover, he had prospered enough to take on a journeyman clockmaker to expand the products he could offer. A year later he used

---

[6] There is no direct evidence of the family's financial position in Philadelphia, but
Faris's apprenticeship in a luxury trade, these purchases of land, his ownership of a
costly silver tankard (see Figure 22 on page 43), and the apparent success of his
mother's shop all suggest that Abigail Faris brought resources beyond the clocks
when she arrived in Philadelphia or acquired them subsequently and that Faris himself was making a success of his career. Philadelphia Land Records, H 13/362–73,
and U 18, 329–31.

[7] As the town's buildings had no numbers, newcomers or those who changed their
place of business had to provide guides to their location in the form of recognized
businesses and landmarks.

the 4 December 1760 issue to inform the public that he now had an excellent workman to carry on a silversmith's business. The Annapolis tax assessors apparently noticed Faris's success as well. In 1759 and 1760, he paid the tax on bachelors[8] in the higher category of estates of £300 or more.[9]

In 1761, the thirty-two-year-old Faris took another step to establish himself in the Annapolis community, when he married twenty-two year old Priscilla Woodward on 29 March. Priscilla was the daughter of Abraham Woodward (1685–1744), and his second wife Priscilla Ruley (1690–1773), the widow of James Orrick. The Woodwards had eleven children (four sons and seven daughters) of whom Priscilla, born 27 February 1739, may have been the youngest. We do not know how William Faris and Priscilla Woodward became acquainted. The Woodwards lived near the head of the Severn River, not in Annapolis, but their kinsman William Woodward, a goldsmith, lived in town and may perhaps have been the means of their introduction.

Marriage to Priscilla represented a socially advantageous step for William Faris. The Woodwards were an established planter family in Anne Arundel and Prince George's counties with kinship ties to others of equal or higher status. Priscilla's uncle Henry, a London resident, had several ties to Annapolis. He married Mary Garrett, a sister of Amos Garrett, a successful Annapolis merchant who was the town's first mayor and its wealthiest citizen when he died in 1728. Two of Henry and Mary Garrett Woodward's sons emigrated to Annapolis. The eldest son, William, the goldsmith, was in London in 1738 but emigrated to Annapolis sometime before 1758.[10] The youngest son, Amos, arrived in Annapolis by 1728.[11]

The children and grandchildren of Priscilla Faris's siblings appear fre-

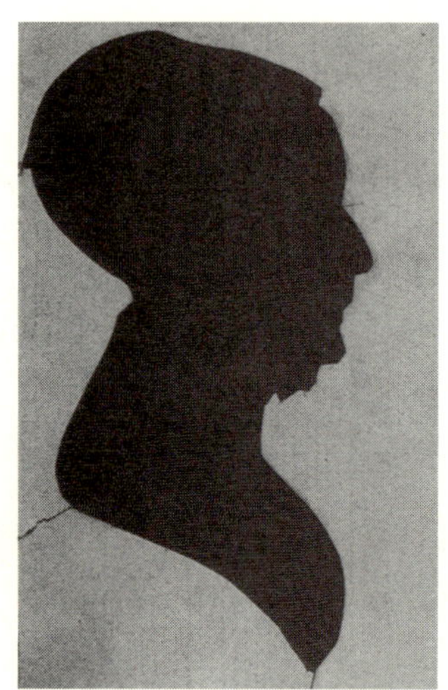

12 ⚘ Priscilla Faris

This silhouette of his wife may well have been made by Faris himself, as he owned a physiognotrace when he died.

---

[8] As a revenue measure enacted to raise money during the French and Indian War, the government taxed all bachelors owning property worth more than £99; those with property over £299 paid a higher rate.

[9] Faris was not taxed in 1757 or 1758, whether because he did not meet the £100 threshold or because he had not been in the parish long enough to be recognized as a taxable bachelor, there is no way to know.

[10] Woodward may never have practiced his craft in Annapolis, being referred to in the local records as a "gentleman." He sat on the St. Anne's vestry from 1761 until 1764, during which time Faris was a churchwarden, but spent his last years in Baltimore, where he died in 1774.

[11] In 1728 Amos Woodward (Priscilla Woodward Faris's cousin) married Achsah Dorsey, member of a prominent gentry family, with whom he had one son, Henry, and three daughters. Henry Woodward, who married Mary Young, daughter of Col. Richard Young, was a large property owner in Annapolis. After Henry's death in 1761, his widow Mary married limner John Hesselius. Faris notes the marriages of three of the Hesselius girls in his diary, one of whom, Charlotte, is linked to Faris through "The Will," which enters Faris's story in 1790 (see "The Will of William Faris" on page 26).

quently in the diary, visiting or being visited by members of the Faris family, and more distant Woodward connections are also noted. Faris sat on the St. Anne's vestry with Priscilla's nephew William. In 1772, when a slave belonging to her brother William ran away and was believed by his owner to be heading back to Philadelphia, Woodward placed a runaway notice in the *Pennsylvania Gazette* (9 July 1772). After describing Joe, he offered a reward to anyone who delivered the slave to him at the head of the Severn River or to William Faris in Annapolis. Woodward presumably named Faris as his agent because of their kinship tie, but Faris also acted in a similar capacity in 1773 for a Philadelphia resident whose runaway slave had formerly lived in St. Mary's County.[12] In this instance, the owner may have known Faris from his days in Philadelphia or the connection may have come through Faris's circle of friends among ship captains.

The first of William and Priscilla's nine children, a son, was born in January 1762, but died shortly after birth. A second son, William, Jr., followed within the year, on 5 December 1762. Charles was born on 29 September 1764 and a daughter, Rebecca, on 29 November 1766.[13] Priscilla was pregnant with Hyram when Rebecca died on 14 October 1768; Hyram was born the following January, on the 18th. The birth of the last son, St. John, took place on 27 December 1770. Three daughters completed the family: Ann, born 9 May 1773; Abigail, born 10 March 1775 and named for Faris's mother; and a second daughter named Rebecca, who was born on 11 December 1778. For a period of nearly twenty years, Priscilla Faris was either pregnant or nursing a new-born baby, and through the 1770s the household always included a few toddlers or young children.

Eight months after his marriage, Faris purchased the lease of a house and lot on West Street, although he had probably moved in about a year earlier.[14] The property belonged to the Vestry of St. Anne's as the glebe land for the parish church.[15] Hatter and innkeeper William Reynolds, who held a larger portion of the land on a long-term lease from the vestry, sold Faris a section of his leasehold in November 1761. The two subsequently extended the length of Faris's tenure in January 1763 and enlarged the size of the leased property in 1770. Fifteen years later Faris negotiated a new lease with Reynolds' daughter Margaret and her husband, Alexander Trueman, for a lot

---

[12] *Pennsylvania Gazette*, 18 August 1773.

[13] The eighteen-month to two-year birth interval was the typical pattern in the eighteenth century.

[14] A December 1760 advertisement now described the Sign of the Crown and Dial as "near the Church."

[15] Land allotted to the church for its support. In rural areas, this land might be farmed by the rector, but in Annapolis the vestry rented it to tenants for residential use.

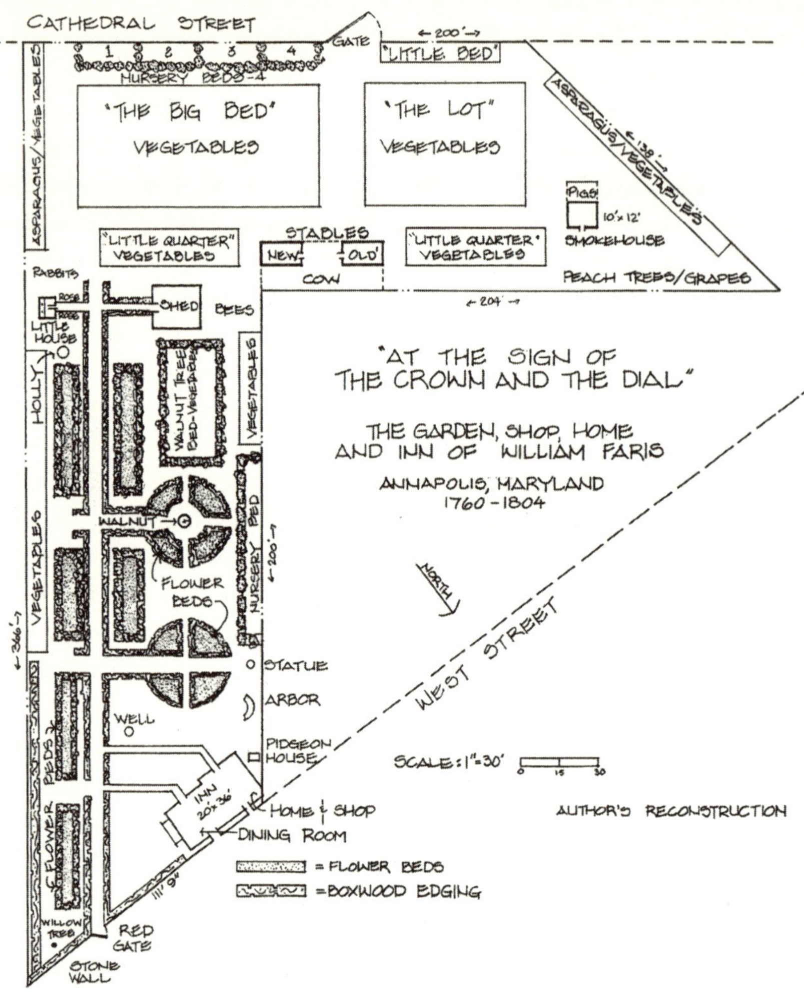

 Layout of William
Faris's Annapolis
Home and Garden

*William Faris's property
as reconstructed by
Barbara Wells Sarudy.*

that extended 111 feet, 9 inches along West Street. On this lot stood the family's dwelling house consisting of two brick sections — a one-story, 18' square main block and an 18' by 20' two-story addition; a 12' by 10' brick smokehouse; and a 16' by 20' frame outhouse, which may have been Faris's shop. The tax assessor who listed these buildings in 1798 did not include several more that appear over time in the diary, such as the old and new stables, the pigeon house, and the necessary.

We know little of the layout of the Faris home. Faris mentions only the "big room," the "little room," a dining room, Mrs. Faris's bedroom, and the room in which Rebecca slept. As Mrs. Faris went one night to sleep in Rebecca's room, it appears that William and Priscilla normally occupied "Mrs. Faris's room." Most likely the boys slept in one room and all the girls in another. The family's slaves may have slept in the kitchen or in the house (no Annapolis household had a separate slave quarter). Any apprentices or journeymen might have shared the boys' room or slept in the shop. While the accommodations seem cramped by modern standards, many eighteenth-century families of similar size lived in much smaller houses. Nevertheless, the crowding could have been one cause of the tensions that Faris occasionally notes and of the recurrent arguments between father and adult sons.

Scattered pieces of evidence attest to the presence of other adults in the Faris household during the 1760s and 1770s. In March 1762 Faris sued Thomas Wilson, an Annapolis merchant, for dealing with Faris's servant without his permission. In 1764 and 1765 Faris paid levies for three taxables — his own and probably those of two workmen, perhaps the "very compleat SILVERSMITH" from Philadelphia whose arrival he had announced in August 1763 and the "excellent Workman" through whom he carried on the jeweler's business.[16] In March 1769, Faris offered for sale the remaining time — between six and seven years — of another servant "by Trade a Gardiner" who could also knit seines.[17] In November 1768 the court judged that Faris's servant woman Mary Hodgkin serve an additional twelve months for the expenses of two illegitimate mulatto children and her runaway time.[18] In October 1769 Faris announced the acquisition of two journeymen to assist in the clock and watchmaking business, as well as a third workman who made chairs. Court Minute Sheets refer to three other servants: Anna Purser in 1774 and Phebe Roberts and William Jones in 1775. Finally, in 1778 Faris advertised in the *Maryland Journal* the sale of a "likely young Negro fellow, by trade a *Silversmith, Jeweller* and *Lapidary*." The women would have been domestic workers, helping Priscilla Faris with childcare, cooking, laundry, and other household chores, while the men worked in one or another facet of Faris's shop or assisted in his garden. Thus, throughout these decades the household appears to have included, in addition to the infants and children, as many as three adult male workers and at least one female domestic worker.

[16] During the colonial period, all heads of households paid an annual poll tax on the labor in their households: adult white males, sixteen and over, and all slaves, male and female, sixteen and over. Although accounts of taxables were compiled every year, those for Annapolis survive only for these two years. There are no entries in the Anne Arundel County court records in which Faris assumes responsibility for an apprentice, so his extra workers most likely were indentured servants or journeymen. The jeweler may have been Gabriel John Legier, who was identified by that skill when Faris posted a £50 bond in March 1763 guaranteeing Legier's court appearance.

[17] This may have been William Jennings, whom Faris brought before the court in March 1768 to be sentenced to serve five additional years for his time as a runaway and the expenses Faris incurred in recovering him. Both Legier and Jennings were English-born convicts whose sentences had been commuted to transportation and servitude.

[18] Hodgkin appears to have received a much less severe penalty than that imposed on Jennings, but Faris may have retained her children until the age of thirty-one and thus gained an additional form of compensation through their labor.

In 1764 Faris expanded his business activities to include tavern keeping, announcing on 2 August in the *Gazette* that he had "supplied himself with the best of Liquors," and that "Gentlemen Travellers and Others" would "meet with the best Entertainment, and the kindest Usage." The county court licensed all persons wishing to operate taverns, requiring each prospective tavern owner to appear in court with two individuals willing to stand surety, or be financially liable if the tavernkeeper failed to meet the required standards.[19] Although Faris advertised his tavern in 1764, his first appearance in the list of license holders occured in August 1768, with Allen Quynn and John Campbell as his sureties. Quynn, who began his career in Annapolis as a shoemaker, was a neighbor of Faris; John Campbell was a tailor with a shop on Church Street.

William Faris had appeared before the justices of the Anne Arundel County court a number of times before his first request for a tavern license. Several of the suits most likely involved unpaid debts; Faris was both defendant and plaintiff in these cases. A number of appearances represented the cases of assault that usually took up court time at every session. In March 1762 Faris was prosecuted for assaulting and beating Dr. John Shaw. Faris protested his innocence but the justices, after hearing the allegations, fined Faris five shillings. Two years later, Faris and his neighbor Allen Quynn were the victims. In March 1770 and August 1772 he appeared before the grand jury on charges of assault, but neither case appears to have come to trial. Similarly, in August 1773 Faris posted a £50 recognizance bond to guarantee his good

---

[19] The court periodically set rates for liquor and meals as well as minimum requirements for accommodations of both humans and horses. See Figure 15.

behavior until the November court, particularly toward his neighbor Abraham Claude, but the two men apparently resolved their dispute before the court met. Faris was not the only family member involved in these altercations. In March 1789, both William and Charles gave evidence to the grand jury, probably regarding an incident of assault for which the court subsequently fined Hyram 2*s.* 6*d.* As the recorded proceedings do not include any of the testimony presented in these cases, the circumstances of the fisticuffs remain unknown. Nor is it possible to say whether or not Faris and his sons were more argumentative than the average Annapolis resident.

Faris also appeared occasionally in the Mayor's Court, whose jurisdiction included violations of Annapolis ordinances and other local misdemeanors. In January 1767, Faris was brought before the court for a chimney fire — a potential threat to the safety of the town that officials monitored diligently. Should sparks from the chimney set other buildings on fire, considerable property damage and possibly loss of life could result. In the same month, Faris faced three charges of "suffering filth to lye on the street," another common offense.

Faris did not appear in court solely as a plaintiff or defendant. He sat on the grand jury a number of times (and lacunae in the records probably understate his service). In 1783 he served as a grand juryman in both March and August and sat again in November 1788, deliberating each time with one or more of the townsmen he later mentions in the diary.

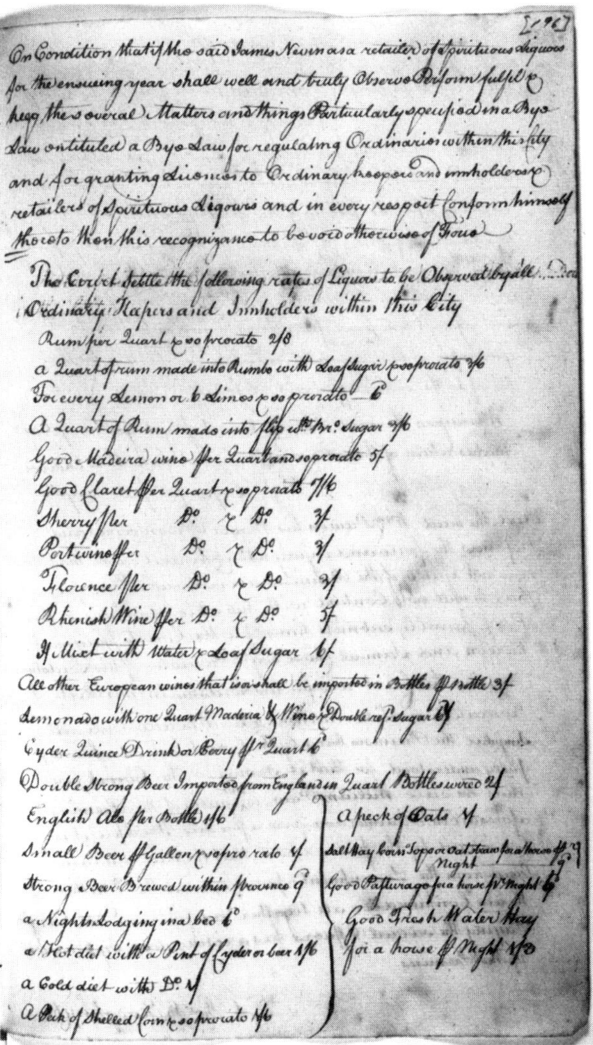

15 ☞ *Prices set by the Annapolis Mayor's Court soon after Faris opened his tavern.*

There is no evidence that Faris held political office in Annapolis, nor did he ever hold office at the county or provincial level. Because the Annapolis records are not complete, it is possible that he served as a common councilman or perhaps even as alderman. St. Anne's parishioners elected Faris to the vestry (the administrative body of the parish) in 1779, a position he held until 1783, when he became churchwarden for one year. Faris's vestry service suggests that he might have held public office, as the position of vestryman was an important one generally conferred on men who also served on the city corporation, on the county bench, or in the assembly.

In the course of writing his diary, Faris included one or more references to about five hundred individuals, but only twice does he appear as an actor in someone else's account. In the first instance, the artist Charles Willson Peale recorded in his own diary on 20 October 1775 that "Yesterday I left Mr. Benn: Dulanys miniture Picture with Mr. Farris to be Set" in an appropriate frame, as well as leaving "also a Glass for him to polish for it." The second reference occurred during the Revolutionary War (see below).

Faris was perhaps too old to take an active part in the Revolutionary War effort, but the records of the local committee of observation suggest that he did — eventually — take his place in the militia. Faris petitioned the local committee of observation in 1776 for the return of his guns, stating that although he had neglected to enroll himself in the militia when first called upon to do so, he had acted from a dislike of the Annapolis officers and not from any hostility to the patriot cause. On the third of July his firearms were returned and he was considered "fully enrolled" as of that date.[20] Faris later took the oath of allegiance before Thomas Worthington on 28 February 1778 along with his fellow townsmen.

A letter written in May 1779 by a planter in northern Anne Arundel County offers a different perspective on Faris's role during the Revolution. The correspondent wrote to alert Dr. Howard to a "plan carrying on by the Citizens of Annapolis against the country people in general." "The principal persons concerned in leading the mob are Chas Wallace, McHard, William Faris, Jack Chambers, the three Middletons &c and all their followers are the lower class. Their determination is to examine all corn houses, bacon lofts, &c, & where they think any person has to spare they will offer their own price & if the person refuses their price, they will put it under a guard & send it to Annapolis there to be stored until they have finished their plunder & then distribute or rather divide it amongst themselves...." A party of about 150 armed men, according to the writer, "set out on a plundering party," seizing grain at the head of the South River, and intended to visit settlements along the Severn, at Elk Ridge, and elsewhere "until their savage appetites are satisfy'd...." With the usual sources of supply either cut off by blockades or superseded by army

---

[20] The Provincial Convention set up at least fifty-four militia battalions in January 1776, including three in Anne Arundel County; ordered all eligible men to enroll in a militia unit by March 1; and authorized militia officers to confiscate the firearms (except pistols) of all who did not enroll. Those who actively encouraged non-enrollment could be arrested and tried. Surviving records do not list any Annapolitans receiving commissions at this time, so it is not possible even to speculate about the individuals to whom Faris objected. Officers as of 1777 (who might have been appointed in 1776) included John Brice, John Callahan, John Davidson, William Goldsmith, Benjamin Harwood, Charles Wallace Howard, Samuel Harvey Howard, Nicholas Maccubbin, and Gilbert Middleton; all but Middleton and Charles Wallace Howard appear in the diary.

provisioning agents, Annapolitans evidently felt impelled to take direct action to ensure adequate food supplies for town dwellers who did not have enough land to feed themselves.

The portrait of William Faris that emerges from the surviving bits of evidence is that of a respected and successful, although feisty, individual, not very different in general terms from many of the friends and neighbors who appear in the diary. After all, it was Allen Quynn, not Faris, who beat a neighbor's wife because he thought she gossiped about him.[21] Faris's appearances in court, whether as defendant or plaintiff, are not out of the ordinary in number or cause. The opinions of people that he records in his diary are usually temperate in tone, far more moderate than the comments that Georgetown merchant Samuel Davidson (whose brother John was a neighbor of Faris) left scattered in his account book.[22] Yet sometime about 1791, a poem entitled "The Will of William Faris" (see page 26) circulated in Annapolis and elsewhere.

The "Will" has appeared in print three times, first in the January 1879 issue of *Scribner's Monthly*, as part of an article "Old Maryland Manners;" next in Elihu Riley's *The Ancient City*; and finally in Pleasants and Sill, *Maryland Silversmiths*. "Old Maryland Manners" (attributed by Riley to artist Francis Blackwell Mayer) states that the "Will" was found in the "dusty pigeon-hole of a dead lawyer's office, legally indorsed, 'W. Farris, watch-maker at Annapolis, Maryland, his will,—composed by Miss Charlotte Heselius.'"[23] Lockwood Barr states that Faris himself believed the "Will" to be the work of his competitor Abraham Claude,[24] but presents no evidence for this assertion.

Beyond the occasionally negative characterizations of Faris, the existence of his "Will" implied that Faris had died, an implication that Faris felt sufficiently damaging to himself to cause him to place a notice in the 24 July 1791 *Maryland Journal and Baltimore Daily Advertiser* informing the public that he still "remains in good Health, and full Vigour of Life," continuing to do business at his home on West Street opposite Abraham Claude. That Faris's business would be harmed by a premature report of his death is undeniably true. Anyone reading the "Will" or hearing an account of its contents would

---

[21] See 30 July 1794 entry.

[22] For example, on the account of Pierre L'Enfant: "by profit loss knowing you now to be a pitiful dirty fellow and very poor, I give up the debt."

[23] Lockwood Barr, in his article on Faris that appeared in the December 1941 *Maryland Historical Magazine,* states that Charlotte, the nineteen-year-old daughter of John Hesselius, was a friend of Faris's daughters. But this assertion seems unlikely. Nancy, Faris's oldest daughter, was just sixteen and still a schoolgirl, and Faris's few references in the diary to any of the Hesselius family do not suggest a close relationship to his own family.

[24] Claude was also an Annapolis watchmaker and silversmith.

To the PUBLIC.

WHEREAS certain evil-disposed Persons have knowingly, wickedly, and maliciously counterfeited the Subscriber's last Will and Testament, which was introductive of an erroneous Propagation, in several Counties of this State, that he departed this Life some Time in June last; and, as a farther Indication of their malicious Disposition, they published, or caused to be published, a Funeral Sermon (possessed of very injurious Contents) to be delivered over his Body; both of which Circumstances, combined together, tend to very pernicious Consequences to the Subscriber's Trade and Manner of obtaining a Livelihood, by the Desertion of a considerable Degree of Custom which would otherwise have resorted to him—To detect Falsehood, disappoint Malice, and prevent farther Injury to himself, he hereby certifies the Public, that such Propagations are not true, and hopes that no Person will pay the least Degree of Attention whatever to them, as they were only circulated to impair and injure the Subscriber's Trade; and the Public may rest assured, that he now remains in good Health, and full Vigour of Life, in *West-Street*, *Annapolis*, opposite Mr. ABRAHAM CLAUD's, where he means to persevere in the Business of WATCH and CLOCK-MAKING, in all its various Arts and Branches, and solicits, once more, the Patronage of a generous Public.

WILLIAM FARRIS.

Annapolis, July 24, 1791.

16 ☞ *Although the poem "The Will of William Faris" was probably intended as a prank, it circulated widely enough to lead Faris to place this announcement that he was alive, well, and still in business.*

have no reason to believe it false unless they saw Faris with their own eyes. Annapolitans would know that he still lived, but out-of-town customers with no contrary information would take their business elsewhere. Thus the assumption that Faris made, according to Barr, of a malicious motive for its composition. Those writing about the "Will," particularly Barr, have also argued that the *content* of the will, as well as its existence, reveals that malevolence, but this conclusion seems less evident from a careful reading of the document. The writer, who certainly did know Faris and his family, paints a portrait of a frugal man who has cared for his possessions during his lifetime, taking equal care to distribute them to those who would most benefit from or appreciate the bequests, and doing so with a great deal of affection and concern for his family. And if the "Will" accurately expresses Faris's opinion of Quynn and Claude as his enemies, that is an opinion he failed to record in his diary.

Faris placed the announcement of his continued existence in the newspaper in July 1791 and started his diary in January 1792. We will never know if there was a connection between the "Will" and the decision to begin keeping a diary, but in his journal Faris has left us a far more revealing portrait of himself than the one created by the anonymous poet. Read them both and form your own judgment.

Dramatis Personae – 1 January 1792

WILLIAM FARIS, age 63

PRISCILLA FARIS, age 51

WILLIAM FARIS, age 29, probably living in Havana
(see 7 April 1792 entry)

CHARLES FARIS, age 27, living at home and
working in his father's shop

HYRAM FARIS, age 22, living at home and
working in his father's shop

ST. JOHN FARIS, age 21, living at home but soon
to go to sea with a mate's berth

ANN (Nancy) FARIS, age 18, marries William Pitt in 1796

ABIGAIL (Abee) FARIS, age 16, marries Archibald Kerr in 1802

REBECCA FARIS, age 13

SYLVE, age unknown, slave in Faris household

Priscilla Faris

Charles Faris

St. John Faris

Ann (Nancy) Faris

The Will of William Faris

25 Hypochondria.

Old Faris one day, as he sat in his shop
Revolving the chances of dying or not,
The hyppo[25] so seized him he tho't it was best
To divide his estate ere his soul went to rest,
So to work went the goldsmith: — Dreadful the task!
But first, for advice, he applied to his flask.
The gin, ever generous, fresh spirits afforded
And the will as I heard it was nearly thus worded,
I, William Faris, being well as to health,
Knowing Death often comes to old people by stealth
And without giving caution, or caring for fears,
Will take whom he pleases, regardless of tears;
So I now think it best to be thus on my guard,
To forsake all the gains I have made all my life
And, God knows, I have made them with trouble and strife,
Many nights have I watched, dread want to defy:
Now I make my last will and prepare me to die,
Then, I give and bequeath to my dear loving wife;
In case she's a widow the rest of her life:
The plates, spoons and dishes, pots, kettles and tables,
With the red and white cow that inhabits the stables,
The landscape, and "Judith" that hangs on the wall,
And the musical clock hind the door in the hall.
My buckles and cane to son William I give.
And no more, because he's got substance to live,
His road I took care in his youth to instruct him.
Tho' I say it myself, a princess might trust him.
The dog grew ungrateful, set up for himself,
And at Norfolk, they say, he has plenty of pelf.
Since he's gone away 'twill be best for his brother.
I give Hy[r]am his portion to comfort his mother,
All the tools in my shop to said Hy[r]am I give
And, if he minds work, he'll make out to live.
My coat, which I turned, is a very good brown
And may serve many years to parade in the town.
'Twill be good as ever if he take my advice,
And the buttons of silver will make it look nice,
And the place in the back which is greased by my club[26]

26 A club-shaped
knot or tail in which
the hair was worn at
the back of the head,
fashionable in the
second half of the
eighteenth century.

26

Would come out if he'd take good care to rub
It with soap and with brush or good spirits of wine
Which will freshen the cloth and make it look fine.
The coat he must wear with my corduroy breeches
When Abbey has given them a few odd little stitches.
And Ab' will be kind, I know, to her brother
Because he's the favorite of me and his mother.
A pair of silk hose I had when a boy
Intend shall be his; 'twill give him much joy.
To own these said hose he has begged for so often
But they n'er shall be his till I'm safe in my coffin.
I had always a mind to give them to Saint
'Till he like a fool, turned Methodist quaint.
I swore at the time he never should have them;
And I know Saint would *wear*, the other would *save* 'em.
For the reasons here mentioned, I leave them to Hy
To wear if he pleases when walking is dry.
To my son, Charles Faris, I give and bequeath
My watch and bird organ, and also I leave
To said son, as he pleases, a black ring or pin;
They're the first that I made, rather clumsily done,
But good, in all conscience, enough for my son.
The teeth he may have, rather clumsily strung;
Every tooth that I've drawn since the time I was young;
Six pair of thread stockings; two cotton, two yarn;
That my wife, poor dear woman, sat up all night to darn,
These will last him, with care, a very great while
And so money he'll save to make the pot boil.
To Saint Faris, my son, who is now on the seas
I will that he has any roots that he please;
All my garden utensils; "Swift's Polite Conversations";
And I wish he'd leave sea to live with his relations.
I know all their minds, and they all love poor Saint,
And his brother has promised to teach him to paint.
The "History of China" and "Swift" sometimes lend
When your business or pleasure requires a friend;
Such acts, my dear children, I very well know
Are of much greater service than making a foe.
Thank God! I've but two that I hate from my heart.
And, as ill luck would have it, they're not far apart.
I've the greatest dislike; God forgive me the sin;
But indeed there's no bearing that old Allan Quynn,
There's another I hate bad as Quynn for the fraud

That his heart is so full of that's Abraham Claude.
This sin, as I die, I hope will be forgiven;
Or, else, I am sure, I shall ne'er get to heaven,
My sons, if you heed me, beware of such friends;
They'll destroy all you're worth, if they have but the means.
To Nancy, the darling of me and my wife.
I give and bequeath the spinnet for life.
Once I thought she would play with the help of a master,
But, it grieves me to say, she learned not a bit faster,
Harry Woodcock I trusted to teach her to play,
But I soon found out 'twas money and time thrown away;
So she did what was right, made me save all my pelf
And picked out a tune here and there by herself.
All the town knows that Harry's a very great liar
And music from him she should never acquire,
What a time there has been for his making of money;
Like a puppy he's missed it, like a puppy he's funny,
Poor devil, sometimes, in the midst of a gloom,
For a dinner he's forced to play the buffoon;
But I still like old Woodcock I vow and declare;
As a proof I shall leave him a lock of my hair.
To Abigail next; my trunk, desk, and papers,
That's therein contained and a large box of wafers.[27]
The "Spectator" for her, as she reads very well,
And she'll soon learn to write, for now she can spell,
For Abb is the girl that would take the most learning.
And, I flatter myself she's a girl of discerning.
A negress, named Sylva, I leave to my Nancy,
For Sylva she'd always a very great fancy.
That woman's first child, about fifteen years old,
I give to my Ab lest for debt she be sold.
Poor thing 'twas a fool from its birth, I well know,
But her mistress will teach her to spin, knit, and sew.
I leave to Sol Mogg for tolling the bell,[28]
My old hat and pipe which he knows very well.
To my nephews and nieces my blessing I give
And entreat they will mind and learn how to live.
My thanks to the public I cannot express;
Their goodness to me has been quite to excess,
My feelings are many but words are too few
To tell how it pains me to bid them Adieu.

[27] A small colored disk of flour mixed with gum or gelatine which, when moistened, was used to seal letters, attach papers, or take the impression of a stamped seal.

[28] The bell of St. Anne's, rung to announce Faris's death.

Reflections on William Faris's Diary

W E   D O   N O T   K N O W   W H Y William Faris kept his diary. There is
no suggestion in the prose that he expected anyone else to be reading it. On
the other hand, Faris made no effort to encrypt his observations so that if he
did not keep the diary hidden, anyone picking it up could read its contents.
That may be one reason why the diary is in many ways both highly personal
and almost completely impersonal. Its entries are Faris's notations about the
events of *his* day, which occasionally — but not often — encompass his feelings about the things that have happened. The comings and goings of other
members of the family are included — as are the illnesses that befall them —
but judgments are rarely recorded, just the occurrences themselves. It is
telling, for example, that Faris always notes the day of his birth — but never
makes reference to the birth day of anyone else in the household. Moreover, the
diary reveals almost nothing of the domestic routine of the family and only
rarely even for Faris himself. Mrs. Faris began making currant jelly on 21 June
1803 and Faris thought an unusual noise on 30 May 1798 might have been
the girls dropping the dinner they were bringing up from the kitchen, but
little else of daily life that does not take place in the garden is captured in the
pages of the diary. Family members generally appear when they help Faris in
the garden, fall ill, travel, or quarrel.

The diary did serve some practical purposes. Its foremost function may
simply have been to record, for the consummate gardener that Faris was, the
daily weather, the one constant in virtually every entry and often the only subject. Nothing in the diary suggests that Faris referred back to his previous
notations for a sense of continuity or change in weather patterns, but his
entries do reveal that he was closely attuned to variations in the weather, aware

of its being particularly hot or cold, unseasonably warm or chilly, excessively dry or unusually wet. In a closely related purpose, the diary served as a garden journal — the most extensive entries occurred during the months when Faris was busiest in his garden and recorded, often in minute detail, the activities of everyone engaged that day in garden chores. Comments scattered throughout the diary definitely indicate that Faris referred back to it to keep track of what he planted, when he planted it, and from whom he obtained the plant material or seeds. He used his notes to determine how long it took seeds to germinate or seedlings to start bearing flowers or fruit. When he transplanted seedlings or planted roots or bulbs, Faris marked each different specimen with a numbered stick and listed the plants and the accompanying number in the diary.

Faris also used the diary to record milestones — births, marriages, deaths, journeys — in the lives of his acquaintances. It might at first appear that he merely copied into the diary items that he read in the *Maryland Gazette,* but a careful comparison of the two sources clearly demonstrates that this was *not* the case, as there was very little overlap between the two. The diary contains many more entries of this type than found space in the *Gazette* while omitting quite a number printed in the paper. Moreover, the *Gazette* appeared only once a week, on a Thursday, but Faris's recordings occur on every day of the week. Faris was writing down not what he read in the newspaper but what he learned by word of mouth as he did his marketing, talked to friends he met while walking to and from the market house or other shops, or entertained guests or tavern customers in his own home. The marriages of which he took note were generally those of people with whom he had some personal connection: friends of his children or the children of his friends, his customers, his neighbors, his kin. Births and deaths followed a similar pattern. While these were usually discrete entries, Faris sometimes referred to new mothers by their maiden name as well as their married name, and occasionally took note of births that occurred less than nine months after his notation of the marriage.

Not only do we not know why Faris kept a diary, we also do not know why he decided to begin his diary on the first of January in 1792. It does seem clear that the diary transcribed here represents everything that Faris wrote[1] in the way of a journal. Faris's cash book of the same period — January 1792 — contained occasional entries similar to those that appear in the early journal, but these notes quickly disappear from the cash book. At the same time, it took Faris until the end of November 1792 to settle on the format that he used almost without exception for the next twelve years: the year at the top of each page, the month given for the first entry on each page, the day of the week and day of the month for each individual entry. Had there been earlier volumes, there would have been no irregularity of form over the first year that we have

---

[1] There are some unexplained gaps in the later years that may indicate lost pages.

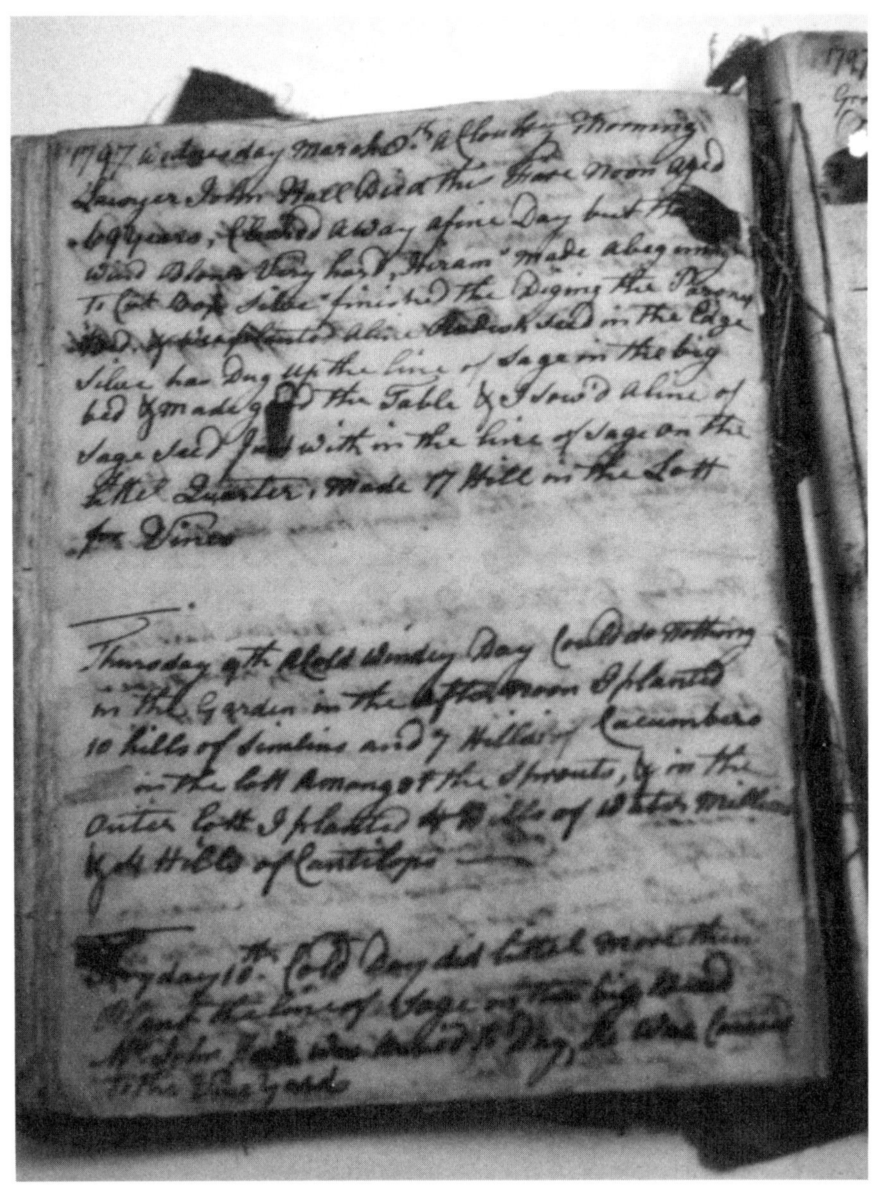

17 ⚘ Diary Page

On this page, Faris recorded his gardening successes and failures.

of the diary. Faris had not been keeping a journal for years — for whatever reason, he began on 1 January 1792. The diary opens with three brief daily notations of the weather; the first substantive entry, on January 4th, concerns the arrival home of a friend's son with news of acquaintances who were part of the forces sent west to fight Indians. If any unusual circumstances in Faris's life at the time prompted his decision to keep a journal, there is no trace of them in the diary itself. Throughout the years that he kept his diary, Faris does show a great interest in the other elderly members of the Annapolis community, recording conversations in which birth dates and ages are exchanged among the "long-livers." A sense that by age sixty-three he had already lived a full life may have prompted Faris to begin the diary, but that would seem more reason to start on his birthday than on 1 January — and in 1792 he fails to note the occasion of his birth, August 16th passing like any other day.

The diary could rightly be called an *Annapolis* diary, as very little of the outside world intrudes, and usually only with a local connection. Disturbances in western Maryland, particularly in connection with the Whiskey Rebellion in Pennsylvania, required that Annapolis contribute troops to the state's share of the effort to counter the insurgencies. Raids on American shipping by Barbary Coast pirates posed a danger for Faris's son, St. John, when sailing to the Mediterranean. The yellow fever epidemics that began with the 1793 outbreak in Philadelphia could threaten the lives of Annapolitans if the infection spread southward. With the exception of a brief mention of the Citizen Genêt affair and of an embargo placed on overseas shipping in March 1794, the French Revolution passed without comment. The death of George Washington and the election of Thomas Jefferson were the only national events of which Faris took notice. His world was in Annapolis, and a relatively small portion of the city at that: from the dock up Church Street, around Church Circle, and up West Street to the city gate, except for the occasional excursion — fish feast, sailing in the harbor, or trip to Baltimore — and the odd visit to Mr. Stier's garden at Strawberry Hill or a walk down Northeast Street (now Maryland Avenue) to see the fence being built at Edward Lloyd's. Yet, although Faris's physical world appears circumscribed, the scope of his personal world was quite large. For example, the 1798 federal direct tax record lists about ninety households in Annapolis and nearby Middleneck Hundred — and members of eighty of them appear in the diary. Faris also enjoyed a wide circle of acquaintances in Baltimore, particularly in the maritime community of Fells Point, with the ship captains and Bay pilots frequently calling upon him as they made their way up and down the Chesapeake.

The diary entries offer a revealing portrait of family life in the Faris household. The tensions that existed between Faris and his children erupted periodically in arguments and silences, punctuated by dramatic departures. Charles and Hyram both left home more than once after disputes with their father, at least one of which apparently originated in an argument between the two in which their father intervened. Although Faris appears to have been on much better terms with his daughters, particularly after first Ann and then Abigail married, there are hints of discord there as well: In February 1798 Faris wrote that "Madam & Miss have not spoken to me" and in October 1799 that Abee had gone off to her brother Charles's home to complain about her father. The next month found Faris without a plate for his broth at dinner; while Faris gave no indication of who failed to provide the plate, there is no doubt but that he felt aggrieved and mistreated.

While his children may at times have been a source of anxiety or anger for Faris, they also provided the household with much of its energy and sociability. The early years of the diary are filled with accounts of balls, races, militia assemblies, sailing excursions, gatherings of friends for tea or dancing, and other convivial group activities. In the later years, after the marriages of Ann and Abigail and the deaths of their siblings, life in the Faris household became much quieter. Before 1800, Faris routinely wrote about the fall racing season, recording the owners of the winning horses and the purses they collected. But no mention of the races occurs after Charles died. William may either have gone to the races with Charles or written his diary entries on the basis of Charles's account of the days' events. In the same way, the July 4th celebrations and the accounts of the militia musters vanish from the pages of the diary. Friends still called to visit, but larger gatherings became much rarer and generally were associated with visits by the couple's daughters and their families. One senses that William and Priscilla Faris keenly anticipated and enjoyed the regular exchange of visits with the Baltimore households and particularly the extended stays of their grandchildren. Two of the most poignant moments in the diary — brief but nonetheless telling — are Faris's accounts of the death of granddaughter Priscilla Ann at the age of fourteen months in July 1798 and Marriah's tearful departure for Baltimore after a stay of many months with her grandparents.

Faris filled the pages of the diary with information about some aspects of his life (gardening, in particular) but maintained almost complete silence on others. He served as a vestryman of St. Anne's Church from 1779 to 1783 and as churchwarden from April 1783 to April 1784. Yet the diary makes no mention of Faris's religious practices. He occasionally noted that the Masons processed to church (that is, marched to church in a procession) as part of their annual celebration on December 27 of the feast day of St. John the Evangelist, but not that he was part of the procession. On the other hand, Sunday was definitely a day of rest — with very rare exceptions, usually involving the activities of others, the Sunday entry contained only an account of the day's weather. When Faris does explicitly mention religion, it is not his own Episcopalian faith. In October 1792, he listened to "the best preacher" he had ever heard, Duncan McLane, a Universalist who gave several public addresses in the State House. A birthright Quaker (although not himself a member of a meeting), Faris maintained ties to the Society of Friends through local Quakers, particularly the Cowman and Hopkins families, received traveling Friends as visitors in his home, and attended their public lectures. Hyram appears to have been a Methodist, as his father recorded several visits he made to the Methodist chapel on the Severn River and attendance one year at the annual meeting on Kent Island. On some of his trips, other members of the Faris family accompanied Hyram, and the Pitts became members of the Methodist church in Baltimore. On one occasion, Mrs. Faris and "the girls" went to hear a Mr. Lyell preach, probably at the Methodist church nearby on the grounds of the State House.

Nor does the diary indicate any regular observance of religious holidays.

The 25th of December passes without notice, with the single exception of 1803, when Nancy sent some mince pies and mince meat as well as confections for her daughter Rebecca Maria, who was living with her grandparents — gifts possibly associated with the observance of Christmas. The account book does record a "Christmas box," or cash gift, given to apprentice William McParlin on the first Christmas that he spent in the Faris household. And Charles, during one of the periods that he lived apart from his parents, had a twelfth night party at his home. The holidays that did receive frequent mention were secular and patriotic. Nancy attended a birthday ball in honor of George Washington; the militia paraded on May Day with patriotic songs; and in the early years the fourth of July witnessed parading, feasting, and a ball.

Faris, who may have had little or no formal schooling of his own, obviously valued education for his children, sending both his sons and daughters to school for tuition in the standard grammar school curriculum and engaging private instruction for other subjects. It is worth noting, therefore, that the only references to St. John's College occur in connection with events taking place on the college grounds that were unrelated to the institution itself or in accounts of deaths of St. John's students or faculty. His own sons were too old when the college first began accepting students for their attendance to be a practical step, and his daughters, of course, were not eligible to attend. A number of Faris's acquaintances, who appear in the diary, taught at the college, and others whom he mentions, such as the Courtenay boys who were rumored to have drowned, attended St. John's — but their college connection never warranted his attention, nor did any aspect of the college's affairs.

Historians of the colonial and antebellum period have considered preparation of medicines and treatment of the ill one of the responsibilities of the mistress of the household. Faris's diary reveals, however, that at least in his household, it was the master who attended to the sick. A number of physicians practiced in Annapolis around the turn of the century and Faris regularly consulted several of them — primarily James Murray and his two partners, first John T. Shaaff and later Reverdy Ghiselin. He administered the medicines or other treatments recommended by the doctors, but often he diagnosed and treated family members on his own, particularly for the recurrent fever and ague of malaria. In several instances, he also inoculated individuals against smallpox. The remedies imposed on the ailing members of the Faris household often sound worse than the illness itself, but they conformed to the theories of disease and bodily disorder of the time. For the worst scourge, yellow fever, there was no understanding of the cause of the illness and no effective method of treatment or even of prevention through sanitary measures. The best protection was a strong constitution or, in the case of infectious diseases, immunity acquired through mild exposure to the same or a related pathogen. Throughout his diary, Faris displays a keen interest in scientific matters, and his familial practice of medicine undoubtedly stemmed from that interest. He was not averse to second-guessing the physician or to trying out his own remedies.

One might speculate as to whether Faris would have known Benjamin Franklin while he lived in Philadelphia. The question arises because it is not far-fetched to think of Faris as Annapolis's Franklin (leaving aside Franklin's role as a political figure). Faris was always experimenting, always interested in the newest inventions or ideas, whether lead pencils, pianofortes, inflammable air, silk reels, a physiognotrace, or an electrifying machine. Faris owned navigator's instruments and charts; they might originally have been the property of St. John, but his father kept them. He possessed a library of more than one hundred volumes, adding to his collection as estate sales made new titles available. It is regrettable that the appraisers of his estate did not take the time to itemize his books, thus depriving us of additional evidence of the range of Faris's interests. When Faris's property was offered for sale after his death, the account of purchases listed only four titles: seven volumes of *The Spectator*, five volumes of Cato's *Letters*, five volumes of Sterne's works, and four volumes of Goldsmith's — politics and literature. Certainly there would have been books on gardening and agriculture, perhaps Faris's own copy of the *Dictionary of Arts*

18 ⚘ Physiognotrace

It did not take Faris long to try his hand at this new apparatus, invented by John Isaac Hawkins in 1802. The device was found among Faris's possessions when he died in 1804. Silhouettes could be cut by placing the sitter's cheek on the side and using the apparatus to trace the profile. Silhouettes were an inexpensive form of portraiture that met with great success through to the mid-nineteenth century. More experienced hands could even create them with the use of scissors. Faris himself may have made the silhouette of his wife (Figure 11 on page 13).

and Sciences (a massive, multi-volume tome), maybe some religious writings, and more of the Roman and Greek classics, almost surely in translation. Faris took great pains to provide a multi-faceted education for his children, sending all of them to school and providing French and shorthand lessons. There is no way to know what kind of formal schooling Faris himself might have had. His master had an obligation to supply some education during Faris's apprentice-ship, but it is probable that, like Franklin, he acquired much of his knowledge on his own.

The journal entries that describe the movements of the Faris household and their friends and relatives attest to a remarkable degree of mobility that encompassed both young and old, male and female, white and black. Journeys to Baltimore, Philadelphia, and the Eastern Shore are commonplace, under-taken by the elderly, unmarried young women, and enslaved children, as well as able-bodied adult males, and carried out by packet, stage, or carriage, or on horseback or foot. Within the Faris household, Charles was the most frequent traveler. He went back and forth to Baltimore on a regular basis, often to escort other family members; made a trip of nearly two weeks as far north as Harford County, for reasons which his father did not record; and once visited the "federal city" of Washington — an early tourist of the nation's capital. Hyram was the walker of the family, traveling on foot to Prince George's County to visit his mother's kinsman, Thomas Woodward; at least once to Baltimore, a journey of more than thirty miles that required crossing the Severn, Magothy, and Patapsco rivers by ferry; and on several visits to the Severn chapel. Charles was the more likely to travel by horse, although his sis-ters also visited their Woodward relatives and other friends on horseback. The senior Farises traveled to Baltimore by stage and packet. It is a testimony to the deplorable conditions of road travel that they generally elected to go by packet boat even during the winter months, resorting to the stage mainly when the packet was not operating because of ice or unfavorable winds. Faris owned no carriage of his own, but occasionally a friend sent a carriage for him (see 11 June 1797 entry) or came by carriage to collect one of his daughters for a visit or to take them to the evening's ball.

On 29 January 1803 the Farises sent Charity, a young slave girl, to Baltimore by herself on the stage to join the Kerr household as a maid for Abigail. Charity probably belonged to Faris, although she was not listed among his possessions when he died; she may have become part of the Kerr household after this date. That she traveled independently was not unusual — slaves had considerable mobility as conveyers of goods and messages (Faris recounted elsewhere, for example, the dispatch of a slave to fetch a doctor when a shooting occurred). What is surprising are the frequent occasions when young white women traveled on their own (generally as twosomes, but often alone) or escorted by men who were unrelated to them. On one of her visits to the Cowman family, Nancy Faris was accompanied by George Johnson, a neighbor and friend about five years her senior. In 1796, Charles escorted seventeen-year-old Nancy Ashmead, one of his sisters' good friends, back from Baltimore. Nancy Ashmead traveled frequently, including trips to Philadelphia, on one of which she was accompanied by Major John Davidson, another Faris neighbor and friend. Other friends of the Faris girls, such as Polly, Becky, and Betsy Gassaway or Fanny and Sally Whetcroft, traveled by themselves to Baltimore and to the Eastern Shore.

During the years covered by the diary, all the members of the Faris family journeyed regularly to Baltimore, generally staying in Fells' Point. They appear to have been visiting friends in the maritime community concentrated in that part of the city (and received frequent visits in Annapolis from the same friends). St. John, not long after his father started keeping his journal,

19 ↞ Plan of the Town of Baltimore and its Environs, 1792

Faris's trips to Baltimore usually took him to Fell's Point (shown in the center), home of the city's ship captains and of Faris's daughters, Ann and Abigail, after their marriages.

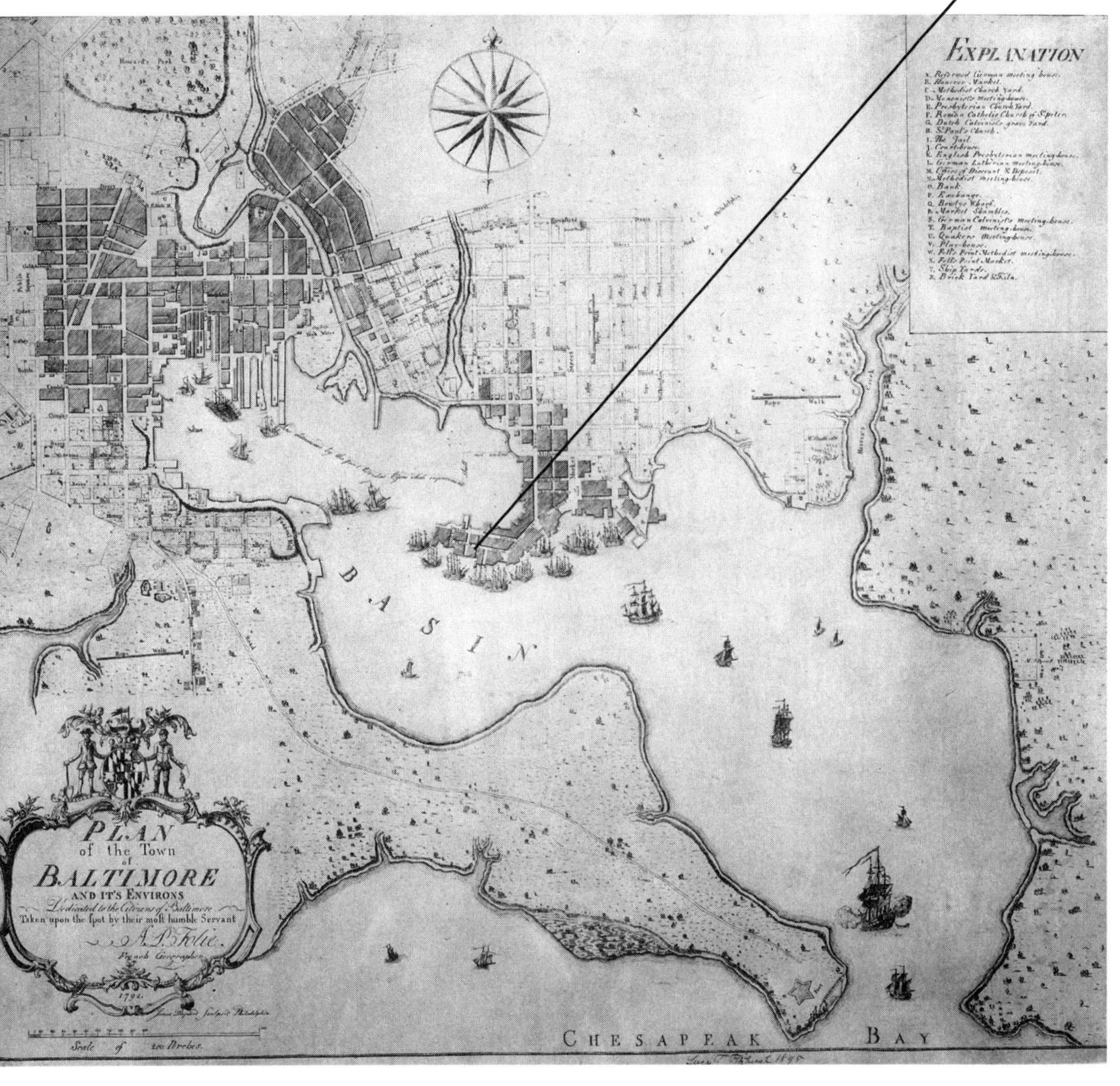

obtained a position as a mate on the snow *Commerce* and most likely had been at sea with a lesser rank for some time before that. Faris himself had many good friends among the ship captains who visited Annapolis, most of whom lived in Baltimore. Whether his acquaintances developed after St. John went to sea, or his father's friends influenced St. John's choice of career, we do not know. Faris's home, which was also his tavern, was not located on the waterfront, where it would have been easily accessible to anyone coming off a ship in the harbor — but perhaps the captains preferred a more remote place to drink and dine where they might be less likely to have their crew as tavern companions. One of Faris's neighbors in the 1760s and 1770s was Captain John Pitt (whose son William would eventually marry Faris's daughter Ann), and it may have been through Pitt that Faris became a part of the maritime milieu.

20 ☞ *Sea Captains Carousing in Surinam*

William Faris entertained ship captains throughout his life in Annapolis, both as customers in his tavern and as friends in his home. This scene, although painted in South America in mid-century, provides an idea of what a rowdy group of drunken mariners could look like once the "punch" started flowing.

The diary reveals nothing directly of Faris as a tavern keeper and it not clear how actively he pursued this aspect of his business during the last years of his life. Faris recorded payments in his cash book for a "glass" at 3/9 each, but never troubled to include the names of his customers with these entries. No other tavern related charges appear there, but could have been kept in a different ledger. The visitors whom Faris did mention were personal friends. The diary does take great note, however, of the political world that existed within a block or two of Faris's home. Faris recorded the election or installation of every governor who serving during the diary years, entered the names of men appointed to the executive council and other posts, and followed local elections for corporation offices and the legislature. We also learn from the diary when the general court met and when the petit jury ended its deliberations. Other than the Baltimoreans, the largest group of non-residents to appear in the pages of the diary consists of men who served in the legislature, sat on the bench, or held appointive state office. We can safely surmise that these men probably received mention because Faris knew them personally — most likely as patrons of his tavern during their attendance at sessions of the legislature or court. Whether or not he ever served in public office himself, Faris evidently had a strong interest in the political life of his community.

Historians take note of gardening as a serious avocation of the Chesapeake's planter elite, arguing that the gentry used their demonstration of power over nature to justify their exercise of political power. Faris's diary reveals that men of the middling (like himself) and lower sort (to use the contemporary term) also took gardening to be a serious activity, demonstrating their own control over nature. No landscape could have been crafted more carefully than the intensive garden that Faris maintained on his small Annapolis lot — the West Street plot exhibited as much order as the terraced gardens of Charles Carroll and William Paca. Faris, who never exercised political power, planned his landscape to allow room for the vegetables and fruits his family consumed and the ornamental flowers that gave him such delight.[2] Moreover, as the diary demonstrates, serious gardeners in late eighteenth-century Annapolis included more than just elite men, not only middling artisans but older married women, young single girls, free blacks, and slaves all participated. Faris traded not only vegetable seeds (from the kitchen gardens traditionally assigned as a woman's sphere) with women and girls, but also ornamental flowers, shrubs, trees, even silkworms. Smith Price exchanged plants with Faris, while Jack Wheeler reported on frost damage to his beans. Old William, a slave belonging to Richard Ridgely, who assisted Faris in the last years of the diary, scoured the nearby woods for holly trees that he dug up and brought to Faris to be added to the garden. Faris's gardening colleagues included fifty white men, but he also shared plants and seeds with twelve married women, five single girls, and five black men and women, at least two of whom were slaves.

The diary does not suggest that Faris viewed black Annapolitans primarily through the prism of race (although there is also no suggestion that he saw any reason to question one person's holding another in bondage). A number of entries complain of the feckless behavior, as Faris saw it, of the blacks (whether free or enslaved[3]) whom he employed to assist in his garden, but nowhere does he suggest an association between their actions and their race. Had his gardeners been white and exhibited the same behavior, the reactions expressed in

---

[2] Faris's manipulation of nature extended beyond his careful plantings to more scientific aspects of the garden's life, whether the use of procedures like inoculation, grafting, and distilling, or experimentation with different techniques for planting peas or purifying beeswax.

[3] The slaves might have been hired out by their masters or allowed to hire their own time.

the diary would almost certainly have been exactly the same. One would never know from the diary that Smith Price, who operated the stage and exchanged plants with Faris, or John Wheeler, another neighbor with whom he exchanged garden news, were free black men. They pass through the pages of the diary on the same terms as their white Annapolis neighbors. Old William, who dug up holly trees in the wild and brought them to Faris for his garden and who carted dung from Richard Ridgely's stable, could be white except for the lack of a surname. Faris reacts to the murder of a young black girl by the baker's assistant with the same degree of dismay that he would have shown had she been white, to judge from other entries. At the same time, an alarm of some sort prompted the town authorities to search the homes of the city's black residents looking for weapons, but no such search was ever made of white households. Faris reports several incidents of brutality by whites toward blacks, even murder, that would have resulted in criminal charges had the victims also been white. The diary generally portrays racial inequalities in the macrocosm of the city and shared humanity in the microcosm of Faris's own household.

The extensive kinship ties that bound together the Chesapeake gentry remain one of the salient features of the eighteenth-century. For example, the builders of the dozen most impressive mid-century Georgian mansions in Annapolis had multiple connections to one another by birth and marriage. Yet such a density of linkages did not result in an insular and exclusive society. William Faris himself had no claim to membership in that group, whether by birth or marriage, but nevertheless was still a participant, having friendships with men like William Fitzhugh, Richard Sprigg, Alexander Contee Hanson, Richard Harwood, William Paca, Thomas Jennings, and others. The family never penetrated the highest stratum — the Lloyds, Ridouts, Carrolls, Ogles, and others — on a social level, but in a small town no one remained isolated from the local community. Social strata existed, but the boundaries were permeable to varying degrees in different contexts. Whether as a craftsman repairing a piece of silver or winding a clock, a tavern keeper offering a drink, a gardener trading seeds, a parishioner serving on the vestry, or a client seeking legal help, Faris knew everyone in Annapolis, from the governor to a neighbor's slave.

We read his writings, then, because they provide a door into a different world. We enter the eighteenth century through the pages of the diary, worrying about the danger of a sparking chimney or the damage caused by a severe wind, experiencing the anxiety generated by an epidemic of yellow fever or the pain of a child's death, delighting in the company of friends for an evening of dancing or simply in the pleasure of "a fine day."

Clockmaker and Silversmith

"WILLIAM FARRIS, Maker, Annapolis — such is the inscription on the old face of an old clock standing in an old hall in old Annapolis. And pray who was William Farris? — the maker of this stately time-piece that in measured cadence still records the creeping hours, marking the day of the month and showing the phases of the moon by the appearance and disappearance of that ever rubicund and amiable countenance which, in obedience to the mysterious mechanism, peers over and dodges behind the dial-plate with lunar punctuality. He must needs have been an oddity."[1] This excerpt, written in 1879 by Francis Blackwell Mayer, is the first printed reference to the versatile clockmaker who would craft these timepieces during Annapolis's "golden age." A half-century later, in 1930, J. Hall Pleasants and Howard Sill, in their monumental work on Maryland silversmiths, wrote: "The most picturesque figure among eighteenth-century Maryland silversmiths is William Faris of Annapolis. Silversmith, watchmaker, clock maker, designer, portrait painter, cabinetmaker, tulip grower, tavern keeper, dentist, diarist and gossip, he arrests and deserves our attention."[2]

No work on William Faris would be complete without taking a close look at that for which he is best known today: his craft. Although Faris's early period in Philadelphia does not shed much light on his activities and development in the crafts, there exists a fairly large body of information for him in this regard once he reached Annapolis in the middle of the eighteenth century. We do not know exactly when or how Faris first arrived in Annapolis, but it must have been sometime in 1756 or early 1757, for his first advertisement

---

[1] "Old Maryland Manners," *Scribner's Monthly*, 12 (January 1879), 315–16.

[2] J. Hall Pleasants and Howard Sill, *Maryland Silversmiths: 1715–1830* (Baltimore: privately printed, 1930), 257.

appears in the *Maryland Gazette* on 17 March 1757. In this notice Faris refers to himself as a watchmaker who also makes clocks.

WILLIAM FARIS,

WATCH-MAKER, *from* PHILADELPHIA,

At his Shop near the Church, next Door to Mr. Wallace's, in Church-Street, ANNAPOLIS,

CLEANS and REPAIRS all Sorts of WATCHES and CLOCKS, as well and neat as can be done in any Part of *America:* And takes the fame Prices for his Work as are taken in *Philadelphia.*

He alfo makes CLOCKS, either to Repeat or not, or to go either Eight Days or Thirty, as the Purchafer fhall fancy, as good as can be made in *London,* and at reafonable Prices. And all Gentlemen who fhall be pleafed to employ him, may depend on having their Work done with all poffible Difpatch, by *Their humble Servant,*
WILLIAM FARIS.

21 ☛ *Maryland Gazette*
17 March 1757

To understand the work of William Faris we must look closely at his advertisements, for it is through them that we learn of his activities and to what degree either he or his apprentices and journeymen were responsible for the products coming out of his shop. We have developed a very romanticized notion of colonial craftsmen's lives. Many of us envision the colonial silversmith working alone in his shop, melting the material, forging and casting the object, chasing and engraving it according to his fancy. In reality, it is more likely that several artisans played a part in the creation of an object according to the demands of a customer. The finished object was then marked with the initials or name of the shop master, who may not have actually taken part in the creation of the piece.[3]

When analyzing Faris's work, we need to look at the evolution of the products that came out of his shop. In 1757, when he advertised as a watchmaker, we infer that his training was in this field. Although we have found no apprenticeship records for Faris in Philadelphia, information about his early life with his mother provides some clues to his training. As Faris was born in 1728 and reportedly came to the colonies with his mother Abigail[4] as a six-month-old infant and settled in Philadelphia, she must have placed him in the hands of a master craftsman to learn a particular trade. Tradition states that the elder Faris was a London clockmaker, so perhaps that was the obvious choice for young William. Being apprenticed to a clockmaker or a silversmith was not a simple process, however, as these were considered among the most elite of the crafts. As a result, an apprenticeship was expensive for the boy's parents or guardians, as they had to pay the master to take on the young boy as an

---

3 Jennifer Goldsborough, *Silver in Maryland* (Baltimore: Maryland Historical Society, 1983), 4.

4 See Figure 11 on page 13, a portrait of Abigail Faris, which has previously been attributed to William Faris, c.1750, through an entry in the Pitt family Bible. Recently some scholars have questioned this attribution, finding the portrait to be in the manner of Gustavus Hesselius (1682–1755) of Philadelphia. The portrait is virtually identical to that of Hesselius's wife Lydia, painted by the artist c. 1740 (Figure 10 in *Gustavus Hesselius, Face Painter to the Middle Colonies,* by Roland E. Fleischer, 68). Also see Carolyn Weekley, "Portrait Painting in Eighteenth-Century Annapolis," *The Magazine Antiques,* CXI (February 1977), 347.

apprentice.[5] Nevertheless, because Faris's first advertisements related to clock and watch making, we can safely assume that he was trained in these fields. Apprenticeships were usually served for a seven-year term (for a privately-arranged apprenticeship), beginning when the boy was fourteen years old and ending at his coming of age at twenty-one; Faris would have reached his majority in 1749.

The training of apprentices benefited the master craftsmen, who were able to produce more of their product and generate greater revenues through this "free" labor. The apprentice began his tenure by performing simple tasks and acquiring more skills throughout the period of training until he himself was adept in the "art and mystery" of the trade. Apprentices were treated as members of the master's family — fed, clothed, disciplined, and nurtured as any child would be in that family. When the apprentice had reached the age to be released, his master provided him with a suit of clothes and with some tools to begin his own trade.[6] At this stage, the young trainee could become a journeyman and be paid by the piece wherever he could find work. Because Faris probably did not come to Annapolis until sometime in 1756, there is a gap of seven years in which he most likely worked as a journeyman in the shop either of his former master or of another of the many clockmakers and tradesmen in the Philadelphia area.

Although no information about Faris's childhood in Philadelphia has come to light, we do know that his widowed mother married twice after arriving in Philadelphia. Her marriages may have helped to establish William financially as he not only purchased property in Philadelphia as a twenty-one year old but also owned pieces of silver (see Figure 22) and china[7] that would have been very unlikely for a recently-trained apprentice to acquire while establishing himself in his craft.[8] Scattered fragmentary evidence suggests some Philadelphia masters to whom Faris might have been apprenticed. In 1755 Faris mortgaged his Spring Garden property to merchant Robert Greenway for £108.50.0;[9] clockmaker Isaac Stretch, a member of the Philadelphia clock-making family, witnessed the mortgage. An unsubstantiated tradition holds that Faris was associated with Henry Flower, another successful Philadelphia

22 ☞ *This was William Faris's personal tankard, probably acquired when he lived in Philadelphia. We do not know how Faris could afford such an expensive item as a journeyman or perhaps while still an apprentice. Possibly he received it in trade for other services in a master's shop, or his mother may have owned it and passed it on to him. Note that the shape of this tankard is almost identical to the shop drawing of a tankard in Faris's design book (Fig. SD10 on page 439). Tankards can be identified regionally, and this Philadelphia example characteristically echoes those being produced in London in the middle of the eighteenth century. This tankard was cherished by six generations of one family.*

---

5 See Catherine B. Hollan, "Baltimore Apprenticeships in Silversmithing and Its Related Branches," in Goldsborough, *Silver in Maryland*, 40.

6 Hollan, 38.

7 According to Charles Faris Pitt's memorandum, the family had two china "fluted" bowls that "belonged to my Grand Father Wm Faris & [were] bought by him the day he became of age."

8 Correspondence from Carl M. Williams to Lockwood Barr, 1940–41, Filing Case A, Maryland Historical Society [hereinafter MHS].

9 This mortgage may have financed Faris's move to Annapolis.

clockmaker and silversmith. Although there is no concrete evidence of their relationship, Flower is reported to have witnessed legal papers for Faris in 1747,[10] before William was of age, suggesting that Faris might have been his apprentice. Furthermore, one of Faris's musical clocks is almost identical to one manufactured by Flower, a similarity to be expected if Faris trained under Flower.

As stated earlier, we do not know the reason that Faris left Philadelphia and moved to Annapolis. One would think that Philadelphia, the largest city in British North America, would have provided abundant patronage for a talented craftsman even in a very competitive market. Perhaps moving to Annapolis afforded him a chance to establish himself as a newcomer with the decided advantage of introducing new ideas and perhaps new techniques from a larger metropolitan area.

Faris continued to advertise sporadically in the *Maryland Gazette*, published in Annapolis. We hear from him again on 13 April 1758:

> SOME Time ago, a plain Silver WATCH, which wanted a Chrystal, was left at my Shop in *Annapolis*, by an Officer of the Army, who told me it was delivered to him by a Gentleman in *Baltimore* County, whose Name he could not then recollect; nor afterwards, when I apply'd to him on that Account. The Gentleman who brought me the Watch being now gone to the Northward, and the Owner unknown to me, I hereby give Notice, that he may have it again, on convincing me of his Property, paying the Charge of Repairing, and for this Advertisement, from
>
> WILLIAM FARIS

We do not know if this watch was ever claimed, but the notice does show that Faris was engaged in watch making rather consistently from the beginning of his time in Annapolis.

We find Faris once again in the *Gazette's* issue of 8 November 1759 informing the public that he had moved his shop:

> WILLIAM FARIS, WATCH-MAKER, *from PHILADELPHIA*, HAS Removed from *Church Street*, to the House late in the Occupation of Andrew Buchanan, the Sign of the CROWN and DIAL, opposite Mr. *Creagh's*; where he continues to Repair and Clean WATCHES as neat and well as can be done in any Part of *America*, and at reasonable Prices.
>
> He has also procured a CLOCK-MAKER, who makes CLOCKS of all Sorts, which he will warrant to be good.
>
> *N.B.* He gives the best Prices for old Brass.

---

[10] Williams to Barr, 21 March 1940, MHS.

After three years in Annapolis, Faris continued to advertise his trade as a watch and clock maker. This notice also represents the first instance when Faris hired someone to help in his shop. He was at this point beginning to form a group of workers who would carry on the business of his establishment for the rest of his career. It is also noteworthy that he still refers to himself as from Philadelphia, rather than Annapolis.

It was not until 4 December 1760 that Faris's first notice appeared identifying silver as a product of his enterprise. In this instance the clockmaker stated:

> WILLIAM FARIS,
> WATCH and CLOCK-MAKER, at the Sign of the Crown and Dial, near the Church in ANNAPOLIS,
> Makes or Repairs Clocks and Watches as usual, in the best and cheapest Manner.
> He also, having procured an excellent Workman for that Purpose carries on the SILVERSMITH BUSINESS, Large, Small, or Chas'd Work, in the neatest, best and cheapest Manner.
> Also JEWELLING of any Kind.
> All Gentlemen or Ladies who shall be pleased to employ him, may depend on good Dispatch, from Their humble Servant,
> WILLIAM FARIS
> N.B. He gives the best Price for old Gold and Silver.

Although it was not unusual for clock makers to execute work in silver and vice versa, Faris hired someone to do the silver work for him. The clock and watch advertisements make it very clear that Faris executed the craft work himself, whereas Henry Flower, mentioned earlier, advertised himself as a clock, watchmaker, *and* silversmith.

Faris must have been doing exceedingly well in his business, for in the *Gazette* of 25 August 1763 we find him again advertising.

WILLIAM FARIS,
WATCH-MAKER, in ANNAPOLIS,
HAVING procured from *Philadelphia* a very compleat SILVERSMITH, who has served a regular Apprenticeship to that Business, hereby informs the Public, that he can now supply them, on the most reasonable Rates, with all Kinds of SILVER WORK, in the most genteel and fashionable Manner, and with the greatest Dispatch. He also carries on, as usual, the JEWELLER's Business, having an excellent Workman for that Purpose; and will give the best Prices for old Gold and Silver, and all Sorts of precious Stones.

23 ⚓ *Maryland Gazette* 25 August 1763

At this point Faris had at least three workmen in his shop: one clockmaker, two silversmiths, and perhaps one jeweler. Some of these tradesmen may have been doing more than one job, and one or another could have left between notices. But it is important when trying to identify the work of a craftsman to understand that it might, as noted earlier, involve the skills of more than one person. To state that a piece of silver with Faris's touch mark was made by him is not necessarily accurate, inasmuch as William Faris may never have actually hammered silver. He clearly was an entrepreneur and knowingly tells us that in his advertisements. He only ever referred to himself in his *Gazette* notices as a clock and watchmaker and never as a silversmith. This is not to say, however, that he was not intimately involved in the process, for it was his shop and the work executed in it had to be of a standard that measured up to his reputation.

The choice of a business location was no less important in the eighteenth century than it is today. Faris's 1760 *Gazette* notice announced not only his expansion into the silversmith's business but also his relocation to the first block of West Street. Faris's choice of West Street is not surprising, in that many of the town's craftsmen and innkeepers were already congregated at or near the land entrance to Maryland's capital, with the town gate on West Street just one block from Church Circle. His decision to move from Church Street to West Street was a financially astute one for it placed him directly in the path of anyone coming to Annapolis by land. Faris consistently demonstrated business acumen that served him well throughout his life and that gave him an advantageous position in the community.

Having placed himself in a suitable location, Faris did what many other craftsmen of the period found necessary: he opened a tavern. We learn this again from the *Gazette*, on 2 August 1764.

Once again Faris had diversified his economic activities. He now operated a tavern, but made sure that the public knew that all of the previous "branches" of his business were still ongoing.

In the 5 October 1769 issue of the *Gazette*, Faris advertised yet another facet of his establishment in his last craft-related notice:

WILLIAM FARIS,

CLOCK AND WATCHMAKER,

At the CROWN *and* DIAL, *near the Church,
in* West Street, ANNAPOLIS,

BEGS Leave to inform the Public, that he has engaged Two exceeding good Workmen, (one of whom has been a Finisher several Years to the celebrated Mr. *Allam*[11]) and carries on the above Businesses in all their various Branches.—The Gold, Silversmiths and Jewellers Businesses he still carries on in the neatest and best Manner.—He also executes

WILLIAM FARIS,

WATCH-MAKER,

HAVING supplied himself with the best of Liquors, hereby gives Notice to the Public, That he has now open'd TAVERN at his House opposite to where the late Mrs. M'Leod lived. Gentlemen Travellers and Others, favouring him with their Custom, will meet with the best Entertainment, and the kindest Usage, from
Their humble Servant,
WILLIAM FARIS.
N. B. The Watchmaker's, Jeweller's, and Silversmith's Businesses, are carried on in all their various Branches as usual.

24 ☞ *Maryland Gazette*
2 August 1764

---

[11] James Allam advertised in the *Gazette* on 2 February 1753 as a hatter living on West Street near Mrs. Elizabeth McLeod (who was also mentioned in Faris's tavern notice), but there is no information on his "finishing" nor do we know the extent of his trade. A "Mrs. Allam" frequented Faris's establishment in the 1770s to borrow small amounts of money; she most likely was the wife of James Allam. Faris/McParlin Daybook, MS 353, vol. 1, MHS.

any Orders he may be favoured with for Chair Work, having lately supplied himself with a good Workman, and now has for Sale, several Dozens of very neat black Walnut Chairs.—Those who shall please to honour him with their Commands, may depend on being faithfully served on reasonable Terms, and with the utmost Dispatch.—He continues to keep Tavern, having supplied himself with the best of Liquors, Hay and Oats, where Gentlemen will meet with polite Treatment and the best Accommodations for themselves and Horses, from

Their very humble Servant,

WILLIAM FARIS

N.B. He gives ready Money, and the best Prices for old Gold and Silver[12]

Faris had now incorporated chair making into his enterprise. By adding this new facet to his already very busy shop, he again endeavored to expand his overall business and establish himself as a successful Annapolis entrepreneur. We know of no surviving examples of these walnut chairs.

Before looking directly at Faris's craft work, two other aspects of his career deserve attention. The first concerns a series of notices that appeared in the *Maryland Journal and Baltimore Daily Advertiser* in 1792 and 1793.[13] A William Faris lived in Baltimore from 1792 through 1804, residing at 36 South Charles Street in 1799 and at 38 Calvert Street after 1800.[14] This Faris advertised as a gilder, picture frame maker, and looking glass manufacturer. The situation is further confused by the disappearance of the Baltimore Faris at the same time the Annapolis craftsman died. Nevertheless, the Annapolis Faris was in his late sixties at this time, making it unlikely that he would have engaged in new lines of business in Baltimore unrelated to the ones that he had already mastered. Moreover, as the diary fully accounts for Faris's time and whereabouts during the years that the Baltimore Faris was making picture frames and looking glasses, it is unlikely that they were the same person.[15]

---

[12] Faris placed this same notice in the *Gazette* through early 1770. It was his last series of advertisements regarding his trade.

[13] See *Maryland Journal and Baltimore Daily Advertiser* for 9 November 1792 and 17 September 1793 for advertisements by a William Faris in Baltimore.

[14] *Baltimore City Directories.*

[15] There exist two patents issued to a William Faris of Maryland in the 1790s, one for a carriage propeller (29 April 1797) and the other for a water elevator (17 May 1799). Although it is not clear which Faris was responsible for these inventions, they are consistent with the inquisitive and experimental nature of the Annapolis Faris. On the other hand, the patents were issued during the years covered by the diary, which contains no mention of them.

Secondly, we are fortunate that several account books have survived to shed light on Faris's business practices.[16] Two books covering the years 1790 through 1804 provide a glimpse into the daily life of the Faris household — what he and his family were consuming and wearing — as well as expenses related to the operation and maintenance of the household. Faris also kept a daybook, covering the years 1773 to 1784, which lists all of the patrons of his tavern as well as some shop work. At the back of the daybook Faris listed all of the people for whom he did clock work on a yearly basis, including winding and/or repairing their clocks. He also had an annual contract with the state of Maryland to wind and clean the clocks in the governor's residence.[17] Faris did work for some of Annapolis's most renowned citizens during the 1770s and 1780s. He maintained clocks at thirty shillings per year for William Paca, Samuel Chase, and Charles Carroll of Carrollton (all signers of the Declaration of Independence), as well as for General William Smallwood, Doctor James Murray, Doctor Upton Scott, and merchant James Dick of London Town. His

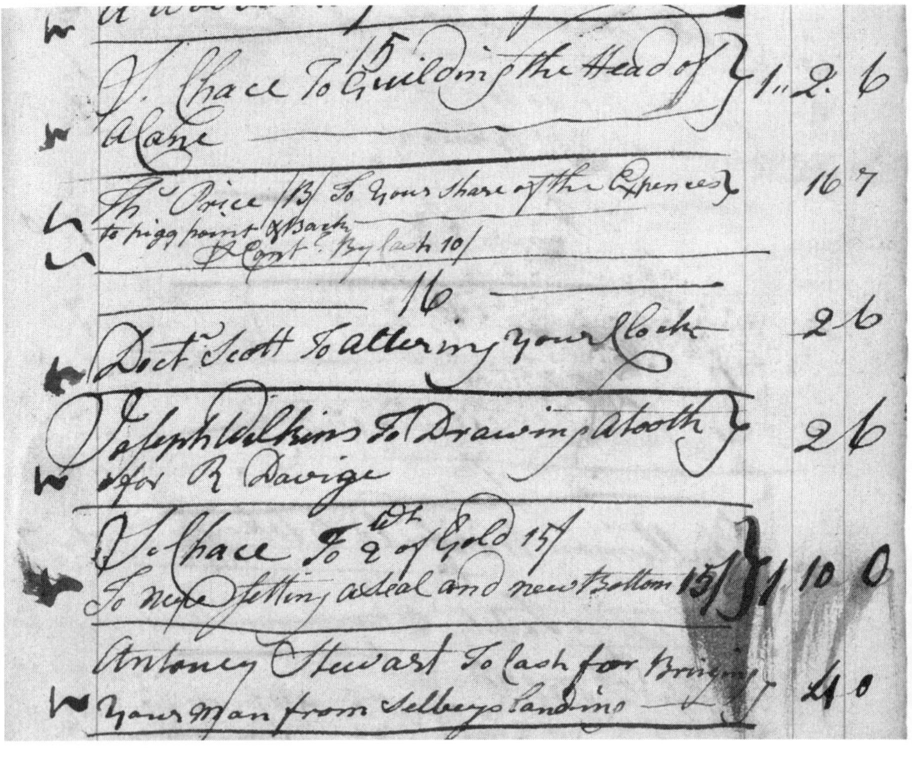

25 ☛ Entry from Faris's Daybook, 1774

This page records entries for a number of Faris's well-known customers, including Samuel Chase, Dr. Upton Scott, and Anthony Stewart, as well as an example of Faris's work as dentist, pulling a tooth for R. Davidge.

---

16 Faris-McParlin Account Books, "Daybook, 1773–1784," (vol. 1) and "Memorandum Book, 1790–1800," (vol. 2), MS 353, MHS; William Faris Account Book, 1800–1804, Maryland State Archives, MSA SC 345.

17 "Repairs of clocks at Government House, November 1788–November, 1791," William Faris Account Books and Diaries, MS 1104, MHS.

shop and tavern customers included political leaders, noted attorneys, and successful planters such as Charles Carroll the Barrister, James Tilghman III, Benjamin Ogle, and Edward Lloyd IV.[18]

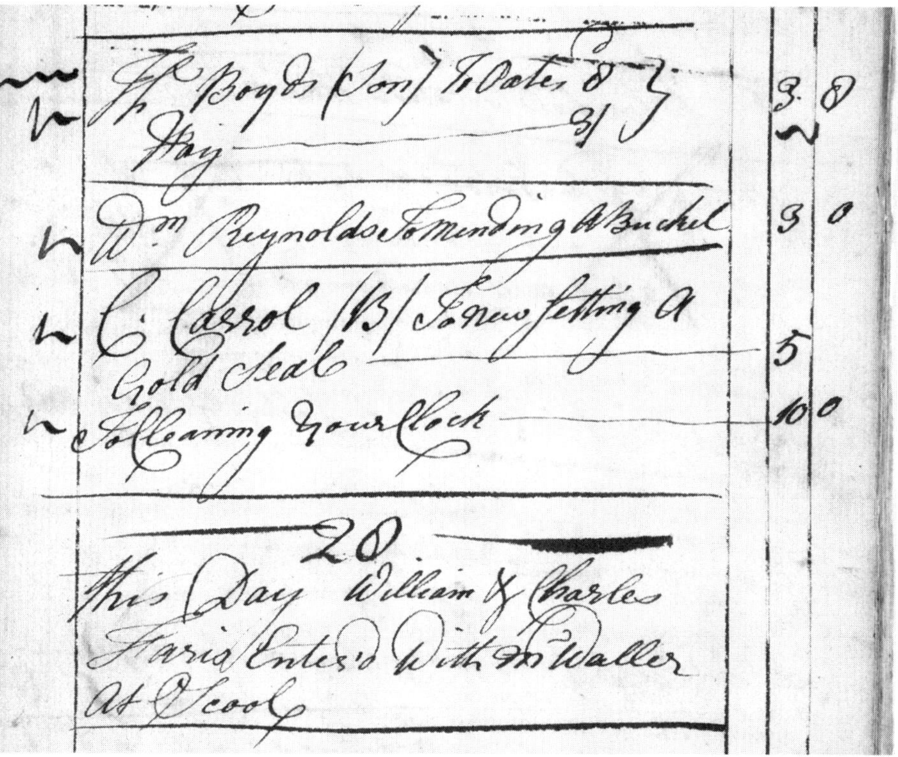

26 ☛ Entry from Daybook, October 1776

Faris charged Charles Carroll the Barrister ten shillings for cleaning his clock. See Figures 33 on page 53 and 34 on page 54 for photographs of the Barrister's clock.

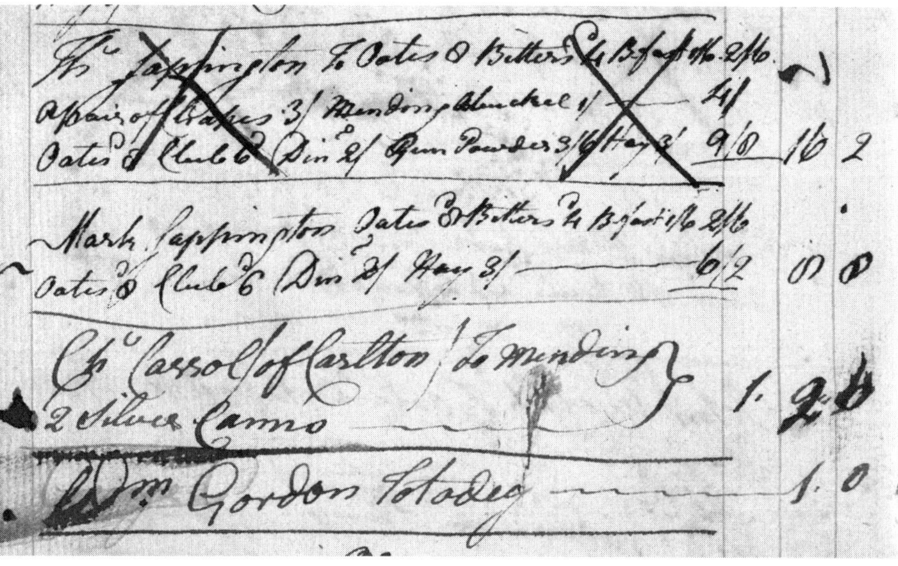

27 ☛ Entry from Daybook, December 1774

On December 24, 1774 Faris charged Charles Carroll of Carrollton £1.2.6 for mending two silver canns. Although members of the gentry engaged local craftsmen for repair work, they usually ordered their new silver items from England.

---

[18] Daybook.

28 ❧ Brass Dial of Tall
Case Clock, ca. 1760

*All of William Faris's
known clocks have brass
dials. The elaborate
engraving of his
name in the
tympanum boss points
to the masterly skill of
this craftsman.*

29 ❧ Brass Dial of Tall
Case Clock, ca. 1770

*This moon dial has the
same corner spandrels as
those found in Figures
28 and 30, the same
molds having cast these
parts for all three clocks.
Note the elaborate
engraving in the tym-
panum arch as well as
the accomplished ren-
dering of the
moon dial.*

30 ❧ Brass Dial of Tall
Case Clock, ca. 1760

*This dial is almost
identical to the one in
Figure 28, having the
same cast spandrels in
the tympanum arch as
well as on the corners of
the dial plate. These
pieces were cast from the
same mold. The only
difference lies in the
engraving of Faris's
name in the tympanum
boss, in this case with
block letters instead of
script.*

It is unlikely that all the clocks that
Faris wound and repaired were of his own
manufacture. Some may have been made
by other colonial clockmakers or perhaps
imported from London. People of means
in colonial Maryland were inclined to
purchase their wares from England, where
the best and latest fashions could be
found, and engaged local craftsmen primarily for repair work. Even when importation embargoes forced colonists to
patronize their local craft people, they
insisted that the objects continue to be
fashioned in the latest English taste.[19] In
fact, Faris earned much of the income
recorded in his account books from repairs
and from making small objects such as
buttons, thimbles, watch glasses, and
keys.[20]

Because Faris considered himself primarily a clock maker, we will begin
examining his craft work with a discus-
sion of clock making in colonial America.
The tall case clock was one of the most
expensive individual items that a person
could buy for his home in the eighteenth
century. The manufacture of a case clock
was a complicated undertaking due to
the involvement of at least two separate
artisans. This assemblage necessitated a
clockmaker for the dial and the movement and a cabinetmaker for the case.[21]

---

[19] Thomas K. Ford, *The Silversmith in
Eighteenth-Century Williamsburg: An Account of
his Life & Times & of his Craft* (Williamsburg,
Va.: Colonial Williamsburg Foundation,
1956), 12.

[20] Memorandum Book, 1790–1800; Account
Book, 1800–1804.

[21] Although some sources state that Faris made some of his own cases, we have failed
to find any evidence for this assertion. See Figures 29, 35, and 36 for a clock whose
case we know to have been made by specific cabinetmakers.

Brass dials and their attached movements were often made in the same shop, but sometimes yet a third craftsman or another shop made the dial. In the early period of colonial clock manufacturing, clock makers used brass dials. They forged, cast, turned, and engraved the dial using techniques learned either in England or from an English-trained master.[22] The Philadelphia school exerted a great influence on clock making in Maryland, and many Maryland clockmakers, including Faris, received their training in the neighboring metropolis.[23] Craftsmen used skills common to both the trades of clock making and silversmithing in making the silvered chapter rings and engraved disks (or bosses) in the tympanum area, as well as the cast spandrels in most dials.[24] In fact, the spandrels on the dials in Figures 28, 29, and 30 were all cast from the same mold. This is understandable as molds were expensive; when a clockmaker invested in them, he was going to make sure they were used. Brass was also in short supply prior to the Revolution;[25] as early as 8 November 1759 Faris told readers of the *Gazette* that he "*gives the best prices for old brass.*" Scarcity of the metal made it difficult to produce these dials, especially in the days before painted dials provided an alternative.

Another interesting aspect of Faris's manufacture was his practice of numbering his clocks. Not all clockmakers numbered their movements, suggesting that Faris's penchant for this practice may have been acquired through his master's training. There were Philadelphia clockmakers known for their numbering, among them John Wood Sr. Not all of Faris's clocks are numbered,[26] however, so that the numbering cannot be used to determine the order in which he made his clocks. This practice does, however, provide one more idiosyncratic aspect of Faris's personality.

Faris advertised both eight-day and thirty-day clocks, and his shop drawings included a *"month-clock"* movement (See Fig. SD19 on page 448). Eight-day clocks are the most commonly found of the early clocks, while thirty-day clocks are rare. Faris's musical clocks stand as one of the most advanced features of his creativity. Musical clocks, never common, involved a degree of sophistication and resources not available to the average clockmaker. Faris's probable connection to Henry Flower in Philadelphia is strengthened by the

---

[22] Chris Bailey, *Two Hundred Years of American Clocks & Watches* (Englewood Cliffs, N.J.: Rutledge, Prentice-Hall, 1975), 17–18.

[23] Bailey, *Two Hundred Years*, 73.

[24] Jane Webb Smith, "Clock and Watchmaking in Maryland," in Goldsborough, *Silver in Maryland*, 49.

[25] Smith, "Clock," 51.

[26] The extant numbered Faris clocks are one, six, eleven, twelve, and thirteen. The clocks are numbered behind the dial plate, on the pendulum, on the movement, and behind the moon dials. Numbering should be investigated whenever a new clock of Faris's making is discovered.

fact that Flower made musical clocks.[27] In his diary, Faris mentions clocks on three separate occasions, two of which involve musical attachments. In the first reference, Faris commented on polishing a four-tune clock; the other entry involved a seven-tune clock that he had given to his son-in-law Archibald Kerr.[28] One of Faris's four-tune clocks, purportedly with a thirty-day movement, descended in the McParlin family of Annapolis and could perhaps be the one referred to in the diary; this clock plays the tunes: "A March," "Lovely Nancy," "Foot's Minuet," and a Cotillion.[29]

Faris's estate inventory contains several clocks both complete and in the making. Of these we know the history of a particular musical clock purchased for $36.00 by William Pitt for his wife Ann Faris Pitt at William Faris's estate sale in 1805.[30] (Figure 31) This clock descended in the Pitt family through Charles Faris Pitt (Faris's grandson), was purchased in 1939 by Martin B. Faris of New York, and descended in his family.[31] The clock plays one tune, "Robin Adair," an ancient Celtic song. This clock has a brass dial, a strike/silent and music/silent mechanism, and is signed *William Faris, Annapolis* in flowing script. Above the arch, engraved in block letters, is the phrase "AS THE HOURS PASS SO PASSETH THE LIFE OF MAN." We are left to ponder the philosophical message that Faris engraved over two hundred years ago; perhaps the same thought processes led him to record the daily occurrences of his life in his diary many years later. This clock is perhaps the *musical clock hind the door in the hall* from the satirical poem *The Will of William Faris.* Although the case of this particular clock appears to be a nineteenth-century replacement, there is a note on the inside of the door which states:

31 ☛ Brass Dial of Tall Case Clock, ca. 1765

This musical clock, which plays the Celtic tune "Robin Adair," was purchased by William Pitt for his wife Ann at the sale of her father's property in 1805; he paid $36.00. This may have been the clock which "stood behind the door in the hall" in the poem "The Will of William Faris." (See page 26)

---

27 Barr, *Annapolis Clockmaker*, 176.

28 See entries for 24 September 1793 and 28 November 1802.

29 "The Editor's Attic," *The Magazine Antiques*, XLI (February 1942), 136. The music book in the Faris Music Book Collection (MSA SC 2551) contains the music for "Lovely Nancy" as well as a number of marches and minuets.

30 Anne Arundel County (Inventories), 1805–1808, JG 6/734, MSA.

31 Barr, *Annapolis Clockmaker*, 175.

FARIS C. PITT, Jr.

FROM HIS FATHER, 1910

This Clock Was Imported From England

By William Faris of Annapolis, Md.

Great-Grand Father of the Donor

It seems unlikely that Faris would have imported this clock from England, given that the dial work and the matting (the area within the chapter ring) are entirely consistent with his other dials.[32] The movement, hidden behind the dial, is another matter. Nevertheless, the movements and dials that have been examined to date all point to a single maker, and it would be inconsistent considering the amount of tools and the advanced shop that Faris possessed, for this clock to have been imported. The plaque inside the door points to the fact that it was his clock and descended in his family.

Determining the provenance of individual pieces is often a very difficult process. Case clocks, however, have always been held in such high esteem that they tend to follow a clear line of descent, being willed from generation to generation. The most ornate of Faris's clocks, made for Charles Carroll the Barrister, of Mount Clare near Baltimore, descended from the Barrister's wife, Margaret Tilghman Carroll, through the Tilghman, Earle, and Hollyday families, and is still in Maryland.[33] (See Figures 32, 33 and 34) The clock has a particularly attractive case, with great, carved embellishments and decorations, indicative of the Barrister's attraction to the rococo style. Faris recorded in his daybook the occasional cleaning and repair of this particular clock.

32 ☞ Charles Carroll, Barrister (1723–1783)

Charles Carroll the Barrister patronized Faris's shop in the 1770s. Faris "lengthened two brass rods for curtains," made the clock in Figures 33 and 34, and charged him for cleaning this clock in October 1774.

33 ☞ Brass Dial with Hood of Tall Case Clock, ca.1770

This clock originally belonged to Charles Carroll the Barrister, of Mount Clare near Baltimore, and descended in the Tilghman, Earle, and Hollyday families. This clock is housed in the most elaborate case of all of Faris's clocks. Note the particularly fine engraving of "Annapolis."

---

32 Edward LaFond, personal communication, 25 January 2001.

33 William Voss Elder, *Maryland Queen Anne and Chippendale Furniture of the Eighteenth Century* (Baltimore: Baltimore Museum of Art, 1968), 92–94.

Another outstanding Faris clock, featuring a moon dial, shows the working relationship between Annapolis craftsmen of the period. The case of the clock (Figure 35) carries a "Shaw & Chisholm" label. John Shaw and Archibald Chisholm, two Annapolis cabinetmakers, were in partnership a very short time, permitting this clock to be dated more accurately than is often the case. The label (Figure 36) in the case corresponds with their first period of partnership before the Revolution, roughly 1772–1776.[34] The mahogany case is in the Chippendale style with brass-fluted columns and brass capitals with lattice fretwork above the door and in the bonnet.[35] This collaboration between Faris and the Shaw & Chisholm workshop has never before been recorded. Two other eight-day Faris clocks (Figures 28, 30, 37 , and 38) show similarities of casework and brass dials, but the cases are much simpler in overall construction with restrained ornamentation — and therefore less expensive. If a patron's taste favored a more elaborate case, he could obtain one for a higher price. The case of the Barrister's clock (Figure 34), for example, is typical of the Chippendale high style of the period.

All of the extant William Faris clocks that have been studied have brass dials. Clockmakers engraved their name and place of manufacture on the tympanum boss in the arch of the dial, unless it had a moon dial, in which case the plate would either be placed directly on or engraved inside the chapter ring. The clockmaker engraved his name as a mode of advertising throughout the period.[36] A signed clock dial also provided a standard by which the maker could be judged

---

34 William Voss Elder and Lu Bartlett, *John Shaw: Cabinetmaker of Annapolis* (Baltimore: Baltimore Museum of Art, 1983), 47.

35 James B. Whisker, Daniel David Hartzler, and Steven P. Petrucelli, *Maryland Clockmakers* (Cranbury, N.J.: Adams Brown Company, 1996), 138–39.

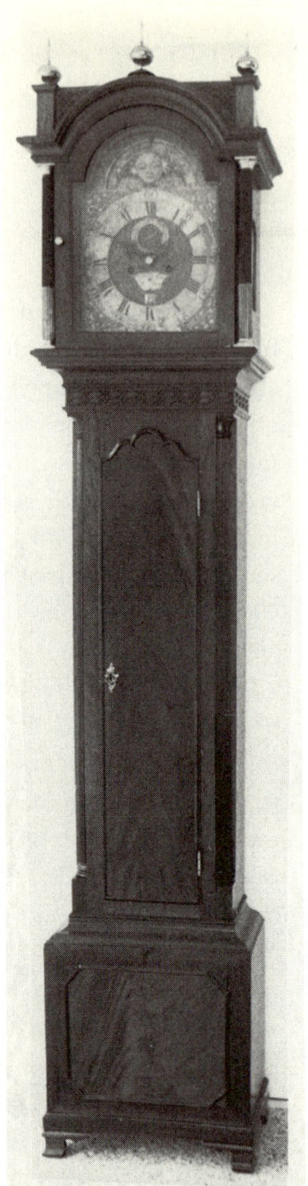

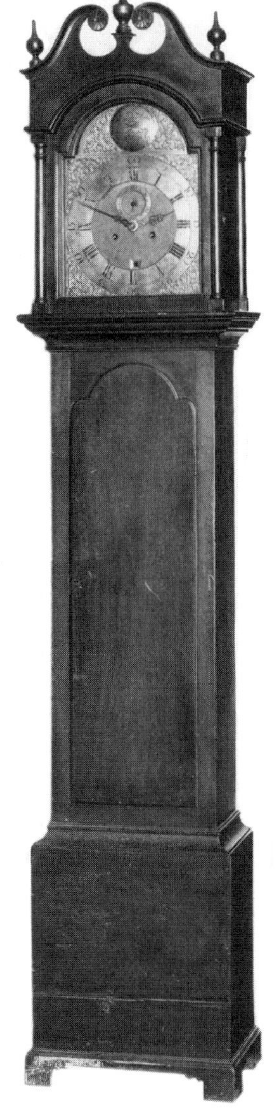

38 ✒ Tall Case Clock
(Full view of Figure 30)

*This walnut clock case
is similar to the one in
Figure 37 with its plain
design. The simplicity
could be indicative of the
personal taste or of the
financial limitations of
the customer who
commissioned the clock.*

36 ✒ John Shaw and Archibald
Chisholm Cabinetmaker's Label
Inside clock case, ca. 1772–1776

*The label allows us to date the
clock in Figure 35 relatively
accurately as Shaw & Chisholm
were in business together only a
short time. The clock dates to
the early period of their first
partnership, which lasted from
1772 to 1776.*

37 ✒ Tall case Clock
(Full view of Figure 28)

*The case of this clock is
representative of the simple
lines of Annapolis furniture.*

39 ✒ White painted
dial of Tall Case Clock,
ca. 1790–1800
Signed:
**HYRAM FARIS/
ANNAPOLIS**

*Hyram Faris worked in
his father's shop until he
moved to Baltimore after
a quarrel with his father
in April 1799. White
dials began to replace
brass dials in the last
quarter of the eighteenth
century.*

and held accountable for his work. Moon dials, which involved more sophisticated movements, were more complicated to make. The phases of the moon were kept in tandem with the time by the clock itself. Faris recorded the sale of a moon clock to Benjamin Sprigg in March 1775 for £15.0.0.[37] The location of this clock today is unknown. The clock in Figure 35 is the only Faris moon clock with its original case known to survive. This clock is numbered No.11 behind the front plate and in the pendulum, and the name *Moore* is inscribed behind the pendulum as well.

Painted, or white, dials began to make their appearance toward the end of the Revolution, but did not become popular in America until the close of the

---

[36] James Biser Whisker, *Pennsylvania Clockmakers, Watchmakers and Allied Crafts* (Cranbury, N.J.: Adams Brown Company, 1990), iii.

[37] Daybook.

55

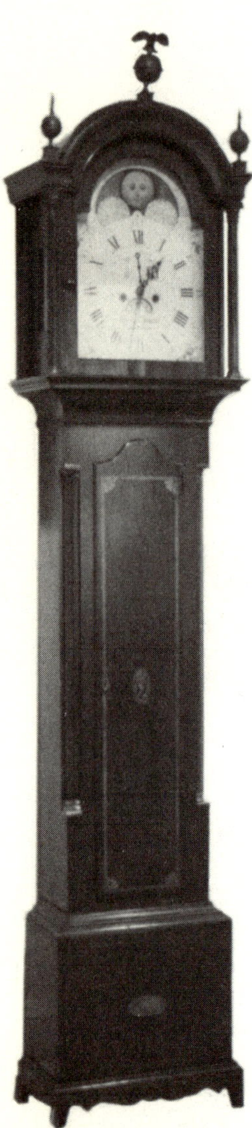

40 ☛ Tall Case Clock
(Full view of Figure 39)

Although not labeled, this case, with its elaborate inlays and beautiful proportions, shows all the characteristics of a very talented cabinetmaker.

eighteenth century.[38] Painted dials allowed the use of much more ornamentation as well as the introduction of a new aesthetic. The dial could also be seen more easily in low light conditions. The clock in Figures 39 and 40, signed *"Hyram Faris, Annapolis,"* is the only extant Hyram Faris clock known to date. Hyram, who trained in his father's shop, was particularly talented as an artist and may have been responsible for some of the drawings in Faris's book of shop drawings (Figs. SD1–SD21 on pages 430–50). The case is also very attractive, showing a high degree of sophistication in the inlay and proportions. It is unlikely that Hyram made the dial as white dials were imported in great numbers both from London and also from certain New England centers of manufacture. Many of them were identical, the only difference in the finished clock dial being the signature of the clockmaker across the face of the dial. Nevertheless, William Faris's inventory listed "1 Tin Box for Baking clock faces." Because painted dials (sheet iron that was then painted and enameled) were crafted using a heat-induced process, the presence of this apparatus suggests that painted dials may have been produced to some extent in Faris's shop. These new dials, which became available after about 1780, provided a less expensive alternative for those wishing to purchase a case clock.[39] The advent of the painted dial actually marked the beginning of the period when case clocks became commercially available.[40] Hyram may have made the movement of this clock in his father's shop; one of the Faris shop drawings is of a clock face with the name *"Hyram Faris*, ANNAPOLIS (Fig. SD17 on page 446) written on the dial in script. Hyram's untimely death in August of 1800 allows the clock to be dated rather precisely to the 1790 to 1800 period.

William Faris's inventory listed all of the clock-related material found in his shop at the time of his death:

9 silver watches	1 clock Reel
3 gilt watches	Sundry Articles for clock and
2 Quarter clocks with cases	watchmakers tools
3 Plain clocks without cases	1 clock graving tool
1 time piece	1 Large case with clock and
2 clocks with cases	watchmakers tools
1 set of clock and	1 box clockmakers patterns
watchmakers tools	1 glass funnel and 2 clock springs
1 watch engine	Sundry articles for clockwork
1 drawer of watch glasses	1 musickel clock with case
2 clockmakers Brackets	1 tin box for Baking clock faces
1 drawer with sundry	Sundry disorted clock and
clockmaker's tools	watch tools

---

[38] Whisker, *Pennsylvania Clockmakers*, 141–42.

[39] Bailey, *Two Hundred Years of Clockmakers*, 25.

[40] Whisker, *Pennsylvania Clockmakers*, 144.

In the 9 November 1778 issue of the *Maryland Journal and Baltimore Daily Advertiser*, Faris announced:

> TO BE SOLD, a likely young Negro fellow, by trade a *Silversmith, Jeweller* and *Lapidary;* there is very few, if any better workmen in America. Any person inclining to purchase the said Negro, may know further, by applying to the subscriber, living in Annapolis.
>
> WILLIAM FARIS
>
> November 7, 1778

Although we do not know the identity of this accomplished black silversmith, his significance for the story of Faris as owner of a workshop is twofold. First, it provides evidence that Faris undoubtedly no longer needed to keep additional workmen because his sons were of an age to be useful in the shop. Equally, if not more important, is the fact that Faris made the investment of training a slave in such highly-skilled crafts. Although skilled slaves could be found in many craft fields in the colonial period, their work generally took place in more utilitarian trades, such as blacksmithing, carpentry, cooperage, ship building, and shoemaking. Slaves who practiced any of the crafts Faris mentioned were rarely found. It is regrettable that we do not know who purchased this slave and whether the man developed his craft any further.

There is no written evidence that Faris formally apprenticed his four sons in his shop although it appears obvious that he provided training for them.[41] Three of his four sons worked with the crafts of watch making and silversmithing to one degree or another. William Jr. left Annapolis sometime prior to 1792, corresponding initially with his family from Norfolk. Faris mentions sending watch-making tools to William Jr. in Havana, Cuba, in January of 1793, and later corresponds with him at his new location in Edenton, North Carolina, where he reportedly had forty or fifty watches in his shop window. Charles Faris, William's second son, stayed in Annapolis, where he moved into his own shop in 1793. We will look at Charles at a later point as he became a talented silversmith in his own right. Hyram was a frequent garden helper as well as an accomplished artist. The miniature of his brother, St. John Faris (See Figures 41 and 42), is attributed to Hyram. Miniature watercolors on ivory were a delicate undertaking, as the painting was done with a hatched or stippled touch rather than the flowing brush strokes of an oil portrait. Hyram's artistic efforts may also have included some of the drawings in the Faris workshop. Saint John never became involved in any of the shop work, although he undoubtedly was familiar with the processes; he took to the sea early in his life.

---

[41] A formal apprenticeship agreement with one's own child would be highly unusual, however.

41 ✒ Saint John Faris
(1770–1796)

St. John Faris was the youngest son of William and Priscilla Faris. He was the only one of the male children not to follow his father's craft.

42 ✒ *Reverse side of Saint John Faris Locket Inscribed:*
St. John Faris. Ob, July 27th, 1796 AE 25 Years & 7 Months

43 ☞ Silversmiths in an 18th century workshop Plate I from Denis Diderot, *Encyclopedie, Dictionaire des Sciences,* Paris, 1763

The silversmiths in this image are pouring molten silver into a mold, battering a piece of sheet silver from an ingot, and forming various vessels. Faris's shop, although much smaller, would have had similar tools and materials with which to form his silver objects.

When Faris first advertised the use of a silversmith in 1760, he must also have had all of the necessary equipment as well as a forging area with a furnace — a large capital investment.[42] A silversmith had to amass substantial capital to purchase the necessary tools and equipment to begin his business, much more equipment than would have been given him by his master at the end of his apprenticeship. He would also have had to be readily accessible to an adequate market for his services.[43] Faris would not receive the money from the sale of his Philadelphia property until April of 1763, leaving us to wonder how he managed to set up such an involved operation when he had only been in Annapolis for three years.

Faris owned an extensive collection of silversmith's tools and related raw materials and equipment at the time of his death:

1 set of silversmiths cutting tools	1 oz 9 dwt gold
1 stand of scales and weights	1 oval lathe
6 plated Teaspoons	1 plate Basket
Sundry Silversmiths Tools in the forge	1 old scale with silversmiths tools
1 Large lathe	1 pair large scales
2 Sand Troughs	1 Large laythe with wheel and
4 Anvils with Blocks	apparatus
1 Mill for silver work	1 show case
18 Silversmiths hammers	1 lapidary mill
1 pair Bellows	6 books silver leaf
1 Large brass mortar and pestle	2 books gold leaf
6 Lead Rings for silversmiths	Sundry blk lead pots crusible &c.
5 Ingot Moulds	1 sett tooth instruments
3 Large Hammers	62 pair cock heels
4 pair forging tongs	155 oz, 10 dwt plate
1 Large Silversmiths Anvil	1 lott punches

---

42 Goldsborough, *Silver in Maryland,* 2.　　43 Ibid., 2.

44 ☞ Frontispiece
and Intent of the
Frontispiece from
*A Touchstone for Gold
and Silver Wares*
William Babcock,
London, 1677
(2 images) A & B

*This view of a silver-
smith shop shows all
the elements, from the
forge to the tools,
needed for a successful
operation. Although
Faris would not be
working until almost
eighty years later, the
"art and mystery" of
the trade had con-
tinued unchanged.*

As mentioned earlier, it was not unusual for a clockmaker also to be involved with silver, because the skills needed to cast, finish, and assemble clockworks and brass dials were not dissimilar to those needed by a silversmith.[44] With the hiring of a *"compleat silversmith"* in 1763, Faris began the one endeavor that would immortalize him in the annals of colonial craftsmanship, especially due to the surviving silver drawings from his shop. Unfortunately, we do not know who this first "compleat silversmith" was, nor to what degree silver was actually made in Faris's shop. One potential candidate for this role was Thomas Sparrow. Faris loaned Sparrow £15 in 1777, for which Sparrow mortgaged a set of silversmith's tools as well as anvils, files, pliers, and even some furniture.[45] Sparrow set up his own silversmith's business in Annapolis on Southeast Street at the "Sign of the Silver Coffee Pot" on 21 March 1765, according to the *Gazette.* If he ever worked for Faris, it was not for very long, although Sparrow was an occasional patron of Faris's tavern. One writer has suggested that because Sparrow advertised in the *Maryland Gazette* on 13 December 1764, in reference to a land sale, that he was at "Mr. Green's in Annapolis" and had just recently returned from his apprenticeship in Philadelphia in September, that he could not have been the newly hired silversmith to whom Faris refers. Sparrow had apparently left Annapolis in 1759 for Philadelphia to undertake his apprenticeship there,[46] but there are no records to corroborate

---

44 Smith, "Clock," 49.   45 Anne Arundel County (Land Records), IB5/375, MSA.

46 Helen Arthur, "Thomas Sparrow: An Early Maryland Engraver," *The Magazine Antiques,* LV (January 1949), 44–45.

that Sparrow left Annapolis in 1759 and returned in September of 1764. Nor is there any evidence to suggest anyone else as Faris's workman.

Historically, silver has been a coveted metal due to its ductility, malleability, and reflective nature.[47] For centuries the very wealthy have valued silver as a sign of status and breeding. Colonial gentry imported most of their luxury items directly from London in the latest fashions. Charles Carroll of Carrollton, for example, wrote on 14 November 1785 "Gentlemen I send by Captain Johns of the *Nonesuch* an old silver tankard which I would have melted into one of the same size and shape with my coat of arms and crest engraven on it as the old one."[48] Charles Carroll the Barrister also ordered silver from England for his estate, Mount Clare, near Baltimore. Twenty years earlier, in October of 1764, he too had written to his London agent asking for "one silver server or waiter to suit a small Company about 8 or 10 persons, one Black Shagreen case with a Dozen Silver Handled Table Knives and Forks and one Dozen Spoons; one Plain Silver three Pint Chocolate Pot, and one Cream Pot of middle size I suppose the Fashion to be Chased."[49] The two instances provide only a minute sampling of the many articles imported from England. It is also interesting to note that purchasers placed complete confidence in their London agents to choose their silver articles. Customers apparently did not demand particulars apart from requiring the "latest fashion."

Because silver wares served as status-defining objects, the gentry more often employed eighteenth-century American craftsmen to repair such objects rather than to fashion new ones. This is true of Faris's shop as well. Carroll ordered his new tankard redone in London, but on one occasion employed Faris for repair purposes. In his daybook for 24 December 1774, Faris charged Charles Carroll of Carrollton £1.2.6 for mending 2 silver canns.[50] Faris also recorded work in his daybook for Samuel Chase, charging him the same sum for "guilding the Head of a Cane" on 15 June 1774 (See figure 25 on page 48).[51] When wealthy southern townspeople employed local silversmiths, other than for repair, they engaged them primarily to fashion spoons or an occasional cream pot or cann; vessels of larger size were mostly imported.

Before one can look at the different pieces of plate (as silver was customarily

---

47 Gregory R. Weidman and Jennifer F. Goldsborough, *Classical Maryland, 1815–1845: Fine and Decorative Arts from the Golden Age* (Baltimore: Maryland Historical Society, 1993), 141.

48 Quoted in Goldsborough, *Silver in Maryland*, 1.

49 Quoted in Michael F. Trostel, *Mount Clare, Being an Account of the Seat Built by Charles Carroll, Barrister, upon his Lands at Patapsco* (Baltimore: The National Society of the Colonial Dames of America in the State of Maryland, 1981), 26.

50 Daybook.

51 Daybook. This cane, an English example dating from 1746/47, is in the collection of the Maryland Historical Society.

referred to in the eighteenth century) associated with Faris, one needs to understand the origin of the raw material available to the smith. Silver was not easily found in North America. In fact, the only way a silversmith could create a new object was by reusing old silver, as extremely high British duties prevented American smiths from importing silver bullion from England.[52] The smith melted old pieces and coins, supplied by the customer,[53] and then poured the molten metal into an ingot mold, or directly into a sand mold, to make cast parts. When an object was completed, the customer had at his disposal a piece that he could use and enjoy but that could also be converted back into ready cash should the need arise. Not all of the pieces of plate brought in by customers to be refashioned, however, necessarily wound up in the melting pot. There are examples of Faris's personal pieces with English origins, such as the small chased creamer (Figure 45) made in London in 1771 by Thomas Sheppard. This piece is engraved **WAP** for William and Ann Faris Pitt, but was actually made before Ann's birth. Faris perhaps received this piece to be melted down and refashioned or in some other trade. Moreover, because of the shortage of the metal, silversmiths were always ready to purchase old silver, as their advertisements tell us.[54] Throughout Faris's daybook, there are entries where he provided cash to customers in exchange for old silver. If a customer needed ready cash the local silversmith was the place to turn. Keeping these odd pieces also provided a way for silversmiths to have prototypes of popular forms to use as models for later work.

The most common silver item commissioned by a local customer would have been a set of spoons. These were traditionally ordered in sets of six or a dozen. Faris records sets of six teaspoons sold to William Noke, one of the builders of Edward Lloyd's house in Annapolis, for £1.18.0 in April 1773 and to Patrick Burke in January 1777 for £1.5.0.[55] Spoons were very versatile tools; forks, although used by more sophisticated people in the eighteenth century, did not become standard table accoutrements until well into the nineteenth century. Faris did, however, record in his daybook that on 18 June 1774 he charged Anthony Stewart, owner of the brig *Peggy Stewart* of Annapolis tea party fame, 7/6 for polishing twelve knives and forks.[56] The knives were most

---

52 Goldsborough, *Silver in Maryland*, 1.

53 The silversmith had the option of retaining the customer's piece for his own purposes in exchange for an equivalent weight of silver. Faris might have chosen to keep a piece as a prototype or for use in his own household.

54 Occupations such as banking and pawn brokering derived from this enterprise.

55 Daybook.   56 Daybook.

45 ☞ Cream Pot
Thomas Shepherd, London,
1771/1772
Fully marked under rim
with lion passant, leopard's
head crowned,
letter Q for 1771/72 and
TS maker's mark for
Thomas Shepherd.
Engraved: *WAP* for
William and Ann Faris Pitt

This rococo cream pot, with its scrolled handle and elaborately chased body, was probably acquired by William Faris from a customer in the 1770s. It may have been brought to him for repair, to be melted down and refashioned, or in trade for something else. The cream pot remained in his family, passing through his daughter Ann, for over two hundred years.

46 ↜ Six Tablespoons
William Faris,
ca. 1760–70
Marked **WF** twice on back
in rectangular reserve on
underside of handle

*Patrons generally ordered
spoons like these
tablespoons in
sets of six or
twelve. The
monogram
V*S*R appears
on the underside
of the spoons, but
the purchaser
has not been
identified.*

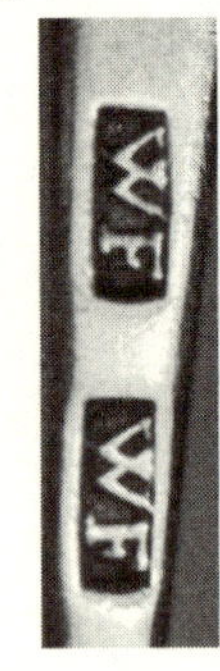

likely bone or ivory-handled with steel blades, and not silver. Spoons were the silver of choice for most people, the bread-and-butter work of silversmiths, and the most common form of colonial silver found today. Spoons were valuable and were occasionally stolen. Charles Carroll of Annapolis advertised in 1753 that a convict servant man belonging to him ran away from the Baltimore Iron Works and that a "silver Table Spoon—stampt on the Back with the Letters I.I. was missing."[57] The illustrations of Faris spoons show the diversity of the pieces coming out of his workshop during the Revolutionary period and afterwards.

47 ↜ Pair of Tablespoons Attributed to William Faris, ca. 1760–70. Marked **WF** in rectangular reserve with chipped lower right corner on underside of handle. Engraved: **IHC** on underside

*The **WF** mark on these spoons has been the object of considerable confusion for silver scholars. For a number of years this mark has been attributed to William Garret Forbes of New York, whose career overlapped Faris's. Louise Belden (Marks of Early American Silversmiths in the Ineson-Bissell Collection), for example, attributed this mark to Forbes. New research, particularly with the Sauceboat (Figure 52 on page 65) in the collection of the Baltimore Museum of Art, has determined that this may in fact be a Faris mark. The sauceboat was purchased by Mrs. Miles White from Mr. Pitt in 1920 for her collection of early Maryland silver. Although a provenance of this nature is usually a fairly positive indicator as to the identity of the maker, there remains some concern as to its attribution, here used with care and referred to as attributed. This mark has appeared on silver with a possible New York background.*

---

57 Quoted in Pleasants and Sill, *Maryland Silversmiths*, 58.

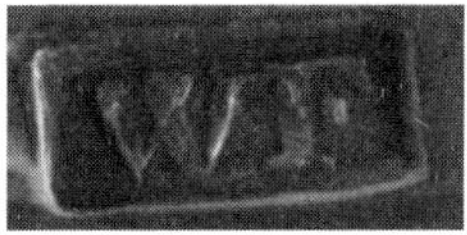

48 ✒ Teaspoon
William Faris, ca. 1775
Marked **WF** once in rectangular reserve on underside of handle

*This shell-backed teaspoon is one of a set of six which belonged to
Ann Faris Pitt. Other examples from this set are in collections of the
Baltimore Museum of Art, the Maryland Historical Society, and private
collectors. This is the only example engraved with the names of all the women
directly descended from Ann Faris Pitt.*
**Engraved Pitt, A. Faris Pitt May 9, 1793/ H.Pitt Littig Jan. 18th, 1820/ A.M.L. Stran
Oct. 9th, 1845/ E.J.S. Jones Oct. 10, 1878/ N.S.J. Johnston Sept 29, 1909.**
Note that the original **P** *on the front of the handle was later expanded into* **Pitt.**

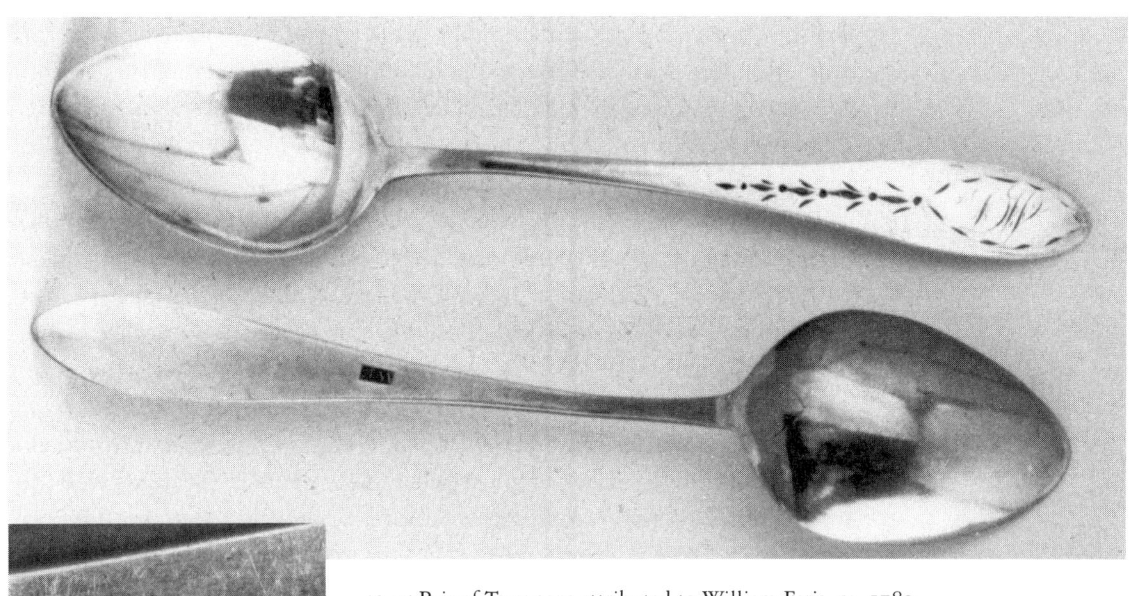

49 ✒ Pair of Teaspoons attributed to William Faris, ca. 1780
Marked **WF** once in serrated rectangular reserve on underside of handle.
Engraved: **DW**

*These bright-cut engraved teaspoons are examples of a style that became popular in
America after about 1780 and therefore date from a later period in Faris's career. The
engraved bellflower design is similar to the inlay found on furniture of the period.*

51 ☞ Cream Pot William Faris, ca. 1775
Marked **WF** twice on bottom. Engraved: **I*Y*F**

This cream pot, almost identical to the preceding example, was probably made at about the same time. The cast parts of both pieces are from the same molds: note the similarities between the legs and the handles. Cream pots of this type were often the first piece of hollow ware purchased by an American customer from a local silversmith.

50 ☞ Cream Pot
William Faris, ca. 1775
Marked **WF** once on
bottom in rectangular
reserve
Engraved: *WAP* for
William and Ann Faris
Pitt

More than any other piece of Faris hollow ware, this cream pot is vital to the identification of Faris's marks because of its documented descent in his family. The piece belonged to William and Ann Faris Pitt, Faris's daughter and son-in-law. It was made in the rococo manner in the 1770s and exemplifies a favorite mid-eighteenth century style. The pear-shaped creamer, on three legs with scrolled handle and feet along with a scalloped rim, was popular throughout the colonies.

The next most frequently purchased silver item was a cream pot, a necessary component of the fashionable ceremony of tea drinking. Cream pots, especially in the mid-eighteenth century, were of the three-footed pear-shaped form and often accompanied a china tea service.[58] Examples of these rococo-style cream pots, as seen in Figure 50 and figure 51 above, were made in Faris's shop in the 1760s and 1770s. The scroll handles and scalloped rim are indicative of this graceful style.

Both of the illustrated cream pots marked with the **WF** of Faris's shop share parts cast from the same molds. The ribbed upper part of the handle is somewhat different in the one engraved **WAP** (for William and Ann Faris Pitt), although still in the same fashion. This raises an important point. The making of molds and formation of cast parts were expensive and time-consuming processes because the smith had to make or buy the master mold. The master mold, which could be made of hard wood, brass, steel, or some other durable material, was then pressed into a wooden frame holding fine sand. Next, the molten silver was poured into the wooden frame and allowed to cool. Once the silver had solidified, the cast pieces, such as the legs and handles on a cream pot or sauceboat, or the spout and finials on a coffee or teapot, were filed, polished, and ultimately soldered onto the body of the piece, which usually had been raised by hammering and forming a sheet of silver into the desired

---

58 Philippa Glanville and Jennifer Faulds Goldsborough, *Women Silversmiths, 1685–1845* (Washington, D.C.: National Museum of Women in the Arts, 1990), 60.

52 ✒ Sauceboat attributed to William Faris, ca. 1780

This Georgian sauceboat was derived from a typical rococo design. The cast C-scroll handle and legs hark back stylistically to the 1750s and 1760s. The reinforced smooth rim and design of the engraving are harbingers of the neoclassical style. American silversmiths often retained molds for cast parts that were going out of fashion because the master molds were expensive and difficult to obtain. The raised parts such as the body or cover could be made in a newer style and combined with older cast parts. This piece, in the collection of the Baltimore Museum of Art, closely resembles the sauceboat illustrated in his book of shop drawings (see Figure SD2 on page 431).

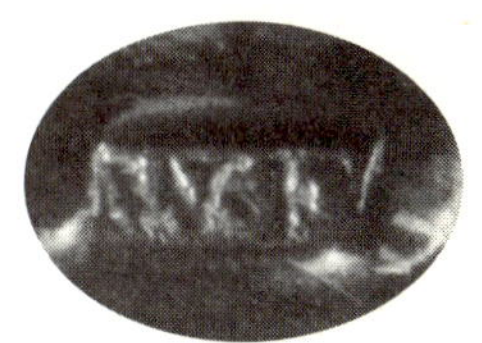

53 ✒ *The mark above, with chipped lower right corner, is found on the sauceboat in Figure 52. Previously attributed to William Garret Forbes, it is here attributed to William Faris on the basis of the Pitt family history of the piece. Mrs. Miles White purchased this sauceboat from a Mr. Pitt in 1920. Both this and the piece in Figure 54 were marked with the same* **WF** *mark on the rim to the right or left of the handle.*

shape.[59] The master molds for these cast parts would then be reused, even when stylistically they were no longer in fashion. This is the reason why pieces such as Faris's sauceboats (Figures 52 and figure 54) have rococo-style handles and legs attached to neoclassical style bodies. The reader will notice that the sauceboats have plain molded rims (one of which is beaded) and not the scalloped ones typical of the rococo period in which the cast parts were designed. These transitional pieces show the versatility and adaptation of American craftsmen. Because colonial silversmiths were not engaged to create pieces of hollow ware like coffee pots, sauceboats, and cream pots on a regular basis, the smith would keep the old master molds and continue to use them long after the period in which they first became fashionable.

54 ✒ *This sauceboat is nearly identical to that in Figure 52 except for the applied beading to the molded rim. Beading was a typical feature of the neoclassical style popular toward the end of the eighteenth century.*

---

59 Henry J. Kauffman, *The Colonial Silversmith: his Techniques and his Products* (Camden, N.J.: Thomas Nelson, 1969), 91.

At any given time, Annapolis did not have more than a handful of working silversmiths.[60] Of these men, certain individuals stand out as particularly important from an historical perspective. Cesar Ghiselin, the earliest known goldsmith (a commonly used alternative for silversmith), arrived in Annapolis from Philadelphia in 1716 and stayed until 1726.[61] Samuel Soumaien came to Annapolis in 1740 and left around 1753. Faris's competitors during the second half of the century included John Inch, William Whetcroft, James Chalmers, and Chalmers' sons James Jr. and John. Not many of these men survived the economic struggles in Annapolis during this period. One reason lay in their inability to diversify sufficiently to withstand the economic depression of the period leading up to and immediately following the Revolution.[62] Of those listed, John Inch, who was among the most successful, was—like Faris—able to generate many sources of income. Inch, who worked as a silversmith in Annapolis from 1743 to 1763, was also a watchmaker, jeweler, tavern keeper, painter, and glazier, as well as operator of a ferry.[63] William Faris, however, had a longer working career, from 1757 to 1804, than any of the above men. Although Faris was active in Annapolis for forty-eight years,

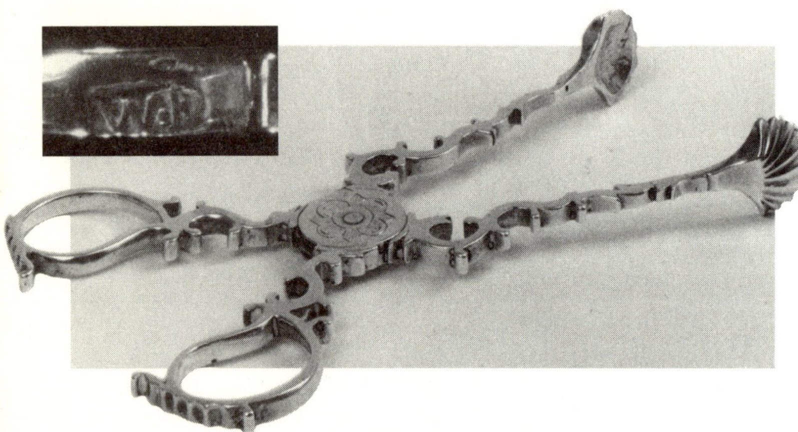

very little from his shop survives today for our examination. None of the other goldsmiths left much silver either. The oldest extant major piece of Annapolis silver is the racing trophy made by John Inch in 1743 and awarded to Dr. George Steuart when his horse *Dungannon* won the Annapolis races that year.[64]

Although relatively few pieces of Faris's silver have come to light, we are fortunate to know of a variety of forms that originated in his shop. Apart from pieces of hollow ware, like cream pots, teapots, and sauceboats, other smaller pieces survive. Sugar tongs were an important addition to any well-set tea

55 🠒 Scissor-type
Sugar Tongs.
William Faris,
ca.1765
*This is the only example
of this style of tongs
known to have been
marked by Faris, but see
Figure 71 on page 76
for an illustration of a
pair that belonged to him
that were made by
Phillip Syng Sr. of
Annapolis in the 1730s.*

---

[60] Nancy Baker, "Silversmiths in Colonial Annapolis," in Goldsborough, *Silver in Maryland*, 19.

[61] His great-grandson, physician Reverdy Ghiselin, appears frequently in the diary.

[62] Baker, "Silversmiths," 18.

[63] Ibid., 19.

[64] Pleasants and Sill, *Maryland Silversmiths*, 38. This trophy, typical of Annapolis silver in its plain design and lack of ornamentation, is now in the Baltimore Museum of Art.

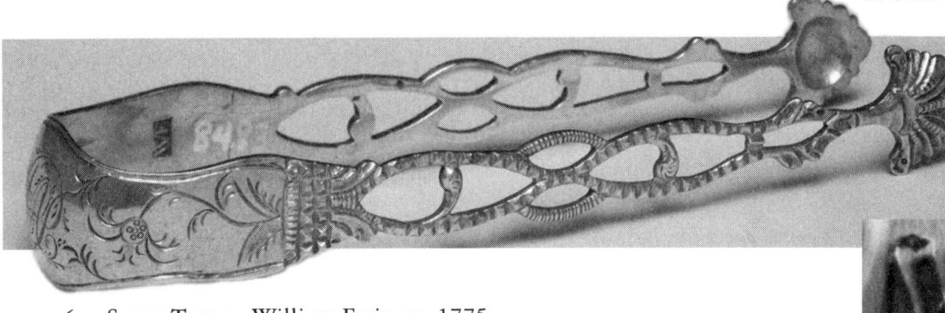

56 ⬥ Sugar Tongs. William Faris, ca. 1775.

This pair of pierced tongs adorned with engraved flowers belonged to William and Ann Faris Pitt. Family history states that William Faris gave them to William Pitt when he married Ann Faris on 7 July 1796.

57 ⬥ *The piece, known to have belonged in the Faris family, is particularly important because the way in which the letter* **W** *is crossed in this mark is different from the marks of other pieces attributed to Faris—thus offering the possibility that more work might be attributed to Faris and his shop.*

table and we have illustrated examples of two types from Faris's shop. Scissor-type sugar tongs (Figure 55) were popular during the middle of the eighteenth century; they were replaced in fashion by the cast-arm style of tongs, and ultimately by the U-shaped solid-arm form. Silversmiths crafted these last two kinds of tongs by carefully tempering the curved end so that it would retain its spring.[65] One example of a pierced cast-armed tongs survives from Faris's shop, made between 1775 and 1790 and engraved **WAP** for William and Ann Faris Pitt (Figure 56).

Faris wrote a list of prices for certain items in the back of his daybook, including fluted soup ladles such as the example in Figure 58. This particular piece has an onslow-pattern handle, which shows the fashion awareness of the craftsman who made it. American silversmiths rarely made the high-style English onslow pattern.[66] Faris charged £3.13.4 for Fluted "Soop" Ladles in his daybook. The design book also contains a drawing of a "soop ladle" (Figure **SD6** on pages 435).

58 ⬥ Ladle. Attributed to William Faris, ca. 1770. *Onslow pattern handles, such as the one on this ladle, are very rare in colonial American silver. This soup ladle testifies to a great degree of sophistication in the work of Faris's shop before the Revolution. Faris recorded two fluted soup ladles in his daybook, charging 27 shillings for fashioning them and 5/7 for the actual weight of 8 oz. 6 dwt. of silver for a total charge of £3.13.4. See Figure* **SD6** *on page 435 for Faris's illustration of a "Soop" Ladle.*

---

[65] Glanville and Goldsborough, *Women Silversmiths*, 68.

[66] Ian M.G. Quimby, *American Silver at Winterthur* (Charlottesville, Va.: University Press of Virginia, 1995), 356.

59 ↙ Strainer
William Faris,
ca. 1765

*Punch was
the most fashion-
able alcoholic
drink of the eigh-
teenth century.
Strainers were
useful for the
filtration of the
spices, coarse
sugar, rinds and
other fruit parts that
were necessary ingredi-
ents. The intricate
handle of this strainer is
a common English and
American rococo design
that was cast in a mold
and the body was pierced
in a very simple pattern.
Compare this strainer
with the later one
marked by Charles Faris
(see Figure 60 below.)*

Coral and bells with whistles were small children's teething trinkets that were extremely expensive luxury items in the eighteenth century. Several paintings of the period show children wearing such pieces hanging from a chain around the neck. The child would teethe on the coral, while the bells and whistle would make a pleasant sound. Coral was considered to possess magical powers and to bring good luck. Coral and bells appear to have been the only silver or gold item made at this time for the sole use of children.[67] Faris charged £1.0.0 for chased examples and from 16/6 to 19/6 for plain ones according to the price list in his daybook.

Strainers were an integral part of eighteenth-century entertainment. Punch was the staple of every tavern and of other social gatherings throughout colonial and early nineteenth-century America. Strainers filtered out the pulp and rind of fruits like lemons, as well as chunks of refined sugar and spices, all of which were used in the process of making punch. They were not necessary implements but rather a luxurious, single-use item. The strainer in Figure 59 shows an intricately cast handle attached to a rather simple bowl. See Figure **SD4** on pages 433 for an illustration of a similarly-shaped strainer in the Faris book of shop drawings.

Funnels were another instrument used for partaking of beverages. Funnels were used in decanting wine; like punch strainers, they were a luxury item.

60 ↙ Strainer   Charles Faris, ca. 1790

*This elegant punch strainer descended in the Pitt family of Baltimore. The mark **CF** is the only initialed punch mark known for Charles Faris, but see Figure 114 on page 237 for an example of a non-silver artifact marked by Charles. All other marks bear his name in script, in keeping with the post-Revolution custom of American silversmiths to spell out their surname.*

---

[67] Glanville and Goldsborough, *Women Silversmiths*, 107–11.

The wine funnel shown in Figure 61, which has come down in the Pitt family collection, is anecdotally attributed to Faris but is unmarked. This example is engraved with the initials **WAP** for William and Ann Faris Pitt and with the initials of their children and grandchildren. Decanting funnels are a rare form in American silver; this one may have been imported, but it is worth noting that American silversmiths sometimes did not mark pieces made for their own use.

There are several forms of silver that appear in Faris's account books for which we have no surviving examples. Snuffboxes were a common but luxurious accessory, part of a gentleman's personal belongings, used to store his tobacco or snuff. Faris made one for Steven Hyland in July of 1774, charging him a total of £1.7.2 for the box and another £2.5.0 for fashioning it. Other recorded forms include knee and shoe buckles, thimbles, cock spurs, temple spectacles, silver coat buttons, pepper boxes, pencil cases, and salts.[68] Indeed, these forms were the most common items sold in American silversmith shops of the period. They were easily lost or broken, as witnessed by the many entries that appear in the account books for the items themselves or for their repair.

There is no way to determine the contribution of the various components of Faris's business activities to his total income over the course of his career. For the last five years of his life, however (bearing in mind both that his tavern keeping was limited to an occasional drink and that his diary makes little mention of time spent in his shop), his two cash books allow us to assess the relative importance of serving a glass of toddy, mending an earring, and making a watch. Faris collected about £500 during this period, just about half of which came from the many watches that he sold, the much smaller number that he repaired, the clocks that he wound and maintained, and the four that he sold. These activities also accounted for about one-third of the slightly more than one thousand entries that Faris recorded. About one hundred and seventy glasses served in the tavern, on the other hand, brought in £37, at 3/9 per glass. The same number of rings, earrings, beads, and brooches — made, repaired, and altered — earned him £61, almost twice as much. Thirty pairs of spurs for gentlemen's fighting cocks garnered £19, or an average of better than half a pound for each pair. Only thirty-two entries dealt with silver: a baker's dozen entries for mending bowls, cups, spoons, and tea tongs, and nineteen each for a set of six teaspoons. Yet these few tasks, 3 percent of the total performed, brought in more than ten percent of Faris's income. His signature skill as clock and watch maker represented the bulk of his craft work, but the luxury craft of silversmith earned him his highest financial reward.[69]

William Faris had a ready supply of sons whom he could apprentice to the arts of silversmithing and clock making in his shop. For the three sons who

61 ⌖ Funnel
Attributed to William
Faris by family
descent, ca. 1775.

*This funnel has a long
history of descent in
William Faris's family,
having belonged to
William and Ann Pitt
and then descending
through the Pitt family
to Mr. C. Gordon Pitt.
Funnels were used in the
decanting of wine from
the barrels in which it
was stored. Funnels are
quite rare in American
silver; although we
cannot disprove its manu-
facture by Faris's shop,
we need to be cautious in
attributing it to Faris
given the large amount of
English silver that he
owned.*

---

[68] Daybook.　　　[69] Account Book, 1800–1804.

entered these crafts, the only surviving pieces represent Charles's work, with the exception of one clock signed by Hyram. These products give us a clear picture of second-generation Annapolis craftsmen. Curiously, Charles began advertising as a watchmaker and clockmaker, but we know him today only by his silver — there are no extant Charles Faris clocks that have come to light. What does survive are four tablespoons, a punch strainer (Figure 60 on page 68), a ladle (Figure 62) made for Chancellor John Johnson and his wife Deborah Ghiselin Johnson, and a striking coffee service in the Metropolitan Museum of Art. This service comprises a coffee pot, covered sugar basin, and cream pot.[70] Each piece of the service is engraved with a crest of a boar or a wolf's head within an oval shield (Figures 63 below, and 64 and 65 on page 71).

62 ☞ Ladle
Charles Faris,
ca. 1790–1800
Marked *Cs
Faris* twice
in oval
reserve on
underside of
handle.
Engraved: **JDJ**
for Chancellor
John and
Deborah
Ghiselin
Johnson

*Chancellor
Johnson prob-
ably commis-
sioned this ladle
from Charles
after he opened
his own shop in
1793.*

63 ☞ Coffee Pot
Charles Faris, ca. 1795
Marked *Cs Faris* script
twice in oval reserve on
inside of foot.

*This is the only coffee pot known by
either Charles or William Faris. Coffee
pots were noteworthy commissions in any
American silver shop. This example is particularly interesting because it has many rococo
elements such as the double-bellied body, the C-
scroll handle, and the cast spout and handle
sockets. The pineapple finial, octagonal base,
and engraving are neoclassical in style.
Pieces such as this that combine
almost equal parts of two styles are
often called transitional.*

---

70 Goldsborough, *Silver in Maryland*, 111.

64 ↜ Cream Pot
Charles Faris, ca. 1795. Marked *Chas Faris* script
once in oval reserve on foot.

*This cream pot is neoclassical in style. Like its
companion sugar basin, the beading around the
perimeters of the spout, base, and middle, as well
as the elongated pedestal on an octagonal
plinth, are characteristic of the Federal
period. Considering the rarity and
scarcity of early Annapolis silver,
it is remarkable that a complete
coffee service survives bearing
Charles Faris's mark.*

Charles seemed to move in and out of the family's West Street
home rather regularly, depending on the current relationship with his
father. Throughout the diary, Faris portrays a difficult relationship with
his next-to-eldest son. Being a bachelor, Charles may have found it advantageous in some ways to remain in his parents' home and work in his father's
shop. When his relations with his father became particularly strained, he
apparently had no other recourse than to move out. In 1793, we find him
striking out on his own by opening his own shop. His first notice in the
Gazette on 12 September reads:

CHARLES FARIS,

Clock and Watch-Maker,

Church-Street, Annapolis,

RESPECTFULLY informs his friends, and the
public, that he has opened shop next door below Mr. Nicholas Brewer, and directly oppofite the
General Court Office, where he carries on the above
bufineffes in all their branches. He likewife carries on
the SILVER-SMITH's and JEWELLER's bufineffes.
Thofe ladies and gentlemen who pleafe to employ
him, may depend on having their work done in the
beft and neateft manner, and on the moft reafonable
terms.
The higheft price will be given for old gold and
filver.

*65 ↜ This sugar basin is
in the neoclassical style of
the late 1790s, unlike its
accompanying transi-
tional coffee pot (Figure
63 on page 70). The
finial may be a replace-
ment or may differ from
the coffee pot because the
three pieces of this service
were probably made at
different times; note the
dodecagonal base on this
sugar basin compared to
the octagonal base on the
other two pieces.
Matching services as we
know them today were
not yet standard and
were too costly for even
most wealthy Americans
to acquire all at once.*

*66 ↜ Maryland Gazette
12 September 1793*

Charles kept this location until January 1796 when there was a fire in his shop. At this time he moved to another location on Church Street, where he would remain, intermittently, until his death in 1800. Charles's announcements echoed his father's notices: he began by identifying himself as a clock and watch maker and then added that he also worked in silver. Of the pieces mentioned earlier, the strainer (Figure 60 on page 68) is probably the only extant piece that can be attributed with much certainty to Charles's independent period, as the bright-cut engraved decoration on the handles dates it approximately to 1795. The other pieces may have been made earlier, while Charles still worked in his father's shop. In fact, Charles was probably responsible for a good portion of the silver coming out of his father's shop. We do not know whether or not William Sr. allowed Charles to strike silver with his own mark, but because some of Charles's pieces do appear to be stylistically earlier than 1793, we must at least consider this a possibility.

Charles found himself starting out in business in a town that had now been eclipsed by Baltimore. He sought to resolve this problem by beginning to import and retail a variety of goods. On 26 May 1796, he again begs our attention in the *Gazette*:

CHARLES FARIS ,

Clock and Watch-Maker,

HAS received an assortment of gold and silver warranted Watches, gold, gilt, and steel Watch Chains and Seals, plated Castors, Candlesticks and Salts, with many other articles in his line, which he will sell low for cash.

Annapolis, May 11, 1796.

Charles advertised abundantly in the *Gazette,* unlike his more reticent father. Evidently this form of repetitive marketing in the local newspaper brought him more patronage even in a town where everyone would have known who he was and where he was located. Charles must have indeed been doing very well, for some time in 1795 or thereabouts he commissioned Charles Willson Peale or his brother James to paint a bust-length portrait of himself. We learn about the origin of this handsome painting (Figure 67) from his nephew and namesake Charles Faris Pitt in a memorandum in the Pitt family Bible: "My Uncle Charles Faris' likeness was painted at Annapolis by Mr. Peal, Elder Peale."[71] This portrait would have been a symbol of success for Charles

67 ✒ Charles Faris
(1764–1800)

Charles Faris was the third child of William and Priscilla Faris and apprenticed as a silversmith in his father's shop.

---

71 In a letter from Charles Coleman Sellers to Lillian Miller, Sellers states that since Charles Willson Peale's work was so thoroughly documented in this period, the portrait was more likely by the hand of his brother James Peale, who painted in the Annapolis area in the 1790s. Files of Historic Annapolis Foundation.

in the Annapolis community, a position that the community itself acknowledged with his election in 1799 as a common councilman.

Charles's next logical step was to expand his operation. In order to do this,
he brought an Irish-born apprentice by the name of William McParlin
(1780–1850) from Baltimore in 1799. It is not known in what capacity
McParlin arrived in Baltimore, whether as an indentured servant or an apprentice. McParlin worked for Charles for just about one year before Charles suc-
cumbed to yellow fever on 1 September 1800. With Charles's death, William
Sr. had no other recourse than to bring the young twenty-year old to live and
train with him. McParlin gave Faris a difficult time, managing to get into all
sorts of trouble, especially with his fondness for drink. On more than one occasion Faris wrote about the escapades of "Billee," as he referred to the young
man. We hear mostly of Billee going to wind the clocks of Faris's customers,
as was customary for Charles before him and for any apprentice in his early
stages, or working in the garden with the old man.

When William Faris Sr. died in 1804, McParlin took over the shop,
although all we have today to bear witness to his proprietorship are a watch
and a few spoons. There is no evidence that McParlin actually did any significant work in silver once Faris died. In fact, despite purchasing some silversmith tools and other sundry articles at Faris's estate sale in 1805, McParlin
does not appear to have produced much silver. Apart from some fiddle-pat-
terned spoons and sugar tongs with the **WMcP** mark that McParlin used on
his silver, no other pieces have come to light. Most of these spoons were probably mass-produced elsewhere and retailed by McParlin. It was a common
practice of the period for one silversmith to take the work of another and place
his mark on it; Faris himself probably retailed quite a lot of silver that he did
not make in his own shop, particularly toward the end of his career. In his
account books, Faris recorded paying Chestertown and Annapolis silversmith
Peter Kirkwood in November of 1799 for making six silver teaspoons.[72]
Whether he practiced this retail habit early in his career, as well, we do not
know. Several pieces that bear the Faris mark and that have been attributed to
his shop may actually have been made in Philadelphia or in Baltimore and
then sold under his mark. By the 1790s Faris may have been winding down
his business, but in order to satisfy his customers' demands for silver and
retain their loyalty for other work, as well as to remain competitive, found
himself filling their orders with the work of other craftsmen.

When Faris died on 15 August 1804, William McParlin wasted no time in
placing his first notice in the *Gazette* on 22 August (Figure 68 on page 74)
stating that he was still engaged in the work of silver and clock and watch
making at the place of the late William Faris. McParlin remained at this location on West Street, married Cassandra Woodward (Priscilla Faris's great-

---

[72] Account Book, 1790–1800.

niece) in 1816, and purchased the property outright from the Faris heirs in 1818 after Priscilla's death in 1817.[73]

WILLIAM M'PARLIN,
CLOCK AND WATCH-MAKER,
RESPECTFULLY informs the citizens of Annapolis, and its vicinity, that he has commenced BUSINESS at the shop lately kept by WILLIAM FARIS, in West-street, where clocks and watches of every description may be repaired in the most approved manner, and on the most moderate terms, also gold and silver work made, sold, and repaired; engraving, such as cyphers, seals, &c. neatly executed, and he assures those who please to honour him with their commands, that the utmost of his abilities shall be exerted to give general satisfaction.
N. B. Old gold and silver bought as usual.
August 22, 1804.

68 ☞ Maryland Gazette
22 August 1804

William McParlin placed this notice in the Gazette within a week of Faris's death.

William Faris, like other silversmiths of the period, marked the silver coming out of his shop with his initials, **WF**. As the master or proprietor of the shop, his initials would have been struck on the silver using a steel die, carved in reverse with the smith's initials or name. This die would be held with one hand, while the other hand used a hammer to strike and impress the mark on the piece. The American colonies did not have a hallmarking system to regulate a standard of purity in their silver as in England, a custom that never changed throughout the colonial period. The English guild system required a series of marks to appear on all silver items, indicating the purity of the alloy itself, the year in which it was made, the city where the item was made, and the mark of the smith who presented it for testing. The masters of American silver shops generally used only their initials or, toward the end of the eighteenth century, their initial and surname. Because many customers were used to the hallmarked examples on the English silver, American smiths often stamped their marks two or more times on a piece of silver.

Unfortunately, initialed punches, such as **WF**, are very difficult to attribute to a particular maker with any known certainty unless the provenance of the piece leaves no room for error. Historically, scholars engaged in silver research have tentatively ascribed marks based on newspapers notices, city directories,

---

[73] Any products manufactured by McParlin after that date are beyond the scope of this book.

and other documentary evidence by matching names and conjectured dates to initials. Other than by using the rare document, such as a letter, inventory, or shop record, that lists the name of the maker of a specific piece, the best way to authenticate attributions of initial punches is to find pieces that have descended in the family of the original maker or owner. This can be done for William Faris because several pieces of Faris silver descended from his daughter Ann to her son Charles Faris Pitt and then to the eldest son of each generation thereafter. Pieces of silver that have both the **WF** mark and the engraved initials of the Pitt family provide a virtual confirmation of the mark. Comparison of an unattributed mark with marks of verifiable family-owned pieces narrows the margin of error in identifying the undocumented mark.

Most of the Pitt family silver pieces are available for study at the Maryland Historical Society. Many of these pieces were not of Faris's crafting—in fact only two pieces currently in this collection are from his shop—but some of the others undoubtedly belonged to him. This important group of silver allows the scholar ample opportunity to study one family's collection of silver from the eighteenth and nineteenth centuries. The Pitts were obviously interested in preserving their family heritage because they engraved their collection with the initials of each succeeding generation. William and Ann Faris Pitt not only obtained most of William Faris's personal silver but also purchased at least one if not more silver items of their own, which they passed down in their family. Most of the remaining pieces were either made by Faris or obtained by him for his own use. The neoclassical cream pot in Figure 69 shown above, marked by John Walraven of Baltimore, may have been acquired from Charles Faris's estate.[74]

Other pieces that belonged to Faris and descended in the Pitt family are the caster by John Delmester made in London in 1762/63 (Figure 70 on page 76) and later engraved with **WAP**, which is very similar to one of the shop drawings, and a large bright-cut engraved ladle, marked by William Skinner, a silversmith from Easton on the Eastern Shore, also later engraved **WAP**. Another important piece from the Faris home is the small scissor-type sugar tongs marked by Phillip Syng Sr. that dates from the 1730s (Figure 71 on page 76). These are marked on the inside of the grips with the maker's mark and engraved on the outside of one grip with the initials **P*W**, most likely for Priscilla Woodward, and **T*W*S** on the other bowl, perhaps for another Woodward couple. They are earlier than the example mentioned above by

---

74 Charles had dealings (unspecified) with Walraven, which William Sr. had to
    resolve after Charles's death. Charles owned 36 ounces of plate when he died.

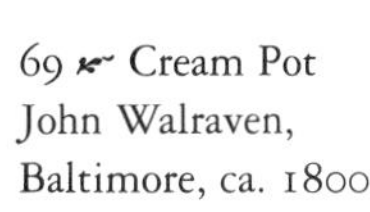

69   Cream Pot
John Walraven,
Baltimore, ca. 1800

This elegant tall fluted cream pot was made by Baltimore silversmith John Walraven ca. 1800. Although we cannot be certain how it came into the family, John Walraven did have business dealings with Charles Faris that his father had to settle after Charles's death in 1800. This cream pot could have been part of Charles's estate or perhaps was purchased by William and Ann Faris Pitt when they were living in Baltimore.

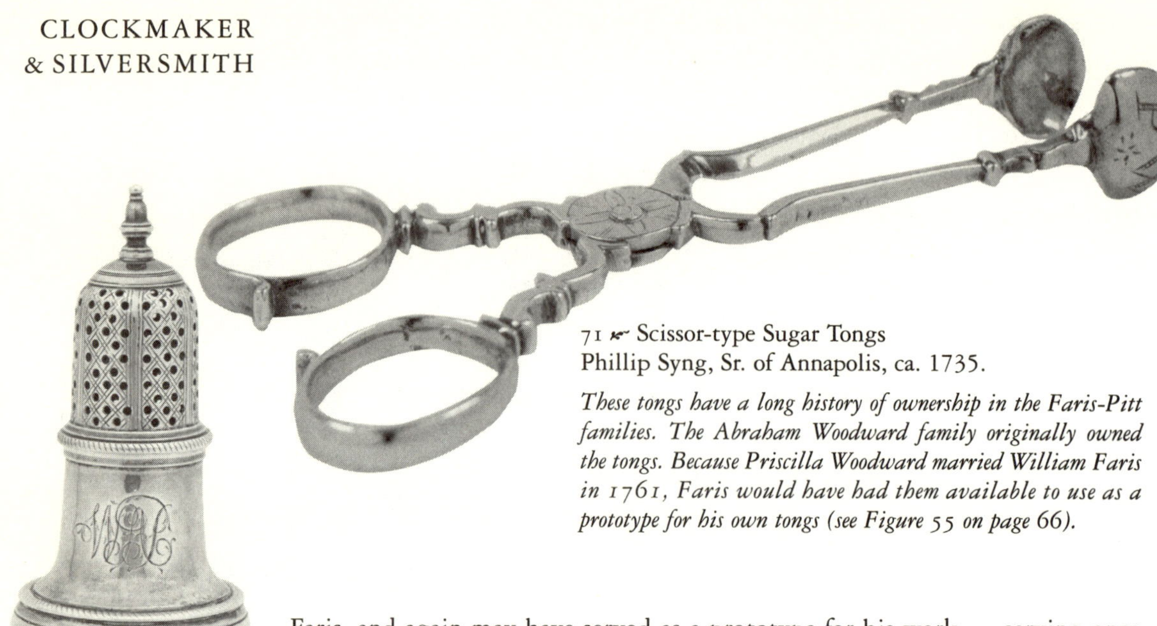

71 ✒ Scissor-type Sugar Tongs
Phillip Syng, Sr. of Annapolis, ca. 1735.

These tongs have a long history of ownership in the Faris-Pitt families. The Abraham Woodward family originally owned the tongs. Because Priscilla Woodward married William Faris in 1761, Faris would have had them available to use as a prototype for his own tongs (see Figure 55 on page 66).

70 ✒ Caster marked by John Delmester, London, 1762/1763 Fully marked on base with Lion passant, leopard's head crowned, gothic letter G for 1762/63, makers mark ID, lion passant also on lid.
Engraved: *WAP* for William and Ann Faris Pitt

This caster, which probably belonged to William Faris, is very similar to one of his shop drawings (Figure SD4 on page 433). This English example shows the extent to which the local population depended on and favored English goods in the eighteenth century.

Faris, and again may have served as a prototype for his work — serving once more to acknowledge the interrelationship of different goldsmiths in the colonial period.[75]

Perhaps the piece of silver most associated with Faris's personal collection is the tulip-shaped tankard, marked by Peter David of Philadelphia in the 1740s, bearing the initials **WF** on the handle (Figure 72 on page 77). This tankard is particularly interesting as it was acquired for Faris's own use yet his means of obtaining it remains a mystery. In the late 1740s, when Faris was ending his apprenticeship in Philadelphia, it would have been unlikely that as a journeyman he could have purchased such an extravagant piece. A tankard was a large and important piece of silver even for a gentleman of means. Perhaps his mother Abigail gave this to her son before he left Philadelphia, or he may have obtained it in trade for other services. The fact that Faris also purchased property in the same town in 1749 allows us at least to speculate as to his financial solidity. This tankard passed to his daughter Ann, engraved *WAP 1801*, and down through the Pitt family. Silversmiths of this period hardly ever died owning more than a few spoons, let alone a collection of the magnitude of the 155 oz. of plate that Faris possessed at the time of his death.[76] Silver was often inventoried by weight and not itemized individually. It is unusual but fortunate that so much of Faris's personal silver collection is still

---

75 Similarly, there is a private collection today that includes three nearly identical tablespoons with marks by as many different makers: William Faris, Samuel Soumaien, and James Chalmers. They were made for the same family at different times and have the same engraved set of initials; the collection also includes a soup ladle made by Thomas Sparrow for the same family.

76 Jennifer Goldsborough, personal communication, 25 January 2001.

72 ☛ Tankard
Peter David
(1707–1755),
Philadelphia, ca.
1740–1750. Marked **PD**
in oval reserve in lip on
each side of handle.
Engraved **WF** on ter-
minal end of handle for
William Faris;
WAP/1801 for William
and Ann Faris Pitt on
one side; **CCP/1848** for
Charles and Catherine
Pitt and **HP/1884** for
Herbert St. John Pitt on
other side; **FCP Jr./1912**
for Faris C. Pitt Jr. on
cover; **EGP/1914** for
Ethel Gordon Pitt on
handle.
Height: 7 1/8"

*William Faris probably
acquired this tankard
when he lived in
Philadelphia. Note that
the shape of this tankard
is almost identical to the
shop drawing of a
tankard in Faris's design
book (Fig. SD10 on page
439).*

known; its extent should generate new thoughts and ideas in the interpretation of this craftsman's status.

It is not always possible to establish the origins and provenance of indi-
vidual artifacts. One of the best documented pieces in the Pitt collection is the
two-handled cup made in 1702/03 by Robert Peake of London. This cup
(Figure 73 on page 78) was originally imported from England by Abraham
Woodward in the early eighteenth century, according to notes by Charles Faris
Pitt in the family Bible. Pitt claimed that the"Silver chased cup, now with
mother, belonged to same [Abraham Woodward] and by him imported [from
England], being one of those cups, for his 3 daughters." This cup originally
belonged to Priscilla Ruley Orrick Woodward (Abraham's wife) who
bequeathed it to her daughter Priscilla Faris in her will dated 18 October
1771, proved 9 March 1773. The will states: *"I give and bequeath to my daughter
Priscilla Farris one silver cupp one best bed and furniture and one saddle and my
wareing apparel to her disposal."*77 The cup remained in the Faris house until
1804 when William and Ann Faris Pitt obtained it after Faris's death. The

---

77 Prerogative Court, Wills, 39/254, MSA.

73 ☛ Two-handled Cup marked by Robert Peake, London, *1702/1703*

Fully marked under rim with Britannia standard, lion's head erased, PE in shield for Robert Peake and date letter for *1702/1703*.

According to the Pitt family Bible, Abraham Woodward imported this cup for his three daughters. Priscilla Woodward Faris received it from her mother, Priscilla Ruley Orrick Woodward, at her death in 1773. William and Priscilla Faris owned the cup until Faris's death when it went to their daughter Ann. The cup then descended in the Pitt family. Another important aspect of this piece is that it was repaired and possibly engraved in the early nineteenth century by George Aiken, a proficient Baltimore silversmith. This is one of only a handful of pieces bearing an American silversmith's mark as well as the English hallmarks of its origin. This piece was already one hundred years old when George Aiken made his repairs and has a history of three hundred years of Maryland ownership.

piece is inscribed with a series of initials on the bottom of the cup: *PW 1746* for Priscilla Woodward, *AP 1804* for Ann Pitt, *FCP 1876* for Faris Chappell Pitt, and *NKP 1898* for Nita Kurtz Pitt. The cartouche on the front of the cup is engraved with the frequently encountered *WAP* for William and Ann Faris Pitt. Another intriguing feature is the touch mark of George Aiken, a Baltimore silversmith who did some repair work on the piece around 1810 and probably engraved it. This is one of the few examples of English silver also stamped with an American mark.[78] When Aiken worked on this piece he was perhaps aware that it was already one hundred years old.

As important as the silver pieces are that originated in Faris's shop, equally if not more significant are his surviving shop drawings. These twenty-one bench drawings are the only extant drawings from a colonial American silver shop. These pen and ink drawings, in some places overlaid with pencil, were unquestionably working shop drawings, showing compass marks and other signs of actual use. Some scholars have speculated that they might have been imported or otherwise acquired.[79] It is just as likely that they were created in Faris's shop because the pieces represented evolve stylistically. That is to say, some of the drawings are of early styles and some of later fashions; they are not a group that could have been assembled at one time. Whether acquired elsewhere or created in Faris's shop, they are representative of an advanced operation in a fascinating place and time in American history. The shop drawings provide one more example of the versatility and ingenuity of one eighteenth-century man. William Faris was one of Annapolis's most captivating citizens, a renaissance man, whose diary opens for us a world to discover and explore.

78 Goldsborough, *Silver in Maryland*, 68.

79 Hugh Honour, *Goldsmiths & Silversmiths* (New York: G. P. Putnam's Sons, 1971), 215.

William Faris's Garden

SHOULD YOU HAVE FOUND YOURSELF on a springtime stroll in
Annapolis, Maryland during the third quarter of the eighteenth century, you
would have been struck by a most pleasant aromatic and visual display coming
out of a local clockmaker's garden, just a short walk along West Street from
St. Anne's Church. Your eyes would indeed have strayed past the front gate
toward the rear of this property, longing to see more. The song of a pet mock-
ingbird and other caged birds would have added aurally to the already over-
loaded senses. Had you knocked on the door of this inveterate gardener, you
likely would have been welcomed as a friend, especially if your intent was to
see the myriad of blooming tulips and other colorful flowers arranged within
the geometrically-edged boxwood beds with their crushed oyster-shell and
grass-lined pathways. A tour through this garden would have been a walk
through a veritable Eden.[1]

William Faris was passionate about his garden, and its care provided the
main theme that permeates his thirteen-year diary. If one had to choose the
subject nearest to his heart throughout the period he wrote in his journal, it
would have to be his garden. In the busy gardening seasons, a day hardly went
by without Faris recording some facet of planting, weeding, grafting,
dividing, hoeing, or harvesting in his West Street lot. He was intimately
aware of his surroundings, and knew what to expect year in and year out from
his plantings. He recorded the weather on a daily basis and took note of the

---

[1] This essay is based in part on the following works by Barbara Wells Sarudy: "The
Gardens and Grounds of an Eighteenth-century Chesapeake Craftsman" (M.A
thesis, University of Maryland, 1988); "A Chesapeake Craftsman's Eighteenth-cen-
tury Gardens," *Journal of Garden History,* 9 (July–September 1989): 141–52; and
Gardens and Gardening in the Chesapeake: 1700–1805 (Baltimore: Johns Hopkins
University Press, 1998).

temperature as part of his gardening practices. His penchant for repetition and experimentation over the years he kept his diary was also typical of the horticulturist. Faris looked over his gardening entries not only for the current season's progress, but to compare with the results of previous years and the development of particular plants.

Walking through an eighteenth-century garden would probably not have been too foreign to what we know today as many of the plants in cultivation at that time are still favorites with today's gardeners. In this visit to Faris's garden, we will look systematically at the way he laid out the garden, as well as consider the individual flowers, vegetables, and other items he cultivated in the 1790s, the only period for which he left documentation.

We are not certain when Faris began to lay out his Annapolis garden, but it must have been in the mid-1760s, for a notice appeared in the *Maryland Gazette* on 18 March 1769 announcing that Faris was selling the remaining *"time of a servant MAN, who has got between Six and Seven Years to serve — He is by Trade a Gardiner."* By this time the skeleton of the garden may have been completed, making the services of this individual no longer necessary.

In planning his garden, Faris used a grid-like pattern to separate the beds in which he planted his flowers and vegetables. (See Figure 74 on page 81)[2] He may have adopted this geometric style from the gardening manuals of his day, or perhaps from observations made during his walks through the town, studying and recording the gardens of his neighbors.[3] This geometric framework created practical pathways that provided access not only for the different beds but also for the stables, smokehouse, shed, and privy, which Faris called his "temple" or "little house." He built these composition pathways of crushed oyster shell (which would harden into a firm surface with constant use and rain), pulverized brick, and sand.[4] Faris alternated intersecting boxwood-lined grass walkways with the composition ones in his design. Faris and his garden helpers, who were many and varied, carefully weeded and tended the walkways. Faris constantly picked up debris from the composition walkways, keeping them in immaculate condition.

Faris's most frequent garden hand was his female slave Sylve. We find Sylve throughout the span of the diary performing many of the chores and much of the maintenance in the yard. She hoed, weeded, swept, and planted alongside Faris during the entire year. They worked outside in the garden at all times of year as long as the weather permitted, being most active in the early spring

---

2 We are grateful to Barbara Wells Sarudy for granting permission to use her map depicting the layout of William Faris's garden. And, of course, the garden undoubtedly evolved over the forty years that Faris tended it.

3 Mac Griswold, *Washington's Gardens at Mount Vernon* (Boston: Houghton Mifflin Company, 1999), 43

4 Sarudy, *Journal of Garden History*, 143

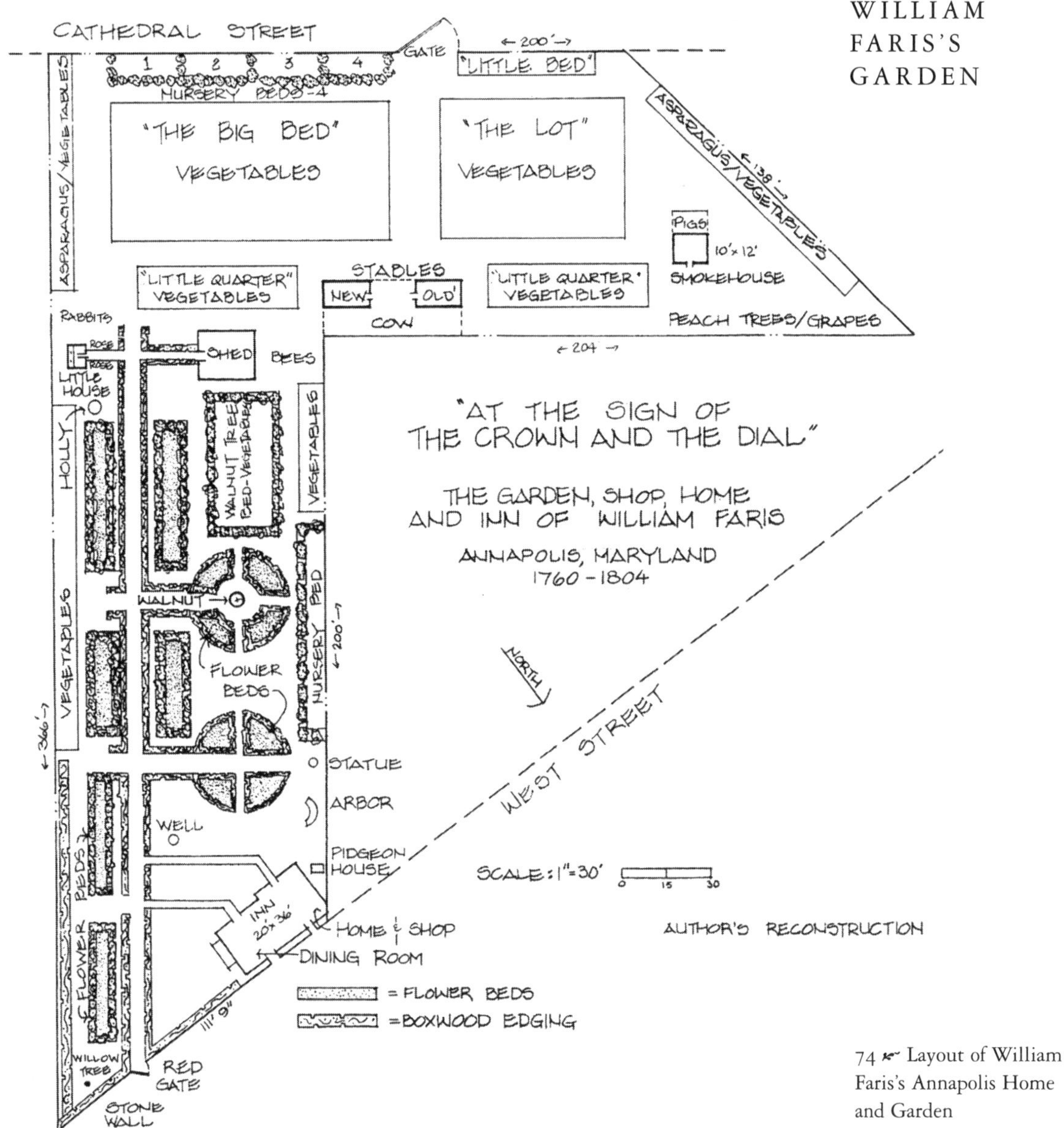

74 ↞ Layout of William Faris's Annapolis Home and Garden

and tapering off in their activities as summer progressed. Sylve was not alone, however, being one of many enslaved blacks (mostly hired from his neighbors), free blacks, and white indentured servants, as well as Faris's family members, who worked assiduously in the garden. Faris also recorded one occasion when his wife, Priscilla, planted peas.

The labor-related aspect of the garden involved many facets. Faris had dung delivered, wheeled in, and spread to augment and fertilize the beds. He also collected dung from his pig enclosure for this purpose. He supervised the troweling of the beds as well as the raking and leveling of the walkways. Trimming the boxwood, which outlined the many beds, was a labor-intensive chore that occupied many of his garden helpers in the spring. Faris ensured that the boxwood would not exceed a certain height, in keeping with the uniformity of the edged beds. Physical work in a garden, no matter how small, is demanding, and more so in Faris's time when one considers how many technological advances used today were not yet available to the eighteenth-century gardener. Faris recorded hiring many laborers during the diary years: when they began, the fact that they never stayed long, and how he consistently paid them the same salary of £12 per year.[5]

Faris's property was small compared to the established seats of wealthy Annapolitans, but nonetheless it was a sizeable plot of land to cultivate. His lot extended three hundred sixty-six feet from West Street to Cathedral Street, bounded on the east side by two of the neighbors with whom he sometimes exchanged seeds: William Goldsmith, until his death in 1797, and then by Eleanor Davidson. At the far end near Cathedral Street Mary Mann had a garden plot. A stone wall formed the first part of this boundary, where neighbor John Riegel lived, but opened up about a third of the distance to a picket fence that extended as far as Cathedral Street. Fences were important elements of eighteenth-century properties, not only used to demarcate property lines but also to keep out unwanted wildlife as well as trespassers.[6] Two hundred feet into the west side of his garden, the property made a sharp right turn, extending another two hundred four feet toward the boundary with neighbor Vachel Stevens, who exchanged more seeds and plants with Faris than anyone else in the diary. The property was in effect a large inverted L-shape. From the West Street vantage point, the garden extended perpendicularly, providing a vista of carefully planted flowers and ornamental plants. This would have been the view of which passersby on West Street would take note and the one of which Faris would have been most proud. The Cathedral Street side of Faris's property was the area where he kept the more utilitarian aspects of his establishment, such as the stables, smokehouse, hog enclosures, and his kitchen garden.[7] This was no accident; Faris carefully placed the ornamental view of his garden so that its aesthetics would prevail. This is not much different from our proclivity today to landscape our houses with the more elaborate foundation plantings of our gardens in conjunction with the street facades of our homes.

If you entered the garden through the West Street gate, a willow tree would have been the first presence encountered in the narrow space. This tree stood until March of 1801, when Faris wrote that it *fell the wrong way against the playhouse yard.* The path gave way to the first of six rectangular flowerbeds in

---

[5] A minimum of thirteen male laborers worked for Faris at different times during the years of the diary.

[6] Sarudy, *Journal of Garden History*, 141.

[7] Ibid., 144.

this axis, where Faris planted flowers surrounded by boxwood edging. In these beds he raised crown imperials, anemones, tuberoses, tulips, and larkspurs among many other varieties.[8] Faris propagated many of the same flowers that were raised by George Washington and Thomas Jefferson in their pleasure gardens.[9] Against the wall that bordered his neighbor John Riegel's property, Faris planted some vegetables, apparently the only such bed in this ornamental area of his garden. Leaving behind the first of these flowerbeds, visitors then encountered another series of rectangular beds, also filled with flowers, which flanked the path in pairs. Next came the well that supplied water for Faris and his family as well as for irrigation of his plants. The well was placed in an advantageous location, facilitating the ancient technique of carefully flooding dirt channels that ran throughout the garden.[10] Faris referred to these channels as his "water tables." He continually recorded the maintenance of these tables, concerned especially for the survival of his not-yet-established plants and seedlings.

The walnut tree, with its surrounding boxwood-edged semicircular quarter-shaped beds, provided the dominant feature in this central part of the garden. Faris mentions planting his tulips, bleeding hearts, and other tender perennials in these beds. He wrote on 6 September 1794 that he *"Beeat the walnuts off the Tree and got I supose a Bushel of nutts,"* and on 16 June 1804 that he *"picked 320 wallnuts of the Tree."* This was one of two circular beds laid out in the same format; the second one, opposite the walnut tree in the direction of West street, was the "Circle bed," which did not have a tree in it until 1 April 1797 when Faris *"took up the Tree called the Pride of Chiney & planted it in the middle of the circkel in the garden"* and on 17 March 1800 when he *" planted a pear Tree in the midel of the scircel."* It is not always clear, however, to which circle Faris refers. He planted this circle bed profusely with India pinks, polyanthus, tuberoses, wall flowers, asters, and tulips. Proceeding past the walnut tree, toward the rear of the property, was the "walnut tree bed" where Faris planted vegetables and some flowers. Faris did not usually mix his ornamental plants with the vegetables, although he occasionally did place a tulip bulb in one of these beds. He positioned a statue in the center of the garden next to the wall that separated his garden from neighbor Thomas Grayham's property.[11] To the right of the statue Faris placed the arbor where he planted beans, no doubt due to their climbing habit and graceful flowers. To the right of the arbor stood the pigeon coop, where Faris bred pigeons for consumption by his family and

---

8 See Appendix pages 451-61 for a complete listing of all the flowers, trees, shrubs, and vegetables that Faris grew.

9 Ann Leighton, *American Gardens in the Eighteenth Century* (Boston: Houghton Mifflin, 1976; repr. University of Massachusetts Press, 1986), 387–489.

10 Sarudy, *Journal of Garden History*, 144.

11 Faris never recorded exchanging plants or seeds with Grayham.

tavern customers; he noted that he installed this coop in 1777 and that it blew down in 1798.

Behind the walnut-tree bed was the dividing line where the utilitarian side of Faris's garden began. His "little quarter" was the first bed encountered immediately across from the shed. Here he planted onions, cabbages, peas, carrots, different varieties of beans, and spinach. Directly in front of the "the little quarter" was the "garden" or the "big bed," which lay at the extreme rear of his property and was bordered with sage and rosemary. Faris clipped these herbs much in the same way he did his boxwood edging, with the intent of defining the borders of the beds in his kitchen garden. He grew vegetables exclusively in this bed for his family and inn patrons, including cucumbers, corn, cantaloupes, watermelons, cauliflower, and cabbage. Faris augmented his vegetable production by shopping at market for items he did not grow or did not have in sufficient quantity.[12] Directly adjacent to the big bed was "the lott." In this large bed he planted more cantaloupes, watermelons, simlins (squash), cucumbers, and muskmelons. These two beds provided room for the spreading and space-absorbing varieties; when space was a consideration, maximizing it was essential. Facing "the lot" were the two stables, both the new and the old where Faris kept his cow and where the boarders in his inn could keep their horses. To the right of "the lot" Faris placed yet another vegetable bed, a few feet from the smokehouse where he hung the meat that he purchased and branded as well as the pigs he had slaughtered. The pig enclosure lay directly behind the smokehouse, very near to his peach trees and grape vines. Faris not only distilled his peaches to make brandy, which became a staple like cider,[13] but fed the peaches to his pigs to increase the flavor of their meat when slaughtered.[14] Faris kept other fruiting trees in this area of the garden, including plums, almonds, cherries, pears, apples, and mulberries. On 5 September 1799 Faris received *some plums from Mrs. N. Carrol thay call them the Magnum Bonum . . . I have made some of them in wax.* George Washington received this same variety in 1760 from his friend George Mason of Gunston Hall.[15] Faris's pressed botanical studies, which he kept in the back of his design book, included the leaves of his white mulberry tree. (Figure 75 on page 85) He wrote in his diary that he fed these leaves to his silkworms, a gift from a friend. The gooseberry and currant bushes, whose fruit he gathered and bottled, also grew in this area of the garden.

Faris kept two rectangular beds on opposite ends of the Cathedral Street side of his property where he planted asparagus ("asparagrass") as well as other

---

[12] Sarudy, *Gardens and Gardening*, 115–16.

[13] Leighton, *American Gardens in the Eighteenth Century*, 237.

[14] Sarudy, *Journal of Garden History*, 138. Faris also distilled mint (see 15 July 1802) but did not indicate his purpose in doing so.

[15] Griswold, *Washington's Garden*, 121.

75 ⚘ Pressed Tulip and
Mulberry Leaves

*See also Figure 14 in color
insert.*

vegetables. He placed these beds against the two fenced boundaries of his
neighbors. At the rear of his property, a second gate provided access to this
area. This entrance was probably the one used by workers delivering his tan
and dung as well as the entrance used by the horses boarded in his stables.

Backing up to the fence directly along Cathedral Street, Faris kept a series of four nursery beds where he rooted boxwood cuttings as well as other flowers. He would root the cuttings from the spring boxwood trimming until they were established, transplanting them to the mature beds once a root system formed. On 30 September 1799 Faris planted 847 Tulip roots in these beds. Faris kept a second boxwood-edged nursery bed adjacent to the boundary with his neighbor Thomas Grayham.

Opposite the shed where Faris kept his garden tools (consisting of his rake, hoe, trowel and spade)[16] stood the privy. He planted flowers in boxwood-lined beds leading to this necessary structure, as well as holly trees transplanted in 1799 and 1800 by one of his laborers, "old William," from the nearby woods.[17] Although Faris wrote that he *trimed the Holley Tree in the garden,"* on 1 April 1797, we have no evidence as to the shape in which he kept them. These holly trees would have provided year-around greenery when so many of the deciduous plantings lay dormant. The boxwood edging also maintained the structural impression of the beds when no flowers bloomed.

William Faris obtained many of his ornamental plants and vegetables from exchanges with friends in the Annapolis community. There was apparently an extensive bartering system within and across all social barriers. Faris traded seeds and plants with gentlemen, single and married women, and many of his neighbors.[18] Faris not only exchanged seeds and plants with his neighbors in Annapolis, but in Baltimore as well. He recorded in his diary receiving plants shipped by the packet and delivered to his home. Maximilian Heuisler, who owned a nursery near Baltimore, was Faris's most frequent contributor of plants and seeds outside Annapolis. This plant exchange system provided a means by which gardeners could vary many of the plantings in their garden as well as introduce new species and cultivars. Faris routinely recorded new kinds that he had not seen before. Gardeners continued to be introduced to new varieties still relatively unknown in cultivation.[19]

In the spring of 1793 William Faris received a hive of bees as a gift from his friend Henry Sibell, a local baker. Honeybees were an important con-

---

[16] Sarudy, *Journal of Garden History,* 147.

[17] Transplanting native trees and shrubs was not peculiar to Faris. Many gardeners, among them George Washington, routinely transplanted native flora to incorporate into their landscapes. Griswold, *Washington's Gardens,* 70. One of the original holly trees attributed to Faris's planting was not taken down until c.1985.

[18] Six different people exchanged seeds or plants with Faris on more than five occasions during the span of the diary: Joseph Brewer, Eleanor Davidson, Alexander Contee Hanson, Maximilian Heuisler, Upton Scott, and Vachel Stevens. The breakdown in gender and race for all exchanges is as follows: fifty white men, twelve married women, five unmarried women, and five black men and women (both free and enslaved).

[19] Griswold, *Washington's Gardens,* 65.

stituent of a well-kept garden, not only for their pollinating contributions but also for the practical products of honey and beeswax that could be collected from their hives. Bee keeping has been practiced since at least the seventeenth century when man began to attempt domesticating these insects.[20] By establishing hives to keep the bees in a controlled environment, beekeepers are able to use the insects in an economically advantageous way. Faris diligently recorded hiving his bees and cleaning out the wooden hives that he built for them. When Faris referred to the "swarming"and "hiving" of his bees, he was taking advantage of the periodic process by which bees abandoned one hive and moved into a new one, allowing Faris to harvest the honey and beeswax from the old hive. This phenomenon occurred because of overcrowding in the original hive.[21] That Faris would keep bees is a predictable facet of his personality and the regimentation that he exercised is evident in his success with their husbandry.

Faris used pots, probably of earthenware or clay, as containers to plant his more unusual flowers, which he could then move at his whim and place wherever he felt they would be most attractive. In these pots he planted some of his more prized species such as Jerusalem cherry trees, chrysanthemum, ice plants, polianthus, mignonettes, impatiens, ivy, tuberoses, hyacinths, sensitive plants, and tulips. He moved these containers along with the plants into the cellar for the winter, leaving the wooden containers, which he referred to as barrels or casks, outside all year. He refilled all his containers with additional dirt when the previous year's soil had settled. Faris also used flower boxes to plant his prized botanical specimens.

Faris tried his hand at different scientific techniques that were part of the horticultural practices of the period. He experimented with grafting (usually referred to as inoculating or budding at this time), the technique of joining the budded end of one variety of plant, called the scion, onto another established plant, called the stock. The joined seam is then coated with a waxy substance until the desired union is obtained. This technique developed as a means of propagating a sterile species onto the trunk of an established plant.[22] On 23 March 1801 Faris *"grafted 5 or 6 Black Curran siances with the Rose grafts."* George Washington grafted and planted hundreds of fruit trees over many years at Mount Vernon.[23] Faris also white washed the trunks as well as

---

[20] *Encyclopedia Britannica, Macropaedia*, 15th ed. (Chicago: University of Chicago, 1976), 2:791.

[21] Swarming usually takes place in the middle of a warm day when the queen bee leaves the old hive, followed by many of the worker bees. She then alights on a tree branch or other surface with the swarm clustered around her, while a group of scout bees searches for a new site. *Encyclopedia Britannica, Macropaedia*, 2:792.

[22] Ibid., 4:663.   [23] Griswold, *Washington's Gardens*, 121.

76 ᴇ Alexander Contee
Hanson (1749–1806)

scraped the bark off his peach trees.[24] Whitewashing the trunks during the winter months may have been done to deflect the reflection of the sun, thereby preventing the splitting of the trunk as it warmed during the day and froze at night. One possible reason for scraping the bark off the peach trees was to prevent insects from burrowing and thereby damaging the trunks of the trees.[25] Faris may also have hybridized his own flowers, as he raised large quantities of both balsam and tulip hybrids; however, he did not claim to name the list of tulip hybrids recorded in his diary on 13 May 1799 but gave credit to his friend and gardening colleague Alexander Contee Hanson. Hanson named some of the tulips after Revolutionary War heroes, classical personages, and contemporary authors. Faris pressed some of the following tulips in his scrapbook: General Green, General Smallwood, General Montgomery, the Brunette, and the Grayhound. (See Figures 77–80 on page 90)

We have no evidence that Faris owned gardening books, as only a few books were listed by title in the record of his estate sale. Nevertheless, given the size of his library and the importance of his garden to him, he must have had access at the very least to some volumes and more than likely owned gardening books himself.[26] The sophistication of his garden leads one to believe he read at least moderately on the subject. A garden of this complexity would have been very difficult to execute exclusively by observing other gardens and exchanging advice with fellow gardeners.

---

[24] Faris also recorded topping his peach trees, using composition on the pruned areas, and tarring the bases as well. All of these practices are facets of proper fruit tree arboriculture.

[25] Rollin Woolley, Colonial Williamsburg Foundation, personal communication, 7 February 2001.

[26] Some of the gardening books which Faris may have used were: Philip Miller's *Gardener's Dictionary,* first published in London in 1731 and subsequently printed in many editions throughout the eighteenth century. Many planters and gardeners in the Chesapeake region particularly and throughout the American colonies in general used this book as a principal source of botanical information. Batty Langley's *New Principles of Gardening,* published in London in 1728, was popular and was turned to especially in the architectural designing of one's garden. Toward the end of the eighteenth century, Londoner William Curtis's *Botanical Magazine,* was a periodical first published in 1787 and continued until Curtis's death in 1799. The magazine continued to be published long after Curtis's death and well into the twentieth century. Many of the plants found in Faris's garden were illustrated in hand-colored copper plate engravings in this periodical. It was not until after Faris's death, however, that the first American book on gardening was published in 1806 by Bernard M'Mahon in Philadelphia and titled *The American Gardener's Calendar.* Batty Langley, *New Principles of Gardening* (London, 1728); Philip Miller, *The Gardener's Dictionary* (London, 1731); Bernard M'Mahon, *The American Gardener's Calendar* (Philadelphia, 1806); William Curtis, *The Botanical Magazine or Flower Garden Displayed* (London, 1797–1800).

By the time Faris kept his garden, tulips had been in cultivation since the
sixteenth century. During the seventeenth century, particularly from 1634 to
1637, ownership of tulip bulbs occasioned such upheaval in Holland that they
became the most coveted of flowers, their possession and display a sign of great
prestige. The fury that developed coupled with the insanely high prices these
bulbs reached — some worth as much as a town house — manifested itself in
a frenzy that became known as "Tulipomania"[27] We do not know when Faris
began planting tulips in his garden, or when he was first introduced to them,
but John Custis IV (1678–1749), a Virginia planter and burgess, and possibly
the best known gardener in colonial Virginia,[28] cultivated tulips in his
Williamsburg garden as early as 1725. Custis memorialized both himself and
his affection for tulips in a portrait painted ca. 1725 in which he posed with
his self-published volume, *"Of the Tulip,"* and a cut specimen of a cat tulip that
rested next to the book.[29] Tulips were undeniably Faris's favorite flower. He
cultivated them by the thousands, making his garden one of the showcases of
Annapolis in April and May.[30] Faris recorded on a yearly basis the number of
tulip stalks he broke off (removing the spent flower stalks once the bloom has
faded). He not only planted tulips in his main ornamental beds, but tucked
them in wherever he could fit them, even in pots or with some of his vegetables. During the spring, visitors to Faris's garden chose the varieties they
wished to purchase, which he marked with a notched stick. In the summer,
when he could divide the bulb, Faris sold the offsets to the individuals who
had marked the plant while in bloom. When Faris died, his fine collection of
tulip bulbs was auctioned off in his estate sale.

William Faris's garden was unique due to its complexity, fastidiousness,
and the faithful record that remains in the diary. Although gardening journals
have been thoroughly studied covering aristocratic landscapes such as George
Washington's Mount Vernon and Thomas Jefferson's Monticello, the elaborate
and finely-tuned garden of a craftsman enables us to appreciate this gentle-
manly pursuit from a different perspective. When one considers that avoca-
tions such as gardening were actually within reach of all segments of society,
one can begin to appreciate the evolution of a social system which, albeit divi-

---

[27] Anna Pavord, *The Tulip* (New York: Bloomsbury Press, 1999), 6.

[28] M. Kent Brinkley and Gordon W. Chappell, *The Gardens of Colonial Williamsburg.*
(Williamsburg: The Colonial Williamsburg Foundation, 1996), 56.

[29] Peter Martin, *The Pleasure Gardens of Virginia* (Princeton: Princeton University
Press, 1991), 63.

[30] Faris recorded breaking the stalks of the tulips after they had bloomed. He listed
the following numbers in May of each respective year: 1,490 in 1792, 1,900 in
1795, 1,956 in 1797, 1,645 in 1798, 3,945 in 1801, 3,656 in 1803, and 2,339
in 1804; a total of 16,931 individual blossoms in the seven years Faris recorded
his work.

sive in many respects, remained open to all who desired to participate in this activity.

77 ⚭ *Pressed Tulip No. 6 Gen'l Green*

78 ⚭ *Pressed Tulip No. 9 Gen'l Smallwood*

79 ⚭ *Pressed Tulip No 60 The Brunette*

80 ⚭ *May 20th: 1799: No. 46 The Gray Hound*

*Plants Grown by William Faris**

Flowers

Name	Alternate Name	Scientific name[31]
Globe Amaranthus		*Gomphrena globosa*
African Marigold	Aztec Marigold	*Tagetes erecta*
Anemone		*Anemone Sp.*[32]
Aster		*Aster Sp.*
Female Balsam	Garden Balsam	*Impatiens Balsamina*
Balsam Apple		*Momordica balsamina*
Bleeding Heart		*Dicentra spectabilis*
Calamus	Sweet Flag	*Acorus calamus*
Carnation	Pinks or Dianthus	*Dianthus caryophylus*
Caterpillars		*Scorpiurus Sp.*
China Aster	Chinese Aster	*Callistephus chinensis*
Chrysanthemum		*Chrysanthemum indicum*
Columbine		*Aquilegia canadensis*
Cockscomb	Tres Coleurs	*Celosia cristata*
Crocus		*Crocus vernus*
Crown Imperial		*Fritillaria imperialis*
Crusula		
Daffodil	Narcissus	*Narcissus Sp.*
Dwarf Morning Glory		*Convolvulus tricolor*
Evening Primrose	Tree Primrose	*Oenothera biennis*
Fleur de Lis	Dwarf Flower de Luce	*Iris pseudacorus*
Garden Primrose	Polyanthus	*Polyanthus X*[33]

* See Appendix pages 451–461 for more detailed list of plants.

[31] The scientific names included in this section are based on the following sources: Sarudy. "The Gardens and Grounds"; Brinkley and Chappell. *Gardens of Colonial Williamsburg*; Leighton. *American Gardens*; and Griswold, *Washington's Gardens*. Scientific names have been included only for the ornamental plants, shrubs, and trees but not for the fruits and vegetables, which are more generally known by their English names.

[32] *Sp.* follows the genus of a particular plant when the genus is known but not the exact species cultivated by Faris.

[33] "X" denotes a cross or hybrid between two or more forms and not a true species.

34 An asterisk denotes
a possible species
candidate, but one
not entirely
confirmed.

Name	Alternate Name	Scientific name
Geranium		Pelargonium Sp.
Hedgehog	Medic	Medicago intertexta
Hollyhock		Alcea rosea
Hyacinth		Hyacinthinus orientalis
Iceplant	Fig Marigold	Mesembryanthemum aureum
Impatiens	Female/Garden Balsam	Impatiens balsamina
Iris		Iris Sp.
Jasmine	Jessamine	Jasminum officinale
Jerusalem Cherry Tree		Solanum pseudo-capsicum
Job's Tears		Coix altissima
Jonquil		Narcissus jonquilla
Lady in Green	Lady's Smock	Cardamine pratensis *34 or Alchemilla vulgaris
Larkspur	Delphinium	Delphinium exaltatum or D.carolinianum
Lily		Sprekelia formosissima or Lilium Sp.
Marigold	Pot Marigold	Calendula officinalis
Mignonette		Reseda odorata
Nasturtium		Tropaeolum majus
Passion Flower	May-pop	Passiflora incarnata
Flowering Pea		Lathyrus latifolia
India Pink	Pinks or Dianthus	Dianthus chinensis/sinensis
Polyanthus	Garden Primrose	Polianthes X
Poppy	Common or Oriental	Papaver somniferum or P. orientalis.
Primrose	Common Primrose	Primula vulgaris
Ranunculus		Ranunculus or Anemonella Sp.
Reason		**Unidentified**
Rose		Rosa rugosa and R. alba
Satin Flower	Honesty	Lunaria annua
Sensitive Plant		Mimosa pudica or Dionaea muscipula
Snails	Medic	Medicago scutellata
Snapdragon		Antirrhinum majus
Stock	July flower or Gilliflower	Matthiola incana
Ten Commandments	Prayer Plant	Maranta leuconeura *
Tuberose		Polianthes tuberosa
Tulip		Tulipa gesnerana
Wallflower	English Wallflower	Cheiranthus Cheiri

Shrubs, Trees, Vines, and Grasses

Name	Alternate Name	Scientific Name
Althea	Rose-of-Sharon	*Hibiscus syriacus*
Boxwood	Box/Edging Boxwood	*Buxus sempervirens 'suffruticosa'*
Holly	American Holly	*Ilex opaca*
Horse Chestnut		*Aesculus Hippocastanum*
Ivy	English Ivy	*Hedera helix*
Formoso		***Unidentified***
Lilac	Common or Persian	*Syringa vulgaris or S. persica*
White Mulberry		*Morus alba*
Pride of China tree	Chinaberry/Pride of India	*Melia Azedarach*
Ribbon Grass	Ornamental Grass	*Phalaris Sp.**
Snowball	Guelder-rose	*Viburnum opulus*
Strawberry tree		*Arbutus unedo*
Sweet-scented shrub	Sweet shrub or Carolina Allspice	*Calycanthus floridus*
Tallow tree	Wax Myrtle	*Myrica cerifera**
Walnut	Black Walnut or White Walnut/Butternut	*Juglans nigra* or *Juglans cinerea*
Willow	Black Willow*	*Salix Sp.*
Golden Willow	Yellow Willow	*Salix vitellina*

Vegetables

Asparagus	Corn	Parsnip
Beans	Cucumbers	Peas
Beets	Eggplant	Pepper
Broccoli	Garlic	Pumpkin
Brussel Sprouts	Kale	Radish
Cabbage	Leeks	Shallots
Cantaloupe	Lettuce	Squash (Simlins)
Carrot	Musk Mellons	Spinach
Cauliflower	Okra	Turnip
Cherry Peppers	Onion	Watermelon
Colewort or Kale	Orach	

Fruits and Nuts

Apple	Gooseberry	Pear
Almond	Grapes	Plum
Cherry	Mulberry	Walnut
Currant	Peach	

Herbs

Bergamot Balm	Mint	Rosemary
Catnip	Nutmeg (Indian)	Saffron
Ginger	Parsley	Sage
Horseradish	Pickling Lime	Thyme

81 ☛ *Detail of
William Faris's
garden.*

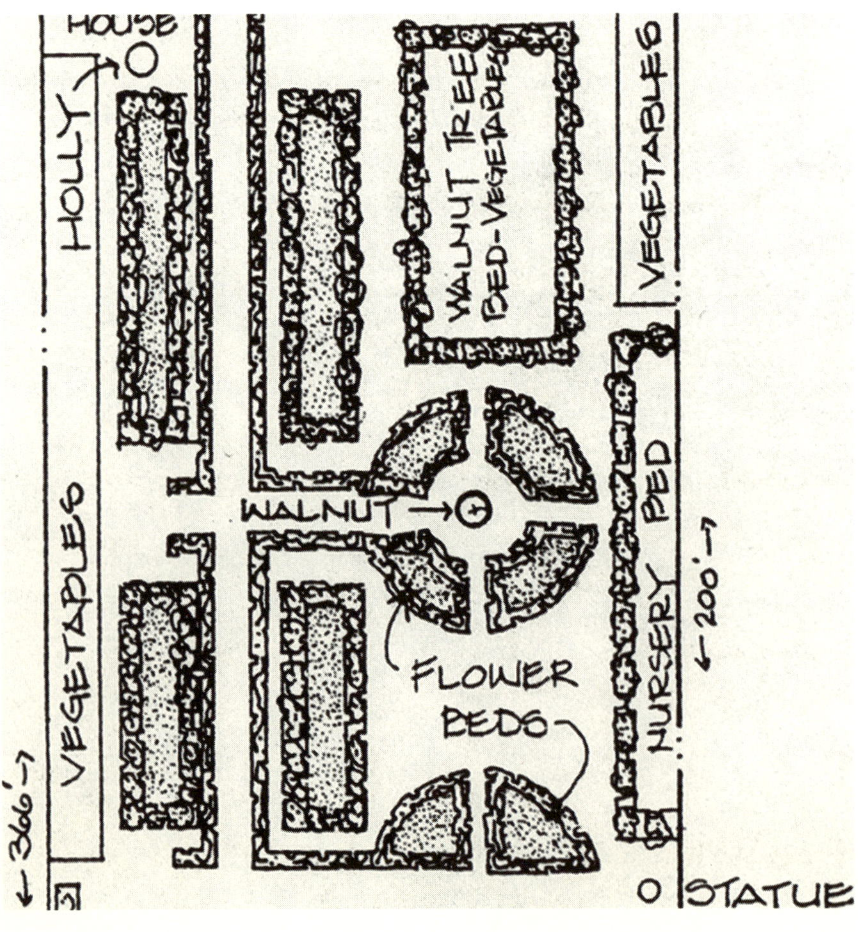

Children and Grandchildren

82 *~* Charles Faris

WHEN WILLIAM FARIS DIED on 15 August 1804, only three of
his nine children survived. This aspect of his life had been very difficult. One
son had been lost as an infant and his first daughter Rebecca had died young,
but the remainder of his losses were of adult children. Saint John had died in
1796, followed by Rebecca, Charles, and Hyram in the summer of 1800.[1]
Faris thus outlived at least six of his offspring. William Jr., remained in
Edenton, North Carolina, apparently never returning to Maryland. He married a widow by the name of Kesiah Hoskins O'Neil in 1803, who already had
grown children from a previous marriage.[2] To date, there are no known
descendants through William Faris Jr. Even in the Pitt family Bible, there is
a blank for the death date of William Jr.; only a space remains leaving us to
wonder about the rest of his life. This does not mean necessarily that the
family did not try remain in touch, but he may have just drifted away.
William received a share of his father's estate in 1808, but did not take part
in the sale of the family home to William McParlin in 1818. He may have
died by that time, or his sisters may have been unable to locate him to obtain
his agreement to the transfer. All four of the Faris sons having died without
known heirs, it is thus only through Faris's daughters Ann and Abigail that
any Faris descendants can be traced.

83 *~* St. John Faris

When Ann Faris married William Pitt on 7 July 1796 and the couple
moved to Fells Point in Baltimore, they began forming their large family
which would eventually consist of nine children. Ann and William would
reach an advanced age together, William dying almost at the age of 81 on 29

84 *~* Ann (Nancy) Faris

---

[1] Charles Faris Pitt recorded all of the Faris-Pitt family dates in the Pitt family Bible.

[2] Lockwood Barr, "Family of William Faris (1728–1804)," *Maryland Historical
Magazine* 37 (1942): 425.

85 ✍ Rebecca Maria
Pitt Chappell
(1798–1834)

December 1848, and Ann living to the age of 87, dying on 17 March 1860. Their first child, Priscilla Ann, was born in Annapolis on 13 May 1797 and died there on 17 July 1798, at the tender age of fourteen months, as her grandfather recorded in his diary. Before Priscilla Ann's death, however, Ann had given birth on 8 June 1798 to Rebecca Maria. Rebecca, known affectionately as Marriah by her doting grandfather, was the one grandchild who lived with him in Annapolis and therefore appears most often in his diary. Rebecca married John George Chappell, owner of a counting house, in Baltimore on 17 July 1817. Rebecca and John George had eight children before she died after eleven weeks of intense suffering from a disease of the spine, in her thirty-sixth year, on 1 January 1834.[3] As was typical of the period, Chappell quickly tried to replace his deceased wife, and turned to Rebecca's youngest sister, Priscilla Eliza. Priscilla, not mentioned in her grandfather's diary as she was not born until 8 December 1809, married her brother-in-law Chappell on 4 September 1834, nine months after Rebecca's death, and had five children of her own. She died in 1881.

Hannah Williams Pitt, born on 16 January 1800, was the third child of William and Ann Faris Pitt. The Pitts named her after her father's first wife, Hannah Williams, who died after just nine months of marriage. This child is an ever-present character in her grandfather's diary as she traveled back and forth with her family between Baltimore and Annapolis. Hannah married Frederick Shaffer Littig on 17 February 1820 and had six children before she died of consumption (tuberculosis) on 23 July 1837, after an illness of twenty-one months.[4] Frederick Shaffer Litttig, who changed his name in 1845 to Frederick Littig Shaffer in order to inherit his step-grandfather Frederick Shaffer's fortune, married Catherine Smythe ten months later and had several more children.

William Faris Pitt, whose Annapolis christening, with his sister Hannah's, Faris very proudly recorded, was born on 11 December 1801 and died at sea on a voyage to Santiago, Cuba on 18 October 1821, having never married. The same fate befell his brother Joseph Henry in New Orleans on September 8th of the following year. Joseph had been born in Baltimore on 12 June 1805 and was just seventeen years old when he died. Although we have no information as to either cause of death, we might assume the culprit to be yellow fever, still rampant at this time in the Caribbean islands and the American gulf states.

John Charles Pitt, born on 2 August 1803, was the last Pitt grandchild whom Faris mentioned in his diary. John Charles was barely a year old when his grandfather died. He grew up in Baltimore and married twice. His first

---

3 See *Baltimore American* newspaper (hereafter *BAN*), 29 January 1834, for Rebecca Pitt Chappell's obituary.

4 *BAN*, 24 July 1837.

marriage to Mary Hedrick on 7 September 1830 ended with her premature death on 6 February 1836.[5] The couple lived in Indiana at the time and had an infant child. John married Mary Ann Champlain in Baltimore on 7 March 1837 and had several more children. He died in Baltimore on 16 June 1876.

The last child of William and Ann Faris Pitt, who was never known by Faris but who would become the steward of most of the family heirlooms as well as its history, was Charles Faris Pitt, the namesake of his uncle Charles Faris, born on 7 February 1808. Charles was a free spirit who decided to sail around the world, first on the brig *Adele,* owned by John Lafitte, to Argentina and next to Mocha on the Red Sea coast on the ship *Lafayette*, also belonging to Lafitte. Upon returning to Baltimore, he opened his own house of business after working for a time in his brother-in-law Chappell's counting rooms. Charles founded his firm under the name of "Charles F. Pitt & Sons, Importers and Commission Merchants" on 116 Lombard Street and dealt in soda ash, caustic soda, sal soda, rosin, indigo, and jute butts.[6] Charles married Catherine Chappell, the sister of John George Chappell, on 3 September 1839. (Thus, three Pitt siblings married two Chappells.) Charles and Catherine had four children, including Faris C. Pitt, who would become the first curator of the Walters Art Gallery in Baltimore as well as a prominent art and antiques dealer.[7] Charles inherited most of the family silver, portraits, and furniture. He also was sufficiently aware of his heritage at an early age to proceed to record all the family dates and stories from the Faris and Pitt families in his Bible. It is only because of Charles's efforts that we have so much early information on these families today. Charles died in Baltimore on 8 April 1887.

When Ann died in 1860, only three of her children survived: Charles Faris, John Charles, and Priscilla Eliza. There had been one more daughter, Eliza, born on 4 July 1812 but she lived only nine days.

It is especially rewarding to conduct research on a family where anecdotal fragments of the past come down to us by way of letters or memoranda. The Pitt family Bible, enclosing the memorandum written by Charles Faris Pitt in 1853, has long provided an exceptional example of family stories recorded and passed down through the generations. We are truly fortunate, however, when hidden pearls of information appear unexpectedly to offer another window into the past. One such document[8] is a letter written by one of Ann Faris Pitt's granddaughters to one of Ann's great-great-grandchildren in the early years of

---

[5] *BAN*, 18 February 1836.

[6] George W. Howard, *The Monumental City* (Baltimore, 1889), 682.

[7] William R. Johnston, *William and Henry Walters: The Reticent Collectors* (Baltimore: Johns Hopkins University Press, 1999), 178.

[8] We are indebted to Mr. and Mrs. McEvoy Cromwell for allowing us access to the papers of the late C. Gordon Pitt, where this letter was found.

the twentieth century. In this letter her granddaughter states:

> . . . as my Mother told me, Grandfather [William Pitt] came to Annapolis in a ship, fell in love with Ann Faris, who would not marry any one or leave her Pappy. He married someone else, and later when his first wife died, came back and Ann changed her mind. He owned ships and must have been well off for those times, and evidently were in society, for Grandmother told me she had been fond of dress, and loved dancing, and one night at a ball, suddenly she was "converted" and never danced again and wore only black clothes. . . . As I remember her she was not very tall, but dignified and distingue [sic]. She always sat straight up, never in an arm or rocking chair, beautiful hands folded in her lap. I never saw her knit or sew.

86 ✎ Faris Chappell Pitt
(1842–1922)

Faris C. Pitt, the great-grandson of William Faris, was the first curator of the Walters Art Gallery and may have helped Henry Walters install the collection. He was also a board member of the Peabody Institute. Pitt was one of the owners of the cellarette illustrated in Figure 122 on page 267 and Figure 123 on page 268. See also Figure 11 in the color insert .

Her granddaughter went on to say that there were two portraits of her,[9] both with a child in her lap, one of them "Mrs. Shaffer" (Hannah Pitt) and the other "Mrs. J. G. Chappell" (Rebecca Maria). She then continued: "After Grandfather died, G. M. lived on Aisquith Street, with two colored women who had been her slaves and refused to leave her; she had other slaves. They were freed after the civil war. I think at one time they had either cotton or tobacco property."

The writer mentions Abigail Faris, William's mother, and some family furniture that had belonged to her, including a "large four post bed, with pineapples carved on the posts, and a gateleg table, and lovely old chairs. She had a 'Spinnet' that we children were not allowed to touch. (of course this furniture I saw when it had descended to my Grandmother) It was sold after her death. I think in 1864 or 65."

The information in this letter, although anecdotal, is filled with fragments of truth. William Pitt had indeed frequented Faris's establishment prior to 1795 when he married Hannah Williams. After Hannah's death nine months later, he returned to Annapolis and married Ann Faris. Ann was fond of balls and dances, as we see from the activities noted in her father's diary, and did indeed become a devout Methodist, being a regular member in good standing at the Fells Point Methodist Church.[10] Although they never did live on Aisquith Street, William and Ann Pitt moved to Exeter Street in Fells Point, where William Pitt died in 1848. They owned two slaves, Nancy Pottinger and Lucretia Sprigg Pottinger (mother and daughter), according to William Pitt's will and to the Pitt family Bible. Nancy Pottinger died in 1860 and Lucretia, who was freed during the Civil War, chose to hire herself to Priscilla Eliza Chappell until her death in 1872.[11] William Faris did have two spinets in his inventory, one of which may have been the spinet of Abigail Faris that the children were not allowed to touch. This may also have been the spinet men-

87 ☞ Ann Faris Pitt
(1773–1860) and her
daughter Hannah
Williams Pitt
(1800–1837).

*Ann Faris was William
Faris's oldest daughter.
She married Captain
William Pitt on 7 July
1796 and moved to
Baltimore. Hannah
Williams Pitt was the
couple's third child,
named after William
Pitt's first wife,
Hannah Williams.*

---

9 Papers of the late C. Gordon Pitt.

10 Records of the Fells Point Methodist Church, located at the Lovely Lane
Methodist Museum in Baltimore.

11 Information also recorded in the Pitt family Bible.

tioned in the "Will": "To Nancy the darling of me and my wife, I give and bequeath the spinnet for life."

Ann's younger sister, Abigail, married Captain Archibald Kerr on 21 January 1802. They had five children, but only one was living when Faris died. Their first child, Alexander, was born on 16 November 1803 and died of yellow fever in St. Thomas on 14 May 1825.[12] Faris noted Alexander's birth in the diary and the trips that he made with his parents back and forth to Baltimore. A second son, Archibald Jr., was born in 1807. Archibald Jr., married Anna Olivia Rutter, daughter of Captain Solomon Rutter, on 20 May 1830 and died on 10 October 1834,[13] leaving one child, Archibald (known as Alexander before his baptism). Anna, who never remarried, died on 27 April 1851.

Three more siblings followed these two. Georgiana Washington, who married Henry Donnell Hunter, Captain of the Revenue, on 11 August 1835, died not long after her marriage.[14] Washington Kerr, the next-to-last child, was born in 1811. He moved to Mexico sometime after his father's death and died there, apparently unmarried, on 6 April 1878.[15] The last child was Isabella Ann, who married William H. Steuart on 2 July 1829 and had two daughters, Abigail Kerr Steuart and Georgiana.

Archibald Kerr and Abigail Faris did not have a very long life together, as Abigail died on 1 August 1821 in her forty-seventh year.[16] After her death, Archibald married a second time, to Henrietta Maria Sterett on 30 November 1825 in Annapolis. This union lasted until Henrietta's death on 8 November 1836.[17] Archibald remained a widower until his own death three years later.

William Faris's legacy is alive and well today, with his progeny spread out over the United States and overseas, his diary and shop drawings safely preserved, and his clocks and silver the prized possessions of collectors and museums. The Baltimore and Annapolis area still holds some of his descendants very near to the neighborhoods where he once lived, gardened, crafted beautiful tall clocks, forged gleaming silver, and wrote faithfully in his beloved diary.

---

[12] *BAN*, 3 June 1825.

[13] *BAN*, 10 October 1834.

[14] Her father, Archibald Kerr, who died on April 29, 1839, provided in his will only for his son-in-law and his heirs; Georgiana was no longer living.

[15] *Baltimore Sun*, 23 May 1878.

[16] *BAN*, 7 August 1821.

[17] *BAN*, 8 November 1836.

The Diary of William Faris

The Daily Life of an Annapolis Silversmith

PART ONE
1792–1793

THE COMPLEAT GAMESTER:
Will:
Bish:

William Faris

January 1th 1792 ✎ a rayney day ✎ (2th) ✎ dull
& rainey ✎ (3th) ✎ dull cloudey weather

4 ✎ clear wather. in the evening, John Davidson's[1]
son William came to Town from the west ward[2] and
informs that Capt. Allexander Truman[3] is a re covering of his wounds and is like to gett well and that
Joseph Allen[4] is on his way home

5 ✎ a dull morning. in the after noon snow and
turned cold. this afternoon had 4 cart Loads of dung
from George Manns.[5] in the evening Nancy &

---

[1] John Davidson (1737–1794) was born in Inverness, Scotland, the son of William and Mary Grant Davidson. He married Eleanor Strachan (1746–1815), daughter of Capt. William and Mary Simpson Strachan, in September 1769 in All Hallow's Parish. Faris records the marriages of their son William and daughters Eleanor and Mary. William attended St. John's grammar school briefly in 1790 and Samuel (b. c.1782) was a student from 1793 to 1795. In 1794, for £1,020, Davidson purchased the Reynolds/Trueman property on Church Circle between West and Franklin Streets that bordered one side of Faris's lot (see entry for 22 April 1794), making him and his family neighbors of the Farises. The Davidsons appear frequently in the diary. § Faris collected 6/6 from Mrs. Davidson in May 1801 as administrator of Charles's estate and £1.2.6. from William.

[2] Troops from Maryland, Virginia, and Pennsylvania, under the command of Colonel Henry Lee of Virginia, in the fall of 1791 took part in an expedition against certain western Indian tribes. In early November, the contingent of about fourteen hundred men suffered a devastating attack that routed the soldiers and killed or wounded more than half the force.

[3] Alexander Trueman married Margaret Reynolds in May 1781. Margaret was the daughter of Faris's former neighbor William Reynolds, a hatter who also kept a tavern in his home on Church Circle until his death in 1777. Margaret and her mother inherited the property, in which Trueman briefly operated a boarding house by 1785. Promoted to major in the spring of 1792, Trueman was part of the military force sent to the Ohio Valley to deal with the Indian problem and was killed there in May, soon after news of his promotion appeared in the *Gazette*. The paper's account of Trueman's death did not appear until August, in a report from Fort Pitt.

[4] Possibly the son of Dr. John and Eleanor Brewer Allen, who was born 27 October 1768. Faris was well acquainted with many members of the Brewer family.

[5] George Mann (1753–1795) arrived in Annapolis soon after the start of the Revolutionary War. He married Mary Buckland (d.1811), daughter of architect William Buckland (1734–1774). Mann operated his tavern, located near the corner of Church and Conduit Streets, in the house of Lloyd Dulany, a loyalist whose property had been confiscated and sold by the state. In the 1780s Mann built an addition to his inn, located on Conduit Street. His establishment hosted many notable visitors and events, particularly those surrounding Washington's resignation of his commission in December 1783. Mann was a councilman from 1791 until his death. He left an estate valued at nearly £2,500. In 1798, Mary Mann lived on the corner of Market and Shipwright Streetss and rented the tavern buildings, consisting of the main building and its brick wing, a large brick kitchen, and an even larger stable, to James Wharfe. § Faris noted in November 1785 that Charles had responsibility for maintenance of George Mann's clock. He collected £3.7.6 from Mary Mann in September 1801 as administrator of Charles's estate and owed Mann's estate 2/3.

88 ✎ FACING PAGE
Frontispiece of *"The Compleat Gamester"*
Charles Cotton, London, 1680.

This image, although portraying a period one hundred years before Faris's time, comes from a manual for tavern games, most of which were played at Faris's West Street tavern. Faris also made spurs for cockfights (shown here) and owned a backgammon table when he died.

Jan., 1792

Abigal[6] in Mr. Wallaces's[7] carriage, snow'd fast

6 🖛 clear and cold morning. in the afternoon Harry Woodcock[8] died at Mr. Hansons

7 🖛 a cold morning with fine snow. continued snowing all day

8 🖛 a cold cloudey morning with fine snow & fine rain

9 🖛 cold & cloudey. about 10 oclock the sun came out. the wind at north and cold. in the after noon, Robert Couden[9] died. in the evening Joseph Allen came to Town from the westward

10 🖛 a fine clear & cold day

11 🖛 a cold day   12th 🖛 a cloudey morning. about 12 oclock began to snow and In the evening Robert Johnston was married to Miss Kitte Ghislin.[10] a very Bad snowe night

13 🖛 a fine clear morning. in the after noon clouded up & in the evening a littel snow but clear'd away a fine night

14 🖛 a fine clear cold morning (15th) 🖛 a fine morning

16 🖛 a fine clear cold morning (17th) 🖛 clear & cold

---

6 The two oldest of the Faris daughters. Nancy was a few months short of her nineteenth birthday and Abigail was nearly seventeen.

7 Charles Wallace (1727–1812) was the son of John and Anne Wallace of Annapolis and the brother of Mary Howard, wife of Cornelius (see entry for 31 March 1792). Wallace's first wife, Catherine, died in August 1795 at the age of 63; his second wife was Mary Ranken (see 26 April 1798). Wallace began his career as a staymaker, kept a tavern until 1756, and by 1763 had opened a store selling imported goods. In 1769 Wallace bought land in the center of town, originally set aside for the governor, and developed it by laying out streets and selling lots. He was the contractor to build the third (present) state house in the early 1770s. Early in 1771 Wallace formed the firm of Wallace, Davidson, and Johnson to engage in tobacco trade. In 1793 Wallace purchased the Tasker family's confiscated estate on Market Street, with its elegant "falling garden," and owned a number of other properties in town, as well as a plantation in Middle Neck Hundred. Wallace was a common councilman, alderman, member of the St. Anne's vestry, visitor of St. John's in 1792, and a member of the executive council for two terms from 1783 to 1785. The *Gazette* reported that Charles Wallace, Esq., died on 13 February 1812 at the home of [his stepson-in-law] Leonard Sellman, in his 84th year. § Wallace belonged the Homony Club, a social club of the early 1770s, which met in Faris's tavern in June 1771.

8 The 19 January *Gazette* noted the death of Mr. Henry Woodcock on Friday in his 56th year; he was a "native of England," but had resided in America "since early manhood." Woodcock was appointed organist for St. Anne's Church in June 1779. He might have been living with William Hanson (see 5 September 1795) or with Alexander Contee Hanson (see entry for 17 July 1793). The "Will" has Faris trusting Woodcock to teach Nancy to play the piano, but deciding that there was no hope of Nancy's ever learning from him. § Woodcock patronized Faris's tavern in November 1775, indulging in wine and oysters.

9 Robert Couden (d. 1792) was born in Scotland. He advertised in December 1750 that he was carrying on Robert Swan's tanning business, but for most of his career he was a merchant. He first advertised the sale of goods at a Church Street store in March 1752, and in 1760 moved to a new store nearer the dock. Couden was a justice of the peace in the 1760s and 1770s, and assistant intendant of revenue during the Revolution. He served in the 1780s first as councilman and then as alderman, and was elected mayor in September 1789. His daughter Mary married future governor John Hoskins Stone (see 5 March 1793) in 1781.

10 Robert Johnson (1766–1798) was the son of innkeeper Robert Johnson (d. 1773) and his wife Ann Golder, the widow of John Golder (see entry of 7 April 1793), and was the brother of George (see 20 January 1793) and John (see 9 January 1794). Catherine Ghiselin was the daughter of Reverdy and Mary Ghiselin (see 21 January 1792). Robert's brother John married Catherine's sister Deborah in January 1794. The Johnson family home was on School Street, the "house on the hill" to which Robert Johnson moved on the 21st. § Robert Johnson Sr. patronized Faris's tavern in the 1760s, where he played billiards and skittles.

1792 18 ✒ this morning awakened about 7 oclock by the ringing of the Bell and the cry of Fire.[11] Mr. Nicholas Carrols[12] House was on Fire but Happiley putt out with out a grate deal of damage. a cold snowey morning. in the afternoon hung up 10 gammons, 10 shoulders & midlings and 5 Joles.[13] still snowing

19 ✒ a clear cold windey morning (20th) ✒ clear & cold

21 ✒ a cloudey morning. Robert Johnston's amoveing from Mrs. Ghislins[14] to his House on the Hill. betwen 1 & 2 oclock it began to snow. in the evening still snowing

22 ✒ still snowing. betwen 1 & 2 oclock lift of snow and the sun out. in the evening died His Excelency George Plator Esqr of violent attack of The Gout in the stomach. a fals report. his Excellency is much better and I am in hopes he will recover & get well

---

[11] Fire posed an ever-present threat in colonial towns. Although Annapolis had a high proportion of brick homes, there were still many houses constructed of wood, as well as numerous wooden outbuildings. Even the brick houses had roofs of wooden shingles that could catch fire from wind-born sparks and interior wood framing and furnishings that would burn easily. City regulations required homeowners to have fire buckets and ladders on hand to help in combating fires, and the Mayor's Court fined homeowners whose chimneys were "blazing," or sending forth sparks that could start a fire (see 25 January 1796 entry for such a fire in Charles Faris's shop). Although there were by this time companies offering fire insurance, few homeowners were protected. A fire that destroyed a home could bring a devastating loss of virtually all possessions, particularly in the days before householders might own intangible assets like bank accounts or stocks.

[12] Nicholas Maccubbin Carroll (1751–1812) was the son of Nicholas (1709–1787) and Mary Clare Carroll Maccubbin. His uncle Charles Carroll the Barrister (1723–1783), having no living children, willed his estate to his nephews Nicholas and James Maccubbin on the condition that they take the name of Carroll. Nicholas Maccubbin Carroll married Ann Jennings, daughter of Thomas, in 1783; the couple had three sons and two daughters. Her sister Julianna married James Brice (see entry for 17 July 1793). Carroll held the offices of councilman, alderman, mayor, and justice of the peace, as well as serving in the legislature. He lived on Green Street, which he had cut through the large lots he inherited from Carroll. § Faris bought turnips and potatoes from Carroll in the winter of 1790–91 and six hogs weighing 1,177 pounds in December 1795. The administration account for Faris's estate included a debt owed by Carroll of £182.19.0.

[13] Urban homeowners, like Faris, kept a cow or two, perhaps some chickens, and a hog for fattening, and cultivated a kitchen garden if they had enough land, but they still relied on the market and neighboring planters for the bulk of their food. Faris bought beef, veal, and lamb from local butchers but usually purchased pork that he smoked, as he does here, for use during the winter from nearby planters.

[14] Mary Ghiselin, the widow of Reverdy Ghiselin (d.1775), who had been a justice of the peace, clerk of the provincial court, and commissioner of the land office. After her husband's death, Mrs. Ghiselin operated a boarding house at her home across West Street from Faris. In the winter of 1783–84, when Congress met in Annapolis, Thomas Jefferson and James Madison boarded at Mrs. Ghiselin's. Her son, Dr. Reverdy Ghiselin (see entry for 13 April 1793), appears frequently in the diary.

89 ✒ John Callahan (1753–1803)

23 ✒ a fine morning. last night was the coldes night this winter

24 ✒ a cold morning (25th) ✒ clear & cold this morning. Lent my Pistoles and Holsters to Jesse DuWees,[15] who is going to Baltimore to defend him self as thare is Highway men on the road. 3 or 4 persons has been robed. one of the persons robed was littel Richard Chew[16]

26 ✒ a cloudey cold {day} ✒ (27th) ✒ at times cloudey all day

28 ✒ a cloudey morning & like for snow. at noon it did snow a littel ✒ (29th) ✒ a fine cold day

30 ✒ a cold cloudey morning. about 1 or 2 oclock snow'd then turn'd sleat & rain

31 ✒ a dull cloudey morning. did not frees last Night. very sloshey walking. thaw'd all day. in the evening it rained

1792 Febry 1 ✒ a dul morning. excessive bad walking from the freesing last {night}

2 ✒ a fine day but cold ✒ (3th) ✒ a fine day still cold

4 ✒ a cloudey morning. about 11 oclock began to rain and continued a small rain all day & carried off a grate deal of the snow

5 ✒ a fine day ✒ (6th) ✒ a fine day ✒ (7th) ✒ a dull cloudey morning like for snow or rain. about 1 oclock began to snow, and wee ware allarmed with John Callahorns[17] chimeney being on fyer, it snow'd all the afternoon (Mrs. Faris went over to

---

15 In 1793, the *Maryland*, homeward bound to America, was taken into Bermuda by a British warship. Owner John Mason (see 11 February 1796) dispatched DeWees to Bermuda as his agent to save the ship and its cargo from condemnation. The *Maryland* sailed from Bermuda for Georgetown in July 1795, but DeWees had not been able to save the cargo or obtain a license to take on goods in Bermuda. DeWees was the secretary of the Jockey Club, which held races in Annapolis every fall, during the years of the diary. George Mann's estate (see 5 January 1792) included among its debts DeWees's bond for £195.14.11, as well as a much smaller debt due from the Jockey Club.

16 The Chews were a long-established family in Anne Arundel County, particularly in the area around Herring Bay at the southern end of the county. It is not possible to be sure whom Faris meant in this entry, although he might have been referring to the son of Maj. Richard Chew (1753–1801) or this might have been the Richard Chew who was a student at the St. John's grammar school in 1790.

17 John Callahan was the son of James and Sarah Callahan. His father was a tailor who died in 1759, leaving his widow, two sons, and two daughters. Callahan married Sarah Buckland (d.1839), daughter of William Buckland, architect of Mathias Hammond's house, in June 1782. His wife's sister Mary was married to innkeeper George Mann (see 5 January 1792). Callahan served in a number of local offices but his most important position was the appointive one of register of the western shore land office, which he held from 1778 to 1803. He and his wife had six children, the marriage of one of whom Faris records on 29 March 1803. In 1798, the family lived in a two-story brick dwelling with several outbuildings, valued at $1,300 and located between State Circle and College Avenue. § Faris collected £0.12.3 from Callahan in December 1800 as administrator of Charles's estate.

Mrs. Brices[18] and came home with a
pair of Boots on). at night it snow'd &
Hailed and Blew very Hard. a very Bad
night & cold

8 ✍ a dull morning & snows a littel and
continued snowing at times all day ✍
(9th) ✍ a fine sun shiney day. it Blew
[very] Hard last Night. the wind
mill[19] had one of her arms carried away

10 ✍ a fine day. this fore noon died his
Excelency Georg Plater[20] Esqr Govenor
of the State of Maryland in ye 57 year of
his age after a long and Painfull Illness
✍ (11th) ✍ a dull morning. betwen
12 & 1 oclock the Hers with the corps
of the govenor went out of Town on its
way to the famely Burying ground at
his seat in St Marys County. in the after
noon it snow'd & Hailed. a cloudey
evening

12 ✍ a cloudey drissely dissagreeable day

13 ✍ a cold dull day. it drisseld rain & snow &
Hail'd at times all day ✍ (14th) ✍ a cloudey dull
dissagreeable day. in the evening fine snow ~~or small
rain~~

90 ✍ George Plater (1735– 1792)

[20] George Plater was born at Sotterly, the
Plater estate on the Patuxent River in St.
Mary's County, the son of George Plater and
his wife Rebecca Addison Bowles. He was a
graduate of William and Mary College and,
like his father, a lawyer. He married first
Hannah Lee, whose first cousin was Thomas
Sim Lee (see 3 April 1792), in December
1762, and second, in July 1764, Elizabeth
Rousby, the stepdaughter of William Fitzhugh
(see 19 January 1793). William Fitzhugh Sr.
and George Plater Sr. were partners with
Robert Chesly in a mercantile firm in the
1760s. Plater's daughter Ann (c.1774–1834)
in 1790 married Philip Barton Key (see 6
October 1800) and his son John Rousby married Elizabeth Tootell, daughter of James and
Ann Tootell (see 26 September 1794), in the
same year. Plater served in both houses of the
general assembly from 1757 to 1790, on the
council of safety, as a delegate to the
Continental Congress, and as president of the
Ratification Convention in 1788. A funeral
procession took his body from Annapolis to
Sotterly for burial. § Faris supplied him with a
pair of rowels (a small wheel that formed the
extremity of a spur) in January 1777.

[18] Probably Frances Wilson Bryce, the widow of Capt. Robert
Bryce, who died c.1771. Bryce owned a lot on the opposite side of
West Street, where his widow operated a boarding house after his
death. In 1784 she advertised a boarding house on Church Street, in
the former Mann's Tavern (see 5 January 1792), but in September
1788 a new advertisement stated that she had moved to Mr.
Quynn's new house opposite the theatre, where she accommodated
boarders by the day or year. Thus, Mrs. Faris only had to cross the
street to visit her.

[19] Located on the point where Spa Creek meets the Severn River.
This land became the site of Fort Severn, which was sold to the
United States Government for the establishment of a Naval School
in 1845—now the United States Naval Academy.

91 ☞ William Smallwood (1732–1792)

15 ☞ still bad weather. snow'd all day. in the evening Nancy went to the Presedents Birth Day Ball[21] at Mr. Manns

16 ☞ a fine day. it is reported that Genl. William Smallwood[22] died on Sunday last ~~at his seat in~~ at the wood yard in Prince Georges County in {blank} year of his age

1792 Febry 17 ☞ a fine day. carried off a grate deal of the snow. I this day finished and glased the frame for Nanceys shell work[23] ☞ (18th) ☞ a fine sunshine morning. about 11 or 12 oclock and about one it be gan to snow at times all the after noon. in the evening still snowing

19 ☞ a clear cold windey day

20 ☞ a clear cold morning. about 12 oclock snow'd about ½ an Hoar. clear in the evening ☞ (21) ☞ clear and cold

22 ☞ a fine clear day and thaw'd a littel

23 ☞ a fine day and thaw'd a littel

24 ☞ a fine day but the wind raw and coole. this day Nancey finished her shell work and had it Brought Home

25 ☞ a fine modarate day. 13 sail of square rigg'd vessels Laying off the Dock.[24] in ye evening foggey

26 ☞ soft foggey morning. in the after noon a moderate rain and continued so in the evening and came on to Blow hard at West ☞ (27) ☞ a fine morning. about noon turn'd cold the wind still continuing to blow hard and freesing

21 From the time of the Revolution, Americans viewed George Washington as a national hero. In urban centers like Annapolis, the elite celebrated Washington's birthday with dinners and balls. Home libraries contained biographies of Washington and his portrait hung on the walls of private homes, including that of Charles Faris, while towns frequently had a "Sign of General Washington" tavern. The greatest outpouring of adulation for Washington occurred following his death in December 1799; see 17 December 1799 entry for Faris's report of the arrival of the news in Annapolis.

22 William Smallwood was born in Charles County, the son of Bayne and Priscilla Heabeard Smallwood. Smallwood lived at the family home, Smallwood's Retreat, on Mattawoman Creek. Educated in England at Eton, he was a career military officer who never married. After serving in the French and Indian War, he represented Charles County in the general assembly and convention from 1761 to 1776. He had a distinguished career during the Revolutionary War, participating in the Battles of Long Island, Trenton, and Princeton, among others, and finished the war with the rank of Major General. Smallwood served three terms as governor from 1785 to 1788. § When Smallwood became governor in November 1785, Faris assumed responsibility for the care of his clocks.

23 The advertisement Mrs. Jones placed in the *Washington Spy* after her removal to Hagerstown suggests the curriculum offered to girls attending urban schools: instruction in "Reading, writing, and arithmetic, Tambour and Dresden, English, and French embroidery, drawing and painting in water colors, geography, filigree and riband work, plain and colored needle-work of all kinds, instrumental music, seed, shell, and paper-work." Academic subjects were not neglected, but there was a strong emphasis upon decorative needle and craft skills, such as Nancy's shell work.

24 The "dock" is the basin of water presently enclosed by Market Space, Compromise Street, and Dock Street. Although much larger in Faris's day, the dock was not big enough to permit large ships to unload at its wharves. Such vessels anchored in the outer harbor and smaller boats carried passengers and cargoes to shore.

28 ☞ frose Hard last night, its a fine day but cold. the Boys ascaiting and sliding on the Ice in the street

29 ☞ a fine day. this day Mrs. Jones is so unwell sent scollors home not being able to attend the school[25]

March 1 ☞ this Morning the Boys are aslyding and skeating on the Ice in the streets and thay ride over South River. its been a very fine day and carried off a grate deal of snow

1792 March 2 ☞ a fine warm day. drisseld & rain'd all day

3 ☞ a fine warm clear day ☞ (4th) ☞ a fine modarate and drislin day

5 ☞ Rain'd thunder'd & rain'd very Hard before day this morning. a fine day after wards. Mrs. Stone[26] died last Night

6 ☞ a very fine day. this day got a root of Polianthus from George Mann and planted it on the Circul Bed nex to Grayhams[27] a stick marked VIIII

7 ☞ a fine day. this day Mrs. Stone was Buried

8 ☞ a rainey day and about 4 oclock snow'd

9 ☞ a fine day. took the fence from the Rabbet Yard and began to take up the Bricks. the Ice is not yet gone from the mouth of the dock but the vessels comes in with wood. it sells at 15/ pr cord. this day the vessels mooved off for Baltimore but Rossetor[28] says thay cannot get higher up the river then Sparrows point[29]

---

[25] Faris noted in his account book on 2 January 1792, that "Nancey faris began going to school to Mr. & Mrs. Jones. A rainey dull day" Joseph Jones advertised in 1790 that he would open a singing school and teach vocal music. On 22 September 1791, Mrs. Jones placed a notice in the *Gazette* that "a boarding school for young ladies will be opened on the 13th of next month." The Faris girls attended as day students.

[26] The *Maryland Gazette* reported on 8 March that Mrs. Mary Stone, wife of John Hoskins Stone, Esq. of Annapolis, died on Sunday, 4 March, at the age of 32.

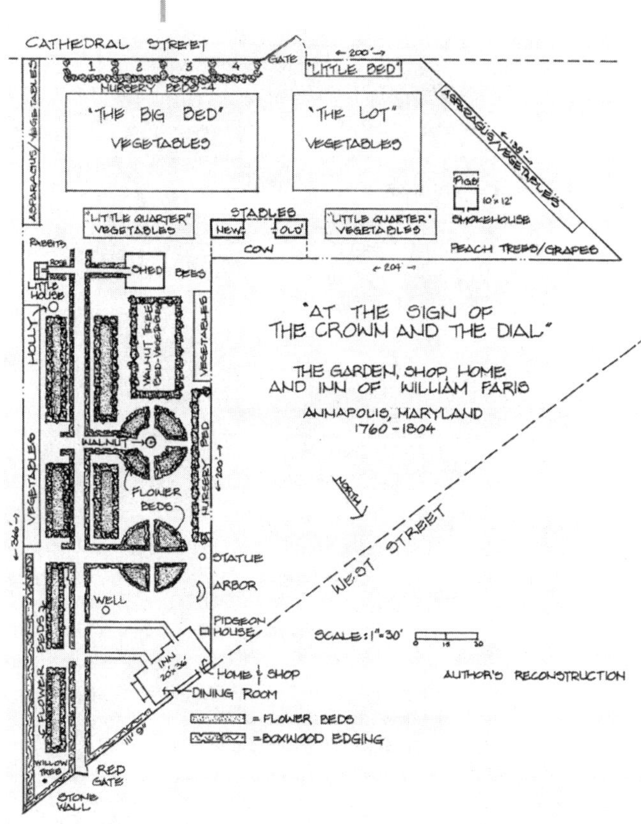

92 ☞ *William Faris's garden as reconstructed by Barbara Wells Sarudy.*

[27] Thomas Grayham (d.1795) may have been the son of Thomas and Keziah Pennington Grayham, born in 1728 in St. Margaret's Parish. He was a shopkeeper in 1783 and operator of a tavern, the Sign of the Green-Tree, near the town gate, in the 1790s. He leased a lot from Allen Quynn (see 9 September 1792) that bordered the west side of Faris's property. At his death he left an estate valued at only £1.9.6, the bulk of it coming from his Bible, valued at 15 shillings. § Grayham served on a grand jury with Faris in August 1783.

[28] Storekeeper Thomas Rossiter and his wife lived in Baltimore in the 1790s, and occasionally exchanged plants with Faris.

[29] Sparrows Point is on the north side of the mouth of the Patapsco River.

30 Catherine may have been the daughter of Richard Fleming, who appears as a shoemaker in the 1780s, had an ordinary license from the mid-1780s to the mid-1790s, and whose bake shop fire, in 1790, destroyed much of the first block of Church Street, including his own home.

31 Probably Susannah Peale Newton Brewer (1746–1809), widow of storekeeper John Brewer V (1738–1788), who lived on Cornhill Street in a substantial two-story brick house with separate kitchen. Faris records the marriage of at least one of their children, Ann Odle, to William Marbury (see 16 June 1798). With the opening of St. John's College in 1789, Susannah Brewer advertised that she could provide lodging for ten students. § The entry in Faris's account book for 13 March read "Mrs. Brewers Neagro man Harry began his month at 22/6 pr month."

32 Probably the wife of John Guyer, who operated a store in partnership with Jonathan Pinkney from 1791 to 1797.

33 A seizure, possibly due to a stroke or the result of a heart attack.

34 The first appearance in the diary of Hyram Faris, born 18 January 1769. Hyram, who never married, lived at home and was his father's most constant gardener among the family members, until they quarreled irrevocably in April 1799 and Hyram moved to Baltimore.

10 ✎ a rainey day. in ye evening a littel snow

11 ✎ a fair day but windey. Blew very hard. Upset Miss Kittey Fleming30 on the Stad House Hill, carryed away all her top riging & brused her face & made her nose bleed

12 ✎ a fine day ✎ (13th) ✎ a fine day. this evening Mrs. Brewers31 neagro man Harrey came to live with me at 3 Dollors pr month

14 ✎ a fine day. this day finish'd takeing up the Bricks of the Floor of the Rabbit Yard and mooved them away and made a begining to carry dung in the Lott

15 ✎ made a begining to digg in the Lott but it rain'd and snow'd so all day that we could do but littel. Mr. Rosetor brought me ½ oz of Large Winter Cabbage cost 1s/

1792 *March 16* ✎ a cloudey dull disagreeable day. the snow on the ground and so wett could do nothing out of doors. piled the shingles in the stable

17 ✎ a fine day. dugg up one half the Lott

18 ✎ rained all day. Majr. Allexander Truman arrived in Town Last evening from Philadelphia and dine'd with me too day. he looks very fatt and harty but complains of a Hurt in his shoulder from an accedent of the stage's over setting on his way down, betwen Chester & Wilmington

19 ✎ a very foggey morning. this morning Mrs. Guyer32 died suddentley in fitts.33 still adigging in the Lott, sowed a border next the dining room, with Radish & Large Winter Cabbage Seed, and Hyram34 began in the after noon To plant parsnip seed 6 Inchs apart and lines 8 Inchs distant, and Harrey Broke the spade, I was obliged to buy another which cost 7/6. it turned out a fine day but at night it rained

20 ✎ Rain'd Hard all last night, a fine morning but windey. finished planting ye parsnups and finished the assparagrass Beds. while at work at the assparagrass Beds two peopel I took to be girls climbed up on the fence (I declare I did not know who thay ware). I desire'd them to gett off the fence. the Biggest reply'd shee would not. she would sett thare as long as she pleas, I told her she should get

down. she replyd she would not get down for me. I
told her she was an impudant slut and get down or I
would make her and went to wards whare s[h]e was
on the fence. as I lifte my hand to put her hand off
the fence she said you Impedant scoundrel tuch me
if you Dare. I pushd her hand off the fence. she
stept down and call'd me an Old Dog Old Dog, I
told her she was a strumpit. how dare you to call
me so, she reply'd, you are an Old Dog, and that
her Husband should call me to an accot for [i]t I
curs'd her & her Husband and I told she was an
Impudant Bitch and I went back to whare the man
was at work, and she and the girl call me several
approbious names

21 ☞ a fine morning. Harrey's carrying dung on the
Bigg Bed in the garden, I sow'd a drill of spiniage
Betwen the assparagrass Beds and Hyram's sowing
ye carrots in drills 8 Inchs asunder.   Harrey Began
to digg the Bigg Bead about a 11 oclock. Mrs.
Guyer was Buryed this after noon

22 ☞ a fine day. Harrey still adigging ye Bigging ye
bigg Bead

1792 March 23 ☞ a cloudey morning. Mr.
Rositer Brought me ½ oz of earley York cabbage
seed cost 1/. sow'd some of it on the first aspaara-
grass bed on the end nex to Mr. Stevens's[35] & on the
other endend the large cabbag and on the other Bed
sow'd Collwort Seed and Lettice on all whare cabbage seed is sow'd — finished digging ye Big Bead
and sow'd 7 rows of Peas 5 rows of them that came
from the Dutch man & 2 rows of Mrs. Sand's[36] and

---

35 Vachel Stevens (c.1754–1811) married Jannella Russell Neilson,
the widow of William Waller, in July 1780. (She married Waller in
June 1778; her name is also spelled "Jenella" and "Jannetta".) He
must have been related to John Stevens (d.1781), who had a son
Vachel (1747–1788), but there is no documentation to confirm
their connection. Stevens advertised in September 1789 that he
could provide lodging for twenty St. John's students, and held an
ordinary license in the 1790s. Stevens, who appraised the estate of
William Hanson with Faris, bought Hanson's house and lots on
Cathedral Street, across from the back of Faris's property, in 1796.
Stevens was also a surveyor, having been paid by the Corporation for
surveying the city's streets in February 1790; he purchased Hanson's
surveyor's instruments at the same time that he bought the real
property. And he succeeded Hanson as examiner general of the
Western Shore, holding the position until his own death in 1811. §
Faris exchanged plant material more frequently with Stevens than
with anyone else mentioned in the diary, beginning in March 1798;
the last exchange took place the April before Faris's death.

36 Anne Graham Sands was the widow
of John Sands (1731–1791), a retired
ship captain who kept an ordinary at his
home on Prince George Street; his
widow continued the business after
Sands' death. § Sands purchased six
silver tablespoons from Faris in the
early 1770s.

37 Elisha Berry (1755–1813) was a planter living in Prince George's County who owned thirty-five slaves in 1790. During the Revolutionary War he was an ensign in the Middle Battalion of the county militia. Berry married twice, first to Eleanor Eversfield and second to Mrs. Jane Ferguson, and had one child by each wife, William and William Ferguson.

38 A tall case clock; one of the few references in the diary to Faris's work as a watch and clock maker.

39 Miss Cook was the daughter of William Cooke (1746–1817) and his wife Elizabeth Tilghman (1749–1836). An attorney, Cooke was a loyalist who left the colonies during the Revolution but returned to Maryland in 1787, resumed his law practice, and sat in the senate in 1794 and 1795. The Cookes had nine children, including daughters Catherine and Anna Maria, both mentioned elsewhere in diary. His daughters' new clothes elicited comment in the early 1790s: "I have not had the curiosity to go to see the Miss Cookes clothes yet, but hear they are very beautiful." Cooke was one of the managers of the lottery to raise funds for completing St. Anne's Church in 1790 and was a pew holder in the new church. For many years until his death, Cooke served as attorney and business agent for Henri Stier (see 27 April 1797) and his daughter Rosalie Calvert. § Cooke represented Faris in his settlement with DeDrusina, Ridder and Clerk in February 1793 (see 4 February 1793).

40 Christopher Love was a seventeenth-century Presbyterian clergyman, executed during the English Civil War by Cromwell's forces because of his loyalty to the Solemn League and Covenant (Scottish support for the Parliamentary cause had been contingent upon the English Puritans signing the Covenant). Love's sermons and prophecies are still in print.

Planted carrotts & parsnups that Mr. Wallace sent me for seed, cloudey & like for rain. Mr. Elish Berrey's[37] been hear & tells the clock[38] has went well ever since he has had her. carryed dung on the small quarter next ye new stable. planted a Hill of musk melleons seed from Miss Cook[39]

March 23 ✍ The Prophecies of Christopher Love[40] which are shortly to be made Public, are of a very extraordanary Kind. he is said to have foretold the American independency the French Revolution and other events which have been confirmed. of those yet to come he speakes in the following words: God will be known to man in the year 1795. This will produce a grate man. The stars will wander and the moon turn as Blood in 1800. Africa, Asia and America will tremble in 1803. A great earthquake all over the world in 1805. God will be universally known by all — then a general reformation and peace for ever, when the peopel shall Learn war no more Happy is the man that Liveth to see this day

24 ✍ Rain'd very hard last night and this morning. clear'd away about 11 oclock. the ground too wett to digg. Harry clear'd the grass out of the Seedling Tulups and cap at cleaning the garden of stones & shells & weeds. I planted 7 hill of musk & water mellons in the Lott and sow'd a drill of spinage the off side the assparragrass Bed. in the evening looks like more Bad weather

25 ✍ some person gumpt the Bigg Gate of the Lott and went through part of the parsnup Bed and gumpt the fence {of} Goldsmith's[41] Lott and Broke off the top of one of the pales and threw it in the garden, and thare is an appearance as if thay went throught the garden and either went in to Mr. Stevens's garden or came from that way and wee Lost a Tabel Cloth out of the Kitchen. a cloudey dull morning and continued so all day

41 William Goldsmith (d.1797), a tanner and shoemaker, lived on Church Circle, adjacent to Faris, at the time of his death. He was the manager of the state tannery during the Revolutionary War, as well as a councilman for Annapolis in 1779 and the early 1780s, and Anne Arundel sheriff from 1792 to 1794. In 1794, Goldsmith bought the lease to the house originally built by William Reynolds on Church Circle. At the time of his death, Goldsmith was a lieutenant in the militia's artillery brigade. § Faris served on the St. Anne's vestry with Goldsmith in the 1770s to early 1780s, and the two men stood surety for William Simpson's tavern license in August 1783. Faris bought a pair of shoes for Charles from Goldsmith in May 1790.

26 ☛ a foggey morning. Harrey's began diging ye
littel qarter next the new stabel, Charles[42] cut the
sage round the Bed. finished digging the littel
qurter & planted 7 rows of Beens. finished the Table
of the Big Bed at the sage & dugg part of the Border
joyning the nurssery of Box to plant more cuttings
of Box. cloudey & small rain

27 ☛ dull cloudey morning with thick mist & small
rain. dug a peace of the Border next to Grayhams &
sow'd it with Parceley. after diner the sun came out
and Looks like to be a fine after noon. Bengan cutting the Box and Hyram aplanting ye cuttings &
Charles's making a stretching frame for Nancey's
picture

28 ☛ a fine morning. Harry's sick, complains of a
pain across his Brest. the large winter cabbage &
radish seed sow'd in the lott the 19th of March are
now makeing thare appearance and the Lettice on
the assparagrass are makeing thare appearance.
Hyram acutting Box and Charles a planting. a fine
warm day. Harrey cept his Bed all day

1792 March 29 ☛ a cloudey foggey morning &
small rain at times. Harry got up this mornig but
was not well. I sent him home to his mistress. still
going on acutting of Box, about the midel of the
after noon Harry's mistress sent him back again and
said nothing ailed him, he's at work, wright March
weather. finish'd planting ye Box

30 ☛ a fine morning. finished cutting ye Box about
11 oclock and Harry Began Troweling the flower
Beds. in the evening cloudey

31 ☛ rain'd hard Last night, a cloudey rainey
morning. clear'd away about 9 oclock. Harry went
in the garden dugg the ribbin grass and then went
to work on the flower Beds and about 5 oclock finish'd six of the Beds next the gate and one up by the
Coffee House[43] and then [to] aplanting of Turnups
betwen the greens. a clear evening but rather raw
and windey

Apl 1 ☛ a fine day but rather coole for the season

2 ☛ a fine day. agreeable to the Govenors
Procclamation the Assembley was to meet this day
and an Instance that was never known be fore thare
was members anough to from [form, or make a

[42] The first appearance in the diary of Charles
Faris, who was born on 29 September 1764.
Charles, who never married, set up shop for
himself in September 1793. He lived at home
except periodically when quarreling with his
father. Charles occasionally helped in the
garden, especially after Hyram left home, but
more often appears in the diary accompanying
family members or traveling by himself back
and forth to Baltimore and on other trips.
Charles served as an ensign in one of the
Annapolis companies of the 22nd militia regiment from August 1797 until his death, and
in 1799 was elected a common councilman for
Annapolis.

[43] The Coffee House was located on upper
Church Street, a few doors below the Maryland
Inn. The proprietor was Cornelius Howard
(1728–1771), the son of Cornelius Howard
(?–1730) and his wife Elizabeth Howard,
widow of his cousin Samuel (d.1724).
Cornelius Jr. married Mary Wallace, the sister
of Charles Wallace (see 1 January 1792). The
Coffee House, which opened in April 1767, on
property leased by Charles Wallace, contained
"24 rooms excluding the garrets." After
Howard's death, his widow operated the business for a time and then rented the property to
a succession of tavern keepers, including John
Ball, his widow Sarah, and Frances Bryce (see
7 February 1792). The Howards had two
daughters: Rebecca, who married Alexander
Contee Hanson (see 17 July 1793), and
Catherine, who married Randolph B. Latimer
(see 2 March 1795).

44 Annapolis was the seat of government for three polities: city, county, and state. Faris was very attuned to the meetings of the General Assembly and of the various state and local courts as well as to the results of state and local elections, although he himself apparently never held elective political office. During the years when Faris kept his tavern, the meetings of the assembly and courts—both located within blocks of Faris's home—meant business for his establishment from the delegates, justices, lawyers, and others who came to town on official business. Even after Faris stopped keeping a tavern, court and legislative sessions brought old friends to Annapolis.

45 Only rarely did urban slave owners own more than a few slaves, making it uncommon for husbands and wives to live together.

46 Possibly William Chapman, who sold mutton to Faris in October 1794, according to the day book. He may have been the William Chapman who married Susannah Gassaway in March 1791.

47 Thomas Sim Lee (1745–1819), a native of Maryland, was a member of the large Lee family whose branches included the Virginia Lees. Lee married Mary Digges (d.1819), daughter of a prominent Catholic family of Prince George's County with ties to the Carrolls. Lee served in both the lower and upper houses of the legislature before his three terms as governor from 1779 to 1782. Lee was elected as governor again for two terms from 1792 to 1794 but declined to serve when elected for the sixth time in 1798. He died in Frederick County, where he lived from 1811 until his death. George Plater (see 10 February 1792), whom he succeeded, had been married to Lee's cousin Hannah.

quorum of] Both Houses44 met this day — man Harry went on Saturday night to see his wife and has not found the way Home to day45

3 ☞ a fine morning. man Harry crawled Home this morning betwen 6 & 7 oclock. went to weeling dung on the side of the bed by the Walnutt Tree & digg a border round it to plant Beens. Mr. Chapman46 gave me some cabbage seed & I sow'd some of it on the assparagrass Bed next the old stable. this day Thomas Sim Lee47 was chose Govenor by the House of Assembley in the room of G. Plater Esqr deseased

4 ☞ a fine morning. Mrs. Brewers Harry behaved Badley and's gone Home. this morning planted the following Beens Arber Beans, the white beens from over the Bay the flower d[itt]o the Irish Beauty and some that Mr. Price48 gave me come from Chaces's.49 in the evening clouded up & rained a littel and looks as if we should have a good deal of it

5 ☞ a fine day. about 2 oclock Thomas Sim Lee Esqr came to Town and was quallifyed as Govenor. the Flag was Hoisted and the guns Fiered and at night a supper at Manns. this evening Mrs. Faris, my self and children all went to see the wax work50 ~~this day planted the arber beens, the Beens from over the Bay~~

48 Probably Thomas Pryse, a saddler and coachmaker who drowned en route to Baltimore in February 1793, leaving a widow and six children. Faris notes the marriages of two children, Letitia (b.1777) and Elizabeth (b.1771), but not those of Harriet (b.1780) in December 1799 to Richard Tootell, Edward (b.1774) to Elizabeth Crist, and Thomas (b.1783) to Ann Griffith of Kent Island in 1800. From c.1788 until c.1794, the family lived in the Reynolds/Trueman property adjacent to Faris on Church Circle, where they operated a tavern. Pryse, whose first *Gazette* ad appeared in November 1774, came to Annapolis from London. § Pryse patronized Faris's tavern from 1773 to 1778, and Faris received twenty pounds of butter from him as payment in March 1776. Faris and Pryse stood surety for James Kelso's license as ferry keeper on the Patapsco River in April 1791.

49 Probably the garden of Jeremiah Townley Chase (see 7 October 1793).

50 The *Gazette* announced the opening on 22 March of a waxworks at the city ballroom, to be seen daily from 10 a.m. to 9 p.m. except on Sundays through the 13th of April.

1792 Apl 6 🖎 a fogey morning. this fore noon the
the Assembley broke. a fine day. in ye evening like
for rain

7 🖎 a cloudey drisley morning. turned out a fine day
and planted the following Roots & Seeds — the
Double Tube Rose 6 Roots on the beads round the
grass & the single ones in the Beads next the Temple

Polianthus from Mr. G. Mann planted the 6th of March

No. 1 Glorey of Canton   2 Mrs. Gassay
       Both from Baltimore

3 Double Cullimbine   4 Sensitive Plant

5 Varigated palmach

6 Coxcomb   7 Affrican Marygold   8 pickeling Limes

9 primrose - India pink & asters & poppeys

10 female Balsom

this day receivd a Letter from Bille dated Havanna
    March 9th 92[51]

8 🖎 a fine day — 🖎 9th 🖎 a cloudey drisley
morning. uncovered the Peas & Hilled them — this
day Abbee bgan going to school to Mrs. Jones

10 🖎 a fine day. fine growing weather

11 🖎 a rainey & drissel'd all day. stuck 1 Row of
Peas

12 🖎 rain'd all most all Last night and all most all
day. in the evening clear'd away but raw & coole

1792 Apl 13

🖎 a dull cloudey drisley day

14 🖎 a cold windey disagreeable day 🖎 (15th) 🖎 a
clear day but cold

16 🖎 a dull cloudey cold morning. about 10 oclock
St. John Faris sett off to Baltimore, and I finished
sticking one half the pea Bead and had no more
sticks

17 🖎 a fine warm day with a littel shower of rain in
the evening 🖎 (18th) 🖎 a cloudey rayney
morning. a rainey disagreeable day 🖎 (19th) 🖎 a
rainey day. this day Abee and Rebecka[52] Left Mrs.
Jones's school on accot. of that dirty fellow Jones's Ill
behaveour[53]

20 🖎 still rainey weather and very cold for the season

[51] This is the first diary reference to William
Faris Jr., the couple's oldest son. His brother
Charles implies that William left home after a
quarrel with his father (see 10 September
1797) and the "Will" refers to William Jr. as
"ungrateful," but Faris does not indicate here
that the letter from William was in any way
unusual or unexpected. William continued to
correspond with his family throughout the
diary, first from Havana and then from
Edenton, North Carolina.

[52] The first appearance of Rebecca Faris, the
youngest daughter of William and Priscilla.
Born on 11 December 1788, she was thirteen
years and a few months old.

[53] Mr. and Mrs. Jones left Annapolis not long
after this incident. By 1793 they had relocated
to Hagerstown, where Mrs. Jones opened a
boarding school for young women and Mr.
Jones, in a separate house, advertised to teach
a few "gentlemen, English grammar, reading,
writing, arithmetic and bookkeeping." Jones's
"ill behavior" perhaps consisted of inappro-
priate attention to one or both of the girls.

54 John Towers, a sea captain, lived on Albemarle Street in Old Town, Baltimore, in 1796. The *Maryland Journal* reported the arrival of the *Commerce* from Grenada, at the southern end of the Caribbean archipelago, on 7 April and her departure for the same port on the 27th, both times under the command of Capt. Towers.

55 St. John Faris's older brother Hyram would sail on the *Commerce,* possibly (but not necessarily) the same vessel, in 1800.

56 Nicholas Harwood (1748–1810) was one of the eleven children of Capt. Richard Harwood (1707–1754) and his wife Ann Watkins (1719–1804). He and his wife, also named Ann, had at least six children before her death. Four of Harwood's brothers appear in the diary, as well as his three daughters and four of his nephews. The Harwood girls were good friends of Faris's daughters. Harwood was clerk of the Anne Arundel County court from 1777 until his death. He was also one of the managers of the lottery to raise funds to complete St. Anne's. In 1798, Harwood leased a home on Cornhill Street, but in 1802 he bought a house at the corner of North Street and College Avenue and the adjoining lot in 1806. § Faris collected £0.17.6 from Harwood in November 1800 as administrator of Charles's estate.

21 ✍ this morning it Hailed & rained allmost all day and very cold for the season. Saint John's returned from Baltimore this after noon and has got a Mate's Birth in a Brigg to the West Indes Capt. Towers[54]

22 ✍ a dull cloudey day

23 ✍ about 10 oclock Saint sett off for Baltimore to go on Bord the Brigg Commerce[55] Capt. Towers Bound for the Island of Grenado. a fine day but rather cool. sow'd a few radish seed on the Border next to Grayhams

24 ✍ a fine day

25 ✍ a cloudey rayney day

26 ✍ a cloudey day and some rain

1792 Apl 27 ✍ a fine day. this evening receiv'd a letter from St. who says he likes his Capt. very well as yet

28 ✍ a fine day. in ye evening rain

29 ✍ a cloudey morning. in the after noon Mrs. Harwood the wife of Nicholas Harwood[56] was Buryed. a very Large cumpaney attended the funeral

30 ✍ a fine morning. fine weather

May 1 ✍ a fine day. Sylve[57] dug the Littel Quarter by the nursery — I melted two small cakes of Beeswax with an intent to whiten them. the one I Laid on the grass the other I put in a Bowl of Water in the sun[58]

---

57 Sylve was a slave belonging to Faris, the only slave still his property when he died in 1804. Although Sylve does not appear in the diary until May 1st, for most years she was the garden's most consistent worker, hoeing the beds, cleaning the walks, setting out plants, and doing myriad other garden chores, as well as working in the house. Sylve had a son Adam, born 2 August 1793, who died on 1 October 1795. The diary mentions no other children of hers, but the "Will" leaves Sylve to Nancy and Sylve's first child, a girl about fifteen years old (in c.1791), to Abigail. Faris mentions no one in the diary who appears to be Sylve's daughter. And nowhere is there any mention of the father of Sylve's children. He and Sylve were unlikely to have been married—slave marriages had no legal sanction—but they might have lived together as husband and wife, had Faris owned both. The children may also have had different fathers; the many years between their births suggests this possibility. In any event, the children may well have had little contact with their father, and Sylve may not have enjoyed much in the way of companionship from her mate. Priscilla Faris retained ownership of Sylve after her husband's death.

58 In one of the many examples of Faris's inquisitive mind, he appears to be experimenting to see which method will bleach the wax most effectively.

2 ✒ a fine day. in the evening a littel rain

3 ✒ a fine day

4 ✒ a fine day. planted out Onions in the littel bed
by the nursery. in the evening a fine rain

5 ✒ a fine day. Doctr Scott[59] sent me some cornation
or rather pink plants & I sent him some evening
primrose plants

1792 May 6 ✒ a fair day but coole & windey. Mr.
O Donal[60] marked a number of Tulips with plain
sticks[61]

7 ✒ a fine day. this day I Hiered a neagro fellow by
the name of Peter Shorter[62] at the rate of Twelve
pounds pr year. he dug the ground betwen the Peas
and mad abegining to clean the walk. I ground the
scythe, hes agoing to mow the grass in cirkel in the
morning. a littel rain in the evening

93 ✒ Dr. Upton Scott (1724–1814)

*Upton Scott was an avid Annapolis
gardener with whom Faris exchanged
plants and seeds.*

59 Dr. Upton Scott was born in Ireland, served in the British army,
and acquired a medical degree in Scotland. He came to Maryland in
1753 as the personal physician of Governor Horatio Sharpe. Scott
married Elizabeth Ross (d.1819), the younger daughter of John
Ross, Esq. (d.1766) and his wife Alicia Arnold, on 5 September
1756. She was the aunt of Philip Barton Key (see 29 May 1792)
and the great-aunt of Francis Scott Key (see 19 January 1802).
Scott served as Anne Arundel sheriff and county doctor, sat on the
council, was an alderman, and replaced his father-in-law in several
provincial offices, including that of clerk of the council. Scott built
a handsome Georgian mansion on Shipwright Street, adjoining the
property of Charles Carroll of Annapolis, about 1765, with large
formal gardens extending to Southeast Street on one side and Spa
Creek on the other. By 1798, the brick outbuildings included a
greenhouse, carriage house, smoke house, stable and cow house, and
poultry house. Scott was a founder of the Medical and Chirurgical
Faculty of Maryland in 1799 and served as its first president. A visitor to Annapolis in 1811 wrote of Scott: "He is fond of Botany, and
has a number of rare plants & shrubs in his green house & garden."
§ Faris charged Scott 2/6 for altering a clock in June 1774, 5/ for
mending a pair of temple spectacles in December 1774, and 17/6
for a man to take his clock and set it up at Scott's plantation
(Belvoir) on the Severn River in July 1776.

60 Capt. John O'Donnell (1749–1805) was an Irish sea captain who
married Sarah Chew Elliott, daughter of Capt. Thomas Elliott of
Fells Point, in October 1785. O'Donnell's ship, *Pallas,* arrived in
Baltimore in March 1785 as the first vessel to bring goods directly
from China (prior to the Revolution all imports from China had to
come through a British port). He acquired a fortune through trade
with China and India, which he acknowledged by naming his
Baltimore country estate "Canton" after his favorite overseas port.
Two accounts by English visitors provide descriptions of the extensive estate and its gardens.

61 Gardeners used marked sticks to indicate
plants or bulbs that would be given or sold to
particular individuals at the proper season.
Different combinations of notches served to
distinguish among recipients. Rosalie Stier
Calvert wrote to her father of the difficulties
that could arise if plants were not marked
carefully: "Poor Dr. Scott (see 5 May) has
gotten his [tulips] in such disorder that I truly
believe he does not have a single one now
whose name he hasn't mixed up." Scott
requested a particular variety from Rosalie and
the following year gave her back the same
tulip, calling it by a different name and
describing it as a rare flower imported by a
ship captain from London.

62 Peter Shorter was probably not a free man,
judging from the entry of 9 May, or even
allowed by his master or mistress to hire his
own time. But he may have been the father of
carpenter Charles Shorter, who was free in the
nineteenth century and who named a child
Peter.

8 🖎 a fine day. Mr. Thomas Harwood[63] mark'd 7 Tulips with a stick with one notch and peter made a poore hand at mowing. then went to digging the tabel round the grass

9 🖎 finished the tabels, and discharg'd peter as he had no wright to hire him self . a find day. in the evening Capt. Kilty married Kitty Quynn[64] and the Town Talked that he should have marryed her sooner as she as she's with child

10 🖎 a fine day 🖎 11th 🖎 a fine day

12 🖎 a fine warm day. in the evening a fine rain

1792 *May 13* 🖎 a fine day 🖎 (14th) 🖎 fine growing weather. this Planted some Peas Mr. Sprigg[65]

94 🖎 Thomas Harwood
(1743–1804)

One of several Harwood brothers whom Faris knew and mentioned in his diary.

63 Thomas Harwood, another of the sons of Capt. Richard Harwood (1707–1754) and his wife Ann Watkins (1719–1804), married Margaret Strachan (1747–1821) in 1772. Harwood was a merchant in Annapolis in partnership with his brother Benjamin (see 20 May 1804). He was appointed treasurer of the western shore in 1775, an office he held until his death. Harwood was sheriff in 1783, a manager in 1790 of the lottery to raise funds to complete St. Anne's, and a commissioner of loans in 1791. Harwood lived in a three–story brick home fronting on the dock. His son Richard married Sarah Callahan, daughter of John (see 29 March 1803).

64 John Kilty (1756–1811) was the son of Capt. John Kilty (?–c.1785) and his wife Ellen Ahearn (?–by 1782). Kilty was born in London and immigrated with his mariner father by 1771. Kilty, a Roman Catholic educated at St. Omer's in France, married Catherine Quynn, daughter of Allen Quynn (see 9 September 1792). Following his service in the militia and regular Maryland line during the Revolution, Kilty was a founding member of the Society of the Cincinnati. He served on the executive council from 1785 to 1793, and as councilman, alderman, and mayor. During his tenure as register of the western shore land from 1803 to 1811, Kilty wrote *The Land-holder's Assistant and Land Office Guide* (1808), a history of the colonial land system and the operation of the land office since independence. The Kiltys lived in Baltimore during part of the period covered by the diary. § In April 1778, Faris lent Kilty £7.10.0, which he repaid, and in March 1781 charged for board of Kilty and his horse.

65 Richard Sprigg (1739–1798) was the son of Thomas Sprigg and his wife Elizabeth Galloway (d.1790). He married Margaret Caile (d.1796), the daughter of John Caile, clerk of the Dorchester County Court, in August 1765. A lawyer, Sprigg lived at his Annapolis estate, Strawberry Hill, across College Creek from St. John's College, and also at Cedar Park, on the West River in Anne Arundel County. Both estates were known for their formal gardens. Sprigg's daughter Sophia married John Francis Mercer (see 9 November 1801 entry) in February 1785 and Rebecca (d.1798) married Dr. James Steuart (see 19 May 1792) in November 1788. Faris notes the marriage of a third daughter, Elizabeth, in the diary (see 19 January 1794). § Sprigg patronized Faris's tavern a number of times in the 1770s.

gave me, and the French consol[66] gave them to him and says thay make the best supe he ever eate. thay are called {blank}. Sylve How'd the Bunch Beens & wed the parcely, & the Border next Grayhams & began the nursery. I sow'd a bed of radishes in the lott. sow'd the peas I got of Mr. Sprigg in rows 3 feet and a ½ asunder

15 ✍ fine weather. this day I got one of the Ice Plant & 2 mininett Plants of Mrs. Neth.[67] in the evening a litter rain

16 ✍ a fine rain this morning. planted out a few early York plants. in the after noon Sylve wed part of the parsnip Bed

17 ✍ a fine day. the Grand Jurey's discharged about noon and I Broke the tops of the tulips which amounted to 1490

18 ✍ a very cold day for the season

1792 May 19 ✍ very cold this morning. Doctr James Murray[68] cut a littel peace off Charles Faris's

---

[66] Chevalier Charles Francois Adrien Le Paulinier d'Annemours (c.1742–c.1809), who traveled in the American colonies and the West Indies between 1768 and 1773. In 1777 the French government appointed him as a liaison with the rebellious colonies. After a treaty of alliance was concluded, in 1778 M. Gérard, the French minister, named d'Annemours consul for Maryland because of the number of French ships calling at Baltimore. In October 1779, his district was extended as far as Georgia. An expanded consular service in 1784 left d'Annemours as the representative for Maryland and Virginia, a post he held until the arrival of Genêt (see 5 September 1793), who suppressed the Baltimore consular service. D'annemours retired to his estate, Belmont, in Baltimore County, which he subsequently sold in 1796, spending the last years of his life in New Orleans.

[67] Annapolis merchant Lewis Neth (1752–1825) was born in Germany and came to Annapolis, by way of Philadelphia, by 1781. He married Elizabeth Adams (d.1830), daughter of blockmaker Nathaniel Adams (d.1770) and his wife Grace, and owner of five houses on Fleet Street inherited from her father. By 1790, the Neths lived at the corner of Church and Green Streets, where Neth sold imported goods and where his wife had her garden; they were tenants of Frederick Grammar (see 27 July 1800). In 1802, Thomas Jennings' estate (see 17 July 1793) sold Neth the Prince George Street home and terraced gardens originally built by William Paca (see 7 November 1797). § Faris paid Mrs. Neth for a coat for Hyram in December 1794, Abee paid her for a pair of shoes in April 1797, and in November 1801 Faris paid for "sunderies as per bill for self & Bille." Faris's estate paid Neth £9.2.2 for funeral expenses.

[68] James Murray (1739–1819) was born in Chestertown, the son of Dr. William Murray and his wife Ann Smith. He received his education at the College of Philadelphia and the University of Edinburgh, returning to practice medicine in Annapolis in 1769. He married Sarah Ennalls Maynadier Nevett (c.1752–1837), the daughter of Rev. Daniel Maynadier (1724–1772) and his wife Mary Murray (1729–?) and the sister of Henry Maynadier (see 11 May 1795). The Murrays lived on Prince George Street in a two-story brick dwelling with a brick kitchen, medical shop, and smoke house. Faris records the marriages of two of Murray's daughters: Anna Maria to John Mason in February 1796 and Sally to Edward Lloyd V in November 1797. A third daughter married the son of Dr. Benjamin Rush of Philadelphia, one of the signers of the Declaration of Independence. Murray, one of the founders of the Medical and Chirurgical Faculty of Maryland, practiced in partnership with John T. Shaaff (see below) until March 1797, and then with Reverdy Ghiselin (see 13 April 1793). § Murray patronized Faris's tavern in 1774, paid 2/6 for a nut for a brass lock in November 1774, borrowed six bushels of oats in September 1775 and one pound of saltpetre in August 1777, and paid £1.5.0 for a pair of "sheo chapes" (most likely, shoe buckles) in April 1778. Charles Faris's estate paid Murray and Reverdy Ghiselin £3.13.9 and Faris collected £3.5.3 from Murray in January 1801 as administrator of Charles's estate. When Faris died, Murray owed him £94.19.7.

Tongue[69] present Doctrs W. Murray[70] Shoff[71] & J. Stewart.[72] it was done in about 2 minuets.   colder this evening then yester day evening. thare was a frost this morning at William Aquarts[73]

20 ✍ a clear day but still cold for the season

21 ✍ Sylve began to digg the Bed in the lott. very cold for the season. Mr. Shryock[74] left Town to day & promis's to send me the Bees wax[75] as soon as possible by the way of Baltimore to be left with Mr. John Griffith to be sent by the packett[76] to me in Annapolis. Mr. Benjamin Griffith desired me to have it left with Mr. Griffith[77] on Baltimore Town

22 ✍ finished diging ye Bed in the lott & finished weeding the parsneps. a fine day, this day was sold by the Shriff W. Goldsmith a runaway neagro man nam'd Jerrey (for fifty five pounds,) who says he Belongs to a man in Carrolina.[78] struck off to Gasper Tille[79]

23 ✍ a fine day ✍ (24th) ✍ a fine day, this day the pettet Jurey was discharged

---

69 Most likely a tumorous growth, as a second surgery was necessary in 1796; see entry for 20 May.

70 William Murray was Dr. James Murray's brother. He married Harriet Woodward Brice (1762–1840), daughter of Henry and Mary Young Woodward (see 5 June 1792) and the widow of Edmund Brice (d.1784), in November 1788, and was guardian of Brice's son, James Edmund, when the boy entered the St. John's grammar school in 1793. Harriet's grandfather Amos Woodward was a cousin of Priscilla Woodward Faris. Murray was also a founder of the Medical and Chirurgical Faculty.

71 Dr. John T. Shaaff (c.1763–1819) was the partner of Dr. James Murray until the partnership dissolved in March 1797. Shaaff, born in Frederick, received his medical education in Europe, and began his practice in Annapolis after his return in July 1790 on the *Integrity*. Shaaff's first wife, Mary Sydebotham, died at the age of 33 in September 1810; he married Mary Stewart in February 1812. Shaaff, another of the founding members of the Medical and Chirurgical Faculty of Maryland, was the organization's first treasurer.

72 Dr. James Steuart, a graduate of the University of Edinburgh in 1779, was the son of Dr. George Hume Steuart and his wife Ann Digges (1718–1814). He married Rebecca Sprigg (1767–1806), daughter of Richard Sprigg (see 13 May 1792), in November 1788. A member of the Medical and Chirurgical Faculty of Maryland, he practiced first in Annapolis and then moved to Baltimore.

73 William Urquhart was the son of William and Jane Urquhart (d.1808). William Sr., who died some time prior to February 1785, lived in Prince George's County, but his widow and son appear to have lived outside Annapolis along General's Highway. Urquhart's mother obtained a license as a tavern keeper in August 1787, which William assumed by September of that year. He married Maria Deford in April 1808 and was the administrator of her father Benjamin's estate in April 1816. Faris may have learned of the frost in conversation with Urquhart at the market house.

74 John Shryock, a pump borer, lived on Pitt Street, in Old Town, Baltimore, in 1796.

75 Faris used the beeswax to make casts of fruit. In the diary he mentions casting both plums and cantaloupes and had a case of wax objects in his parlor when he died.

76 After the Revolution, as Baltimore became the economic center of Maryland, packet services developed to link smaller towns around the bay with the metropolis. George and John Barber operated one packet service that Faris used extensively, but there were others of which he made occasional use. None advertised in the *Gazette* at this time, so they cannot be further identified.

77 Although there were Griffiths in Anne Arundel County, these were probably John Griffith of "Baltimore Town," who died in 1794, and his brother Benjamin, who lived in Philadelphia. John named two Baltimore merchants as his executors, and may have been a merchant or storekeeper himself.

78 Goldsmith placed a notice in the *Maryland Gazette*, 20 March, that he had committed to his custody as a runaway, Negro Jerry, who claimed to belong to a Mr. Peter Richardson of Fairfax County, North Carolina. In lieu of a claim for his recovery by his master, Jerry was sold at auction to the highest bidder.

79 Jasper E. Tilley (d.1817), the son of Ann Tilley, married Elizabeth Higgins in May 1793. Tilley lived on the South River, where first his mother and then he kept the ferry. § Faris's estate paid him, in his capacity as sheriff, £3.9.7 for fees and the 1803 city tax, and £5.4.6 for fees on the estate.

25 ⚓ Lamb[80] came to work about 9 oclock. Joynted 900 shingels & naild on 2 courses. a fine day

1792 *May 26* ⚓ Lamb finish'd the shed about 1 oclock and after diner put a peace under the front of the portch and finished about 3 oclock. it has been a very warm day but now has clouded over & looks as if wee should have some rain which is very much wanted

27 ⚓ it rain'd a littel Last night and this morning but did not wett the ground half an Inch

28 ⚓ a fine clear day but rather coole. Hyram came home in the evening very unwell and went to Bed

29 ⚓ Hyram's very unwell this morning. did not get up till allmost noon, in the after noon Mrs. Sprigg[81] came hear and went to Mr. Keys.[82] returned & drank coffee. mounted her Horse & went off down the countrey. Hyram's bravely this evening. very dry Weather. every thing's all but burnt up in the garden

30 ⚓ Hott & dry ⚓ (31) ⚓ very Hott day the Hottest we have had this spring, a meeting of the Cleargy to chuse a Bisshop

80 Possibly John Lamb, who obtained a marriage license in Anne Arundel in 1778. He may also have been the John Lamb, son of John and Sarah Gordon Lamb, who was born in 1745 and married Hamutal Moss in 1770.

81 "Down country" suggests that this might have been Deborah Sprigg (see 14 May 1794), visiting Annapolis to consult with attorney Philip Barton Key, but it might have been Margaret Sprigg, wife of Richard (see 13 May 1792) or the wife of one of the Prince George's County Spriggs.

82 Philip Barton Key (1757–1815) was the son of Francis Key (c.1732–1770) and his wife Ann Arnold Ross (1727–1811), and the nephew of Upton and Elizabeth Ross Scott (see 5 May 1792). His sister Elizabeth Scott Key married Henry Maynadier (see 11 May 1795) and his nephew Francis Scott Key married Mary Tayloe Lloyd (see 19 January 1802). Key was educated in England and entered the British army after the colonies declared their independence. He served in Jamaica and Florida, where he was taken prisoner. After his release on parole, Key went back to England, but returned to Maryland in 1785 and began the practice of law, being admitted as an attorney in the Anne Arundel County court in November 1786. He married Ann Plater (1774–1834), the daughter of George Plater (see 10 February 1792). Key served as a councilman, alderman, and mayor, and represented Annapolis in the lower house from 1794 to 1799. He moved to Georgetown in 1801, where he practiced law with his nephew Francis Scott Key. The *Maryland Gazette* reported his death on 28 July 1815: "at his seat near Georgetown. As a lawyer he stood in the first rank of his profession; as a gentleman he was greatly respected, even by those who admired him least as a politician." Although he and Faris never exchanged plants or seeds, Rosalie Calvert wrote to her father of Key in 1806, that "your old friend from Annapolis, the lawyer Key, is now one of the best gardeners in the neighborhood." § Faris collected £4.6.7 from Key in January 1801 as administrator of Charles's estate.

83 Thomas John Clagett was the seventh rector of St. James Parish at Herring Bay. Clagett was consecrated Bishop of Maryland at Trinity Church in New York on 18 September, the first Episcopal bishop consecrated on American soil. He died in August 1816 and was buried at his estate, Croome, but his remains were reinterred at the National Cathedral in Washington, D.C., in 1919.

95 ✒ Bishop Thomas John Clagett
(1743–1816)

A minister in Anne Arundel County, Clagett was the first Episcopal bishop consecrated in the United States.

1792 June 1 ✒ very hott & dry. it clouded up and appear'd as if wee should have had rain but it went over, the Reverend Mr. Cleggett's[83] chose Bisshop

2 ✒ a cloudey morning but it broke away Hott & dry

3 ✒ a cloudey close warm morning

4 ✒ cloudey and like for rain, began to take up the Seedlin Tulips

5 ✒ clear Hott and dry. in the after noon clouded up like rain, in the evening two of the Miss Hesselious's was married. Mr. Walter Addison to Miss Charlot and Mr. Thomas Johnston to Miss Betsey[84]

6 ✒ Hier'd a Black man by the name of Daniel at the rate of 12£ pr year. very Hott and dry — finish'd takeing up the Seedling Tulips. began to clear the walks. in the evening water'd the cabages betwen the peas

7 ✒ wee had a littel rain last niqht, but not anuf to do any servis. cleaning the walks and gathered the seed peas. looks cloudey and like for rain. in the evening it began to rain and looks as if we should have a fine rain

1792 June 8 ✒ very cold and cloudey, very littel rain last night. I am Told that on Elk Ridge thay had on Wednesday last a very heavey fall of very large Hail as large as pulletts eggs. the ground at the Walnutt Tree's so hard that its Impossible to digg it. it looks very likely that wee shall have a fine rain to night. it has missild small rain several times to day

---

84 Faris mixed up the brides and grooms in this entry. Walter Dulany Addison married Elizabeth Hesselius and Thomas Johnson married Charlotte Hesselius. The two brides were daughters of limner John Hesselius (1728–1778) and his wife Mary Young Woodward. Mary Hesselius was daughter of Col. Richard Young and the widow of Henry Woodward (1733–1761), whose father Amos was a cousin of Priscilla Woodward Faris. John Hesselius was born in Philadelphia and settled in Annapolis in the 1760s. He died at his plantation, Bellefield, on the north side of the Severn River, leaving a son and four daughters. Walter Dulany Addison (1769–1848), was the son of Thomas and Rebecca Addison (see 17 July 1793). Ordained as an Episcopal minister in Easton in 1793, he served from 1809 until his retirement in 1827 as rector of St. John's Church in Georgetown, D.C. Thomas Jennings Johnson was the son of Thomas Johnson (see 5 November 1795), first governor of the state of Maryland, and his wife Anne Jennings. § Faris altered a pocket pistol for John Hesselius in January 1777.

9 ✍ cold dry & windey. Daniel's not come to work to day. I have planted on the Border whare the Seedling Tulips ware the seed of the Jerusalom Cherrey. in the evening very cold & windey and like for rain

10 ✍ last night very cold and the wind Blew very Hard. a cloudey mornind and very cold. about 10 oclock it began to rain and the wind continues to blow very Hard, and cold

11 ✍ made a begining to plant cabbage plants in the lott and Hyram athining the carrotts and gott 98 early York Plants from Wikins's.[85] Jack planted part whare the seedling tulips stood and the rest betwen the peas from Mr. Sprigge. Daniel came to see us this morning and complains of a pain in his side. I let him have half a crown to get him self Blooded. 9 oclock it began to rain. we quitt and came in the shop

1792 *June* 11 ✍ finished planting. very cold and raind at times all day. this evening receiv'd a litter from Saint John Faris dated the 2d of May from Mobjack Bay[86]

12 ✍ a very windey cold night, morning very cold, cloudey and drisseley, made a fire in the House with charcole for want of wood and should have had a fire in the House these several days past but am out of wood and no wood comes to the dock,[87] I suppose on accot. of the winds Blowing so very hard at north & the eastward of north. in the evening the sun came out clear. at night clear and starr light but still cold and windey

13 ✍ a cloudey morning. about 12 oclock the sun came out and looks as if wee should have a fine after

---

[85] William Wilkins (1737–>1814) was the son of William Wilkins (c.1700–1761) and his wife Deborah Maccubbin (1700–?), the widow of Nathaniel Palmer. William's father was an innkeeper, a business that his mother continued after William Sr.'s death. Wilkins was a merchant, who placed his first advertisement in the *Gazette* in 1763. Two years later he married Sarah Conant (1741–1814), with whom he had at least four children. Wilkins was a churchwarden for St. Anne's in 1780 but by 1789 he and his son, William Jr., were trustees of the Methodist Church built on the grounds of the State House. Wilkins lost his home on Church Street, near the dock, to the same fire that destroyed Richard Fleming's property (see 11 March 1792). Wilkins relocated farther up the street on the opposite side. § A slave belonging to Wilkins swept Faris's chimney in August 1802 and Faris bought two ounces of red bark from Wilkins in September of that year.

[86] A large bay on the west side of the Chesapeake Bay, between the Piankatank and York Rivers.

[87] Town dwellers needed a steady supply of wood to heat their homes through the cold months as well as to cook year-round. While some wood must have come overland by cart, this is the second entry to record the difficulty of obtaining enough wood when the waterways iced over. According to his account book, Faris was able to buy a cord of wood on the 16th for fifteen shillings. He paid another two shillings to the carter who delivered it to his house and six pence to the wood corder who measured it.

88 Faris's "Will" left Sol Mogg, "who tolls the bell"—presumably the church bell at St. Anne's—his hat and pipe. Joseph Mogg may have been a relative or perhaps the same person, given the eccentricities of handwriting and spelling.

89 James West (c.1738–1812) was a tavern keeper on property he rented from Absalom Ridgely on Church Street, consisting of a two-story brick dwelling and brick stable. He held a tavern license in the 1780s and 1790s but eventually moved to Baltimore, where he died in June 1812. Three of his sons, James, Nicholas, and Wilmot, attended the grammar school at St. John's. After the death of his first wife, West married Margaret Whitaker (see 31 December 1795). According to Edward C. Papenfuse (*In Pursuit of Profit*, 145), "James West never made money at anything he did, although his father may have been a prosperous planter. James chose to open a tavern and whiled away his time at cards or tried to prevent damage as his customers brawled."

---

noon. began to take the Tulips up for Mr. O Donal and Mr. Harwood. a fine evening

14 ✒ a fine day. finished takeing up the roots for Mr. O Donal and Mr. Harwood

15 ✒ a fine day ✒ (16th) ✒ a fine morning

17 ✒ a fine day but a littel rain would be of servis

1792 June 18 ✒ a fine day but rain's much wanted. thare is a report and Joseph Mogg[88] says he realy beleaves its true that Mrs. West the wife of James West[89] cruelly Killed a neagro by stomping & Beating. it was buryed this evening

19 ✒ Hott and dry ✒ (20th) ✒ Hott & dry ✒ (21th) ✒ Hott & dry. this morning Mr. Thomas Hyde[90] & Miss Salley sett off for the springs.[91] in the evening a very Black cloud rose in the north and Thundered and lightened a grate deal and Blew very Hard, and wee had but very littel rain

22 ✒ very Hott and dry. in the evening look'd gustey but I am afraid we shall have no rain

23 ✒ wee had a littel rain Last night and a littel this fore noon but scarcely anuff to lay the dust

---

90 Thomas Hyde (1722–1795), the son of Isaac (d.1734) and Mary Hyde, was baptized in All Hallow's Parish. As a penniless orphan, he was apprenticed to learn the trade of shoemaker, and had established himself in that craft by 1745. He married Elizabeth Bishop in July 1749 and had one son, William, born in Annapolis in 1750; William died in 1786 of wounds received in the Revolutionary War. Hyde was also fined and paid surety for a bastard child born in 1768. In 1764 Hyde built a store on Church Street, where he operated as a merchant; beginning in 1772 he also built the Maryland Inn on the corner of Church Street and Church Circle. When he died, Hyde left his estate to his sister Elizabeth Wall and her daughters, Mary, who married Jesse Ray, and Sarah, the Miss Sally who accompanied him to the springs (see 1 March 1795 entry for her marriage). § William Hyde visited Faris's tavern in October 1775.

91 It was quite common for those who could afford the expense to travel to one of several springs in western Virginia to take the waters for their health. In his *Notes on the State of Virginia*, Thomas Jefferson described a variety of hot, warm, and medicinal springs. John Ridout (see 6 October 1797) wrote in August 1786 of his plans to make a similar trip, having experienced symptoms of gout: "I am just now tolerably well & have thoughts of going next week to pass a fortnight at the Virg[ini]a Springs which I think have been in former seasons of service to me." He planned to take his son Samuel (see 17 July 1793), "who has lately had the ague & fever . . . in hope he will be also the better for the change of air & exercise."

24 ✒ a fine day. in the evening looks like rain

25 ✒ a fine day. Hott & dry. Sylvea begant to digg the Walnutt Tree Quarter and I began the frame of the Electrefying Masheen.[92] I have got the frame all-most Plain'd up ready to go to Mortis & Tennenting[93]

26 ✒ a fine day but Hott & dry. Sylve finished digging the walnutt tree quarter

1792 June 27 ✒ Hott & dry. pulled up the peas and sticks in the big Bead and began to digg ware the peas was and cut the Baum

28 ✒ Very Hott and dry ✒ (29th) ✒ a very Hott day. in the evening we had a littel shower of rain not anuff for a season ✒ (30) ✒ hott and dry

July *1* ✒ a very hott day

2 ✒ a very hott morning but a fine wind ablowing. Abee & Rebecka began going to school to Mrs. Leech[94] at 15/ pr quarter. in the after noon Abee carryed Mrs. Leech on dollor in part in hand

3 ✒ very Hott and dry. in the after noon clouded up and looked as if wee should have rain, but it went by but the air's changed and it is more plessent

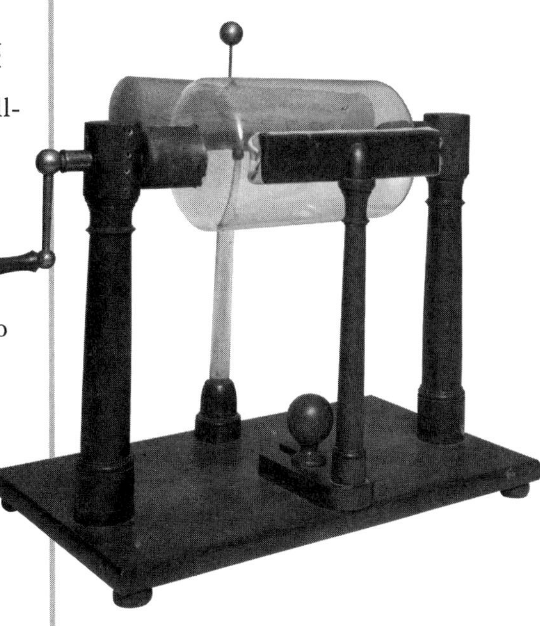

96 ✒ Electrostatic Generator/Electrical Machine

Faris used an apparatus similar to this electrical machine as a form of electric shock therapy for a variety of ailments.

---

92 Faris still owned the electrifying machine when he died in 1804. Appraisers valued the machine, with its "apparatus compleat," at $30.00; Priscilla Faris purchased it for $18 at the sale of the estate. John Long, a hatter on Church Street, had advertised the use of an "Electrifying Machine" in 17 May 1792. It is unlikely that Long's announcement inspired Faris to build his own machine but it is possible that the two men exchanged information about the construction and use of the equipment. Static electricity generators, first used as therapy for paralyzed patients in 1745, produced a shock, or stimulus, that could be confined to a specific area and could be graduated in intensity. Faris several times in the diary mentions the use of electrical stimulus as treatment for various ills, but he never advertised the availability of his machine.

93 Having finished shaping the framing pieces of the electrifying machine, Faris was ready to attach them to one another with mortise and tenon joints. The mortise was a rectangular cavity of considerable depth near or on the end of one piece of wood, into which was fitted a corresponding projection, or tenon, on the end of a second piece, so as to form a secure joint.

94 Mrs. Leech did not advertise in the *Gazette,* but she may have been the wife (or, more likely, the widow) of Nicholas Leeke who opened a school on Cornhill Street in June 1788 and who relocated to South-East Street in September 1789. Nicholas Leeke married Mary Farrell in October 1778.

4 🙠 a cloudey morning. about noon began to rain and continued raining all the after noon and turned cold

5 🙠 a cloudey morning. planted all the ground Intended for plants and Planted Beens on the littel quarter

1792 July 6 🙠 a fine day

7 🙠 I was this day call'd on by a young man from Philadelpia on his way to Oxford or Cambridge who says his name is Charles O Neal, that hes a mason[95] & in distress. I lent him a dollor & a half which he promises he will return it to me. a fine cool day

8 🙠 a fine day 🙠 (9th) 🙠 a very Hott day

10 🙠 a very Hott day, this day receiv'd a letter from Saint informing us of his arrivel at Baltimore. the vessel went by hear last Satarday nigh. and that on the 26 of June near Bermuda thay had a gale of wind which over sett them. thay caut away thare masts and s[h]e righted with 6 feet and ½ water in her Hold

11 🙠 hott & dry 🙠 (12th) 🙠 dry weather

13 🙠 a cloudey morning 🙠 (14th) 🙠 dry weather to the 🙠 (16th) 🙠 in the evening & night a fine rain

17 🙠 this morning rain. replanted the ground with plants and worked the ground

1792 July 18th 🙠 a fine day

19 🙠 Hott & dry 🙠 (20th) 🙠 Hott and dry

21 🙠 a fine day

22 🙠 a cloudey morning. in ye after noon and night rain'd and turn'd cold

23 🙠 a cloudey drisley morning and continued so all day and very cold for the season

24 🙠 a rainey morning and continued till about 12 oclock and then clear'd away and was a fine afternoon & Sylve a weel'd dung on the two new Beds for Tulips by the Walnut Tree

25 🙠 a fine day cutt the sage

26 🙠 a fine day 🙠 (27) 🙠 good weather

28 🙠 a cloudey morning. about 9 oclock began to

95 A freemason, as was Faris (see 27 December 1792).

rain and continued raining a sober moderate rain all day

29   a cloudey morning and rain'd at times all day

30   a fine day   (31)   a fine day

1792 *Augt* 1   whee had a smart shower of rain last night attended with a High Wind and sharp Thunder and Lightening — clear'd away and whee had a fine day rather warm

2   whe had a shower of rain last night, clear'd away and a fine day. in the evening look'd cloudey

3   a fine day but rather cool   (4th) & (5)   good weather

6th   cloudey. dung'd & dugg the Border nex the dining rome in the Lott and sow'd the following cabbage seeds

    No. 1 Early York or Battesey of our owne raising

       2 Early York from Mr. Wallace

       3 d[o] [ditto] from Mr. Pettey[96]

       4 Loaf cabbage from Mr. Chapman

       5 Real Loaf d[o] from Mrs. Onion[97]

7th   a fine rain Last night, a fine day

8   very warm   (9th)   very warm

10   a very Hott day. in the after noon St. J. Faris came Home from Baltimore. in the evening wee had a littel rain which cool'd the aire a littel

1792 *August* 11   very Hott

12   still very Hott. either last night or this morning Kitte Kilty was deliverd of a daughter. I think thay have not been Idel, being only marryed the 9th of May last

13   a fine day

14   thare was a fine rain this morning, cleard a way. in the evening look'd cloudey. this evening I saw Vine Hounsworth[98] who Told me he was discharge by Majr. Gathor[99] and on accot. of his having fitts. he left Fredrick Town on fryday evening last and that a Mr. Allcock paid ten dollors for him to pay for his Provisions

15   a fine day but too cold for the season. thare's been a grate deel of rain or hail some whare in the neighbour hood

96 John Petty came to Annapolis to collect debts owed to the firm of Petty and Yates, wine merchants of London, by Thomas Rutland, who went bankrupt in 1785. With Richard and Joseph Yates, he advertised in August 1792 the dissolution of John Petty & Co., but he continued to operate stores in Maryland. When he wrote his will in September 1793, he identified himself as a merchant of Annapolis, and left all his land to his nephew William and his personal property to his nieces and nephews. His inventory included £1,199 in an Easton store, £1,259 in a Baltimore store, and £573 in Annapolis.

97 John Barrett Onion married Julia Mayberry, daughter of Capt. Beriah Mayberry (see 1 August 1799). The Onions, who socialized with the Faris family on a number of occasions, lived on Cornhill Street in the two-story brick dwelling that was the Mayberry family home. Their son, Beriah Mayberry, age ten, entered the St. John's grammar school in November 1799. § Onion borrowed a half cord of hickory wood from Faris in March 1791. Charles Faris's estate paid Onion £5.1.7 but collected £9.13.0.

98 No one by this surname appears in the standard Anne Arundel County sources. Hounsworth must have been a regular soldier in the militia that had been sent to western Maryland.

99 The War Department announced the appointment of Henry Gaither of Montgomery County as a major in the Maryland infantry in May 1792. Gaither, who served in the Continental Army, died in Georgetown in 1811, at sixty-one. He was probably the Major Gaither who arrived in Annapolis in July 1790 on board the *Integrity* from London; Doctor Shaaff (see 19 May 1792) and Mr. Wilmer (see 19 September 1794) traveled on the same ship.

[100] Jeremiah Yellott (d.1805) arrived in Baltimore from Yorkshire in 1774 and parlayed his wartime activities as master of several privateers into a position as one of the city's most prominent merchants. He married Mary Hollingsworth, daughter of Jesse Hollingsworth, in February 1781. With his father-in-law, ship owners Charles Ridgely (see 8 October 1793) and John Sterrett, and financier Robert Oliver (see 27 December 1798), he formed one of the most powerful shipping interests controlling Baltimore commerce. Yellott is also credited with introducing the topsail schooner, a fast, maneuverable vessel that evolved into the Baltimore clipper. Yellott's activities also touched on other entries in Faris's diary: he was member of the committee to provide relief for the refugees from Saint Domingue in 1793 and served on the committee to found the Bank of Baltimore, whose shares Faris purchased in August 1796. When he died in February 1805, Yellott left a fortune of nearly $382,000—making him one of the wealthiest men in Baltimore. Yellot was one of the owners of the *Hebe*, the ship of which St. John Faris was master on his last voyage, and may have been an owner of the *Commerce*, on which St. John would shortly sail.

[101] Capt. Taylor could have been one of a number of men, all listed as ship captains or mariners in the Baltimore City directories or in newspaper notices: Giles, who married in 1802; James, who married in 1815; Jesse, who died in Alexandria in 1800; John, who lived in Fells Point in 1799 and who may have been the same John who married in 1809; or Thomas, who married in 1806. § Faris acquired a barrel of flour from Mr. Taylor in February 1792.

The Diary of

16 ⚘ still cool. a message from Mr. Yellcott[100] of Baltimore to come thare

1792 Augt 17 ⚘ a fine morning. about 9 oclock my son St. John ~~set off~~ left home to go to Baltimore in Taylors[101] Boat

18 and 19th ⚘ Hott and dry.   this morning Miss Betsey Gassa[wa]y[102] & Mrs. Hamelton[103] & Capt. Mays[104] came from Baltimore. saw St. he's well but did not get up till yesterday morning

20 ⚘ Hott & dry. How'd over the 2 cabbage Beds and began to clean the walks. looks as if wee should have rain in the evening

21 ⚘ cloudey morning and cool and like for rain

22 ⚘ a drisley morning and continued a cloudey day

23 ⚘ a fine day

24 ⚘ a fine rain this morning and continued cloudey & drisley all day. in the evening look'd as if wee should have a gust from the N:W. about 8 oclock it began & rained Hard

25 ⚘ a fine morning

26 ⚘ a fine day ⚘ (27th) ⚘ a fine day but rather cool

1792 Augt 28 ⚘ a rainey morning. I got a Box of pipes of 3 grose from Baltimore cost 13/6 and 2 glass Handels from d⁰ cost 4/6. in the after noon Charles run a drill in his thum which pained him so much that he fainted

---

[102] Elizabeth and her sisters Rebecca and Mary, three of the daughters of Elizabeth Brice Gassaway (c.1758–1798), were friends of the Faris girls and appear frequently in the diary. Their mother Elizabeth was the widow of Thomas Gassaway (1747–c.1788), who had been Anne Arundel's register of wills. She lost her youngest daughter, Catherine, in June 1794 and she (at age forty) and Rebecca both died in 1798. Faris recorded the marriage of her daughter Mary to Ninian Pinkney on 13 April 1802. Thomas Gassaway was the half-brother of John Gassaway (see 27 December 1792), who succeeded him as register of wills. § Charles Faris paid £4.11.0 for a bedstead and curtains that he bought at the sale of Thomas Gassaway's property.

[103] William Hamilton, a pilot, lived at 30 Queen Street in Fells Point in 1796. Mrs. Hamilton may have been his wife, but if she was, she died in late 1798 or early 1799 as Hamilton married Mrs. Maria Sullivan, also of Fells Point, in May 1799.

[104] Possibly Capt. William May, a pilot, who lived at 6 Shakespeare's Alley in Fells Point in 1796.

29 ✒ a fine day. in the morning it rained a littel

30 ✒ a fine morning. wind at W.N.W. Charels sett off in Capt. Barbers[105] Boat about 9 oclock for Baltimore and harford[106]

31 ✒ a fine day

Sept 1 ✒ a fine morning. in the after noon turned cloudey and look'd look'd like for rain

2th - 3th - 4 ✒ fine weather the mornings & evenings turn coole ✒ 5th & 6 ✒ fine weather. in the evening a littel rain and looks as if thare was bad weather comeing ✒ 7th & 8th ✒ good weather

9 ✒ a cloudey day. in the after noon rain. this after noon, Richard Beard[107] was buried aged 72 and Mr. Thomas Hyde told me that he should be 71 in Janary next and Mr. Charles Wallace said he should be 66 in May next. cloudey dull evening. Blows Hard and looks as if wee should have a Harrican. the pall Bearers to Mr. Beard's Burial, Messrs. Thomas Hyde, Charles Wallace, A Quynn,[108]

---

[105] George Barber (1761–1836) operated a number of businesses in town with his brother John, including a packet service between Baltimore and Annapolis. The Barbers also owned a store on the corner of Church and Compromise Streets and a warehouse on Pinkney Street. George also owned Horn Point farm, now part of Eastport. At his death in August 1836, he was survived by two sons and four daughters. § Faris's daybooks record payments on account as well as for specific passages, and freight charges for goods brought from Baltimore. When he died, Charles Faris owed the Barbers £6.16.11 for his own trips to Baltimore.

[106] Charles's trip to Harford County was very unusual, most of his travels being to Baltimore or to visit friends in Anne Arundel or Prince George's Counties. Faris gives no reason for this journey, which takes him two weeks.

[107] Richard Beard (1720–1792) was the son of Matthew and Mary Beard, and the husband of Mary Jones. In 1783 he was a tenant of Charles Wallace living on Cornhill or Fleet street, in a household consisting of himself, his wife, and one slave. His son Richard, who died in 1796, left a substantial estate, including goods at the Beards Point Warehouse, scales and weights for tobacco inspection, and surveying instruments, which must have represented, at least in part, an inheritance from his father.

[108] Allen Quynn (c.1726–1803) was probably a native of Maryland, but his parents are unknown. He and his wife Elizabeth married between 1760 and 1765. Quynn was a shoemaker who attained the status of a gentleman, with a long career in politics. In Annapolis, he held variously the offices of constable, councilman, alderman, engine keeper, port warden, and mayor. In addition, he had a commission as justice of the peace from 1777 to 1803 and represented Annapolis in the general assembly from 1777 to 1802. Quynn owned seven rental properties on Southeast and West Streets as well as a plantation on the South River. Quynn had at least eight children, a number of whom appear in the diary. Of his daughters, Elizabeth was the second wife of Abraham Claude (see 26 January 1795), Mary married John Gassaway (see 27 December 1792), Catherine married John Kilty (see 27 October 1792), and Faris notes Harriet's death in April 1803. Three other children, Allen Jr., John, and Ann all appear in an incident recorded in July 1796. Quynn's son William studied medicine in Edinburgh, where he died in 1784. Quynn died in November 1803 in his 77th year, "long a resident of Annapolis, and for twenty-five years a member of the House of Delegates." His estate, which included seventeen slaves (one of them a shoemaker) and an extensive collection of books (including *Forsythe on Fruit Trees*), totaled $4,523 on his plantation and $3,760 in Annapolis. § In November 1768, Faris and Quynn served as special bail for cabinetmaker Philip Williams. Quynn served on the St. Anne's vestry with Faris in the 1770s and early 1780s, and Faris bought an iron rake for the garden from him in April 1790 for 7/6.

109 Isaac McHard was the market clerk, who had been elected the previous month and resigned the office in November 1793. A tavern keeper, he leased the house at 10–12 Francis Street from 1774 to 1782. He also held a lease on a Market Space property and occupied a house on East Street in the 1790s. McHard married Ann Thompson (?–c.1785), widow of John Thompson Jr. In November 1783, the corporation paid McHard for lodging members of Congress, who were meeting in Annapolis that winter. § During the Revolutionary War, he and Faris were part of a group of Annapolitans described as "requisitioning" scarce supplies from nearby plantations.

110 Jubb Fowler (1735–1827) was the son of Benjamin Fowler (1708–1774) and his wife Helen Brigdell, the widow of Edward Mortimer. In 1783 he owned no real property but did have five slaves, and a household of eight people, four male and four female. Frances Fowler (see 5 October 1795) may have been an unmarried sister (Fowler had a daughter, Frances, who died in August 1830, never having married; she might have been named for an aunt). Fowler's son Robert, age thirteen, entered the grammar school of St. John's in May 1790 and the French school from October 1793 to August 1795. He was described as the son of Jubb, a mechanic, and received his education gratis. In 1797, the levy court met at Fowler's house, although he did not have a tavern license.

111 On the 8th, Faris had laid in a larger supply of firewood, four cords and five feet, for which he paid, in addition to the cost of the wood, charges for carting and cording (measuring).

112 Indian Landing, located on the west shore of the Severn River near the head of its navigable waters, was the site of a tobacco inspection warehouse, where planters brought their tobacco to be evaluated. Tobacco that met export standards would be prised into hogsheads and eventually collected by ship captains for transport to an overseas market.

Isaac McHeard,109 Jubb Fowler110 & William Faris Senr

10 ✍ a cloudey, windey, very cold day

11 ✍ clear and cold morning. a fire in the Big Roome111

12 ✍ a fine morning

13 ✍ a fine day. this morning Charley returned home from Harford

14 & 15th ✍ good weather ✍ (16th) D[itt]o

16 ✍ a cloudey morning & raind most all day & it look'd as if thare would be more rain before morning

17 ✍ dull cloudey day ✍ 18 & 19 ✍ coole. in the evening clouded up and turn'd cold. Blew hard

20 ✍ a cold windey day

21 ✍ a fine day. dissopointed in going to Baltimore. Taylors packet went to the Indian Landing for Tobbacco112

1792 *Sept* 22 ✍ a fine morning. the saffron croccus's is just makeing thare appearance acuming up. I expect to sett off to Baltimore this morning with Capt. Massey.113 Massey did not go, I got a a passage in the East Town Packett, left the dock about 12 oclock and arriv'd at fells Point114 betwen 7 & 8 oclock. I went on board the Snow, and found no one on board. I left the thing for Saint at Capt. Hammeltons, and I went to Town and found St. at Mr. Rosetors who Insisted on my staying thare while I stay'd in Baltimore. on Tusday evening the Snow Commerce finish'd her Loading and shiped her Hands and is to sail on fryday next for London and Liverpool. I left fells point on Wednes day 1/4 after 1 oclock for Annapolis and between Sandy point and

113 A merchant, Joseph Massey lived at 101 Hanover Street and had a store and counting house at 89 South Street, Bowleys Wharf, Fells Point, in 1796.

114 Fells Point lies on the north shore of the Northwest Branch of the Patapsco River and takes its name from Edward Fell, who established a store there in the 1720s. Fell's brother William, a carpenter who emigrated from Lancashire in 1730, built a shipyard, starting the industry that dominated the area for more than a century, as Faris's diary confirms. The settlement, comprising about eighty acres, was annexed to Baltimore in 1773.

Hacketts[115] the Boat run aground and thare stick fast for near 3/4 of an Hour before she was got off. we arrived at Annapolis about 8 oclock in the evening. wee have had very fine weather all the time I have been from Home

1792 Sept 27 ✍ a very cold day compair'd with the weather wee have had

28 ✍ a fine clear day. this evening Mrs. Oner Wilkins[116] was Buried.   this day the Snow Commerce went by Annapolis Bound for London[117]

29 & 30 ✍ fine weather. Mrs. Faris is very unwell

Octr 1 ✍ a fine day. Mrs. Sprigg,[118] Mrs. Perrey[119] & Miss Sprigg came heare to day & dined. Mrs. Faris very Ill. ceeps her bed, the Ladeys went away after diner, in the evening thar was a man Preach'd at the Stad House   one of the best preacher I ever Heard in my Life. hes a Uneversolist[120]

2 ✍ a cold disagreeable day. Mrs. Faris rather worse then yesterday. sent for Doctr. Murray. advis'd parogorick[121] & wine drops at bed time. this evening the Universelist preach'd again

3 ✍ Mrs. Faris very Ill this morning. sent early for the Doctor. thay both came. thay sent her a small Cordal draft,[122] she is something better, she's takeing the decoction of the Bark[123]

---

[115] Sandy Point lies on the western shore of the Chesapeake Bay, between the Magothy and Severn Rivers, and just north of Hacketts Point, at the mouth of the Severn River, between Whitehall Bay and the Chesapeake Bay.

[116] Honor Elder Howard (1740–1792) was the daughter of Henry Howard (1703–1773) and his wife Sarah Dorsey (1715–1791). She married three times, her first husband being Rezin Warfield (d.1767), her second being John Davidge (d.1770) and the last being Joseph Wilkins (d.1785). She had at least one daughter, Sarah Warfield, who received a legacy from her maternal grandmother. Honor Wilkins left an estate of £237, including four slaves, plus real estate in Annapolis.

[117] The *Maryland Journal* reported that the *Commerce* had sailed, under the command of Capt. Compton.

[118] Probably Margaret Caile Sprigg, wife of Richard Sprigg of Strawberry Hill (see 13 May 1792), and one of her unmarried daughters, either Elizabeth or Margaret.

[119] Possibly the wife of William Perry (see 24 March 1796).

A Front View of the State-House &c. at ANNAPOLIS the Capital of MARYLAND.

97 ✍ A Front View of the State House &c at Annapolis. Engraving from *Columbian Magazine*, February, 1789

Faris attended a number of public lectures on religion that were held in the State House. (see enlarged view in Figure 102 on page 169).

[120] Universalists believed that all souls will eventually be saved and restored to God, denying the Calvinist doctrine of salvation only for the elect and eternal damnation for all others. The preacher was probably Duncan McLane (see 13 December 1792).

[121] Paregoric is a preparation of powdered opium, anise oil, and benzoic acid camphor, used as an antiperstaltic, particularly in the treatment of diarrhea.

[122] An aromatized alcoholic liqueur.

[123] A medicine prepared by boiling bark, in this case most likely of cinchona bark, used to produce quinine for the treatment of malaria.

Octr 3 ✍ a fine morning. this fore noon I planted out 415 Seedling Tulips in 2 Beads and 2 roots of the Garden Primrose or Polyanthus's

4 ✍ a fine day. Mrs. Faris a grate deel better then she was

5 – 6 ✍ fine weather. Mrs. Faris something better

7 ✍ a fine day. Mrs. Faris came down stairs. Old Mr. Husk,[124] commonly call'd the Pedler died Last night & was Buried this evening

8 ✍ a fine day. Mrs. Faris is Better but very weeak

9:10:11 ✍ three days raceing.[125] very fine weather

12 ✍ a cloudey dull morning. a littel rain and the appearance of more. Rain'd all most all day. in the clear'd away & starr light

13 ✍ Miss polley Kelley[126] from Baltimore was T[r]yd and acquitted for the suppos'd murder of her child

14 ✍ a fine day

1792 Octr 15 ✍ a rainey morning. Abee has taken with her 3 dollors to pay Mrs. Leech for her's and Rebeck's last quarter and Abee begins her Second Quarter this morning and Rebeca has got the augue & feaveour[127] tharefore dont go till she gets well. the weather clear'd away and a fine after noon

16 ✍ a fine day ✍ (17th) ✍ a fine day

[124] Faris refers to Jacob Hurst as a peddler, but he was a successful merchant who owned a number of properties in town, along Church Street and on Market Space. Hurst was one of the proprietors who in 1784 gave up his rights to a lot near the dock for use of the site by the city for the new market house. When he died in 1792, Hurst was survived by his wife Margaret and son John, to whom he left his real estate. § John Hurst was one of the two creditors to sign the inventory of Charles Faris in 1800 (collecting £4.0.6 from the estate) and bought sixty-six files, one box of "sundries," two hand vices, a string of seine weights, a gun, and four books at the sale of Faris's estate.

[125] John Tayloe III (1771–1828), of Mt. Airy plantation in Virginia and the builder of Octagon House in Washington, D.C., owned both Nontoaka, winner of the 40 guineas purse on the 9th, and Seringaptam, winner of the 20 guineas purse on the 10th. Tayloe was the son of John Tayloe II (1721–1779) and his wife Rebecca Plater (1731–1787), sister of Governor George Plater (see 10 February 1792). Tayloe's sister Elizabeth was married to Edward Lloyd IV (see 19 November 1792). In 1792 Tayloe married Ann Ogle (1772–1855), daughter of Benjamin and Henrietta Ogle (see 14 November 1798); Faris notes the marriage of her sister Mary in July 1804. § Faris received 18/9 from Tayloe in April 1800 and perhaps £1.4.4 in June 1799 as well (the daybook entry looks like "Taylor," but Faris wrote the name that way in the diary when he clearly meant "Tayloe"). (See Figure 118 on page 249)

[126] Mary Kelly's case was heard first in Baltimore County, where she lived, but was brought before the general court of the western shore because it involved a capital crime. Testimony presented in the Baltimore court stated that Kelly had delivered an illegitimate female child on 26 July 1792 and that after the birth she had placed her hands around the child's throat to suffocate and strangle her; that she had stabbed the child in the abdomen with a knife; and that she had struck and beat her with mortal blows. Despite not one but three methods of homicide, the jury that heard the case in Annapolis found Kelly not guilty. Dr. John Shaaff (see 15 May 1792) appeared as the sole witness for the defense; John Barrett Onion (see 6 August 1792) was the foreman of the jury; and three of Kelly's four defense attorneys were William Pinkney (see 30 August 1793), Philip Barton Key (see 29 May 1792), and Edward Hall (see 5 October 1797). The court record gives no personal details about Mary Kelly, but it is possible that she lived in the Fells Point area and that Faris made note of the acquittal because he knew her.

[127] Probably malarial fever, although the term ague was also used more generally to describe chills.

18 ✒ a cold rainey morning. in the afternoon clear'd away. a fine afternoon

19 ✒ clear & cold. this morning I took a walk down by Col. Lloyd's.[128] he has a fence aputing up with pine Posts and Pine rails

20 ✒ a dull cloudey day. William Pitt[129] told me that Snow Commerce lef the Capes[130] the 29th of Septr.

21 ✒ In the night rain'd hard. a clear day but cold. Capt. Taylor came from Baltimore this afternoon and says he saw a Boat that over sett off Hawkins point in patapsaco river[131] and he saw Boats take up the things belonging to the Boat and that the peopel ware all drownded, he belives thare was a famely on board

1792 Octr 22 ✒ a clear coole day ✒ (23th & 24th) ✒ clear and coole. this day the pettet Jurey's discharg'd

25 ✒ a fine day ✒ Omited ✒ (22th) ✒ Rebbecca Faris enter'd her Second Quarter with Mrs. Leech

26 ✒ a fine day.

27 ✒ the General Court determen'd the dispute betwen Mr. Gant[132] & Capt. Kilty in regard of the office at the Federal City. Determined in faveour of Mr. Gant,[133] and the court Broke up, a fine morning

98 ✒ The Edward Lloyd Family
Several members of Edward Lloyd IV's family appear in the diary.

[130] Capes Henry and Charles at the mouth of the Chesapeake Bay, with Charles on the north side and Henry on the south. Vessels traveling the bay picked up or dropped off pilots at the capes; in bad weather ships often went aground on the shoals around the capes or were "overset" there. Faris also notes acquaintances who traveled to the capes for their health.

[131] Hawkins Point is on the south shore of the Patapsco River, east of Baltimore, at the south end today of Key Bridge.

[132] Attorney John Mackall Gantt lived in Georgetown in the early 1790s, part of the Maryland territory ceded to the District of Columbia. Gantt was appointed a judge in Prince George's County in 1806 and was listed in the 1806 account of John Gwinn's estate (see 13 September 1794) as a resident of Prince George's.

[133] When Maryland ceded land to form the District of Columbia, the legislature passed an act in 1791 creating an office for recording deeds and for other purposes within the ceded territory. The executive council in 1792 assumed the right to appoint the office holder and unanimously selected John Kilty, signing and sealing his commission. John Mackall Gantt had been fulfilling the duties covered by the new post, and continued to do so despite having been notified of Kilty's appointment. Kilty sued to establish his right to the office but the general court ruled on 9 October in favor of Gantt and ordered Kilty to pay one thousand pounds of tobacco to cover Gantt's court costs.

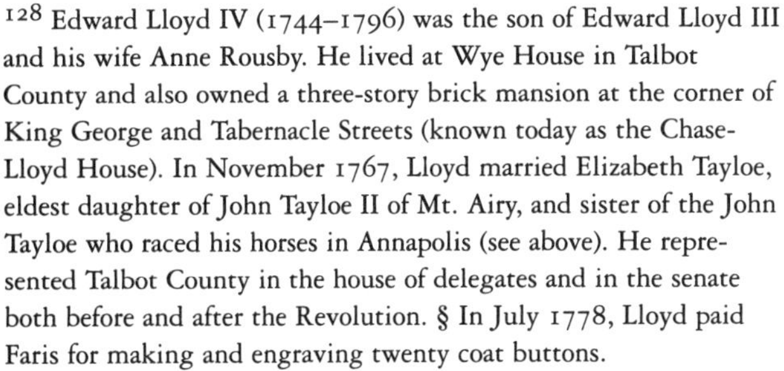

---

[128] Edward Lloyd IV (1744–1796) was the son of Edward Lloyd III and his wife Anne Rousby. He lived at Wye House in Talbot County and also owned a three-story brick mansion at the corner of King George and Tabernacle Streets (known today as the Chase-Lloyd House). In November 1767, Lloyd married Elizabeth Tayloe, eldest daughter of John Tayloe II of Mt. Airy, and sister of the John Tayloe who raced his horses in Annapolis (see above). He represented Talbot County in the house of delegates and in the senate both before and after the Revolution. § In July 1778, Lloyd paid Faris for making and engraving twenty coat buttons.

[129] The first appearance in the diary of William Pitt (1768–1848), whose second wife will be Ann Faris (see 19 June and 7 July 1796 entries). Pitt was the son of John (d.1790) and Ann (d.1801) Pitt, former neighbors of the Faris family who lived at the corner of Cathedral and West Streets. In March 1788 both John and William Pitt asked for and obtained from the Anne Arundel County Court certificates attesting to their character as pilots. Pitt's brothers Richard and Joseph and his sister Magdalen also appear in the diary. § In May 1798 Pitt brought Faris a bag of coffee sent by William Faris Jr. from the West Indies.

[134] Hollond never advertised in the *Gazette* and does not appear in any of the standard sources. Not only did all seven of Faris's children attend grammar schools, but their father encouraged a variety of other instruction as well. In addition to the shorthand lessons mentioned here, three of the children later studied French (see 12 September 1793) and Rebecca took dancing lessons (see 15 January 1796). As all of the children who lived at home attended dances and balls, it is likely that at some point each of them had received dancing lessons. Such instruction not only taught the steps of the dances, but also more general lessons about deportment and social graces.

[135] Sarah Worthington (1770–?) was the daughter of Nicholas Worthington. Nicholas (1734–1793), the son of Thomas Worthington (c.1691–1753) and his wife Elizabeth Ridgely (d.1734), married Catherine Griffith, daughter of Capt. Charles Griffith and his wife Catherine Baldwin, in November 1751. His wife's cousin Ann married Samuel Chase (see 7 October 1793) and her cousin Hester married Jeremiah Townley Chase (see 4 April 1792). Worthington was commissioned a justice of the peace in November 1770 and served as a colonel in the Anne Arundel militia during the Revolutionary War. He represented Anne Arundel in the general assembly from 1777 until his death and was an orphans' court justice from 1777 until 1792. The Worthingtons died within a month of each other at their plantation, Summer Hill, near Annapolis. § Faris bought three feet bare measure of oak wood and three-quarters of a cord of wood from Worthington in January 1777, and served on the St. Anne's vestry with him.

[136] William Goldsborough was the son of Robert Goldsborough (1733–1788) of Dorchester County and his wife Sarah Yerbury. See 23 July 1793 for the marriage of his brother Richard to Sarah's sister Achsah.

[137] Cathedral Street.

28 ☛ a fine day ☛ (29th) ☛ a fine day ☛ (30th) ☛ fine weather

31 ☛ a cloudey rayney day. in the evening received a Bundel of close and a Letter from Saint John Faris dated Cape Henrey Septr. 28th

Novr 1 ☛ raind & Blow'd hard last night. a fine morning. Charles & Hyram began to learn the Short Hand Wrighting with Mr. G. Hollond[134]

2 ☛ a cloudey drisley day. in the evening clear'd away and looks as if wee should have clear weather

3 & 4 ☛ fine weather

5 ☛ cloudey morning. in the after noon & evening rain

6th & 7th ☛ fine weather

8th ☛ a fine morning. in the afternoon cloudey and rain. one of Nicholas Worthington's[135] daughters was married to Mr. William Goldsbura[136] from the Estern Shore

9 ☛ rain'd hard the grates part of Last night. a cloudey drisley morning but clear'd away a fine after noon. this day put on my Winter shoes

10 ☛ a fine day

11 ☛ a fine morning. in the after noon clouded up & in the evening rain

12 ☛ a coole windey day

1792 Novr 13 ☛ coole weather. planted the remainder of the seedling tuleps on the Border nex the Back street[137]

14 ☛ cool weather. planted on the Border nex to Mr. Grayhams the Tuleps that Mr. Harwood mark'd

15 *Thursday* ☛ a fine day. in the evening cloudey. the two girls and Rebecka Gassaway went to the Colts Ball[138]

16 *Fryday* ☛ a fine day

17 *Saturday* ☛ a fine day. in the evening Capt.

[138] The Colts Ball was an annual event, held in conjunction with the fall races, and perhaps took its name from the Colts Purse, one of the prizes offered to competitors. Faris's daughters attended in most years, but the assemblies were never mentioned in the newspaper.

Daniel Campbell[139] and David Geddis[140] supt'd
and spent the evening with me

18 Sunday ✍ a fine day

19 Munday ✍ a cloudey rainey day. Last night or
rather this morning about 4 oclock, sum person
attempted to Brake open my shop window. thay
rench'd the shutters so as to brake a pain of glass,
Hyram heard the noise & got up, I suppose thay
heard him and made off — I heard a noiss and gott
up, and Charles also got up, thay ware gone — last
night, Williams[141] that rob'd Samuel Davidson[142]
Broke gaile and's gone with his Irons on

20 Tuseday ✍ Blew very Hard at N.W. last night.
Capt. D. Campbell's sloop drag'd her ancer and was
this morning aground on Greenberrey point[143] and
it continued Blowing hard all day

Wednesday 21 ✍ this morning betwen 1 and 2
oclock whe ware allarmed by some person Brakeing
open the shop window. Charley & Hyram persu'd
him, Hyram found him in the play house yard,[144]

---

[139] The 1799 Baltimore Directory identified Daniel Campbell as a
partner with Thomas Yates (see 15 January 1794) in the firm of
Yates & Campbell, auctioneers.

[140] David Geddes was born in Scotland and emigrated to Maryland
in 1784; he carried with him a letter from William Quynn to his
father (see 9 September 1792): "This will be delivered to you by
Mr. Giddis A Young Gentleman from Scotland who means to reside
some time in your City." Geddes took the oath of allegiance in
1785. He became a partner in the firm Steuart & Geddes, but by
1789 was lamenting his lack of business to a friend in Philadelphia.
In April 1790 Geddes advertised in the *Gazette* that he intended to
move and wished to collect the debts owing to him. In June 1791
he opened a ferry and house of entertainment in Georgetown, where
his wife died in November 1792 at the age of twenty-nine. By 1796
he was a revenue officer living in Fells Point, just a few doors away
from William and Ann Faris Pitt. According to the *Maryland
Gazette*, Capt. David Geddes died on Friday, March 6, 1807, in
Baltimore where he lived, "an old inhabitant of Fell's Point."

[141] The *Gazette* contains no account of the jail break and no court
records exist for this period. John Williams was recaptured and sent
to Baltimore on the 2nd of December.

[142] Probably the son of John Davidson (see 1 January 1792),
although possibly Davidson's brother Samuel, a merchant in
Georgetown.

[143] Greenbury Point is located on the north shore of the Severn
River, just west of Whitehall Bay. It was the site of Providence, the
first settlement in the Annapolis area.

[144] The brick play house, located on West
Street adjacent to the east side of Faris's property, was built in 1771 under the direction of
David Douglass of the American Company.
Douglass leased the lot from William
Reynolds, who in turn held it by lease from
the St. Anne's vestry. William Eddis, writing
in November 1771 of its opening that fall,
reported that "The structure is not inelegant
. . . the boxes are commodious and neatly dec-
orated; the pit and gallery are calculated to
hold a number of people without incom-
moding each other; the stage is well adapted
for dramatic and pantomimical exhibitions;
and several of the scenes reflect great credit on
the ability of the painter." During the years of
the diary, the American Company, now under
the direction of Lewis Hallam Jr. and the actor
John Henry, visited Annapolis regularly.

145 The original St. Anne's Church, completed in 1704, was soon too small for its congregation but remained in use until 1775, when it was razed. A larger church of a more sophisticated design was planned but the Revolutionary War and the postwar depression of the 1780s delayed construction and the building was not completed until 1792. The new church was 110 feet long and 90 feet wide, with an "elegant Altar" and frescoed interior. The 22 November issue of the *Gazette* informed readers that "on Sunday next a divine service will be performed in the new church." Of the ninety-two individual pew holders of the new church, as recorded in 1797, seventy-one are mentioned in the diary; William Faris, however, is not listed as a pew holder. Similarly about fifty members of the St. Anne's vestry (serving over a period of seventy years) appear in the diary.

146 The Rev. Ralph Higginbotham (d.1813), vice principal of St. John's College, was a native of Waterford, Ireland and a graduate of Trinity College, Dublin. He was ordained in Waterford in 1774 and served as rector of St. Anne's for twenty years, from 1784 until 1804. His wife Margaret died in 1797 at the age of forty-one; his daughter Mary became the second wife of Samuel Harvey Howard (see 31 October 1794). Higginbotham officiated at the marriages of both of Faris's daughters.

147 Possibly Rev. Thomas Scott, who was the minister of St. James Parish in southern Anne Arundel County from 1794 to 1796.

148 The *Gazette* makes no specific mention of Aspenwall's visit to Annapolis, but the 29 November issue does contain an article describing the use of white mulberry for silkworms and identifying Connecticut as a source. In May 1795, Faris received a gift of silkworms from the daughter of a friend and tried feeding them mulberry leaves, but says nothing further about the success of his efforts (see entry for 25 May). In May 1799 he pressed white mulberry leaves into his design book.

order'd him to stand or he would shute him, not with standing he push'd for it, hyram's gun miss'd Fire. he follow'd him withe cuting knife and made a stroke at him as he turn'd the corner and by that means the fence catched the stroke and the fellow got off. when day light appear'd I found he had ingeard the window in such a maner that I was oblig'd to have a new molding to one angel & the Bottom lining to repair

1792 Novr 22 Thursday ☞ a disagreeable day of snow & rain. in the evening Mrs. Faris unwell something like the ague — Charley and I Fix a gunn at his Board with strings to the Back door in to the yard, Back Window & the door to the Back Shop that should wee be attackt at either of them places that it may go off and give the allarm

Fryday 23th ☞ a rainey day

Saturday 24th ☞ a cold cloudey & windey day

Sunday 25 ☞ a fine day. this day our new church was opened, and consocrated,145 by Bisshop Clegett and Parson Higgenbottom,146 Parson Scott147 & [crossed out]. this morning Capt. D. Campell sail'd for the West Indies. a fine wind at N

Munday 26 ☞ a fine day

Tuseday 27th ☞ a very fine day

1792 Novr Wednesday 28 ☞ a warm day, the wind blowing hard at S and looks as if wee should have bad weather. in the evening a man came heare from Connecticut and had with him sowing silk and some wove silk and says it's the groth and manufactor'd in Connecticut. his name is Daniel Aspenwall148

Thursday 29 ☞ rain'd very hard last night. a fine day

Fryday 30 ☞ Last night Maynards149 shop was attempted to be Broke open. one of the shutters thay got down & Broke open the seller door. he heard them and thay ran off — a fine day but coole

---

149 The shopkeeper may have been John Foster Maynard (1742–?) or his son James Pelham Maynard. James married Elizabeth Wilmot in January 1790; Faris records her death on 25 December 1800; Maynard then married Julia Owen (b. 1774), the daughter of Richard and Elizabeth Owen (see 4 November 1795), in January 1806. Maynard for a time operated a tavern, probably in the building that had been the Coffee House. § Charles Faris's estate paid him £3.19.1.

Saterday Desr 1th ✍ Last night I dremt that my son St. John Faris was with me and that thare was a weding and that the Bride went about and licked the ground and dust with her mouth. the ground was very soft and light. thare appear'd a grate deal of mirth and rejoyceing — a dissagreeable day with snow

1792 Desr 2 Sunday ✍ John Williams was Taken up last night and this morning was sent off for Baltimore Gole under the care of Thomas Goldsmith[150] & B. Welsh[151] in a chair.[152] a cloudey cold disagreeable day like for snow

Munday 3th ✍ clear & cold

Tuseday 4th ✍ dull cloudey cold rainey day

Wednesday 5th ✍ a warm cloudey Foggey day. in the evening Constantine Bull[153] was Buried. he was in his 78 year

Thursday 6th ✍ a cloudey drisley day

Fryday 7th ✍ a cloudey morning. in the after noon turn'd cold & in the evening began to frees smartley. Charley sett off for Prince G's County, William Woodwards[154] daughter that married Mr. Con sett off Home to the Back Countrey[155]

Saterday 8th ✍ a fine day

1792 Desr. Sunday 9th ✍ a dull cloudey dissagreeable day and looks likely that whee shall have bad weather

Munday 10th ✍ a fine day

Tuseday 11th ✍ a fine day. Charley return'd from Pr. G's County

Wednesday 12th ✍ a cloudey day. looks as if wee should have bad weather

Thursday 13th ✍ a cloudey disagreeable day. in the evening Mr. McClain[156] the Universilist Preacher came to Town and Preach'd in Stad House

---

[150] Thomas Goldsmith was appointed a constable in August 1792. At the age of ten, in November 1764, he had been bound to Thomas Hyde (see 21 June 1792) as a shoemaker, but in August 1773 petitioned the court to be rebound, as he had for some time been helping Hyde as a store or shopkeeper and wished to learn that trade.

[151] Benjamin Welch (1753–1802), the son of Dr. Robert and Frances Peacock Welch, married Sarah Lee (d.1787) and lived on the South River. Their daughter Katherine (1783–?) married Nicholas Zachariah Maccubbin (see 15 May 1802). § In April 1799 Faris received cash from Welch to be credited to the account of Samuel Chew.

[152] Goldsmith and Welch were taking their prisoner to the Baltimore jail in a carriage.

[153] Constantine Bull (1719–1792) was the son of Edward and Mary Bull of Norwich, England. He and his wife Catherine Walker had four children, including two sons born in Annapolis and a daughter, Mary, whose second marriage Faris records (see 26 April 1798). Bull advertised dry goods for sale in July 1748, but in 1760 was identified as a schoolmaster when he appeared as a defendant during the November court session.

[154] William Woodward (1747–1807) was the son of William Woodward (1716–1790) and his wife, Alice Ridgely, and the nephew of Priscilla Woodward Faris. He married Jane Ridgely, with whom he had two sons and three daughters. His oldest son, also William, who married Susannah Jacobs in November 1790, moved west sometime after 1798. Faris records Alse's marriage in July 1793, Henry's marriage in February 1797, and this visit to her family of Sarah, who had married Richard Conn, but not the marriage in 1803 of Ann to William Ridgely (the third generation of intermarriage with the Ridgely family). § Faris served on the St. Anne's vestry with Woodward's father in the 1770s and bought hay from him in the winter of 1773–74.

[155] Richard Conn and Sarah Woodward received a license to marry on 27 August 1792. Sarah was the daughter of William and Jane Woodward and the great-niece of Priscilla Woodward Faris. The back country could have been anywhere west of Frederick.

[156] In February 1793 Joseph Clark (see 27 December 1792) advertised that he had published and was selling "Eternal Damnation Reprobated," a sermon by Rev. Mr. McLane.

157 Faris recorded payment on 20 December of £16.13.7 for 966 pounds of "Hogg meat . . . pr HH." HH is probably Henry Hammond, from whom Faris bought a similar quantity of meat in 1799.

158 The two houses had considered an act "to arrange, regulate and discipline" the state's militia, drafted in order to have Maryland's regulations conform to a recent act of Congress designed "more effectively to provide for the national defense, by establishing an uniform militia throughout the United States." The lower house passed the act, but the senate objected to regulations that called for enrolling all thirty thousand eligible men (those between the ages of eighteen and forty-five) and requiring them to drill four times a year. Representatives from the two houses met but could not resolve their differences; the senate then drafted its own amendments but the house would not accept them. As neither side would yield, the session ended without any action.

159 Thomas Woodward (1732–1799) was the son of Abraham and Priscilla Ruley Orrick Woodward, and an older brother of Priscilla Woodward Faris. He married Margaret Waters, the widow of Thomas Ijams, in May 1778, and lived in Prince George's County, where he was often visited by the Faris children. The Thomas Woodward who appears in the diary after 1799 is almost certainly his son.

160 The 3 January issue of the *Gazette* reported that a new Masonic Lodge, of the "Lodge of Antient York Masons," had celebrated St. John the Evangelist's Day at Mr. Vachel Stevens's house. The Lodge, designated no. 12 in the state, received official recognition from the Grand Lodge of Maryland in April 1793. St. John the Apostle and Evangelist was one of the two patron saints of the Masonic order. On his feast day, Masons customarily held a procession from their lodge building to the local parish church, where a special sermon would be preached.

Fryday 14th ☞ cloudey drissley. in the afternoon clear & coole. in the evening Mr. McClain preach'd

Saturday 15th ☞ a fine day in the evening Mr. McClain Preached

Sunday 16th ☞ a fine day but cold. in the after noon Mr. McClain Preach'd his fare well sermond not expecting to come heare aney more

1792 Desr Munday 17th ☞ a fine day

Tuseday 18th ☞ a fine day. this morning Parson Dunn. McClain left this place for Baltimore. intends to be heare again in May next

Wednesday 19 ☞ a fine day

Thursday 20th ☞ a cold cloudey [day]. this day Mr. Chapman brought my hogg meat[157] it did not answer my expectations. it was a grate deeal too light

Fryday 21th ☞ a very fine day

Saturday 22th ☞ a fine day. in the evening cloudey

Sunday 23 ☞ a fine day. in the after noon I receiv'd a letter from my son William in the Havannah — and the Assembly Broke up and did nothing with the melisha Law[158]

1792 December Munday 24 ☞ a rainey night & morning. Thomas Woodward[159] came to Town, in the evening clear'd away. in the evening as Hyram was fixing the gun it went off & made a Hole throw the door & 4 holes in ye Back Window

Tuseday 25th ☞ a fine day. after diner Mr. Woodward went home & Charley with him

Wednesday 26th ☞ a fine day

Thursday 27th ☞ this day the new Lodge was opened by the name of the Amanda Lodge of the City of Annapolis,[160] John Kerr[161] tyler[162] and was raised to the degree of fellow caraft [craft] — Joseph

---

161 Elfreda Fairbrother, the daughter of Francis and Ann Fairbrother (see 21 March 1794), married John Kerr in November 1789. He is the most likely person to have been a fellow Mason of Faris's.

162 *Tiler* was the name given to the two guards or doorkeepers responsible for preventing anyone not a mason from entering.

Clark[163] master and ajurnd to Mr. Stevenson's to diner. present Joseph Clark master Mr. Stevenson[164] David Geddis a French gentlemen Mr. Eastave[165] Rev'd Mr. Ralph,[166] Rev'd Mr. Scott, Capt. Stewart, B. Harrison,[167] J. Gassaway,[168] Barnard Markell,[169] Allen Quynn, William Faris, John Kerr, Thomas Freeman.[170] a clear cold day

1792 Fryday Desr 28th ✒ a fine day

Saturday 29th ✒ a fine day

Sunday 30th ✒ a fine day

Munday 31th ✒ a fine day, Doctr Murray call'd to look at Mrs. Faris's finger. he desired her to take off the poltice she had to it and put a poltice of Bread wetted with sugar of lead dissolved in water[171]

---

[163] Joseph Clark (?–1798) was born in England and probably emigrated to Maryland about 1774. He married Isabella Ferguson, daughter of tailor and tavern keeper Alexander Ferguson and his wife Elizabeth, in 1777. Clark began his career in Annapolis as a merchant, but is better known as an architect, who by 1785 was the superintendent of repairs to public buildings. Clark advertised in that year that he would oversee construction of the new roof and cove ceiling on the governor's house and the repair of the State House roof and dome. In July 1786 he was engaged to finish McDowell Hall, the first building of St. John's College. Clark is also credited with the design of William Paca's second home, Wye Hall, whose construction began c.1790. In April 1792 he announced that the design for the new St. Anne's could be seen at his house. In February 1793 Clark proposed a circulating library for Annapolis, for which he would be the librarian. Two of his sons studied at the St. John's grammar school: Horatio (b. c.1779) and George (b. c.1781). See 1 September 1793 entry for Horatio's death; George died in August 1794. In September 1793, Clark, in his capacity as Masonic grand master, stood by President Washington's side during the ceremony laying the first cornerstone of the capitol building. After working for a time in Washington, D.C., Clark moved to Baltimore in 1796, where he died in April 1798.

[164] Vachel Stevens (see 22 March 1792).

[165] Perhaps the Andrew (André?) Estave who appears in the 1790 census of Anne Arundel and also in the Prince George's County levy book in the 1790s.

[166] Possibly Rev. George Ralph, who died in Baltimore County on 17 May 1813 at the age of 60. He was a native of England, ordained in 1791, who took his first parish in Baltimore in 1791. He never held a position in Annapolis, however. It is more likely that Faris simply omitted Ralph Higginbotham's last name, as the St. Anne's minister was a member of the Amanda Lodge.

[167] Benjamin Harrison was admitted as attorney in the Anne Arundel County court in August 1784 and served one term on the executive council in 1787. In December 1787 he married Deborah Ghiselin, who must have been a cousin of Reverdy Ghiselin (see 13 April 1793). But she would have been Harrison's second wife, as he was probably the father of the John Harrison ("son of Benjamin") who was admitted to the St. John's grammar school in June 1790 at the age of thirteen and who enrolled in the college in December 1795.

[168] Probably Col. John Gassaway, who became register of wills upon the death of his half-brother, Thomas Gassaway (see 18 August 1792). The son of Henry Gassaway and his second wife, he married Mary Quynn, daughter of Allen Quynn (see 9 September 1792), in January 1788. The couple had two children, a daughter Eliza, and a son John, who entered the St. John's grammar school at the age of nine in 1799. Gassaway was a lieutenant colonel of militia in 1795, on the committee for the defense of Annapolis in 1798, and on the committee to build a fort in 1799. Faris noted both the death of Mary Gassaway in 1795 and the subsequent remarriage of John Gassaway to Elizabeth Price in 1799. Gassaway lived in a house owned by his father-in-law across the street from Faris. § Priscilla Faris listed a debt of £10.16.3 due from Gassaway to Charles's estate.

[169] Perhaps a relative of Conrad Markell, a baker who had an ordinary license from 1762 to 1766. There were also Markells in Frederick County.

[170] Thomas Freeman, a schoolmaster, advertised in May 1790 that he was opening "an ENGLISH and MATHEMATICS SCHOOL . . . to teach reading, writing, and accounts, Euclid's Elements of geometry and trigonometry, with their application to all branches of mathematics." § Faris noted in his account book on 11 April 1791 that "This day Rebecca began to school to Mr. Thomas Freeman." Rebecca had turned twelve the previous December.

[171] A poultice was a soft, moist mass (about the consistency of cooked cereal) that was spread between layers of cloth or toweling and applied hot to a given area to create moist local heat. In this case, the poultice was probably being used to treat an infection.

172 No Capt. Sinnett appears in the Baltimore City directories. Faris's reference suggests that he did not know Sinnett, so he may have been the captain of a foreign vessel.

173 Captain Stephen Vickery (c.1765–1809) was listed in the 1800 census as living in Fells Point, with a household consisting of three whites and one free black. He subsequently appeared in the city directory under Stephen Vickery and Co., tobacconists, at 44 Granby Street and 29 Bond Street, Fells Point. In 1803, he was still at Granby but the business was described as a Still House and Laboratory. Vickery's obituary, nonetheless, listed him as Capt. Vickery.

174 Hay scales were erected outside the town gate, not far from Faris's home, in 1784. They were used to weigh hay, fodder, and straw purchased by residents or shipped out of the port to Baltimore. As Faris notes, the Corporation had decided to relocate them to the waterfront.

175 Joseph Burneston, a felt maker and hatter, was in Annapolis by 1788, when he took on an apprentice. He opened a shop on Church Street, just down from Church Circle, in 1790 and had another shop near the market house in 1792. In July 1794 he placed a notice in the *Maryland Gazette* that he intended to move to Baltimore.

176 Annapolis, which received a charter of incorporation in 1708, was governed by a Corporation consisting of the mayor, aldermen, councilmen, and recorder (city attorney).

177 The market house, at the head of the dock, was built between 1785 and 1790. It was regulated by a market master and contained stalls leased to vendors of fresh fish, meat, dairy products, and produce. Faris only once indicates that he did the marketing—on 2 August 1794 he states that he was at the market when Phillis left—but the entries describing slippery walking and the frequent exchanges of information with various acquaintances, as well as the assertions of the "Town's" opinion of events, all suggest that he regularly obtained his news at the market.

Tuseday January 1th 1793 a fine day, the poltice that Doctr Murray directed did not answer. her finger & Hand begant to swell and be very uneasey, took it off and put a poltice of Parceley & Butter. the Doctr did not come hear to day

Wednesday 2th ✒ a fine warm day but cloudey, no Doctor today. Mrs. Faris's finger appears to be better

1793 Janry 3 Thursday ✒ a raw, cloudey, drisley day. at night rained

Fryday 4th ✒ rain'd most all night. a cloudey dull morning, clear'd away about noon. in the evening very foggey

Saturday 5th ✒ a cloudey dull day

Sunday 6th ✒ a fine day

Munday 7th ✒ a very fine day. this evening a Captain Sinnett[172] came heare and told us that he saw my son William in the Havannah+ and that he was well and was doing very well. that he had altered a grate deal for the better.   + about 2 months ago

Tuseday 8th ✒ a fine day. this day wrought to my son William at the Havannah, by Capt. Steven Vickery[173] of Baltimore Town and sent by him some fyles, plyers, cuting knipers, Hand vice, glass's & keys

1793 Wednesday Janry 9th ✒ a cloudey drisley morning. about noon clear'd. a cold wind W by N. the vessels all sett off this morning that ware laying off heare

Thursday 10th ✒ a fine day. about noon thay began to moove the Way House,[174] from whare it stood at the Town gate to the dock. thay got it by the evening oppiset to Mr. Burneston's[175] door and thare thay left it for the night. the Corporation[176] had better left it whare it was, and Built a new one at the dock, but it is Like most of thare other proceeding, a peney wise & a pound Foolish

Fryday 11th ✒ a fine day. in the after noon thay got the Way House to the place intended by the Market House[177]

Saturday 12th ✒ a fine day. Hyram sett off this morning after Brackfast to take a walk to Mr. Thomas Woodwards in prince Georg's County[178]

Sunday 13th ✍ a fine day

1793 Munday Janry 14th ✍ about 4 oclock it Hailed a littel just to show on the ground. a cloudey morning and continued cloudey & drisseley all day. Hyram came Home after 8 oclock in the evening. very dark

Tusday 15th ✍ a dull cloudey day. planted 4 Horse Chestnutts on the Border next Mr. Stevens's. the one next the post had mark'd on it I.O.B. Hyram Brought them from over South River

Wednesday 16th ✍ rain'd & drisel'd all day. Mr. Maxamelion Hisler[179] from Baltimore who ceeps a nursserey, Flower garden & vineyard

Thursday 17th ✍ raind a good deal last night. claear'd a fine day, I gave Mr. Maxamillion Hesler of Baltimore a root of the Passhon flower, some double Bloom'd Almond & passhon Jessemon, & Dwarf Flower Deluce

1793 Janry Fryday 18th ✍ a fine day

Saturday 19th ✍ a fine day. in the evening Messr. William Fitzhew[180] & G. Plater[181] was here & Drank appel Todey, Mr. Fitzhew told me that his father would be 71 years of age some time this month

Sunday 20th ✍ a fine day. last night Mrs. Geor[g]e Johnson's[182] was Brought to bed of a fine girl

Munday 21th ✍ a fine day. in the after noon turned cold. last night old Mrs. Wilmot[183] died and was Buried this evening

---

[178] Hyram's route would have taken him across the South River ferry at London Town and then down southern Anne Arundel County to another ferry crossing over the Patuxent River before he reached Prince George's County, a distance of about ten to fifteen miles (depending on his choice of crossing) to which would be added the remainder of the way to Thomas Woodward's plantation.

[179] Maximillian Heuisler (d.1816) emigrated to Maryland from Munich, Bavaria, first appearing in the Baltimore County records when he married Mrs. Marie Bernard on 3 August 1791. Within two years, he opened a nursery just outside of Baltimore on the road to Philadelphia, and advertised the sale of fruit trees, shrubs, and seeds for kitchen and flower gardens. In 1803 he moved his nursery to a branch of the Patapsco River, south of Baltimore and closer to Annapolis. Faris several times mentions exchanging or purchasing plants or seeds with Heuisler.

[180] William Fitzhugh Jr. (1761–1839), the son of Col. William Fitzhugh (see 18 November 1794), lived first in Calvert County, then in Washington County by 1790s, and in Genesee, New York from c.1800 until his death. He married Ann Hughes of Hagerstown, the daughter of Col. Daniel Hughes.

[181] George Plater (1766–1802) was the son of George and Elizabeth Rousby Plater (see 10 February 1792). Plater served three terms in the lower house in the early 1790s.

[182] George Johnson (1768–?) was the son of innkeeper Robert Johnson (d.1773) and his wife Ann Golder, the widow of John Golder (see 7 April 1793). He was the brother of Robert (see 12 January 1792) and John (see 9 January 1794). Johnson married Miss Van Deren of Philadelphia in May 1792.

[183] Probably Dinah Brewer Wilmot (b.1729), the daughter of John Brewer IV (1709–1754) and his wife Elizabeth Maccubbin (1708–1779), and the widow of John Wilmot (b.1726). Her husband, a schoolmaster, taught all four of the Faris boys in the 1770s. Her son John (1752–1807), a storekeeper, married Ann McClellan, the daughter of Elizabeth McClellan (see 27 June 1800), in 1774. Her grandson John (1778–1858) attended St. John's grammar school from May 1790 to May 1793, and his brother George, age thirteen, was "educated gratis" in 1800. § John Wilmot Sr. patronized Faris's tavern frequently in the early 1770s, but it was probably John Jr. who served on a grand jury with Faris in November 1788. Faris recorded in his daybook on 23 June 1777 that "Hyram and St. John Faris Began Schooling with Mr. John Wilmot" and on 6 July 1777 that "William and Charles Faris entered with Mr. Wilmot."

Tuseday 22th ☞ a fine day but cold

Wednesday 23th ☞ a fine day but cold

Thursday 24th ☞ snow'd a littel this morning, cold & cloudey all day

1793 Fryday January 25th ☞ a fine day. in the evening Abbey and Rebacka Left Mrs. Leech's school

Saturday 26th ☞ a fine day

Sunday 27th ☞ a cold cloudey drisley morning with a spit of snow, in the after noon and evening snow & Hail

Munday 28th ☞ a cloudey morning, in the after noon cleard away very fine & warm

Tuseday 29th ☞ a fine day

Wednesday 30th ☞ the first day we have had this winter that look'd much like winter, for it snow'd all day and cold. the winde Blew very Hard at night

Thursday 31th ☞ a clear cold day

1793 Fryday February 1th ☞ a fine day, in the evening turned cloudey like for snow

Saturday 2th ☞ a rainey day & not so cold as yesterday

Sunday 3th ☞ a fine day, but in the evening turned cloudey. I sow'd some seeds of the Jerusalom Cherrey in the pott round the root of the Tree

Munday 4th ☞ Mr. Cook sent a notice to me to meet the arbetrators in Baltimore at Mr. Grants[184] on Munday the 18th of this month to settel the afair of Rdder, Druceney & Clark's[185] — this has been a fine day

Tuseday 5th ☞ a fine day

Wednesday 6th ☞ a rainey day

Thursday 7th ☞ a fine day the snow all gone

Fryday 8th ☞ a fine morning. after noon & evening cloudey

1793 Febry 9th Saturday ☞ a fine day, dug a peice of ground in the lott next the dining room and sow'd some early York seed from Mr. pettey & some Lettice & Redish Seed

Sunday 10th ☞ a cloudey day

---

[184] In 1796, Daniel Jr. and Hezekiah Grant were merchants with a store and counting house at 99 South Street, while Daniel Grant [Sr.?] was listed at 10 Light Street. The latter was probably the tavern keeper whose son, James Stewart Grant, age ten, entered the St. John's grammar school in 1793. The arbitration meeting could have been scheduled for either establishment, but such meetings more commonly took place in a tavern. Daniel Grant died in his 83rd year in July 1816, while Daniel Jr. died in his 24th year in October 1796.

[185] The London firm of Messrs. DeDrusina, Ridder & Clerk. Letters written in 1784 and 1785 reveal that Faris sent a consignment of watches to the firm for "finishing." Faris objected to the size of the bill for this work and also to the length of time that it had taken. Presumably these were the issues to be settled during this visit to Baltimore. A new firm, DeDrusina & Co. entered the Annapolis market after the Revolution; by the 1780s, it had become DeDrusina & Clerk but failed during the depression of the mid-1780s. Reconstituted as DeDrusina, Ridder & Clerk by the 1790s, its representatives may have been attempting to recover debts owed to the earlier establishment.

Munday 11th ☞ a cold cloudey day. in the evening began to snow

Tuseday 12th ☞ snow'd all night, this morning & all day, a day of snow and like to be

Wednesday 13th ☞ snow'd a littel all night and this morning the [snow] cleard away. the [sun] came out

Thursday 14th ☞ a fine day

Fryday 15th ☞ a fine day. the stage that went off on tusday did not get to Baltimore till Thursday the rodes so bad. no stage to day. the mail was Brought on horse back. therefore I am dissopointed in my intended jurney on the stage, but am in Hopes that Taylor will set off to morrow for Baltimore. I intend going with him

1793 Febry 16th Saturday ☞ this morning I sett off a littel after 9 oclock in Capt. Barbers boat with several passinger for Baltimore.   whe had a very fine passage, got thare a littel after 4 oclock.   a fine day

Sunday 17th ☞ rained all day. I dined at Mr. Rossetors

Munday 18th ☞ a cloudey day. very Bad walking. I mett the arbetrators according to appointment at Mr. Grants, whare a young gentelman from Mr. Thomas Smith,[186] produced the accot. of Rider, D. Deceny & Clark, I made my objections to the accot., and adjurned till the after noon, in the after noon mett and the arbetraiters went on the Business. thay brought in that I should pay Ninety Eight Pounds two Shillings and six pence, with out aney Intrist and brok up

1793 Tuseday Febry 19th ☞ a rainey day and no wind. Brackfast'd dined & drank Tea at Mr. Rosetors. then went to Mr. John Leopold's,[187] who gave me several roots of the Double Tuber Rose, for which I am to send him some of the Passion Flower Roots and some Jassemin and like some of each to Mrs. Rosetor

Wednesday 20 ☞ a cloudey morning. sett off at 20 minits after nine oclock in Capt. Barbers Boat and ariv'd in the dock in Annapolis 20 minits after 2 oclock, we should have been much sooner had wee not met with the accident of carreying away our fore gaff

[186] Thomas Smith was probably the attorney representing the plaintiffs. He may have been the Thomas Smith who lived at 101 Bond Street, Fells Point (the same address as that of hatter George Smith) in 1796, and who died in April 1797 at the age of fifty-seven.

[187] John Leypold was a baker in Annapolis as early as August 1771, but later moved to Baltimore, where he appeared in city records first as a sugar refiner and then as a "gentleman." In September 1792, the Baltimore firm of Gart & Leypold sued baker Henry Sibell (see 23 March 1793) in the Anne Arundel County court.

188 Thomas Gaston, one of the owners of the Annapolis packet, drowned off the mouth of the Magothy on Friday last, according to the *Maryland Gazette*. He married Susannah Hanslift (c.1760–1808) in March 1785 and had one daughter, Ann, born in April 1787. Faris noted her marriage on 29 September 1803. After Gaston's death, his widow married William Wells (son of Daniel Wells Sr., see 24 February 1801) in January 1794. § William Wells does not appear in the diary, but Faris bought sugar from him in 1791, a peck of meal in 1795, and a pair of shoes in 1797.

189 The Magothy River, on the western shore of the Chesapeake Bay, between the Severn River (Annapolis) and the Patapsco River (Baltimore).

190 According to the *Gazette*, it was John Ross, a cabinetmaker, who drowned. Ross married Magdalen Pitt, the daughter of Capt. John and Ann Pitt, in December 1786. She was, therefore, the sister of William Pitt (see 20 October 1792), who would marry Faris's daughter Ann on 7 July 1796. Magdalen was the administrator of her husband's estate, which totaled £50, and included a schooner worth £22.10.0, six silver tea spoons, a tool chest and tools valued at £5.5.0, and two work benches and turning lathes at £4.

191 Mr. Thomas Coats, of Greenbury's Point, according to the account in the *Gazette*. The probate of his estate was administered by John Mitchell of Calvert County, who reported that Coats, who left property valued at £56, had no kin in the state.

192 The *Maryland Gazette* recorded the death of William Lockerman, the owner with Thomas Gaston of the Annapolis packet.

193 According to the *Gazette's* report of the accident, Benjamin Buckland was a cabinet-maker. There is no evidence to suggest that he was related to architect William Buckland.

194 The *Gazette* identified John Hammond as a cabinetmaker. His inventory totaled only £25.9.0, and a chest with tools accounted for £10.19.9 of that amount. A Charles Robinson was the administrator of Hammond's estate, the entire balance of which went to Sophia Minskie. Sophia must have been either Hammond's mother or his sister, as only a parent or sibling should have inherited his estate in the absence of a will.

Thursday 21th ☛ variable wather rain & sun shine. this day Charles differ'd with Hyram and used him and myself very ill, with out any cause

Fryday 22th ☛ a cloudey morning. snow'd a littel. clear'd away a fine day after wards

1793 Febry Saturday 23th ☛ yesterday as Thomas Gastin[188] was on his passage in his boat for Baltimore with a number of passengers, the Boate over sett and sunk off the mouth of Magethy[189] and the following persons ware drownd'd. Thomas Gasting, Thomas pryce sadler, N. Ross,[190] Mr. Coats,[191] Mr. Lockerman,[192] B. Buckland,[193] J. Hammond[194] & a neagro man & James Jenings.[195] Matcalf[196] saved himself by clinging to the mast whare he was about 2 Houres before he was taken up by a Rock Hall[197] Boat. the accident Happen'd about a 11 oclock, and too day {Thomas} Dance the plasterer fell from one of the upper scaffels of the doome of the Stad House and* is dead or a dying.[198] a cloudey dull day.   *supp{ose}d. to be about 90 feet high from whare he fell

Sunday 24th ☛ a rainey drisley day

Munday 25th ☛ a cloudey dissagreeable day. in the evening rain moved the greens & stalks out of the Big bed in to the bed at the Walnutt Tree

---

195 James Jennings may have been the son of Thomas and Juliana Jennings (see 17 July 1793). He was a student at the St. John's grammar school from November 1789 until May 1792 and was enrolled in the French school from October 1792 until January 1793.

196 The diary mentions a number of otherwise anonymous individuals who may have lived their entire lives in Annapolis without appearing in the census, tax, church, or probate records, leaving the diary as perhaps the only record of their presence. Matcalf (fortunate not to have died of hypothermia before his rescue) appears to have been one of those men—many more women, of course, left no recorded trace of their lives.

197 A town on the eastern shore of the Chesapeake Bay, in Queen Anne's County. Boats ferrying passengers across the bay generally went either to Rock Hall or to Kent Island.

198 Thomas Dance, employed to finish the interior of the State House dome, died as the result of his fall, as described by Faris. The death was reported in the *Maryland Gazette* on 28 February: Thomas Dance, of Annapolis, plasterer, died Saturday last, being at work on the inside of the dome of the Stadt-house. He made a false step, and fell to the floor.

William Faris

1793 Febry Tuseday 26th ☛ a drisley rainey day

Wednesday 27th ☛ a disagreeable day, rain, snow &
sun shine and in the evening came on to blow hard

Thursday 28th ☛ Blewd very hard all last night
and turned very cold, a clear day but cold & windey

Fryday March 1th ☛ a fine day but coole

Saturday 2th ☛ a fine day

Sunday 3th ☛ a very fine day

1793 Munday March 4th ☛ ☛ a fogey
morning. Hyram went in the garden a made a
begining. planted Box round one of the nurssery
Beds the one nex the Walnutt Tree. Mr. Pryce's
Dick[199] Hawled 5 Loads of dung from Mr. G.
Mann's.   betwen 3 & 4 oclock it began to rain and
Sylve was taken up the greens in the Lott and I
intend to have them planted in the garden

Tusday 5th ☛ a right March day. in the morning it
rain'd a shower & clear'd away the[n] came on to
Blow Hard. Sylve planted the stawks & greens and
went to diging in the lott for carrotts and parsneps
and Hyram has been planting Box round the
nursserey Beds

Wednesday 6th ☛ a fine morning. planted and
sowd in potts vizt. 1 pott of mininet. 2 d⁰ Tube
Rose and sencitive plant seed, 1 d⁰ Ice plant, 1 d⁰
egg plant, 1 d⁰ aster, and Hyram's Finish planting
ye Box round the nurssery Beds. Sylve finished
digging the Carrot and Parsnep beds

1793 March 7th Thursday

   ☛ a fine warm day but gustey. Hyram began to plant
the parsneps the rows 9 Inchs wide & 6 Inchs from
seed to seed. Charels came to him self to day in
part. he is gone to work

Fryday 8th ☛ a rainey morning, continued planting
parsneps, and began and sow'd 3 rows of carrots,
lines 8 Inch apart, but was oblig'd to leave off on
accot. of its raining, clear'd away. finished planting
the Parsneps. it came on to Blow so hard that wee
could not finish the carrotts, this after noon John
Shaw's[200] wife died

Saturday 9th ☛ froze very Hard last night, and Blew
very Hard, thare was Isesickels 9 Inchs long this
morning, wind continued Blowing hard. in the afternoon it Luled a littel, I finished sowing the carrots

[199] Dick was a slave belonging to Thomas
Pryse, but may have been able to hire his own
time, for Faris paid him in 1795 and 1796 for
carting bricks and wood.

[200] John Shaw (1745–1829) was born in
Scotland and immigrated to Maryland about
1763. A cabinetmaker, Shaw was a partner in
the firm of Shaw & Chisholm from 1772 until
1776. Shaw did considerable work for the state
in fitting out and furnishing the new State
House and was the state armorer from 1777 to
1819. He made the city's hay scales, repaired
the fire engines, and finished the public necessary on the State House grounds. Shaw married Elizabeth Pratt in September 1777, with
whom he had seven children before her death;
his second wife was Margaret Stewart
(d.1806), the widow of Capt. John Stewart (see
27 December 1792), with whom he had one
child. In 1784 Shaw purchased a home on
State Circle, a one-and-a-half story brick
dwelling with a brick smoke house and frame
shop. § Charles Faris's estate paid Shaw
£2.1.3. Shaw bought a number of tools, the
cannon stove (see 21 October 1793), a pair of
scales and weights, and three books at the sale
of Faris's property.

1793 March Sunday 10th 🖎 a fine day, this after noon Mrs. Shaw was buried. the corps was carried in to the church. a grate number of Peopel attended

Munday 11 🖎 a rayney morning. Mr. T. Pryces Dick Hawled a Load of dung from Mr. G. Mans, a cloudey drisley after noon

Tuseday 12th 🖎 a cloudey morning. in the fore noon it snow'd. in the after noon clear'd away & the sun shined

Wednesday 13th 🖎 a fine day but cold. Sylve began diging the Big Bead

Thursday 14th 🖎 a fine day. Sylve finished diging ye Big bed

1793 March Fryday 15th 🖎 a fine morning. planted the big Bed with 7 rows of Peas, 4 rows next to Steven's of 6 weeaks 2 rows Dutch man, 1 row from Sands's. opened the assparagrass Beds but did not finish them. in the evening looks like for rain

Saturday 16th 🖎 a cloudey drisley morning. finished the assparagrass Beds & sow'd early York of our owne raising on the first bed on the end nex to Steven's. on the other end seed from Charles Wallace, and on the other Bed end next to Stevens's early York from J. pettey and the other end real cabbage seed from Mrs Onion and Lettice on the whole. clear'd away fine & warm

Sunday 17th 🖎 a very fine warm day

1793 March Munday 18th 🖎 a fine morning. Charley & Hyram digging the flower beds. I receiv'd 2 shrubs from Mr. John Leypold of Baltimore, called the Scented Shrub — finished digging ye flower beds. Sylve dug the littel quarter for Beens. looks like for rain — sow'd radishes & lettice betwen the goosberrey bushes on the pea Bead

Tuseday 19th 🖎 a fine day. planted 4 rows & a peace of Bunch Beens and had not anuff to finish. sow'd on the Border some flower seeds got from Mrs. Rossetor with out names — & sow'd Blew Lettice & Headed Spinige from Mr. Geddis & other spinige further on

Wednesday 20th 🖎 a fine morning. planted 20 Double Tube Rose in the Circel Beds & the Beds leading to the littel House, sow'd a bed of parceley on the border next the old stable, finish'd planting the Bunch Beens & planted the Beens round the arber

1793 March Thursday 21th 🙟 rain'd thunder'd & Light'd very hard last night. rain'd in the morning. in the fore noon clear'd away cold & windey

Fryday 22 🙟 frose hard last night. very cold in the fore part of the day, in the after noon turn'd more modarate

Saturday 23 🙟 a fine day. Henrey Sypels[201] made me a pressent of a Hive of Bees,[202] I Hire'd a neagro man named Nace at the rate of £12-0-0 pr year. He's acleaning the walks

Sunday 24th 🙟 a fine day

Munday 25th 🙟 a fine day. dug the Border at the end of the new stable & planted Cherrey Tree seeds & pott mary gold seeds, dug the Border for the nurssery of Box

1793 March Tuseday 26th 🙟 a cloudey morning. planted a line of Ivy from Mrs. Sands on the Border whare the nursserey of Box is & planted out the Box that was left of planting rond the flower Beds. came on to rain hard. clear'd away in the after noon. sow'd 4 Hills of the pickeling lime & moved the golding willow & planted 3 cutings of the golding willow

Wednesday 27th 🙟 a cold cloudey day, Nace acleaning the walks

Thursday 28th 🙟 a cold day, Nace acleaning ye walks

Fryday 29th 🙟 a fine day. I planted the Burgumot Balm in a Box, and planted the Balsam Appel Majrs. one the side of the Walnut Tree Quarter, Nace clean'd the Balm and scatter'd dung on it & then whent to cleaning the walks

Saturday 30th 🙟 a fine day

Sunday 31th 🙟 a cloudey morning, Charley, Abee & Rebacka sett of to William Woodwards. a fine after noon. Charley came Home in the evening. left his sisters & all well

1793 Munday April 1th 🙟 a fine day

[201] Henry Sibell (d.1797), a baker, held a license in the 1780s as a tavern keeper. He owned property in the first block of Church Street, purchased from the Commissioners for Confiscated British Property; the loyalist Dulanys had been the owners before the Revolution.

[202] This is the first mention in the diary of beekeeping, but Faris's later comments about the habits of bees suggest that this was not his first hive (see 26 June 1793). Bees were used as pollinators of flowers and as a source of honey. Faris kept bees throughout the years covered by the diary, and maintained a careful record of the state of his hives.

Tuseday 2 ✒ a fine day, Charley & Hyram sett off to William Woodward's, Hyram walked

Wednesday 3th ✒ a fine day, Nace's tied up the Hyacenths & in the after noon began to cut the Box, cut 3 lines and planted a few cutting of Box. in the evening Hyram came Home. left his sisters well

Thursday 4th ✒ a fine day. Nace a cuting Box, Charley came Home about a 11 oclock, Hyram's planting Box cutings

Fryday 5th ✒ a right April day. frequent showers of rain. Nace Finished cuting the Box, carryed out the cutings and began to clean the Beds & walks of the cuttings

Saturday 6th ✒ a fine growing weather. Nace's finished cleaning his walks & is a tying the Hyacinths

1793 Sunday April 7th ✒ a fine day. Abee & Rebecka came Home betwene 11 & 12 oclock, Abee with the augue on her. came with William Woodward Junr. & Henrey & Miss Alse staid [to] diner & Tea[203] & went off in the evening. Mrs. Golder's[204] brought to bed of a son this evening. Doctr Schoof call'd in. he told me I should take in the evening 25 or 30 drops of Lodnam[205] and he would call to see me in the morning

Munday 8th ✒ a fine day. sow'd colleflower seed on the Border at ye end of the new stable. came from Mr. Robert Moore[206] No. 1 flower seed from Miss Hood's[207] call the Lady in Green, and a bed in the

---

203 Dinner was a midday meal, eaten between one and two in the afternoon in the Faris household; tea was served late in the afternoon or early evening.

204 Sarah Ashmead Golder, the daughter of Annapolis innkeeper Joseph Ashmead and the wife of Archibald Golder (1760–1808), one of Faris's neighbors. Golder was the son of John Golder, a cabinetmaker who died of mushroom poisoning. Golder's mother Ann then married Robert Johnson (d.1773), whose sons are mentioned frequently in the diary, before becoming the wife of Joseph Ashmead. Golder married Sarah Ashmead in April 1782. Golder was clerk of the city Corporation from 1789 until his removal in July 1801 because he was "incapable due to a loss of reason," although he was appointed hay weigher in February 1805. Golder was also a storekeeper, who announced the opening of his dry and wet goods store in the 21 April 1796 *Gazette*. Golder inherited the lease of a large lot on the corner of West and Cathedral Streets and in 1794 purchased a lease on the opposite side of West Street from Capt. William Pitt, Faris's future son-in-law. Golder also had a tavern license in the 1790s.

205 Laudanum, a preparation of powdered opium dissolved in alcohol, was the preferred drug at this time for treatment of a variety of ills, from nausea and diarrhea to smallpox and tuberculosis, as well as for alleviation of pain. Addiction was a serious side effect of long-term use. Charles Carroll of Carrollton's wife Molly, for example, who in 1776 began to use laudanum for treatment of insomnia, the physical toll of difficult pregnancies, and nervous anxieties, was addicted to the drug for much of the remaining six years of her life.

206 Robert Moore was a Baltimore merchant who shipped cauliflower to Faris by packet in March 1791 and September 1792.

207 Miss Hood was most likely the daughter of John Hood Jr. (d.1795) of Anne Arundel County. Hood had three wives (Hannah Poole, Rachel Howard, and Elizabeth Gaither) and at least three daughters: Hannah, Sarah (who married by April 1799), and Elizabeth (who married in December 1797). There is no way of knowing which daughter exchanged plants with Faris. Hood himself cultivated apples on a grand scale, having about 1,300 productive trees on his plantation when he died.

lott with seed from W. Woodward calld English Lambs Qarter, and in the after noon Nace began to do up the Water Table[208] round the grass walk, which he mow'd in the morning. the wind Blows hard this evening like for rain. I have the siattick or pain in my Hip[209]

Tusday 9th ⚓ I have had the pain in my hip. The leg so bad that I could not sett up. oblig'd to have a bed & Bed sted in the big room[210] & Mrs. Gassaway sent me a pair of crutches. Nace finished the water table. a fine day

Wednesday 10th ⚓ I took a dose of salts this morning. Doctr Shoof call'd in, he told me I should take in the evening 25 or 30 drops of Lodnam and he would call to see me in the morning

1793 Thursday April 11th ⚓ a fine day. Doctr Shoof did not call to see me too day as he promised. I am a grate deal better. I have had the Bed taken out of the room. Nace's cleaning ye walks in the garden

Fryday 12th ⚓ raind this morning. clear'd away. Nace stuck the Peas and Hill'd them, the Pain in my Hipp's much as it was yesterday. I have never seen the Doctor since

Saturday 13th ⚓ a fine day. Doctr R. Ghislin[211] came Home this after noon from London — Nace aclearing the suckers from the goosberrey & curren bushes

---

[208] Water tables served as an aqueduct system to irrigate the garden.

[209] Faris's shaky handwriting in this and several subsequent entries is mute testimony to his suffering. Sciatica was the term used to describe pain, caused by pressure on a nerve root in the lower back, that radiates from the back into the leg.

[210] In houses with two stories, whose bed chambers were on the second floor, beds were often set up on the first floor for family members who were seriously ill. The patient would have no need to climb stairs and would be more conveniently located for those doing the nursing.

[211] Reverdy Ghiselin (c.1765–1822) was the son of Reverdy and Mary Ghiselin (see 21 January 1792). He was the great-grandson of goldsmith César Ghiselin (d.1734) and his wife Katherine Reverdy, from whom he and his father took their given name. Ghiselin married Ann Robosson in February 1798; Faris records both the marriage and the death of Ann and her child in 1801. On Christmas day in 1804, Ghiselin, then a member of the governor's council, married Margaret Bowie, daughter of Governor Robert Bowie. Ghiselin, who studied medicine in Paris, became the city's health officer in September 1793, with duties that included examining all strangers arriving in the city by water or stage to prevent the spread of yellow fever. He served as councilman and alderman and for eleven terms on the executive council from 1801 to 1812. Ghiselin lived across West Street from Faris in the family's two-story brick house that he inherited from his father. § Faris recorded a purchase from Ghiselin on 21 October 1799 of an ounce of red bark. Charles Faris's estate paid Ghiselin £5.11.3 and paid Drs. Ghiselin & Murray £3.13.9. Ghiselin owed William Faris's estate £4.8.1 and collected from it £3.11.3. At the sale of Faris's property, Ghiselin bought five books and one pair of scales and weights.

212 An Episcopalian, Faris served as a vestryman and churchwarden. Several members of his family, however, attended Methodist services, particularly Hyram. Faris's "Will" states that Faris had intended to give his silk hose to Saint John "'Till he like a fool, turned Methodist quaint." But Faris's comments in the diary about visits to Methodist services by Hyram and others do not display any hostility. There was a Methodist meeting house on the grounds of the State House, a small frame building known as the Old Blue Church, originally built on Hanover Street but moved in 1789 by permission of the General Assembly. One diary entry suggests that family members attended services there. Methodism in Maryland grew as a result of the preaching of Francis Asbury (1745–1816), an Englishman who was converted in his teens and became an itinerant preacher when he was twenty-one. In October 1771 Asbury brought his ministry to the colonies, arriving first in Philadelphia. He made numerous visits to Maryland, including frequent appearances in the Annapolis area. In 1777, for example, he preached in the play house, next door to Faris's home, as well as at the homes of John Hesselius (see 5 June 1795) and Catherine (or Charlotte) Small (see 15 October 1793) and at the head of the Severn River—perhaps at the chapel that Hyram visited.

213 None of the Anne Arundel County court judgment volumes survive for the years covered by the diary, so there is no way to determine the circumstances of Hyram's assault. This may have been the John R. Bryce who was an adjutant of the 22nd militia regiment in 1794, who advertised in September 1799 that he would petition for an act of insolvency, and who died in May 1805 at the age of thirty-four. He was the son of Capt. Robert and Frances Bryce (see 7 February 1792).

214 The resin of the tropical hardwood American trees and shrubs of the genus *Guaiacum*, especially *G. sanctum* of the West Indies and Florida, used as a stimulant and as a remedy for rheumatism and other ailments.

Sunday 14th ✒ fine growing weather. several showers to day. Hyram walk'd to the chappel212

Munday 15th ✒ a rainey morning. clear'd away cold

Tuseday 16 ✒ a fine morning. sow'd egg plant seed from Doctr Shoff in the pott whare I sow'd before. Hyram was fined at court 5/ for strikeing John Brice alis Largone213

1793 Wednesday April 17th ✒ a fine day. Nace's a diging up the Lott

Thursday 18th ✒ a fine day. Nace's finished digging ye Lott

Fryday 19th ✒ a fine day. in the after noon a fine shower of rain

Saturday 20th ✒ a rainey morning. planted out 32 early York plants seed from Pettey sow'd the 9th of Feby in the after noon & evening rain

Sunday 21th ✒ rain and mist at times all day and very cold & raw

Munday 22th ✒ a rainey cold dissagreeable day

Tuseday 23th ✒ a fine day

Wednesday 24th ✒ a fine day but coole. I had 2 oz. of Volatile Tincture of Gum Guaiacum214 of Doctr Murray & Shaaff to take for the pain in my hip thigh & leg, Nace went away this evening

1793 Thursday Apl 25th ✒ a fine day. in the evening like for rain

Fryday 26th ✒ a rainey day

Saturday 27th ✒ a rainey dissagreeable day

Sunday 28th ✒ another dull rainey day. Blew very Hard last night

Munday 29th ✒ a cloudey dull morning. dug a littel peace of ground & sow the cabage see[d] I had from Mrs. Onion's. at 11 oclock the sun looks like cuming out. a fine afternoon. thare's a report that William Cayton,215 Charles Cayton216 and William Ross217 are drownded

Tusday 30th ✒ a fine day. in the evening, cloudey and looks like for more rain. this day the Boddey of Benjamin Buckland (one of the unfortunate that was drownded the 22th of Febry) was found near Sandy point — the report of the Caytons and Ross's being drownded is fals. thay come Home safe

1793 Wednesday May 1th ✒ a dull morning but cleard away a fine day. received a letter from my son William dated Havanna March 24th which gives an accot of his being in good Health

Thursday 2th ✒ a dull drisley day

Fryday 3th ✒ a rainey day, William Pitt sent a Boy to Inform us that St. John Faris arrived at Baltimore yesterday — in the evening the sun shined out

Saturday 4th ✒ a very fine day, this after noon Hyram sett off for Mr. H. Welsh's.[218] Nace return'd last night

Sunday 5th ✒ receiv'd a Letter from My son Saint. he is well. he left Liverpool the 7th of March and arrived at Baltimore the 2th of May. he sent his mothers Fann & Mrs. Stevens's silk he carrey'd to be died. a dull cloudey day

1793 Munday May 6th ✒ very cold last night, a cloudey cold mistey day — Nace began his second month this morning

Tuseday 7th ✒ a cloudey morning. mark'd 6 Tulips for Doctr Scott with 1 notch on the stick — a cloudey drisley day

Wednesday 8th ✒ a dull cloudey day but warmer then its been some days pas. John Ross, one of the unfortunate 9 that was drownd the 22th of Febry was found too day. like wise Thomas Price was found

---

215 William Caton was probably the son of Capt. William Caton, a mariner who operated a tavern in the 1770s and who also patronized Faris's tavern in 1774 and 1775. William Caton (Jr.), who probably married Ann Purdey in 1788, advertised himself as a hairdresser for ladies and gentlemen from 1788 to 1793 (at the Sign of the Head Dress on Francis Street). In June 1795 Caton advertised the sale of dry goods, still at the same location, a two-story brick house on the south side of Francis Street. In August 1799 he operated a boarding house at the Sign of the Scales, but by December had taken over the property formerly belonging first to George Mann (see 5 January 1792) and then to James Wharfe (see 2 April 1796), where he operated the Sign of the Indian King. In 1801 Caton bought Richard Sprigg's Strawberry Hill estate across College Creek (see 13 May 1792). Four years later, Caton advertised that he was leaving town, but the following year he was a partner in the mercantile firm of Caton & Neth (see 15 May 1792). § Faris bought tea from Caton in 1791 and sugar and brandy in 1797.

216 In March 1787, the county court bound Charles Caton, then seventeen years old, as an apprentice to Thomas Price to learn the trade of bricklayer. He was discharged from Price's service in November for "incorrigible behavior." In February 1790 the *Gazette* reported that he helped to put out a fire in the governor's residence. He may have been William Caton's brother, being too old to be his son.

217 William Ross was a chair and cabinet maker located on Church Street in June 1791. He married Rachel Allen (b.1766?) in June 1783, who may have been the daughter of John and Eleanor Allen (see 4 January 1792). In 1798, Ross rented an old brick house on Shipwright Street from Charles Carroll of Carrollton, and shared with Benjamin Fairbanks the rent of a small house on Cornhill Street—this may have been a workshop. It is possible that John Ross, the cabinetmaker who drowned in February 1793, and William Ross were related, given that they practiced the same craft.

218 Henry O'Neal Welch, who died within the year, leaving an estate valued at £1,613. Welch's will, written in 1784, left his property to the sons of his brothers Thomas and John and of a sister. He apparently never married although he may have had one son, as he also named John Welch, the son of Mary Jacobs and grandson of John Jacobs, as one of his heirs. § Welch patronized Faris's tavern in 1773 and 1774.

Thursday 9th ⚬ a fine morning, James Jenings one of the unfortunate nine that was drownded the 22th Febry was found by one of the Kent Island Boates & Brought to the dock

Fryday 10th ⚬ a fine day

Saturday 11th ⚬ a fine day

1793 Sunday May 12th ⚬ a fine warm day. in the evening a pritey littel rain. this evening Mr. Charles Maccubbin was married to Miss Sarrah Allen[219]

Munday 13 ⚬ a fine day, thined & replanted the Carrots and Parsneps, & Broke of the Tulep stalks ~~Mr. Charles Maccubbin was married to Miss Sarah Allen this evening~~[220]

Tusday 14th ⚬ Mr. Hissler from Baltimore brought me 6 roots of the Double Anemonies & 2 roots of Double Tube Rose planted 3 in potts & 3 in the Bed round the grass

No. 2 Anemonies

No. 3 tubee Roses on the Border next Grayhams

a fine day

Wednesday 15th ⚬ a fine day

Thursday 16th ⚬ a fine day

Fryday 17th ⚬ a fine day

1793 Saturday May 18th ⚬ a fine day. my son Saint came home last Night about 10 oclock fron Baltimore. he is right well & Harty

Sunday 19th ⚬ a fine warm day

Munday 20th ⚬ a fine warm day but very dry. rain's much wanted

Tuseday 21th ⚬ warm & dry. watered part of the garden this evening — my son St. John Faris left Home this morning for Baltimore about 9 oclock

Wednesday 22th ⚬ Nace has been sick all day, cept his room. a fine day. in the after noon a fine rain

Thursday 23th ⚬ a fine day. Nace went off this morning before I was up

Fryday 24th ⚬ a fine day. in ye evening turned cold & cloudey

1793 Saturday May 25th ⚬ a raw cold day

[219] Merchant Charles Maccubbin (1756–1799) was the son of Nicholas Maccubbin (1709–1787) and his wife Mary Clare Carroll (1756–1799), and the brother of Nicholas Maccubbin Carroll (see 18 January 1792) and of Mary Clare Maccubbin, wife of John Brice (see 23 April 1795). Sarah Allen (1774–1836) was the daughter of Dr. John and Eleanor Allen, and the sister of Joseph Allen (see 4 January 1792). § Abbe and Nancy attended a party given by the Maccubbins on 10 November 1795. Faris collected £0.11.3 from Maccubbin's estate in September 1801 as administrator of Charles's estate.

[220] This crossed-out entry suggests that Faris learned of the wedding some time after it took place and initially wrote the news down on the wrong date.

Sunday 26th ✍ a rainey morning. in the after noon cloudey & coole

Munday 27th ✍ a cloudey morning, clear'd away a fine after noon & very warm

Tuseday 28th ✍ a fine warm morning. in the after-noon clouded up and turned raw & cold like for rain

Wednesday 29th ✍ a cold raw rainey day

Thursday 30th ✍ a rainey day. p[l]anted the wal-nutt tree square full of plants, and the square in the lott in the evening made a fire in the House

Fryday 31th ✍ a rainey morning, continued cloudey. in the evening fine rain. still a fire in the House

Saturday June 1th ✍ a fine day but raw & cold. gathered & Botteled the goosberreys. a fire in the house in the evening. the Genaral Court broke up this forenoon

1793 Sunday June 2th ✍ several showers of rain to day

Munday 3th ✍ pulled up the peas & pea sticks and dugg the ground & began to digg the littel quarter by the old stable. a fine day

Tuseday 4th ✍ morning & fore part of the day r[a]in. in the after noon clear. planted cabbage plants whare the peas grew, and planted colleflower plants in the littel quarter

Wednesday 5th ✍ a fine day. in the evening cloudey and like for more rain

Thursday 6th ✍ rain'd last night & this fore noon in the after noon a shower. in the evening starr light

Fryday 7th ✍ a fine day

Saturday 8th ✍ a fine day

1793 Sunday June 9th ✍ a very Hott day. William Pitt left heare this day on his voige in his Pilot Boat loaded with Flower for the West Indias

Munday 10th ✍ a very Hott day

Tuseday 11th ✍ a very Hott day

Wednesday 12th ✍ a very Hott day. in the evening a fine rain

Thursday 13th ✍ a fine day. in the after noon a shower of rain

Fryday 14th ☙ receiv'd a letter from my son William dated the 9th of May — a fine day

Saturday 15th ☙ a fine day. in the afternoon Hyram went off for H. Wilsh's, in the evening like for rain

Sunday 16th ☙ a fine day

1793 Munday June 17th ☙ a very warm day. about 10 oclock the Bees swarm'd. in the after noon a fine rain

Tuseday 18th ☙ a very Hott day, cutt the sage

Wednesday 19 ☙ a very Hott day. Doctr Shoff's thorometor was up as hygh as 96, James William's[221] at 94[222]

Thursday 20th ☙ a very Hott day. in the evening wee had a littel shower which cooled the aire a littel

Fryday 21th ☙ a fine day. in the evening wee had a fine shower

Saturday 22th ☙ rained a good deal Last night and this morning and continued till after noon. in the evening the sunn sett clear

Sunday 23th ☙ a fine coole day

Munday 24th ☙ a fine coole day. cutt the Baum

1793 Tuseday June 25th ☙ a dull drisley morning and rained at times all day. finished the colleflwers and a row of plants in the bigg bed

Wednesday 26th ☙ a rainey drisley day, about 10 oclock the Bees swarmed, I never knew an instance of bees swarming of a wett day before. it drisseld when thay came out

Thursday 27th ☙ a cloudey morning. about noon clear'd away. a fine after noon

Fryday 28th ☙ a warm clear day, I made the Black Phosphorus and gave Charles & Hyram. each had some of it

Saturday 29th ☙ a clear warm day

Sunday 30th ☙ a very Hott day. in the evening a littel refreshing shower

1793 Munday July 1th ☙ trimed the Rose Bushes the side nex to Grayhams. a very Hott day

Thuseday 2th ☙ a very Hott day. in the evening wee had a littel sprinkel of rain

---

[221] James Williams (c.1741–1818?), the nephew of Revolutionary-era merchant Thomas Williams, took over his uncle's store with his brother Joseph. In 1798 he owned a two-story frame dwelling, with kitchen, stable, milk house, and smoke house, on the dock. Between 1789 and 1805 he held the offices of councilman and alderman and served three terms as mayor of Annapolis. In April 1791, Williams posted bond as the new sheriff of Anne Arundel County. Williams also kept a racing stable, and offered the stud services of his stallion Pitt (named for British statesman William Pitt, see 11 January 1795) in April 1792. § Faris bought a barrel of flour from Williams in January 1796 and a quarter of beef in December 1798. He collected sixteen shillings from Williams in September 1801 as administrator of Charles's estate. Williams bought eighteen files, a brass globe, and a number of hammers at the sale of Faris's estate.

[222] One of the instances in the diary that reveal the daily exchange of information among the men of the town.

Wednesday 3th ๛ a Hott day. David Geddis told me that my son St. saild from Baltimore the 22th of May

Thursday 4th ๛ a Hot day

Fryday 5th ๛ a fine day

Saturday 6th ๛ a fine day. in the after noon Mr. James Maccubin's[223] vessel was to have been Lanched but by some accident she stopt in her ways and did not go off. in the evening a littel shower of rain. Mrs. Faris was taken to day with the Ague & Feveour

1793 Sunday July 7th ๛ a fine day, Hyram walked up to the Severon Chappel, Mr. Maccubbin's Brigg was Lanched this morning

Munday 8th ๛ a fine day. Mrs. Faris has had a very sevear fitt of the Ague and Feveour

Tuseday 9th ๛ a fine day. about noon thare was a fine rain. Mrs. Faris took Bark, in the evening cloudey like for rain. a good deal of Lightening

Wednesday 10th ๛ a fine day. yesterday & too day thare has been betwen 30 & 40 vessels went to Baltimore the most of them full of French peopel from Cape Fransway.[224] thay say that one vessel had near 1200 on bord. the Town's Burnt down[225]

Thursday 11th ๛ a fine day in the after noon I Buded[226] a wite rose on the Holley on the right hand going to the littel house[227] & a red rose on the other

1793 Fryday July 12th ๛ a fine day

Saturday 13th ๛ a fine day

Sunday 14th ๛ a fine coole day. thare has been a grate deel of gun Fireing at Baltimore to day & yester day evening[228]

Munday 15th ๛ a cloudey cool day. in the after noon I Planted two cherrey trees in potts

Tuseday 16th ๛ a fine rain Last night. a fine warm day

Wednesday 17th ๛ a fine day. in the evening the citicens met at the Stad House in consiquence of a message from the committee of Baltimore relaiting to the French Peopel, the citicens met and chos a

[223] James Maccubbin (c.1759–1834) was the son of Richard and Elizabeth Maccubbin (see 10 June 1800) and a second cousin of Nicholas Maccubbin Carroll (see 18 January 1792) and Charles Maccubbin (see 12 May 1793). A merchant, he lived in a three-story brick building at the corner of Cornhill Street and Market Space. He was briefly secretary of the senate in 1781 and 1782, served as a councilman from 1789 to 1793, and was the chief judge of the orphans' court. § Charles Faris's estate paid him £1.10.5 and Faris collected £0.19.5 1/2 from Maccubbin in January 1802 as administrator of Charles's estate.

[224] Cap Français (now Cape Haitien, Haiti). The passengers were refugees fleeing the revolution in Saint Domingue.

[225] The *Gazette* the next day reported that Capt. Joseph White brought news that the port had been set on fire by a rebellion of Negroes and mulattoes, and that "near forty sail of vessels" had passed Annapolis on their way to Baltimore.

[226] Grafted.

[227] Necessary or privy.

[228] The *Gazette* contains no account of the gunfire, but it was probably related to the arrival of the refugees. See the entry for the 17th.

committe to corres[p]ond with the committe of Baltimore. the committee whare as follows viz. Thomas Jenings[229] Allexander C. Hanson[230], N. Carrol, James Brice,[231] S. Ridout,[232] J. Kelty, James Williams

1793 Thursday July 18 ↙ this morning Capt. Kelty & Mr. James Williams two of the committe went off for Baltimore. a fine day

99 ↙ Alexander Contee Hanson (1749–1806)

Chancellor Hanson was one of Faris's most frequent gardening colleagues.

229 Thomas Jennings (c.1736–1796) immigrated to Maryland c.1759 from England, where he had studied law, and was admitted to practice in the Anne Arundel County court in June 1761. He and his wife Juliana had ten children, including Juliana, who married James Brice (see 17 July 1793) and Anne, who married Nicholas Maccubbin Carroll (see 18 January 1792). In 1780 Jennings bought William Paca's Georgian mansion on Prince George Street. Jennings served in the house of delegates and senate and as councilman, orphans' court justice, and attorney general. § Jennings represented Faris in his first lawsuit in the Anne Arundel County court, when Faris was sued by John Inch; Inch defaulted, giving the verdict to Faris. Jennings patronized Faris's tavern in 1773 and 1774, drinking punch and toddy. In January 1775 Faris charged Jennings for a key and for the silver content and labor of making a pair of spectacles, and in 1784 charged thirty shillings for a year of winding and otherwise caring for Jennings' clocks.

230 Alexander Contee Hanson was the son of John Hanson Jr. (1721–1783) and his wife Jane Contee (1728–1812) of Mulberry Grove in Charles County. He received his education at the College of Philadelphia and was admitted to the Maryland bar about 1772. He married Rebecca Howard (1758–1806), daughter of Cornelius and Mary Howard (see 31 March 1792) in June 1778. Hanson was an associate judge of the general court from 1778 to 1789 and chancellor and judge of the land office from 1789 until his death. In 1798 he was a tenant of William Campbell on Church Circle, not far from Faris's home, living in a two-story stone house with a brick addition, brick stable, and coach house, all valued at $2,200. § Faris collected ten shillings from Hanson in April 1801 as administrator of Charles's estate.

231 James Brice (1746–1801) was the son of John Brice II (1705–1766) and his wife Sarah Frisby (1714–1782), and the younger brother of John Brice III (see 23 April 1795). He built the imposing Georgian mansion at the corner of East and Prince George Streets on lots he inherited at the age of twenty. In 1781, at the age of thirty-five, he married his next-door neighbor, Julianna Jennings (c.1764–1837), daughter of Thomas Jennings (see 17 July 1793). Brice was a lawyer and planter who served almost continuously on the executive council from 1777 to 1799, as acting governor upon the death of George Plater (see 10 February 1792), and as mayor of Annapolis for two terms, among other offices.

232 Samuel Ridout (1765–?) was the son of John and Mary Ogle Ridout (see 6 October 1797) and the brother of Horatio (see 21 November 1793). Samuel was educated in England, under the supervision of his grandmother Anne Tasker Ogle. The two were still in England when the Revolutionary War broke out and spent most of the war years in France, only returning to Maryland after the war ended. Samuel married Mary Grafton Addison (d.1807), the daughter of Thomas Addison (d.1775) and his wife Rebecca Dulany, daughter of Walter and Mary Grafton Dulany (see 5 August 1801). Her brother Walter Dulany Addison married Elizabeth Hesselius (see 5 June 1792) and her brother Thomas married Henrietta Maria Paca, daughter of William Paca and Sarah Joice (see 7 November 1797). An attorney, Ridout was admitted to practice in the Anne Arundel County court in August 1789. He served on the executive council in 1800 and from 1813 to 1815 and was elected mayor of Annapolis in 1802 and 1805. The Ridouts lived on Southeast Street, in one of the three-story brick townhouses Samuel's father built in the early 1770s.

Fryday 19th ✍ a very Hott day. in the evening looks as if wee should have rain. it did rain at night

Saturday 20th ✍ a fine day. Mrs. Faris told me that Charles Intended to go away on Munday, he has not spoke to me of it as yet

Sunday 21th ✍ a fine day

Munday 22th ✍ Transplanted the earley York plants on the Border next to Grayhams, dug part of the border & planted a row of Beens the sort I got from Mr. Man. a fine day

Tuseday 23th ✍ a very Hott day, one of Mr. Nicholas Worthingtons daughters was married to Mr. Goldsberey[233]

1793 Wednesday 24th ✍ Hyram & his sisters went over to Mr. Mitchels.[234] a very Hott day

Thursday 25th ✍ Henrey Woodward & his sister Also dined here, she came to Town to buy her weddin close. she's to be married to Mr. Watkins,[235] a fine pleasant day

Fryday 26th ✍ yesterday Robert Pinkeney[236] shott him self near to Mr. Ogel's Folley plantation.[237] this morning a Jurey of Inquest was summond and went down and brought in thare verdict that he did it willfully — and it's reported that on Wednesday last that the wife of Mr. John Davidson Hanged her self, it is told as follows, a neagro woman observed her to be very melloncolly, saw her take the key of the garrot and go up thare (an thing s[h]e never k[n]ew her to do before). after she went up a littel wile, the woman followed her very softley. when s[h]e came to the garrot doore it was shut. shee peep'd through the key hole and saw her mistress hanging clear of the flore. she Immediatly Burst open the doore, and luckely haveing a knife, she cut her down, and for the Pressent saved her Life — Mr. John Davidson was from home. he and one of his daughters was gone to dine at Mr. Nicholas Worthington's, wose daughter was married the day before — this has been a fine pleasant day

1793 Saturday July 27th ✍ a fine day

Sunday 28th ✍ a very Hott day

Munday 29th ✍ a cloudey morning, the Beens I sow'd the 22th of this month are acuming up. a Hott after noon. in the evening looks cloudey like for rain

233 Richard Goldsborough was the son of Robert Goldsborough (1733–1788) of Dorchester County and his wife Sarah Yerbury, and the brother of William, who married Achsah's sister Sarah. Achsah Worthington was the daughter of Nicholas and Catherine Griffith Worthington (see 8 November 1792).

234 There were three Mitchell households in Anne Arundel in 1790, headed by Hugh, David, and Thomas, but no way to know which Hyram and his sisters visited.

235 There were a dozen Watkins households in Anne Arundel in 1790, but in 1800 Stephen and his wife and their three young boys lived in their own household with one slave. Watkins advertised in September 1797 that he was going to file a petition for insolvency. Such a move generally resulted in the appointment of trustees to manage the debtor's assets and attempt to settle with creditors. Alse Woodward was the daughter of William Woodward and his wife Jane Ridgely (see 7 December 1792). Her grandfather, William Woodward (1716–1790), was the oldest brother of Priscilla Woodward Faris.

236 Robert Pinkney was probably the son of the tailor by that name, who died in a fall from his horse in 1773, leaving a widow and three children. Robert Sr.'s estate was administered by his widow Priscilla and son Jonathan, known as Jonathan of Robert to distinguish him from the son of Jonathan Pinkney. Given the recurrence of the same names in both families it is likely that Robert Pinkney (d.1773) and Jonathan Pinkney (emigrated 1755) were related, both having arrived in the colony from England. § Robert Sr. patronized Faris's tavern in 1773. Jonathan Pinkney signed the inventory of Charles Faris as one of the creditors, and received £6.7.11 from the estate to settle the debt.

237 Faris may have been mistaken about either the plantation or its owner. Folly quarter belonged to Charles Carroll of Carrollton, part of the estate at Doohoragen Manor in western Anne Arundel (now Howard) County.

100 ✒ William Whetcroft (c.1735–1799)

William Whetctoft was an Annapolis silversmith and friend of Faris who lived nearby on West Street.

[238] William Whetcroft was born in Ireland and emigrated to Annapolis in 1766. Whetcroft advertised himself at various times as a goldsmith, jeweler, lapidary, and clockmaker. He had a shop in Baltimore from 1767 to 1769, but returned to Annapolis after his marriage to Frances Cudmore Knapp, the widow of William Knapp and sister-in-law of John Knapp (see note 242). The Whetcrofts and their children, of whom there were eight recorded births (at least five of whom lived to be adults), were good friends of the Faris family and appear often in the diary. There were other branches of the family in Annapolis, perhaps headed by brothers or nephews of William Whetcroft (see 18 August 1793 and 22 July 1795). Faris does not record the marriage of Whetcroft's fourth daughter, Ann (b.1778), in Philadelphia to Alexander Kerr on 20 April 1796; Alexander may have been related to Archibald Kerr, who will marry Abigail Faris in 1802 and name his first child Alexander. The Whetcrofts lived across West Street from Faris from 1776 until 1798. § Whetcroft patronized Faris's tavern in 1776, paying mostly for oats and hay, and paid fifteen shillings for two days hire of a horse in April 1777.

Tuseday 30th ✒ Hott and dry

Wednesday 31th ✒ cloudey morning. in the fore noon thare was a fine shower of rain which cooled the air

1793 Thursday Augt 1th ✒ a coole plessant day

Fryday 2th ✒ a fine pleasant day

Saturday 3th ✒ a fine pleasant day

Sunday 4th ✒ Mr. Whitcroft[238] told me that it was a fals and mallishous storey rais'd on Mrs. Davidson. it's true that thare was some words in the famely. she did not want Mr. Davidson & daughter to go to Worthingtons to diner — this has been a warm day. rains much wanted

Munday 5th ✒ a warm day

Tuseday 6th ✒ a warm day

Wednesday 7th ✒ a warm day

1793 Thursday Augt 8th ✒ a warm day. in the evening rain and looks as if thare would be a fine rain. Wrought to my son William & Capt. Campell, who promises to get an opertunity of sending it safe

Fryday 9th ✒ a fine rain Last night and this morning a littel. planted a singl row of Beens in the big bed. a fine day

Saturday 10th ✒ a fine day

Sunday 11th ✒ Last night William Wilkins's[239] daughter polley died and was buryed this morning — a fine day. Nancey's very unwel

Munday 12th ✒ I planted 3 rows of Beens in the big Bed. a Hott day. Nancey has a Hott feveour all day

Tuseday 13th ✒ a fine day but Hott and dry. Nancey is a littel better

1793 Wednesday Augt 14th ✒ a fine morning. I cast a cantilope mellion in wax.[240] in the after noon thare was a fine rain

---

[239] The *Maryland Gazette* noted on 15 August that "Miss Mary Wilkins, only daughter of William Wilkins, merchant of this city, died 10th instant, in her 16th year."

[240] Twice in the diary Faris describes casting fruit in wax. His inventory listed "One case wax work" (valued at $5.00) among the furnishings of his parlor, so he probably did the casting for display and enjoyment.

Thursday 15th ↝ cloudey & rain at times most of the day

Fryday 16th ↝ a fine day. this day I enter'd into my 65th years of age. this evening I took the Polianthis out of the Pott and Parted the roots. it mad 5 plants

Saturday 17th ↝ a fine day. Hyram's complaining of a pain in his Brest Neck & Head. I gave him a dose of salts in the morning and it did not work. I intend giveing him peregorick ellixr and wine drops this evening and a purge of salts in the morning

1793 Sunday Augt 18th ↝ a very Hott day. young Mr. & Miss Mitchel & Miss Moss[241] dined and drank Tea. this morning Mrs. Elizabeth Whitcroft[242] was Brought to bed of a fine Boy

Munday 19th ↝ this morning clear'd the pigen House[243] of dung & Hill'd 3 rows of the beens. a very Hott day. in the evening a fine rain

Tuseday 20th ↝ a fine day. parted the old root of Polianthis in four and made good the front row of Box and cut the top to the line — Doctr Murray call'd for his spectacle case, I ask'd him to look at Charles, he told me to give him cream atarter[244] & water for his common drink

Wednesday 21th ↝ a fine day. in the evening look like rain

Thursday 22th ↝ a fine day. in the evening sow'd a few radish seed & planted the small Leek roots

Fryday 23th ↝ a fine day

1793 Saturday Augt 24th ↝ a fine day. in the evening a fine rain.

Sunday 25th ↝ rain'd most of the night last night. a drisley rainey day

Munday 26th ↝ a drisley cloudey day. this after noon sow'd earley York & cabage from Mr. Chapman & sow'd spinage seed all on the Border next Grayham and planted a row of beens in the big bed next the new stabel — a french 44 gun ship came

---

241 Several branches of the Moss family included daughters who might have been the Miss Moss who visited with the Mitchells. This could have been either Rachel or Sarah, daughters of Nathan Moss (1742–1786) and his wife Delilah Conway. Miss Moss could also have been Sarah, the daughter of Robert (d.1796) and Elizabeth Moss. Or she could have been Elizabeth, the daughter of Samuel Skidmore (d.1780) and Monica Moss, who was born in 1773.

242 Elizabeth Knapp (c.1760–1809), who married Burton Whetcroft in April 1789. She was the daughter of William Knapp, an Annapolis watchmaker in the 1760s, and the sister of John Knapp (see 21 October 1793) and Mary Knapp (see 7 September 1794). Burton Whetcroft (c.1754–1822), a native of Ireland, came to America at about ten years of age and settled in Maryland. He may have been a nephew of William Whetcroft (see 4 August 1793) and perhaps of James Whetcroft. Whetcroft's Annapolis offices included councilman, alderman, and mayor, and he was clerk of the Court of Appeals. In 1813 he moved to Washington, D.C., to live with his only daughter, Frances E. Clark, and her husband. He died in Utica, N.Y., at the age of sixty-eight. § Faris collected £2.14.10 from Whetcroft in May 1801 as administrator of Charles's estate. Whetcroft bought one piece of ribbon, for $.50, at the sale of Faris's property.

243 Dovecotes, called pigeon houses in Britain and colonial America, date back to antiquity, doves having been among the first domesticated creatures. Pigeons and doves were a practical food supply: they could forage for most of their food and produced four to six broods of two eggs each year. Four to six weeks after hatching the squabs were ready to leave the nest—or to be eaten. The guano that accumulated in the dovecote could be used as fertilizer for flower beds. Removing it regularly was good practice as the birds were known to prefer a clean cote.

244 Cream of tartar is the purified form of potassium bitartrate, found in the lees of wine. Faris may have been referring to potassium antimonial tartrate, a salt used in medicine as a cathartic.

245 The 29 August issue of the *Gazette* reported the arrival last Monday of the French frigate *L'Astree*, in about twenty days from Port au Prince, Saint Domingue. During her passage, she captured a ship in ballast, bound from Jamaica to New York, which also arrived in Annapolis. No mention was made in the paper of the fate of the captain. The *Maryland Journal* stated on the 27th that the ship was in the Patapsco but was not allowed to anchor in the harbor as a number of those on board were sick with a malignant fever.

246 Gabriel Duvall (1752–1844) was the son of Benjamin Duvall (1719–c.1801) and his wife Susanna Tyler (1718–94). He served as the city corporation's recorder (attorney) from 1789 to 1802, was a delegate from Annapolis to the general assembly from 1787 to 1793, and sat in Congress from 1792 to 1797. In 1802 Duvall moved to the District of Columbia, where he was the first comptroller of the treasury from 1802 to 1811; from 1811 until 1835 he was an associate justice of the Supreme Court. His first wife, whom he married in 1787, was Mary Bryce (c.1762–1790), daughter of Capt. Robert Bryce and his wife Frances Wilson (see 7 February 1792). In May 1795 Duvall married Jane Gibbon (1757–1834), daughter of Capt. James Gibbon of Philadelphia. Duvall lived across town from Faris on Northeast Street, near the intersection with King George Street. § In August 1783, Duvall defended Faris in a suit in the Anne Arundel County court.

too in the Bay off the harbor.245 the peopel on boar either threw the captain over bord or put him on shore in the West Indies

Tuseday 27th ✒ a dull cloudey drisley day

Wednesday 28th ✒ a cloudey morning. cleard away fine and warm. began to replant the Box took up one Line & replanted it and cut the top of the end line

1793 Thursday Augt 29th ✒ a fine day. replanting the Box at the nursserey

Fryday 30th ✒ a very Hott day, finis'd replanting the Box, Gabriel Duvall246 & William Pinkeney247 both came to Town to day. Duvall from Philadelphia, and say that thare is a Feveour rageing thare that carreys off 40 or 50 of a day. thay are well and ded in 6 Hours248

247 William Pinkney (1764–1822) was the son of Jonathan and Ann Rind Pinkney and the brother of Ninian Pinkney (see 13 April 1802). His father emigrated to Annapolis from England by 1755. William was educated at King William's grammar school, read law with Samuel Chase, and was admitted to practice in the Anne Arundel County courts in August 1785. In 1789 he married Anna Maria Rodgers, daughter of Col. John and Elizabeth Rodgers of Harford County. Pinkney served as councilman, alderman, and mayor, and for three terms on the executive council from 1793 to 1795. He sat in the lower house of the general assembly and was attorney general of Maryland from 1805 to 1806. Pinkney drafted the declaration of war against Great Britain in June 1812 and was wounded at the Battle of Bladensburg during the ensuing War of 1812. He served as a representative and senator in Washington, as minister to both Great Britain and Russia, and as U.S. attorney general from 1812 to 1814. Pinkney died in Washington, D.C., and was buried in Congressional Cemetery. Pinkney was a charter member of the Amanda Lodge, to which Faris belonged (see 27 December 1792).

248 This is the first reference in the diary to the yellow fever epidemic experienced in Philadelphia in 1793. Yellow fever, an infectious tropical disease transmitted by a specific species of mosquito, began to appear in the North American colonies in the late seventeenth century, brought by ships that had been in the Caribbean. Although Philadelphia experienced repeated outbreaks, John Duffy (*Epidemics in Colonial America*) does not list any for Baltimore before 1793. The epidemic of that year was the first in Philadelphia for thirty years, so its reappearance must have been particularly alarming. The 19 September *Gazette* carried an extract from a letter describing the effects of the epidemic: "Carts are constantly employed to carry the dead to the different burying-grounds, where they are buried sometimes five or six in a grave, especially in Potter's Field, where the graves can scarce be dug fast enough to receive the dead."

Saturday 31th ✒ a smart gust of thunder, Lightening and rain Last night. a fine day. in the after noon Oliver Weeden[249] put the window in Mrs. Gater's[250] House for Charles Faris

Sunday September 1th ✒ a fine day. Last Wednesday night Joseph Clark's son Horatio[251] was taken Ill and died this morning, & Buried in the afternoon. he died of a Puter'd sore throte[252]

1793 Munday Septr 2th ✒ a fine day

Tuseday 3th ✒ Oliver Weeden's finished the Board and Partition in Charles's shop, a fine day

Wednesday 4th ✒ a fine day

Thursday 5th ✒ a fine day. in the evening the citecens mett and an adress was drawn up by the Chancellor, at the request of the peopel, to his Excellency the President on accot of his Proclamtion[253] and the French minester Citicen Gennetts conduct[254]

Fryday 6th ✒ a fine day. Charles has moved his tools, Bed & Bagage to his shop.[255] it looks as if wee should have rain this evening — as Dick's Boy that rides post was going out of town Blowing his Horn a man at Mr. Golders door shook his stick at him, the boy said nothing to him but was call'd to Mr. Stevens's. the man follow'd him and beat him badley

1793 Saturday Septr 7th ✒ a fine day — this day about 10 oclock Mr. John Pettey died

Sunday 8th ✒ about 9 oclock this morning Mr. John Pettey was buried, a cloudey rainey day

---

249 Oliver Weeden was a carpenter and joiner, who in 1783 owned no property and whose household consisted only of himself and his wife. In 1798, his widow Catherine owned a small frame dwelling but did not live there.

250 Ann Gaither (d.1808) was the widow of Samuel Burman and of Samuel Gaither, who died in 1762. She was licensed for many years to operate an ordinary, probably located on the south side of Church Street. She owned a number of properties in town; Faris's entry suggests that Charles was renting one of her houses.

251 According to the 5 September issue of the *Maryland Gazette*, Horatio Clark died Sunday, 1st inst., aged 14, eldest son of Joseph Clark, architect. He had been enrolled in the St. John's grammar school at the age of ten.

252 Diphtheria.

253 Washington's 22 April proclamation of impartial conduct during the war that had broken out between Britain and France in the aftermath of the French Revolution. The proclamation was opposed by the pro-French Jeffersonians but supported by Federalists. As Edmond Genêt (see following note) made his way north from Charleston, the proclamation and the government's position with regard to the fighting elicited demonstrations and counter-demonstrations. The meeting in Annapolis, chaired by Alexander Contee Hanson (see 17 July 1793), approved the proclamation and denounced "the intervention of any foreign minister to correct supposed abuses in our government" (*Gazette*, 26 September).

254 Edmond Charles Edouard Genêt was named minister plenipotentiary to the United States in November 1792 by the Girondin government, which hoped to strengthen ties to the United States, obtain payment of the American debt owed for funds loaned during the Revolutionary War, and secure credit for supplies needed to prosecute war in Europe. Genêt's practice of outfitting American privateers to raid British shipping and of appealing to the American public, coupled with the execution of Louis XVI, whom Americans viewed as a former ally, turned the government against Genêt, to the point of requesting in August that he be recalled. When the Jacobin faction took over in France, beheading the Girondins and the queen, they also recalled Genêt. The minister fled to Philadelphia and remained out of sight until Robespierre himself had been executed. Genêt then married Cornelia Clinton, daughter of the New York governor, in November 1794 and settled in New York, where he lived until his death on Bastille Day, 1834.

255 Charles Faris's first advertisement as a watch and clock maker appeared in the 12 September issue of the *Gazette*. He identified his shop as being on Church Street, next door below Mr. Nicholas Brewer.

Munday 9th ✒ a cloudey morning. clear'd away very warm

Tusday 10th ✒ a cloudey morning. in the evening rain

Wednesday 11th ✒ a fine day

Thursday 12th ✒ a fine day. I agreed with the French Teacher to teach Hyram, Nancey & Abbee French at 4 dollors pr month, the three to begin to morrow evening

Fryday 13th ✒ a fine day. Mr. Griffin[256] Began to teach Hyram, Nancey & Abbee French

1793 Saturday Septr 14th ✒ a fine day. in the evening cloudey

Sunday 15th ✒ a fine day

Munday 16th ✒ a very warm day

Tuseday 17th ✒ raind Last night. cloudey this morning. clear'd away cold, wind at north

Wednesday 18th ✒ a fine day but very cold for the season

Thursday 19th ✒ a fine day, more modarate then yesterday

Fryday 20th ✒ a fine day

Saturday 21th ✒ a fine day. thare's been a grate deel of Fireing a guns to wards Baltimore all day. Charles Wallace Broke the smallest of the two large electurel jars[257]

1793 Sunday Septr 22th ✒ a fine day

Munday 23th ✒ a fine day. in the evening cloudey

Tuseday 24th ✒ a dull day. pollished the under coating of the 4 Tune Clock[258] and laid on one coate of the finishing coating

Wednesday 25th ✒ a dull cloudey day

Thursday 26th ✒ a fine day, dined on Board the French ship,[259] a 3 decker, had a very ellegant diner

Fryday 27th ✒ a fine day

Saturday 28th ✒ a fine day. Hyram & my self dined on board the French ship

Sunday 29th ✒ a fine day. the French ship set off for Baltimore

1793 Munday Septr 30th ✒ a fine day

---

256 Griffin may have been the French teacher at Mr. Randall's mentioned in Jane Higginson's advertisement (see 4 June 1797).

257 This may have been part of the apparatus of the electrifying machine.

258 A musical clock that Faris was making.

259 Possibly the *L'Astree*.

Tuseday Octr 1th ✒ a fine day. this evening the citicens mett at the State House & came to a resolution of ceeping gard with an Intent of Preventing peopel's comeing to Town from Philladelphia either by Land or water.[260] 20 mounts gard to night

Wednesday 2th ✒ a fine day

Thursday 3th ✒ a fine day. this morning 8 oclock Hyram went on gard. 2 Hours on & 2 Hours off

Fryday 4th ✒ a fine day. 7 oclock this morning Hyram came off gard

Saturday 5th ✒ a fine day, about 12 oclock Capt. Henrey Baldwin died[261]

1793 Sunday Octr 6th ✒ a fine day

Munday 7th ✒ a fine day. none of the Judges are come to Town.[262] Mr. Chace[263] is sick in Baltimore, Mr. Goldsberrey[264] is not come over the Bay & thay say that Mr. Jerrey Chace[265] is sick

101 ✒ Samuel Chase (1741–1811)

Samuel Chase commissioned Faris to gild the head of a cane for him on 6/15/1774

[260] An effort to establish a quarantine to keep the yellow fever epidemic from spreading to Annapolis.

[261] Capt. Henry Baldwin (1754–1794), an Annapolis tavern keeper, fought in the Revolutionary War. He married twice, first to Sarah Hall Rawlings in January 1784 and second in January 1790 to Maria Graham Woodward (d.1835), the granddaughter of Priscilla Woodward Faris's cousin, William Woodward, the Annapolis goldsmith. Baldwin died in 1794, survived by his widow and three children.

[262] Faris refers to the General Court, the state's chief trial court, which heard both civil and criminal appeals from the county courts and original suits between residents of different counties. The court met twice a year, in Annapolis and in Easton. Samuel Chase was appointed chief justice in August 1791; his colleagues on the court were Robert Goldsborough and Jeremiah Townley Chase (see following notes).

[263] Samuel Chase, who was living in Baltimore at the time. Chase was the son of Rev. Thomas Chase, a minister in Somerset County. He married first Ann Baldwin (?–1766), daughter of Thomas and Agnes Sanders Baldwin, an Annapolis innkeeper. Ann's sister Hester married Jeremiah Townley Chase (see 4 April 1792), Samuel's second cousin. Chase's second wife, Hannah Kitty Giles, was an Englishwoman (?–1848), whom he married in 1784 while in England on state business. Chase had nine children, including his son Thomas, who

married a daughter of Jeremiah Townley Chase. A man of great talent and inordinate ambition, Chase had a long and distinguished but controversial career as an attorney and public official. With his good friend William Paca (see 7 November 1797) and others, he was a leader of the Revolutionary movement in Annapolis. Chase was a delegate and senator in the General Assembly, signer of the Declaration of Independence, Anne Arundel County justice, councilman, alderman, and recorder, and associate justice of the Supreme Court from 1796 to 1811. § Chase had a long association with William Faris. In the years for which Anne Arundel court records survive, Chase represented Faris more frequently than any other attorney. In addition, he was one of two securities for Faris's 1772 ordinary license, and also visited the tavern as a patron. In June 1774, he bought two ounces of gold and paid Faris £1.2.5 for "guilding the Head of a Cane." Chase also bought twelve dozen round bottles from Faris in March 1781. Faris and Chase served on the St. Anne's vestry together in the late 1770s and early 1780s.

[264] Robert Goldsborough (1740–1798) was born at Myrtle Grove in Talbot County, the son of Robert Goldsborough (1704–1777) and his wife Sarah Nicols (?–1740). Goldsborough was educated at the College of Philadelphia and was a member of the American Philosophical Society. He married Mary Trippe in September 1768. A lawyer, Goldsborough served in the lower house and was one of the judges of the general court from 1784 until his death.

Sept. / Oct., 1793

163

265 Jeremiah Townley Chase (1748–1828) was the son of Richard Chase (d.1757) and his wife Catherine. In June 1779 he married Hester Baldwin (d.1823), the daughter of Thomas and Agnes Sanders Baldwin, whose sister Ann was the first wife of Samuel Chase (see above). His wife's cousins were married to Nicholas Worthington (see 8 November 1792) and Thomas Johnson (see 5 June 1792). The couple had four daughters, including Frances, whose marriage Faris records on 1 October 1803. A lawyer, Chase qualified to practice in the Anne Arundel County court in August 1771. In the 1780s Chase was an alderman and mayor of Annapolis for one term. He served on the executive council, as judge of the general court from 1789 to 1805, and as chief judge of the 3rd judicial district and court of appeals from 1806 to 1826. Chase lived, first as a tenant and then as owner beginning in 1811, in the Georgian mansion built on the corner of King George and Northeast Streets by Mathias Hammond. § Chase appears as a patron of Faris's tavern in 1776, the same year in which he purchased a pair of knee buckles from Faris. In February 1799 Faris received £3.1.11 from Chase but did not specify the origin of the debt in his daybook, and collected £3.7.1 1/2 from Chase in September 1801 as administrator of Charles's estate.

266 Charles Carnan Ridgely (1760–1829) was born in Baltimore County, the son of John Carnan and his wife Achsah Ridgely. He changed his name legally in 1790, to comply with the terms of his uncle Captain Charles Ridgely's will. He married Priscilla Dorsey, daughter of Caleb Dorsey Jr. of Belmont, in October 1782; the couple had three sons and eight daughters. He served three terms as governor, from 1816 to 1819, and was undoubtedly the richest man elected to the office, having inherited his uncle's estate, including the Northampton Iron Works and Hampton plantation in Baltimore County. Rosalie Calvert wrote of his election, "They wanted to make my husband [George Calvert] Governor of Maryland this year, but I persuaded him to refuse this honor and it was conferred on General Ridgely who has a large fortune and nothing to do." (See Figure 127 on page 298)

Tuseday 8th ✎ a fine day. this after noon the race was won by Mr. Carnan Ridgley's[266] Bay Horse. thare was only 2 started, the Bay & a gray belonging to Mr. James Williams, thay ran but 2 Heats[267]

Wednesday 9th ✎ a fine day

Thursday 10th ✎ a fine day

Fryday 11th ✎ a fine day

Saturday 12th ✎ a cloudey morning

1793 Sunday Octr 13th ✎ a fine day. in the evening Mrs. George Johnston sent for Nancey to sleep with her Mr. Johnson's from Home[268]

Munday 14th ✎ a fine day, Nancey is at Mr. Johnstons to night

Tusday 15th ✎ a cloudey cold day. in the after noon a littel rain. this morning Mrs. Small[269] died in the 64 year of her age. this after noon, wee made a Fire in the shop with stone coal for the first time this Fall

Wednesday 16th ✎ a clear cold day, this after noon Mrs. Small was buried, her corps was attended by a grate number of peopel

Thursday 17th ✎ a fine day. more modarate then yesterday & the day before

---

267 Ridgely's horse Trimmer won the Jockey Club purse.

268 Mrs. Johnson may simply have wanted another adult in the house while her husband was absent, or she might literally have wanted Nancy to share her bed, or at least her room. It was customary for people to share beds and so rare to sleep in a room without other occupants that when the usual roommates were absent, substitutes would be sought.

269 Charlotte Small was a midwife, who wrote her will in October, leaving her small two-story frame house on Green Street to Bishop Francis Asbury and a legacy to Margaret Peacock, who lived with her. Margaret "Peacock" is undoubtedly the Margaret "Peaco" who married Methodist minister Joseph Wyatt in 1795 (see 29 May 1802). The Wyatts were tenants in Asbury's house in 1798. The history of Calvary Methodist Church identifies Catherine Small, a Scottish woman, as one of leading Methodists in the early years, but this individual may have been Charlotte Small. In the accounting of her estate, William Paca, Mrs. Ogle, and Col. Stone all owed Small £1.10.0 each, and Mrs. Ridout owed her £5.0.0—charges that undoubtedly stemmed from her work as a midwife.

Fryday 18th ✍ a fine day. Majr. Joseph Simm[270] was with me this after noon and in conversaticion told me that he was born in June 1728, so that he is two months older than I am as I was born in Augt the same year

Saturday Octr 19th ✍ a fine day, in the evening turn'd cold and cloudey

Sunday 20th ✍ a fine day. its reported that the printer of the dayley paper in Baltimore[271] has been to Philada. and return'd with the Feavour to Baltimore and is sent out of Town

Munday 21th ✍ Mr. Whitcroft receiv'd a Letter from John Knapp[272] in Philada. in froming him that he has had the Yellow Feveour and has recoverd and is right well and that Knapp's Father in Law is now down with it. a fine day. my poor Mocking Bird died Last night.[273] I fixt a grate in the stove in the House and mad a fire in it. answers mighty well and the cole is very good & Burns well[274]

Tuseday 22th ✍ this morning the citicens war allarm'd at seeing at seeing the marks of the graves in the church yard[275] a fine day

1793 Wednesday Octr 23th ✍ a fine day

Thursday 24th ✍ a fine day. part of the Pettet Jurey was discharged this fore noon

---

[270] Joseph Sim (1728–1793) was the son of Dr. Patrick Sim, a native of Scotland, and his wife Mary Brooke. He was born in Prince George's County but moved to Frederick by 1781. He was an uncle of Thomas Sim Lee (see 3 April 1792) and a cousin of Jane Hanson, the mother of Alexander Contee Hanson (see 17 July 1793). His daughter, Mary Brooke Sim (d. ca.1794), married Roger Nelson (see 22 April 1799). Sim was a delegate from Prince George's, a provincial court justice, a member of the executive council, a major in the militia by 1751, and a colonel in the Prince George's militia during the Revolution. He died in Frederick County one month after his visit with Faris.

[271] There were three daily papers at this time: the *Baltimore Daily Repository*, published by David Graham, Leonard Yundt, and William Patton; the *Baltimore Daily Advertiser*, published by Philip Edwards; and the *Maryland Journal*, published by James Angell. Faris identifies Angell by name on 22 July 1794, so he may be referring here to Edwards (the other sole proprietor). Edwards established his paper in July 1792, when he was about nineteen years old. When he died, at the age of twenty-seven in October 1800, the *Federal Gazette* identified him as the proprietor of the *Maryland Journal*, formerly Angell's paper.

[272] John Knapp (d.1820) was the son of William Knapp, a watchmaker in Annapolis in the 1760s. He married Mary Phile, the daughter of Frederick Phile of Philadelphia, in August 1792. The Knapps came to Annapolis for the wedding of John's sister Mary (see 7 September). The other Knapp siblings married before Faris began keeping his diary: Deborah to John Randall in January 1783 (see 15 January 1795), Elizabeth to Burton Whetcroft in April 1789 (see 18 August 1793), and Ann to James Shaw in December 1789 (see 15 January 1795). Their brother William's widow married William Whetcroft (see 4 August 1793). The *Gazette* reported the death in the city of Washington of John Knapp, "for many years a clerk in the office of the Comptroller of the Treasury," on 31 July 1820.

[273] On the 25th, Faris notes the death of two "yellow birds." Although these are the only references to birds in the diary, his inventory listed eleven bird cages. Period portraits, particularly of children, frequently show pet birds in cages.

[274] Faris had bought 100 bushels of James River coal, at a cost of £9.7.6 plus 8/4 for carting, on 4 October. This is the first time that Faris writes of making a fire in a stove, a heating device that was beginning to replace the fireplace as it provided a more efficient means of heating a room. When he died, Faris owned a cannon stove (a form of cast-iron stove, so named because it resembled a cannon resting on its breech), valued at $.12 1/2.

[275] Presumably Faris means that they were alarmed by the number of recent graves, visual evidence of the yellow fever epidemic.

Fryday 25th ☞ a fine warm day. in the evening turn'd cloudey and like for rain. Last night the 2 yallow Birds died

Saturday 26th ☞ a very warm day. Mr. Griffin did not teach to day. he called & appologised that he was aprepairing to go to Baltimore. in the evening clouded up like for rain, and turned cold

Sunday 27th ☞ Blew very hard last Night and this morning, a cloudey cold disagreeable day and snow'd two or 3 Times, and at night it snow'd and looks as if it was a going to be very bad weather

Munday 28th ☞ a cold Blustering night and has continued cold & Blowing all day

1793 Tuseday 29th ☞ cold cloudey windey dis-sagreeable day

Wednesday 30th ☞ a cold cloudey day. looks like for snow

Thursday 31th ☞ Last night Steven Beard[276] (the Taylor) died — a cold cloudey drisley day

Novembr Fryday 1th ☞ a raney drisley day

Saturday 2th ☞ a fine day. last night Mr. Nicholas Warthan[277] died

Sunday 3th ☞ a cloudey drisley day

Munday 4th ☞ a fine day

Tuseday 5th ☞ a cloudey drisley day

Wednesday 6th ☞ rain and fair weather at times like March or April all day

Thursday 7th ☞ a fine day

1793 Novr Fryday 8th ☞ a fine day

Saturday 9th ☞ I receiv'd a note from Mr. Henrey Stockett[278] in forming me that my son Saint arrived at Baltimore yesterday and that he is right well — this has been a fine day

Sunday 10th ☞ a fine day, but it Blew very Hard last night and rain'd a littel

Munday 11th ☞ a fine day

Tuseday 12th ☞ a fine day. in the evening turned cloudey. look like for snow or rain

Wednesday 13th ☞ a rainey cloudey day, receiv'd a letter from my son Saint from Baltimore. he right weell & Harty

[276] Stephen Beard appears occasionally in the records in the 1780s, as a defendant in a court case in August 1788, as a grand juror—with Faris—in October 1788, and in John Davidson's 1785 store account for William Paca. Beard left only a small estate, valued at £56, which was divided between his brother Joseph and his sister Catherine, wife of John L. Ray, the administrator. He was not a son of Richard Beard (see 9 September 1792) but may have been related, as Richard Beard named his eldest son Stephen.

[277] Nicholas Warthan does not appear in census records or in the *Gazette* (although other members of the family can be found there), nor in the probate records.

[278] Possibly Henry Stockett (1759–1808) of All Hallow's Parish, son of Lewis and Katherine Stockett.

Thursday 14th ✒ a clear cold windey day

1793 Novr Fryday 15th ✒ this after noon I had John Hides[279] warren try'd before Mr. James Maccubin.[280] he dock'd hides accot in the shoes but allow'd his price for soaling. thare fore I have the cost to pay and I accordingly super ceeded it — this has been a fine day

Saturday 16th ✒ a fine day. planted 7 colleflowers & Hung 7 by the stock root upwards in the celler

Sunday 17th ✒ a cloudey morning. in the afater noon & night rain

Munday 18th ✒ clear and cold after a very Blustering night

Tuseday 19th ✒ a fine day

Wednesday 20th ✒ a fine morning. in the after noon clouded up. in the evening rain'd

Thursday 21th ✒ a bad rainey & Blowing night and rained most of the day. in the evening the ellections closed and Horatio Ridout[281] was ellected

1793 Fryday Novr 22th ✒ a fine day. Mr. McClain is in Town & is to preach this evening in the Stad House

Saturday 23th ✒ a cloudey dull day

Sunday 24th ✒ Blow'd & rain'd Hard last night, a fine day

Munday 25th ✒ a fine day

Tuseday 26th ✒ a fine day. I planted 3 slips of Rosemary in the pot, with the egg pland and 2 slips in the garden by the side of the Smoke House

Wednesday 27th ✒ a fine day

[279] John Hyde (1765–1819), a boot and shoemaker, was probably related to Thomas Hyde (see 21 June 1792) but the exact relationship is not clear. He married Sarah Jane Wells (d.1826), the daughter of Daniel Wells Sr. (see 24 February 1801) in February 1789. Hyde's shop was located on Conduit Street, opposite George Mann's tavern. In the 1790s he leased the tanyard of Thomas Hyde on Spa Creek between Bishop and South Streets. Hyde served as a councilman and as a commissioner for the city. § Faris purchased many pairs of shoes and slippers from Hyde for his family, as well as 22 1/2 pounds of butter, between 1791 and 1793, but bought none after this date. Charles Faris's estate paid him 8/5 and Faris collected £1.9.1 from Hyde in September 1801 as administrator of Charles's estate.

[280] In this episode, Hyde and Faris were in disagreement over Hyde's charges, and Faris had the suit heard before James Maccubbin (see 7 July 1793), a justice of the peace. Small suits could be heard by a single justice. Maccubbin eliminated Hyde's charge for shoes, but not the expense of resoling, leaving Faris liable not only for that debt but also for the costs of trying the suit. Faris consequently appealed the case to the full court.

[281] Horatio Ridout (1769–?) was the son of John and Mary Ogle Ridout (see 6 October 1797) and the brother of Samuel (see 17 July 1793). He married first in 1791 Rachel Goldsborough, the daughter of Robert Goldsborough (1733–1788) and sister of the Goldsborough brothers who married Nicholas Worthington's daughters (see 8 November 1792 and 23 July 1793 entries). After her death in June 1811 at Whitehall, Ridout married, in October 1812, Ann Weems, daughter of Col. John and Mary Weems (see 15 October 1795). A lawyer, Ridout was admitted to practice in the Anne Arundel County court in April 1791, and served as a councilman in 1793. In this instance, Ridout was elected to the lower house as a delegate from Anne Arundel, replacing Nicholas Worthington, who had died while in office; he held the seat through 1796. The Ridouts lived on Southeast Street, in one of the three brick town houses that Horatio's father built in the early 1770s. § Faris collected 9/4 from Ridout in September 1801 as administrator of Charles's estate. Ridout owed Faris's estate 11/2.

Thursday 28th ✒ a cloudey drisely day

1793 Fryday Novr 29th ✒ rain'd hard last night, this morning drisley & cloudey, I have concluded to go to Baltimore in the French Town packett Capt. Thomas[282] and am readey am readey only waiting for thare seting off. 11 oclock the Boat went away with out me for which I am not very sorrey as it is a dull drisley disagreeable day and the wind at NE and very littel of it

Saturday 30th ✒ a cold windey day. I think it was not unluckey for me that I did not go in the french Twon packet for I was taken with a bad gripeing and Lax

Sunday Desr 1th ✒ a fine day. I took last night some Hott todey when I went to bed and had my feet washt & I think I am better to day

Munday 2th ✒ a fine day. sett off for Baltimore about 3/4 after 9 oclock. wee had an agreeable passage. thare was several passangers, wee arriv'd to Baltimore about 8 oclock or a littel after and a Mr. Williams and my self whent to a Mr. Speck's,[283] had a glass of todey each & our supers and went to bed

1793 Tuseday morning Desr 3th ✒ got up earley & went down to the point, to see my son St. Brackfast'd with him at whare he Boards, and after Brackfast went to see Capt. Francis DeCross[284] in a Large 3 deckd ship call'd The Gift of God — of Burdux, but last from St. Dominqo. I dined with him & several other gentlemen, in the after noon I left them. the Capt. made me promis to come next day — I went to Saint, with him went to super and return'd on Board the snow (at this time it was snowing very hard it began to snow about 12 oclock) whare we made a good Fire by wich wee satt talking till about 11 oclock. I then went to bed in the Capts cabbin

Wednesday Desr 4th ✒ still snowing a littel. the snow was nearly 18 inchs deep, bad traveling. about 4 oclock St took a turn with me up to town, its very bad traveling. I went to a few places in town and return'd to the point, and din'd at the same plase as yester day, call'd and seed Mrs. Berry[285] & Mr. & Mrs. Steel[286] in the evening. sup'd and Lodg'd as yesterday

Thursday 5th ✒ a fine day. Brackfasted with Saint & Capt. Travers[287] at his house. about 9 oclock the

[282] Capt. Thomas could have been William Thomas who lived at 5 Shakespeare Street in Fells Point in 1800, or pilot Robert Thomas, who lived on Fleet Street in the same year, or Capt. Barton Thomas who married Mary Probart, both of Baltimore, in November 1805.

[283] Henry Speck, tailor and operator of the Indian King Tavern, lived at 2 Water Street in 1796. The tavern was a boarding and lodging house complete with livery stables.

[284] Capt. DeCross, who does not appear in any Baltimore City directories, was almost certainly a French citizen.

[285] Lucy Rhodes Berry, wife of Capt. Robert Berry, was born in Virginia on the James River. The Berrys lived in Fells Point at the corner of Wolfe and Alisanna [Aliceanna] Streets. The minister of old St. Paul's Church in Baltimore married their daughter Ann and Richard Pitt, brother of Ann Faris's husband William Pitt, in 1801 (see 17 April). Faris often visited the Berrys on his trips to Baltimore.

[286] Capt. John Steel and his family lived in Fells Point, where the household in 1790 contained four adult white males, six white females, and six slaves. Steel's wife Henrietta died at age fifty-three in November 1800, and he died in his 71st year in September 1809.

[287] Probably William Travers, a ship captain who lived at 29 George Street in Fells Point in 1796. He may also have been the Capt. Traverse of the *Antelope*, who cleared out of Baltimore in 1785.

boat call'd for me. I went on bord. thare was several passangers and did not get to Annapolis till a 11 oclock at night & Kittey Cook was married to Jonas Clapham[288]

Fryday 6th ✒ a cloudey day

Saturday 7th ✒ a foggey day & very bad walking

Sunday 8th ✒ a fine day but very Bad walking

Munday 9th ✒ a fine day

Tuseday 10th ✒ a cloudey day like for snow

Wednesday 11th ✒ a fine day

Thursday 12th ✒ a fine day

1793 Fryday Desr 13th ✒ Doctr Schoff gave me a Riceipt to prepair a medican [medicine] for my daughter Nancey, who has been out of order for some time — a fine day

Saturday 14th ✒ a fine day

Sunday 15th ✒ a fine day

Munday 16th ✒ a fine day. in the after noon clouded and in the evening rain'd a littel

288 Jonas Clapham (1763–1837) was one of eleven children, the son of John Clapham, a government clerk, and his wife Rebecca Green. Jonas was named after his maternal grandfather, Jonas Green, printer of the *Maryland Gazette* and public printer for the province. Clapham's death was noted in the 31 August 1837 issue of the *Maryland Gazette*: died in Baltimore City, 28th inst., in his 75th year; he was a native of Annapolis, but for the last forty years a resident of Baltimore. Catherine Cooke (d. 1849) was a daughter of attorney William Cooke (see 22 March 1792). On 17 May 1795, Faris recorded, but then crossed out, a false rumor of her death. In 1817, Rosalie Calvert wrote of Clapham, who had replaced his father-in-law as the Calverts' business agent, that "he is our agent, a very haughty man and Mr. Cooke's step-son." § John Clapham patronized Faris's tavern in 1773 and 1776.

102 ✒ A Front View of the State House &c at Annapolis, the Capital of Maryland.

Faris attended a number of public lectures on religion that were held in the State House.

A Front View of the State-House &c. at ANNAPOLIS the Capital of MARYLAND.

Tuseday 17th ✒ a fine day

Wednesday 18th ✒ raind Hard this morning & about 10 oclock it thunder'd & lightened. in the afternoon clear'd away and the sun shined out in the evening

Thursday 19th ✒ a fine day

1793 Fryday Desr 20th ✒ a cloudey day

Saturday 21th ✒ Hyram sett off to walk to Baltimore this morning at 10 oclock to see his brother St. John and to endeavoure to stop him from going the voyge to Amsterdam on accot of the Algereens[289] — a fine day

Sunday 22th ✒ a fine day

Munday 23th ✒ a fine day

Tuseday 24th ✒ a fine day in the evening about 10 oclock Hyram returned home from Baltimore, he left Saint right well, he expects to sail to morrow and intends wrighting to me from the Capes he laughfs about the Algereens

Wednesday 25th ✒ a rainey morning in the after noon clear'd away

1793 Thursday 26th ✒ snow'd a littel last night and this morning, but cleard away the coldes day this winter

Fryday 27th ✒ clear & very cold

Saturday 28th ✒ a fine clear day but cold

Sunday 29th ✒ this morning the House of Assembley Brok up, and the members thare off push'd for the track Home as quck as possible — a fine day

Munday 30th ✒ a fine day and more modarate

Tuseday 31th ✒ a cloudey drisley morning. in the after noon clear'd away

[289] The Barbary states of North Africa—Morocco, Algiers, Tunis, and Tripoli—demanded protection money from countries whose ships sailed the Mediterranean Sea. Ships of countries refusing to pay faced attack and possible capture. In 1801, the Pasha of Tripoli would declare war on the United States, President Jefferson would send a naval squadron to protect ships already in the Mediterranean, and a treaty in 1805 would end payment of tribute in return for a large ransom to secure the release of imprisoned sailors. The report in the 19 December issue of the *Gazette* of a truce between Portugal and Algiers must have prompted Hyram's alarm: "Our vessels will now be exposed to the most imminent hazard of capture, as it was the Portuguese squadron alone which hitherto prevented the Algerines from cruising in the Atlantic against them."

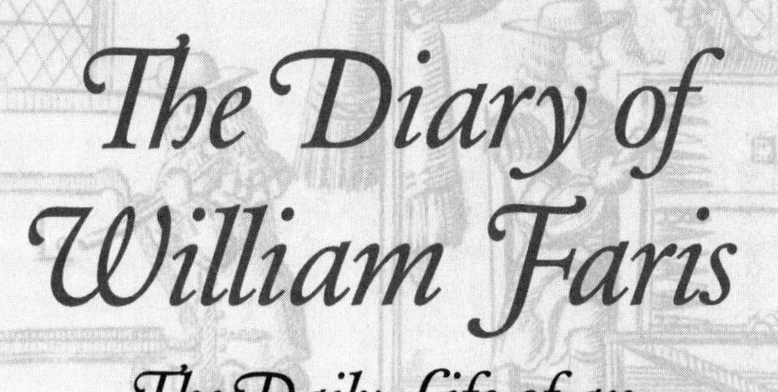

The Diary of William Faris

The Daily Life of an Annapolis Silversmith

PART TWO
1794–1795

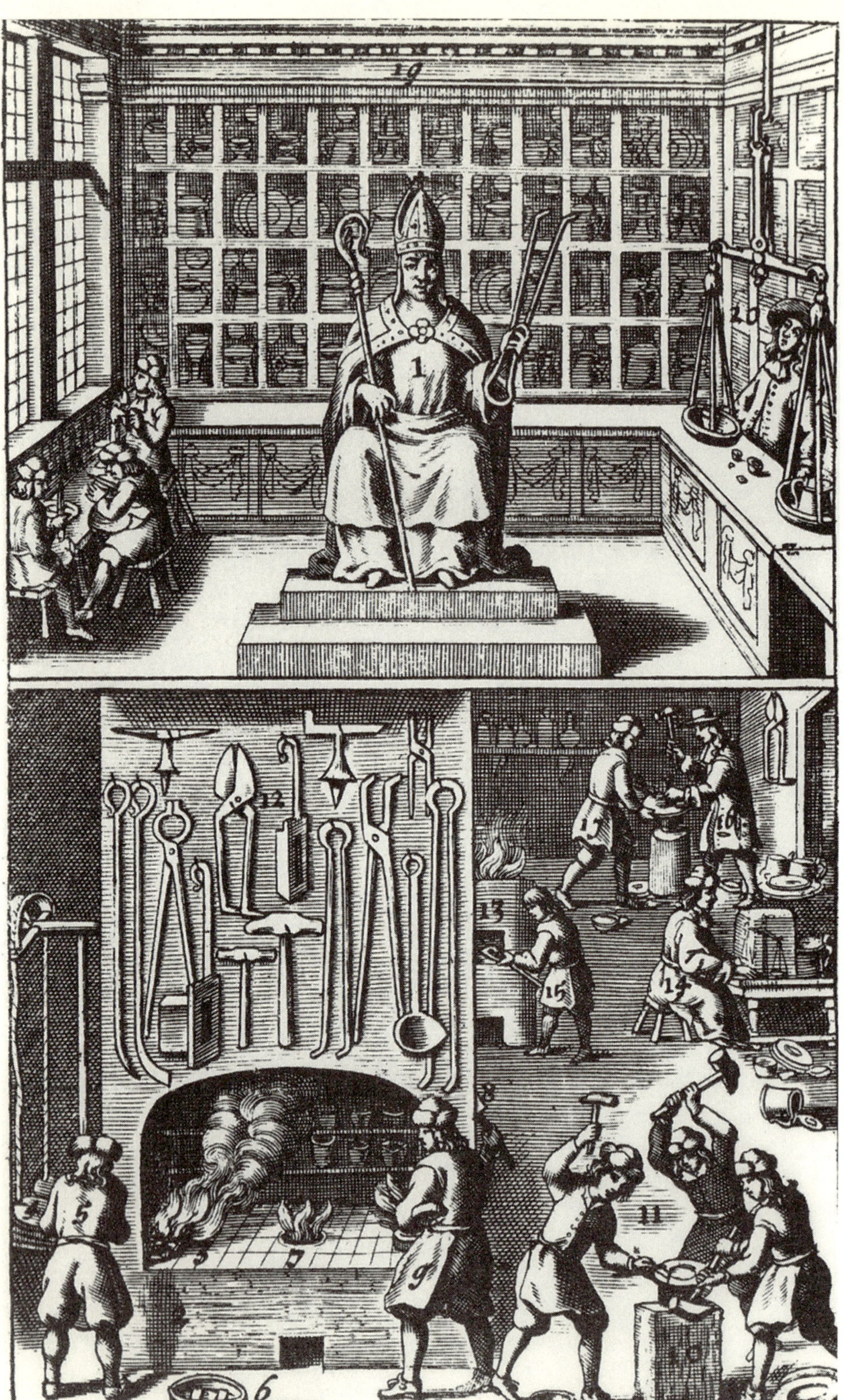

103 ☞ *This view of a silversmith shop shows all the elements, from the forge to the tools, needed for a successful operation. Although Faris would not be working until almost eighty years later, the "art and mystery" of the trade had continued unchanged.*

1794 Wednesday January 1th ❧ a very fine day. Mr William Wimes[1] dined with me. after diner Mr Warfield[2] & Mr Baker call'd in & spent an Hour or two

Thursday 2th ❧ a fine day

Fryday 3th ❧ a cloudey day. in the evening rain

Saturday 4th ❧ a warm fine day

Sunday 5th ❧ a fine day

Munday 6th ❧ a fine day

Tuseday 7th ❧ a cloudey day & looks like for snow

Wednesday 8th ❧ a fine day

1794 Thursday January 9th ❧ a dull cloudey morning. in the after noon drissley and small rain. in the evening Miss Deberoug Ghislin marryed to Mr. John Johnston[3]

Fryday 10th ❧ a cloudey day

Saturday 11th ❧ a drisley cloudey day

Sunday 12th ❧ Blew very Hard last night. a cold morning. a fine day but cold

Munday 13th ❧ a cold cloudey drisley day

Tuseday 14th ❧ a clear cold day. this after noon Mr Mackubins's Brigg arriv'd from the West Indies after being out 5 or 6 months and given over

Wednesday 15th ❧ a clear cold day. this morning Thomas Yates[4] came heare from Baltimore very unwel with a Lax and vomiting. I went with him to Mr Williams's and got him an order to go to the poor House[5]

---

[1] Probably William Weems (1758–?), the son of David Weems (1706–1779) and his second wife, Esther Hill (1717–1776), and a younger brother of Col. John Weems (see 15 October 1795). The family Bible notes that he committed suicide through an overdose or overuse of laudanum. § Faris collected £1.2.6 from Weems in April 1802 as administrator of Charles's estate.

[2] There were a number of Warfields in Anne Arundel, making it difficult to identify Faris's visitor. He might have been the father of Henry Warfield (see 15 February 1796), who attended St. John's briefly and whose death Faris reports (see 15 February 1796). § At least five different Warfield men patronized Faris's tavern in the 1770s.

[3] John Johnson (1770–1824) was the son of innkeeper Robert and Ann Johnson (see 7 April 1793) and the brother of Robert (see 12 January 1792) and George (see 20 January 1793). Deborah Ghiselin (1771–1847) was the daughter of Reverdy and Mary Ghiselin (see 21 January 1792). Her sister Catherine married Robert Johnson in January 1792. Johnson was a councilman, alderman, and mayor for two terms. He also served two terms on the executive council, in the senate from 1801 to 1805, and as attorney general, judge of the appeals court, and chancellor following the death of Alexander Contee Hanson (see 17 July 1793). Chancellor Johnson died in Hancock, Maryland, while on his way to meet with Virginia's commissioners to establish a boundary line between the two states at the head of the Potomac. § Sometime between 1794 and 1800, Charles Faris made a silver ladle, engraved with the monogram "JDJ," for John and Deborah Johnson (see Figure 62 on page 70). Faris collected £1.0.10 from Johnson in June 1801 as administrator of Charles's estate.

[4] Thomas Yates (c.1751–1815), an army officer during the Revolution, was an auctioneer in Baltimore. He married Mary Myers in August 1778; she died in January 1802. Two of their sons, Thomas (age eleven) and Charles (age nine), entered the St. John's grammar school in 1798.

[5] "An Act for the relief of the poor" (1768, Ch. 29) provided that "there shall be an alms and work-house erected in the several counties," levied an assessment of fifteen pounds of tobacco per taxable for three years, and appointed five trustees for Anne Arundel County: Thomas Beale Worthington, Nicholas Worthington, Thomas Dorsey, Lancelot Jacques, and Upton Scott. A subsequent act (1771, Ch. 36), noting that the trustees had not been able to find land for sale convenient to Annapolis, extended the suitable area to a ten-mile radius. In February 1775, Nathan Hammond, then one of the trustees, placed a notice in the *Gazette* looking for cedar posts and rails to fence the property, so the poor house must have been built or nearly completed by that time. It was located about a mile outside of Annapolis, near the present-day intersection of West Street and Taylor Avenue. James Williams, as a justice of the peace, could authorize admission to the poor house, which also provided medical care.

1794 Thursday 16th ✍ a fine day. receivd a Trunk with his close and a Letter from my son St dated Cape Henrey Janry {9?}th by Mr. William pitt. he left Baltimore the day after Christmas day

Fryday 17th ✍ a dull cloudey day. the 3 girls went to the Play this evening for the first time[6]

Saturday 18th ✍ a dull cloudey day

Sunday 19th ✍ a very fine day. in the evening Miss Elizabeth Sprigg is Married to Mr. [blank] of Baltimore marchant[7]

Munday 20th ✍ this morning betwen 9 & 10 oclock a companey of about 26 Ladeys besides gentlemen (in that companey was my self, Mrs Faris, Nancey & Abee and Charles & Hyram). wee had a very agreeable day and came ashore betwen 4 & 5 oclock. a fine day

1794 Tuseday Janry 21th ✍ rain'd last night. a cloudey morning, but clear'd away a good day

Wednesday 22th ✍ a very foggey morning and a warm day

Thursday 23th ✍ it rain'd & snow'd and Blew very Hard last night. Blew Mr. Wallaces's ~~stable down & kiled 2 Horses~~ had an old House Blown down & a sulkey mash'd. a clear windey day

Fryday 24th ✍ a cold windey day with flying clouds of snow and very squaley

Saturday 25th ✍ a clear cold windey day

Sunday 26th ✍ a cloudey snowey day

1794 Munday Janry 27th ✍ a clear cold day

Tuseday 28th ✍ a clear cold day

Wednesday 29th ✍ snow'd & Hailed all day

Thursday 30th ✍ a fine day after a very bad night of Hail & Wind

Fryday 31th ✍ clear and cold

Saturday Febury 1th ✍ a very cold clear day

Sunday 2th ✍ a cold day

Munday 3th ✍ a cloudey day

1794 Tuseday Febry 4th ✍ a fine day cold

Wednesday 5th ✍ a clear cold day

6 The bill of fare that evening included the comedy *Road to Ruin* (its first Annapolis performance), *The Caledonian Frolick,* and *The Deserter.*

7 Hugh Thompson (1760–1826) was a Baltimore merchant, living at 20 North Frederick Street in 1796. Elizabeth Sprigg was the daughter of Richard and Margaret Caile Sprigg (see 13 May 1792).

Thursday 6th ✍ a cloudey morning. in the afternon began to snow

Fryday 7th ✍ a cloudey morning. clear'd away about 11 oclock, a fine afternon

Saturday 8th ✍ a fine day

Sunday 9th ✍ snow this morning and looks as if it would turn to rain. it continued snowing & raining all day

Munday 10th ✍ a foggey morning and continued so all day

Tuseday 11th ✍ a fine day

Wednesday 12th ✍ a warm cloudey day. in the evening rain

Thursday 13th ✍ a fine day

Fryday 14th ✍ a cloudey day

1794 Saturday Febry 15th ✍ a fine day

Sunday 16th ✍ a fine morning. in the afternoon clouded up and snow'd

Munday 17th ✍ a fine day

Tuseday 18th ✍ a fine day but cold

Wednesday 19th ✍ like to March weather, flying clouds of rain & sunshine. put the frame of the Bee House to geather

Thursday 20th ✍ a cloudey drisley day. I rought to my son William by Capt. Griffith[8] who is Bound to the Havannah — Mrs. Faris is very unwell. she went to bed after diner. in the evening I think she is a littel better, she swetted a littel. in the evening rain

Fryday 21th ✍ cold & the wind Blows very hard. Mrs Faris is still very unwell. Doctr Murray was to see her to day & sent her a Bolos[9] to take at bed time

1794 Saturday Febry 22th ✍ a fine day. the Vollenter Companey peraded in thare new close & cutt a good Figure and went through the fireings very well.[10] Mrs. Faris's is still very unwell but I think something better. Doctr Murray call'd to see her and told me to give her some Perigorick ellexer & wine drops at night and make a decockcion of Barke for her to take to morrow

[8] Possibly Owen Griffith, who lived in Fells Point in 1790.

[9] From the Greek word for lump, a pharmaceutical preparation ready to be swallowed in the form of a pill.

[10] The parading marked the observance of Washington's birthday. After the maneuvers of the volunteer company led by Capt. John Gassaway, the participants retired to Archibald Golder's tavern—across West Street from Faris—for dinner. The revelers drank sixteen toasts, including one to the officers of the French frigate, *L'Astree*, which would stop in Annapolis again the following month.

Sunday 23th ✍ a disagreeable morning, snows very fast. about 10 oclock changed to rain & snow in the evening clear'd away. Mrs. Faris still very Ill, her feveour's High. nither of the Doctrs called to day. in the evening I gave her some salt of Tarter sugar & water

1794 Febry 24th Munday ✍ a very cold day and snow'd. Mrs. Faris's something better but has a bad cough. she's taken bark twice to day. Doctr Murray called in to day and said she might take some Bark. Doctr Murray sent Mrs. Faris a small vial of stuff to take at bed time to allay her cough

Tuseday 25th ✍ a very cold day. Mrs. Faris still as she was. she's troubled with a nasty Hacking cough. Doctr Murray sent her a small viol of drops & a littel spemarcity & sugar, in the evening he desir'd me to put a Blister to Mrs. Faris's side & give her 20 drops of Lodnum & 30 drops of Antimonil wine. I sent to Doctr Shoff's shop for a littel Diaccalum[11]

Wednesday 26th ✍ a fine day. Mrs. Faris's littel or no better. the blister put on last night did not draw, Doctr Murray sent her 3 or 4 pill to take and a Blister to be put on to night — I think this evening Mrs. Faris's a little better. I warrented Joseph Clark and had it try'd this afternoon before Mr. James Maccubin at Archibald Golder's. Judgent went in my faveour for dept and cost. Clark appeald to the County Court[12]

Thursday 27th ✍ a fine day. Mrs. Faris is much better to day. her blister drew very littel. Doctr Shoffe sent her some vinagar of squills[13] & Honey

Fryday 28th ✍ a fine day. this morning Mrs. Faris appear'd to be good deal better, but in the afternoon her feveour came on & she's very poorley. Doctr Shoof was heare this morning & ~~desired~~ order that she's to have no medicen but the vinagar of squills

Saturday March 1th ✍ a fine day. Mrs. Faris's still very poorley. Doctr Murray sent her 3 Bolles's, she took one about 3 oclock. he call'd again about 5 and forbid giving any more until 9 oclock and no more all night unless she should be very restles

1794 Sunday March 2th ✍ a very fine morning. Mrs. Faris is better. took no medicin to day. in the evening clouded up & rain. Mrs. Faris is to take a bolos to night at bedtime

[11] *Spermaceti*, a waxy substance obtained from the head of the sperm whale, was used in preparation of ointments such as cold cream and rose water ointment. *Antimony* in a powdered form was used as an emetic. *Diachylon* is an adhesive plaster whose primary ingredients are lead oxide and oil.

[12] As in his suit with John Hyde, Faris sued Joseph Clark and had the case tried before a single magistrate, in this case James Williams. The loser of the case again had the right to appeal the verdict to the full court, as Clark did. Faris's account book does not indicate the nature of Clark's debt. On 18 September Faris notes that he won his case in the full court.

[13] The fleshy inner scales of the white variety of the bulb *Urginea maritima*, used as a diuretic, emetic, expectorant, and cardiotonic.

Munday 3th ✒ a gustey day, right March weather. Mrs. Faris's much better. Doctr Murray sent her a Boles to take at bed time

Tuseday 4th ✒ a fine day but cold. Mrs. Faris is much Better. Doctr Murray call'd this morning and said he thought she would not want aney more medicen

Wednesday 5th ✒ snowing all day. Mrs. Faris is much Better. she complains of her Blister hurting her. otherwise shes in a fair way of geting well

Thursday 6th ✒ rain'd most of the night and all day till the evening. Mrs. Faris is Braveley to day and am in hopes she will be down stairs as soon as the weather comes good

1794 Fryday March 7th ✒ a cold cloudey morning. about noon clear'd away a fine afternoon. Mrs. Faris is Braveley but cant come down stairs on accot of the weather

Saturday 8th ✒ a cold disagreeable day. in the evening turn'd more mild. Mrs. Faris is braveley and would be down stairs onely the weather is so cold

Sunday 9th ✒ a fine day

Munday 10th ✒ a very fine day. Sylve a began to digg in the lott for parsnips

Tuseday 11th ✒ a very fine day. Sylvea's finished digging the ground for the parsnips and began to clear the litter out of the garden

1794 Wednesday 12th ✒ a fine day. dress'd the assparagrass beds and on the near one sow'd earley York and Lettice and on the other, on the end next Steven's I sow Cabbage. the other end Brocklo & Cabage and Lettice on the wole and betwen the beds Spinage

Thursday 13th ✒ a fine day. in the after noon clouded up like for rain. Phil has finished the Bee House

Fryday 14th ✒ a cloudey drisley morning, sow'd the Ice plant & sencitive plant in potts — betwen 12 & 1 oclock Hyram began to plant Parsneps rows 9 inchs wide & 6 inches from seed to seed — thare has been a Quarrel at G. Man's betwen Capt. Kelty and the French officers.[14] it seems that Kelty struck one of them. thare was 2 or 3 drew thare swords but

[14] Officers of the French frigate, *L'Astree*, whose arrival in Annapolis Faris recorded on 29 September 1793, and whose departure he notes on the 23rd of March. The vessel wintered over in Baltimore, calling in at Annapolis again on her way down the Bay.

by the interferrence of the By standers thare was no mischief don. Kelty was got away and carried home. I got a small Box of Turner's Cerate of Doctr Murray to dress Mrs. Faris's Blister — Phil began to repale the fence betwen the garden and lott for which I am to give him 5/

1794 Saturday March 15th ☞ a drisley cloudey day. Phil could not work nothing don in the garden. Capt. Kilty & french officers have mad Frinds

Sunday 16th ☞ a very warm fine day. Hyram sow'd som of the Tree or Pershion Tobbacco seed

Munday 17th ☞ a fine warm day. this morning I move'd the stacks out of the lot intend puting vines thare. Silve weel'd som dung on the Border next to Grayhams. she's diging it up. I have Planted the Burgomott Baulm out and sow'd Loaf Spinege in drill to the Peach Tree, the rest of the Border I sow'd with Radishes, Cabbage and Lettice. in the after noon, Sylvea made Hills in the lott and I Planted Simmilins, Cucumber, Watermellens and Cantilope seeds & Silvea's began digging part of the littel quarter next the old stable for carrots

1794 Tuseday March 18th ☞ a fine day. Miss Betsey Wright is married this day to a French officer whose name is [Nicholas Gremel].[15] he has been in Town 8 or 10 days. he courted her or rather was in her companey 6 or 7 Times and cannot speake one word of English nor she one word of French — Sylve has begun the big bed

Wednesday 19th ☞ a fine day. Hyram finished planting the parsneps, [h]as sowed a bed of carrots the rows 8 inchs apart. Phil has finised the fence, and Sylve has not quite finished the big bed

Thursday 20th ☞ a fine day. Sylve's finished the big bed and Hyram's made a begining to cut the Box. the General & Capt. of the frigat has came down and the officers & women & Betsey Wright that was are all gon on Bord & its expected the Frigett will sail this evening or to morrow. several of the officers called & took leave of the Famely

1794 Fryday March 21th ☞ a fine morning. Hyram Finish'd the Box the lower part and has began the Box by the littel House. it came on to rain in the after noon, he left off. I planted egg plant seed in a pott — Last night Mrs. Fairbrother died ~~76~~ 56[16]

---

[15] Nicholas Gremel and Elizabeth Wright received a marriage license on 18 March 1794.

[16] Probably Ann, the widow of Francis Fairbrother (c.1729–c.1785). Fairbrother was a councilman, Annapolis tax assessor, and justice of the peace in the early 1780s. The Fairbrothers leased a red house and its lot on the south side of Church Street, just above Green Street. The couple had one child, Elfreda, who was married to John Kerr (see 27 December 1792). § Fairbrother served on the St. Anne's vestry with Faris in the 1780s.

Saturday 22th ✍ a fine day. Hyram finished cuting the Box about a eleven oclock and came out of the garden, whe had something to do in the shop. this after noon Mrs. Fairbrother was Buried

Sunday 23th ✍ a fine day in the after noon the French Frigett, "Les Astree" sett off for Hamton Road[17]

Munday 24th ✍ a fine day . this morning I made the trenches and Becky[18] sow'd the peas. Sylve covered them with pea sticks. Bob came betwen 7 & 8 oclock.   made up the tabel round the Bed and Hyram to troweling the flower beds. I Had some business that call'd me down town. when I came back Bob was gone. in the afternoon Sylve went to taking up the Baum which I had told Bob to do and I replanted it in the evening. John Johnston and wife sett off this fore noon for Alleganey County

1794 Tuseday March 25th ✍ a fine day, Sylve weel'd dung on the littel quarter and dug it up and went to cleaning the walks and I replanted the sage and planted the Tube Rose Roots and Hyram finished digging the flower beds

Wednesday 26th ✍ a clear cool morning.   planted the littel quarter with 6 rows of Bunch Beans, Hyram's a digging and doing the Water Table round the grass walk, Sylve's cleaning the walks

Thursday 27th ✍ a coole raw day. Hyram finish'd the tables round the grass. in the evening looks as if it would rain, it would be of service

Fryday 28th ✍ a raw cold day, nothing done in the garden to day except marking some of the Blew Hyacinths. orders are come to naval officers to lay an Imbargo on all vessels from going to furren ports[19]

1794 Saturday March 29th ✍ continues coole disagreeable weather

Sunday 30th ✍ still cool disagreeable weather. in the evening looks likely for rain. its much wanted

Munday 31th ✍ a fine morning with small rain. the Cucumbers and Water Melleons are acuming up that ware planted the 17th of March, this afternoon the citizens mett and chose a committe to do something in regard of haveing the citee fortifyed. a clever littel rain this evening

[17] Hampton Roads, the channel in southeastern Virginia between the mouth of the James River and the Chesapeake Bay. It provides the last protected anchorage for ships leaving the bay.

[18] The first occasion on which Rebecca helped her father in the garden.

[19] The embargo came in response to British seizures of American ships engaged in trade with the French West Indies. Britain and France were at war, with American opinion strongly divided: Federalists supported Britain, Republicans favored France. Congress adopted the embargo after rejecting a Republican plan for commercial retaliation against Britain, and sent John Jay to England to negotiate a settlement of the maritime dispute that would avert a war. Annapolitans obviously feared that the embargo might lead to hostilities with Britain and that Annapolis might be attacked, hence the desire expressed over the next week to have the city fortified.

March, 1794

Tuseday April 1th ~ a cold windey day, Sylve has dug the littel Border next the Lott & I planted the following things. Viz No. 1 the strawberrey tree see[d] 2 the Hedge Hog. 3 Snails. 4 Caterpillars — and in the evening sow'd a short row of Tip up on Tipto peas, on the end of the littel quarter next to Stevens's. Mrs. Boardley's Jacob[20] brought me some cutings of the strawberrey Tree. I planted 4 in the garden and 3 in the lot

1794 Wednesday April 2th ~ a fine day. Sylve acleaning the walks. in the evening the citizens ware to have mett at the Stad House to heare the report of the committe. a few did meate, the report was read and agreed to. it was requesting the Govenor & Council to petition Congress to reconsider the matter and fortify Annapolis — I sow'd Jobe's tears on the Border next the lott & on the end of the bed next the old stabel

Thursday 3th ~ a rainey morning. I sow'd the following things on the Border next the Lott. No. 5 the Satten Flower No. 6 India pinks — and at the end of the stable the Flowering pea, and Convolvalis Miner at the peach Tree by gate. Bob came about 10 oclock and went for been sticks.[21] he brought a parcel of sticks that ware too small. in the after noon he brought 9 in the course of the after noon & thay war as much too big. a fine evening

Fryday 4th ~ a fine morning. Bob's Bringing poles. he makes a poore Hand of it

1794 Saturday April 5th ~ a cold windey day. Bob has not made his appearence to day

Sunday 6th ~ a fine morning. cut 6 stocks of assparagrass. in the after noon, turn'd cold. clouded up like for rain

Munday 7th ~ a cold day

Tuseday 8th ~ still cold. this evening the citizens met and drew a pettition to Congress praying that Annapolis may be Fortifyed and put in a state of Defence[22]

Wednesday 9th ~ a rainey day

Thursday 10th ~ a dull drisley cold day

Fryday 11th ~ a cold raw morning. about noon clear'd away more modarate. I planted 13 seeds of the Pride of the East. No. 7. got them from William Weems

[20] Probably the slave of Sarah Fishbourne Mifflin Bordley (1733–1816), the Philadelphia-bred second wife of John Beale Bordley (1727–1804). Bordley owned a house located between Tabernacle and Northeast Streets, off State Circle, but preferred to live on his Wye Island estate (acquired through his first marriage to Margaret Chew) and rented the Annapolis property.

[21] Faris sent Bob to gather sticks and branches that he could use as bean poles.

[22] The 17 April issue of the *Gazette* reported that on the 8th, senator William Vans Murray (representing an Eastern Shore district) had requested appointment of a committee to bring in a bill to fortify Annapolis. The fort would protect "the safety of the records and state papers . . . the state treasury . . . the wealth of the city, and . . . the navigation of the bay of Chesapeake." The motion carried and a committee was appointed.

1794 Saturday April 12th ✒ a cold rainey day. this morning old Jenney came heare at [blank] shillings pr month[23]

Sunday 13th ✒ a cloudey morning, William Whitcroft sett off, for George Town in his sulkey for George Town & Jossiah King[24] on horse Back with him

Munday 14th ✒ a fine morning. Sylve cleaning the walks. a fine day

Tuseday 15th ✒ a fine day. replanted the cimelin hills & cucumbers & melleons. in the evening water'd them

Wednesday 16th ✒ a fine warm day. Mrs. Faris was taken very Ill this morning with chill & Feaveour. Doctr Murray sent her a bottel of medicen to take 2 Table spoon fulls every 3 Hours. it came about 4 oclock. he & Shoff ware both out of Town. in the evening I planted out satten flower plants and took the sticks off the peas this morning

Thursday 17th ✒ a dull cloudey day, phil took plank to make the Bee Hives, Mrs. Faris is braveley to day. she is down stairs. Mr. James Williams's wife died[25]

1794 Fryday April 18th ✒ Charles sett off for Baltimore this morning about 8 oclock. a fine day. Mrs. Williams was Buried this after noon

Saturday 19th ✒ a fine day. Charles returned from Baltimore betwen 5 & 6 oclock this afternoon

Sunday 20th ✒ a fine day

Munday 21th ✒ this morning Sylve Hill'd the peas & Beens and soon after came on to rain and rained at times all day. Old Jenney went off this morning with out biding fare well, Mr. John Callahorn's wife gave her more wages

104 ✒ Sarah Buckland Callahan (1763–1839) and her daughter Anne Callahan (1785– ?)

Sarah Buckland married John Callahan in 1782; Anne was one of her three daughters.

25 The 17 April issue of the *Maryland Gazette* reported that Mrs. Eliza Williams, wife of James Williams, Esq., of Annapolis, died on the 16th inst.

---

23 Faris noted in his account book for this date: "Old Jeney began her month this morning at [blank] shillings pr month."

24 Josias W. King was William Whetcroft's son-in-law, having married Whetcroft's oldest daughter Letitia (b.1771) in July 1791. King was the clerk of the committee of grievances and of the courts of justice in the mid-1790s. The wedding was described in a contemporary letter as "a very merry wedding in our neighborhood: Miss Letty Whetcroft to a Mr. King—Miss Lowry was at the ceremony, and all the entertainments which were very numerous, in ten days there were five Balls etc. etc."

[26] The theater on West Street was first mentioned in the *Gazette* in August 1772, when the American Company of Comedians performed there. In 1775 the St. Anne's vestry agreed to equip the playhouse for church services until the new St. Anne's Church was built. The land itself remained part of William Reynolds' leasehold and thus was inherited by his daughter and her husband, Alexander Trueman. A 1794 Chancery Court case involving Trueman's estate indicates that William D. Beall bought the theater lot lease for £130. Trueman's own house and lot, formerly Reynolds' tavern and currently occupied by William Goldsmith, Esq., were sold by decree of the Chancery Court in April 1794. John Davidson bought the property for £1,020 but died in October before completion of the sale. In August 1798, trustee Gabriel Duvall transferred title to Eleanor Davidson, who was already living in the house.

[27] Cornelius Mills (c.1755–1823) was for forty years sergeant-at-arms for the House of Delegates. He married Elizabeth Goldsmith in January 1775; after her death (see 30 September 1797), in January 1800 he married Anne Blackwell Wischam, whose death Faris reports in February 1801. She was the widow of John Wischam, a cavalryman during the Revolutionary War and a storekeeper, who died in 1798. A carpenter and joiner, Mills was also a tavernkeeper in the 1780s and 1790s. For a few years he operated in William Reynolds' former home on Church Circle adjoining Faris's property. The establishment mentioned here was described in the *Gazette* as "Mill's Garden;" this name and other references by Faris suggest that this tavern was on the outskirts of the city. Mills' son Washington entered the St. John's grammar school in 1794 at the age of sixteen; when his younger brothers enrolled in 1800, they did so under the patronage of Philip Barton Key (see 29 May 1792). Mills' stepsons William and John Wischam, eight-year-old twins, also enrolled in 1800. When Mills died in 1823 at the age of 67, the *Maryland Gazette* described him as "a patriot, and an active participator in our revolutionary struggle." § Mills patronized Faris's tavern in 1779 and Faris paid him £22.10.0 in May of that year. Faris collected £5.1.2 from Mills in October 1802 as administrator of Charles's estate. Expenses for the administration of Faris's estate included £3.15.0 paid to Cornelius Mills, auctioneer, probably for handling the sale of Faris's personal property. At that sale, Mills bought fifty-four files, one lot of musical instruments, and two books.

Tuseday 22th ✒ a raney morning. cleared away in the after noon. Mr. John Davidson Bought Majr. Trums House for £1025, & Maj. Beal Bought the ground rent of the Play House[26]

1794 Wednesday Apl 23th ✒ a cloudey morning. in the evening clear'd away

Thursday 24th ✒ a cloudey drisley day

Fryday 25th ✒ cloudey. I planted 4 rows of earley York plants. about noon & in the after noon rain, in the evening clear'd away fine. Mr. W. Pitt brought Tickets to Nancey & Abee and thay went to the Show

Saturday 26th ✒ a fine day

Sunday 27th ✒ a fine day

Munday 28th ✒ a fine day. Sylve stuck the peas and Hilled them & How'd the ground betwen them

Tuseday 29th ✒ a fine day but rather coole

Wednesday 30th ✒ a fine morning. about noon wee hired an old neagro woman by the name of Phillis at 15/ pr month. a fine day

1794 Thursday May 1th ✒ a fine morning. earley this morning the Vollenteer Companey march'd out of Town to Mills's[27] and dance'd round the Liberty Tree and returned to Town. I marked the following Flowers

No 1 Best Tulips	48	11 White Hyacinths	66
3 Red d⁰	200	12 Red d⁰	278
4 White d⁰	32	13 Blew d⁰	75
5 Black d⁰	8	14 Winged d⁰	
6 Yallow d⁰	62	15 Red Crown Imperel	7
7 Parrot tails d⁰	21	15 Yellow d⁰	7
8 Doubel d⁰	61	16 John Quills	3
9 Red & White d⁰	32	17 White Nercess	18
10 Seedlings d⁰		18 Yallow d⁰	9

about 10 oclock the Vollenter Companey met and march'd out to the ground by the Collage and went through thare exercise & Fireing. about 12 oclock thay ware dismis'd, the Govenor was with them.

the Companey & a large dined at Mills's and in the evening a Ball at George Manns.[28] a very fine day

1794 Fryday May 2th ✒ a fine day. in the evening receiv'd a Letter from my son Saint John dated Texel Road[29] March 3th 1794. he arrived at the Texel Road the 28 of Febry

Saturday 3th ✒ a fine day

Sunday 4th ✒ a fine day

Munday 5th ✒ a fine day. in the evening looks like rain

Tuseday 6th ✒ a drisley cloudey cold day. No. 7 sowed some seed from Mrs. French Thomas[30] which is called [blank]. thay are good for sore eyes by puting the Leaves in cold water which will turn it like thin starch, then wash your eys with it, then apply the leaves to the eyes. its like wise good in the flux by puting the leaves in cold water & makeing a glister[31] off it

1794 Wednesday May the 7th ✒ a fine day

Thursday 8th ✒ a fine day but too cold for the season

Fryday 9th ✒ still cold for the season. phill has Finished the Bee Hives

Saturday 10th ✒ still cold for the season

Sunday 11th ✒ a fine warm day

Munday 12th ✒ a very warm day in the evening looks as if thare would be rain

Tuseday 13th ✒ a fine day but very warm

Wednesday 14th ✒ a fine warm day. in the evening thare was a fine shower of rain. Mrs. Deborah Sprigg[32] was heare to day. she tells me that my accot has pass'd the commissary but she could not convenientley pay me at this time

1794 Thursday May 15th ✒ a fine day

Fryday 16th ✒ a fine day

Saturday 17th ✒ a fine day

Sunday 18th ✒ a fine day but very cold for the season

Munday 19th ✒ very cold for the season

Tuseday 20th ✒ a fine day but cold for the season

28 The *Gazette* described the day's events in very much the same terms as Faris used, although Faris omitted the liberty cap that accompanied the liberty pole and the fourteen toasts, many of them expressing support for France. Faris's account brackets his list of marked flowers and is complete only when his two descriptions are combined: marching on the college green with review by the governor, entertainment at Mills with liberty pole and toasting, and evening ball at Mann's Tavern. The volunteer company was led by Capt. John Gassaway (see 29 December 1792).

29 Texel Island, part of the Netherlands, is located on the North Sea, guarding the entrance to Amsterdam.

30 There are no records of a French Thomas during this time period, but it is possible that Faris meant the wife of Capt. James Thomas (see 25 May 1795), with whom he exchanged seeds in 1797.

31 A medicinal liquid, in this case perhaps to be administered in an enema; Faris's inventory contained "one box with glyster pipe compleat," used for that purpose. Fuller's *Pharmacopoeia Extemporanea* (1710) provides recipes for a wide variety of glysters, some to be administered externally and others internally, both by mouth and by means of an enema.

32 Deborah Woodward Sprigg was the widow of Frederick Sprigg (1749–1791) of Montgomery County. She may also have been related to Priscilla Woodward Faris. Her husband's estate owed money to Faris, the commissary's office (responsible for supervising probate matters) had approved payment, but she lacked the funds to settle with Faris at this time.

Wednesday 21th ☞ a fine day

Thursday 22th ☞ a warm day

Fryday 23th ☞ this morning I planted some seeds of the reasons on the Border next Grayhams. a fine day. in the evening a clever littel shower of rain

1794 Saturday May 24th ☞ wee had a clever rain Last night. a fine day with little showers. I planted out plants this morning & some in the evening

Sunday 25th ☞ a cloudey morning. Mr. G. Johnston & Mrs. Johnston & Nancey went off this morning to Mr. Hopkins's.[33] returned in the evening all well. littel Susan was heare all day. this evening its reported that one of the young Courtneys[34] is drownded in crossing the creek from Mrs. Hesselious's. the report is contridicted, its not true, he is well at Mrs. Hesselious's

Munday 26th ☞ a fine rain Last night. a cloudey day, painted nine of the Bee Hives

Tuseday 27th ☞ a fine day

1794 Wednesday May 28th ☞ a rainey day

Thursday 29th ☞ a fine day. Phill dugg the walnutt tree bed

Fryday 30th ☞ a cold cloudey morning. in the after noon and night windy cold & rain. the pettit jurey of the General Court's discharged to day

Saturday 31th ☞ Mrs. Bernard's[35] dead, the wife of a french man that lives in George Johnston's House. rained at times all day

Sunday June 1th ☞ a cloudey morning. about 10 oclock Mrs. Bernard was Buried. the weather clear'd away a fine after noon

Munday 2th ☞ a fine day. planted the walnut tree quarter with plants, gathered the wallnuts and goosberreys. Sylve Pull'd up 2 rows of Peas and dug the ground and wed the littel quarter of [torn]

1794 Tuseday June 3th ☞ this morning planted 2 rows of Bunch Beans in the Bigg Bed. Capt. John Kelty's wife's Brought to bed of a fine Boy about 8 oclock this morning, a fine day

Wednesday 4th ☞ a fine morning. in the after noon a fine rain

33 Probably Elijah Hopkins, the son of Gerard Hopkins (d.1778) and his wife Mary Hall (d.1788), whose sister Sarah was married to John Cowman (see 9 June 1794). The two families, both friends of the Farises, were members of the Society of Friends, as was Faris's father William. Elijah married first Hannah Howell, of Philadelphia, in 1777 (see 6 December 1795), and second Sarah Snowden, daughter of Samuel and Elizabeth Snowden of Prince George's County. Faris appears to have maintained ties to the Quaker community—not only by his friendships with the Cowmans and Hopkinses but also by visits from Philadelphia and English Quakers.

34 These were undoubtedly the two sons of Hercules Courtenay, a Baltimore merchant, who were enrolled in the St. John's grammar school—Edward, age thirteen, and William, age eleven—from April 1793 until April and June, respectively, of 1796. In 1796 Courtenay was secretary of the Maryland Insurance Company at 16 South Street.

35 The wife of Pierre Bernard. Bernard and his family were "late of the Cape François," that is, refugees from the revolution in Saint Domingue. In April 1797 Pierre, age twelve, and Alexander, age eight, enrolled in the St. John's grammar school; Joseph, age seven, joined them in 1800. Pierre Bernard also appeared as a creditor of Abraham Claude in January 1800 (see 26 January 1795).

Thursday 5th ✒ a rainey day

Fryday 6th ✒ a fine day

Saturday 7th ✒ a fine morning. about noon rain, in the afternoon cloudey like for rain. Nancey's gone to Mr. Johnstons to be redy to sett off earley in the morning to Mr. Hopkins's

1794 Sunday June 8th ✒ rained a good deal last night and this morning earley. Mr. G. Johnson & Nancey went off this morning ½ after 7 oclock. appears to be clear & be a fine day. in the after noon cloudey and in the evening rain after 8 oclock and Mr. G. Johnson's not come to Town

Munday 9th ✒ Mr. George Johnson & Mrs. Vandering[36] came to Town about 6 oclock this morning. lefft Nancey well at Mr. Cowmans[37] — a fine day

Tuseday 10th ✒ a fine morning. planted 3 rows of Bunch beens in the big bed. in the after noon gustey, in the evening was brought from the Head of Severon two 18 Pounders in a flat[38]

Wednesday 11th ✒ a fine day

Thursday 12th ✒ a fine day. in the afternoon a fine rain. in the evening cleared away

Fryday 13th ✒ a fine morning. in the after noon gustey

1794 Saturday June 14th ✒ a fine morning. in the after noon rain

Sunday 15th ✒ Chares went of to Messrs Cowman's and Hopkins's to see his sister Nancey. a fine day

Munday 16th ✒ Charles came home last night after I went to bed. he tels me Nancey's braveley and that he left her at Mr. Elijah Hopkins's whare shes to stay till Wednesday. a cloudey showerrey day, this evening thare was a dust cicked up. thare has been 1100 catriges taken out of the armery, thar was gards and Protroling the Town all night

Tuseday 17th ✒ this fore noon thare was partey went through the Town & sarch'd every House for guns & armes and several was found amongst the neagroes. several neagroes ware taken into custodey and some commited

1794 Wednesday June 18th ✒ a fine day

36 Mrs. Vandering, or Van Deren, was George Johnson's mother-in-law (see 20 January 1793). Faris mentions her three times and spells her surname differently each time.

37 John Cowman (1737–1808) was a Quaker who lived near Governor's Bridge, on the far side of the South River. He married Sarah Hopkins, daughter of Gerard and Mary Hopkins (see 25 May 1794). Both families were friends of the Faris family, with whom they often exchanged visits. § Faris bought a quarter of beef from Thomas Cowman in January 1801; the account of Faris's estate listed a debt of £1.8.17 from the estate of Thomas Cowman.

38 Cannon, perhaps brought to Annapolis in response to the petition for fortification.

105 ✒ Antoine Laurent Lavoisier (1743–1794) and His Wife (Marie Anne Pierrette Paulze), (1758–1836)

Jacques Louis David's painting depicts the same apparatus for experimenting with hydrogen ("inflammable air") that Faris was using in the 1790s.

39 Faris's inventory listed "one large bottle for inflamatory air," valued at $3.00. Inflammable air was the name first given to hydrogen, whose discovery is credited to Henry Cavendish. The *Philosophical Transactions of the Royal Society* contain a number of papers in the 1780s by Cavendish, Joseph Priestley, James Watt, and others describing experiments designed to determine the properties and behavior of inflammable air. There is no evidence that Faris read the *Philosophical Transactions* but he was clearly aware of the experiments. Faris's vitriol was probably oil of vitriol, or sulphuric acid, with which he hoped to fill his bottle with hydrogen, through the reaction of the acid upon an unspecified metal.

40 Hyram had joined one of the Annapolis militia companies. In September 1797, he received an appointment as a lieutenant.

41 This may have been Richard Giles Brewer, who died of dropsy in June 1799. Brewer advertised goods for sale in June 1794, and was also a constable and clerk of the market from 1795 until his death. In July 1797 he was appointed sheriff. Although undoubtedly a member of the extensive Brewer family, his exact relationship is not documented.

Thursday 19th ✒ a ffine day

Fryday 20th ✒ a fine day

Saturday 21th ✒ receivd a letter from Nancey by Mr. Cowman's son, she is well & he dined with us. I finished my Bottel to hold Inflamable Are[39] but could not fill it for want of Vittrol. I got some from Charles but it's good for nothing, it would not do. it has been a fine day. Mrs. Elizabeth Gassaway's yungest daughter Kittey was taken unwell last night or this morning and is this evening very Ill

Sunday 22th ✒ Mrs. Gassay's daughter died ~~last~~ about 1 oclock. this has been a fine day

1794 Munday June 23th ✒ a cool cloudey dull day. this evening Mrs. Gassaways daughter was Buried

Tuseday 24th ✒ a fine day

Wednesday 25th ✒ a fine day

Thursday 26th ✒ a rainey day. in the evening clear'd away but the weather dont look setteled

Fryday 27th ✒ a cloudey drisley day. white washed the big room. in the after noon Mr. John Onion & wife drank Tea with us

Saturday 28th ✒ a dull driseley fore noon. in the after noon clear'd away. this evening the 4 Compeny mett, Hyram in his ridgementels for the first time[40]

1794 Sunday June 29 ✒ a fine day. Mr. & Mrs. Onion dined with us. in the evening look gustey as if wee should have rain

Munday 30th ✒ a fine day

Tuseday July 1th ✒ a warm day

Wednesday 2th ✒ a cloudey morning. Nancey came home about 10 oclock & Mr. Cowman with he[r]. he dined with us. in the after noon and evening it rained

Thursday 3th ✒ a fine day

Fryday 4th ✒ the companey met about 9 oclock at the church and march'd to the collage green & went through thare menuvers & Fireings & dispersd about 1 oclock. a grate maney went to Mills's & dined. a very Hott day. in the evening Richard Brewer[41] drunk had a difference with one of the young Mills who gave him a nock & Hurt him a good deel. in the evening a fine rain[42]

1794 Saturday July 5th ✍ rained allmost [all] night. this morning cloudey and came on to rain. it rain allmos all day

Sunday 6th ✍ raind & Blowd very Hard all last night. cloudey drisley morning. cleared away about 10 or 11 oclock. a fine afternoon

Munday 7th ✍ a fine day. made abegining to take up the flower roots

Tuseday 8th ✍ a fine day. Hyram's been all day takeing up roots & Sylve a Howing the walks of the garden

Wednesday 9th ✍ rained Last Night and this morning. a cloudey driseley day

Thursday 10th ✍ a fine day. Phil Norris came about 10 or 11 oclock to taking up the flower roots. he has done one Bed & begins another

1794 Fryday July 11th ✍ a cloudey drisley day. Phil did not come to work to day

Saturday 12th ✍ a rainey morning. phil's sick, not come to work. William Goldsmith came from Baltimore to day and says that the snow Commerce went up this morning. a clear after noon

Sunday 13th ✍ a fine day. this morning I receivd a letter from Baltimore & 1 doz of Pattent Led pencils.[43] he[44] is well & Hyram went to Kent Island to the Methodist quarterley meeting. he came back in the evening

Munday 14th ✍ this morning sent Saint's Trunk & close to him by John Barber.[45] a very warm day

Tuseday 15th ✍ a very Hot day. Hyram's been in the garden taking up roots

Wednesday 16th ✍ a warm day. Phil came to work to day

1794 Thursday July 17th ✍ a warm day. Phill did not make his appearance to day

Fryday 18th ✍ a very Hot day

Saturday 19th ✍ this morning Saint John come Home from Baltimore right well & Harty. a very Hott day

42 This is the first entry for July 4th that records events celebrating the day. The *Gazette* on 10 July reported that "To celebrate the Anniversary of America's Independence on Friday last . . . in the evening there was a ball at the assembly room." Although Faris frequently mentions balls attended by one or more of his daughters, apparently none of the girls went to this one.

43 N. J. Conté in 1795 first produced pencils—using a graphite core, mixed with certain clays, pressed into sticks, and fired in a kiln—by the method that still forms the basis for the manufacture of all lead pencils. Faris, always a man ahead of his time, may have obtained pencils produced by the German firm of Faber, which used a variety of different methods beginning in 1760, none of which produced satisfactory pencils. Faris does not comment on the utility of his box of pencils.

44 St. John Faris, who returned home on the *Commerce*.

45 John Barber (c.1771–1822) married Catherine Taylor in February 1794 and Susannah Rawlings in October 1796. He and his brother dissolved their partnership in 1821 and John died the following year, on the 6th of April, in his 51st year. He was survived by his widow Susan[nah].

46 Although the Faris children have already made a number of visits, either for the day or for longer periods of time, to Woodward relatives and old family friends in the countryside around Annapolis, this is the first record of an excursion to Baltimore. Long before any family members settled in that town, Nancy and her siblings made extended visits, often in the company of friends. The Faris children may have stayed with relatives of their traveling companions or in the homes of the many sea captains in the port city who were friends of their father.

47 James Angel, one of the proprietors of the *Maryland Journal*, sold the paper in December 1794 to Francis Brumfield. By 1796, Angel was an officer of the revenue in Baltimore, living at 119 Baltimore Street. He died in September 1797.

48 Thomas Wilson was an Annapolis merchant, who leased a house just down the block from Faris at the corner of West and Cathedral Streets in 1775, but sold the lease three years later to Capt. John Pitt, father of William (see 20 October 1792). The Chancery Court judged Wilson insane in 1789. § In March 1762, Faris sued Wilson for "dealing with" one of his servants without Faris's permission, but Faris defaulted by not appearing in court when the case was heard.

Sunday 20th ✒ a fine day. Mrs. Vandren & Mrs. Johnson dined with us. in the after noon a littel shower of rain. my daughter Rebecca complains of a pain in her Head & Has a fevour

Munday 21th ✒ this morning Mrs. Hamelton, my daughter Nancey, Betsey & Rebacka Gassaway sett of about 9 oclock in the packett for Baltimore.46 a fine day

Tuseday 22th ✒ this morning about 8 oclock Saint sett of For Baltimore in the stage in companey with Mr. Angel the printer47 — to take the snow Commerce as Captain, a fine day

1794 Wednesday July 23th ✒ a fine day

Thursday 24th ✒ receiv'd a letter from Nancey, she's well. thay did not get to Baltimore till 2 oclock in the morning. a fine day

Fryday 25th ✒ a fine rain this morning before day. Charles went off for Baltimore at 9 o'clock in the packett. it drisseled at times all day, in the evening a fine rain

Saturday 26th ✒ rained hard last night and allmost all day

Sunday 27th ✒ rained all most all day till about 4 oclock then it left off, but looks cloudey as if wee should have more rain before the weather gets set-teled, Hyram took a dose of salts to day

Munday 28th ✒ a warm Fine day. Hyram's still unwell, he has got a feveour. I called in Doctr Shooffe. he order that his feet be bathed in warm water when going to bed & take some wine dropps & Lodnum

1794 Tuseday July 29th ✒ Charles & Nancey returned home from Baltimore this morning about 3 o'clock. hyram's very Ill. the doctor sent him 3 doses of James's Pow[d]ers. he began taking them at 9 oclock, about 5 he sweet a very littel. in the evening the doctr sent him som salts to be taken in the of the night. it has been a fine day

Wednesday 30th ✒ Hyram is still Ill, he had a very sever chill to day abut 3 oclock. in the evining he's something better — Allen Quynn went from Stevens's doore over to Thomas Wilson's48 and Beat Wilson's wife for telling him some Truth of him self and Famely — a fine day

Thursday 31th ⚓ Hyram is clear of his Feveour to day, he is taking Bark. a fine day

Fryday Augt 1th ⚓ Hyram's braveley to day but week, he's taking Bark. a fine day

1794 Augt Saturday 2th ⚓ Phillis went off with her self this morning before Mrs. Faris got up and while I was at market. in the after noon about 3 oclock Sylve was brought to bed of a fine Boy.[49] a fine day but very Hott

Sunday 3th ⚓ a fine day but very Hott

Munday 4th ⚓ a very Hott day

Tuseday 5th ⚓ a very Hott day

Wednesday 6th ⚓ a fine coole day

Thursday 7th ⚓ a fine pleasant day. Hyram's taking up the roots in the beds by the Littel House

Fryday 8th ⚓ a fine pleasant day. in the evening looks cloudey and like for rain

Saturday 9th ⚓ a rainey day

1794 Sunday Augt 10th ⚓ this morning about 9 oclock Mr. George Johnson & wife & Mrs. Vanderen and Famely sett off for the Hed of the Bay on thare way for Philadelphia.[50] a fine morning — an express came in from the President to the Govenor that thare should be a darft of 2500 of melisha of this state to be sent out against the Insurgents of the frontier of Pensylvania[51]

Munday 11th ⚓ raind, thunder'd & Lightened Hard last night. a fine day but very Hott and sulterey

Tuseday 12th ⚓ a fine day but rather coole

Wednesday 13th ⚓ a fine Pleasant day

Thursday 14th ⚓ a fine pleasant day

1794 Fryday Augt 15th ⚓ this evening I receivd a letter from my son William (by Capt. Rock) from the Havanna dated the 22th of July, he's well. this has been a pleasant day

Saturday 16th ⚓ this is my Birth day. I am 66 & now enter into my 67 year. a fine morning, in the after noon rain

Sunday 17th ⚓ a fine day

49 Sylve's son Adam.

50 The family evidently moved to Philadelphia (see 8 April 1795).

51 The insurgency is known today as the Whiskey Rebellion. In 1791 Congress levied a moderate excise tax on distilleries, an act that met its strongest resistance in western Pennsylvania, where farmers profited from distilling their excess corn into whiskey. Thomas Mifflin, governor of Pennsylvania, refused to enforce the law, despite low levels of violence from 1791 to 1793. In July 1794, when federal officials tried to bring some of the protestors to trial, rioters burned the tax collector's home, killed a soldier, and threatened to secede from the Union. In response, Congress authorized the president to call out the militia. On 7 August Washington called out about 13,000 militia men from four states, including Maryland. Accompanied by generals Daniel Morgan and Henry Lee, Washington led the troops over the Allegheny Mountains, whereupon the insurgents dispersed and the rebellion ended. See also entries for 27 August, 13 to 16 September, and 26 to 27 September. The Annapolis troops apparently went no farther than Frederick.

Munday 18th ✍ a fine day

Tuseday 19th ✍ this morning Miss Betsey & Rebecka Gassaway returned from Baltimore — a fine day

Wednesday 20th ✍ a fine morning. in the after noon rain

Thursday 21th ✍ a fine day

1794 Fryday Augt 22th ✍ a fine day

Saturday 23th ✍ this morning about 4 oclock Hyram sett off for Baltimore to see his Brother Saint. a fine day

Sunday 24th ✍ rain'd very Hard in the Night and at times all day. tharefore it may be sett down as a rainey day

Munday 25th ✍ a cloudey morning. dug & sow'd on the Border next to Grayhams at the end next the Burgandy Baum cabbage seed from Mrs. J. Davidson & further on early York seeds. a fine day

Tuseday 26th ✍ I was taken very unwell last night owing to suden change of weather. it turned very cold in the nighit. I took cold & it fell on my bowels which put me very much out of order that I did not get up scarcely the whole day. a cloudey drisley day

1794 Wednesday Augt 27th ✍ a fine day. Hyram was drawn yesterday to serve in the millitia to go to the west ward — he returned this evening from Baltimore. left his Brother Saint well

Thursday 28th ✍ a fine day. I find my self very poorley, a gripeing in my Bowels

Fryday 29th ✍ a fine [day]. I find my self a good deel Better

Saturday 30th ✍ a fine day

Sunday 31th ✍ a fine morning. Charley went of to prince georges county to try after a substitute[52]

Munday Sept 1th ✍ a fine morning. in the after noon a very seveare gust of rain thunder & Lightening

1794 Tuseday Septr 2th ✍ a very warm day. in the evening clouded up like for rain

Wednesday 3th ✍ a cloudey drisley day

[52] Someone who, for a fee, would be willing to take Hyram's place in the draft.

Thursday 4th ✒ a receiv'd a Letter from my son St. who Informes me that thay are very sickeley at Fells point. thay die 10 or 12 of a day. Mrs. Maggey Ross[53] is dead, she died the 2d of Septr. this was a cloudey morning & rain'd at times most of the day. in the evening clear'd away fine

Fryday 5th ✒ a fine day. in the evening John Knapp and wife came to Town from Philadelphia

Saturday 6th ✒ a fine day. in the after noon Beeat the walnuts off the Tree and got I supose a Bushel of nutts. in the evening looks like rain

1794 Sunday Sept 7th ✒ a rainey morning. in the after noon clear'd away and coole. this evening Miss Polley Knapp's to be married to a Mr. Dobbins of Allexandria in Virginia[54]

Munday 8th ✒ a fine day but rather coole. on Saturday Last William Goldsmith told me that he saw my son Saint and that he was well and that he would be home on Munday, by some accident he has not come, his mother is very unhappy on the dissopointment for fear that he should be either sick or dead, as thay are so very sickeley at the point in Baltimore

Tuseday 9th ✒ a fine day

Wednesday 10th ✒ Charles sett off this morning for Baltimore. a fine day

1794 Thursday Septr 11th ✒ a fine day. in the evening Charles returned home from Baltimore. left his brother St. well

Fryday 12th ✒ a fine day

Saturday 13th ✒ this morning Charles was taken very Ill with a Billious Feveour[55] I gave him some wine drops which puked & Brought of a grate deal of Boyl {bile?} . I sent for Doctr Shoof, he came and orderd him 3 papers of Antimonial Powders. the first he puked up Immediatly, I gave him another which stay'd on his stomack. in the after noon he began to swet and it Puked him. in the evening he got better and I hope it will go off & he'l be Bravely. the Artillerey Companey is order'd to march to Fredrick Town & Capt. Guym[56] & severel of his Companey turned out as Vollenteers to go guard the Armerey & magazeen in Fredrick Town.[57] it has been a fine day

53 Most likely Magdalene Pitt Ross, widow of John Ross (see 23 February 1793). The wording of Faris's entry suggests that Mrs. Ross lived in Baltimore rather than Annapolis; she may have moved there after her husband's death to live with her widowed mother, Ann Pitt.

54 Archibald Dobbins was the son of Archibald Dobbins Sr., a native of Ireland who died in Baltimore in May 1808 in his seventy-second year. Mary Knapp was the daughter of William Knapp, an Annapolis watchmaker (see 21 October 1793).

55 A complex of symptoms that included nausea, abdominal discomfort, headache, and constipation; formerly attributed to excessive secretion of bile.

56 John Gwinn (c.1756–1809) was the clerk of the general court of the western shore from June 1791 until his death. He was also a manager of the orphans' school lottery, a councilman, and an alderman, as well as captain of the first volunteer company of the militia. He owned several lots on Franklin Street, just south of Faris's home on West Street, which he acquired in 1794. In 1798 he was a tenant of John Hoskins Stone (see 29 September 1794), living in a three-story brick house on Church Street. In 1805 and 1806 he operated the City Tavern, but in January 1807 Mary Mann (see 5 January 1792) advertised the two houses for lease again. § Faris received $40 (£15) from Gwinn in October 1799 for tulip roots and collected 17/9 from him in November 1800 as administrator of Charles's estate.

57 The *Gazette* reported on 18 September that General Smith gave a speech in Baltimore trying to recruit three hundred infantry volunteers to defend the Frederick arsenal.

1794 Sunday Septr 14th ✍ Charles is something better. I gave him Bark twice this morning, after wards his feveour came on. the doctr directed me to give him some thing and give him Bark which I did. he complains of a pain in his Head. it's been a fine day

Munday 15th ✍ this morning another draft of the melletia took place in Blew & Buff, the shirts & Artillerey Companeys, one man in four was drafted. Capt. Guym's and other Vollenteers marchd to day. Charles is Braveley. a fine day

Tuseday 16th ✍ Lieutenant Davidson brought Hyrams substitute and I paid him 35 Dollors. 9 of the Light Horse went of for Fredrick this after noon. I am in hopes Charles will be well now, to night he is Braveley. it rain'd this morning but cleared away a fine day

Wednesday 17th ✍ a fine day

1794 Thursday Septr 18th ✍ I defeat'd Joseph Clark, I obtained a judgment against him in court. a fine day. in the evening it Lightened very much to the north ward

Fryday 19th ✍ a very warm day. Mr. Jonathan Willmore[58] & Mr. A. Golder both promisd to wright to Joseph Clark to pay the money[59]

Saturday 20th ✍ a fine day

Sunday 21th ✍ a fine day but cold

Munday 22th ✍ a fine day

Tuseday 23th ✍ in the fore part of the day it rained, in ye afternoon cloudey & cold

1794 Wednesday Septr 24th ✍ a cloudey cold day. this evening Majr Wright, Doctr Shooff & a nother came in George Town, whare Genral Lloyd[60] and Majr Wright[61] whent & Fought a duel. Lloyd receivd two wound, one slite in the neck the other in the arm & Wright a slight wound in the arm

Thursday 25th ✍ a cloudey drisley day

Fryday 26th ✍ rained, Thundered & Lightened very hard Last night. a fine day. in the after noon the Vollenteer Companey returned to Town from Fredrick, all well except John Tootel[62] who thay left in Fredrick Town sick, in the evening the Fiffer was Buried with Honors of War. he had been sick some Time

[58] Jonathan R. Wilmer (d. 1805) served as a member of the executive council for three terms from 1797 to 1799.

[59] Clark had moved to Washington, D.C., by this time.

[60] The *Gazette* carried no report of the duel and Lloyd is not listed as a militia officer, although his title of "general," like Wright's "major," may stem from service in the Revolutionary War.

[61] Robert Wright (1752–1826), of Queen Anne's County, served with distinction during the Revolutionary War. A lawyer, he was a delegate from Queen Anne's in 1784 and from Kent County in 1786. Wright served in the U.S. Senate from 1801 until 1806 when he was elected governor of Maryland. He resigned in 1809 during his third term in expectation of election to fill a vacancy on the court of appeals but was not selected for the post. Wright sat in the House of Representatives from 1810 to 1816 and from 1820 to 1823, when he was appointed associate district court judge, a position he held until his death.

[62] Probably the son of James and Ann Tootell (see 16 July 1797). When James Tootell, John's brother and a purser in the U.S. Navy, died in 1809, his estate was divided among his five surviving siblings, but John was not among them, indicating that he had died.

William Faris

1794 Saturday Septr 27th ✒ a fine day.
in the after noon his Excelency the Govenor
and Troop of Light Horse returned from
Fredrick and at night Capt. Guym's
Companey Parraded through the Town with
a Cap of Libberty[63] with several Lights
round it and the Companey (singing the
Carmanol[64]). thay cut a figure and looked
well

Sunday 28th ✒ a fine day but in the
evening clouded up like rain

Munday 29th ✒ a very Hott day — in the
evening the grate & mighty General J. H.
Stone[65] call'd a meeting of the Town in
regard of the disorder in Baltimore.[66] thay
did littel, few met, thay adjurned till to
morrow morning

Tuseday 30th ✒ a few of the peopel met at
Stathouse this fore noon and went into
resolves to endeveour to prevent the disorder
from being Brought to Town. about 2
oclock the Packett arrived from Baltimore with several Passengers on bord. thay ware not sufferd to
come on shore till thay took an oath that thay had
not been ware the disorder was & then permited to
come on shore — thare is guards fixed at Sandy
Bottom, at Rutland's warf & at Severn ferrey —
thare is a grate change in the weather, since
morning it has Turned very cold

October 1th Wednesday ✒ a very cold rainey day.
oblig'd to have a fire in the House

Thursday 2th ✒ cleared away this fore noon.
became a fine day & modarate. my sone St. John

106 ✒ John Hoskins Stone (1750–1804)

*Faris described Stone as "the grate & mighty
General J. H. Stone" in September 1794.*

---

[63] Based on the cap given to a freedman in ancient Rome at
the time of his manumission and used as a contemporary
symbol of liberty.

[64] A dance and song popular during the French Revolution.

[65] John Hoskins Stone was born in Charles County, the son
of David and Elizabeth Jenifer Stone. Stone was a descen-
dant of William Stone, governor of Maryland from 1649 to
1654, and brother of Thomas, one of Maryland's signers of
the Declaration of Independence. Stone married Mary
Couden (1760–1792), daughter of Annapolis merchant
Robert Couden (see 9 January 1792), in February 1781. He
held a commission in the Maryland Line from January 1776
to November 1779, serving as a captain in William
Smallwood's regiment (see 16 February 1792) and participating with distinction in the battles of Long Island,
White Plains, and Princeton, before being seriously
wounded at Germantown. Stone resigned his commission
when chosen as a member of the executive council, a position he held until 1785 when elected a delegate to the
General Assembly from Charles County. Stone served
three terms as governor from 1794 to 1797. After his last
term expired, he made his home in Annapolis, where he
died in October 1804.

[66] An outbreak of yellow fever.

67 A heavy, white, odorless powder, used as a cathartic.

68 The 16 October issue of the *Gazette* reported Davidson's death: "died in Annapolis, on the 11th instant, in his 57th year; he was a tender husband, a good father, the uniform patriot, and an honest man. At his sad shrine the poor, the fatherless, and the widow, will weep for the loss of their benefactor."

69 Across the South River in All Hallow's Parish, London Town was a thriving community in the early eighteenth century, but it faded away after failing in 1747 to be designated as a tobacco inspection site. It remained the southern terminus of a ferry across the river.

70 Nicholas Hannah appears neither in the census nor the probate records but does occasionally surface elsewhere. In March 1779, Hannah was the fourth sergeant of Annapolis's Independent Company of Militia; the use of "Capt." in the diary entry may indicate a militia rank rather than any naval status. The probate of William Whetcroft's estate in 1800 listed a July 1779 debt of John Lampe and Nicholas Hannah in the amount of $1,535.16. (John Lampe was a watch and clock maker who worked in Annapolis before his move to Baltimore in October 1780.) Hannah witnessed the will of Henry Oneal Welch (see 4 May 1793) in December 1784 and proved the will in May 1794. § Hannah frequently patronized Faris's tavern in 1775 and 1779.

---

came home from Baltimore the fore noon. he has had a tutch of the feaveour in Baltimore. he was taken last thursday week. he's quite well but looks thin to what he did

Fryday 3th ☞ a cold disagreeable day

Saturday 4th ☞ clear & cold. I gave Abee 8 grains of callomell[67] by Doctr Shooffs directions, at bed time

1794 Sunday Octr 5th ☞ the callamell I gave Abee worked her very much in the night. she's very poorley. she has kept her bed all day but am in hopes she will be abel to take Bark to morrow. a fine clear cold day

Munday 6th ☞ Abee is Poorley. I gave her some few doses of Bark but she could not take maney. a fine day but cold. Charles complains he's a feveour

Tuseday 7th ☞ Charles has been very unwell all day and Abee is still very poorley. shee dont get clear of her Feveour. a fine day not so cold as it was

Wednesday 8th ☞ I gave Charles a vomit this morning. he continues unwell. Abee is better, a fine day

Thursday 9th ☞ Charles & Abee's much better, thay are taking Bark a fine day. thay nither of them took aney midson from the doctor

1794 Fryday Octr 10th ☞ this morning about 2 oclock Mr. John Davidson[68] died & about 12 or 1 oclock his corps was carried out in the Herse to London Town[69] to be Buried. a fine clear cold windey day, Charles is at his shop to day

Saturday 11th ☞ a fine day. Mrs. Davidson Buried a littel neagro to day

Sunday 12th ☞ this morning an express came in with an accot of Capt. N. Hannah's[70] death. he died yesterday morning about 4 oclock. a fine day

Munday 13th ☞ Mr. William Whitcroft went of this fore noon for Allexandria. a fine day

Tuseday 14th ☞ I got a neagro man to wheel in dung and dig the flower Beds, he has dung'd & dug up the Beds next to the grass — a fine day

1794 Wednesday Octr 15th ☞ finished planting the flower Bed round the grass walk & circel. a fine day

Thursday 16th ✒ finish'd planting the flower roots in the Lower part of the garden. a fine day

Fryday 17th ✒ a fine day finished planting the flower roots

Saturday 18th ✒ a fine day

Sunday 19th ✒ a fine day

Munday 20th ✒ a fine day

Tuseday 21th ✒ a fine day

1794 Wednesday Octr 22th ✒ this morning a littel after 9 oclock Capt. Saint John Faris sett off in Capt. John Barber's boate for Baltimore, from thare he's to go to St. Michels on the Eastern Shore to take charge of a new ship, and take her to Baltimore[71] — a fine day

Thursday 23th ✒ a fine day. in the evening Mrs. William Whitcroft & daughter Fanney came to Town from Allexandria

Fryday 24th ✒ a fine day

Saturday 25th ✒ a raw disagreeable day. looks like for rain

Sunday 26th ✒ it Blow'd very Hard a near Harrican and rained all night. its Blow'd & Rained all day and looks as if it would continue to do so for some time

1794 Munday Octr 27th ✒ Blowed very Hard last night & Rained till about 9 or 10 oclock. left of raining but continues Blowing and cloudey and is turning cold

Tuseday 28th ✒ a cloudey raw cold day

Wednesday 29th ✒ Charles sett off For Baltimore about 10 oclock this morning. a fine day

Thursday 30th ✒ a fine day. Charles returned home in the evening from Baltimore

Fryday 31th ✒ a fine day. in the after noon the companey Belonging to the Town were to have mett. the Blew and Reds mett. Capt. Golder went to the grounds but his men would not meet, a few of Capt. Howards[72] companey mett but with out officers — in the evening a littel shower of rain

1794 Saturday Novr 1th ✒ a fine rain last night. a fine day

71 A notice in the 5 September *Maryland Journal* stated that the *Commerce*, with all her equipment, would be sold on Thursday next by Yates and Campbell, auctioneers. St. John would now be the captain of the *Hebe*, also owned by Jeremiah Yellott.

107 ✒ Samuel Harvey Howard (1750–1807)

Samuel Harvey Howard and his family were good friends of the Faris family.

72 Samuel Harvey Howard was the son of Samuel Howard Jr. (1717–c.1766) and his second wife Ann Harvey (1723–1774). Howard's first wife was Susannah, the niece of Charles Wallace (see 5 January 1792), by whom he had four children. In April 1789 he married Mary Higginbotham (d.1828), the daughter of Rev. Ralph Higginbotham (see 25 November 1792), with whom he had two children. Howard was a captain in the Independent Company of Militia during the Revolutionary War. He served as Anne Arundel coroner, councilman, and alderman, and was the register of the Court of Chancery. Faris recorded the marriages of three of his daughters in the diary. § Howard patronized Faris's tavern in 1775, 1776, and 1779. Faris collected £0.15.11 from Howard in May 1801 as administrator of Charles's estate.

73 Rosalie Calvert wrote of Tayloe in 1819, "You are mistaken, dear Father, about [Mr. Tayloe's] character—there are few people as frugal as he, and his wife is positively stingy. He has not been preoccupied with horseracing for some years now. They have handsome equipages and cut a fine figure in society, but they manage all this with the greatest thrift."

74 John Tayloe's gray, Diomed, won the purse of 40 guineas. James Williams' horse was the only local entry.

75 The Howards were another Anne Arundel family with several branches, all of which included men named John. This John Howard was perhaps the son of Samuel Howard Jr. (1717–c.1766) and his first wife Patience Dorsey, who were married in 1740. John, who was born in January 1747, was the older (half-)brother of Samuel Harvey Howard (see above).

Sunday 2th ✘ a cloudey day with rain at times

Munday 3th ✘ a windey cloudey day

Tuseday 4th ✘ this day Messrs. Washington, Ridgly Tayloe[73] & Williams's horses run for the Jockey Club purs, and was won by Mr. Tayloe's Horse, Williams's horse was distance'd the first heat.[74] a clear coole windey day

Wednesday 5th ✘ this day the City purs was run for by Messrs. Tayloe, Carnan Ridgley & James Williams's ho[r]ses & the Purs was won by Mr. Ridgley Hores. he won the 2 first heats, Williams's Horse was distanceded — a fine day

1794 Thursday Novr 6th ✘ a fine day

Fryday 7th ✘ a fine day

Saturday 8th ✘ this morning Mr. Gaberal Duvall went off in the stage for Philada to Congress and took his daughter Polley (that used to live at Oliver Weeden's) with him. in the evening I receiv'd a Letter from my son Capt. Faris. his ship is called the Hebe. he is right well & Hartey. a fine day

Sunday 9th ✘ a fine day

Munday 10th ✘ a dull cloudey [day]. looks like for bad weather

1794 Tuseday Novr 11th ✘ a cloudey day

Wednesday 12th ✘ a fine day

Thursday 13th ✘ a fine day

Fryday 14th ✘ Snow & Hail this morning, about 8 or 9 oclock turn'd to rain & rain'd & Blow'd hard all day

Saturday 15th ✘ a clear cold day. John Howard[75] died this fore noon about 10 or 11 oclock

Sunday 16th ✘ rained hard in the night. a fine day. in the after noon John Howards corps was taken out in the Hers to the Famely Burying ground at the Plantation that belonged to his Father to be Buryed

Munday 17th ✘ this fore noon John H. Stone was ellected govenor, the artillery compy & vollenteer ware under arms and Fired. in the evening thay march through the Town with the Cap of Liberty & drum & musick playing. a fine day

1794 Tuseday Novr 18th ✍ this day my old frind Coln. Fitzchew,[76] his son William & Mr. Hughs[77] dined with me. the Colln. & son went off in the evening. Mr. Hughs staid till near 8 oclock — a fine day

Wednesday 19th ✍ a fine day

Thursday 20th ✍ a dull cloudey rainey day. in the evening the Colts Balls to Mrs. Onion came here to dress and go with the girls. I could wish that Abee would not go for fear of her being sick. it rained & Blew very Hard

Fryday 21th ✍ a fine cold day. the Insurgents ware turned over to the Federal Court & the pettit jurey discharged[78]

Saturday 22th ✍ a fine day

1794 Sunday Novr 23th ✍ a clear & cold day

Munday 24th ✍ a fine day

Tuseday 25th ✍ a fine clear cold day

Wednesday 26th ✍ a fine day. Miss Betsey Goldsmith's to be married to Capt. Gardner this evening[79]

Thursday 27th ✍ a fine coole day

Fryday 28th ✍ a fine day

Saturday 29th ✍ a warm cloudey day & in the evening looks like for rain

108 ✍ Col. William Fitzhugh (1721–1798)

Fitzhugh, an old friend of Faris, and two of his sons visited Faris at different times.

---

[76] William Fitzhugh was the son of George Fitzhugh (c.1690–1722) and his wife Mary Mason, daughter of Col. George Mason (c.1697–1728) of Gunston Hall, Virginia. Fitzhugh was born in Virginia but moved to Maryland about 1752, settling first at Rousby Hall in Calvert County until 1793 and then in Washington County. Fitzhugh was a planter and owner of grist and fulling mills, as well as a distillery in Calvert. He was a good friend of George Washington and the owner of thoroughbreds that he raced in Annapolis. A colonel in the French and Indian War, he served as a delegate to the General Assembly from 1754 to 1783, member of the council, treasurer of the western shore, commissary general, and justice of the peace. His first wife was the daughter of Richard Lee and widow of George Tuberville; his second wife was Ann Frisby (1729–1793), daughter of Peregrine Frisby and widow of John Rousby (1728–1751). Faris noted visits from two of Fitzhugh's sons in the diary.

[77] William Fitzhugh Jr., the son of Col. William Fitzhugh, married Ann Hughes, daughter of Col. Daniel Hughes of Hagerstown (d.1818). It is probable that it was William's father-in-law who visited Faris with the Fitzhughs.

[78] Faris's final report on the Whiskey Rebellion.

[79] Obediah Gardner was a ship captain who lived in Baltimore. Elizabeth was his second wife, as the *Maryland Gazette or Baltimore Advertiser* reported his marriage to Miss Deborah Gottier of Fells Point in June 1791. Elizabeth Goldsmith was probably the daughter of William Goldsmith (see 25 March 1792).

80 Probably Frances Whetcroft, wife of William, and Elizabeth Whetcroft, wife of Burton. Sally, born 6 March 1773, and Fannie, born 19 April 1774, were the daughters of William and Frances. See 14 August 1796 for their marriages.

81 Matthew Simmons Bunbury was a ship master living in Fells Point. When he died in January 1820, his obituary described him as "long a respectable inhabitant of this city" and captain of the Sea Fencibles in the War of 1812.

82 In order to supplement the inadequate salary Chase received as chief justice of the General Court (£600), the legislature created the position of chief judge of the Baltimore County criminal court, to which post it then appointed Chase. Opponents, acting both on principle and for political reasons, eventually introduced resolutions in the House of Delegates arguing that Chase's plural office holding violated the state constitution and formally requested his removal. The House, after hearing Chase argue in his own defense, narrowly declined to consider the resolution and by a wider margin defeated the request for removal.

83 James Frazier and Anne Duckett obtained a license on 6 December 1794. James Frazier was a sea captain who lived in Baltimore in 1796. Anne Duckett was probably not a sister of Allen Bowie Duckett (see 10 November 1801), but may have been related through another branch of the family.

84 The county jail stood on Cathedral Street, one block northeast of Faris's home.

85 Palsy is a disorder of motor function, such as weakness or tremor, and pleurisy is a painful inflammation of the pleura, the membrane enveloping each lung. It is usually accompanied by chills, fever, and coughing.

Sunday 30th ✍ a warm day. in the evening the two Mrs. Witcrofts & Misses Fanney & Sallie Whitcrofts[80] and Mr. W. Pitt & Capt. Bumberrey[81] drank tea, Capt. Bumberrey's bound to the West Indies. it rains & looks like bad weather

1794 Munday Desembr 1th ✍ Mr. Samuel Chace spoke in the House of Assembley upwards of 3 Hours in vindication of his holding 2 places of Proffitt that's Judge of the General Court & Judge of the Crimenal Court of Baltimore.[82] a very rainey day

Tuseday 2th ✍ Mr. Chace carryed his point in the House. thay determened in his Faveour. a very Fine day. about 8 or 9 oclock at night it began to rain & thunder & Lighten & rain'd a good part of the night

Wednesday 3th ✍ this fore noon Capt. Gardner sett off for the West Indies. a fine day but Blows hard

Thursday 4th ✍ clear & cold

Fryday 5th ✍ this morning Charles went off to Baltimore & Miss Salley & Fanney Witcrofts went to Easton on the Eastern Shore. a fine day, in the after noon the Miss Witcrofts returned. the wind came a Head

1794 Saturday 6th ✍ a fine day. the Miss Whitcrofts went off again for East town on the Eastern Shore

Sunday 7th ✍ a fine warm day. in the after noon about 5 oclock Capt. James Frazer was married to Miss Duckett.[83] in the evening Charles returned from Baltimore

Munday 8th ✍ a cloudey morning like for rain or bad weather. turn'd cold & windey

Tuseday 9th ✍ a fine day. this morning the carpenters began to shingel the roof of the Prisson[84]

Wednesday 10th ✍ a fine day. finished shingeling the prisson

Thursday 11th ✍ a fine day. last night Mrs. Goldsmith was struck with the Palsey and Plurisey[85] and she is very Ill

1794 Fryday Desr 12th ✍ a fine day

Saturday 13th ✍ a fine day

Sunday 14th ❧ a fine day. Kittey Johnson's[86] very ill with either the yaws or Kings Evel[87] in her throte. it was thought she would have died about 1 oclock to day

Munday 15th ❧ a fine day

Tuseday 16th ❧ a fine day. it is said that Nathon Waters[88] is ded over South River. soon after I went to bed I felt a disagreeable pain in my groyne. I put my hand to the part and found that my guts had come out through a Hole in the rim of my {illegible}

Wednesday 17th ❧ a fine day. receiv'd a letter from St. he sent for his gun, and is to sail on Sunday next but dont say whare he's bound to

Thursday 18th ❧ I sent St. his gun by J. Barber. a cloudey day. Looks like bad weather cuming

1794 Fryday Desr 19th ❧ a dull cloudey raney day

Saturday 20th ❧ a cloudey Foggey morning. about a 11 oclock came onto rain & about 3 oclock clear'd away a fine evening

Sunday 21th ❧ snow'd this morning, Lawrance Oneal[89] one of the House of Assembley was Impeach'd yesterday and Try'd before the House for an offence as follows. a man had Taken up a Trackt of Land and paid every thing on it. pattenon had Issued but Govenor Edon when he went away carryed off the pattron, tharefore the Land became liable to be taken up. to prevent that and save expences the man Pettitioned the House to make good his right. ONeal seeing the Pettition in the committee room went to the Land office and Pray'd a warrant on the Land with an intent to deprive the man of it. the House acquited him with passing sentance of disgrase on him

1794 Munday Desr 22th ❧ a fine day

Tuseday 23th ❧ a fine day

Wednesday 24th ❧ a fine day

Thursday 25th ❧ a very fine day. Mrs. Gassaway and her daughter Rebacka dined with us. in the evening it rained. Mr. Gale[90] one of the members of the Assembley from the Eastern Shore died this morning & Buried this after. and Mr. Thomas Merricks[91] died this morning

86 Catherine Ghiselin, the wife of Robert Johnson (see 12 January 1792).

87 Yaws is a tropical disease characterized by raspberry-like sores on the skin. King's Evil was tuberculosis of the lymph glands.

88 Nathan Waters was a saddler, who first appeared in Annapolis in 1761 and who married Catherine, daughter of Jonathan and Martha Wilson. In 1767 he identified himself as a hatter, and as an Annapolis merchant and planter. Waters owned property in the block between School and Church Streets. His daughter Elizabeth married Archibald Chisholm, the business partner of John Shaw (see 8 March 1793), in 1777.

89 Lawrence O'Neale (1738–1815) was probably born in Pennsylvania and emigrated to Maryland with his family in 1744. He represented Montgomery County in the House of Delegates from 1780 until 1796. As Faris recounts in this entry, the House voted down a resolution to expel him on its second reading but a resolution of censure did pass. John Hamilton, the petitioner to whom Faris refers, had completed all the legal and monetary requirements necessary to obtain a patent for his land but when Governor Eden left the colony in June 1776, he took the patent with him. Hamilton's petition sought a legislative act to confirm his title, but O'Neale attempted—using the information contained in the petition indicating that the land remained legally vacant in the absence of a patent—to acquire the tract himself. The General Assembly judged that "such conduct is a violation of the rights of the people, of this state, and the duty of a representative." Despite his censure, O'Neale continued to hold office, serving as a justice of the peace, for example, from 1787 to 1797.

90 Robert Gale, who represented Somerset County only in that one year.

91 Thomas D. Merrick, Esq., of Charles County. He was probably the Thomas Merrick admitted to practice in the Anne Arundel County court in March 1787.

92 John Baker advertised himself as a tailor and habit-maker in November 1782. The 1790 census listed one John Baker in Anne Arundel, with a household of one adult white male, two white females, and thirteen slaves— *possibly* the same man.

93 Probably La Coruña, on the northwest coast between the Atlantic and the Bay of Biscay.

94 Possibly Setúbal, on the Bay of Setúbal in Portugal, just south of Lisbon. Ships imported salt from "St. Ubes," carried as ballast, during the Revolution.

95 Although St. John had been captain of the *Commerce* on his last voyage, the position as captain of the *Hebe* on its maiden voyage appears to be far more momentous for his family.

96 Capt. John Rogers lived in Fells Point in 1790. The 1796 Baltimore City Directory stated that he had a boarding house at 56 Pitt Street.

97 Schoolmaster James Crosby, whose administrator advertised on 15 January for settlement of claims against the estate.

98 Death by drowning was a common mishap. Because few people knew how to swim, any accident that resulted in immersion in deep water could mean death for the individual involved. In the winter months, cold water temperatures compromised the chances of survival even for those who could swim.

Fryday 26th ✍ Mr. Merrick's corps was carried out of Town this morning for Charles or St. Mary's County to be Buried. Mrs. Merrick & children followed in a chair with her brother on horse Back. a fine day

1794 Saturday Desr 27th ✍ the Assembley Broke up about a 11 oclock this fore noon, and in the after noon Miss Salley & Fanney Witcrofts returned from the Eastern Shore. a fine day

Sunday 28th ✍ a fine day

Munday 29th ✍ a fine day

Tuseday 30th ✍ a cloudey dull drissley day. John Baker the Taylor92 died to day

Wednesday 31th ✍ a dull cloudey Foggey day

1795 Thursday Janry 1th ✍ a dull cloudey day

Fryday 2th ✍ in the night it snow'd a littel so as to be seen on the ground in places. a fine morning, afterwards clouded & turned cold. in the evening, Capt. St. John Faris came home from Baltimore. his ship at anker in the Bay Bound to Croney93 in Spain, then to St. Tubes,94 from thare to Lisborn, then Petersburgh in Rusha

Saturday 3th ✍ a fine day

Sunday 4th ✍ a fine day. Mrs. Faris & the girls & Boys & Mrs. Gassaway & Beckey Gassaway set off to go on Bord Capt. Faris's ship.95 wee went allmost to Greensburey's point. the wind came on to Blow so hard that the women & girls all got sceard very much, Beckey Gassaway Fainted. we found the women & girls ware in such a fright we put about & came Home again about 1 oclock

1795 Munday Janry 5th ✍ this morning about 11 oclock Capt. Faris & Capt. John Rogers96 took leave of my Famely and went on bord thare ships. thay Both got under way about 2 oclock, Capt. Rogers Bound to Amsterdam & Capt. Faris to Croney in Spain a fine day

Tuseday 6th ✍ Mr. Crosbey97 was drownded last thursday. was found yesterday and Buried to day. he went over Severon aguning and by some means he was drownded.98 a fine day

Wednesday 7th ✍ rained allmost all last night. a cloudey day

Thursday 8th ✒ a dull cloudey cold
day

1795 Fryday Janry 9th ✒ a cloudey
drisley day

Saturday 10th ✒ a fine day but cold to
what it has been

Sunday 11th ✒ about 12 oclock the
Picture of William Pitt[99] fell down
from whare it hung & Broke the frame
and did not hurt the glass, and about 4
oclock in the after noon Mrs. Polley
Gassaway[100] died, a dull cold cloudey
day

Munday 12th ✒ Blow'd very hard last
night and snow'd a littel. a fine day
but cold

Tuseday 13th ✒ a cloudey morning
and very cold and looks like fallng bad
weather. about 10 oclock it began to
snow, a fine after noon but cold.
betwen 4 & 5 oclock Mrs. Gassaway
was Buried on the hill

1795 Wednesday 14th ✒ clear and
cold

Thursday 15th ✒ a fine morning. at
Brackfast Charles brought the news of James
Shaws[101] death, he died yesterday morning of a

109 ✒ Mezzotint of William Pitt

*This engraving is most likely the one that
Faris mentions as falling off the wall and
breaking its frame.*

99 Probably a mezzotint by Charles Willson Peale of William Pitt
(1708–1778), Earl of Chatham and defender of American resistance
to the Stamp Act. Edmund Jennings commissioned Peale to paint a
portrait of Pitt as his gift to the gentlemen of Westmoreland
County, Virginia. Peale's portrait, painted in 1768 using a recent
bust as a model, depicts Pitt as the friend of Liberty, in Roman
attire with classical symbolism. Peale produced a mezzotint version
of his portrait in an attempt to capitalize on Pitt's popularity in
America, but that popularity had diminished once Pitt took office
as head of the government from 1766 to 1768. Peale lamented that
he had not sold enough impressions of the mezzotint "as would pay
him the cost of the paper." That Faris owned a copy suggests that
he was a strong supporter of the patriot cause.

100 The daughter of Allen Quynn (see 9 September 1792), who
married Col. John Gassaway in January 1788. She was survived by
her husband and two children.

101 James Shaw, a merchant in Dorchester
County, married Ann Knapp (c.1764–1826),
daughter of Annapolis watchmaker William
Knapp (see 21 October 1793), in December
1789. Deborah Knapp, the wife of John
Randall, was Ann's sister (see following note).
Shaw had two sons who attended the grammar
school at St. John's: William, age 12 (the son
of a first wife), entered in 1792 and John
Randall—named for Shaw's brother-in-law—
entered at age nine in 1799 with his uncle as
his guardian.

110 ✒ Deborah Knapp Randall
(c.1763–1852)

John Randall's wife Deborah. Faris records the births of two of her children.

102 Deborah Knapp Randall, daughter of watchmaker William Knapp and sister of James Shaw's widow. Her husband, John Randall (1750–1826), was born in Virginia, the son of Thomas and Jane Davis Randall. Randall was apprenticed to William Buckland, who became his guardian in December 1766 upon the remarriage and move of his mother, and came to Annapolis when Edward Lloyd IV (see 19 October 1792) hired Buckland to complete the unfinished house he had bought from Samuel Chase (see 7 October 1793). After achieving his majority, Randall became a merchant, eventually acquiring (by 1793) Middleton's tavern fronting on Market Space, with its kitchen, stable, dairy, salt house, and terraced garden down Prince George Street to the water. Randall held numerous Annapolis offices, including councilman, port warden, alderman, mayor, and commissioner, between 1801 and the 1820s. § Faris made several dozen purchases from Randall between 1791 and 1801, including an iron tea kettle, a garden spade, shingles, plank, nails, sugar, salt, and a pair of stockings for himself, as well as numerous barrels of corn meal and flour. Randall patronized Faris's tavern in 1774 and 1775. With Vachel Stevens (see 22 March 1792), he appraised Charles Faris's estate in 1800, and acted, with John Davidson (see 2 June 1795), as surety for the administration of William Faris's estate. He collected £31.4.4 from Charles's estate and owed William's £10.5.4.

mortification in his Bowels. Mrs. Randal[102] has gone over the Bay to ye Widdow. a dull dissagreeable day, in the evening it rained

Fryday 16th ✒ a very bad night. it hailed and snow'd and Blew very hard and cold. a fine morning. clear & the sun shines very fine but cold

Saturday 17th ✒ a fine clear cold day

Sunday 18th ✒ the wind Blowed very hard last night. a fine clear day but very cold

Munday 19th ✒ a very cold day

1795 *Tuseday Janry 20th* ✒ a very cold clear day

Wednesday 21th ✒ I was overperswaded by the girls to buy a carpett for the big room in the House for which I gave £5.5.0 which money I think I had better have laid out other wise.[103] a fine day

Thursday 22th ✒ a dull cloudey day like for snow. it did snow a littel once the the course of ye day

Fryday 23th ✒ a cloudey morning. in the after noon it beg to snow and continues snowing till about 10 oclock & then turn'd to rain & raind very hard

Saturday 24th ✒ it raind & Blow'd very hard all night, this morning and all day continued raining & Blowing

1795 *Sunday Janry 25th* ✒ in the night & this morning it snow'd till a 11 or 12 oclock then seemd to clear a way but soon clouded up and continued cloudey the rest of the day

Monday 26th ✒ a fine day. not so cold as has been. a disagreeable affair happened to day to a neagro girl

---

103 The cash book entry for the 21st reads, "To a carpet for the house 5.5.0", with no identification of the seller. But as he paid cash, Faris probably acquired the carpet from a local merchant.

104 Abraham Claude (d.1800), who was a watch maker, silversmith, dry goods merchant, and grocer, advertised his first shop in September 1772 in partnership with Charles Jacob. Although family tradition states that Claude was Swiss, the *Gazette* notice stated that he had come from London. His first wife was Ann Stevens (d.1784), the daughter of John Stevens (d.1781) and his wife Elizabeth Mercer, by whom Claude had four children; in 1785 he married Elizabeth Quynn (d.1811), daughter of Allen Quynn (see 9 September 1792). The Claudes lived on the opposite side of

belonging to Abraham Claud.[104] he had hired her to Sweaney the Baker.[105] a man that he had thare as a Baker wanted to ly with her, she would not let him. he at different times threetened that if she would not that he would kill her. she told her master of it — too day he attackt'd her again while she was makeing the Bed up stairs and she would not let him do as he wanted. he took up a gun and snapt it at her. then said she was not loaded but that he would do for her, then got another gun and shott her in the arm and Head in a Terrebe manner that it is a grate chance if it is not the cause of her deth

1795 Tuseday Janry 27th 🖛 a fine day

Wednesday 28th 🖛 a fine day

Thursday 29th 🖛 a rainey day

Fryday 30th 🖛 it Blow'd exceedingly hard last night. Blew down part of my garden fence next to Mr. Grayhams — I got the fence repaired. a fine day but windey

Saturday 31th 🖛 a fine day

Sunday Febuary 1th 🖛 a fine clear cold windey day

Munday 2th 🖛 a cloudey morning but clear'd away. a fine day

1795 Tuseday Febry 3th 🖛 a rainey morning. in the afternoon clear & windey

Wednesday 4th 🖛 clear and cold

Thursday 5th 🖛 clear & cold

Fryday 6th 🖛 clear & cold

Saturday 7th 🖛 a cloudey cold day. in the evening snow'd a littel

Sunday 8th 🖛 a cloudey disagreeable day, it spitt of snow at times all day

---

West Street, in a two-story brick dwelling with a frame smoke-house, purchased from Quynn in 1779. § In August 1773 Faris entered a recognizance bond for his good behavior toward Abraham Claude. Whatever the cause of that dispute, Claude was a tavern patron in 1779. Faris purchased five pounds of sugar from Claude in July 1799 and a quart of vinegar in March 1802. Faris never mentioned Claude in connection with his garden, but Claude's inventory included $20 in garden utensils and produce.

[105] Sweeney never advertised in the *Gazette* and does not appear in the census or probate records.

Munday 9th ⚬ snow'd in the night and continues snowing very fast till about noon, still cloudey like more bad weather. I receiv'd a letter from St. John Faris dated the 8th of Janry from the Capes

1795 Tuseday Febry 10th ⚬ a fine day

Wednesday 11th ⚬ a fine day

Thursday 12th ⚬ a fine day. Mr. Thomas Woodward dined with us to day, hes looking after his man Shedreck[106]

Fryday 13th ⚬ a fine morning but cold. in the evening cloudey

Saturday 14th ⚬ a clear cold day

Sunday 15th ⚬ a very cold day

Munday 16th ⚬ very cold

Tuseday 17th ⚬ snow'd in the night. a cloudey morning. snowd at times in the course of the day, cold & Blustering weather

1795 Wednesday 18th ⚬ clear & cold

Thursday 19th ⚬ a fine day

Fryday 20th ⚬ a fine day

Saturday 21th ⚬ Charles went of to Baltimore this morning about 8 oclock. a fine day

Sunday 22th ⚬ a very fine warm day. in the evening clouded up looks like rain

Munday 23th ⚬ a cloudey morning. Sylve began to digg the side of the lott next Mrs. Davidson's but about noon it began to rain and continued raining a littel all the after noon. in the evening about 8 oclock Charles returned from Baltimore

Tuseday 24th ⚬ rain'd hard last night. a fine day. Sylvia will finish to ground for the parsneps

1795 Wednesday Febury 25th ⚬ snow'd a littel this morning, a cold very windey day

Thursday 26th ⚬ a cold dull day

Fryday 27th ⚬ a very cold windey day

Saturday 28th ⚬ a very cold windey day

Sunday March 1th ⚬ clear & cold. this evening Miss Sallee Wall is married to Mr. Clemments[107]

[106] Woodward placed a notice dated 22 December 1795 in the *Maryland Journal* offering a $50 reward for "Negro SHADRACH, 31 years of age," who had run away in November 1794, so his search on this day was clearly unsuccessful.

[107] Francis Thomas Clements (d.1817), who had a farm on the south side of the Severn River, was elected councilman in October 1801. Chosen as mayor in September 1806, he declined to serve. Sarah Wall (d.1826) was the niece of Thomas Hyde (see 21 June 1793). Clements died in Annapolis on 31 March 1817 and his widow, "at an advanced age," on 26 January 1826, both deaths being reported in the *Gazette*. § Faris made two purchases of potatoes from Clements in December 1797, while Clements owed Faris's estate 3/9.

Munday 2th ☞ a fine day. this morning filled a Barrel with dirt & planted 6 simlin seeds in it from Mr. Lattimore.[108] Silve's acleaning the walks & I a Triming the goosberrey & current Bushes & trimmed the line of Sage next Grayhams

1795 Tuseday March 3th ☞ a fine day. could do nothing in the garden, the ground is too hard to digg

Wednesday 4th ☞ a fine day

Thursday 5th ☞ about noon Sylvea began to digg the big Bed. a very Fine day. this evening Miss Hesselius's to be married to Mr. Cleggett[109]

Fryday 6th ☞ Sylvea's allmost finished diging the Big bed. a very Fine day

Saturday 7th ☞ a cloudey morning. Sylvea finish'd the big Bead. I sow'd 5 rows & ½ of peas from Mr. Hopkins begun next to Grayham's, and one row & ½ of my owne, and Planted 2 rows of earley York plants next Grayhams. about 12 oclock it began to rain so that I was oblig'd to leave off & come in. in the afternoon finished planting ye Bed with cabbage plants

31th ☞ the peas is now beginning to make thare appearance {sideways in margin}

1795 Sunday March 8th ☞ thunder'd and light-en'd and rained very Hard last night — planted in the Barrel, the Doubel White Wall Flower seed from Miss Nelley Davidson. a cold windey day

Munday 9th ☞ a cold day

Tuseday 10th ☞ a cold day. in the evening Miss Walker,[110] Miss Green, Miss Polley Gassaway & Miss Kittey Witcroft[111] & Messrs S Green[112]

---

108 Randolph Brandt Latimer (d.1805) lived in Annapolis between 1790 and 1798. In March 1790 he married Catherine Howard Rutland, the widow of Thomas Rutland and daughter of Cornelius and Mary Wallace Howard (see 31 March 1792). In 1792 Latimer was the agent for the sale of state land, following two terms on the executive council from 1789 to 1791. § Faris bought an iron fire-back from him in June 1802.

109 Judson Magruder Clagett (1769–1800), a Georgetown merchant, was the son of Thomas Clagett (1741–1792) and his wife Mary Meek (c.1746–1809) of Prince George's County, and the step-brother of Allen Bowie Duckett (see 10 November 1801). Caroline Hesselius was another of the daughters of John and Mary Young Woodward Hesselius (see 5 June 1792).

110 Probably Rebecca Walker, who would marry William Davidson on 8 October. She may have been the daughter or sister of the William Walker whose death Faris notes on 9 January 1801.

111 The youngest daughter of William and Frances Whetcroft, who was born on 8 July 1779.

112 Samuel Green (1757–1811), the son of Jonas and Anne Catherine Green, was the Annapolis postmaster from 1791 to 1811. Jonas Green, who had revived the *Maryland Gazette* in 1745, published the paper until his death in April 1767. His widow Anne Catherine continued as both publisher of the paper and official printer for the colony until her death in March 1775. Samuel and his older brother Frederick published the paper together during the years that Faris was writing his diary. Frederick married Anne Sanders in 1775, with whom he had four children, three sons and one daughter, Anne Catherine, whose marriage Faris records on 23 November 1798. She is probably the Miss Green referred to in this entry. There is no record of a marriage by Samuel. When both men died in January 1811, the *Gazette* noted that they were "never separate in life"either, which suggests that Samuel may have lived with Frederick and his family.

[113] Thomas Harris Jr. was the son of Thomas and Ann Harris. Eleanor Davidson (1777–1802) was the daughter of Faris's neighbors, John and Eleanor Davidson (see 1 January 1792). § At the sale of Faris's estate, Harris bought two large books for $8.00.

[114] Charles Wayman may have been the son of John Wayman, a farmer and tavern keeper in Anne Arundel County in 1785. When John died in 1793, Charles signed his inventory as one of the nearest kin. Charles attended St. John's grammar school from October 1790 to August 1791, where he might have met the Faris children and become part of their social circle. In July 1795, he was an ensign in one of the Annapolis companies of the 22nd militia regiment—the same post that Charles Faris held from August 1797 until his death.

[115] The first smallpox inoculation of Sylve's son, Adam. Inoculation, or variolation, involved transplanting pus from the eruptions on a smallpox victim into an incision or puncture in the skin of an uninfected person. If a case of smallpox developed, it was generally mild and carried a greater chance of survival than ordinary contact provided. This procedure was first used about 1720 and continued into the early nineteenth century, even after the introduction of vaccination as the preferred treatment. Vaccination, using cowpox virus, did not become an accepted practice until the early 1800s, following Edward Jenner's development of the technique in 1796. Faris inoculated a number of people, including his grandchildren.

[116] A medicine, especially a cathartic. In this instance, the doses of physic appear to be related to the smallpox inoculations.

Thomas Harris,[113] W. Davidson, Charles Wayman[114] drank Tea & after Tea they had the Fiddel & danced till ½ after 9 oclock. Miss Gassaway had a Fitt

Wednesday 11th — a fine day but cold

Thursday 12th — made up the assparagas Beds & sow'd on the near one No. 1 Earley York 10 d⁰ No. 2 cabbbage from Mrs. Davidson on the other No. 3 cabbage from Mr. Woodward, No. 4 Battissee 5 Winter Leaf No. 6 cabbage from Mr. Sipels & lettis on both. in ye after noon began to rain

1795 Fryday March 13th — Hyram's made a begining to plant parsnips, & Sylve a diging the Border next to Grayhams, & I cutt one Hedge of Box. abut a 11 oclock began to rain fast, it was cloudey and drisled at times all the morning. this morning about 9 oclock I ennockalated the littel neagro child about 7 or 8 months old for the small pox[115] — betwen 12 & 1 oclock it rain'd & snow'd, in the afternoon it clear'd away & turned very cold. I made abegining to Plant a line of Box on the Border nex to Mr. Grayhams but it was so cold I was obligd to leve off

Saturday 14th — a very cold windey morning. the grounds Frose very Hard. gave Silve & Addam a dose of Phissick[116]

Sunday 15th — this Fore noon Beckey planted gord seed in the lott next the garden Fence. a cold windey day

1795 Munday March 16th — snow'd this morning till 12 oclock then turned to small rain, in the evening cloudey — this after noon a neagro Lad came hear to hire. Doctr Ghislin's to ennockculate him, & he's to serve me a month after he gets well for nursing himm & Trouble of the House. his name is Clem

Tuseday 17th — this morning I gave Silve & Addam the 2d dose of Phissick & Clem was ennockculated. a fine day, not so cold as yesterday, still windey. this after noon Clem was planting parsneps a littel wile & I ennockculated Addam thee 2d Time

Wednesday 18th — a cloudey morning. Clem took a dose of Phissick, I finish'd Planting the line of Box nex to Grayhams & Hyram made abegining to cut the Box. cutt 3 or 4 rows & it began to rain and rained all the after noon & evening

1795 Thursday March 19th ↜ a very cold windey night, & this morning cold & windey & continued to Blow hard all day

Fryday 20th ↜ a coole windey day but not so cold as yesterday, I sow'd 30 rows of Parsley on the Border next to Grayhams, & Clem will finish planting Parsneps this after noon — in the evening sow'd a Bed of onions seed on the Border at the further end nex to Stevens's

Saturday 21th ↜ sow'd spinige in drills next the Burgomott Baum, then went to cutting Box

Sunday 22th ↜ this morning I ennockculated Adam the 3d time.   a mild day but cloudey & drisseld at times. in the evening look'd as if it would sett in to rain

1795 Munday March 23th ↜ finished cuting all the Box except the nursserey Box. a very fine day

Tuseday 24th ↜ Finished cuting the Box and Troweled 4 of the Flower beds & I planted the shallotts on the Border & planted Wall Flowers on the Circel Bed. a fine day

Wednesday 25th ↜ rained in the morning. in the fore noon I sow'd Radishes & Lettice on the Border next to Grayhams & Sylve dug up the littel bed at the end of the new stabel. in the after noon Planted radish seed on the end of the Parsnep Bed. in the evening came on foggey

Thursday 26th ↜ planted 6 rows of Beens in the littel quarter, sow'd spinige on the Border next to Grayhams. sowed 6 sorits of chiney asters on the flower Bed next the grass walk & planted the Tubee Rose Roots & sow'd India pink seed in the Barrel, turnd windey & cold. this evening looks like for rain. Hyram's diging the nurssery Beds, ennockculaited Addam again the 4 time

1795 Fryday March 27th ↜ rain'd & Blew hard all night. this morning the ground was cover'd with snow. it snow'd, rain'd & Hailed & the wind Blows hard & is very cold and continued snowing & Hailing all day & Blows very hard at N:E & very cold. Clem's small pox has made thare appearence as if he would have it preetey thick. thare's Isesickels to the eves of the house 8 or 9 Inches long

Saturday 28th ↜ the wind Blew very hard all night and raind this morning & all day it rain'd & the wind Blew hard. in the evening the clouds seem'd to brake away & the wind changed to the N & dont blow so hard

Sunday 29th ☞ a fine day to what the 2 or 3 last have been but its cold. the snow's alaying in several Places this evening

Munday 30th ☞ made hills in the Lott & planted No. 1 cucumbers No. 2 cantilopes No. 3 water mellions, the rest of the Hills with simlins. Sylve's do up the Border of the littel quarter & cleaned the walk & Hyram has finished digging ye flower Beds. a very fine day

1795 Tuseday March 31th ☞ the peas that ware sown the 7th of March are now begining to make thare appearance. William Biggs's[117] daughter died at Chester Town, brought her over the Bay & she was Buried this after noon. a cold raw cloudey drisley day ~~Littel Addam has the small pox just a coming out~~

Wednesday April 1th ☞ sow'd Ice plant seed, d⁰ Egg d⁰ and gegery in potts, this morning or Last night Mr. Thomas Hyde died aged 73 last January. a fine day

Thursday 2th ☞ I ennockculated littel Addam this morning for the 5 Time, Clem's a cleaning ye walks in the gardin. this afternoon Thomas Hyde was Buried. a fine day. in the evening it rained

1795 Fryday April 3th ☞ rained very Hard last night. a fine day

Saturday 4th ☞ a fine day, Clem went of with himself yesterday fore noon & has not found the way back

Sunday 5th ☞ a very Fine day, in the evening looks as if it would rain

Munday 6th ☞ a sharp gust of Thunder Lightening and Rain last night, a fine warm morning. How'd the peas & cabbage plants, & for the first time this spring saw the Martins about. a fine warm day

Tuseday 7th ☞ cloudey like for rain. planted radishes in the Hills in the lot the seed from Govenor Stone. still continues cloudey & like for rain. the wind has got to N:E

1795 Wednesday April 8th ☞ a cloudey rainey morning, in the after noon clear. Hyram began to

117 William Biggs was a storekeeper in the early 1780s, a partner of Biggs & Eastman. He was unmarried, owned no real estate, and held one slave. Biggs operated a tavern in Annapolis in the late 1780s, but then took up farming in Kent County on the Eastern Shore.

1A ✒ Ann Faris Pitt (1773–1860) and her
daughter Hannah Williams Pitt (1800–1837)
Attributed to Joshua Johnson, ca. 1800

1B ✒ Charles Faris (1764–1800)
Attributed to Charles Willson Peale, ca. 1795

1C ✒ Saint John Faris
(1770–1796)
Attributed to Hyram Faris,
ca. 1795

1D ✒ Abigail Faris
Attributed to Gustavus Hesselius, ca. 1740

1E ✒ Rebecca Maria Pitt Chappell
(1798–1834)
Jacob Eichholtz, 1819

I

2A ✍ William Paca (1740–1799)
Charles Willson Peale, ca. 1772

*Faris visited the garden shown in this painting when he
called on Henri Stier in April 1798.*

2B ✍ Charles Carroll, Barrister (1723–1783)
Charles Willson Peale, 1788

*Charles Carroll the Barrister patronized
Faris's shop in the 1770s.*

2C ✍ Henri Joseph Stier (1743–1821)
Rembrandt Peale, 1799

*Stier, a Belgian aristocrat who came to Annapolis
from Philadelphia in 1795, exchanged plants
and seeds with Faris.*

2D ✍ Alexander Contee Hanson (1749–1806)
Attributed to Rembrandt Peale, ca. 1798

*Chancellor Hanson was one of Faris's most
frequent gardening colleagues.*

3A ✒ Dr. Upton Scott (1724–1814)
Unidentified Artist, ca. 1770

*Upton Scott was another Annapolis
gardener with whom Faris exchanged
plants and seeds.*

3B ✒ The Edward Lloyd IV Family
Charles Willson Peale, 1771

Several members of the Lloyd family appear in the diary.

3C ✒ View of Annapolis, Maryland
Anonymous, after a drawing by Charles Cotton Milbourne, ca. 1800

*St. Anne's Church, just a short distance down West Street from Faris's home,
and Church Circle, around which he walked on his trips to the market.*

3D ✒ William McParlin
(c.1780–1850)
David Boudon, 1807

*William McParlin came to Annapolis
in 1799 as an apprentice to
Charles Faris.*

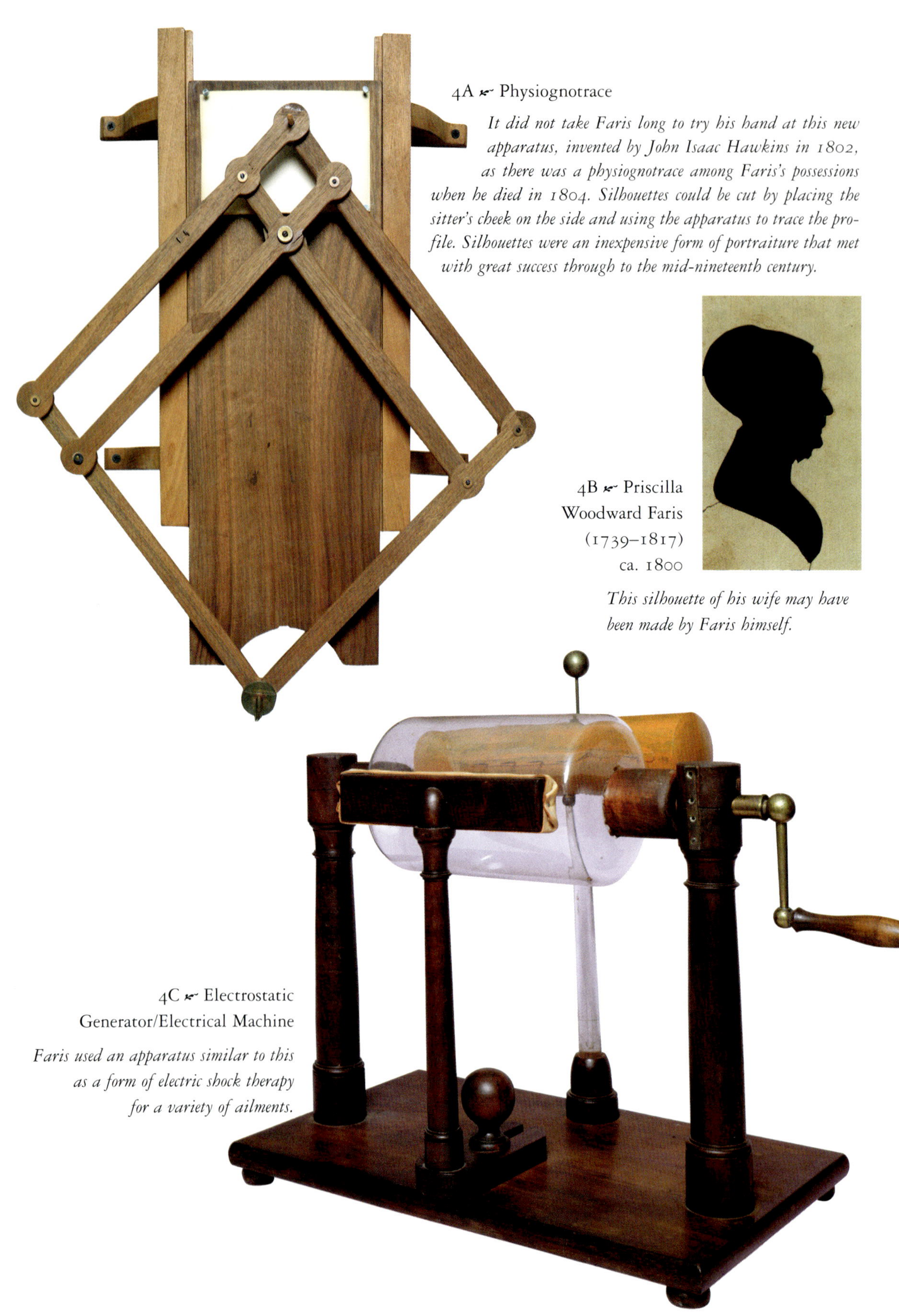

4A ✒ Physiognotrace

It did not take Faris long to try his hand at this new apparatus, invented by John Isaac Hawkins in 1802, as there was a physiognotrace among Faris's possessions when he died in 1804. Silhouettes could be cut by placing the sitter's cheek on the side and using the apparatus to trace the profile. Silhouettes were an inexpensive form of portraiture that met with great success through to the mid-nineteenth century.

4B ✒ Priscilla Woodward Faris (1739–1817) ca. 1800

This silhouette of his wife may have been made by Faris himself.

4C ✒ Electrostatic Generator/Electrical Machine

Faris used an apparatus similar to this as a form of electric shock therapy for a variety of ailments.

4

5A ✌ Shop Drawing for a **Sauceboat**, ca. 1760

5B ✌ Shop Drawing for a **Teapot**, ca. 1760–1775

5C ✌ Shop Drawing for:
1) **Caster**, ca. 1760–1770
2) **Cream pot**, ca. 1770
3) **Strainer**, ca. 1760–1770
4) Section of **strainer**, ca. 1760–1770

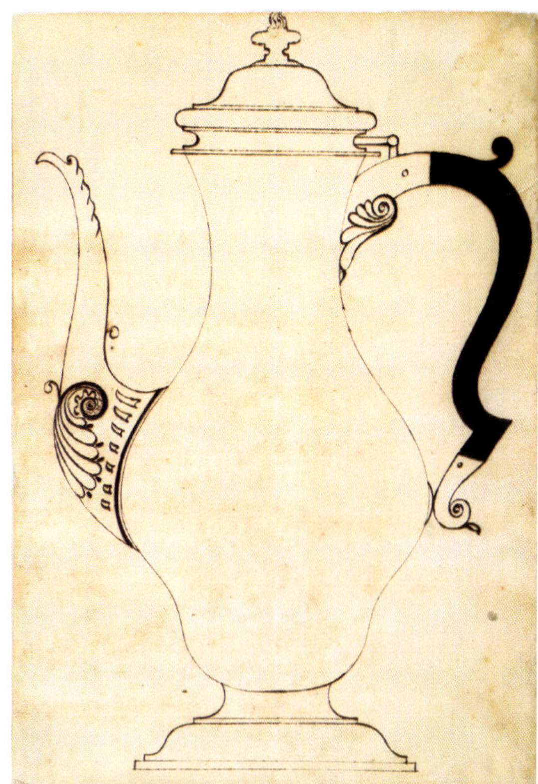

5D ✌ Shop Drawing for a **Coffee Pot**, ca. 1770–1780

5

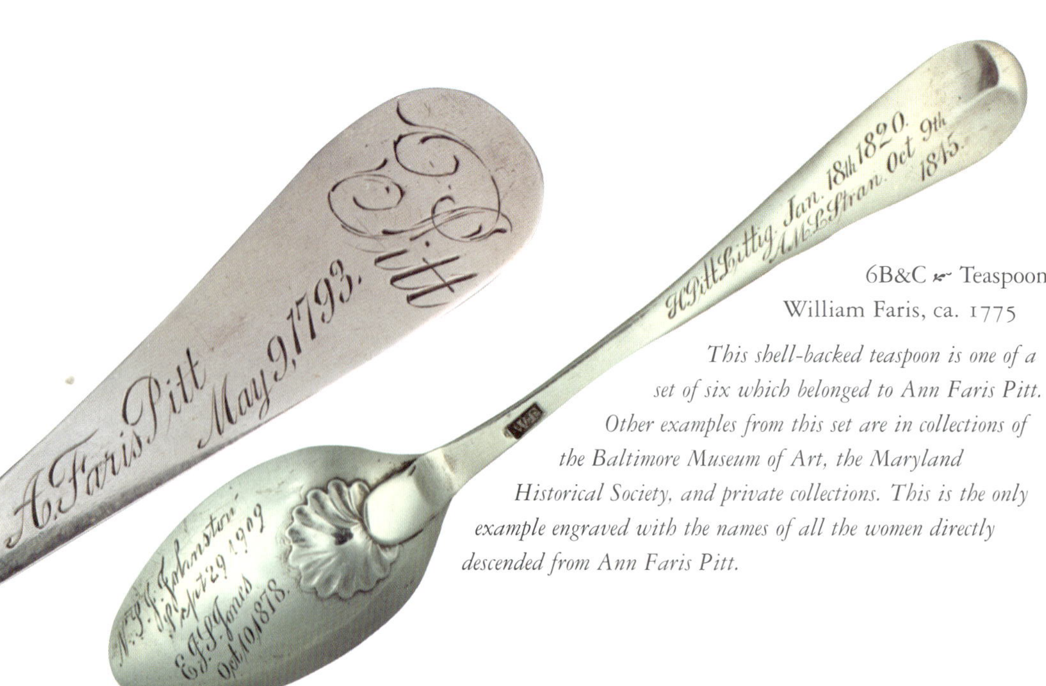

6A ☙ Six Tablespoons by William Faris, ca. 1760–70

Patrons generally ordered spoons like these tablespoons in sets of six or twelve.

6B&C ☙ Teaspoon
William Faris, ca. 1775

*This shell-backed teaspoon is one of a
set of six which belonged to Ann Faris Pitt.
Other examples from this set are in collections of
the Baltimore Museum of Art, the Maryland
Historical Society, and private collections. This is the only
example engraved with the names of all the women directly
descended from Ann Faris Pitt.*

7A ✒ Two-handled Cup
marked by Robert Peake, London, 1702/1703

According to the Pitt family Bible, Abraham Woodward imported this cup for his three daughters. Priscilla Woodward Faris received it from her mother, Priscilla Ruley Orrick Woodward, at her death in 1773. William and Priscilla Faris owned the cup until Faris's death when it went to their daughter Ann. The cup then descended in the Pitt family.

7B ✒ Funnel
Attributed to William Faris, ca. 1775

This funnel has a long history of descent in William Faris's family, having belonged to William and Ann Pitt and then descending through the Pitt family. Funnels were used in the decanting of wine from the barrels in which it was stored.

7C ✒ Caster
marked by John Delmester, London, 1762/1763

This caster, which probably belonged to William Faris, is very similar to one of his shop drawings (Figure SD4 on page 433). This example shows the extent to which the local population depended on and favored English goods in the eighteenth century.

8A 🠣 (INSET) View of Annapolis in 1797

This watercolor, painted in 1797 by Comte de Maulevier Colbert from the vantage point of Richard Sprigg's planta-tion, Strawberry Hill, shows Windmill Point, the State House dome, and the spire of St. Anne's Church.

8B 🠣 A Ground Plot of the City of Annapolis
James Callahan, 1743, after John Stoddert, (1718)

The plan of Annapolis as laid out when it became the capital of Maryland in the 1690s; with minor changes the survey shows the town that Faris knew.

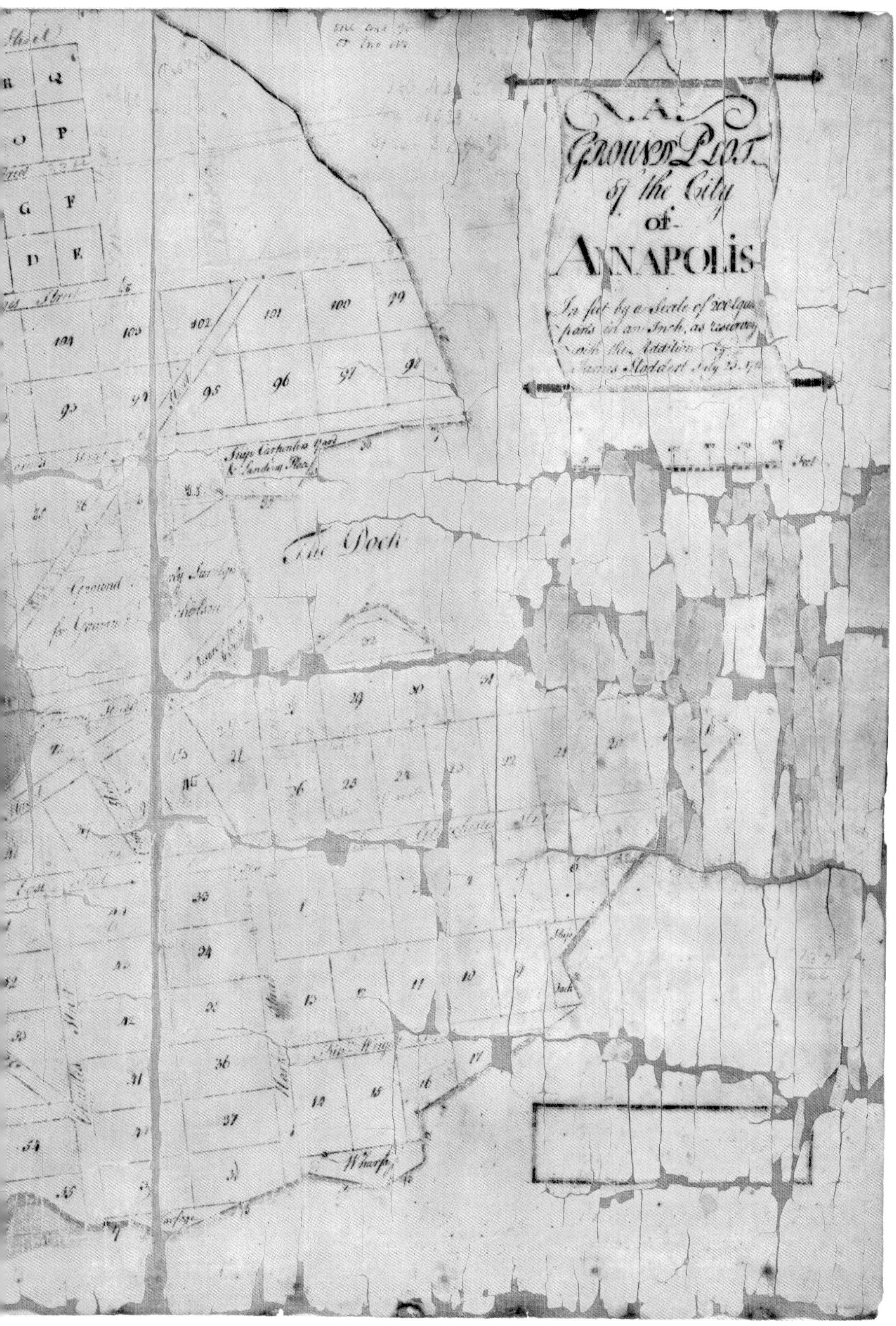

GROUND PLOT
of the City
of
ANNAPOLIS
The Dock
Wharfe

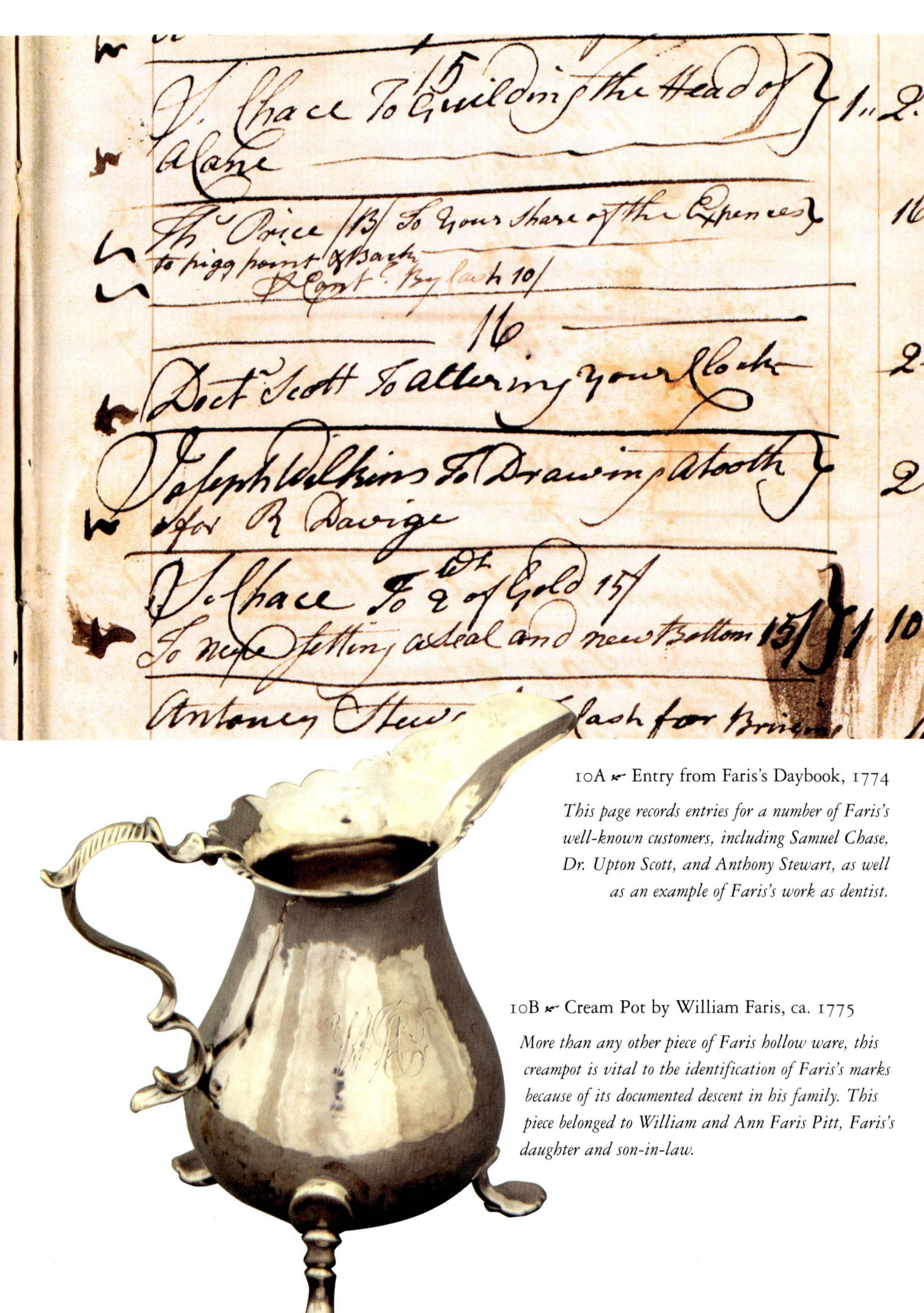

10A ☛ Entry from Faris's Daybook, 1774

This page records entries for a number of Faris's well-known customers, including Samuel Chase, Dr. Upton Scott, and Anthony Stewart, as well as an example of Faris's work as dentist.

10B ☛ Cream Pot by William Faris, ca. 1775

More than any other piece of Faris hollow ware, this creampot is vital to the identification of Faris's marks because of its documented descent in his family. This piece belonged to William and Ann Faris Pitt, Faris's daughter and son-in-law.

11A ✒ Escutcheon of Cellarette
English, ca. 1795

11B&C ✒ Cellarette with view of
open cellarette showing gilded bottles

*The number of original bottles that have survived is
testimony to the careful stewardship given to the cellarette.
All the bottles are partially gilded.*

*It is quite remarkable that William Faris owned this elaborate piece of furniture. Although he acquired it in
1797, he never mentioned its origins either in his diary or in his account books. Family legend states that it came
from a vessel, presumably as a gift.*

12 ✒ White painted dial of Tall Case Clock, ca. 1790–1800. Signed: **HYRAM FARIS/ANNAPOLIS**

Hyram Faris worked in his father's shop until he moved to Baltimore after a quarrel with his father in April 1799. White dials began to replace brass dials in the last quarter of the eighteenth century.

13 ✒ Brass Dial of Tall Case Clock, ca. 1765. Engraved: *William Faris*/ANNAPOLIS. Musical Movement

This musical clock, which plays the Celtic tune "Robin Adair", was purchased by William Pitt for his wife Ann at the sale of her father's property in 1805; he paid $36.00. This may have been the clock which "stood behind the door in the hall" in the poem "The Will of William Faris."

14 ✒ Pressed Tulip   *No. 3 Gen'l Montgomery
and White Mulberry Leaves.*

15 ☞ Plan of the Harbor and City of Annapolis
drawn by Major Capitaine, aide to the Marquis de Lafayette, 1781

WILLIAM FARIS,

WATCH-MAKER, *from* PHILADELPHIA,

At his Shop near the Church, next Door to Mr. Wal-lace's, in Church-Street, ANNAPOLIS,

CLEANS and REPAIRS all Sorts of WATCHES and CLOCKS, as well and neat as can be done in any Part of *America:* And takes the same Prices for his Work as are taken in *Philadelphia.*

He also makes CLOCKS, either to Repeat or not, or to go either Eight Days or Thirty, as the Purchaser shall fancy, as good as can be made in *London,* and at reasonable Prices. And all Gentlemen who shall be pleased to employ him, may depend on having their Work done with all possible Dispatch, by *Their humble Servant,*
WILLIAM FARIS.

16A ✒ *Maryland Gazette*
17 March 1757

WILLIAM FARIS,
WATCH-MAKER, in ANNAPOLIS,

HAVING procured from *Philadelphia* a very compleat SILVERSMITH, who has served a regular Apprenticeship to that Business, hereby informs the Public, that he can now supply them, on the most reasonable Rates, with all Kinds of SILVER WORK, in the most genteel and fashionable Manner, and with the greatest Dispatch. He also carries on, as usual, the JEWELLER's Business, having an excellent Workman for that Purpose; and will give the best Prices for old Gold and Silver, and all Sorts of precious Stones.

16B ✒ *Maryland Gazette*
25 August 1763

WILLIAM FARIS,
WATCH-MAKER,

HAVING supplied himself with the best of Liquors, hereby gives Notice to the Public, That he has now open'd TAVERN at his House opposite to where the late Mrs. M'Leod lived. Gentlemen Travellers and Others, favouring him with their Custom, will meet with the best Entertainment, and the kindest Usage, from
Their humble Servant,
WILLIAM FARIS.

N. B. The Watchmaker's, Jeweller's, and Silversmith's Businesses, are carried on in all their various Branches as usual.

16C ✒ *Maryland Gazette*
2 August 1764

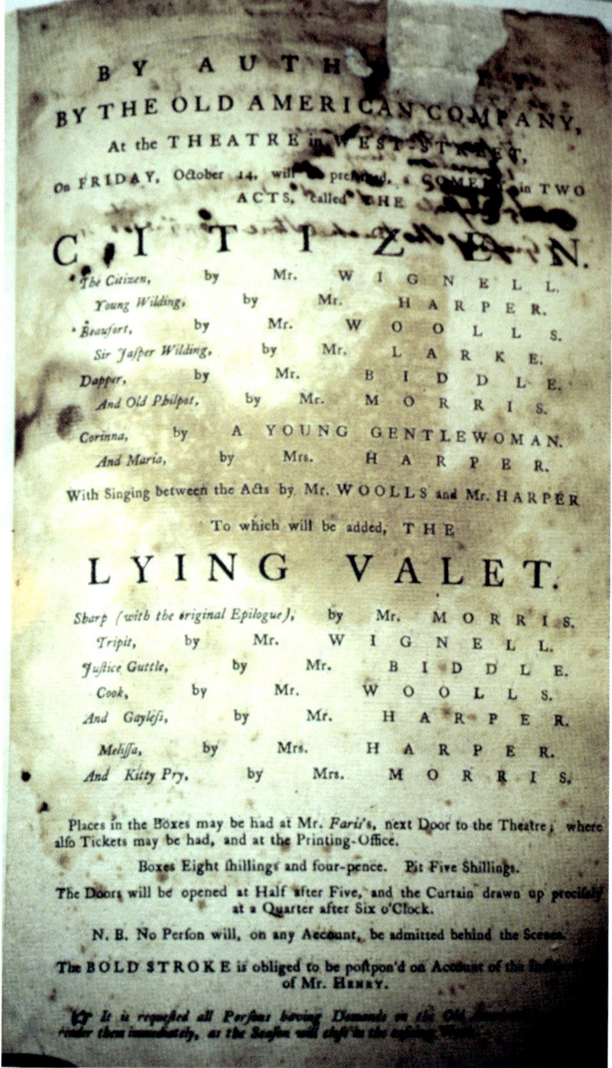

16E ✒ Playbill for *The Citizen* and *The Lying Valet*

Faris never missed an opportunity for free advertising, as shown in this playbill with its notice: "places in the Boxes may be had at Mr. Faris's, next Door to the Theatre."

16D ✒ *Maryland Gazette*
22 August 1804

William McParlin placed this notice in the Gazette within a week of Faris's death.

WILLIAM M'PARLIN,
CLOCK AND WATCH-MAKER,

RESPECTFULLY informs the citizens of Annapolis, and its vicinity, that he has commenced BUSINESS at the shop lately kept by WILLIAM FARIS, in West-street, where clocks and watches of every description may be repaired in the most approved manner, and on the most moderate terms, also gold and silver work made, sold, and repaired; engraving, such as cyphers, seals, &c. neatly executed, and he assures those who please to honour him with their commands, that the utmost of his abilities shall be exerted to give general satisfaction.
N. B. Old gold and silver bought as usual.
August 22, 1804.

do up the water tabel round the grass walk. in the evening Mr. George Johnston from Philladea call'd to see us

Thursday 9th ✒ a very cold windey day, Hyram has been about the Tabels in the garden

Fryday 10th ✒ very cold. the Crown Imperiel's look'd very badley. this morning it so cold can do nothing in the garden. Mr. G. Johnston drank Tea & spent the evening with us, Last Night G. Mann died[118]

Saturday 11th ✒ a cold day. in the after noon Mr. George Mann was Buried

1795 Sunday Apl 12th ✒ a fine day but too cold for the season but not so cold as some days past. in the evening rain

Munday 13th ✒ rained hard last night. this morning cloudey but am in hopes it will clear away & be a fine day, planted the senssitive plant seed in 6 places, the stick mark'd No. 1 — Sylve's dug the littel quarter by the old stabel & Hyram's been cuting the grass & doing up the tabel round the grass walk

Tuseday 14th ✒ Hyram's finished round the grass, took up the Iives & replanted them round the littel qurter & sowed carrot seed & planted onions on part of the littel quarter, took up the thime & replanted it. a very fine day

Wednesday 15th ✒ a very fine day. the Beens that ware planted the 26 of March are coming up finely, sow'd red globe seed & Sylve finish cleaning the walks, this evening John Barbers wife was Buried

1795 Thursday April 16th ✒ the simlins & cucumber are cuming up that ware planted the 30th of March — I planted Jobe's Tears on the Border next the lott. a very Fine day

Fryday 17th ✒ a fine day

Saturday 18th ✒ a cold raw day

Sunday 19th ✒ a raw cold day

Munday 20th ✒ still raw & cold. I stuck the peas to day

Tuseday 21th ✒ a fine [day] but rather cool

1795 Wednesday April 22th ✒ this day Neagro Ned was try'd, for Kiling his Master Mr. Dorsey of

[118] The 16 April 1795 *Maryland Gazette* reported the death of George Mann on the 10th instant, in Annapolis, aged 43 years. His widow Mary, whose garden plot adjoined one of Faris's, died on 6 July 1811.

119 The *Gazette* reported on 14 May that Negro Ned was hanged on Friday last for the murder of Mr. Vachel Dorsey, son of John (1734–1779), of Elk Ridge. Dorsey was survived by his widow, Anne Poole Dorsey, a son, and a daughter.

120 John Brice III (1738–1820) was the son of John and Sarah Frisby Brice and the older brother of James Brice (see 17 July 1793). He married Mary Clare Maccubbin (1749–1806), sister of Nicholas Maccubbin Carroll (see 18 January 1792), in 1766, the year of his father's death. John also inherited a lot on Prince George Street, but built a far more modest home than his brother's. Brice was a lawyer, a merchant in partnership with Thomas Harwood III from 1769 to 1778, and a planter. He served as a clerk of the Anne Arundel County court, delegate to the General Assembly, member of the executive council, justice of the peace, alderman, and mayor of Annapolis for one term in 1780.

121 The two Annapolis militia companies were apparently distinguished by their regimental colors—red and blue for one, and buff and blue for the other (see 15 September 1794).

122 Luce may have been a slave owned or hired by Faris.

123 At this time, the governor's official residence was a house facing the harbor just northeast of King George Street, a location that is now part of the Naval Academy grounds. The house was built by Edmund Jennings who rented it to Governor Horatio Sharpe and then sold it to Sharpe's successor, Robert Eden. The State of Maryland confiscated the property during the Revolutionary War, along with much of the other property owned by British subjects or loyalists, and made it the governor's residence. In 1866, the state sold the house and its grounds to the United States government for incorporation into an expanded Naval Academy and built the present Government House between State and Church Circles.

Elkridge[119] and was found gilty. a raw cold day. in the evening like for rain

Thursday 23th ✒ this morning Neagro Ned receivd sentence of death to be Hang'd — and a neagro of Mr. John Bryce's[120] was tryed and found guilty of Killing a neagro man. a fine day but cold

Fryday 24th ✒ a fine day but coole

Saturday 25th ✒ a cloudey day & small rain at times

Sunday 26th ✒ a fine day

1795 Munday Apl 27th ✒ rainey morning, hill'd the Beens in the littel quarter & Hill'd the peas planted 6 rows of Beens, from the Govenor who says thay wil be fit to gather in 6 weaks. the girls are all Busiley imploy'd in makeing collers for the Red & Blew Companey[121] against the first of May — in the afternoon about 2 oclock Luce[122] died — rain'd smartley all the after noon

Tuseday 28th ✒ a cloudey morning. sow'd 25 rows of carrot seed on the end of the onion Bed. clear'd away fine. in the after noon Luce was buried. cloude up & wee had a shower of rain the[n} clear'd away a fine evening

Wednesday 29th ✒ the girls has finish'd the coullors. Hyram planted out India pinks & China asters round the Circel Beds & Beds by the littel house. a fine day, and marked the White Red & Blew Hyacinth & John Quills

1795 Thursday April 30th ✒ how'd the parsneps in the lott, a cloudey day & drisel'd at times

Fryday May 1th ✒ the Compy of Blew & Reds arrected a may pole with a cap of Liberty on the top. beneath that the Amurican Flag under that a circel with 3 Flags the Amurican, the French & Duch, this circel was surrounded with transparrant paper & at night was Illuminated— after the Companey was don exercising at noon the Govenor invited them to his House[123] & gave them a drink & a snack & dismis'd them. a fine day

Saturday 2th ✒ a dull cloudey day, this evening Miss Nelley Davidson sent me a peace of snapdragon, I planted it on the border next the lott

1795 Sunday May 3th ✒ a fine day

Munday 4th ✍ sow'd lettice seed on the far end of the Border next Stevens's. a fine day, Charles went to bed unwell this morning

Tuseday 5th ✍ a cloudey morning, thunder'd & look'd like for rain. clear'd away & turned cold, Charles is still very unwell & ceeps his bed

Wednesday 6th ✍ a fine day. Charles has got bravely. he has been up allmos all day

Thursday 7th ✍ a fine warm day. Charlis has not been abel to sett up to day. he's been very bad all day

1795 Fryday May 8th ✍ a warm day. in the evening we had a gust of rain and the wind Blew very hard. it blew down one of the chimneys at the Poor's house. it broke through the roof & 2 flours and did a good deal of mischief such as throwing low the fences — and the neagro was Hanged to day — Charles is very poorley

Saturday 9th ✍ a fine warm day. marked marked the following flowers in the nursserey Beds. No. 1 Bad tulips such as I dont mean to plant again No. 3 Reds No. 4 White No. 7 Double Seedlings No. 5 purpel No. 6 Yellow No. 8 Red & White — Charles seemed better in the fore part of the day & took 2 or 3 doses of Bark, but in the latter part of the day his feaveour came on again and is very ill

1795 Sunday May 10th ✍ a cloudey day. Charles's much Better to day

Munday 11th ✍ a fine rain this morning. planted plants in the pea bed, howd the Beans. in the after noon planted 6 hills with mellions from Mr. Mannadear.[124] the 3 hills next the lot are nutmeg mellins & the 3 next the streat are Polynac mellins. Charles is something better but very weak & poorley

Tuseday 12th ✍ a fine warm day

Wednesday 13th ✍ a fine day. in the evening a shower of rain

1795 Thursday May 14th ✍ Charles has been to his shop to day. in the evening cut the sage by the stabel, a fine day but rather coole

Fryday 15th ✍ a fine day, Broke of the tops of 1900 Tulips the Doubbel ones are not quite Blown open yet, and thare is still several to brake off yet that's not out of flower

[124] Colonel Henry Maynadier (1759–1849) was the son of Rev. Daniel Maynadier (1724–1772) and his wife Mary Murray (1729–?) and the owner of the estate on the Severn River. He married Elizabeth Key (c.1759–1832) in July 1781. His sister Sarah's second husband was Dr. James Murray (see 19 May 1792). His wife was the niece of Elizabeth Ross Scott, the wife of Upton Scott (see 5 May 1792); the sister of Philip Barton Key (see 29 May 1792); and the aunt of Francis Scott Key (see 19 January 1802). Maynadier served as a councilman, commissioner, and alderman. David Bailie Warden, visiting Annapolis in 1811, wrote in his journal: General M[ason] (see 11 February 1796), & Colonel M[aynadier] carried me to dine at the Seat of the latter, seven miles from the City, situated on a rising ground from where there is a view of a portion of the *Severn*, where the Banks of this river are high, wild, and striking. Col. M. is fond of farming & of Gardening." § Faris bought 14.5 pounds of veal from Maynadier in May 1795.

Saturday 16th ✒ a fine day

Sunday 17th ✒ I took notice of the Beans in the littel quarte by the old stabel's being very much frost bit, thay certainly got it a Thursday night, this has been a very cold day for the season, the wind blows Fresh. should it fall calm, wee shall certainly have a frost — ~~Mr. Cook's daughter that marryed Mr. Clapham died this after noon~~

1795 Munday May 18th ✒ it thundered & Lightened very hard Last night and rain'd some. a very cold raw dul day

Tuseday 19th ✒ very cold dull raw day

Wednesday 20th ✒ not so cold to day as it has been

Thursday 21th ✒ a very warm day. in the evening a fine rain

Fryday 22th ✒ a cloudey rainey warm day

Saturday 23th ✒ a cloudey rainey morning. about noon clear'd away a fine afternoon, gathered peas to day

1795 Sunday May 24th ✒ a fine day

Munday 25th ✒ a fine morning. sow'd on the Border next Grayham's stable the following seed Brussels sprout seed from Mr. Maynadier 3 sort of cabbage seed from the Govenor. Miss Marriah Thomas[125] made me a pressent of betwen 20 or 30 silk woorms. I put them in a drawer on white paper & gave them Mulberey Leaves — Charles went off for Baltimore this morning, in the afternoon Mrs. Goldsmith died. a fine day but coole

Tuseday 26th ✒ a fine day

Wednesday 27th ✒ a fine day but rather coole. in the after noon Mrs. Goldsmith was Buried

1795 Thursday May 28th ✒ a fine day. in the evening it rained

Fryday 29th ✒ a fine morning. began to weede the flower beds next the grass walk. about a 11 oclock began to rain — and continued raining all the after noon

Saturday 30th ✒ a fine day. in the evening wee had a smart rain — Thomas Hammon Brother to William Hammon[126] was Buried this after noon

---

[125] Mariah Thomas was one of the daughters of Capt. James Thomas (d.1810), the son of William Thomas (1705–1767) of Talbot County. He married Hannah Coward of Talbot County c.1777. Thomas moved to Annapolis in 1791, and served on the executive council for six terms, from 1795 to 1801. The Thomases were good friends of the Faris family—particularly the Thomas and Faris girls—and appear frequently in the diary. Faris reports Mariah's marriage to Thomas Goldsborough on 26 September 1801 and her sister Betsy's marriage to James Williams on 21 February 1802.

[126] William Hammond (c.1760–1807) advertised in the 14 May 1795 *Gazette* for settlement of his brother John's estate. Only William appeared in the 1790 census, with a household of four adult white males (the remainder of the record is illegible), suggesting that John may have lived with him. They were probably the two sons of John Hammond (1735–1784) and his wife Ann. William Hammond, who owned part of Acton on Spa Creek not far from Faris's house, died in 1807 in his forty-seventh year. § Charles Faris's estate paid him £1.2.6.

Sunday 31th ☛ a grate deal of rain fell nast light. a fine morning but very cold and continued so all day

Munday June 1th ☛ a very cold day. I am apt to think that thare was a frost last night — a Fire would not have been disagreeable to day

1795 Tusday June 2th ☛ Pulled up the pea vines and am digging the ground. a fine day but several showers of rain and too cold for the season. Miss Nancey Ashmead[127] went of for Philadelphia with Mr. Davidson[128]

Wednesday 3th ☛ finished digging whare the peas grew and filled the ground with plants. a fine day

Thursday 4th ☛ a fine rain last night. the Bees swarmed about 12 oclock & setteled on the appel tree. wee cut of som lims which I suppose disturbed them, thay sett of and went back from wence thay came, a fine day but still too coole

Fryday 5th ☛ about 12 oclock the Bees swarmed and wee hived them cleverley. a very large swarm the larges that I allmost ever saw. a very fine day & in the evening Place'd them in the new Bee House

1795 Saturday 6th ☛ a fine day

Sunday 7th ☛ a fine day

Munday 8th ☛ a fine day

Tuseday 9th ☛ a fine day. Abee's gone to sleep with Mrs. Golder, Arch is gone to Baltimore. yesterday evening Mrs. Quynn went in to the cow pen to milk, and one of cows pokeed her and Broke her thigh[129]

Wednesday 10th ☛ a fine day

Thursday 11th ☛ several showers of rain & warm a fine growing day

1795 Fryday June 12th ☛ a cloudey, dull, cold day

Saturday 13th ☛ a cold cloudey day

Sunday 14th ☛ a fine day but coole

Munday 15th ☛ about 1 oclock the Bees swarmed. a fine day and warm but turned cool in the evening

Tuseday 16th ☛ this morning Mrs. Davidson made a begining to put up a string of Fence betwen her garden and mine. a fine day

[127] Anne Ashmead, born on 7 April 1779, was the daughter of Joseph and Ann Ashmead, innkeepers in Annapolis. Her mother was the widow first of John Golder (d.1760), whose son Archibald was a good friend of Faris's (see 7 April 1793), and second of Robert Johnson (d.1773), whose sons are mentioned frequently in the diary. The Ashmeads were also good friends of the Faris family and socialized with them often. Faris frequently noted Nancy Ashmead's travels to Philadelphia and to Baltimore, the latter trips often in the company of members of his family.

[128] John Davidson (1754–1807) was probably born in another colony and immigrated to Maryland before 1776. He married Anna Maria Grason (c.1775–1815), daughter of Thomas Grason (see 2 October 1796), with whom he had three children. Davidson lived a few blocks away from Faris on Charles Street in the house known today as the Adams-Kilty house. Davidson reached the rank of major during the Revolution and was a brigadier general in the militia in the 1790s; Faris refers to him in the diary as both General and Major Davidson. He served on the executive council from 1783 to 1801, was a councilman and alderman, and was elected mayor in September 1799. Davidson's death was reported in the 5 February 1807 *Maryland Gazette*: Gen. John Davidson died in Baltimore on Monday. An old inhabitant of this city, his remains were brought here and interred with military honors. § With John Randall (see 15 January 1795), Davidson was a surety for the administration of William Faris's estate.

[129] Well into the nineteenth century, many Annapolitans kept a cow or two on their property to provide milk for the household. Similarly, residents kept pigs which would be slaughtered in the fall and the meat smoked for use over the winter months. See 2 July for Charles Faris's purchase of a pig.

Wednesday 17th ↜ a cloudey morning & a mist of rain. about 10 oclock clear'd away. a fine after noon

Thursday 18th ↜ this morning began to make a silk reel from the Dictionary of Arts & Siences,[130] a fine warm day

1795 Fryday June 19th ↜ a fine day. the carpenters have finished the fence this evening with old posts, rails & old pails

Saturday 20th ↜ a cloudey drisley day. in the evening the wind Blows very hard and looks as if wee should have rain

Sunday 21th ↜ a fine day. in the evening it's reported that Majr. Davidson is marryed to Miss Kittey Johnson,[131] and that Nancey pinkeney's[132] maryed to Mr. [blank] Bond[133] the evening looks gustey like for rain — a fals report of both. NB its a fals allarm, nither of the above girls are married

Munday 22th ↜ pull'd up the Been Vines. dugg the ground & planted 5 rows of Beens & Sylve's digging the walnut tree Bed. a fine day. in the evening waterd the Beens that was planted to day

1795 Tuseday June 23th ↜ sow'd Brussell sprout seed, on the Border next Stevens's the seed from Mr. Samuel Howard. a fine day

Wednesday 24th ↜ a dull drisley cloudey [day] and at time raind. at night looks as if wee should have a fine rain

Thursday 25th ↜ rained very hard last night. I planted out 160 Brussel sprout plants of the seed from Mr. Mannadear and fill'd up the other beds with cabbage plants. it was drissiling & cloudey all day

Fryday 26th ↜ a fine day

Saturday 27th ↜ a fine day, Hyram's complaining Doctr Shoof directed him to take 12 gs of callamil at night & a dose of Jallop[134] in the morning

1795 Sunday June 28th ↜ Hyram took a dose of Jallop this morning betwen 5 & 6 oclock. he heve it up diretly. about an Hour after I gave him another, it like wis came up. about 9 oclock he went to Doctr Shoof and informed him how it was with him. he gave him 8 pills to take in about 3 or 4 Hours. he got 5 down but could take no more with out heaving. I then gave him Sena tea which procured

---

[130] At least eight different authors published dictionaries of the arts and sciences during the eighteenth century, from Ephraim Chambers' *Universal Dictionary of Arts and Sciences* (1728) to William Henry Hall's *Complete Modern Universal Dictionary of Arts and Sciences* (1791). John Harris's 1736 work contained neither a description nor an illustration of a silk reel; early editions of Chambers had a lengthy description but no illustration. The Rev. Temple Henry Croker's *The Complete Dictionary of Arts and Sciences . . .* (1766) contained not only the description that appeared in Chambers, but also several illustrations, from different angles, of the complicated apparatus. The reel was used to draw silk from the balls wound by the silkworms and form it into thread. In addition to the reel, the process also required a furnace with a copper bath for heated water into which the balls were placed to loosen the silk. By this method, two men could produce three pounds of silk a day. While it is unlikely—if Faris's silkworms produced any silk at all—that he would have had enough to justify the effort of constructing the complete apparatus, his inventory does list "one silk reel" valued at $.50.

[131] A Kitty Johnson did marry David Robinson in April 1800.

[132] This may have been Ann Pinkney (c.1755–1835), the daughter of Jonathan Pinkney and his wife Ann Rind, and the sister of William Pinkney (see 30 August 1793). She never married.

[133] There were four Bond households in Anne Arundel in 1790 and one, with a different head, in 1800, providing no way of identifying the supposed bridegroom, who may not even have been an Anne Arundel resident.

[134] Jalap is a purgative drug obtained from plants of the morning glory family.

him 3 or 4 stools and I think he better — it has been a fine day

Munday 29th ☞ Hyram's poorley to day but better then yesterday. a fine day

Tuseday 30th ☞ a fine day

1795 Wednesday July 1th ☞ a raney day

Thursday 2th ☞ a dull drisley rainey day. Charles Bought a pigg & Brought home. fitted the sty up and put him in

Fryday 3th ☞ Charles Faris sett of in the packett this morning for Baltimore. a cloudey day

Saturday 4th ☞ no perading to day. every thing very ded & dull except the Flag's being hoisted & the cannon Fired one oclock and a Ball at night. Nancey's gone to * — it has been a very fine day *Mr. Greens to dress & go to the Ball, but no Ladeys went except the 3 Miss Gassa[wa]ys & 2 Miss prices, so she did not go but came home from Mr. Green's betwen 9 & 10 oclock

Sunday 5th ☞ this morning after Brackfast Hyram sett of over South River on horse Back. a fine day. in the evening it rained

1795 Munday July 6th ☞ a fine day. in the evening thare was an accot of the arrival of the vessel that Poor John Tootel went out in and that he died in the West Indes — Charles arrived from Baltimore Last night about a 11 oclock

Tuseday 7th ☞ John Cowman Junr & Mr. Plumer[135] dined with us. Mr. Cowman brought a Horse for Nancey Faris to go to his Fathers. thay sett of about 5 oclock. a fine day

Wednesday 8th ☞ Hyram began this fore noon to take up the Tulep Roots in the nurssey Beds. a fine day

Thursday 9th ☞ a fine day

1795 Fryday July 10th ☞ a very warm day. in the evening looks cloudey as if we should have a gust

Saturday 11th ☞ a very warm day

Sunday 12th ☞ a sulterey warm day, Charles went to Thomas Woodward's & thare saw his sister the Fameley & she are all well

[135] Joanna Hopkins, daughter of Gerard Hopkins (see 7 March 1795), married John Plummer (1750–1789), the son of Jerome and Mary Harris Plummer, of the West River Quaker community, in December 1772. Faris's visitor may have been one of his sons, probably either Jerome (b.1775) who married Elizabeth Hopkins in 1796, or Gerard (b.1775) who married Mary Hopkins in 1802.

Munday 13th ✎ a sulterey hott day

Tuseday 14th ✎ very Hott, in the evening cloude & look like rain

Wednesday 15th ✎ a fine rain this morning & continued cloudey all day. in the evening a littel more rain

1795 Thursday July 16th ✎ a fine day

Fryday 17th ✎ a fine day

Saturday 18th ✎ this morning Nicholas Carrols Brigg arrived, that was run ashore to southward of the Capes, Capt. Thomas Moore[136] went down and got her off & Brought her up, a very warm day, in the evening cloudey as if it woul rain

Sunday 19th ✎ a warm day. this evening Robert Parker was married to a young woman that lived with Samuel H. Howard[137]

Munday 20th ✎ this evening was buried a young man by the name of Williams,[138] a student of the Collage, a sober sollid well be Haved young man. a very warm day

1795 Tuseday July 21th ✎ a very Hott day

Wednesday 22th ✎ this after noon about 1 oclock Mrs. Dorrethey Whitcroft[139] dide. a very Hott day. I this day mad abegining or rather an attempt to make a forty Piano[140]

Thursday 23th ✎ Mrs. Whitcroft was Buried this morning about 6 oclock. a very Hott day. in the evening a littel shower of rain

Fryday 24th ✎ a fine rain last night. a very hott day. in the evening cloudey, look as if wee should have rain to night

Saturday 25th ✎ thare was a cleaver rain last night. a very Hott day

1795 Sunday July 26th ✎ this morning Hyram sett of to Mr. Cowmans to see his sister Nancey. a fine pleasant day. he returned betwen 9 & 10 oclock in the evening. she's right well & the fameley whare she is is well

Munday 27th ✎ the Corporation whare to have met this after noon in regard of the man that wants to show Fire woorks in the Play House, but it rained so very hard most of the day and all the after noon that they could not meat

---

136 Thomas Moore was a ship captain who lived at 16 Wilkes Street in Fells Point in 1796.

137 The only license for a Parker at this time was issued on 18 July to Jonathan P. Parker and Elizabeth Ann Owings. Jonathan Parker was a coach maker in 1783, but this may have been a son. Jonathan Parker lived on the west side of Green Street in 1801 as a tenant of Nicholas Carroll. There was a Robert Parker in Annapolis as well, who supplied bread to Faris in 1794 and 1795, and who appears in probate records in 1798.

138 Alexander Williams, the son of planter Francis Williams of Calvert County, who entered the St. John's grammar school in April 1792 at the age of eighteen and the college in August 1793.

139 Possibly the wife of James Whetcroft. Henry Whetcroft, James's son, married his cousin Sarah in 1796; William's wife was Frances, and Burton's wife was Elizabeth. None of the males in the next generation appear to have been married in 1795.

140 Faris is making himself a pianoforte. The instrument (whose name would eventually be shortened to piano) was relatively new and an improvement over the older harpsichord in that it could be played both softly (piano) and loudly (forte). The pianoforte was invented c.1700, the first references to pianos imported into the colonies occur in the 1760s, and the first advertisement (in the *Pennsylvania Packet*) for a commercially-available American-made piano dates from 1783 (David Hildebrand, pesonal communication, 29 September and 18 December 2000). Few pianofortes are listed in eighteenth-century inventories. Where they are recorded, the owners tend to be wealthy members of the gentry, such as Edward Lloyd IV (see 19 October 1792), who owned two, one valued at £22 and the other at £75, when he died in 1796.

Tuseday 28th ✍ could not make up a Corporation, J. Bullen[141] went to Baltimore & Nicholas Carrol went out of Town so that thare could not be any thing do[ne]. in the evening no peopel met at the Play House so he did not preform. a warm day

1795 Wednesday July 29th ✍ a fine day. in the evening the Fire man made another attempt but no bodey came so he did not preform

Thursday 30th ✍ a rainey day

Fryday 31th ✍ a dull cloudey day. in the evening looks as if wee should have more rain

Saturday Augt 1th ✍ a fine day. in the evening French man Fiered off his fire works in the collage green

Sunday 2th ✍ a cloudey day. in the afternoon & evening rain

1795 Munday Augt 3th ✍ rained very hard all last night and Blow'd a Harrican[142]   Blow'd down the Willow Tree in the lot and a grate many trees about and has certainly done a great deal of damage about. the tide was so high this morning that one could not get to the Market House with out a Boat. several vessels Blow'd ashore. cloudey & rain at times all day, in the evening looks like for more rain

Tuseday 4th ✍ a fine day and very hott

Wednesday 5th ✍ a very warm day. in the evening looks as if wee should have more rain

1795 Thursday Augt 6th ✍ a very Hott day

Fryday 7th ✍ a Hott day

Saturday 8th ✍ a very hott day. in the evening looks like rain. I receiv'd a Letter from Nancy, she well. talks of being home on Munday or Tuseday

Sunday 9th ✍ a fine shower of rain last night. a very warm day

Munday 10th ✍ a very warm day. in the evening wee had a fine rain

Tuseday 11th ✍ a fine morning. in the afternoon and evening raind hard

1795 Wednesday Augt 12th ✍ a rainey night last night. a cloudey rainey day. in the evening looks like for more rain

Thursday 13th ✍ rained last night. a cloudey raney drisley day

[141] John Bullen, the son of John (d.<1764) and Sarah Bullen, was an alderman at this time, but also served several terms as mayor of Annapolis, both earlier and later. In 1783 he was the owner of two lots and three slaves. He was unmarried in that year and probably never married. When he died in 1798, leaving an estate appraised at £617, he devised his property to his Jennings niece and nephews.

[142] The storm drove six ships ashore at Ocracoke Bar in North Carolina and a Spanish fleet of eighteen vessels onto the Hatteras shoals. Heavy flooding occurred as far west as Winchester and Martinsburg, Virginia. "The center probably orbited in over eastern North Carolina like a comet and then headed east-northeastward out to sea again after dousing the entire tidewater and Piedmont in a tropical deluge." David Ludlum, *Early American Hurricanes: 1492–1870* (Boston: American Meteorological Society, 1963), 34–35.

Fryday 14th ↩ the wind Blew hard all Last night & rained,¹⁴³ a rainey morning and continued rain & cloudey all day till the evening the sun came out and looks like clear weather

Saturday 15th ↩ a fine clear day

Sunday 16th ↩ this day I enter in to the 68 year of my age. a fine day

1795 Munday Augt 17th ↩ a fine coole morning but to wards noon turned very warm

Tuseday 18th ↩ a very Hott day. Mrs Faris Abee & Beckey & several girls & Charles rode out in the stage this morning to meet Nancey but thay ware dissoopinted, she did not come home to day. I afraid some thing has happen'd to her that prevented her coming

Wednesday 19th ↩ a fine morning. about a 11 oclock Nancey came home & young Mr. Cowman with her. she's very fatt & harty. in the after noon shee with her brother Charles & sisters went over the creek to a Tea party with Mrs. Kilty & several other. a very Hott day

Thursday 20th ↩ a very warm day. in the evening a fine rain

1795 Fryday Augt 21th ↩ a rainey Night last last night. a cloudey morning and continued cloudey & drisling all day

Saturday 22th ↩ a dull cloudey day

Sunday 23th ↩ a dull cloudey day. in the evening the sun came out & look as if wee should have good weather

Munday 24th ↩ rained at times all day & looks as if it would be a rainey night

Tuseday 25th ↩ a fine day

Wednesday 26th ↩ a Hoot day

1795 Thursday Augt 27th ↩ a Hott day

Fryday 28th ↩ a very warm day

Saturday 29th ↩ a very Hott day, Mr. Samuel Green & Charles Faris sett of this morning about 4 oclock for Baltimore

Sunday 30th ↩ a very Hott day. in the evening clouded up and looks as if wee should have rain

Munday 31th ✎ a cloudey morning and rained at times all day

1795 Tuseday Sept. 1th ✎ rained hard at times all Last night. this morning cloudey and rained at times all day. in the evening sow'd earley York seed on the Border next the Burgomot Balm, and next to it cabbage seed a dull evening

Wednesday 2th ✎ a cloudey morning but clear'd away a fine day, Miss Betsey Hopkins & her Brother Jarrad[144] came to see us and dined & stay'd Tea and returned home in the evening. she appears to be a very fine girl. I never had the pleasure of seeing her before

Thursday 3th ✎ a fine coole day

1795 Fryday Septr 4th ✎ cold morning but turned warm in the midel of the day and pleasant

Saturday 5th ✎ a fine morning. about 10 oclock this fore noon Mr. William Hanson[145] Examener of Certificats died — a fine day

Sunday 6th ✎ rain'd very hard this morning Before day and about day Mr. Patrick McGraw one of the Masters of the Collage is dead.[146] he died in the night or this morning. a neagro man came from Baltimore in Capt. Thomas's Boat yesterday is dead & Buried. Mr. William Hanson's to be Buried at 10 oclock this morning. the Buriel was put of till between 12 & 1 oclock on accot of the rain, in the after noon cloudey and drisley and looks as if wee should have more rain

1795 Munday Septr 7th ✎ it has raind hard all last night and it's now 8 oclock and raining and looks like to continue raining. Miss Betsey Pryce was married Last Night to a young dutch man of Fredrick County By the name of Cryst[147] — about 10 oclock Mr. McGraw was Buried a cloudey drisley afternoon

Tuseday 8th ✎ rained hard last night, a cloudey drisley day, in the evening the sun came out & look as if wee should have a fine day to morrow

Wednesday 9th ✎ a fine warm day

Thursday 10th ✎ a fine day

Fryday 11th ✎ a fine day but very warm

1795 Saturday Sept. 12th ✎ a fine day. in the evening turn'd cloudey & look like for rain.

[144] Probably the children of Elijah Hopkins (see 7 March 1795).

[145] William Hanson left his house and lot to his wife, Helen Grey, whom he married in February 1788. The couple had a daughter Mary and possibly other children. The witnesses to his will were Ann, Helen, and Mary Tootell, perhaps neighbors or perhaps relatives of his wife. Although Faris considered his estate very small, it included one slave, a carriage, and mahogany furniture. The examiner general was an official of the land office, responsible for examining and signing certificates of survey.

[146] The 10 September 1795 *Maryland Gazette* noted the death of Mr. Patrick McGrath, Professor of Humanity at St. John's College, last Sunday morning, the 6th instant. McGrath's inventory, which valued his property at £120, stated that he had no kin in this country. § Faris bought two volumes of magazines for 7/9 and a small looking glass for £1.12.9 at the sale of his goods.

[147] Henry Crist was a tavern keeper, operating for a time in the property formerly owned by George Mann (see 5 January 1792). An August 1797 notice in the *Gazette* announced that French engravings would be exhibited at his ballroom, but by January 1799 he applied for relief as an insolvent debtor. Elizabeth Pryse was a daughter of saddler Thomas Pryse, one of the drowning victims on 22 February 1793.

Abraham Claud has been unwell with the gout in his stomack but to day he was very Ill, it was expected that he would have died, but he's better

Sunday 13th ✒ a cloudey morning but cleared a way at times. the sun sett clear in the evening

Munday 14th ✒ a very close sultrey morning. (Doctr Scott called to see me and in conversation he told me that he was Born in December 1724). a close sulterey Hott day, this day receiv'd a Letter from my son Capt. Faris dated Lisborn May the 20th

Tuseday 15th ✒ a fine day

1795 Wednesday Sept. 16th ✒ Mr. John Cowman and Mr. Richard Hopkins[148] dined with us. Mr. Cowman is and has ben very poorley. it's been a very Hott sultery day

Thursday 17th ✒ a fine day but very warm

Fryday 18th ✒ a fine day. in the after noon seems cloudey like rain

Saturday 19th ✒ rained Last night. a clear morning but has turned cold. betwen a 11 & 12 oclock Charles & his sister Abee sett of for Thomas Woodwards in Prince Georges County

Sunday 20th ✒ a fine cool day

Munday 21th ✒ very cold. I am afraid thare will be a frost to night

1795 Tuseday Septr 22th ✒ clear & cold for the time of year. had a fire in the grate room in the evening

Wednesday 23th ✒ a fine day about 9 oclock Capt. James West's wife died, a fire in the morning and evening in ye grate room

Thursday 24th ✒ a fine Pleasant day

Fryday 25th ✒ a fine pleasant day

Saturday 26th ✒ a fine day. in the evening the wind got round to the East and looks like rain

Sunday 27th ✒ rained hard last night. continued raining and Blowing very diard all the fore part of the day. in the evening the sun sett clear

1795 Munday Septr 28th ✒ a fine day

Tuseday 29th ✒ a fine day but has turned rather coole

[148] John Cowman's brother-in-law, one of the sons of Gerard Hopkins (see 7 March 1795).

Wednesday 30th ✒ a fine day

Thursday Octr 1th ✒ about 2 oclock this morning Sylvea called her mistris & the girls. thay got up. Adam was very sick, and betwen 9 & 10 oclock he died. in the evening he was buried — Mrs. Faris & the girls took on very much Perticularly Beckey — a fine day,[149] Miss Nancey Ashmead's returned from Philladelphia

Fryday 2th ✒ a fine day. in the evening the wind got round to the N.E. and has clouded up and looks like rain

Saturday 3th ✒ this fore noon betwen 10 & 11 oclock Abee came home & Thomas Woodword with her. she very harty. a fine day, in ye evening looks like rain

1795 Sunday Octr 4th ✒ it is reported that Risdon Harwood[150] is drownded in South River. some say he fell over board & others say that he threw him self over bord on purpos, it's been a fine day — Mr. Owens[151] the school master's wife died this after noon

Munday 5th ✒ Miss Fowler died this fore noon. a fine warm day. in the evening rain — I received a Letter from my son Capt. Faris dated Hamburgh Augt 9th

Tuseday 6th ✒ rained allmost all night. a fine morning. in the after noon Mrs. Owens was Buried. it has been a fine day

Wednesday 7th ✒ this after noon Miss Fanney Fowler was buried. a fine day, Charles sett off this morning for Baltimore in Barber's packett

1795 Thursday Octr 8th ✒ a fine day. in the evening Mr. William Davidson is married to Miss Rebecka Walker[152]

Fryday 9th ✒ a fine day. in the evening Nancey & Abee's gone to Mr. Greens to Tea and spend the evening, thare was a card for Charles[153] but he's in Baltimore

Saturday 10th ✒ a fine day. in the evening rained a littel

Sunday 11th ✒ rained hard this morning before day. clear'd away a fine day

Munday 12th ✒ a fine day

[149] Faris frequently follows the report of someone's death or burial with the phrase "a fine day," but the latter has no relationship to the events that he records. "A fine day" refers only to the weather, and is not an evaluation of anyone's experience of the day.

[150] Risdon Harwood was undoubtedly a member of the extensive Harwood kinship network composed of the grandchildren and great-grandchildren of Richard (d.1712) and Mary Harwood, but there are no records that locate Risdon within the group.

111 ✒ Richard Owen (ca. 1744–1822)
St. John's professor Richard Owen and his family were good friends of the Faris family.

[151] Elizabeth Pinkney, the wife of Richard Owen (c.1744–1822), who immigrated to Annapolis from Wales. The Owens family, which lived on School Street in a one-story frame house, contained four children, three of whom appear in the diary. Owen, at the time a master of writing and arithmetic at St. John's College, died in Baltimore County in March 1822 at the age of seventy-seven. § When Faris died, Owen owed his estate £1.6.3.

[152] The son of John and Eleanor Davidson (see 1 January 1792), who died in 1802, leaving an estate appraised at $2,908.

[153] Each of the three Faris children received a card of invitation to the tea.

154 Richard Weems was the son of Capt. Richard Weems (1740–1780) and his second wife, Mary Ward, whom he married in April 1768. Richard was born 17 March 1769 in St. James Parish in southern Anne Arundel County, the eldest of his parents' five children and the older brother of James Nicholson Weems (see 24 September 1802). If Richard did shoot Col. Weems, he did not kill him (see following note).

155 Col. John Weems (1727–1794) was the son of David Weems (1706–1779) and his wife, Elizabeth Lane (d.1738). He lived at Portland Manor in St. James Parish, in southern Anne Arundel. Weems, who was a colonel in the county militia during the Revolution, was a justice of the peace from 1757 until the 1770s and a county commissioner of the tax in the 1780s. His second wife (the name of his first is unknown) was Mary Dorsey (d.1816), whom he married in December 1781. Her sister Eleanor married John Hall (see 8 March 1797). John and Mary had eight children, including a daughter, Ann, who married Horatio Ridout (see 21 November 1793). § Faris bought four barrels of corn from Weems in 1791, through John Randall (see 15 January 1795).

156 Probably Helen Hanson, the widow of William Hanson (see 5 September 1795).

157 Deborah Ghiselin, the wife of John Johnson (see 9 January 1794).

Tuseday 13th ✍ a fine day

1795 *Wednesday Octr 14th* ✍ a fine day. in the evening cloudey like rain

Thursday 15th ✍ rained last night & this morning. cleared away about 12 oclock, it is reported that Richard Weems[154] son of Richard willfully shot Mr. John Weems[155] in the Lower part of his Body. Doctr Ghislin has gone down to see what he can do for him. a neagro came up for him — a fine after noon

Fryday 16th ✍ a fine day

Saturday 17th ✍ a rainey morning. about noon clear'd away a fine afternoon but cold

Sunday 18th ✍ Frind Smith of Philada & Deberow Darby & Liddia Young from England Travelling frinds came to town this morning & Mrs. Darby & Mr. Smith preached & Mrs. Darby pray'd to a large congregation in the Stat house. thay ware accompaney by John Cowman & some of the hopkins's — a fine day

1795 *Munday Octr 19th* ✍ a fine day but cold

Tuseday 20th ✍ a fine day

Wednesday 21th ✍ this day a Neagro Man was tryed in the General Court and found gilty of commiting a rape on a yung girl of a 11 years of age. the crime was committed in Prince Georges County — a fine day

Thursday 22th ✍ a fine day

Fryday 23th ✍ a fine day, Mrs. Ellener Hanson[156] died last night betwen 12 & 1 oclock

Saturday 24th ✍ this evening Mrs. Hanson was Buried. it's been a cold dissagreeable day. looks likely for snow, or falling weather of some cind

1795 *Sunday Octr 25th* ✍ a fine day

Munday 26th ✍ a fine day

Tuseday 27th ✍ a fine day. Mrs. Debero Johnson's[157] come to Town from Cumberland

Wednesday 28th ✍ a fine day

Thursday 29th ✍ a fine day

Fryday 30th ✍ a fine day

Saturday 31th ✍ a fine day. in the evening turned cloudey & cold. about 12 oclock this fore noon Mrs. Wallace died[158]

1795 Sunday Novr 1th ✍ a cold cloudey day. looks as if wee should have snow or rain, this evening Miss Ellenor Davidson's to be married to Mr. Thomas Harris

Munday 2th ✍ a fine morning. I went to planting the Tulips. I have planted the first two Beds with seedling tulips. Mrs. Wallace is Buried this after noon. Mrs. Kelty & Nancy Howar[159] came to Town in the stage from Baltimore a fine day

Tuseday 3th ✍ a cloudey ugley morning but cleared away. the Jockey Club purs was won by Mr. Ridgly's Horse Easey.[160] 3 Horses started, one was distanced the first heat, Coll. Tayloe's horse was wiped most of the second Heat but could not forse Ridgelys Horse. a fine day, a Ball at night, Nancy Abee & Beckey, for the first time she ever went to a Ball, Mrs. Kelty with them. thay went in Smith's[161] stage

1795 Wednesday 4th ✍ this day's race was won by Mr. Johnson's mare of Virgina,[162] after the race a yung man by the name of Yealdall[163] was comeing to Town. his Horse stumbeled and threw him over his Head by which means the young man died imediatly

Thursday 5th ✍ a fine day, the Colts Race was won by Coll. Tayloe's colt,[164] its reported that Thomas Johnson[165] of the Federal City is dead

Fryday 6th ✍ a fine day

Saturday 7th ✍ finished palanting the Tulip Roots in the nurssery Beds. the senter row with red the next row on each side seedlings & the out side rows with the Best Tulips & next to them Hyacinth rush leav'd Irsisses & some John Quills. a very fine day

1795 Sunday Novr 8th ✍ a very fine warm day. in the evening clouded up & looks like rain

Munday 9th ✍ it both rain'd Blow'd very hard this morning and continued cloudey & raining all day

Tuseday 10th ✍ a very fine day. in the evening Mr.

[158] The 5 November 1795 *Maryland Gazette* reported that Mrs. Wallace died Saturday last in her 64th year, in Annapolis. This was Catherine, the first wife of Charles Wallace (see 5 January 1792).

[159] One of the daughters of Samuel Harvey Howard (see 31 October 1794). Faris records her marriage on 22 September 1796.

[160] Carnan Ridgely's horse Cincinnatus won the race easily and captured the $200 purse.

[161] Perhaps the John Smith who in December 1801 advertised that he was starting a stage line between Annapolis and Georgetown.

[162] William Johnson's mare Virago won the City purse of 20 guineas.

[163] There were several branches of the Yealdhall family in Anne Arundel at this time, making it impossible to be sure whose son died in the accident recorded by Faris. § Benjamin, Gilbert, and William Yealdhall all patronized Faris's tavern frequently in the 1770s.

[164] The *Gazette*, which appeared on Thursdays, did not report the results of this race.

[165] Possibly Faris is referring to Thomas Johnson (1732–1819), the first governor of the State of Maryland. Johnson, the son of Thomas Johnson (1702–1777) and Dorcas Sedgwick (1705–1770), was born in Calvert County but came to Annapolis to study law with Stephen Bordley. He married Anne Jennings, the daughter of Thomas and Rebecca Sanders Jennings, in February 1766 and the couple had seven children, including Thomas Jennings Johnson, whose marriage to Charlotte Hesselius Faris records on 5 June 1792. His brother Joshua was a partner with Charles Wallace and John Davidson in the firm Wallace, Davidson & Johnson (1771–1776) and with Wallace in Wallace, Johnson & Muir (1781–1790). § Faris made a pair of silver spectacles for him in April 1777, at a cost of £3.9.0.

166 Letitia Pryse was one of the daughters of saddler Thomas Pryse (see 23 February 1793) and William may have been the William Caucaud who lived in Calvert County in 1800.

167 The register of wills appointed two individuals to appraise each estate subject to probate (the very poor were exempt and estates so wealthy as to be certain of having sufficient assets to cover outstanding debts often did not go through probate).

168 The Marine Corps dates its history from 10 November 1775, when the Continental Congress ordered that "two battalions of marines be raised." In 1794, in response to the threat to shipping posed by Algerian pirates, Congress authorized construction of six frigates, each of which would carry a complement of marines. Hyram probably had service on one of these ships in mind when he sought a commission. In the end, only three of the frigates were built—the *Constitution*, *Constellation*, and *United States*—and recruiting for the marines did not begin until 1797.

William Caucord is married to Miss Lettee Price[166] — my dauters Nancey & Abee is goone to spend the evening at Mr. Charles Maccubin's. thare is to be a party thare

Wednesday 11th ☞ a fine day

Thursday 12th ☞ a cold day. in the after noon clouded up. in the evening rained & looks as if wee ware going to have bad weather

1795 Fryday Novr 13th ☞ a cold day. in the evening cloudey

Saturday 14th ☞ I this day with Mr. Vatchel Stevens went to appraise[167] the effects of the late William Hanson and I never saw so littel property in a House in my Life scarcely, as I did in that — a fine day. the amount of the appraisment is £251.18.5 ½

Sunday 15th ☞ a cloudey day. looks like bad weather comeing

Munday 16th ☞ a dissagreeable cold rainey day

Tuseday 17th ☞ a fine day

Wednesday 18th ☞ a fine day

1795 Thursday Novr 19th ☞ a fine day

Fryday 20th ☞ a fine day. receivd a Letter from Capt. Faris. he arrived in Baltimore yester day. had a passage of 60 days from Hamburgh to Fells Point

Saturday 21th ☞ Charles sett of in the stage this morning for Baltimore. a cloudey disagreeable day

Sunday 22th ☞ a cold windey dissagreeable day

Munday 23th ☞ this fore noon Hyram show'd me a Letter wrought by Govenor Stone ~~to the President~~ recomending him to the Pressident and requesting that he would appont Hyram an officer in the Mereen service.[168] a cold windey day

1795 Tuseday Novr 24th ☞ a fine day. mooved the mulberey Trees, in the evening Nancey & Abee went to the Colts Ball in Mr. Whitcrofts carrige

Wednesday 25th ☞ when the girls came home last night they came upstairs & they and Perticularly Mrs. Faris made such a noise with opening and shuting of doors that I got so disturbed that I could not get to sleep again till it was allmost day, and I have been very unwell all day, Mrs. Onions & Miss Charrity Onions dined heare. I did sett at Tabel but could eate but very littel I was so unwell, & diner not till betwen 2 & 3 o'clock, its been a fine day

Thursday 26th ↝ a cold cloudey day. about 2 oclock it hailed. continued cloudey and looks like falling weather

Fryday 27th ↝ a mideling good day

1795 Saturday Novr 28th ↝ a fine day, Charles complains of a pain in the Head. I ellectrifyed him for it, he seems a littel better

Sunday 29th ↝ Charles is very Ill. I went to Doctr Murray, he told me he had a pain in his brest that he could not come out, I then call'd on Doctr Ghislin. he came to see him. his opinion was that he was very Ill and was apprehensive it would turn to a nerves feveour. he sent him 3 papers of powders, & to take 1 every 2 or 3 Hours till they opperated — Hyram's apply'd to Mr. George Dent[169] & he has given a Letter of recomendation to the Secretary of War for a Luftennents commission in the Mareen Service. its been a raney dissagreeable day

Munday 30th ↝ Charles is still Ill — a fine day

Tuseday Desr 1th ↝ Charles is I think a littel better. a fine day

1795 Wednesday Desr 2th ↝ Charles's much as he was yesterday — a fine day

Thursday 3th ↝ Charles is much Better. a fine day

Fryday 4th ↝ Charles is much Better. he's down stairs. a fine day

Saturday 5th ↝ a fine day. the House of Assembley pass'd the Bill for altering the Jeneral Court[170] a mejority 16 Teen

Sunday 6th ↝ a fine day but turnd cold in the evening. Messrs Mifflin, Morris & Howell[171] the Quaker friend from the Dellawar state spent the evening with me

1795 Munday Desr 7th ↝ Charles went to his shop to day. a very dissagreeable cold rainey day

Tuseday 8th ↝ rained very hard the gratest part of the night, a fine day

Wednesday 9th ↝ a fine day

Thursday 10th ↝ a fine day, in the evening clouded up and looks like bad weather coming

[169] George Dent (c.1758–1813) was born in Charles County where he was a justice of the peace, delegate to the lower house, and state senator. From 1793 to 1801 he represented the first district, which did *not* include Annapolis, in Congress. The second district representatives, Gabriel Duvall and Richard Sprigg, were both Republicans, while Dent was a Federalist, which may be why Hyram sought his assistance rather than that of one of the local congressmen.

[170] Although the bill, to confirm an act passed in the previous session "concerning the jurisdiction of the General Court," passed the lower house, on 9 December the senate rejected it after the second reading and it did not become law.

[171] Mr. Mifflin may have been John F. Mifflin, son of Sarah Mifflin Bordley (see 1 April 1794) and Mr. Morris may have been Robert Morris (see 12 July 1804). The Quaker, Howell, may have been a relative of Hannah Howell, who married Faris's friend Elijah Hopkins in 1777 (see 7 March 1795).

Fryday 11th ✎ a fine day

Saturday 12th ✎ a dull cloudey day. in the afternoon & evening it rained

1795 Sunday Desr 13th ✎ rained very hard last night. a cloudey dissagreeable day

Munday 14th ✎ a cloudey dull day

Tuseday 15th ✎ a fine day

Wednesday 16th ✎ this day finished the stand of my Forty pio anio[172] all but painting it. a fine day

Thursday 17th ✎ a fine day

Fryday 18th ✎ a fine cold day

Saturday 19th ✎ a fine day

1795 Sunday Desr 20th ✎ snowd last night & this morning. clear'd away a fine day

Munday 21th ✎ a fine day. I had our 2 Hoggs Killed

Tuseday 22th ✎ the Hoggs I Killed yesterday way'd one 116 the other 112. a fine day

Wednesday 23th ✎ a fine morning. in the afternoon and evening cloudey like falling weather

Thursday 24th ✎ this morning early Hyram sett off on foot to Baltimore to see his Brother. about noon the Assembley Broke up. a fine day

Fryday 25th ✎ a fine day

Saturday 26th ✎ a fine day

Sunday 27th ✎ a fine warm day

1795 Munday Desr 28th ✎ a fine day

Tuseday 29th ✎ a fine morning. in the afternoon clouded and looked like for snow or falling weather

Wednesday 30th ✎ a fine day

Thursday 31th ✎ Hyram returned home from Baltimore this morning. a fine morning but soon clouded over & about 12 o'clock began to rain & continued all the after noon. in the evening rained smartley and looks as it would continue. Capt. James West is to be marryed to Miss peggey Whittecor,[173] Charles is gone to the wedden — Charles returned about 7 oclock, with an accot of the wedden's being broke off on accot of her sister's haveing a mollatto or neagro Husband so says report[174]

---

172 The pianoforte that Faris started making on 22 July.

173 James West (see 18 June 1792) and Margaret Whitaker received a license on this day. Although the wedding did not take place, they obtained a second license on 31 March 1796 and presumably married at that time.

174 Lydia Whitaker, possibly Margaret's sister, and William Rummells obtained a marriage license in 16 October 1792. There were free blacks in Annapolis by the name of Rummells, to whom William may have been related, or there may have been rumors of a kinship that did not in fact exist.

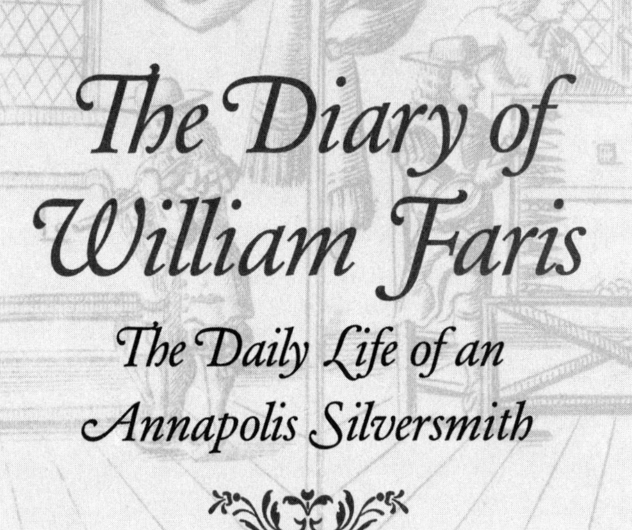

The Diary of William Faris

The Daily Life of an Annapolis Silversmith

PART THREE
1796–1799

1796 Fryday January 1th ✍ a fine day

Saturday 2th ✍ a fine day

Sunday 3th ✍ rained in the night, cloudey morning. about noon clear'd away fine after noon

Munday 4th ✍ a fine day

Tuseday 5th ✍ a very fogge morning & continued cloudey all day

Wednesday 6th ✍ rained grate Part of last night and has raned all day and now rains hard and look likely to continue

Thursday 7th ✍ Blow'd very hard & snow'd last night. a fine day after the bad night

1796 Fryday 8th ✍ a fine coole day

Saturday 9th ✍ a fine clear day for the season

Sunday 10th ✍ a cloudey morning, about a 11 oclock it began to snow and continued snowing all day. the girls ware sent for to dine at Capt. Thomas's and thay went thare. the girls came home about 8 oclock in the evening, it look as if winter was now setting in. it is s[t]ill snowing as fast as aney time to day

Munday 11th ✍ a cloudey, rainey, sleeting Bad day. in the evening Mr. Golder had a party at his House. I suppose thare could not be less then 50 persons men, women & children. thare was 7 Faris's & spent a very agreeable evening & broke up about 1 oclock

Tuseday 12th ✍ a very fine day, the Snow is Intirely gone

1796 Wednesday January 13th ✍ a fine day

Thursday 14th ✍ a rainey day

Fryday 15th ✍ Rebacco Faris & Miss Ashmead commenced going to the Danceing School.[1] a dull cloudey day

Saturday 16th ✍ rained Last night. a dull cloudey day

Sunday 17th ✍ rained in the night & continues. about a 11 oclock it snowd & rained fast for about an Hour. left of snowing but continued raining all day and still continues

Munday 18th ✍ a fine day

[1] Perhaps the school run by Citizen [James] Robardet, who periodically advertised "Robardet's Dancing School" in the *Gazette* (see, for example, 19 July 1792 or 16 October 1794 issues).

112 ✍ FACING PAGE *All of William Faris's known clocks have brass dials. The elaborate engraving of his name in the tympanum boss points to the skill of this craftsman.*

[2] The 1 January 1796 issue of Baltimore's *Federal Gazette* carried a notice of the imminent sailing for Amsterdam of "the Ship *Hebe*, St. John Faris, master." Jeremiah Yellott (see 16 August 1792) was one of the owners of the vessel. On the 13th, the *Hebe*, bound for Amsterdam, was the only ship to clear out of Baltimore.

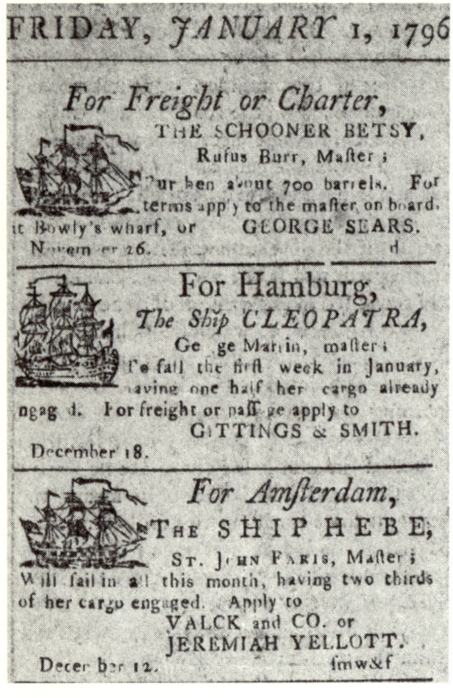

113 ☛ *Federal Gazette and Baltimore Daily Advertiser*
1 January 1796

[3] James Wharfe was the first tenant in Mann's tavern after the death of its original proprietor. As Wharfe witnessed George Mann's will in March 1795, he may have been working for Mann at the time. He was a deputy sheriff in January 1799 and chosen as a councilman in February of that year. Faris notes his marriage to Eleanor Brewer in July 1796, but she must have been his second wife as his sons John, age 7, and Joseph, age 9, entered the St. John's grammar school in 1795. Wharfe moved away from Annapolis in July 1801. § Faris bought two quarters of lamb from Wharfe on 16 August and 2 September in 1795 and nine cart loads of dung in September 1798. Charles Faris's estate paid Wharfe £6.4.4 and Faris collected £4.4.1 from Wharfe in September 1802 as administrator of Charles's estate.

1796 Tuseday January 19th ☛ about 12 oclock my son Capt. St. J. Faris came on shore. his vessel lys of in the Bay Bound to Amsterdam.[2] a fine day

Wednesday 20th ☛ a bad day. it rains hails & sleets, bad walking. in the evening wee had a littel Party & a Dance alltho the badnes of the evening & did not determin on haveing aney companey till betwen 3 & 4 oclock, wee had a companey of 20 odd

Thursday 21th ☛ a fine morning. about 10 oclock Capt. Faris went on Board in Capt. Thomas's Boat & by a 11 oclock was under way with a fine wind bound to Amsterdam. a fine evening but rather cold, a fine N.W wind

Fryday 22th ☛ a fine day but cold & slipery walking. about 9 oclock Charles sett off for Baltimore

Saturday 23th ☛ a fine day

Sunday 24th ☛ a fine day. about 4 oclock this after noon Charles returned from Baltimore

1796 Munday Janry 25th ☛ abut 10 oclock the roof of Charles's shop took fire. its supposed it was occassioned by a spark from the Pipe of his stove. it was put out with but very littel damage, a cloudey dull day

Tuseday 26th ☛ raind hard last night. a fine day but turning cold

Wednesday 27th ☛ a cold snowey day

Thursday 28th ☛ clear & cold

Fryday 29th ☛ a clear cold day

Saturday 30th ☛ last Night was the coldest night & this day the coldes wee have this winter

Sunday 31th ☛ a very cold day

1796 Munday Febury 1th ☛ a cold day

Tuseday 2th ☛ a cold morning. in the after noon turned more moderate. in the evening small rain

Wednesday 3th ☛ a fine day, sup'd and spent the evening at Mr. Golders

Thursday 4th ☛ a fine day, in the evening a large Tea Party at Mr. Warfs,[3] Mrs. Faris, my self and all the Famely was thare & stay'd till near 1 oclock before we got Home

Fryday 5th ✍ a fine day

Saturday 6th ✍ a fine day

Sunday 7th ✍ Charles sett off this morning on horse Back for Baltimore. a fine day

1796 Munday Febry 8th ✍ a fine day, Charles returned from Baltimore in the evening

Tuseday 9th ✍ Mrs. Faris[4] planted peas on the border next to Reigels.[5] a fine day

Wednesday 10th ✍ rainey snow & Hail this morning till about 10 oclock then continued raining all the rest of the day & evening

Thursday 11th ✍ a fine day after the rain. this evening Miss Nancey Murray's to be married to Mr. John Mason of George Town.[6] thare's a Ball at the Ball House[7] the evening, and Charles Hyram, Abee & Rebbecka are gone to it. the girls went in Mrs. Davidson's carriage

Fryday 12th ✍ a fine day but coole like March weather

Saturday 13th ✍ a fine day

1796 Sunday Febry 14th ✍ a fine day

Munday 15th ✍ about 12 oclock at noon, Mr. Henrey Warfield[8] died of a bad Feveour at Mr. Vatchel Stevens's. He was a worthey young man, his death is a loss to community

Tuseday 16th ✍ Capt. Rodgers Brackfasted with me too day & this fore noon went off to his ship to sail for Hamburgh. a fine day. this morning Mr. H. Warfields corps was carried in to the countrey to the Fameley Burying Ground to be interd

Wednesday 17th ✍ a fine day. in the evening cloudey

Thursday 18th ✍ a rainy day

Fryday 19th ✍ a fine day

1796 Saturday 20th ✍ a fine day but cold

Sunday Febry 21th ✍ a fine day. in the evening turned cold & clouded up, looks like bad weather

Munday 22th ✍ this morning the ground's coverd with snow. a fine day

Tuseday 23th ✍ a clear cold windey day

4 This is the only entry in which Priscilla Faris worked in the garden.

5 John Riegle was the sexton of St. Anne's, responsible for routine maintenance of the church and its furnishings. He also had an ordinary license in 1796. Riegle was in Annapolis as early as 1786, when he purchased £5.11.6 of sundries from the estate of Nicholas Maccubbin.

6 General John Mason (1766–1849) was the fourth son of George Mason of Gunston Hall (1725–1792) and his wife Anne Eilbeck (?–1773) of Charles County, Maryland. Anna Maria Murray (?–1859) was the daughter of Dr. James and Sarah Murray (see 19 May 1792). Mason was a merchant in the firm of Mason, Fenwick & Co., which started in tobacco but moved into banking, international commerce, foundries, trade in flour and wheat, and land investment. Jefferson appointed Mason a brigadier general in 1802 and he was commissary general of prisoners during the War of 1812. Mason built a house on Anastolan Island, in the Potomac River—today's Roosevelt Island, but known for many years as Masons Island—after his marriage, and also owned a house in Georgetown.

7 The Assembly Rooms, on Duke of Gloucester Street, built in 1765 for social gatherings, including balls, or "assemblies." The building burned during the Civil War, but the surviving walls became part of City Hall. Ebenezer Hazard, writing of his visit to Annapolis in 1777, noted that "the Assembly Room . . . is Spacious & Neat . . . well calculated to answer to the Purpose for which it was built; the orchestra is elevated in the Manner of a Gallery, & the Musicians go into it by a private Stairs."

8 Henry Warfield attended St. John's grammar school from November 1790 to May 1791. At the time of his death, Warfield was secretary of the senate. He left an estate valued at £79, which included his law books (£10), a desk, clothing (£40), and a horse (£18).

9 Benjamin Ogle (1775–1845) was the son of future governor Benjamin Ogle (see 14 November 1798). Anna Maria Cooke (c.1777–1856) was one of the daughters of attorney William Cooke (see 22 March 1792). § Faris received 11/3 from Ogle in April 1799.

10 Castor oil was a laxative used to treat constipation—Faris's "costive" condition.

Wednesday 24th ⤶ a cold dull cloudey day like for bad weather

Thursday 25th ⤶ a fine day. this evening Mr. Benjamin Ogel Junr is to be marryed to Miss Nancy Cook[9]

Fryday 26th ⤶ a fine day

Saturday 27th ⤶ a fine day

1796 Sunday Febry 28th ⤶ a fine day

Munday 29th ⤶ rained hard last night. cloudey morning. in the after noon it rained

Tuseday March 1th ⤶ snow'd fast this morning and till near noon, a cloudey after noon

Wednesday 2th ⤶ snow'd smartley this morning till 9 or 10 oclock, but continued cloudey all day

Thursday 3th ⤶ hailed & sleeted last night & this morning turned to a mist & continued cloudey all day

Fryday 4th ⤶ cut down the Appel Tree by the littel room & trimed the other, Hyram's trimed the rose bushes & I trimed the line of sage & Sylve's finished digging up the Parsneps & is digging the ground ready to plant more. a fine day

1796 Saturday March 5th ⤶ Sylve has finished the ground for Parsneps this fore noon, and after diner Hyram went planting the Parsnep seeds. a raw cold day

Sunday 6th ⤶ I have been very costive for some time, I took a dose of castor oile to day.[10] it did not work me much. it's been a fine day

Munday 7th ⤶ this morning I hired a neagro man by the name of Charles. I sett him to planting parsneps, rows 9 Inchs wide & 6 Inchs from seed to seed. he finish'd the parsneps & finis the remainder of ground with carrots rows 7 Inchs & ½ apart. a fine day but in the evening clouded up & turnd cold. I like wise put up 3 posts with rails for the grape vines

Tuseday 8th ⤶ snow'd the most of last night and continued snowing all this morning till 12 oclock then cleared away very cold

1796 Wednesday March 9th ⤶ clear & cold. snow on the ground in maney places

Thursday 10th ☞ a clear day. weather's turn'd more moderate. Chares has moved to his new shop,[11] neagro Charles has been helping him, after diner he went down for some Bottels, he brought them home, left them in the shop. went off with him self & I have not seen him since

Fryday 11th ☞ a fine day. not seen aney thing off my man Charles

Saturday 12th ☞ a fine day

Sunday 13th ☞ Nancey & Abee went with Capt. Thomas and his Fammeley a sailing too day, its been a very fine day

Munday 14th ☞ Sylve's began digging ye Bigg Bed & Hyram's began troweling the flower beds. a fine day, in the evening clouded up like for rain

1796 Tuseday March 15th ☞ I cut the line of Box on the right hand side of the grass walk & Sylve has finished digging the Big Bed & Hyram's digging the flowers beds. a fine day

Wednesday 16th ☞ it came on to Blowed very hard in the nigh. continues Blowing excessive hard. Mr. John Brice chimney of his House blew down, I have 6 pannels of Fence down. I expect to heare of much damage being done. a sloop on anker in the harber broke her cabel & is ashore on Horn point.[12] the Seeder Tree by Macnemarrows[13] brok off about 3 feet above the ground. now betwen 9 & 10 oclock at night and its still Blowing extreemlly hard. I dont remember ever its Blowing harder in my life

Thursday 17th ☞ the winde has Blowen extreemly hard all night, and all day till the evening it has abated. I have got Sullivan[14] this evening about the fence, the 3 girls and Hyram's gone to the Ball

1796 Fryday March 18th ☞ a very fine morning, about 10 oclock clouded up & snow'd Haild & rained a littel. I planted the Big Bed with peas & planted cabbage plants betwen the rows and this after noon the carpenter finished puting up the fence. in the after noon it came on to blow prette Hard and got the Lumber from the old Fence put away

Satuday 19th ☞ a cold windey day. nothing done in the garden

[11] Charles's advertisements do not indicate the location of this new shop, but it may have been at Henry Maccubbin's house on Church Street, which he occupied in 1798.

[12] The neck of land between Spa and Back Creeks.

[13] Probably Darby McNemara, who must have plagued Faris for the remainder of his life (see 17 November 1800), for only in September 1805—more than a year after Faris's death—did the *Gazette* carry a notice that McNemara's house was for sale. McNemara died in February 1806, leaving no family, his wife having already died and there apparently being no children. McNemara left his estate to Daniel Fowler (see 3 January 1801).

[14] Possibly joiner John Sullivan, who appears in the Annapolis records as early as 1792, when he witnessed the will of John Henry Maccubbin, signing it with a mark. He also appraised the estate of John Butcher (see 3 December 1796) in 1797 and purchased goods at the 1799 sale of Richard Wells's property. In 1798 he rented a small one-story house with a frame kitchen and stable. His son James, age 11, attended the St. John's grammar school in 1799. § Sullivan received £7.10.0 for funeral expenses as part of the administration of Faris's estate, a charge that may have included Faris's coffin. Priscilla Faris listed a debt of £9.15.7 1/2 owed by Sullivan to Charles's estate.

Sunday 20th ✒ a fine morning & fore part of the day. in the after noon clouded up & looks as if wee should have rain

Munday 21th ✒ a fine day, but cold & raw

Tuseday 22th ✒ a very fine morning. made 23 hills in the lott & planted 7 of cucumbers, 6 of cantilopes & 10 of simmelins of the Bunch cind, Miss Betsey Thomas & her brother William is come to spend the day with us — Sylvea's weeled in dung on the littel quarter and began to digg it, Hyram's digging ye flower beds, in the evening clouded up like for rain

1796 Wednesday March 23th ✒ a fine morning. planted the Tube Roses & sow'd in potts the Sencitive Plants, the Ice Plant & the egg plant seeds. Hyram's finished digging ye flower beds, and Sylvea's dug the littel quarter and beg[an] to fork the asspargrass beds. in the evening looks like for rain

Thursday 24th ✒ Planted the littel quarter with Beens from Mr. Parrea,[15] Hyram's triming the Box, the weather's turn'd cold & cloudey

Fryday 25th ✒ Hiram's cuting Box. I finished puting up the peaces for the vines to run on a windey cold day. sow'd radish seed in the littel quarter betwen the beens

Saturday 26th ✒ very cold Last night, some water in the garden frose better then ½ Inch thick, Hiram is cuting Box. a cold raw day

1796 Sunday 27th ✒ Charles Hiram & my self dined at Capt. Thomas's. a fine day

Munday 28th ✒ Miss Fanney & Salley Whitcroft sett of in Capt. George Barbers boate for Baltimore and went as far as the Bodkins[16] & turned back, the wind Blew so hard & came round to N.W. thay got back again about 3 oclock in the after noon

Tuseday 29th ✒ the Miss Whitcrofts sett of earley this morning in Ellick's stage[17] for Baltimore, a fine day

Wednesday 30th ✒ finished the assparagrass beds and sowed on the near one No. 1 Drum head & No. 2 earley York cabbage seeds & on the far one green Brocklo & cabbage seed & lettice on both, a fine warm day

Thursday 31th ✒ a fine day, very dry. rain's much wanted

[15] This individual was probably Joseph Parrian, a gardener who lived on Pitt Street in Old Town in 1796.

[16] Bodkin Point is the east end of Bodkin Neck, on the south shore of the mouth of the Patapsco River, formed by Bodkin Creek and the Chesapeake Bay.

[17] Regular stage service between Annapolis and both Baltimore and Washington became available by the 1790s, paralleling the availability of packet transportation by water.

1796 Fryday April 1th ✒ a fine day, Hyram cuting Box, the Peas in the big Bed making thare appearance

Saturday 2th ✒ a fine morning, hiram has this afternoon finish'd cutting all the Box except the line of Box next to Rigels, thare was a littel shower of [rain] this after noon & in the evening it looks as if wee should have a fine rain

Sunday 3th ✒ rained but littel last night, a dull cloudey day

Munday 4th ✒ Sylvea's taking the cuttings of Box & litter out of the garden, Hiram has finished the line of Box next to Rigels & is doing up the Tabels round the grass walk & I stuck the Peas on the Border, a fine day

Tuseday 5th ✒ Hiram's doing up the tabels & Sylve is taking the litter out & cleaning the garden, it is rather cool to day

1796 Wednesday April 6th ✒ Sylvea ruffinished [rough finished] cleaning the garden, brought in dung and dug the border whare the vines are & Planted a line of garlick on the front edge. Hyram's Troweling the tabels round the grass walk. a coole day for the season, I planted a young Tree the Pride of Chine a present from Mrs. Davidson

Thursday 7th ✒ Hyram's finished the tabels round the grass walks. Mr. Archibald Golder gave me a Berrey or seed of the Tallow Tree. I planted it at the far end of the Border by the grapes with stick No. 12 a fine day

Fryday 8th ✒ warm & very dry

Saturday 9th ✒ a fine day

Sunday 10th ✒ a cool windey day. in the afternoon turned very cold, I have simlins up, I have covered them for feer of a frost

1796 Munday April 11th ✒ a cold raw day

Tuseday 12th ✒ a fine morning. in the afternoon cloud'd up & Lookd Like for rain

Wednesday 13th ✒ a fine day, cutt assparragrass

Thursday 14th ✒ a cloudey morning, looks like for rain, in the after noon it rained a littel

Fryday 15th ✒ a fine day

Saturday 16th ☞ this morning before day Mrs. Quynn died, a cold raw day

Sunday 17th ☞ a fine day. in the evening Mrs. Quynn was Buried

1796 Munday April 18th ☞ I stuck the peas in the big bed, and waterd the garden, the peas on the Border is in Blossom

Tuseday 19th ☞ a fine day but every thing in the garden's suffering for want of rain

Wednesday 20th ☞ a fine day, but very dry

Thursday 21th ☞ a fine day

Fryday 22th ☞ a fine day

Saturday 23th ☞ a fine day but very dry

Sunday 24th ☞ a fine day. about noon whee had a littel sprinkel of rain, and in the evening it clouded up, wee had a littel sprinkel but looks as if wee should have a fine rain

1796 Munday April 25th ☞ the rain wee expected last night went off. wee had none of it — Mr. Hanson Marked 30 Tulips & 6 Hyacinths with sticks with out any mark at 6 Dolls. pr doz. a fine day but raw & coole

Tuseday 26th ☞ a cloudey cold raw day. in the evening it looks as if wee should have rain. Capt. John Stewart died this morning[18]

Wednesday 27th ☞ a cloudey morning, & the wind Blow'd very hard, in the after noon wee had a fine rain, but not anuff of it. the sun shined out in the evening

Thursday 28th ☞ a fine day but cold

Fryday 29th ☞ a fine day but cold, this after noon Mr. Whitcroft & famely returned home from Philada

Saturday 30th ☞ still cold

1796 Sunday May 1th ☞ a fine day. in the evening my whole Famely drank Tea at Mr. William Witcrofts

Munday 2th ☞ Charles went of this morning in Capt. G. Barbers boat for Baltimore. in the evening Hyram, Nancey, Abee & Beckey's gone to a Ball at Warfs Long Room. a fine day. Sylve's been diging ye littel quarter by the old stable for beens

[18] Capt. John Stewart was the son-in-law of William Brown (d.1794) and was related to Elizabeth McClellan (see 27 June 1800) and her daughter Ann Wilmot, but the exact nature of the kinship is undocumented. § By the late 1700s, it had become a common practice to hold a public sale of a decedent's assets and to distribute the proceeds to the heirs rather than dividing the physical property itself. When Mrs. Stewart held a sale of her husband's estate in August 1797, Faris bought a poplar sacking bottom bedstead for £2.0.6.

Tuseday 3th ↙ planted 7 rows of Beens in the littel quarter by the old stabel. a fine day

Wednesday 4th ↙ a fine day

Thursday 5th ↙ a fine day. the Family spent the evening at Capt. Thomas's. Mrs. Faris & my self came home about 10 oclock & left the rest of thare a danceing

1796 Fryday May 6th ↙ a fine rain last night and this morning and continued raining till noon then clear'd away a fine after noon. Charles came home from Baltimore last night, he and 7 or 8 others walked from Magothey. the wind Blew very hard and a Head

Saturday 7th ↙ a fine day

Sunday 8th ↙ wee had a cleaver littel rain in the night. a fine morning, but turned cold in the afternoon, made a Fire in the House. in the evening came on to Blow very hard & cold

Munday 9th ↙ a fine morning but cold, Sylvea has digg'd up part of the Border next to Rigels and I sowed on the farther part cabbage seed I saved, next Drum head cabbage seed & lettice with both, then Sylve went about thining ye parsneps. in the evening it came on to rain a littel

1796 Tuseday May 10th ↙ a fine day

Wednesday 11th ↙ a fine morning, the chancellor brought me 2 Ice plants. I planted them in the Barrel, in the after noon wee had a shower of rain

Thursday 12th ↙ a fine day. about 1 oclock the Bees swarmed & in the evening moved them in to the Bee House. gather'd Peas to day

Fryday 13th ↙ a fine day. in the evening mooved the old Hive with the Bees & put it on 2 Hives at the end of the Bee House

Saturday 14th ↙ a fine day

Sunday 15th ↙ a fine morning. in the after noon a fine rain. this morning old Mrs. Sands died aged [blank]. Charles setts up with the corps to night[19]

1796 Munday May 16th ↙ a fine day

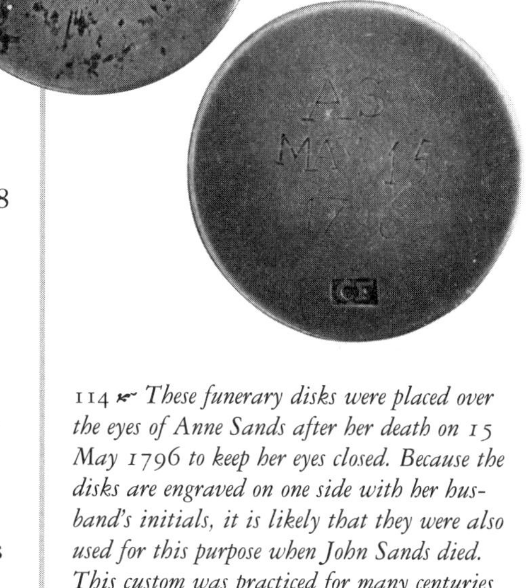

114 ↙ *These funerary disks were placed over the eyes of Anne Sands after her death on 15 May 1796 to keep her eyes closed. Because the disks are engraved on one side with her husband's initials, it is likely that they were also used for this purpose when John Sands died. This custom was practiced for many centuries but usually with coins rather than artifacts specifically made for that purpose. It is telling that Charles not only made and engraved the disks for Sands, but watched over her corpse as well.*

[19] Although the practice was dying out, there existed a long tradition of having one or more people watch over a corpse between death and burial. "Watching" was a mark of respect for the deceased and his or her family, prevented any tampering with the corpse, and ensured that someone would be present if the body unexpectedly revived. There is no indication as to why Charles Faris would have been watching in this instance. When William Paca's niece died in 1766, the expenses charged to her estate included a payment to the person who sat up with her corpse, but there is no indication that Charles was paid for his service. More likely he acted as a friend of the family.

Tuseday 17th ⚮ a cloudey morning. in the after noon a fine rain & in the evening Mrs. Sands was Buried

Wednesday 18th ⚮ a rained the most of last night. continues rainey this morning, this morning Mr. Burton Witcrofts[20] child died. in the evening it was Buried. a fine evening

Thursday 19th ⚮ a raney morning. clear'd away a fine after noon. in the evening raind a littel

Fryday 20th ⚮ a fine morning. after Brackfast Doctr Ghisling cutt my son Charles's Tongue, present the Doctr's 2 young men, Messrs Brewer[21] & Thomas[22] — it is the second time it has been cut Doctr Murray cut it before but did not take it all out but I am in hopes it is all out now — about 11 oclock I sow'd some of the Brussel sprout seed I had from Mr. Hesler Baltimore. a fine day but turn'd cold

1796 Saturday May 21th ⚮ this morning about 2 oclock Mr. John Johnson's wife was Brought to Bed of a Son. a fine day but cold for the season. Mr. Johnson's sones name is to be Reverdy[23]

Sunday 22th ⚮ a fine day

Munday 23th ⚮ a fine day. in the evening wee had a littel rain & looks as if wee should have a fine rain

Tuseday 24th ⚮ a fine day but coole. after the rain this afternoon the old Hive of Bees swarmed. I hived them & the Bees went up into the Hive Immediatly and in less then a Hour I had them fixed in thare place

Wednesday 25th ⚮ a cold raney morning. a fire in the grate in the House. continued rainny all day

Thursday 26th ⚮ a cold raney day. a fire in the grate in the House

1796 Fryday May 27th ⚮ a fine day

Saturday 28th ⚮ a cloudey morning. about 9 oclock Hyram sett of for Mr. Linscums's & about 12 oclock Messrs. Walker,[24] Goldsmith, Cayton & West sett of & about 5 oclock W. Whitcroft sett of for Linsecums. its the old mans Birth Day.[25] thare is to be grate doings thare this evening. in the evening it rained & is cloudey

---

[20] The child who died may have been the boy born in 1793 (see 18 August).

[21] Dr. William Brewer (b.1777) was the son of William Brewer (1732–1811) and his wife Rebecca Newton (d.1802). § He may have been the William Brewer who received 15 shillings from the estate of Charles Faris, but there were at least two other William Brewers in the area.

[22] Most likely the Dr. Thomas who bought two books at the sale of Faris's property.

[23] The choice of his maternal grandfather's name did not follow the usual pattern of naming the first-born son after the father's father. Reverdy Johnson (1796–1876) became one of the foremost attorneys of his day, particularly noted for his skill as a constitutional lawyer. Among a number of significant milestones in his career, his arguments in the Dred Scott case are credited with determining the decision against Scott's freedom.

[24] Possibly the William Walker who married Ann Coale in June 1792 and perhaps the William Walker whose death Faris records on 9 January 1801. He may have been related to Rebecca Walker (see 10 March 1795).

[25] Francis Linthicum (1734–1804) was the son of Francis Linthicum and his wife Eleanor Williams. He married Mary Mayo, daughter of Joseph and Sarah Mayo, in January 1755; the couple had 8 children. Linthicum fought in the 5th Maryland Regiment during the Revolutionary War and owned a plantation, Margaret's Fields, on the South River.

Sunday 29th ✍ this morning at Brackfast time William Witcroft & Hyram & the companey returned to Town from Mr. Lincecumbs very much dissopointed, thay expected to have had a dance but thare was not a woman thare, Miss was gone from home — in the after noon Nancy Abee & Charles & Hyram went with Capt. Thomas & Famely asailing. a fine day. in the evening clouded up & looks like rain

1796 Munday May 30th ✍ rained Hard in the night & this morning & most of the day till the evening. the sun sett cleare

Tuseday May 31th ✍ a rainey morning & continued raining till noon, a fine after noon. Sylve dug the Border whare the Peas grew & I sow'd part of it with radish seed, & drove the Bees out of the Old Hive in to a nother & took the Honey. the Hive was rotten and ready to tumbel to peaces. a fine evening

Wednesday June 1th ✍ a fine day

Thursday 2th ✍ a fine day

Fryday 3th ✍ a fine day

Saturday 4th ✍ this morning Charles, William Davidson & Samuel Green sett of about 4 oclock for Baltimore. a fine day. this after noon Capt. Celty & famely came to town from Baltimore

1796 Sunday June 5th ✍ a fine warm day. in the after noon wee had a fine rain and in the hith of it Charles came home from Baltimore

Munday 6th ✍ rained hard this morning — cloudey & drissiled at times all day. Sylve's been diging in the Walnutt Tree Bed at times to day

Tuseday 7th ✍ rain'd most of the night and continued all day till the evening & then cloudey

Wednesday 8th ✍ a fine day

Thursday 9th ✍ a fine day. in the evening rain

Fryday 10th ✍ a fine day. in the afternoon the Bees swarmed. I hived them, in the evening and Immediatley after it came on to rain and rained very hard all the evening

1796 Saturday June 11th ✍ a cloudey morning and continued cloudey all day

Sunday 12th ✒ last night Mrs. Rebacka Davidson was Brought to bed of a daughter, was marryed the 8th of Octr 95. thare was some preaching friends in the Stadhouse this fore noon. after diner the Friends came to see me & gave me and the Famely a very Frendley exortation. a dull cloudey day

Munday 13th ✒ Sylve Pulled the pea vines & sticks in the big bead and is digging the ground. a midling good day

Tuseday 14th ✒ a fine morning. Sylve finished diging the Big bead. in the after noon it rained & thunder'd verey Hard, it clear'd away. I planted a few plants ware they war missing

1796 Wednesday June 15th ✒ a cloudey morning. about 9 oclock clear'd away a fine day. planted a few cabbage plants this morning — Hyram began to do up the Tabel round the grass walk [page torn] noon

Thursday 16th ✒ Hyram's doing up the tabels. a cloudey day

Fryday 17th ✒ a fine day. Hyram's finished the Water Table round the grass walk

Saturday 18th ✒ a fine day but very warm. in the evening Mr. Pitt came up from Virginia with his two new Boats

Sunday 19th ✒ a fine morning. Mr. Pitt Brackfastd with us and after Brackfast he asked mine & Mrs. Faris's consent for our daughter Nancy. nither of us had aney objection to [page torn] tharefore I suppose it will not be long before thay are married. a fine day

1796 Munday June 20th ✒ a fine day

Tuseday 21th ✒ a fine day

Wednesday 22th ✒ this after noon Capt. Thomas and his Famely went over the Bay. a fine day

Thursday 23th ✒ a fine day but warm

Fryday 24th ✒ a ffine day

Saturday 25th ✒ Hyram's very poorley. I gave him a dose of castor oyle, he's no better. in the evening he went down to Doctr Murray's, he was not at home. Mr. Owens[26] sent a Bolos for him to take at bed Time. a fine day

---

[26] Dr. John Owen (b.1775) was the son of Richard and Elizabeth Owen (see 4 October 1795). He attended St. John's from November 1789 until June 1792, but did not receive a degree. In March 1797 he advertised that he was collecting debts owed to the partnership of Dr. James Murray and Dr. John T. Shaaff. By 1800, Owen had moved to Baltimore City.

1796 Sunday June 26th ✍ this afternoon wee had a fine shower of rain, Hyram's much better. the Doctr has sent him another Bolas. this has been a very hot day

Munday 27th ✍ a fine day. not so hott as yesterday

Tuseday 28th ✍ I have been and am very unwell. a fine day

Wednesday 29th ✍ I am still poorley — a fine day

Thursday 30th ✍ I am Better to day but have had no doctor — a fine day

Fryday July 1th ✍ a fine day

Saturday 2th ✍ a fine day. in the evening, William pitt came to Town from Baltimore

1796 Sunday July 3th ✍ we had some fine showers of rain this fore noon. a fine after noon

Munday 4th ✍ about 10 oclock this fore noon Mr. Goldsmith took Thomas Willson[27] in cusstodey to his own House, but in the after noon carried him to Prisson — this has been an exceeding Hott day

Tuseday 5th ✍ a very Hott day

Wednesday 6th ✍ in the after noon wee took two Hives of Bees. one was swarmed the 12th of May 96 a very fine hive — a very Hott day

Thursday 7th ✍ this evening William Pitt was married to my daughter Nancey by Parson Higginbothom.[28] Present Mrs. Thomas Mrs. Stevens Mrs. Golder Miss Ashmead Mr. Witcroft Mr. McMyers[29] & Capt. Gardner. it has been a very hot day

1796 Fryday July 8th ✍ an excessive Hott day. wee had a grate deal of companey both fore noon & evening

Saturday 9th ✍ a fine day. not so hot as yesterday, in the afternoon wee went to Mrs. Stevens's & spent the evening. thare was the Miss Witcrofts & Miss Thomas's &c — Genl Davidson Plaid the fiddel and thay danced

Sunday 10th ✍ a fine day. in the evening looks as if wee should have rain before morning. this evening Richard Gray the Barber was married to Miss Richardson[30]

Munday 11th ✍ a fine Pleasant day

[27] Possibly the merchant who has already appeared in the diary several times (see 30 July 1794). Nothing in either the diary or the *Maryland Gazette* explains why Wilson was arrested.

[28] Although the Pitts eventually joined the Methodist Church, the ceremony was performed by the rector of St. Anne's, the Episcopal church in Annapolis.

[29] John McMyers, a blockmaker, lived at 46 Philpot Street in 1796, next door to William and Ann Faris Pitt after their marriage. He had a shop at the lower end of Bond Street in Fells Point from 1796 through 1803. In January 1794, he married William Pitt's sister Elizabeth, who was probably his second wife.

[30] Richard Gray and Eleanor Richardson obtained a marriage license on 9 July. Gray opened a tavern in October 1805 near the State House. He may have been the same Richard Gray who married Elizabeth Brewer, daughter of Nicholas, in 1781.

Tuseday 12th ☞ a fine morning. in the after noon a fine rain. in the evening the whole Famely went to Capt. Thomas's

1796 Wednesday July 13th ☞ a cloudey morning. planted cabbage plants in the Big Bead. in the after noon a littel rain. Planted the walnutt tree Bed with Brussel Sprout Plants — this morning Charles and Capt. pitt went of for Baltimore with Capt. Thomas in his Boate

Thursday 14th ☞ a fine rain to day. Mr. Richard Spriggs wife died yesterday

Fryday 15th ☞ rained Hard in the night. Charles came home this morning. it has drisseled a small rain at times all day

Saturday 16th ☞ a fine day

1796 Sunday July 17th ☞ a Hott day

Munday 18th ☞ a fine day

Tuseday 19th ☞ a cloudey day with some rain

Wednesday 20th ☞ rained all day

Thursday 21th ☞ raind most of the night & this morning till near 12 o'clock, then clear'd away. a fine after noon

Fryday 22th ☞ a fine day. Capt. Pitt went to Baltimore this morning

Saturday 23th ☞ a fine day, this morning Miss Nancey Quynn[31] went of in the stage with her Brother Allen for Baltimore from thare to Fredrick whare she's to stay, the Town says she is with child & not of her own couler

1796 Sunday July 24th ☞ a fine day

Munday 25th ☞ a fine day

Thursday 26th ☞ cleaned & dug up the littel quarater by the old stabel & planted it with Beens. a fine day

Wednesday 27th ☞ Sylve has clear'd & dug the littel quarter — a fine day

Thursday 28th ☞ a fine rain this morning, about 9 oclock cleared away, about 12 oclock Charles Hyram, Nancey, Abee & Rebbeka went over the creeck to the big Frying pan to a fish Feast.[32] thare was a large companey thare & spent the day very

[31] The daughter of Allen Quynn (see 9 September 1792). Her name was physically cut out of the diary sometime after the 1930s, but appears in the Pleasants text (*Maryland Historical Magazine*, 28 [1933]: 219). Nancy Quynn was not mentioned in her father's will. On 11 February 1797 Faris records that Nancy Quynn Hunter came to town with her husband and that they stayed with the Claudes, Nancy's sister Elizabeth and her husband Abraham Claude. Both of Nancy's brothers, Allen and John, lived in Frederick.

[32] Possibly one of the necks of land on College Creek.

242

agreeable & in the evening Mr. James Warfe is married to Miss Ellen Brewer[33]

1796 Fryday July 29th — a fine day

Saturday 30th — this afternoon Capt. pitt came from Baltimore. a fine day

Sunday 31th — a very Hott day

Munday Augt 1th — a Hott day in the evening wee had a shower of rain which cooled the aire a littel

Tuseday 2th — a Hott day

Wednesday 3th — a fine day, W. pitt went to Baltimore

Thursday 4th — a fine day. Mrs. Faris has been very Ill with the collick[34] this after noon but she is Better

1796 Fryday Augt 5th — a fine coole day. Mrs. Faris is Better. I gave her a dose of castor oile

Saturday 6th — Last night betwen 11 & 12 oclock W. pitt returned from Baltimore & knocked the Famely up — a rainey morning & continued raining at times all day. I planted out about 100 plants

Sunday 7th — a rainey day

Munday 8th — a fine day. howed the plants in the two Beds, dug up a peace of ground by the nurssery of Box & Planted the Polianthus

1796 Tuseday Augt 9th — distilled 4 Bottels of Peach Leaves water & planted the littel quarter with Beens. a fine day. William Pitt is got a tutch of the Feveour & ague — this evening betwen 8 & 9 oclock Mrs. Ellenor Harris was Brought to bed of a fine Boy

Wednesday 10th — a fine day

Thursday 11th — W. pitt has the ague & Feveour has been taking Bark to day. a fine day

Fryday 12th — a fine day

Saturday 13th — this morning Messrs. Archibald Golder and wife, Capt. Pitt & wife & Mr. Poole[35] sett of for Mr. Cowmans, a cloudey morning. in the after noon rain & a wirl wind that tore Golder's & Wilsons Willow Trees to Peaces & Broke other & threw down an old House by the Town Gate[36]

33 James Wharfe (see 4 February 1796) and Eleanor Brewer obtained a license on 28 July. McIntire, *Annapolis Families*, states that Wharfe married Eleanor Stockett Brewer (b.1757), the daughter of Joseph and Mary Stockett Brewer. It is more likely, however, that he married the daughter of Joseph and Rachel Wootten Brewer, as Eleanor Wharfe, William Wootten Brewer, and Rachel Brewer each received a one-third share of Rachel Wootten Brewer's estate in 1799, indicating that they were Rachel's three children.

34 Acute abdominal pain.

35 Edward Poole (d.1808), whose marriage Faris will record on 4 June 1797. In 1798 he rented a small, single-story frame dwelling house from Benjamin Oden. Poole was a witness in 1799 to the will of Beriah Mayberry (see 1 August 1799) and in 1804 to the will of John Wheeler (see 4 May 1799). He appears as a voter on the poll lists of 1799 and 1800.

36 The town gate, located a short distance up West Street from the Faris home, controlled access to town by land. Benjamin Mifflin, who visited Annapolis in 1762, noted that there "is but one way to it North Leading under an Old Frame Building to which is Fixt a Swing Gate to Keep the Cattle out of the Town."

37 The two women were daughters of William Whetcroft (see 4 August 1793). Henry Whetcroft (c.1765–1837) was the son of James Whetcroft and most likely a first cousin of Sarah. In 1793 he was the register of St. Anne's parish. He moved from Annapolis to Washington, D.C., where he served for many years as an "active and faithful clerk" in the Third Auditor's office before his death in 1837. Thomas Munroe (b.1771) was the son of William Munroe and his wife Marie DeBrass. Munroe served as postmaster of the District of Columbia from 1797 to 1829. Faris purchased shoes for various family members from Thomas's brother John between 1792 and 1802.

38 The fort could have been either Fort Horn, on Horn Point opposite Annapolis where Spa Creek joins the Severn River, or Fort Nonsense, on the opposite shore of the Severn. Either destination would have required a boat, which Capt. Thomas undoubtedly provided.

39 Used at the time to describe any of several diseases characterized by fever and catarrhal symptoms.

115 ✍ *St. John Faris, the youngest son of William and Priscilla Faris.*

116 ✍ *Reverse side of the locket.*

1796 Sunday Augt 14th ✍ a cloudey drisley morning. in the evening cloudey like for rain. Mr. & Mrs. Pitt & the partey are come home from Mr. Cowmans, this evening Mr. Thomas Monrow was married to Miss Fanney Whitcroft & Mr. Henrey Whitcroft to Miss Sarah Witcroft[37]

Munday 15th ✍ a cloudey foggey drisley morning. an account of Capt. Gardner's sloop's being lost. its said that about a mile out side the Cape she filled with water and all hands left her, a cloudey dull day

Tuseday 16th ✍ a fine morning. this day I am 68 years old, & entering in to my 69th year. on the Border joyning ye Horse Radish I sowed No. 1 Parrot Tail Tulip seed and No. 2 Tulip seed of a good sort — & planted {page torn} earley clear stone Peach stones — turned very coole this evening

Wednesday 17th ✍ a fine day but coole. Capt. pitt went to Baltimore this morning

1796 Thursday Augt 18th ✍ this after noon Capt. Thomas's Famely, Nancy, Abee, Rebacka & Charles & several others, went over to the the Fort[38] to a Tea party — a fine day but coole

Fryday 19th ✍ arrivd at New York the ship Atalanta. Capt. Holbrook's Log book. Augt 5th. saw a ship, haveing a signal of distress — bore away for her. we hoisted out our yawl and went on Bord. she proved to be the Hebe of Baltimore that saild from Amsterdam May 7th under the Command of St. John Farrees with 230 passengers bound to Baltimore — when thay had been a few weeks at sea a number of them ware attacked with a contageious distempter[39] of which the Capt. died in a few days, at the time wee board'd her, thare ware 7 dead. the first and second mate and maney of the passengers confined to their births and only 3 hands left capabel of working the vessel. thay had then lost by this sickness upwards of 100 persons & every thing exhibited to the utmost distress. Capt. H put a man on board to assist in taking her into the most convenient port & supply'd them with some stores

1796 Saturday Augt 20th ✍ a fine day

Sunday 21th ✍ a cloudey rainey morning & showers at times through day

Munday 22th ✍ a cloudey drisley rainey day. in the evening W. Pitt came from Baltimore

244

Tuseday 23th ✍ a fine day

Wednesday 24th ✍ about a 11 oclock Capt. pitt sett off in his Boat for Virginia & Archibald Golder with him. Golder goes for his Health as he says — a fine day. in the Tuseday paper I see a further accot of my Poor Son, its from the same vessel, Capt. Richard Holbrook who says that, Capt. Faris was taken sick the 20th of July and died on the 27th 40

1796 Thursday Augt 25th ✍ a fine day

Fryday 26th ✍ a fine morning. in ye after noon thare was a fine rain. after the rain I planted out 207 Brussel sprout plants in the Lot

Saturday 27th ✍ a fine day

Sunday 28th ✍ a fine day. in the evening I had sevear fitt of the ague & a very smart Fever

Munday 29th ✍ Charles sett of this morning in the packett for Baltimore. I gave him a 100 Dollors to day in Part of my share in the Bank.41 a fine day

Tuseday 30th ✍ a fine morning. about 2 oclock I had another fit of the ague. I took 65 drops of Lodnum. I had a smart ague but not much Feveour

1796 Wednesday 31th ✍ a fine morning. in the evening Charles returned home from Baltimore. a fine day

Thursday Septembr 1th ✍ betwen 1 & 2 oclock I had a smart ague & Feveour. a fine day

Fryday 2th ✍ dull cloudey cold morning. I began to take the Bark

Saturday 3th ✍ I miss'd my augue to day. it has been a fine day but rather cold

Sunday 4th ✍ about 3 oclock this after noon Mr. Archibald Golder came to Town, from the capes by the way of Baltimore. left Capt. pitt at the capes. a fine day

Munday 5th ✍ betwen 12 & 1 oclock Capt. pitt returned from the capes. a fine day

1796 Tuseday Septr 6th ✍ this morning sow'd 40 drils of Parceley seed on the border next Mrs. Davidsons. a fine day

Wednesday 7th ✍ Capt. pitt went of for Baltimore this morning. a dull cloudey day. in the evening it rained

40 The account that Faris recorded on the 19th came from the 19 August issue of the *Federal Gazette.* This second report he read in the Sunday, 21 August, issue of the *Maryland Journal.*

41 Faris was buying shares in the Bank of Baltimore, each of which cost $300, payable in installments. No shares were listed among the assets in his inventory, however.

SHIP NEWS.
PORT OF BALTIMORE.
ENTERED,
Ship Swift Picket, Malcolm,   Jeremie
Schooner Peggy, Gorsuch,   Jacquemel
CLEARED,
Ship Willink, Stewart,   Amsterdam

New-York, August 15.
Arrived—ship Atalanta, Holbrook, Liverpool, '86 days; brig James, Watson, Guadaloupe, 22; sch'rs. Two Brothers, Kemberly, St. Croix, 18; Jay, Smith, Port-au-Prince, 18.

August 16.
From the log-book of the ship Atalanta, arrived here on Sunday, 86 days from Liverpool:

August 5, saw a ship, having a signal of distress—bore away for her. We hoisted out our yawl and went on board; she proved to be the Hebe, of Baltimore, that sailed from Amsterdam May 7, under the command St. John Farrier, with 230 passengers, bound to Baltimore.

When they had been a few weeks at sea, a number of them were attacked with a contageous distemper, of which the captain died in a few days At the time we boarded her, there were 7 dead, the first and second mate, and many of the passengers confined to their births, and only three hands left capable of working the vessel; they had then lost by this sickness upwards of 100 persons, and every thing exhibited to the utmost distress. Captain H. put a man on board, to assist in taking her into the most convenient port, and supplied them with some stores, which they were much in need of.

117 ✍ *The* Federal Gazette *announcement of St. John's death that Faris had read when he recorded the news in his diary on the nineteenth.*

Thursday 8th ☞ Charles Faris went this morning in the Packett for Baltimore. a raney day

Fryday 9th ☞ a fine day

Saturday 10th ☞ a fine day. in the evening Capt. Pitt came down from Baltimore

Sunday 11th ☞ a fine day

1796 Munday Septr 12th ☞ about 9 oclock Capt. Pitt sett off for Baltimore. went with him Mrs. Pitt, Abee Faris Nancey Ashmead Mrs. Thomas & Marriah Thomas. a fine morning, the wind at south, a very warm day

Tuseday 13th ☞ a very warm day. in the evening look'd like for rain

Wednesday 14th ☞ a very Hott day. in the evening look'd like for rain

Thursday 15th ☞ a warm day. in the evening Capt. Thomas's Boate came down from Baltimore. Mrs. Thomas Miss Marriah & Charles Faris came down in her, thay left Mrs. Pitt Abee & Nancy Ashmead well

Fryday 16th ☞ a fine day. in the after noon I sow'd cabbage seed on this end of the Border next to Reigels & joyning it I sow'd earley York cabbage seed, & Planted Tulip Roots in the Flower Beds whare thay ware wanting

1796 Sunday Septr 17th ☞ a fine day but has turned very cold

Munday 18th ☞ a cold windey day

Tuseday 19th ☞ this after noon I sow onion & spinige seed on the border next to Mrs. Davidsons. a cold day

Tuseday 20th ☞ a fine day

Wednesday 21th ☞ a fine day

Thursday 22th ☞ a fine day. in the evening Samuel Molds of Baltimore Town's to be married to Miss Ann Howard, daughter of Samuel Harvey Howard of Annapolis[42]

Fryday 23th ☞ a fine day. receivd a Letter from Nancey & Abee. thay are both well

1796 Saturday Septr 24th ☞ a fine day

Sunday 25th ☞ a fine day

[42] Samuel Moale (1771–1857) was a member of the Moale family of Baltimore. He may have been the Samuel Moale who attended St. John's from March 1790 until February 1797. Ann Howard (c.1776–1827) was one of the daughters of Samuel Harvey Howard (see 31 October 1794).

Munday 26th ⚓ a fine day

Tuseday 27th ⚓ a fine day

Wednesday 28th ⚓ a fine rain last night & this morning. left of raining about 10 or 11 oclock but continued cloudey all day

Thursday 29th ⚓ a fine day

Fryday 30th ⚓ a fine day

Saturday Octobr 1th ⚓ a cold raw cloudey day. had a Fire in the grate in the House the first time this Fall

1796 Sunday Octbr 2th ⚓ a rainey day. this evening's to be married Genl John Davidson about 45 years old to Miss Marriah Grissom betwen 20 & 21 years of age[43]

Munday 3th ⚓ a rainey Blustering night & continued so all day

Tuseday 4th ⚓ a fine day

Wednesday 5th ⚓ this morning about 9 oclock Charles sett of in the packett for Baltimore. a fine day. in the evening clouded up looks like for rain

Thursday 6th ⚓ rained last night & this morning. cleared away a fine day

Fryday 7th ⚓ a fine day

Saturday 8th ⚓ a fine day

1796 Sunday Octr 9th ⚓ this after noon a neagro Fellow drownded him self in the poor House creek, a fine day

Munday 10th ⚓ in the after noon, Miss Nancey Ashmead and Charles returned from Baltimore. he lef his sisters & the famely all well. a fine day

Tuseday 11th ⚓ a fine day

Wednesday 12th ⚓ a fine day. in the evening clouded up & rain'd a littel

Thursday 13th ⚓ a fine day

Fryday 14th ⚓ a fine day

Saturday 15th ⚓ cloudey morning. clear'd away a fine fore noon. about 2 oclock cloudey. in the after noon rained a littel & continues cloudey & like for rain

43 John Davidson (see 2 June 1795) and Anna Maria Grason obtained a marriage license on 22 September. Anna Maria was the daughter of Commodore Thomas Grason, the first commodore appointed to the Maryland navy during the Revolutionary War. Grason was killed in April 1782 during an engagement with British ships. In 1800, when Anna Maria's brother William, age twelve, attended the St. John's grammar school, General Davidson was listed as his guardian.

1796 Sunday Octr 16th ↜ raind & Blow'd very hard in the night & this morning, clear'd away about 9 oclock very fine & in the afternoon cloudey

Munday 17th ↜ a fine day

Tuseday 18th ↜ a fine day

Wednesday 19th ↜ a cloudey morning. about 9 oclock Hyram & his sister Rebacka & Miss Anne Goldsmith sett off in the packett for Baltimore. a fine day

Thursday 20th ↜ a fine day

Fryday 21th ↜ a cloudey day

Saturday 22th ↜ a cloudey morning. clear'd away & a fine afternoon

1796 Sunday Octr 23th ↜ a fine day

Munday 24th ↜ Hyram & his sister Abbee left Baltimore yesterday morning about 9 oclock and did not get here till about 6 oclock this morning, thay left thare sisters & fameley well — a fine day. I have had old Terrey's Husband all day a weeling in manure & covering the Flower beds with it

Tuseday 25th ↜ finished covering the Flower beds with manure. a fine day, the pettet jurey of the General Court is discharged this day

Wednesday 26th ↜ a fine day. yesterday Miss Betsey Gassaw[ay] was Brought to Bed of a Son

Thursday 27th ↜ a fine day. in the latter part of the day turned a littel coole

1796 Fryday Octr 28th ↜ this morning about 9 oclock I sett of for Baltimore. arrived at the point about 6 oclock and Mr. Goldsmith with me wee went to Capt. pitts, he was at home & glad to see us. Mr. Goldsmith staid all night. it has been a fine day

Saturday 29th ↜ I called on Capt. Yelliott. I requestd he would draw the account of and let me have the Perticulars,[44] after Rangeling some time he Promised me I should have it — I went to see Capt. Hamelton, and wee went and took a vew of the Frigat. in the evening I returned to Capt. Pitts. he sett of this morning down the Bay with the ship. a fine day

Sunday 30th ↜ went to Capt. Berrey & he's down

44 Probably related to St. John's service as captain of the *Hebe*.

the Bay. Mrs. Berrey's un well abed, in the after
noon Capt. Kelty & wife, Mrs. Moles & Mr. Smith[45]
called at Mr. pitts, stay'd but a littel wile, Kelty nor
wife never asked me to come and see them. a fine
day

Munday 31th ✍ went to town. call'd on Yelliott,
the accot not finished. I went to several Places on
Business & returned to Capt. pitts to diner — a fine
day

1796 Novr Tuseday 1th ✍ I call at Capt.
Hameltons & Capt. Berreys, from thence I went to
town, call'd at Yelliotts and got the accot but it's a
dam'd one, returned to the point, the wind Blew
very hard all day and turned cold

Wednesday 2th ✍ I left daughters Anne & Rebacka
both well this morning betwen 7 and 8 oclock and
went to Town, 9 oclock sett of in the Packett for
home, and betwen 3 & 4 oclock arrived at
Annapolis. my Famely all well. it's been a fine day

Thursday 3th ✍ a fine day

Fryday 4th ✍ a fine day. in the evening clouded up
like for rain

Saturday 5th ✍ a fine day

1796 Sunday Novr 6th ✍ a fine day

Munday 7th ✍ a fine day

Tuseday 8th ✍ the Jockey Club purs was ran for to
day and won by Mr. Tayloe's mare Virago

Wednesday 9th ✍ this day the Colts purs was run
for and won by Mr. Tayloe's mare Calipso. a fine day

Thursday 10th ✍ a fine day

Fryday 11th ✍ a fine day

Saturday 12th ✍ a fine day

1796 Sunday Novr 13th ✍ a dull cloudey day.
look like falling weather

Munday 14th ✍ a dull cloudey day

Tuseday 15th ✍ a cloudey dull morning. abot 12
oclock rain'd a littel, in the after noon clear, in the
evening cloudey. this Fore noon Mr. Vanhorn[46] was
chosen Clark of the Sennett

45 Possibly Robert Smith, the rumor of whose
death Faris notes on 27 December 1798, or
Thomas Smith, with whom he negotiated the
settlement of the DeDrusina, Ridder & Clerk
account in February 1793.

118 ✍ Colonel John Tayloe III (1771–1828)
*Tayloe's horses consistently won during the fall
racing season.*

46 Archibald Van Horn, a delegate from
Prince George's County, was speaker of the
house in 1805. He had been secretary of the
senate from 1796 to 1799, and also served in
the senate and as a member of the House of
Representatives.

47 Henry Ridgely (c.1765–1811) married Matilda Chase (c.1763–1835), the eldest daughter of Samuel Chase (see 7 October 1793), in June 1787. He was the secretary of the senate from 1789 to 1792, served as a councilman and alderman in the 1790s, and sat on the executive council for six terms beginning in 1790. His eldest son, William Greenbury, enrolled in the St. John's grammar school in January 1795. At the time of his death, Ridgely was a judicial district associate judge. Matilda Ridgely died in Georgetown in her seventy-second year. Their daughter Hester was the second wife of Dr. John Ridgely (see 30 November 1799). § Faris collected £1.16.1 from Ridgely in September 1801 as administrator of Charles's estate.

48 Molly Johnson does not appear to have been a relative of Robert, George, and John Johnson, but she may have been a minor child whose birth has gone unrecorded.

49 The inventory of John Butcher's estate (whose surname generally appears in the records as Boucher) included two slaves and a leased half-acre lot. His widow Amelia obtained an ordinary license in 1797; it was not uncommon for a widow needing a means of support to use her home as a tavern. § Faris bought two quarters of beef from John Butcher on the 12th and 18th of November, 1795.

Wednesday 16th ✒ this Fore noon Mr. John Johnson was chose on of the councel in the room of Mr. Henrey Ridgley,47 who resigned — a fine day

Thursday 17th ✒ a fine day

Fryday 18th ✒ a fine day

Saturday 19th ✒ this morning earley Charles sett off on Horsback for Baltimore. a fine day

1796 Sunday Novr 20th ✒ about noon whee had a littel rain, a clear after noon. in the evening Charles returned from Baltimore

Munday 21th ✒ a fine day

Tuseday 22th ✒ fine day but very foggey, in the evening, it rain'd a littel but looks as if wee should have a good deal before morning

Wednesday 23th ✒ last Night Miss Molley Johnson48 died. a fine day

Thursday 24th ✒ this fore noon about 10 oclock Miss Molley Johnson was buried. a clear cold day

Fryday 25th ✒ clear & cold

Saturday 26th ✒ a clear cold day

1796 Sunday Novr 27th ✒ a cold day

Munday 28th ✒ a fine day not so cold as yesterday

Tuseday 29th ✒ a fine day

Wednesday 30th ✒ a fine day

Thursday Dessember 1st ✒ it snowed last night. this morning the ground was covered, cloudey in the afternoon. about 3 oclock began to snow and looks as if wee should have a good deal of it

Fryday 2th ✒ a fine day

Saturday 3th ✒ a fine day, some time last night John Butcher49 died

1796 Sunday Desember 4th ✒ a fine day. in the evening John Butcher was Buried

Munday 5th ✒ a fine day

Tuseday 6th ✒ a dull cloudey rainey day

Wednesday 7th ✒ the wind Blow'd very hard and snow'd in the night & this morning and continued coudey and Blowing hard all day

Thursday 8th ☞ a clear cold day

Fryday 9th ☞ a fine day

Saturday 10th ☞ a fine morning, about 2 oclock this after noon Mr. Thomas Jenings died aged about 60. in the afternoon clouded up, looks like for bad weather

1796 Sunday 11th ☞ a fine day. in the evening William Sands[50] the wood corder's wife was Buried

Munday 12th ☞ a fine day

Tuseday 13th ☞ a cloudey mor[n]ing. about 12 oclock my worthey old Friend Mr. Thomams Jinings was Buried. in the after noon snow & slet

Wedneday 14th ☞ a fine day, this evening I had a letter from Nanchey & Beckey, giveing an accot how thay ware sceard, last Fryday night. thay heard a voice like Mr. Pitts saying O Nancey, Nancey, Nancy, he at the time down the Bay

Thursday 15th ☞ this morning Charles sett of on Horse Back for Baltimore. a fine day

Fryday 16th ☞ a fine day

Saturday 17th ☞ a fine day. Charles returned home this evening & says Capt. pitt & his wife & Rebacca sett of too day for Annapolis. betwen 8 & 9 oclock Capt. pitt Nancy & Rebecca came to home to the House

1796 Sunday Desr 18th ☞ a raney day

Munday 19th ☞ after Brackfast Mr. Pitt & Hiram Faris sett of on Horse Back for West River. a fine day

Tuseday 20th ☞ a cold day, in the evening Mr. Pitt and Hiram return'd Home

Wednesday 21th ☞ a clear cold day but snow'd this morning before day

Thursday 22th ☞ snow'd a littel in the night but clear'd away an exsessive cold day. in the after noon Mr. Golders chimney was on Fire. the wind blew fresh. we were apprehensive of haveing a bad Fire. some of the Flakes of fire from the chimney fel in my Portch

Fryday 23th ☞ a clear & very cold day. its frose a grate ways out side of Greenbureys point

[50] William Sands was appointed wood corder for the city in April 1789. § Faris records payments to Sands for cording wood on the 8th and 9th of January in 1794.

Saturday 24th ✒ a cold day

1796 Sunday Desr 25th ✒ a clear cold day. this afternoon came to Town Capt. Barney[51] & 2 or 3 French officers. he has left his Friggets ~~in hamton rod~~ at Norfolk

Munday 26 ✒ s[n]ow'd in the night & this morning a littel. cleard away a fine day

Tuseday 27th ✒ this morning about 9 oclock Mr. Pitt Mrs. Pitt & Rebecke Faris sett of for Baltimore in Smith's stage. a fine day

Wednesday 28th ✒ a fine day

Thursday 29th ✒ a fine day, Hiram has been complaining this 2 or 3 days — he went down to Doctr Murrays to day. he Bled[52] him & gave him a callomel pill to take to night and a purge[53] to take in ye morning

Fryday 30th ✒ snow'd this morning till about 12 oclock then small rain & cloudey all day. Hiram took his Purge this morning but did not work him but very littel, young Owens call'd to see him but Doctr Murray never came neare Him

1796 Saturday Desr 31th ✒ a fine day. Hiram's something better. Doctr Murray call'd to see him to day and desired I would give him Creem a Tarter water to drink

1797 Sunday January 1th ✒ Doctr Murray called to see Hiram. Hes a grate deel better. he has walked out to day, the Miss Thomas dined with us to day and in the evening Capt. Thomas sent Preemptorey for Marriah to come home betwen sun down & dark. Miss Betsey went home some time before because she has been for some time very unwell. a fine day

Munday 2th ✒ a clear cold day

Tuseday 3th ✒ a cold dissagreeable snowey day

1797 Wednesday Janry 4th ✒ a cloudey cold morning. in the after noon it clear'd away and & the sun came out .

Thursday 5th ✒ a fine day but cold

Fryday 6th ✒ a fine clear cold day

Saturday 7th ✒ a clear very cold day

[51] Joshua Barney (1759–1818) was born in Baltimore County, where his father operated a farm. Barney left the farm to go to sea, becoming a ship's navigator by the age of sixteen. After long service during the Revolutionary War, he accompanied James Monroe to France, where he entered the service of the French government until 1800. After returning to the United States, Barney became the naval commander responsible for the defense of Washington and was wounded at the Battle of Bladensburg during the War of 1812. In December 1796, Barney sailed from Saint Domingue to the Chesapeake Bay with two frigates, *Medusa* and *L'Insurgente,* to obtain food supplies for the island, which had been retaken by French troops. After dispatching several merchant vessels, Barney repaired and resupplied his own ships, and then escaped the British blockade of the mouth of the bay by sailing through it at night.

[52] A treatment designed to release pressure in the arteries by opening a vein and draining off "excess" blood.

[53] A medicine intended to induce vomiting.

Sunday 8th ⟡ a fine clear cold day. in the evening I saw Capt. Farling[54] at Mr. Randals who told me that he saw my son William in ~~the Island of~~ Jackomel[55] in the Island of

Munday 9th ⟡ clear & cold

Tuseday 10th ⟡ clear & cold

1797 Wednesday January 11th ⟡ a clowdey raney morning & continued till 2 or 3 oclock then clear'd away and the sun came out, a fine evening

Thursday 12th ⟡ a fine day. in the evening old Mr. Wall[56] was Buried

Fryday 13th ⟡ a fine day

Saturday 14th ⟡ a rainey day till about 3 oclock. in the after noon continued cloudey

Sunday 15th ⟡ a fine day

Munday 16th ⟡ a cold windey day

1797 Tuseday January 17th ⟡ a fine day

Wednesday 18th ⟡ snow this moring the ground covered. cleared away a fine afternoon and evening

Thursday 19th ⟡ a fine day

Fryday 20th ⟡ the ground was covered with snow this morning and snowing & has continued snowing all day & was a snowing at 9 oclock when I went to bed

Saturday 21th ⟡ a cloudey dull dissagreeable day and looks like for more falling weather. this evening something falls either snow or fine rain

Sunday 22th ⟡ snow'd last night. a cloudey morning. in the evening clear'd awayay & looks as if wee should have some good weather

1797 Munday January 23th ⟡ a midling clear day. I sent by Mr. L. Neth 200 Dollors to pay into the Bank wich makes up the whole amount of my two shares

Tuseday 24th ⟡ a fine day — Mrs. Dickson[57] was buried this after noon

119 ⟡ John Randall (1750–1826)

Randall was a local merchant from whom Faris purchased many of the supplies for his household. Randall appraised Charles Faris's estate after his death.

54 William Furlong, a sea captain, lived at 5 Shakespeare Alley in Fells Point in 1796.

55 Probably the town of Jacmel or Jacquemel on the south coast of Saint Domingue. The name of the island is left blank in the diary.

56 Mr. Wall was undoubtedly related to Sarah Wall, the niece of Thomas Hyde (see 21 June 1792) and may have been her grandfather. He might have been the Henry Walls who rented lot 34 on Market Street, south of Duke of Gloucester Street, from Charles Carroll in 1762 and who was the state armorer.

57 Mrs. Dixon was a long-time resident of Annapolis, having been fined for a chimney fire in February 1784. She appears in the 1790 census but the information for her household is illegible.

Wednesday 25th ☞ a fine morning. about a 11 oclock Parson Higginbottoms wife died — a fine day

Thursday 26th ☞ a fine day

Fryday 27th ☞ a fine day

Saturday 28th ☞ this evening Mrs. Higginbottoms was Buried. a fine day. Charles Bought two Tickets in the Gennel lotterey[58] No. 695 & 696. thay are betwixt him & my self. he gave a 21 Dolloll for them & I paid him Ten Dollors & a ½ for the half of them

1797 Sunday January 29th ☞ a cloudey warm morning. about 12 oclock rained. in the after noon fine sun shiney cloude & rain. in the evening the sun came out fine. its been like an April day. in the evening Capt. Pitt arrived heare from Baltimore. he rode up

Munday 30th ☞ it came on to Blow hard at N.W. in the night and turned cold, a cold day

Tuseday 31th ☞ a cold day

Wednesday Feburay 1th ☞ a cloudey drisley day

Thursday 2th ☞ this fore noon Capt. pitt sett of with 5 or 6 Passengers for Norfolk. a fine day. I trimed the Rose Bushes to day

Fryday 3th ☞ a fine day. finished triming ye grape vines

Saturday 4th ☞ a fine day

1797 Sunday Febry 5th ☞ a fine day

Munday 6th ☞ a fine warme spring day

Tuseday 7th ☞ a fine day, this evening I received Letters from the girls, by a Mr. Hall, thay are well

Wednesday 8th ☞ dunged & dug the Border next to Reigels & planted 17 rows of Peas. a fine day

Thursday 9th ☞ a fine day. in the evening clouded up and looks like for fallng weather

Fryday 10th ☞ Blow'd & rained hard all Last night. a rainey morning. now 12 oclock & still raining. in the after noon rain & snow

Saturday 11th ☞ a fine day. in the evening Miss Nancy Quynn that was & her Husband, a Mr. Hunter, came to Town, thay stop'd at Clauds

1797 Sunday Febry 12th ✍ a fine day. Hiram went over South River this morning in companey with Capt. McCening.[59] in the after noon John Reigle fell down in a Fitt in his yard. in the evening Mrs. Faris Abee & my self drank Tea at old Mr. Witcrofts

Munday 13th ✍ a cloudey drsley day

Tuseday 14th ✍ this morning Charles went of in the Packett for Baltimore. a dull cloudey drisley day

Wednesday 15th ✍ about a 11 oclock this fore noon Mr. John Reigels wife died, and I am informed that Mr. John Worthington died yesterday,[60] finish'd wheeling dung on the Big Bed, a midling good day

1797 Thursday 16th ✍ Hiram went to William Woodwards this morning. his son Henrey[61] was married yesterday. a fine day

Fryday 17th ✍ Hiram return'd home about 11 oclock. a dull rainey day. at night rains Hard. this after noon John Riegels wife was buried

Saturday Febry 18th ✍ this morning Capt. pitts Boat came hear from Baltimore and Brought 14 gammons & 14 shoulders to be smoak'd. I mark'd them with a Hot Iron with a straight line.[62] a cloudey drisley morning. about noon clear'd away a fine after noon. in the evening, Charles & Beckey came Home in the Packett from Baltimore, left Mr. & Mrs. Pitt well

Sunday 19th ✍ a fine day. in the evening clouded up & looks as if wee should have rain

Munday 20th ✍ a fine day

Tuseday 21th ✍ a fine day, Mr. Perrey Fitzchew[63] called to see me. he tells me his Father is well & in fine spirrits

Wednesday 22th ✍ last Night thare was an atempt to sett Mr. Peaco's[64] Howse on fire, thare was a Meeting of the citizens this fore noon at the State House. th[ay] agreed to devid the city in 6 wards and ceep gaurd. a fine day

1797 Thursday Febry 23th ✍ a fine day, this evening Hiram's gone on guard

Fryday 24th ✍ this fore noon about a 11 oclock wee narrowley esscaped haveing a Terrebel Fire. it is supposed some Person sett the stabel of Mrs. Gaters on Fire. it was luckely discover'd and by the gratest

59 When Jacob McCeney died some time prior to 1793, he was survived by four sons: Jacob, Zachariah, Joseph, and Benjamin. Hyram may have been accompanied by Jacob, who was a captain in the 2nd militia regiment by September 1795.

60 John Griffith Worthington (1764–1797) was the son of Nicholas Worthington (see 8 November 1792). John Griffith, an attorney, was admitted to practice in the Anne Arundel County court in March 1786 and served as an Anne Arundel delegate to the General Assembly from 1789 to 1795 and as a councilman from 1790 to 1792. He died at the age of thirty-three at Summer Hill, the family home then owned by his twin brother Brice John Worthington.

61 Henry Woodward (1770–1822) was the son of William and Jane Ridgely Woodward (see 7 December 1792). Eleanor Williams Turner (1774–1850) was the daughter of Col. Thomas and Rachel Duckett Williams, and the widow of Richard Warfield Turner.

62 It is likely that Pitt bought this meat for his own household, and that Faris marked the pieces to distinguish them from his own supply.

63 Peregrine Fitzhugh (b. ca.1760), the fourth son of Faris's friend, Col. William Fitzhugh (see 19 January 1793). At this time Fitzhugh was living in Washington County, but he moved in 1799 to Soder's Bay, Lake Ontario, where he lived for the remainder of his life.

64 Samuel Peaco was licensed to marry Mary Sands in December 1789 and had a son, John Wesley, who entered the St. John's grammar school in 1801 at the age of 10. In October 1801 he leased the "prison lot" fronting on Prince George Street from the Corporation for 99 years. He served as market clerk in 1816, constable in 1821, and market master in 1833. A Methodist, Peaco (whose name appears in one source as Peacock) was undoubtedly related to Margaret Peacock, the legatee of Charlotte Small, who also left her house to Methodist minister Francis Asbury (see 15 October 1793).

65 The 2 March 1797 *Gazette* mentioned only the fire on 24 February: there was a fire set to a small wooden building adjoining Mr. Wharfe's stable and belonging to Mrs. Gaither but it was put out without much damage.

66 Jacob Jenings was not related to Thomas Jennings (see 17 July 1793) but cannot be otherwise identified. He was never mentioned in the *Gazette*, left no traces in probate records, and does not appear in the 1790 and 1800 census records, nor were there any Jenings households in Anne Arundel in either year.

exercion was Pulled down and the Fire extinguised. it was joyning to Warfs stabel.65 a dull cloudey day

Saturday 25th ☞ a cold disagreeable day

Sunday 26th ☞ this morning I took a dose of castor oil. after diner Miss Kittey Whitcrof came her for the firs time after Iillness. she looks bravely considering how Iill she has been, it has been a fine day but rather cold and windey

Munday 27th ☞ about 9 oclock this morning I was taken with a very sever ague, which continued for about 2 hours, then came on the fevour which continued till in the night, Sylve made a begining to dig the Big Bed

1797 Tuseday 28th ☞ I have been but very Poorley to day, Sylve's diging the big bed. a dull cloudey raw disagreeable day

Wednesday March 1th ☞ sow'd the following cabbage seed No. 1 early York from Smith No. 2 Jacob Jenings66 3 large cabbage from Old Terrey 4 Savoys from Smith 5 cabage seed from Mrs. Thomas. Silve's done diging ye Big bed, she doing up the Tabels. I have miss'd my ague to day, in the afternoon I planted the big Bead with Peas, and Silve's made abeging to open the asparagras Beds. a fine day

Thursday 2th ☞ a fine morning. Sylve's fork'd up the asparragrass beds, in the after noon & night snow

Fryday 3th ☞ a dull cloudey day. the snow is all gone

1797 Saturday March 4th ☞ sow'd two lines of spinige betwen the asparagrass Beds. cut the line of Box next to Reigels, Silve dug the littel quarter & took up the sage. in the afternoon I planted 1 line of sage & in the evening sow'd lettice on the asparagrass beds. a fine day

Sunday 5th ☞ last night Henrey Sibell died, a windey day. in the evening Henry Sibell was Buried

Munday 6th ☞ the wind Blew exessive hard last night and has continued so all day, Silve made a begining in the lott to dig the Parsnep bed this after noon

Tuseday 7th ☞ cold cloudey & about a 11 oclock snowed a littel. I sow'd the Beans in the littel

256

quarter & planted some more of the sage but it was so cold I was obliged to quit it. Silve has been a diging a littel in the lott to day, but she left it. its turn'd very cold & cloudey. looks like falling wether & the wind blows Hard

1797 Wednesday March 8th ☞ a cloudey morning. Lawyer John Hall[67] died this Fore noon aged 69 years, cleared away a fine day but the wind Blows very hard, Hiram's made a begining to cut Box. Silve's finished the diging the Parsnep Bed & wee planted a line radish seed in the edge. Silve has dug up the line of sage in the big bed & made good the Table & I sow'd a line of sage seed just with in the line of sage on the littel quarter. made 17 Hill in the Lott for Vines

Thursday 9th ☞ a cold windey day. could do nothing in the garden. in the after noon I planted 10 hills of simlins and 7 hills of cucumbers in the lott amongst the sprouts, & in the outer lott I planted 4 Hills of water millin & 4 Hills of can-tilops

Fryday 10th ☞ cold day. did littel more then Plant the line of sage on the big Bead. Mr. John Hall was Buried to day, he was carried to the vine yard

1797 Saturday March 11th ☞ when I got up this morning the ground looked white with hail & snow, a cloudey cold dissagreeable day. did nothing in the garden. last night about 9 oclock Mrs. Mary Howard[68] died, sister to Charles Wallace

Sunday 12th ☞ a cloudey day

Munday 13th ☞ a fogey morning. I finish'd Triming ye nurserey Box & began that by the littel house & Hiram's digging the Box round the circel Beds. Silve has dig Border & sow'd 36 drills of Parceley seed, then went to takeing up the cuttings & cleaning up the garden and the neagro girl Henney is planting parsneps lines 9 Inchs apart and seed 7 Inchs from seed to seed. in the evening Mrs. Mary Howard was Buried. a fine day

1797 Tuseday March 14th ☞ a fine morning. finished planting parsneps & carrots, Hiram's cuting Box. I had the Litter taken from round the roots of the grape Vines & losened up the erth, Sylve's working in the garden. a fine day

Wednesday 15th ☞ Hiram has finished cuting ye Box and this after noon began to Trowel the Beds

[67] John Hall (1729–1797) was born in All Hallow's Parish, the son of Henry Hall (1703–1756) and his wife Martha Bateman (d.1734). He married Eleanor Dorsey (c.1739–1805), daughter of Edward, in August 1767; the couple had no children. Hall was a lawyer who trained Samuel Chase (see 7 October 1793) among others. He served in the lower house from 1762 to 1785 and in the senate from 1786 to 1795. During the Revolution, when he was a leader of the radical faction, he was a delegate to the Continental Congress. He owned houses in Annapolis and an estate, known as The Vineyard, on General's Highway, a few miles west of Annapolis. § Hall patronized Faris's tavern in 1774 and 1775.

[68] The widow of Cornelius Howard, the first proprietor of the Coffee House (see 31 March 1792).

round the grass walk, a fine day. in the evening came on to drissel & small rain. Abee has been Poorley this 2 or 3 day. Doctr Ghislin advis'd me to give a purg of Jallap, callomel and creem atarter, it work'd her very well. she's still poorely but I am in hopes she will be bravely to morrow

Thursday 16th ✍ Last night Thomas Townsend[69] the carter died, a dull cloudey damp day. Hiram's diging the flower Beds — Abee is still Poorley

1797 Fryday March 17th ✍ a dull cloudey drisley day. littel done in the garden. I finished planting the young Tulep Roots on the Border by the Walnut Tree. this evening Thomas Townsend was Buried

Saturday 18th ✍ I sow'd lettice & redish seed, from Mrs. Thomas's on the Border betwen the stable & littel house, Hiram's has finished diging the flower Beds, & Silve is cleaning the walks of the garden. Hiram has began doing up the Tabels round the grass walks. a fine warme day

Sunday 19th ✍ a cold windey dissagreeable day

Munday 20th ✍ a fine day, Hiram was in the shop to day. a fine day

Tuseday 21th ✍ Hiram is doing up the tabels round the grass walk. a fine morning. in the after noon turned cold & cloudey, looks as if we are going to have Bad weather

1797 Wednesday March 22th ✍ cloudey & rain at times all day. in the evening came on to Blow very Hard

Thursday 23th ✍ Hiram has finished the tabels round the grass walks, a fine day

Fryday 24th ✍ a dull dissagreeable rainey windey day

Saturday 25th ✍ a fine day. Hilled the peas on the Boarder. last night the Norfolk a packet Boat over sett some whare about the Bodkin. cannont tell what has become of the peopel. the vessel has drifted down by Talleys[70]

Sunday 26th ✍ Mrs. Faris & the girls went to the Methodest[71] both fore noon and after noon to heare a Mr. Lile[72] Preach, a fine day. in the evening cloudey like for rain

---

[69] Thomas Townsend, identified as a laborer in 1783, owned no property and had a household of two males (one adult) and two females. The Mayor's Court fined John Townsend in January 1794 for allowing slaves to ride in his carts.

[70] Talley's Point is on the south shore of the Severn River, where the river joins the Chesapeake Bay, about 10 miles south of Bodkin Point.

[71] These meetings may have been at the church on the State House grounds.

[72] Thomas Lyell (d. 1848), a native of Virginia, was ordained as a deacon in the Methodist Church by Francis Asbury in Alexandria, Virginia in November 1797. He spent the period from 1792 to 1799 as a circuit preacher covering the area from Pennsylvania to Virginia; in 1797 his circuit covered Fairfax and Alexandria.

1797 Munday March 27th ↝ a fine day but very windey

Tuseday 28th ↝ a fine day but windey

Wednesday 29th ↝ a fine day. stuck the peas on the Border

Thursday 30th ↝ a fine morning. in the afternoon cloudey & like for rain. this after noon I sow the Ice pla[n]t seed in the Barrel

Fryday 31th ↝ a fine day. in the evening it rain'd

Saturday April 1th ↝ a fine morning, took up the Tree called the Pride of Chiney & planted it in the middel of the circkel in the garden. the carrotts are acoming up that ware sow'd the 14th of March. this afternoon trimed the Holley Tree in the garden. a fine day

1797 Sunday April 2th ↝ this morning cut assparagrass. a fine day

Munday 3th ↝ a very fine morning, sow'd Eggplant seed in a pott, sow'd Jeruselum Cherrey seed in the Barrel by a stick, sow'd India pink seed and Chinea aster seeds round the flower beds, Silve's dug the littel quarter by the old stabel & I planted the onions on the side of the Bed. in the evening wee had to Tea Mr. Lile, Mr. John Ridgley son of Absalom[73] Mrs. Golder & Miss Ashmead, it has been a very fine day

Tuseday 4th ↝ this morning watered the garden and planted 7 rows of Beens in the littel quarter next the old stabel. a fine day. & Hilled the peas in the big Bead

Wednesday 5th ↝ sowed spinige on the Border by the Parseley. Silve stuck the Peas in the big bed and hilled them. the beans in that was planted the 7 of March. a fine day

1797 Thursday April 6th ↝ rained a littel this morning. clear'd away a fine day, in ye evening rained a littel. this morning about 10 oclock William Goldsmith died

Fryday 7th ↝ rained all night, and continues raining and looks as if wee should have a continuance of it — out 12 oclock it left of raining, I gave 2/6 for a 100 plants.[74] I plantd them in the big bed. a cloudey mistey afternoon

73 John Ridgely (1778–1843) was the son of Absalom Ridgely (1747–1818) and his wife Anna Robinson (d.1845). His father was an early Methodist and one of the trustees of the first Methodist church in Annapolis. Ridgely attended St. John's grammar school from July 1793, when he was fifteen, until November 1794. He married Harriet Callahan (c.1790–1828), daughter of John and Sarah Callahan (see 7 February 1793). Ridgely's second wife, whom he married in Georgetown in 1835, was Hester Ridgely, daughter of Judge Henry and Matilda Chase Ridgely (see 16 November 1796). Absalom Ridgely was the son of Henry Ridgely, a modest planter, and his wife Katherine Lusby, and was a distant cousin of the other Ridgelys who appear in the diary. He married Anna Robinson in 1775; the couple had fourteen children. Ridgely settled in Annapolis sometime before 1780 and set up as a small shopkeeper. At the time of his death, Ridgely lived near Faris on a lot (now part of the governor's residence) which he left, with its garden, to his wife. In addition to John, his children included Elizabeth, who married James Nicholson Weems (see 24 September 1802) and David (b. ca.1793), who was the state librarian and author of *Annals of Annapolis*. § Faris bought a pair of shoes for Mrs. Faris from Ridgely in September 1802. Charles Faris's estate paid the firm of Ridgely & Evans £4.3.0 and William's estate paid Ridgely & Weems £2.9.4.

74 Faris occasionally bought plants in bulk when he didn't have enough of his own to fill his beds but generally did not indicate from whom he purchased them.

75 Julia Owen (b.1774) was the daughter of Richard and Elizabeth Owen (see 4 October 1795). She taught school (see 1 May 1804) before her marriage in January 1806 to James Pelham Maynard (see 30 November 1792).

76 There were three Joseph Brewers, all born in the early 1770s, who might have given the seeds to Priscilla Faris. This is possibly the Joseph Brewer who had a store on Conduit Street in 1798 and who moved his business to Cornhill Street in 1800.

77 Perhaps Jonathan Galloway (1748–1810), the son of Samuel and Anne Chew Galloway of Tulip Hill on the West River. Jonathan lived in Annapolis in a modest one-story brick house with a brick shed. His brother John, who married Sarah Chew, inherited Tulip Hill from their father. Samuel Galloway, a merchant, owned the sloop *Greyhound* in 1750. Among the tulips Faris pressed in his design book, he included one named "Gray Hound."

120 ↩ Pressed Tulip
May 20th: 1799: No. 46
The Gray Hound

Saturday 8th ↩ a dull cloudey rainey day, this after noon William Goldsmith was Buried

Sunday 9th ↩ clear, cold windey day

Munday 10th ↩ a clear coole windey day. Mr. R. Johnson sent me som fine cantolope seed & small corn. I planted them both

1797 Tuseday April 11th ↩ I sow'd the Lettice & Radish seed Mrs. Thomas gave me on the end of the Walnutt Tree bed, a fine day

Wednesday 12th ↩ a fine day

Thursday 13th ↩ a cloudey morning. looks like rain. a right Apl day, rain & cloudey at times all day

Fryday 14th ↩ a fine morning. about 9 oclock Mrs. Faris, Miss Owens[75] & Charles Faris sett of in the Packett for Baltimore. a fine day

Saturday 15th ↩ the Peas that was planted the 8th of Feburey are Belling out for Blossom, a dull rainey day

1797 Sunday April 16th ↩ a rainey day

Munday 17th ↩ a clear day but cold for the season in the evening Charles came home in the stage from Baltimore. left his mother & sister well and thay intend heare on Wednesday or fryday

Tuseday 18th ↩ a rainey cold morning, a cold windey day

Wednesday 19th ↩ Mrs. Faris left Baltimore about 12 oclock and arrived heare about 4 oclock. a very cold windey day. left Nancey & Mr. Pitt well

Thursday 20th ↩ a fine morning, Mrs. Faris Brought 2 sorts of seeds that Mr. Joseph Brewer[76] gave her in Baltimore. I have planted them No. 1 is like a coffe Been, the other is red like a crab's eye No. 2 — and on the Border, I sow'd the Brussel sprout, from Mr. Gallow[ay][77] next the Bee house. on the further end I sow'd the Brussel Cale from Mr. Hiseler of Baltimore. a fine day

1797 Fryday April 21th ↩ a fine day, the peas on the Border are in Blossom

Saturday 22th ↩ marked the Hyacinths, and marked 8 Hyacinths with a stick mark'd No. 1 for Mr. Hanson. a fine day. in the evening a littel rain

Sunday 23th ↩ a rainey cloudey day

Munday 24th ✒ How'd the firs crop of Beans for the first time, a dull cloudey mistey dissagreeable day

Tuseday 25th ✒ a cloudey rainey morning. about 10 oclock clear'd away fine & warm after noon

Wednesday 26th ✒ about 3 oclock this after noon my daughter Nancy & her Husband Capt. pitt came to Town from Baltimore. a fine day

1797 Thursday Apl 27th ✒ this morning I went out to Mr. Steers's[78] to see his garden. he has a fine collection of Hyacinths the Best I have seen. a fine day

Fryday 28th ✒ Capt. Pitt whent of this morning about 9 oclock in the Packett for Baltimore. a fine day

Saturday 29th ✒ a fine warm day. in the evening looks like for rain

Sunday 30th ✒ Last night about 9 oclock Mrs. Wilson was taken unwell and died this morning about 8 oclock — and this evening Moses Maccubin,[79] at the Poors House died, I saw him in town within these 2 or 3 days appearantly well, a fine day. in the evening a fine rain

1797 Munday May 1th ✒ a fine day. in the after noon a fine rain, Mrs. Wilson was Buried this evening. Henney unwell & gone to her mothers

Tuseday 2th ✒ a windey cold day. marked the following flowers Viz.

No. 1	Best tulips		o	White Hyacinths
2	Dwarfs d⁰		11	Red d⁰
3	Red d⁰		12	Blew d⁰
4	White & Red d⁰		13	Winged d⁰
5	Black d⁰		14	Red Crown Imperil
6	Yallow d⁰			
7	Parrot Tail d⁰		15	Yallow d⁰
8	Doubel d⁰		16	John Quill
9	White & Red d⁰		17	White Nercess
10	Seedlings		18	Yallow d⁰

121 ✒ Henri Joseph Stier (1743–1821)

[78] Henri Joseph Stier and his family were Belgian aristocrats who fled Europe when French revolutionary troops reached Amsterdam, across the border from their home in Antwerp. They arrived in Philadelphia in October 1794 and in the fall of 1795 came to Annapolis, where they first rented the Sprigg estate, Strawberry Hill, on the Severn across from St. John's. In the fall of 1797, they moved again, renting the former Annapolis home of William Paca (see 7 November 1797) from the estate of Faris's friend Thomas Jennings (see 17 July 1793). Stier's daughter, Rosalie, married George Calvert in 1799 and moved with him to Prince George's County, where they eventually settled at Riversdale. When Stier returned to Belgium in 1803, he announced his departure in the 14 April *Gazette* and advertised the sale of his collection of hyacinths and tulips. § Faris received £2.0.3 from Stier in April 1800.

[79] Moses Maccubbin was the son of Moses Maccubbin (1714–1774) and his wife Mary, and was a second cousin of Charles Maccubbin (see 12 May 1793) and Nicholas Maccubbin Carroll (see 18 January 1792). Maccubbin, who married Sarah Holland in May 1779, was the first hay weigher for the city when the position was created in August 1784. His will refers to his widow and to "children;" Sarah married James Hunter in October. Maccubbin left a very small estate, only £21, but one that included four pictures, six silver teaspoons, a cradle, and four bee hives.

1797 Wednesday May 3th ✒ a dull morning. Mr. Hanson marked 3 doz. & 4 Tulips, with a stick with a notch on the corner at [blank] pr Doz.

in the seedling & nursserey Beds the following flowers

No. 21	General Washington	
22	Ladey	d^o
23	Sweetsented	d^o
1	Best	d^o

a cold disagreeable day. in the evening the sun sett fine.

the midde row in the nurserey Beds I have marked the good ones No. 3 the others of the row I mean to through by

Thursday 4th ✒ a fine day

Fryday 5th ✒ a fine day. in the evening a smart gust of rain

Saturday 6th ✒ a fine day

1797 Sunday May 7th ✒ this morning William Tuck[80] died, with the Gout in his stomack. a cold windey day

Munday 8th ✒ a cold morning. a fire in the Big Room. sowed cardamon seed on the end of the Big Bed by the Time a stick mark'd No. 1 — in the after noon whee had a gust of hail & rain. in the evening William Tuck was Buried, this morning Henney came home from her mothers

Tuseday 9th ✒ a cold day for the season

Wednesday 10th ✒ a fine day. in the evening turn'd cold

Thursday 11th ✒ a fine day

Fryday 12th ✒ a fine warm day

Saturday 13th ✒ a fine morning. about ½ after 6 oclock my daughter Anne Pitt was Brought to Bed of a daugter a fine child. thay are both well & Hartey as possible, a fine day, Samuel Howards wife was Brought to [illegible] daughter this evening

1797 Sunday May 14th ✒ a cold raw dissagreeable day. this fore noon gathered Peas

[80] William Tuck was a painter and glazier, who worked on the Assembly Rooms in the late 1760s and also operated an ordinary in the 1780s. His son Washington, age thirteen, entered the St. John's grammar school in 1795 having been "adopted by the Senate of Maryland per William Cooke" (see 22 March 1792). He matriculated at the college in May 1797 and in 1799 was apprenticed to cabinetmaker John Shaw (see 8 March 1793).

Munday 15th ✒ a fine day

Tuseday 16th ✒ a fine morning, Broke off 1900 Tulip stalks. in the evening turned cloudey & cold

Wednesday 17th ✒ coole dissagreeable day

Thursday 18th ✒ Blowed very hard last night, a dull cloudey morning. in the afternoon a fine rain

Fryday 19th ✒ cloudey & rainey and cold day, Broke of 56 Tulep stalks which was the last of them which made in the wole number 1956

Saturday 20th ✒ a cloudey drisseley day. Charles went of this morning earley for Baltimore

1797 Sunday May 21th ✒ a fine warm morning, in the after noon turned cloudey & wee had a fine rain, in the evening Charles came home from Baltimore

Munday 22th ✒ a fine day. gathered peas out of the Big Bed

Tuseday 23th ✒ a windey day. in the evening looks like rain

Wednesday 24th ✒ a coold morning but turned out a fine day

Thursday 25th ✒ a fine morning, sowd on the Border next to Reigels portsmouth Brocklo, from Mr. Mr. Jos[ep]h Cots.[81] this after noon I sow'd yellow Turnip seed from Mr. Cots on the Border next the seedling Tulips. a fine warm day

Fryday 26th ✒ a fine day

Saturday 27th ✒ a fine day. in the evening it clouded up & thundered and Lightened very much & threatened to be a very seveer gust

1797 Sunday May 28th ✒ a fine day

Munday 29th ✒ this morning Silve weeled dung on the Walnutt Tree Bed & Began to digg it. a fine day. I took up the Crown Impereal Roots round the grass walk

Tuseday 30th ✒ dull cloudey morning & rained at times all day. Silve has finished diging the Bed and I have planted 2 lines of Brussel Cale Plants in it. this evening, a rainey evening and cold. Mrs. Pitt has a Fire in her room up stairs

[81] Faris has clearly written "Joseph" but the census records show only a Jonathan Coats in Baltimore Town in 1790 and 1800 and a John Coates in Anne Arundel in 1790.

Wednesday 31th ✍ Silve's cut down the weeds in the lott and then Pulled up the pea vine in the Bige Bed & went to diging the ground, in the morning I planted the Walnut Tree bed with Brussell Cale Plants & in the evening watered them. I took up the remainder of the Crown Imperel Roots. a fine day

1797 Thursday June 1 ✍ Silve has finished diging the Big Bed whare the Peas grew, & has sp[r]ead the dung on the lot, then went to gethering goosberrey. a very cold day, Nancey pitt had a fire in her room

Fryday 2th ✍ a cloudey dull day. in the evening it rained

Saturday 3th ✍ a fine day

Sunday 4th ✍ a cloudey foggey morning, since Wednesday last Charles has left of Brackfasting heare, ~~and when~~ he comes to his dinner & when he comes he mumbels out something like, how do you do pape in a such a manner, that it appears to me that ~~it is~~ that he would rather not speake at all, to day at diner Charles took it in his head to get up from Table in a pet with out eating his diner, when he came in he never spoke a word to me, either one way or another, nor I to him — a fine day. in the evening clouded up and the wind Blows hard and looks like for rain, this evening Mr. Poole was married to Miss Jane Higgason[82]

1797 Munday June 5th ✍ a fine morning after the rain. I planted the Big Bed with plants whare the peas grew and planted 50 Brussel sprout plants in the lott. Silve watered the plants in the evening. a fine day

Tuseday 6th ✍ a fine day but coole & windey

Wednesday 7th ✍ a fine day

Thursday 8th ✍ henney enter'd into her 4 month this day. a fine day. Hiram's made abegining to take up the flower roots in the Lower beds

Fryday 9th ✍ a cloudey drisseley morning, cleared away a fine warm day

Saturday 10th ✍ a fine warm day. in the afternoon Mr. pitt came heare from Baltimore on Horse Back. in the evening Mr. John Wims's[83] man waighted on me with his masters complyments that I would

[82] Jane may have been the daughter of James Higginson, a merchant who leased property on King George Street in 1774 with William Whetcroft (see 21 October 1793). She was undoubtedly the J. Higginson who advertised in the 3 April 1794 *Gazette* the opening of a school, "at the house of Mr. Randall, for the TUITION of YOUNG LADIES in the useful and ornamental qualifications of the NEEDLE, together with READING and WRITING in the most approved method." Instruction in French would also be available.

[83] This was probably John Weems (1737–1813), son of James and Sarah Parker Stoddert Weems and cousin of John Weems (see 15 October 1795), who originally lived in Calvert County, then moved to Anne Arundel for a time, and finally settled in Kentucky shortly before his death. He married four times and had at least twelve children.

come to his house on Elk Ridge, the carrage was in Town for me

1797 Sunday June 11th ↙ Sett off earley this morning in Mr. Whims's carrage for Elk Ridge. a fine day

Munday 19th ↙ a cold morning. returned home about 1 oclock, left Mr. Weems's at 5 oclock in the morning. thay had a verey seveer gust heare on Saturday after noon last. 6 Bay craft over sett in the river. the peopel ware all saved, like wise thare was a ship agoing to Baltimore. she carried away her fore & main Topmasts, and mizen mast and Mr. Neths kitchen chimney was blown down and Broke in the roof[84]

Tuseday 20th ↙ this morning the neagro girl Henney went of with her self as soon as she got up. Silve Pulled up the Beans in the littel quarter, & dug it up and it is Planted again with Beans. it rained a littel this after noon. its coole for the season. the Beans never came up, thay rotted in the ground

1797 Wednesday June 21th ↙ a coole day

Thursday 22th ↙ a dull cloudey day

Fryday 23th ↙ Last night night and to day Nancey pitts childe has been very Iill, this evening thay had her Privetly Babtized, by the name of Ann Prissila[85] — she is something better to night, it has been a fine day

Saturday 24th ↙ a fine day

Sunday 25th ↙ a fine day

Munday 26th ↙ a fine day

Tuseday 27th ↙ a fine day

1797 Wednesday June 28th ↙ a fine day

Thursday 29th ↙ a fine day

Fryday 30th ↙ a fine day, the Bees swarmed this after noon

Saturday July 1th ↙ Mr. pitt came to Town in his Boat this after noon, a fine day

Sunday 2th ↙ a fine day but very warm

Munday 3th ↙ about 9 oclock the whole Famely left home to go to the Dock to see Mr. & Mrs. pitt & child and Abee sett of for Baltimore. when the Boat

[84] Faris's account anticipates the report in the 22 June issue of the *Gazette*: "Saturday last, about 5 o'clock in the afternoon, we had a most violent storm of wind and hail from the south-west, which, although of a very short continuance, did considerable damage," including, in addition to the loss of the Neth chimney and the capsized boats, the destruction by hail of the crop on Mr. Chase's farm.

[85] According to the Pitt family Bible, the child was baptized Priscilla Ann, named after her maternal grandmother and mother.

left the warf, it wanted 1/4 of 10 oclock, a light Brees of wind but fair, Charls Faris went with them, a very warm day

1797 Tuseday July 4th 🖙 a fine day

Wednesday 5th 🖙 this evening Charles returned from Baltimore, he left Mr. Pitt & his sisters & the child all well, a fine day

Thursday 6th 🖙 I have been very unwell all day. its has been a fine day

Fryday 7th 🖙 a cloudey drisley morning, continued cloudey all day. in the evening it looks as if we should have rain. it is very much wanted

Saturday 8th 🖙 Last night Mrs. Fanney Monrow was Brought to Bed of a fine Boy. thay are both well, a fine day. in the evening clouds up as if wee should have some rain

Sunday 9th 🖙 a fine day

1797 Munday July 10th 🖙 a fine day

Tuseday 11th 🖙 wee had a fine rain last night, a fine morning. Planted Beens in the littel bed at the end of the stabel and in the after noon planted out some Brussel Sprout plants & some portsmouth Brockelo in the lott and watered them & the Beans that was planted in the morning. a fine day

Wednesday 12th 🖙 a fine day

Thursday 13th 🖙 this fore noon Mr. Joshua Frazer[86] call'd to see me. he is just came from Baltimore. he looks very Harty, I think I never saw him look Better. in conversation I asked him how oled he was, he tole me that he was Born in Oct. 23th 1722 — so he will be 75 years old next Octr. this has been a very warm day

Fryday 14th 🖙 a very Hott day

Saturday 15th 🖙 a fine day. in ye evening looks as if wee ware agoing to have a fine rain

1797 Sunday July 16th 🖙 a fine day. in the evening it came on to rain & looks as if wee should have a fine rain. I am inform'd that Doctr Roberts[87] of Kent Island died yesterday. Mrs. Brice & Mrs. Tootel[88] went over thare to day

Munday 17th 🖙 whe had a very prettey rain last night and it has been cloudey allmost all day, this

[86] Joshua Frazier (d. ca. 1799) was in Annapolis by 1765, when he lived on upper Church Street. By 1783 he was working as a carpenter and owned two lots, in the area of Fleet and Cornhill Streets, and seven slaves. When he died in Montgomery County, Frazier left no widow and no children, but was survived by his sister Elizabeth, the widow of Dr. Richard Tootell.

[87] Dr. Jonathan Roberts died the 15th instant at his farm on Kent Island, aged about 65 years, according to the 20 July issue of the *Maryland Gazette*.

[88] Probably Ann Tootell, the widow of merchant James Tootell (d. 1786) who lived at the intersection of Francis Street and State Circle in a one-story brick dwelling. She advertised in September 1789, when St. John's opened, that she could provide lodging for 10 students. She may have been related to either Dr. Roberts or to his widow.

morning wee replanted the Big bed with plants that was wanting & Silve has how'd all the greens & wed the vines, the Beens that was planted the 11th of July are cooming up fineley

Tuseday 18th 🖝 Silve has been howing the lott and geting the weeds out.   in the evening I made 4 rows in the bed by the old stabel & planted them with could not make out the [row] for want of Beens. a fine day

Wednesday 19th 🖝 a fine day

1797 Thursday July 20th 🖝 a very warm day

Fryday 21th 🖝 a fine day

Saturday 22th 🖝 a fine morning. about 12 oclock came on to rain. wee had a very fine rain. clear'd away in the evening. I Planted out the remainder of the Brussel Sprout Plants and fill the bed with Brussel Cail and Portsmouth Brockcalo. a fine evening. Mrs. Faris went & slep with her daughter Rebaca to night

Sunday 23th 🖝 I saw Mr. Henrey Whitcroft this afternoon. he tells me that Mrs. Fanney Monrows child is given over by the Doctrs and that he did not think it could live more then an Hour or two, a fine day

Munday 24th 🖝 a fine day

1797 Tuseday July 25th 🖝 a fine day

Wednesday 26th 🖝 a fine day

Thursday 27th 🖝 a cloudey morning. about 2 oclock wee had a fine rain. this after noon Mrs. Fanney Monrows child died. a cloudey drisley after noon

Fryday 28th 🖝 a fine warm day. in the evening clouded up and looks as if we should have a fine rain

Saturday 29th 🖝 a fine day

Sunday 30th 🖝 a fine morning. about noon clouded over & rained a littel but continued cloudey the rest of the day

1797 Munday July 31th 🖝 a cloudey morning. dug a peace of the Border next Rigels & sow'd onion seed — continued cloudey all day

Tuseday Augt 1th 🖝 a cloudey drisley day

122 🖝 Cellarette

According to family legend, this piece came from a vessel, presumably as a gift. Faris's appraisers listed the cellarette as a "Liquour Case." William Pitt bought the cellarette at the sale of Faris's property in 1805.

See also 11B in color insert.

All the bottles are partially gilded.

See also 11C in color insert.

Wednesday 2th ⚬ a cloudey drisley rainy day

Thursday 3th ⚬ a rainey day

Fryday 4th ⚬ a drisley rainey day

Saturday 5th ⚬ a fine day. in the evening clouded up and wee had a fine rain, accompaney'd with some sharp claps of Thunder & lightening

1797 Sunday 6th ⚬ I belive it rained all night. it has rained all the morning. its now 10 oclock past and is still raining and looks likeley to continue, about 12 oclock it left of raining but continued cloudey

Munday 7th ⚬ this morning Mr. W. Witcroft & son sett of for Virginia. a dull cloudey drisley day

Tuseday 8th ⚬ it rained a grate deel Last Night & this morning, about a 11 oclock I sowd a row of Beens in the Big bed by the goosberrey Bushes. its very cloudey & looks like for more rain — Nancey Howard that was, but now Mrs. Moles was Brought to Bed of a daughter on Sunday last — the weather has clear'd away a fine after noon

Wednesday 9th ⚬ a fine day

Thursday 10th ⚬ a fine day ~~it is reported that Miss Lidia Ridgley daughter of Mr. R. Ridgly, died the day before yesterday at Mr. Daniel Dorseys in Fredrick County~~

1797 Fryday Augt 11th ⚬ a fine day

Saturday 12th ⚬ a fine day. in the evening clouded up and rained a llittel but looks as if wee should have a good deel before morning

Sunday 13th ⚬ it rain'd last night, a cloudey drisley morning, I receivd from Mr. Elisha Hopkins 9 peas of a perticular fine sort. I imediatly planted them in a row on the Border next to Reigels. likewise sent me som plants which he calls the Bleeding Hart, I planted some of them under the Snow Ball tree, some on the Border by the wallnut tree & some in the lott. 12 oclock cloudey like for rain. about 2 o'clock clear'd away a fine after noon

Munday 14th ⚬ a fine day but coole

1797 Tuseday Augt 15th ⚬ a fine day but cold for the season. sow'd spinige on part of the littel quarter next the old stable

Wednesday 16th ☛ this morning I am 69 years old and entering into my 70th year, a fine day

Thursday 17th ☛ a fine day but still coole for the season

Fryday 18th ☛ a fine day

Saturday 19th ☛ a fine day

Sunday 20th ☛ a fine day

Munday 21th ☛ a fine day

1797 Tuseday Augt 22th ☛ a fine morning. about noon wee had a fine rain, & continued cloudey and drisley at times till night

Wednesday 23th ☛ had the Border dug up with an intent of sowing cabbage seed but was dissopointed in geting the seed. I had a littel that I saved. I sow'd that next to ye onions. Oliver Weeden died last night & was buried this evening, he was well & harty yesterday at work, and in the evening was struck at onst with the dead Polsey and died before day — this has been a fine day

Thursday 24th ☛ Nancey pitt & littel nancey and Abee sett of yesterday morning at 9 oclock at Baltimore and did not get heare till this morning. thay nocked us up. thay had a tiresome time of it — a fine day

1797 Fryday Augt 25th ☛ a fine day. in the evening it lightened a grate deal to the N

Saturday 26th ☛ Mr. Miller,[89] at the Plains gave some cabbage seed & I sow'd some of them. a fine fore Part of the day. in the after noon looks very like for rain

Sunday 27th ☛ rained Hard last Night. a fine day

Munday 28th ☛ this morning about 10 oclock the carpenters came. wee went & goot 2000 shingels, two of them went to joynting & Old Harrey got a scaffold up in the front of the House and got out stuff for the cornish and in the morning he intends to begin riping of the old shingels and make abegining to new shingel the Houss.[90] a fine day

1797 Tuseday Augt. 29th ☛ a fine day

Wednesday 30th ☛ look'd like for rain this morning. my head carpenter's sick, has not worked to day. one side of the roof is shut in & the other better then half done. a fine day

[89] This was possibly Samuel Miller, a legislator from Cecil County between 1781 and 1798, who married Rachel Marriott of Anne Arundel in April 1790. Philip Miller and William Miller both appear in Anne Arundel probate records in the early 1800s, and Faris collected debts owed to Charles's estate from John Miller and Peter Miller in the fall of 1800. The Plains might have been either the Plains of Annapolis (a resurvey of Acton on Spa Creek) or Pleasant Plains, a plantation off Whitehall Bay.

[90] Faris purchased 2,000 shingles from John Randall on the 28th, paying 6 dollars, or £4.10.0, for them, and an additional 350 shingles, at a cost of 15/9, on the 31st. He also purchased 26 pounds of nails from Jonathan Pinkney on the same day, but did not note the price. The carpenters received £2 for their labor on September 1st.

Thursday 31th ✒ a fine morning. about 12 oclock
the carpenters finished shingeling the roofe of the
House. a fine day

Fryday Septr 1th ✒ a very warm day

Saturday 2th ✒ a very warm day, in the evening
wee had a smart rain with sharp Lightening and
thunder and some Hail

Sunday 3th ✒ this fore noon about a 11 oclock
Adam Bowyer[91] was taken with the cramp in his
stomack and died a littel before 1 oclock too day —
a fine Plessant day

1797 Munday Septr 4th ✒ a fine day. in the
afternoon Adam Bowyer was Buried

Tuseday 5th ✒ a fine day

Wednesday 6th ✒ Betwen 1 & 2 oclock this
morning Mr. Pitt Nocked Hyram up. he's just from
the capes. a fine day

Thursday 7th ✒ a fine morning. about 7 oclock
Hyram & Mr. pitt sett of in his Boat for Baltimore
to see the Frigate Lanched.[92] a fine day. the Frigate
went off at 9 oclock this morning. she had a very
fine Lanch

Fryday 8th ✒ a fine day

1797 Saturday 9th ✒ a fine day

1797 Sunday Septr 10th ✒ Charles Faris came
heare this morning. he asked me how I did, I
reply'd to him and asked him if he had spoke to his
Brother, and has made up with him. he said he was

[91] John Adam Bayer advertised in the
February 1786 *Maryland Gazette* that he
intended to come to Annapolis in the spring
to carry on the tanning and currying business
at the tanyard of Thomas Hyde (see 9
September 1792), which he would be renting.
In 1791 he moved to another leased tanyard at
the corner of Compromise and Chestnut
Streets bordering on the dock. § In March
1788 Bayer served on a grand jury with Faris.

[92] The U.S.S. *Constellation*, the first of the
frigates authorized in 1794 (see 23 November
1795) to be launched.

124 ✒ *The frigate
Constellation,
launched in
Baltimore.*

willing to make up with Hyram if so be he would
speake to him — I said and not till then, he said
no, I told him he ought and that I expected that he
would for to my certain knowledge he was very
much in the rong and that he had used Hyram very
Ill — and that if he did not speeke to him that I
would never speake to him more, Hah says he I am
not the firs son you have turned out of doors, and
that I had never done aney thing for him and it
appears to me from his pressent and former conduct
to me for 12 months Past that he has been wanting
to quarrel with me.   he took up his hat and went off
— about 10 oclock Hyram came home from
Baltimore. he says that the Peopel at the point are
very sickely and a grate maney die. the doctrs have
declared that it is the Yellow Feaveour. thare is 13
or 14 of a night buried, Mr. pitt is gone down the
Bay with a ship, a fine day

1797 Munday 11th   a fine day

Tuseday 12th   a fine day

Wednesday 13th   a fine day

Thursday 14th   a fine day

Fryday 15th   a fine day. this evening news came
to Town by the stage from Baltimore that Capt.
Gardner is ded and that Mr. Thomas Goldsmith
died on Wednesday last — Mr. Pitt came heare this
morning from down the Bay

Saturday 16th   Mr. Pitts Boat went of for
Baltimore this morning. a fine day

1797 Sunday Septr 17th   Mrs. Johns[93] dined
heare to day. a fine day

Munday 18th   a fine day. in the evening wee had
a fine rain

Tuseday 19th   a fine day

Wednesday 20th   a fine day. in the evening spent
the evening at Capt. Godman's.[94] a largeg & an
agreeable companey of gentelmen & Ladeys

Thursday 21th   a fine day

Fryday 22th   a dull cloudey dissagreeble day

1797 Saturday Septr 23th   a dull cloudey day.
in the evening Mr. & Mrs. Pitt and Abee & Rebaca
went to the Circus to see the Feats of Horsman
ship[95]

93 Possibly the wife of Capt. Richard
Johns, who lived at 28 Bond Street in
Fells Point in 1796, or the wife of pilot
William Johns, who lived on Ann Street,
also in Fells Point.

94 Samuel Godman (d. by 1807) who
would be elected to one term in the House
of Delegates in October. He was a justice
of the peace in 1789, a member of the
committee for the defense of the city in
1798, and of the committee to build a fort
in 1799. In September 1797 he was
appointed captain of a company of the
22nd militia regiment.

95 The *Gazette* carried advertisements for
circuses in 1791 and 1799 but not for this
performance.

96 John Wells (d. 1803) was an Annapolis butcher, one of a family of butchers in town. His daughter Sarah married in 1799, so Elizabeth Shearbutt, whom he married in September 1785, must have been his second wife. In 1798 he owned a one-story frame dwelling, with a brick smoke house and frame slaughter house. The most frequent entries in Faris's day-book, covering the years from 1791 to 1800, were payments to Daniel Wells Sr., Daniel Wells Jr., and John Wells. Faris generally bought lamb, mutton, and veal in the spring and summer and beef in the fall and winter. § Wells's ledgers recorded debts of £2.17.6 owed by Charles Faris and £15.12.9 owed by William Faris. Priscilla Faris listed a debt of £3.11.6 owed by Wells's estate to Charles's estate.

97 There were a number of Edelens living in Prince George's and Charles Counties during this time, but this may have been Edward, who advertised in June 1797 that his stallion Lamplighter would stand at Mt. Airy, an estate in Prince George's County.

98 Probably William Hughes, a ship captain who lived at 80 Pratt Street in Baltimore in 1796.

99 William Brogden (1743–1824), the son of Rev. William Brogden and his wife Elizabeth Chapman, represented Anne Arundel County in the House of Delegates from 1792 to 1799 and was a justice of the peace. § In December 1799, he paid Faris 15 shillings for a watch.

100 John Chew Thomas (1764–1836) represented Annapolis in the General Assembly in 1796 and 1797 and was a member of Congress in 1799. A Quaker and a lawyer, he was born in Cecil County and died in Pennsylvania.

Sunday 24th ⚓ a dull morning. in the afternoon cloudey & rain, I told Mrs. Faris to tel her son Charles that if he did not comply with my request that he should not have his washing done heare aney longer

Munday 25th ⚓ a fine day, Mrs. John Wells[96] died last night

Tuseday 26th ⚓ a fine day, Mrs. John Wells was Buried this evening. the Jockey Club purs was run for & won by Mr. Ridgeleys hors Cincinnatus

Wednesday 27th ⚓ a clear cold morning — a fine day the Colts purs was won by Mr. Edelen[97] mare Tulip

Thursday 28th ⚓ a fine day

1797 *Fryday Septr 29th* ⚓ a fine day

Saturday 30th ⚓ a dull cloudey day N last night Cornelius Mills's wife died

Sunday Octr 1th ⚓ it riained & Blowed hard last night. a dull cloudey rainey day. in the evening Mills's wife was Buried

Munday 2th ⚓ Mr. Pitt sett of in his Boat this morning for Baltimore. a fine day

Tuseday 3th ⚓ a fine day. in the evening Capt. Berrey & Captains Hews[98] & I for get his name, Hews would endeaveour to make out, that Baltimore was as Helthey as it has been for maney years, and that it was not sickeley at the point and that the peopel that moved out ware moveing in again — its clouding up and looks like for rain

1797 *Wednesday Octr 4th* ⚓ rained last Night & this morning. cleared away a fine day but Blow'd hard

Thursday 5th ⚓ a fine day. in the evening the ellection was closed and the Following gentelmen ware ellected, W. Brogdon,[99] Thomas,[100] ~~Hall~~,[101] Samuel Godman, assembley men & B. Welsh had a majority of votes, but thare is a dispute about his being ellegible

101 Although Faris crossed his name out, Edward Hall (?–1813) was also elected. Hall, who married Mary Stevenson in March 1790, lived near the West River, south of Annapolis. He was a delegate to the General Assembly from 1794 to 1801 and speaker of the house in 1800, and served three terms on the executive council from 1801 to 1804. § Faris collected fifteen shillings from Hall as administrator of Charles's estate in November 1800.

Fryday 6th ✍ a fine day. in after noon Mr. John Ridout[102] died aged 67

Saturday 7th ✍ a warm dull cloudey day

Sunday 8th ✍ a fine warm day. Mr. Ridout was Buried to day at White Hall[103]

1797 Munday Octr 9th ✍ dug up the seedling & nursserey Beds and planted the two seedling beds, in the first row next the wallnut tree at this end I planted the sweet sented tuleps, & at the begining of the next row I planted the Genl. & Lady Washington. a fine day. and Silve has dug the 4 beds ajoyning ye circel Bed

Tuseday 10th ✍ I have been very unwell all day that I did nothing in the garden, its been a fine day but coole

Wednesday 11th ✍ a fine day. finished planting the nurssery & seedling beds

Thursday 12th ✍ a fine day

Fryday 13th ✍ a fine day

1797 Saturday Octr 14 ✍ a fine day, Charles went of to Baltimore earley this morning

Sunday 15th ✍ a fine day. in the evening Charles returned from Baltimore

Munday 16th ✍ a fine day, Silve has dug up the circel Bededs

Tuseday 17th ✍ a fine day. Silve has finish'd digging the flower beds and I have been planting, most of the day

Wednesday 18th ✍ a fine day, I have been planting flower roots most of the day

Thursday 19th ✍ a fine day

1797 Fryday Octr 20th ✍ a cloudey morning. I finished Planting the Bulbus roots & flower about 8 oclock — about 12 oclock began to rain and continued drissiling & raining all the after noon and the wind has Blowed very hard all day at N.E

Saturday 21th ✍ the wind continued to Blow very hard all Night and still continues, a cloudey dissagreeable morning, continued a dul cloudey drisley day. in the evening rain and look likely to continue

102 John Ridout (1732–1797) was born in Dorsetshire, England and educated at Oxford University. He immigrated to Maryland in August 1753 as secretary to the new governor, Horatio Sharpe. In 1764, he married Mary Ogle (d.1808), the daughter of Samuel and Ann Ogle and the sister of Benjamin Ogle (see 14 November 1798). Ridout sat in the upper house of the General Assembly from 1761 to 1774 and was naval officer for the Annapolis district from 1762 to 1777. The Ridouts lived on Southeast Street across from the home of Charles Carroll of Carrollton. The Ridouts, who were not enthusiastic patriots, spent the Revolutionary War years at their plantation in Frederick County and at Whitehall, Governor Sharpe's estate, which Ridout eventually purchased. Both Ridouts were buried at Whitehall. § Faris charged Ridout 7/6 for mending a fan in June 1773. He collected £1.2.10 1/2 from Mary Ridout in January 1802 as administrator of Charles's estate.

103 An estate on Whitehall Bay, on the north side of the Severn River, built by Governor Horatio Sharpe, Ridout's patron, who sold it to Ridout in 1782. The central block, constructed in 1764–65, is connected by hyphens to square, hip-roofed wings. The garden facade, visible today from the water, evokes a classical temple and the interior features neoclassical woodwork and plaster work, making Whitehall the first true Classical Revival residence in America.

Sunday 22th ☞ the sun appear'd this morning & lookd as if wee should have a fine day. this has been a fine day after the Bad weather — Moses Maccubbin's widow was marred to day to Mr. Hunter[104] at the Poors House

Munday 23th ☞ a fine day

1797 Tuseday Octr 24th ☞ Mr. Nevett,[105] a Depety Sherref of Prince Georges County told me that he was by & saw the Blows given that kiled Messrs Pollox,[106] and all, at prince georgs ellection[107] and knows the men that did it — a dirty windey rainey day

Wednesday 25th ☞ a fine day

Thursday 26th ☞ a fine day. in the evening Mr. Pitt came heare from the capes

Fryday 27th ☞ a fine day

Saturday 28th ☞ a fine day

1797 Sunday Octr 29th ☞ a fine morning. in the after noon clouded up & looks like bad weather's comeing

Munday 30th ☞ Mr. pitt went of in the packett this morning for Baltimore, to see how the Feaveour is at the point. if it is gone, Nancey's to go to Baltimore on fryday,[108] this has been a cold cloudey day — I took up the Dutch Black Radishes and Buryed them in sand in a Barrel in the celler

Tuseday 31th ☞ a fine day

Wednesday Novr 1th ☞ this morning the General Court adjurned, to the 3d tuseday in Desembr. a fine day

Thursday 2th ☞ a fine day

1797 Fryday 3th ☞ Charles went to Baltimore this morning. a fine day

Saturday 4th ☞ a dull cloudey day. in the after noon and evening rained

Sunday 5th ☞ rain'd and Blowed very hard last night and this morning at South, continued a cloudey drisley day. in the evening the wind came round to N.W and the cloudes appears to brake away to the N.W. looks like for clear weather. Charles came home this evening from Baltimore

Munday 6th ☞ a veriety of weathers. a right March day, snow, Hail, and sun shine

[104] Sarah Holland married Moses Maccubbin in May 1779; Faris recorded his death on 30 April 1797. She must have been the second wife of James Hunter (d.1806), for at the completion of probate, his estate was distributed in 1814 among 7 children, and his son James was twenty when he entered St. John's in 1799. Hunter, an overseer of the poor in 1798, owned a plantation on the South River. Sarah married a third time, in August 1807, to John Smith. § Faris bought 10 bushels each of turnips and potatoes from James Hunter in November 1791.

[105] Perhaps Charles Nevitt, who had been a constable in 1795, or Thomas Nevitt, who was deputy sheriff in 1805.

[106] This may have been William Polluck, whose administrator placed a notice in the *Gazette* in January 1798 concerning settlement of his estate.

[107] This incident did not make the pages of the *Maryland Gazette*.

[108] Nancy Faris Pitt and her children generally spent the later summer and early fall, when yellow fever was most prevalent, in Annapolis rather than in Baltimore. The larger, busier, and more densely settled port of Baltimore was more vulnerable to infection brought in from tropical areas.

1797 Tuseday Novr 7th ✒ 20 minits after 9 oclock the packett went of from the warfe for Baltimore. my daughter Anne pitt & child, Mr. Paca,[109] & several others went in her — a fine day

Wednesday 8th ✒ this fore noon thare was members of the Hous of Assembley anuff in Town, thay made a House — a fine day

Thursday 9th ✒ a fine day

Fryday 10th ✒ a fine day. in the evening the ellection for sherref closed, and John Welsh[110] was ellected by a large majority of voates

Saturday 11th ✒ a dull cloudey day

1797 Sunday Novr 12th ✒ rained hard last night and this morning till about 12 oclock, then cleared away. a fine afternoon

Munday 13th ✒ a fine day. in the evening John Henrey Esqr[111] was chose govenor

Tuseday 14th ✒ this fore noon the following gentelmen were chosen counselers to the govenor Viz. John Davidson, James Thomas, Jonathan Wilmore, Arthur Shoofe,[112] John Johnson, a fine day

Wednesday 15th ✒ this morning the roofs of the Houses looked white with snow, it continued snowing till about 12 oclock, the sun show'd out,

125 ✒ William Paca (1740–1799)

Faris visited the garden shown in this painting when he called on Henri Stier in April 1798.

[109] William Paca was the son of John and Elizabeth Smith Paca, of Baltimore (now Harford) County. Paca received his education at the College of Philadelphia and studied law in Annapolis with Stephen Bordley. In May 1763 he married heiress Mary Chew (c.1736–1774), whose sister Margaret was the first wife of John Beale Bordley (see 1 April 1794), Stephen's half-brother. The Pacas bought two lots in Annapolis, on which they constructed an elegant Georgian mansion, later purchased by Thomas Jennings (see 17 July 1793). With Samuel Chase (see 7 October 1793), Paca was a leader of the Revolutionary movement in Annapolis, and eventually signed the Declaration of Independence. Paca was mayor of Annapolis, served three terms as governor from 1782 to 1785, sat in the house and senate, and was a federal district judge from 1790 until his death. § A lawyer, Paca represented Faris in four suits between 1766 and 1769. Faris sold William Paca and Mathias Hammond 18 bottles of Madeira, 10 bottles of red port, and 8 bottles of punch on 14 May 1773, the day on which Annapolis voters elected the two men as delegates to the lower house—beverages bought either to treat the voters or to celebrate the victory. Faris bought 1,063 pounds of hog meat from Paca in December 1796 and nearly 1,000 pounds from his son, John Philemon Paca, in December 1800.

[110] John Welsh (d. 1802) was the county crier in August 1785 and served as sheriff from 1797 to 1800. He may have been the John Welch who married Mary Hall in August 1782, for he left a widow, Mary, who transferred his property to John Ross as trustee (see 5 October 1803). Welsh owned property on Cornhill Street that had been purchased by his father in 1793. He may also have been a shoemaker, for his estate of $1,683 included a chest of lasts, boot trees and hooks, and other shoemaking equipment. § The John Welsh who patronized Faris's tavern in the early 1770s was probably his father.

[111] John Henry (1750–1798), the son of Col. John Henry and his wife Dorothy Rider, was born in Dorchester County and married Margaret Campbell. He was elected governor in November 1797 and died at his home in Dorchester during his second term.

[112] Arthur Shaaff served four terms on the executive council from 1797 to 1801 and represented Annapolis in the General Assembly from 1803 to 1807.

but soon dissopeard and was cloudey all the after noon and evening, I had a letter from Nancey pitt dated tuseday. she tells me she intends haveing her dear littel Anne annocolated to morrow

1797 Thursday Novr 16th ☛ Last night was the coldest night this fall, a clear cold day

Fryday 17th ☛ a cold windey snowey day

Saturday 18th ☛ clear and cold

Sunday 19th ☛ a clear cold day

Munday 20th ☛ a cloudey Blustering morning. turned out a fine day. in the evening came on to snow

Tuseday 21th ☛ hail sleet & rain all day[113]

Wednesday 22th ☛ a dull cloudey morning. about 8 oclock the clouds appeared to brake and looked as if wee ware agoing to have good weather, at half after 8 Mrs. Faris went down to the packett and went on bord & at 9 oclock sett of for Baltimore, littel or no wind. about 12 oclock the sun shined out and a clever littel Breze of wind from the south, but in the after noon clouded up and littel or no wind

Thursday 23th ☛ a cloudey rainey day. in the evening Beckey went to the Ball, with Mrs. D. Johnston in Mr. Cooks carrage

Fryday 24th ☛ a clear cold day

Saturday 25th ☛ a fine clear cold day. receiv'd a letter from Nancey, littel Ann has been enocolated 3 times and was enocolated again last thursday. Mrs. Faris got to Nancey's about 7 oclock in the evening of Wednesday

1797 Sunday Novr 26th ☛ clear & cold

Munday 27th ☛ clear & cold

Tuseday 28th ☛ a fine day, Betwen 12 & 1 oclock the guns were fired when John Henrey Esqr was swore in govenor

Wednesday 29th ☛ a fine day. this evening I receiv'd a letter from Nancey pitt, she informs me the my littel Ann, was enocolated on Fryday last for the 3d time, but she has now taken the infection. her arm begins to show it

113 Faris recorded a payment in his cash book of 3/9 for cutting and dressing Becky's hair.

276

Thursday 30th ✒ a clear cold day. it frose harder last night then aney night this fall, it Frose the water in my larg bottel that I hold Inflamable aire in — in the evening Mr. Edward Loyde[114] was married to Miss Sarah Murray daughter of Doctr James Murray

1797 Fryday Dessr 1th ✒ a clear cold day

Saturday 2th ✒ a cloudey drissely day. looks like for Bad weather

Sunday 3th ✒ a cloudey morning, Charles & J. Gassaway sett of betwen 9 & 10 oclock on horse Back. Charles to Baltimore & Gassaway for Elkridge Landing.[115] it turned out a drisley disagreeable day

Munday 4th ✒ last night was a very windey bad Night and some littel snow, a clear morning and the wind Blows hard and very cold. it has been the coldest day wee have had this winter, Mrs. Randal's Brought to Bed of a fine daugter

Tuseday 5th ✒ a fine clear day but very cold. this evening Charles came home from Baltimore

1797 Wednesday Desr 6th ✒ a clear cold day

Thursday 7th ✒ clear and cold

Fryday 8th ✒ a cold dull day, looks like for snow or rain, wrought to Nancey by Mr. Nevit[116]

Saturday 9th ✒ snow'd a littel last night, a fine morning. in the evening clouded up & looks like for falling weather

Sunday 10th ✒ a fine clear cold day

Munday 11th ✒ a fine day

Tuseday 12th ✒ a fine day

1797 Wednesday 13th of Dessr ✒ a fine day

Thursday 14th ✒ a fine morning. in the afternoon clouded up & looks like fallaing weather

Fryday 15th ✒ dull cloudey drisley rayney day

Saturday 16th ✒ a fine day

Sunday 17th ✒ a fine day

Munday 18th ✒ a fine day but turned cold

Tuseday 19th ✒ a clear cold day

[114] Edward Lloyd V (1779–1834) was the son of Edward and Elizabeth Tayloe Lloyd (see 19 November 1792). Lloyd served as governor of Maryland from 1809 to 1811, and also sat in both houses of the state legislature and in both houses of the United States Congress. § Faris collected £9.15.7 from Lloyd in January 1801 as administrator of Charles's estate. In 1802 and 1803 Faris hardened four pairs of cock's heels (as well as riveting one) and mended a castor (either a cruet or a stand for a set of cruets) for a total payment of £3.

[115] Elk Ridge Landing is on the western shore of the Patapsco River. At the time it was in Anne Arundel County, but is now in Howard County very near the Anne Arundel border.

[116] This may be the same man who was deputy sheriff of Prince George's County (see 24 October 1797). There were no individuals by that name (or any similar name) in the Baltimore City directories of the period.

Wednesday 20th ✍ a cloudey cold day

1797 Thursday Decembr 21th ✍ the wind Blew extreemly hard & was very cold last night, a fine clear morning but very cold all day

Fryday 22th ✍ snow'd this morning a littel. a cold day

Saturday 23th ✍ last night was a seveer cold night. a fine clear cold day. I sent a letter to day by Mr. William Paca to my daughter Nancey

Sunday 24th ✍ a fine clear cold day

Munday 25th ✍ a cludey morning and Hailed till about 10 or 11 oclock, then cleared away, about 1 oclock Mr. Pitt came heare from below in a schooner, thay broke in through the Ice. thare is several vessels lying heare that cannot go aney further on account of the Ice. a cold day

1797 Tuseday Desr 26th ✍ a fine morning. at ½ after eight oclock my daghter Abee and Mr. Pitt sett of in the stage for Baltimore. thay made 13 in the stage, about 10 oclock it began to cloud up & at 11 it began to rain a littel and continued drisling small rain all day and in the night

Wednesday 27th ✍ this morning Charles sett of for Baltimore. a fine day but cold

Thursday 28th ✍ a fine day but very cold

Fryday 29th ✍ a fine day. in the evening Mrs. Faris returned home from Baltimore in the stage and Charles returned home

1797 Saturday Desr 30th ✍ a fine day

Sunday 31th ✍ a fine day

Munday Janury 1th 1798 ✍ rain'd hard last night. a fogey cloudey day

Tuseday 2th ✍ a fine day

Wednesday 3th ✍ a fine day

Thursday 4th ✍ a dirty disagreeable [day]. rain and sleet all day — in the evening turned to snow betwen 8 & 9 oclock. the ground was covered with snow

Fryday 5th ✍ a dull morning. about 10 or 11 oclock the sun was out fine but in the afternoon, clouded up and looks like for more bad weather

1798 Saturday Janry 6th ๛ a fine day

Sunday 7th ๛ a fine day

Munday 8th ๛ a dull morning. in the after noon Hail and turned to rain

Tuseday 9th ๛ a fine day

Wednesday 10th ๛ a dull day. look like falling weather

Thursday 11th ๛ snow'd a littel last night, a fine day

Fryday 12th ๛ a fine day

Saturday 13th ๛ a fine day

Sunday 14th ๛ a very fine fore part of the day, in the after noon clouded up and looks like Bad weather

1798 Munday Janry 15th ๛ last night betwen 7 & 8 oclock it was luckeley discoverd that the Church was on Fire. the accident happened by Miss Margarett Marree's[117] leeveing her foot stove in the church with fire in it, the fire sett the stove on fire and it communicated to the Floor, as it was discovered before it got to much head it was soon put out — a dull disagreeable day. in the after noon & evening rain

Tuseday 16th ๛ a fine day & warme

Wednesday 17th ๛ a fine warm day. in the after noon Miss Rebbacka Gassaway died

Thursday 18th ๛ a fine day

Fryday 19th ๛ it turned cold & cludey to day and looks as if wee should have snow

Saturday 20th ๛ snow'd a littel last night. a cloudey morning. about 10 oclock clar'd away. a fine day but cold. in the after noon Miss Rebaca Gassaway was Buried

1798 Sunday Janry 21th ๛ a fine day. this evening the House of Assembley Broke up. Mr. William pitt came up in the stage from Baltimore with a parcel of sailors to take a brig to Baltimore

Munday 22th ๛ a fine morning. Silve weel'd dung from Mr. Reigels and put it on the Border & some on the Big Bed then cut up & thined the Snow Ball Bush and althea that had growen into a wilderness. in the the afternoon it rained. this evening Mrs.

[117] There was a family with a surname similar to Marree in Annapolis in the late 1790s, but they were French refugees from the revolution in Saint Domingue and unlikely to have been parishioners at St. Anne's. A. F. A. Marye, age 9, the son of M. Marye, late of St. Domingo, enrolled in the St. John's grammar school in 1799 and M. Marie was a debtor to George Mann's estate in 1796. A Vincent Mayree rented a single-story frame dwelling house on Cornhill Street from Eleanor Davidson in 1798; Margaret might have been his daughter.

Murphey the mother of Mr. Neth was Buried. Mr. Pitt sett of this morning in the Brig

Tuseday 23th ✒ a dissagreeable snowey morning. about 10 oclock clear'd away cold & the wind Blew hard at N.W

Wednesday 24th ✒ a clear cold day

Thursday 25th ✒ a cold dull day. looks like for snow

Fryday 26th ✒ a cloudey drisley morning. to day Colln. John Thomas[118] died, a member for Charles or St. Marey's to the Assembley, he died at Capt. Thomas's. a dull cloudey evening

1798 Saturday Janry 27th ✒ a rainey Night and rained allmost al day. in the evening turned to hail and freesing

Sunday 28th ✒ a littel after 12 oclock Colln. John Thomas was Buried, a clear cold day, Charles Faris went of for Baltimore this morning

Munday 29th ✒ a cloudey morning, cleared away a fine day but cold

Tuseday 30th ✒ a fine day. Charles returned from Baltimore this evening

Wednesday 31th ✒ a fine day

Thursday Febry 1th ✒ a fine day

Fryday 2th ✒ a fine day, in the afternoon Hyram was taken un well & went & laid down. I called in Doctr Ghislin. he advis'd me to give a dose of castor oil. I gave him half of it this evening & I intend to give him the other half in the morning

1798 Saturday Febry 3th ✒ I gave hyram the other half of his castor oile this morning. it did not work him much but he is much better, a fine day

Sunday 4th ✒ Hyram took a dose of Blew Stone[119] this morning. it worked him modaratley, he seems bravely since. it was a cloudey morning but turned out a fine after noon

Munday 5th ✒ very windey. I sett Sylve to digging the Border next to Reigels & in the after noon I Planted 18 rows of Peas, a fine day

Tuseday 6th ✒ a fine day

Wednesday 7th ✒ a dull windey day

[118] John Thomas was the son of Maj. William Thomas (1714–1795) and his wife Elizabeth Reeves (c.1714–1808) and the husband first of Mary Mastin and second of Ann Dent, both of Charles County. Thomas served in the militias of Charles and St. Mary's Counties during the Revolutionary War. Although he died at the home of Capt. Thomas, the two men were not related.

[119] Cupric sulfate, prescribed as a laxative.

Thursday 8th ✒ clear & very cold

Fryday 9th ✒ a very cold day

Saturday 10th ✒ a very cold day

1798 Sunday Febry 11th ✒ a dull cloudey dissagreeable day, Maddam & Miss has not spoke to me to day

Munday 12th ✒ a fine morning. in the afternoon clouded up. its cold and looks like for bad weather

Tuseday 13th ✒ snow'd a littel last night, a cloudey disagreeable day. this evening Miss Polley Turnbull was married to Mr. Young of the Eastern Shore[120]

Wednesday 14th ✒ a dissagreeable snowey morning and snow'd a littel at times all the fore noon, in the afternoon clear'd away & the sun came out

Thursday 15th ✒ the wind Blew very Hard last night. a dull cloudey morning, clear'd away a tolarabel good day

Fryday 16th ✒ a dull cloudey day

Saturday 17th ✒ a cold windey day

1798 Sunday Febry 18th ✒ a clear day but cold & windey

Munday 19th ✒ a cold cloudey dissagreeable day. the wind Blows hard at NE. in the evening came on to Hail and rain

Tuseday 20th ✒ it has been a very bad night, a cloudey drisley cold windey morning, very bad walking, the streets are like glass, a dull cloudey day, but warmer then it was. it has thawed, the Ice & Hail's all most gone — Doctr Ghislin was maried to Miss Nancy Robertson, daughter of the late Elisha Robertson of the N. side of Severon[121]

Wednesday 21th ✒ a cloudey dull day. in the evening and night it rained hard

Thursday 22th ✒ snow'd a littel this morning earley but clear'd away a fine morning. this after noon Doctr Ghislin came home & Brought his wife with him in Smiths stage, a fine day

Fryday 23th ✒ a dull cloudey morning. in the afternoon it began to drissel & rain

[120] John Young, Esq., of Caroline County, married Mary Turnbull of Annapolis, Rev. Ralph Higginbotham officiating, according to the *Gazette*. Young represented Caroline County in the lower house for 7 terms between 1796 and 1812. Mary Turnbull was the daughter of John Turnbull and his wife Sarah Beall, of Prince George's County.

[121] Anne Robosson was the daughter of Col. Elijah Robosson, who died in 1796. Her widowed mother's death occurred in 1815, when the 27 April *Gazette* reported that Mary Robosson had died in her sixty-second year. "Her venerable mansion, situated on the public line from the Severn Ferry to Baltimore was always a receptacle for the wearied traveller; it was under her roof they found repose." See 13 April 1793 entry for Reverdy Ghiselin.

1798 Saturday Febry 24th ✍ a fine morning, in the after noon turned cloudey

Sunday 25th ✍ a cloudey day

Munday 26th ✍ Betwen 12 & 1 oclock last night Abee came home from Baltimore — a fine morning and continued a fine day which is a rarity

Tuseday 27th ✍ Mrs. Key[122] told me this morning that my good old Friend Colln. FitzChew, is dead & that he died the 10th of Febry aged 76, a fine morning. Silve made abegining in the garden. she has dug a peace on the Border and I sow'd earley York & loaf cabbage and a littel lettice seeds adjoining the Baum and she is spreding the dung & takeing up the stalks in the big bed. in the afternoon Sylve complained of a Pain in her head. I told her leave of and go in the House. a fine day

1798 Wednesday 28th ✍ a fine morning. in the afternoon came on to snow

Thursday March 1th ✍ a cloudey drisley rainey morning. in the after noon, it snow'd and turned to a drisley rain

Fryday 2th ✍ a dull drisley morning, in the afternoon the sun shined. in the evening came on to Blow fresh

Saturday 3th ✍ a fine day

Sunday 4th ✍ a fine day. this evening John Shaw was married to Mrs. Peggey Stewart, widdow of Capt. John Stewart

Munday 5th ✍ a fine morning. I have sow some radis seed on the Border nex to Reigels, Silve is digging ye Big bed, Silve has finished digging the big bead. a fine day

1798 Tuseday March 6th ✍ a fine morning, tho a smart white Frost, Sylve opened & did up the aspargrass beds and I sow'd on the near on White Loaf Cabbage seed & Lettice seeds from Baltimore & on the fur one I sow'd earley York seed from Baltimore & 2 sorts of Lettice I raised last year, in the after noon Sylve went to doing up the tabels round the Big bed. a fine day

Wednesday 7th ✍ dug the Border next Mrs. Davidsons and Planted onions and Sylve's cleaning ye garden. a fine day

122 Most likely Ann Plater Key, the wife of Philip Barton Key (see 29 May 1792), whose father, George Plater, had been a close friend of William Fitzhugh.

Thursday 8th ☞ a fine morning. finished planting
the onions. Planted the Big bed with Peas the first
4 rows & a peace of a row next to Reigels in Peas
Mr. Hopkins gave me. he says thay are a very forward sort, the rest of the rows ware our own. in the
after noon it looks dull & cloudey like for rain. its
been the warmest day this spring. in the evening I
took up & parted my Polianthis's roots

1798 Fryday March 9th ☞ planted out the
Roshembole & trimed the sage. a fine day

Saturday 10th ☞ a fine warm morning. I have cut
the 2 lines of Box on each side of the grass walk as
you go in the garden and the peas I Planted the 5 of
Febry are just makeing thare appearance acuming
up, a very fine warm day. about 12 oclock I water'd
the Peas on the Border that's just cuming up

Sunday 11th ☞ the wind has blow'd very hard all
Night and this morning & its very cloudey & looks
like rain. the orris, lettice & cabbage Plants are
cuming up on the Border. in the after noon rain

Munday 12th ☞ the wind Blow'd very hard last
night & too day and is cold, Sylve has begun to
dung & dig the Parsnep & carrot Beds in the lott.
in the after noon I cutt one hedge of Box. a cold raw
day

Tuseday 13th ☞ a cloudey dull day. Hyram's cuting
Box. Sylve's finish'd diging the Parsnep Bed & littel
John Rigel is aplanting of it

1798 Wednesday March 14th ☞ a fine day.
Hyram has finished cutting the Box in the Beds
round the grass walk and the beds by coffe house
and is about the Box in the nurssery beds, Sylve has
dug the littel quarter at the end of the new stable
and is takeing up the cutings and cleaning the
garden, and littel John Reigel has finished Planting
the Parsneps. in the evening turn'd cloudey looks
like for rain. the radishes on the border are acuming
up

Thursday 15th ☞ a cloudey morning. look like for
rain. I have sow'd the carrots and Hyram's cuting
Box and finished cuting about 12 oclock, and it
came on to rain, in the evening clear'd away fine &
the sun sett cleare

Fryday 16th ☞ a cold raw day. Hiram's a
Troweling the Flower Beds

Saturday 17th ✒ a coole raw day, Hiram's diging the Flower Beds

1798 Sunday March 18th ✒ a dull cloudey day

Munday 19th ✒ a cloudey drisley day

Tuseday 20th ✒ I Planted out my Dutch Radishes but I am afraid thay wont do. thay apper to be on the rotten order, I planted on the circil of the big bed by the littel house some Cannadian Corn given to me by Mr. P. McGill[123]

Wednesday 21th ✒ it rained and Thundered Hard this morning and continued raining & cloudey all day. in the evening the wind came on to Blow hard at N.W — about 8 oclock in the evening the Pidgen House Blew down. it was Built in the year 1777[124]

Thursday 22th ✒ a cold windey day

Fryday 23th ✒ a fine day, hoed the Peas on the Border the second time. in the evening clouded up and looks like rain

1798 Saturday March 24th ✒ rained hard last night and this morning betwen 11 & 12 oclock. cleared a way fine after noon. in the evening clouded up and looks like for more rain, the Peas in the Big Bed that was sown the 8th of March are just makeing thare appearance

Sunday 25th ✒ rain'd last night. a fine morning but about 10 oclock it turned cloudey and a shower of Snow, Hail & Rain, and continued cloudey in evening looks very thick & dirty, like bad weather

Munday 26th ✒ a fine morning. sow'd 1 row of Bunch peas from Mr. Rolph[125] and the rest of the Bed with Dwarf Beens & 26 peas that I rais'd from the Peas from Mr. Hopkins. last sumer he gave me 9 and 7 came up, I have planted 12 Hills of the 6 weeks simlin from Mr. Stevens & 5 hills of canitlops & 3 Hills of cucumbers, and Hyram informs me that it is reported that Mr. Pitts Boat is over sett and 2 hands lost, and likewise a white Bottom'd Schooner over sett ~~& 3 hands lost~~. in the afternoon planted the Ice plant seed & Egg plant seed in the Barrel

1798 Tuseday March 27th ✒ about 8 oclock Mrs. Faris and my self, sett of in the stage for Baltimore. a fine day. arrived thare in the evening. found Mrs. Pitt and Famely all well. Mr. Pitt came

[123] Patrick McGill (1744–1796) may have been the son of Rev. James McGill and his wife Sarah Hilleray of Queen Caroline parish. He was the constable for Elk Ridge Landing in 1786 and in March 1794 advertised that the White Horse Tavern at Elk Ridge Landing was for rent or sale. § McGill patronized Faris's tavern in 1774.

[124] Dovecotes, although common in the tidewater, were impermanent buildings—constructed of unpainted wood with post-in-ground foundations—that were not expected to last more than a generation or two.

[125] Possibly John Ralph, an Anne Arundel County resident in 1790.

home on Fryday evening. he has not got his Boat up
yet but expects to get her up. I left Baltimore
Sunday morning 8 oclock and arrived at Annapolis
about 2 oclock in the after noon the first day of
April

Munday April 2th ✒ a cloudey drisley morning.
sow'd the Sencitive Plant seed in a pott and Planted
No. 15 a root the Name for got botth from Mr.
Hesler & 2 roots of the John Quill from Mr.
Leopold, in the after noon came on to rain fast and
looks as if wee should have a good deal of bad
weather. cut assparagrass this morning for the first
time

Tuseday 3th ✒ it rained and the wind Blew very
hard all night and continues to rain & Blow hard all
day

Wednesday 4th ✒ it still continues to rain and Blow
hard

1798 Thursday April 5th ✒ a cloudey mistey
day

Fryday 6th ✒ made 8 Hills in the outer lott and
Planted 4 of them with cantilopes & 4 with cucumbers. a fine day

Saturday 7th ✒ a dull cloudey day

Sunday 8th ✒ a fine day

Munday 9th ✒ this morning took the litter from
the grape vines, dunged & dug the ground and
Planted cantilope seed on the border with the vines
and some on the border of the walnut tree bed. a
fine day

Tuseday 10th ✒ this morning abrought the Potts
out of the seller, a fine day. in ye evening clouded
up and rained

1798 Wednesday April 11th ✒ a dull cloudey
drisley day. planted Cannady corn on the Border at
the far end of the grape vine & assparagrass see[d].
behind it the seed from Mr. E. Hopkins & planted
more corn on the border of the walnut tree bed

Thursday 12th ✒ a right April day. showerrey all
day. about 12 oclock wee had a smart of Hail in the
evening clear

Fryday 13th ✒ a raw cloudey drissley day

Saturday 14th ⚑ an April day, showers of rain & windey & cold & raw, I Planted more Cannady corn on the side of the Parsnep Bed

Sunday 15th ⚑ a clear cold windey day

1798 Munday April 16th ⚑ a very cold windey day. Silve has been sticking ye peas the big Bed

Tuseday 17th ⚑ last night was very cold thare was Ice in the bucket at the Well near ½ an Inch thick, this morning Silve has finished sticking the Peas in the Big bed. a very cold day

Wednesday 18th ⚑ a clear cold day

Thursday 19th ⚑ a fine morning. sow'd the following flower seeds

    No. 1 Sensitive plant

        2 the Indian Nuttmeg

        3 the Parson's Pride

        4 Amaranthus tricolo

a fine day

Fryday 20th ⚑ a cloudey day. in ye evening looks like for rain

Saturday 21th ⚑ a fine warm morning. in the after noon a fine rain, cleared away rather coole

1798 Sunday April 22th ⚑ a fine day. in the evening Mr. John Harwood was married to Miss Mary Brewer daughter of the late John Brewer[126]

Munday 23th ⚑ a dull cloudey morning. Silve how'd and Hilled the Peas in the big bed for the last time. clear'd away a fine day

Tuseday 24th ⚑ a fine day

Wednesday 25th ⚑ a fine day. in the afternoon Mr. Pitt called hear with the Capt. of ship from Chester Bound out and a young man with them. Mr. Pitt drank Tea with us while the Capt. & young man went to walk. in the evening thay went on board the ship

Thursday 26th ⚑ this fore noon I went to see Mr. Steer,[127] he gave me the following seeds which I planted in 3 potts as follows Letter A Hyacinth seed, letter B Emoney d⁰ letter C, arucula seed — Mr. Pitt was heare this after noon. the wind is ahead. he thinks to go to morrow, a fine day this

[126] John Harwood may have been the son of John Harwood (1744–1823) and his wife Mary Hall, and the grandson of Capt. Richard and Ann Watkins Harwood. Mary Brewer was the daughter of John and Susannah Brewer (see 13 March 1792).

[127] Stier was now living in William Paca's former home in Annapolis (See Figure 125 on page 275).

evening Mr. Charles Wallace (who is this day 71 years of age as Samuel H. Howard says) is married to Mrs. Mary Rankin,[128] about 40 or 45 years of age

Fryday 27th ↝ the girls had the big room white-washed to day.[129] a fine day

Saturday 28th ↝ a fine day

Sunday 29th ↝ a fine day

Munday 30th ↝ Capt. Johns Brackfasted with us this morning, he's bound out,[130] a fine day

Tuseday May 1th ↝ a fine day. the peas in ye big bed are in blossom

Wednesday 2th ↝ a fine littel rain this morning. I planted betwen the peas in ye big bed cabbage plants

1798 Thursday May 3th ↝ a fine day

Fryday 4th ↝ a fine day, in ye evening cloudey like for rain

Saturday 5th ↝ a fine day. in the after noon wee had a fine littel rain

Sunday 6th ↝ wee had a fine rain last night, clear'd away a fine day

Munday 7th ↝ Silve has dug up the littel qurter by the old stabel & I sowd one row of Algereen Peas, given by Miss Ashmead, and 4 rows of the Bunch beens. a fine day

Tuseday 8th ↝ a fine day but coole for the season

Wednesday 9th ↝ a fine day but still coole

Thursday 10th ↝ a fine day but still coole

1798 Fryday May 11th ↝ a fine day but very coole John Barber's come from Baltimore and says that George Barber's Boat over sett, in Patapsaco River just by the Rocks[131] on Wednesday last on her way to Baltimore

Saturday 12th ↝ a fine day but still cold. in the after noon Mr. Joseph Pitt[132] called heare on his way to Baltimore from the capes

Sunday 13th ↝ a fine day. in the evening Mr. Pitt came hear. he brought down a parcel of passengers, amongst them ware Messrs. Hamelton & Snider.[133] thay drank Tea with us and Mr. Pitt went of for Baltimore directley. He brought me a letter from

128 Mary Bull (c.1747–1834), the daughter of Cornelius and Catherine Walker Bull (see 12 May 1792). She was the widow of George Ranken, former clerk of the Corporation and of the general court, who died in 1788 with no property. Catherine Wallace, the first wife of Charles (see 5 January 1792), had died in 1795. § George Ranken patronized Faris's tavern in 1773.

129 Faris paid 5 shillings on the 28th for having "ye big room" whitewashed. The following year he paid "George" 3/9 on 11 June for the same task, but did not record the event in his diary.

130 The 27 April issue of the *Federal Gazette* reported that Capt. Johns, commanding the schooner *Sisters*, had cleared Baltimore for the West Indies.

131 Possibly Seven Foot Knoll, in the mouth of the Patapsco just off Bodkin Point, but perhaps a less well-marked obstacle farther up the river.

132 Joseph Pitt, William Pitt's younger brother, was a pilot who lived on Apple Alley in Fells Point in 1803. He married Elizabeth French on 7 January 1802 in a ceremony performed by the minister of the Fells Point Methodist Church.

133 In 1799, there were six Sniders living in Baltimore, including John Snider, a ship chandler, at 41 Fells Street in Fells Point, but none were identified as a ship captain.

Mrs. Faris & one from Mrs. Pitt, thay are all well. wee gathered a good mess of peas to day for the first time

Munday 14th ✍ a fine day

Tuseday 15th ✍ a fine day. Capt. J. Steel, Capt. Snyder & Capt. Cole[134] dined with me to day

1798 Wednesday May 16th ✍ a fine day

Thursday 17th ✍ a fine day. I Broke of 1645 Tulep stalks. the rest I intend to brake of as soon as the flower falls

Fryday 18th ✍ a fine day

Saturday 19th ✍ a fine day

Sunday 20th ✍ gathered Peas in the big Bed. Mrs. Gassaway dined heare. a fine day

Munday 21th ✍ a fine day but very dry, wee have had no rain since the 6th of the month. every thing is suffering for want of rain

Tuseday 22th ✍ a cloudey morning looks like for rain but it want of still dry

1798 Wednesday May 23th ✍ a fine morning. in the afternoon & evening a fine rain, just before the rain I mooved the egg plants out of the Barrel & planted them in potts & took up the Ice Plants, filled up the Barrel, for it had setteled a good deal, I then Put the plants in it again

Thursday 24th ✍ a cloudey morning. in the after noon a clever littel rain

Fryday 25th ✍ a cloudey morning, & rained a littel at times, in the cleared away & the sun came out fine and sett cleare

Saturday 26th ✍ a fine day, the root that Mr. Hesler gave me is come up. its name is, the Lyly of St. Jaego[135]

Sunday 27th ✍ a fine day. in the after noon clouded up and in the evening rained a littel

Munday 28th ✍ rained the most of the night and continued raining all the morning till about 12 oclock then cleared away

1798 Tuseday May 29th ✍ a cloudey morning. at 9 oclock Old Terrey sett of in the Packett for Baltimore, to my daughter Nancey and took with ½ a Bushel of Peas and a Basket of lettice, about 12

134 The 1800 Baltimore City Directory listed 8 Coles, including Thomas, a ship chandler, who lived at 46 Pitt Street in Fells Point.

135 Faris's grandson and namesake, William Faris Pitt, died at St. Jaego in 1821.

oclock the Bees swarmed. I hived them & put them in the Bee House. a fine day

Wednesday 30th ✒ a rainey morning. about 20 or 25 minits after 1 oclock at noon I had called Silve to bring me som fire[136] to light my pipe, she brought it, while I was lighting my pipe I hear'd a crash as if some glass or earther'n whare was brok. I was setting in the big room. I desired her to open the Back doore. I thought the girls ware coming out of the kitchen and let what thay whare bringing up fall down — but on looking about I found that a pain of glass in the window next the Bofett was broke — thare was not a being in the littel room and it appears Impossible for a stone to be thrown from with out to have broke it, thare fore it appears very extrodenary how the accident should have happened. thare was a waiter[137] standing against the Pain of glass that was broke and it was not mooved

1798 Thursday May 31th ✒ a cloudey morning, sow'd the following seds on the Border next to Reigels

No 1 Brussel Sprout, from Mr. J Coats

    2   d^o d^o from Mr. Steear

    3   d^o Coal of my raising

and lettice with them, and further on I sow'd some cabbage seed sent to me by Mr. Jenings Jacob. continued a dull day. in the afternoon Sylve laid down. she complained of being un well

Fryday June 1th ✒ a fine day

Saturday 2th ✒ a fine day. in the evening, Sylve complained of being unwell and went to bed

Sunday 3th ✒ a fine warm day, I gave Silve a Puke this morning. it worked her upwards and down. I am in hopes she will be better, in the evening seems to cloud up and looks like for rain

1798 Munday June 4th ✒ a fine rain last night. a cloudey morning, rain in the after noon. I gave Silve Bark to day. I am in hopes she will get braveley

Tuseday 5th ✒ a fine rain last night, a cloudey morning. clear'd away a finc warm day, Silve's Better

Wednesday 6th ✒ it was cloudey at times all this morning. in the after noon the Bees swarmed. in the evening it rained

[136] A coal or ember, probably from the kitchen fireplace.

[137] A serving tray for food or beverages.

126 ⚜ Rebecca Maria Pitt Chappell
(1798–1834)

As a child, Rebecca Maria Pitt, known to her grandfather as Marriah, lived with her grandparents in Annapolis.

[138] Rebecca Maria Pitt, named after Nancy's younger sister.

[139] William Marbury (1762–1835) married Ann Odle Brewer (1770–1847), the daughter of John and Susannah Peale Newton Brewer (see 13 March 1792). Marbury was a manager of the orphans' school lottery and clerk of the general court of the western shore in 1791, a captain in the first volunteer company of the militia in 1795, and a collector of revenue for the city corporation in 1797. He moved to Georgetown by the early 1800s, where he and his wife lived until their deaths. Marbury is best known as the plaintiff in *Marbury v. Madison*, the Supreme Court case that established the principle of judicial review. Marbury (and three others) sued James Madison, secretary of state in the Jefferson administration, to obtain a commission as justice of the peace authorized by Madison's Federalist predecessor. The Court ruled in February 1803 that Marbury was entitled to his commission but that it could not order its delivery because the power to do so came not from the Constitution but from the Judiciary Act of 1789, an act that the court declared unconstitutional.

Thursday 7th ⚜ a fine morning, sow'd on the further end of the Border, 1^d the green curled savoy, and the 2^d yallow curl'd savoy, from Maj. Davidson. Silve's a pulling up the Peas in the Bigg bed, and dug up the ground.   a fine day

Fryday 8th ⚜ a fine morning. Sylve's cleaning up ye garden. in ye after noon a fine rain. in ye evening clear'd away and I planted the ground whare the Peas grew with Plants

1798 Saturday June 9th ⚜ a fine day

Sunday 10th ⚜ a fine day. in ye evening cloudey

Munday 11th ⚜ this morning I receiv'd a letter from my daughter Pitt dated the 9th, whare in she lets me know that she is as well as can be expected. she was brought to Bed the morning before of a daughter[138] — a cloudey drisley day

Tuseday 12th ⚜ a dull cloudey drissley day

Wednesday 13th ⚜ a fine day. in the afternoon & evening we had a littel rain

Thursday 14th ⚜ a fine day. in the evening sow'd lettice seed on the fur end of the Border next the young tulips

Fryday 15th ⚜ Mr. Green came down in ye stage. he told me that thay ware all well at Mr. Pitts yesterday, a fine day

1798 Saturday June 16th ⚜ a fine day. in the after noon, thare was a meeting of the citizens, & thay appointed 5 Captains, Messrs John Davidson, John Gassaway, John Guynn for the mellitia, [blank] Mawberry[139] Capt. of artilery & James Williams Capt. of Horse and the Capts. are to chuse thare subb^n officers — in the evening clouded up like for rain. I gathered simlins to day

Sunday 17th ⚜ a cold cloudey morning, clear'd away a fine day but continued cold

Munday 18th ⚜ this morning I planted the peas that I got from Mr. Hopkins, this is the 3d time I have planted them. I had 9 peas & 7 only came up, I have now planted 62. a cloudey morning, Sylve's takeing up the seed peas & pea sticks and dig the ground, in the evening I water'd the Peas I planted this morning. a cloudey day

Tuseday 19th ⚜ a cloudey drisley day

Wednesday 20th ☛ a cloudey day, this morning Mrs. Boyle[140] had her right Brest cut of, on accot of a canser in it[141]

1798 Thursday June 21th ☛ a fine day

Fryday 22th ☛ a fine morning, Hiram sett off in the Packett for Baltimore at 9 oclock, a fine day, the warmest wee have had this summer

Saturday 23th ☛ a fine day

Sunday 24th ☛ the peas I planted the 18th are come up. a very Hott fore noon. in the after noon wee had a fine rain. clear'd away in the evening close and sulterey. Crawford[142] dreamed last night that the French had landed in Ireland and that thay had a severe Battel

Munday 25th ☛ a drisley day

Tuseday 26th ☛ a dull cloudey day

Wednesday 27th ☛ a fine day

1798 Thursday June 28th ☛ this morning Hiram Faris came home from Baltimore. left them all well thare and thay say thay will be heare in a fortnight or 3 weeks. a cloudy morning, clear'd away a fine day

Fryday 29th ☛ a fine day

Saturday 30th ☛ a fine day

Sunday July 1th ☛ a very warm day. Mr. Antoney Pinkeney[143] died to day

Munday 2th ☛ a very Hott day. dug the littel quarter whare the Beens grew, and Silve has begun diging the walnutt tree Bed

Tuseday 3th ☛ a very hot [day]. in the even wee had a gust of rain. Silve has not finished diging the bed

---

[140] Mary Brewer, born 3 September 1748, the daughter of John Brewer IV (1709–1754) and his wife Eleanor Maccubbin (1708–1779), married James Boyle in September 1781. She was the sister of Nicholas Brewer Sr. (see 30 May 1803), who mentioned her as his only legatee in a will written in 1786, although he had other siblings. Boyle was a widow when her son James (1784–1854) was admitted to the St. John's grammar school in January 1792; he received an A. B. degree in 1800 and an A. M. in 1806.

[141] The British novelist Frances Burney described in a letter to her sister her own experience of a mastectomy in September 1811. "About August 1810," she wrote, " I began to be annoyed by a small pain in my breast, which went on augmenting from week to week." She consulted leading doctors and was "condemned to an operation by all Three." The operation took place in her home, after her husband had been banished from the house. Burney occupied herself with arrangements: "I had a bed, Curtains, & heaven knows what to prepare—but business was good for my nerves" while she waited for the surgeons. After the "7 men in black" arrived, Burney was given a wine cordial and "compelled . . . to submit to taking off my long *robe de Chambre*, which I had meant to retain. . . . I refused to be held; but when, Bright through the [transparent] Cambric [that covered her eyes], I saw the glitter of polished Steel—I closed my Eyes. . . . The dreadful steel was plunged into the breast—cutting through veins-arteries-flesh-nerves. . . . I began a scream that lasted unintermittingly during the whole time of the incision—& I marvel that It rings not in my Ears still! so excruciating was the agony." The operation removed the entire breast in a procedure that lasted twenty minutes. By ten the next morning, according to the medical student who wrote the case history, "the patient was surprised at the well-being she felt." Despite the trauma of her surgery, Burney was fortunate: her cancer had not metastasized and she lived another thirty years.

[142] Probably *not* David Crauford, Esq., justice of the peace of Prince George's County, although Faris may well have known him, as Crauford served in the conventions of the Revolutionary period and in the lower house in the 1780s. Nevertheless, Faris's reference seems too casual to refer to someone he would not see on a regular basis.

[143] Anthony Pinkney, who married Margaret Gillis in June 1791, may have been the son of Robert and Priscilla Pinkney (see 26 July 1793). Anthony signed the inventory of Robert Pinkney as one of his nearest kin. Ninian Pinkney Jr. witnessed Anthony's will, which made no mention of children.

June / July, 1798

1798 Wednesday July 4th ✍ Planted beens in the littel quarter by the new stabel, promises to be a warm day. Silve's finished the w. tree bed before Brackfast & is howing the cabbages in the big bed. a fine day. in the evening Hiram & Abee & Rebaca went to the Play

Thursday 5th ✍ a fine morning. in the afternoon a fine rain. in the evening Planted Brussel Sprout Plants in the walnut tree bed. the firs 4 rows the seed came from Mr. Steere the other from Mr. Coates, & planted the littel quarter betwen the Beens with yellow & green curled savoy plants

Fryday 6th ✍ a fine day

Saturday 7th ✍ a fine Pleasant day

1798 Sunday July 8th ✍ a fine day. in the evening a cleaver rain

Munday 9th ✍ this morning Charles went to Baltimore in the Packett. a fine day

Tuseday 10th ✍ a fine day

Wednesday 11th ✍ a fine day. about 5 oclock in the after noon Mrs. Faris & Charles & littel Anne pitt came from Baltimore in the Packett. in the evening whee had a fine rain

Thursday 12th ✍ a fine day

Fryday 13th ✍ a fine day but very cold, I put on my worsted stockings & a thick jackett

Saturday 14th ✍ a fine day but but still cold but not so cold as yesterday

1798 Sunday July 15th ✍ last night Mrs. Ann Gastin widdow of George Gastin[144] died, a fine day

Munday 16th ✍ a drissley cloudey day

Tuseday 17th ✍ a cloudey morning. littel Anne has been very Ill all night & is still very Ill. Charles is gone to Baltimore to bring Nancey heare, my Poor dear littel Ann died about 3 oclock this after noon — a cloudey evening

Wednesday 18th ✍ a rainey morning. about 2 oclock, Charles Nancey pitt & her littel strainger Miss Rebaca came heare from Baltimore all in good health but in much troubel for the loss of her dear littel Ann, a fine after noon

[144] Ann Dranc, who married George Gaston (or Garston), either a ship captain or mariner, who held a long-term lease on West Street at the other end of the block from Faris. Gaston may have been a brother of Thomas Gaston (see 23 February 1793), owner of the packet that capsized. Faris notes the marriage of the Gastons' only child, Elizabeth, who inherited the property after her mother's death, on 29 June 1800.

Thursday 19th ☞ this morning about 8 c'clock My dear littel Prissila Ann Pitt was Buried, a clear cold day

1798 Fryday July 20th ☞ a fine day but cold for the season

Saturday 21th ☞ a fine day

Sunday 22th ☞ a fine morning, gathered the yung Roshemboles or Onions of Eagipt,[145] a fine day

Munday 23th ☞ a fine morning, Silve's dug the Border nex the lot by the Bee hives & I sow'd Brussel Cale seed

Tuseday 24th ☞ a very warm day

Wednesday 25th ☞ a warm morning. at 9 oclock Nancey pitt and her dear littel Rebaca, and Abee sett of in the packett for Baltimore. a Hott day

Thursday 26th ☞ a very Hott day

Fryday 27th ☞ a very Hott day

Saturday 28th ☞ very Hott & dry

1798 Sunday July 29th ☞ very Hott & dry. Mr. Warf's waiter died this after noon in conssiqence of drinking cold water

Munday 30th ☞ a cloudey morning, Silve's dug a littel pece next the goosberrey bushes, I holed it & watered it & in the evening I intend Planting plants thare & Silve's ahowing the walnut tree Bed. clear'd away very warm. in the after noon wee had a fine rain

Tuseday 31th ☞ a fine morning. Planted the littel quarter by the old stabel with yallow & green curled savoy Plants, dug a peace on the border next to Reigels & sow'd onion seed, Silve's pulling up the parsnep that's runing to seed in the parsnep Bed. a fine day

Wednesday Augt 1th ☞ a fine day

Thursday 2th ☞ a fine day but Hott & dry

Fryday 3th ☞ Hot & dry

1798 Saturday Augt 4th ☞ a warm day. in the evening whee had a shower of rain, its cloudey and looks as if wee should have more befor morning

[145] It is very unusual for a Sunday entry to record any activity by Faris.

Sunday 5th ✒ a fine rain last night. a very Hott day

Munday 6th ✒ a fine day

Tuseday 7th ✒ a Hott day

Wednesday 8th ✒ a Hott day

Thursday 9th ✒ a very hot day

Fryday 10th ✒ a very Hott day

Saturday 11th ✒ a warm day. in the evening whee had a clever littel rain

1798 Sunday Augt 12th ✒ a fine day

Munday 13th ✒ a fine day. in the evening looked as if wee should have rain, its much wanted

Tuseday 14th ✒ a fine rain last night, & several showers in the day and a fine rain in the evening. I Planted out the plants that ware missing in the garding

Wednesday 15th ✒ Charles is taken unwell this morning with a Pukeing. his mother & Beckey is with him. betwen eleven & twelve oclock wee had a clever shower of rain. cleared away hott & looks gustey. whee have a fine rain this evening

Thursday 16th ✒ this morning I am 70 years of age. wee have had several showers of rain to day. this evening I planted the Peas I got from Mr. Hopkins the 3d time this year

1798 Fryday Augt 17th ✒ wee had a cleaver shower of rain to day

Saturday 18th ✒ last night about 10 oclock my daughter Abee, Mrs. Hamelton, Miss Byas[146] and a littel neagro Boy of Nancey pitts all came heare from Baltimore. I expect thay will be heare about a weak or 10 days — this has a very Hott day

Sunday 19th ✒ a fine day. in the after noon clouded up and look like for rain. Mrs. Hamelton dined at Mr. Stevens's and stays thar

Munday 20th ✒ a fine day

Tuseday 21th ✒ Silve has pulled up the simlin vines in the lot and dugg the ground readey for plants. a fine day. the peas I planted the 16th are cuming up

Wednesday 22th ✒ a fine day

146 Probably Mary Biays, daughter of Maj. Joseph Biays (see 20 June 1800), who would marry Dr. Joseph Allender (see 11 August 1799) in February 1800.

1798 Thursday Augt 23th ✒ a fine Pleasent day

Fryday 24th ✒ a fine day

Saturday 25th ✒ verey Hott & dry

Sunday 26th ✒ a very Hott day

Munday 27th ✒ a very Hott day. in the evening wee had a littel rain

Tuseday 28th ✒ a dull day

Wednesday 29th ✒ a clear cool morning and continued so all day out of the sun

Thursday 30th ✒ a fine day

Fryday 31th ✒ a fine day. in the evening cloudey

1798 Saturday Septr 1th ✒ a fine day

Sunday 2th ✒ a fine day

Munday 3th ✒ this morning, Mrs. Hamelton & Miss Byas went of for Baltimore. a coole, dull cloudey day

Tuseday 4th ✒ last night wee had a clever rain. this morning Sylve Planted the quarter in the lott the first 3 rows, of Brussel Sprout plants the seed from Mr. Steear, the next 2 rows, Brussel Sprout plants, the seed from Mr. Coats, the next 2 rows Brussel Cale plants. a fine day. in the evening it thunders & lightens, and looks as if wee should have rain before morning

Wednesday 5th ✒ wee had a fine rain Last night. a fine day

Thursday 6th ✒ a fine day

Fryday 7th ✒ Peter Jenings[147] was Hanged to day agreeable to his sentence. thare was a repreve sent but the express arrived too late — a fine day but very coole for the season

Saturday 8th ✒ a fine day

Sunday 9th ✒ a fine day

Munday 10th ✒ a fine day

Tuseday 11th ✒ betwen 8 & 9 oclock this morning Mr. Pitt, Mrs. pitt & child came up in thair Boat from Baltimore, all well & Harty. a fine day

Wednesday 12th ✒ a fine day. in the evening Mr. & Mrs. Pitt & girls went to the Play

[147] A mariner named Peter Jennings, who lived on Apple Alley in Fells Point in 1796, may have been this unlucky individual.

Thursday 13th ✏ after diner Mr. & Mrs. Pitt & child sett of in thare Boat home for Baltimore. a fine day

1798 Fryday Septr 14th ✏ a fine day. in the after noon sow'd Parrott tail Tulip seed in a Box in the garden

Saturday 15th ✏ a fine day

Sunday 16th ✏ a fine day

Munday 17th ✏ a fine day

Tuseday 18th ✏ a cloudey day & a littel rain at times through out the day. had draw'd home from Mr. Warfs 9 cart load of dung[148]

Wednesday 19th ✏ very Hott day

Thursday 20th ✏ a fine day

Fryday 21th ✏ a fine day but in the evening turned coole

Saturday 22th ✏ this fore noon Mrs. Faris let a window fall on her fingers & Brused them. a fine day

1798 Sunday Septr 23th ✏ a fine day

Munday 24th ✏ a fine day

Tuseday 25th ✏ a fine coole day

Wednesday 26th ✏ a fine day but cold — this evening Capt. Johns went to the Play with the girls

Thursday 27th ✏ a fine day. in the evening clouded up and looks like Bad weather cuming

Fryday 28th ✏ this morning Capt. Johns & Mr. Hughs sailed from hear for the West Indeas. a clear cold day

Saturday 29th ✏ a clear cold day. in the evening made a fire in the House

Sunday 30th ✏ a fine day

1798 Munday Octr 1th ✏ a fine day

Tuseday 2th ✏ a fine day

Wednesday 3th ✏ a fine day

Thursday 4th ✏ a fine day. this is the last night of the Players, preforming heare this season

Fryday 5th ✏ a fine day. several of the Players are gone & a good deal of thare sceanery

[148] Innkeepers, who provided stables for the horses of their clientele, were good sources of dung for gardeners like Faris.

Saturday 6th 🖙 the Montesuma, that was, Lays of heare on her way down the Bay. a fine day — in the after noon the ship went away down the Bay

Sunday 7th 🖙 a dull cloudey day

Munday 8th 🖙 a fine day

1798 Tuseday Octr 9th 🖙 finished cleaning the walks and scater'd dung over the saffron Plants that's just cuming up. a fine day. this evening Miss Henearetta Lloyd was married to Mr. Richard West[149]

Wednesday 10th 🖙 a fine day

Thursday 11th 🖙 a cloudey foggey morning. clear'd away a fine day

Fryday 12th 🖙 a dull cloudey day

Saturday 13th 🖙 a dull day like for rain

Sunday 14th 🖙 Betwen 7 & 8 oclock this morning Mr. Richard Wells[150] died, and betwen 8 & 9 oclock Miss Nancey Harwood, Abee, Rebacka & Messrs. Reason Rowles[151] & Charles Faris sett of in Smith's stage for the Head of Severon to William Woodward Junr's[152] and the chappel. in the evening betwen 6 & 7 oclock the girls return'd from Mr. Woodwards. a dull cloudey day

1798 Munday 15th 🖙 a cloudey dull day. in the evening Mr. Wells's corps was put in the ground

Tuseday 16th 🖙 a fine day

Wednesday 17th 🖙 a fine day. this morning Thomas Yates came hear from the Eastern Shore on his way to Baltimore

Thursday 18th 🖙 a fine day

Fryday 19th 🖙 a cloudey day. in the evening like for rain. this morning Thomas Yates sett of in the packett for Baltimore

Saturday 20th 🖙 a cloudey drisley day. Silve has been unwell & a Bed all day

Sunday 21th 🖙 Silve's much better this morning. she's up & about her Business. about diner time she was taken un well, eat no diner but went to Bed with a smart feveour on her. I called in Doctr Ghislin, he advised giveing her plenty of Herb tea — a fine day

[149] Richard William West was the son of Stephen West (1727–1790) and his wife Hannah Williams, of the "Woodyard" in Prince George's County. Richard was named after his grandfather, Capt. Richard Williams, a ship captain in the Guinea trade. His father, a highly successful merchant, was a partner in the firm West & Hobson, which operated 9 stores located on both shores of the bay. Henrietta Maria Lloyd (b.1782) was the daughter of Edward Lloyd IV (see 19 October 1792). § Faris collected £7.5.4 from West in June 1801 as administrator of Charles's estate.

[150] When Richard Wells died, he left an estate valued at only £55. Henry Johnson was the administrator and no kin signed the inventory. Wells was a butcher, however, from whom Faris bought a hog, weighing 110 pounds, in January 1795, so he may have been related to John Wells and the two Daniel Wells. § Faris bought a tureen for two shillings at the sale of his goods.

[151] Rezin Rowles married Sophia Myers, both of Baltimore, in June 1803 and married Catherine Wilson, the daughter of William Wilson, in October 1807. He witnessed the will of mariner John Gordon (see 26 January 1803) in November 1797 but was not in Annapolis when the will was proved in February 1803, so he may have moved to Baltimore by that time. He was probably the son of Rezin Rowles of Kent Island, Queen Anne's County, whose estate was sold by his administrator in October 1796.

[152] If Faris's reference is accurate, this should be the son of William and Jane Woodward (see 7 December 1792), who married Susanna Jacobs in November 1790 and eventually moved "west." Priscilla Woodward Faris was his father's aunt.

[153] Joshua Seaney, from Queen Anne's County, was the chief judge of the third district court, appointed in April 1792. Prior to that, he represented the Eastern Shore in Congress from 1789 to 1792. His widow was probably Fannie Nicholson, the daughter of James Nicholson, whom he married in New York in March 1790.

[154] Richard Hall Harwood (1771–1819) was the son of Col. Richard and Margaret Harwood (see 22 September 1801). Anne Catherine Green, named after her paternal grandmother, was the daughter of Frederick and Anne Green (see 10 March 1795). Harwood was a delegate from Anne Arundel to the General Assembly from 1798 to 1803, a member of the executive council in 1804, and a judge of the circuit court.

[155] Tayloe's horse Leviathan won the purse. His horse Florizel also won the sweepstakes.

[156] Ridgely's horse Gunpowder was the winner of the Colts' Purse.

127 ☛ Charles Carnan Ridgely (1760-1829)

Col. Ridgely's horses raced frequently in Annapolis.

1798 Munday Octr 22th ☛ a fine day. this evening its reported that Mr. Joshua Seaney[153] is ded

Tuseday 23th ☛ a fine day. in the evening Mr. Pitt came heare on his way to Baltimore. he left the Montezuma yesterday after noon out side the capes. this evening Miss Anne Green was married to Mr. Richard Harrwod, son of Coln. Harrwood[154]

Wednesday 24th ☛ Mr. pitt left us this morning after Brackfast for Baltimore. a fine day

Thursday 25th ☛ this fore noon littel Suck a fine littel neagro girl belonging to Mr. Quynn died. a fine day

Fryday 26th ☛ a fine day

Saturday 27th ☛ a dull cloudey day with small rain

1798 Sunday Octr 28th ☛ a fine morning but cold. in the afternoon clouded up & looks like Bad weather

Munday 29th ☛ a clear cold day

Tuseday 30th ☛ the Jockey Club purs was run for to day and won by Mr. Taylor's Horse.[155] only 2 Horses run. a clear cold day

Wednesday 31th ☛ the race was won to day by Mr. Ridgley's Horese.[156] a cold clear day

Thursday Novr 1th ☛ a snowey morning. in the after noon turned to rain and looks like a continuence of Bad weather

Fryday 2th ☛ a fine morning. Charles went of in the packett for Baltimore. in the afternoon clouded up & looks like for Bad weather

1798 Saturday Novr 3th ☛ a cloudey drisley day

Sunday 4th ☛ a clear cold day. in the evening Charles returnd from Baltimore. Nancey child was enockalaited last Wednesday. thar are all well

Munday 5th ☛ a fine clear day. planted 4 Fross Nercess's roots by the grape vines from Mr. H. J. Stier

Tuseday 6th ☛ a fine day

Wednesday 7th ☛ this morning at 9 oclock Mrs. went of in the Packett for Baltimore. a fine day but littel wind

William Faris

Thursday 8th ☞ a fine day. in the evening cloudey

Fryday 9th ☞ a fine day

Saturday 10th ☞ a fine day

1798 Sunday Novr 11th ☞ a fine day

Munday 12th ☞ a fine morning. marked the four
flower roots Hyram brought home on Sunday week
last with a stick mark'd 5 — in the evening covering the flower beds, with Leaves & a coat of
manure over that — a fine day

Tuseday 13th ☞ Sylve's finished covering the assparagrass Beds & is diging Parsneps. a fine day. in
the evening turned cloudey

Wednesday 14th ☞ a drisley morning. this fore
[noon] Benjamin Ogel Esqr[157] was ellected govenor
in the room of J. Henrey who resigned. a dull
cloudey day

Thursday 15th ☞ the stabel of Harwoods[158] was by
some acciden on Fire. it was Interly Burnt down &
a Horse burnt to death and another much Burnt. a
cloudey day

1798 Fryday Novr 16th ☞ a fine day, I stoped
up the Bees this evening

Saturday 17th ☞ a fine day

Sunday 18th ☞ a fine day

---

[157] Benjamin Ogle was the son of Samuel Ogle (c.1694–1752) and
his wife Anne Tasker (1723–1817). When Ogle visited the Bladens
in England in 1769, Barbara Bladen (whose husband Thomas had
been governor of Maryland in the 1740s) wrote to his mother that
"he was very well & is really grown & handsome. I believe he will
make sad destruction among the Belles at Annapolis." Ogle married
Henrietta Margaret Hill (1751–1815) on 13 September 1770. His
sister Mary was the wife of John Ridout (see 6 October 1797). Ogle
was elected to three terms as governor from 1798 to 1801. Faris has
already noted the marriage of his son Benjamin in February 1796
and will record the marriage of his daughter Mary in July 1804. In
1792, his daughter Ann married John Tayloe (see 4 November
1794), who regularly visited Annapolis for the fall races. Ogle, a
member of the Jockey Club, also owned a racing stable, as well as a
two-story brick dwelling at the corner of Northeast and King
George Streets in Annapolis and Bel Air plantation in Prince
George's County. § Faris added a silver spout to a china teapot for
Ogle in March 1776 at a charge of £1.7.6. Faris collected £6.17.0
from Ogle in September 1801 as administrator of Charles's estate.
Ogle owed Faris's estate £1.1.6.

128 ☞ Benjamin Ogle (1749–1809)
*Faris records in his diary Ogle's election
as governor in November 1798.*

[158] This may have been Thomas Harwood
(1777–1826) who was the son of Col. Richard
and Margaret Hall Harwood (see 22
September 1801). He replaced Archibald
Golder as clerk of the corporation in July
1801 and remained clerk until September
1806. He may also be the Thomas Harwood
who in 1802 purchased the house on Hanover
Street, lately occupied by John H. Stone (see
29 September 1794), known today as the
Peggy Stewart House.

Oct. / Nov., 1798

299

159 Charles Steuart (d.1799) was the son of Dr. George Hume Steuart (1700–c.1784) and his wife Ann Digges (1718–1814), and the brother of Dr. James Steuart (see 19 May 1792). In 1780, Steuart married Elizabeth Calvert, daughter of Benedict Calvert (c.1724–1788)—the illegitimate son of the 5th Lord Baltimore—and his wife Elizabeth, daughter of Charles Calvert (d.1734); in 1784 he married Mary Waters. His brother-in-law, George Calvert, married Rosalie Stier, daughter of Henri Stier (see 27 April 1797). The owner of a plantation on the South River as well as property in Annapolis, Steuart was a merchant in partnership with his brother William in the 1780s.

160 Richard Ridgely married Elizabeth Dorsey in October 1778. Two of his sons, Richard and Daniel, attended the St. John's grammar school in the 1790s. Ridgely was secretary of the senate in 1777, served as a councilman from 1796 until he resigned in March 1802, and was an Annapolis delegate to the General Assembly in 1801 and 1802. § Ridgely supplied dung for Faris's garden in May 1801, and Faris received cash payments from Ridgely in 1799 (about £40), 1800, and 1801, without specifying the reason for the payments.

Munday 19th ✒ Mrs. Faris came home this morning before I was up, the Boat arrived about 12 oclock last night from Baltimore, last night Mr. John Bullin & Mr. Charles Stewart159 both died. a foggey drisseley morning, continued raining cloudey & foggey all day

Tuseday 20th ✒ a cold, snoweny, windey day. Isesickels, 6 or 7 Inchs Long, in the evening ye sun sett clear, Mr. Stewarts corps was carried out of Town to day

Wednesday 21th ✒ at noon Mr. Bullin was Buried. a clear cold day

1798 Thursday Novr 22th ✒ a fine clear day

Fryday 23th ✒ a fine day

Saturday 24th ✒ a fine day

Sunday 25th ✒ a fine day

Munday 26th ✒ a fine day

Tuseday 27th ✒ a fine day

Wednesday 28th ✒ a fine day

Thursday 29th ✒ Mr. John Steel dined & spent the evening with us. a foggey cloudey day

Fryday 30th ✒ a fine warm foggey day

1798 Saturday Desr 1th ✒ a fogey dull day. in the evening it rained a littel & looks as if wee should have a setteled rain, Charles's gone to Prince Georges to Mr. Thomas Woodwards

Sunday 2th ✒ a rainey drisley day

Munday 3th ✒ this fore noon Charles returned from Prince Georges. a fine day

Tuseday 4th ✒ a clear cold windey day

Wednesday 5th ✒ a clear cold day. Mrs. Richard Ridgley160 was Brought to bed of a son this morning

Thursday 6th ✒ a cold snowey day

1798 Fryday Desr 7th ✒ a fine clear cold day

Saturday 8th ✒ a dull cloudey day

Sunday 9th ✒ rained most of last night & this morning turned to hail & snow till about a 11 or 12 oclock and then turned to rain and rained the rest of the day and looks like a continuance of it

Munday 10th ↜ a clear cold day

Tuseday 11th ↜ this morning a littel snow and
Hail, a clear cold after noon. slipperey bad walking

Wednesday 12th ↜ a clear cold day

1798 Thursday Desr 13th ↜ a dull cloudey
morning. in the fore noon began to rain and rained
all the afternoon & evening

Fryday 14th ↜ a fine day

Saturday 15th ↜ a clear & very cold day. about a
11 oclock this fore noon Mr. Robert Johnson died

Sunday 16th ↜ a clear cold day

Munday 17th ↜ a clear cold day. betwen 12 & 1
oclock Mr. R. Johnson was Buried

1798 Tuseday Desr 18th ↜ a fine day

Wednesday 19th ↜ snow'd last night & this
morning a littel. the ground is cover'd with snow a
cloudey day

Thursday 20th ↜ a clear cold day. the streets are
covered with Ise and snow

Fryday 21th ↜ a fine day. Mr. Weems sent me a
gallon of Peach Brandy, a round of Beef cured in the
New England way, a qr of shote[161] a pott of Butter
and some Buck weeat meal

Saturday 22th ↜ snowing very hard this morning
and continued so all day, now evening its snowing
as fast as ever & look as if it would continue snowing

1798 Sunday Desr 23th ↜ clear & cold

Munday 24th ↜ betwen 11 & 12 oclock Mr. Pitt
came heare from Baltimore. a clear cold day. I this
day lent my littel Pockett stillyards to Mr. William
Witcroft Senr for a month or 6 weaks {noted in a
different pen:} thay are returned

Tuseday 25th ↜ Mr. Pitt dined with us this day. a
fine day

Wednesday 26th ↜ a fine morning, Mr. Pitt &
Abee sett of about 10 oclock in a stage for
Baltimore, in the after noon clouded up & came on
to Hail

[161] A quarter of a shoat,
or young weaned pig.

162 Robert Oliver (1757–1834) was a prominent Baltimore financier who incurred the enmity of the younger Robert Smith (an attorney) when in early December he blackballed Smith for membership in the Baltimore dancing assembly room. In retaliation Smith spread rumors accusing Oliver of forgery in cashing a bank draft, an attack on Oliver's credit and livelihood. Oliver responded by naming his seconds and challenging Smith to a duel. Attempts to resolve the dispute peacefully only resulted in enlarging it, in the process involving Oliver's business partner, Hugh Thompson (see 19 January 1794) and his associate Jeremiah Yellott (see 16 August 1792). By the evening of 26 December, when the duel was to take place, four men had challenged Smith. The city's magistrates intervened at this point, insisting on an exchange of grudging public apologies. No one was killed, but news of the affair had obviously reached Annapolis within twenty-four hours, illustrating the remarkable speed, but not necessarily accuracy, with which news traveled considerable distances at a time when no telegraph, telephone, radio, television, or e-mail existed to aid in its transmission. It is worth noting that Faris had some acquaintance with at least two of the participants.

163 Henry Henley Chapman (d. 1821), speaker of the house in the 1798 and 1799 sessions, was a delegate from Charles County. His first wife, Eleanor, had died in the summer of 1796. Chapman was speaker again in 1814 and 1815 and served on the executive council in 1816 and 1818. Mary Davidson was the daughter of Faris's neighbor Eleanor Davidson (see 1 January 1792). § Faris collected £2.15.7 from Chapman as administrator of Charles's estate in December 1800.

164 William Perry, Esq. (1746–1799), died Thursday last in Annapolis, in attendance on his legislative duties, according to the 17 January *Gazette*. Perry was a senator from Talbot County beginning in 1783 and served as president of the senate from 1792 until his death.

1798 Thursday Desr 27th ✐ a fine morning. about a 11 oclock Mrs. Elizabeth Gassaway died, in her 40th year — its reported that Mr. Oliver has killed Mr. Robert Smith[162] — Both of Baltimore Town. a fine day

Fryday 28th ✐ a fine day

Saturday 29th ✐ Raind hard last night, Mrs. Gassaway was Buried this afternoon, a cloudey day and very sloppey bad walking

Sunday 30th ✐ Blow'd very hard last night — a clear cold windey day

Munday 31th ✐ a fine day

1799 Tuseday January 1th ✐ a cloudey drisley morning and turned to a smart rain. in the afternoon clear'd away, in the evening Miss Polley Davidson was married to Mr. Chapman Speaker of the House of Assembley[163]

Wednesday 2th ✐ a fine day. Hyram has planted the rest of his anemonies in a Bed at the end of the new stabel, a fine day

Thursday 3th ✐ a snowey day

Fryday 4th ✐ a cloudey cold day. looks like for more snow

Saturday 5th ✐ a very cold, cloudey day. in the evening came on to snow

1799 Sunday Janry 6th ✐ last night and to day has been the coldest wee have had this winter. a clear cold day

Munday 7th ✐ a cold day

Tuseday 8th ✐ a cold dull day

Wednesday 9th ✐ snow'd a littel last night a cloudey dull morning. about noon clared away. the sun came out fine & the snow melts away — a fine after noon

Thursday 10th ✐ a fine day

Fryday 11th ✐ died last night or this morning Mr. William Perrey, Speaker of the Senett.[164] a fine day

1799 Saturday 12th ✐ a fine day. this evening Mr. William Perrey was Buried

Sunday 13th ✍ a dull cloudey drisley day

Munday 14th ✍ a foggey dull day

Tuseday 15th ✍ a fine day

Wednesday 16th ✍ Trimed the currend Bushes on the big bed next the new stabel. a fine day

Thursday 17th ✍ a fine day

Fryday 18th ✍ a dull cloudey day. I trimed the goosberey Bushes on the right hand side of the Bigg Bed

1799 Saturday Janry 19th ✍ Mr. Wilmore[165] took the littel room chimney down. a dull cloudey day. Hyram's gone a squrrel hunting

Sunday 20th ✍ a cloudey morning, about noon cleard away a fine afternoon

Munday 21th ✍ last night betwen 10 & 11 oclock the Govenor finished seealing & signing the Laws, and the Assembley Brok up. a clear cold windey day

Tuseday 22th ✍ Sylve's digging up the Border next to Iiams's[166] & I planted 3 potts with the following flower seeds Femal Balsoms, asters or Qeen Margeretts, and Trycolo. a fine day

Wednesday 23th ✍ a fine morning. I have sow'd 17 rows of peas on the Border & betwen the rows I have sow'd orris seed, & I have sow'd a littel earley York seed, and planted out the roshembole onions that bares the increse on the top

1799 Thursday Janry 24th ✍ it snow'd in the night. the ground was white this morning. it continued snowing and at times Hail with it till about noon and then turned a fine Hail the rest of the day and evening

Fryday 25th ✍ Hailed & rained in the night. very bad walking. the streets are all Ice, a dull cloudey cold day

Saturday 26th ✍ a close cloudey foggey morning. continued a rainey drssiley day

Sunday 27th ✍ a drisley, rainey dull morning and continued a dull cloudey day

Munday 28th ✍ a cold raw dissagreeable day

Tuseday 29th ✍ a clear cold day

Wednesday 30th ✍ a fine day, took the roof of the littel room & Hung up the Hogg meat

[165] Probably Thomas Wilmer (c.1744–1812), a bricklayer who lived not far from Faris on West Street as a tenant of Allen Quynn (see 9 September 1792) in a one-story frame house. He bought the house and lot in 1809 and still occupied it in 1812. § Faris made one payment each year, from 1800 to 1802, to Mrs. Wilmer for bread, candles, and butter. On 29 July 1802, Faris recorded that Wilmer whitewashed the big room. Wilmer bought 10 files at the sale of Faris's estate.

[166] Samuel Ijams was a neighbor of Faris, and a tenant of Allen Quynn (see 9 September 1792), living next door in a one-story frame dwelling.

Thursday 31th ✒ a fine day

1799 Fryday Febuary 1th ✒ a fine day

Saturday 2th ✒ a drisley cloudey morning in the afternoon William a Black man brought me a Holley tree & I planted it by the littel House in the garden.[167] a rainey afternoon and evening

Sunday 3th ✒ snow'd in the night. a clear cold day. in the evening Mr. John Wells's daughter was married to Mr. Sherred[168] — who lives on the Eastern Shore

Munday 4th ✒ a fine day

Tuseday 5th ✒ a dissagreeable snowe morning. a clear cold after noon

Wednesday 6th ✒ this fore noon Charles sett of on Horse Back for Baltimore. a fine day

1799 Thursday Febry 7th ✒ a fine day

Fryday 8th ✒ a dull cloudey day looks like for rain. Mr. Pitt called heare this evening on his way down the Bay. staid about an Houre and went on board

Saturday 9th ✒ it rained & Blowed very Hard all last night. a rainey morning. about noon cleared away a fine after noon

Sunday 10th ✒ a clear cold day. in the evening Charles returned from Baltimore

Munday 11th ✒ a clear fine day

Tuseday 12th ✒ a fine day

Wednesday 13th ✒ a fine day

Thursday 14th ✒ a fine day

1799 Fryday Febry 15th ✒ a clear cold day

Saturday 16th ✒ clear & cold day

Sunday 17th ✒ snow'd hard last night & this morning to about 12 oclock, then stoped snowing but continued cloudey till about 3 oclock then cleared away a fine afternoon

Munday 18th ✒ a fine day

Tuseday 19th ✒ a dissagreeable snowey day

Wednesday 20th ✒ a cloudey raney day

Thursday 21th ✒ a cloudey drisley day

[167] According to local lore, the last surviving holly planted by William Faris was taken down c. 1985.

[168] Philemon Sherwood was a member of a well-established Talbot County family. He represented the county in the house of delegates from 1795 to 1798. Sarah Wells was the daughter of butcher John Wells (see 25 September 1797).

Fryday 22th ✒ a cold, snow Hail, rain & drisley all the fore part of the day. in the afternoon clear but very cold, cleaned out the Bee Hives to day

1799 Saturday Febry 23th ✒ last night & to day has been as cold as aney wee have had this winter. this after noon my son Charles, & James Warf ware ellected common counsel men. Samuel Ridout and [blank] Clements[169] stood like wise. Rideout had 7 or 8 & Clements had about 20 votes

Sunday 24th ✒ a clear cold day. the wind Blow'd very hard

Munday 25th ✒ a clear & cold [day]. in the afternoon clouded up & looks like for snow

Tuseday 26th ✒ a dull cloudey cold morning. about noon it began to snow & snow'd hard all the afternoon and looks likely to continue

1799 Wednesday 27th ✒ a seveer night. snow'd and Blowed hard & cold, a cloudey dull morning but nothing falls, a cloudey dull day but not so cold as it has been

Thursday 28th ✒ a dull cloudey day but has thaugh'd a good deal

Fryday March 1th ✒ a snowey morning, and Beckey's complaining of being unwell, continued snowing hard till about noon, then turned to a misselen fine snow. in the evening it appear'd as if it would turn to a rain, this after noon Mr. William Pitt called heare on his way down the Bay

Saturday 2th ✒ a cloudey snowey day

Sunday 3th ✒ the sun came out finely this morning as if wee should have a fine day, about 10 oclock it clouded up and snow'd at different times the whole day

1799 Munday March 4th ✒ a windey cold day

Tuseday 5th ✒ the Baltimore stage did not come in Last night. I don't know the reason rightley. last night was very cold, and a very cold morning and day but clear in the afternoon. I filled a Box with earth and sow'd earley York cabbage seed in it

Wednesday 6th ✒ a clear cold day. about 11 oclock I sett of in the stage for Baltimore and got to Mr. pitts betwen 8 & 9 oclock in the evening

[gap in diary]

169 Francis T. Clements (see 1 March 1795).

Sunday 17th ↜ left the point on Bord the packett betwen 8 & 9 oclock and arrived at Annapolis about 3 oclock. wee had a fine passage. I brought my daughter Abee home with me. a fine day

Munday 18th ↜ a fine clear morning but cold & windey. a clear, cold, windey day

1799 Tuseday March 19th ↜ a clear cold day

Wednesday 20th ↜ Blow'd very hard in the night & snow'd a littel and rained very hard, a drisley morning, after Brackfast Hyram went down to Charles's shop, a dull cloudey drissley day

Thursday 21th ↜ in the night it rained very hard & Blow'd a near Harrican, a cloudey windey morning, continued a dull cloudey day

Fryday 22th ↜ a fine day

Saturday 23th ↜ the peas I sow'd the 23th of January are just makeing thare appearance, I have taken of the dunge covering that was on the Flower beds all winter, a fine day. the cabbage seed that was sown the 22th of January are come up

Sunday 24th ↜ water'd the Box with earley York cabbage seed sown in it. a fine morning, a fine day

Munday 25th ↜ Sylve's digging the big bed & I have been trowelling the flower beds. a fine day

1799 Tuseday March 26th ↜ a fine morning. Sylve's finished digging ye Big [bed] & I have sow'd with 7 rows of Peas, 6 rows the peas ware soaked the other row raw peas, I planted 79 yung rosehemboles on the Border next to Iiams's & I have been digging the flower beds, Charles came & helped me to day, wee have finished diging the flower beds at the circil, it has clouded up this after noon & looks like rain

Wednesday 27th ↜ rained & the winde Bolwed very hard last night & this morning. it Blowd the tin Funnel of the chimney. about noon it clear'd up, Silve & I went in the garden. I trowel'd one of the Beds by the littel house & she made abegining to open the assparagrass beds, but it came on to rain again, wee quitt and came in the House

Thursday 28th ↜ a cold, windey Blustering night, a clear cold windey morning about 10 oclock this fore noon it snow'd a littel. continued a cold windey day. did nothing in the garden. in the evening Mr.

S. Howard's daughter Susan was married to Mr. John Edmonson of the Eastern Shore[170]

1799 Fryday March 29th ↜ a fine morning. Mr. pitt came heare with Mr. Petter Gold[171] to Brackfast. thay are on thare way to Virginia, Sylve's finished doing up the assparagrass beds and I have sow'n on the near bed

Large Dutch Cabbage &

Large Imperial head Lettise

 & on the further bed

Earley York Cabbage &

Large Yellow Hollond Loaf Lettis from Mr. Hesler

and betwen the beds spinige

and Rebaca planted radishes on the border

and 4 roott of Jacobin Lilley from Mr. Hesler No. 15

a fine day

Saturday 30th ↜ a dull cloudey morning. after Brackfast, Charles came and helped me to trowel the flower beds. wee finished troweling of them betwen 10 & 11 oclock, sow'd Ice plant seed on the Barrel. a fine day

Sunday 31th ↜ a fine warm day

1799 Munday April 1th ↜ I have a neagro man Tom a cuting Box. Sylve's dug the littel bed at the end of the new stabel & I planted it with Bunch Beans & betwen radishes & I have been planting Box cutings. Sylve's cleaning the beds of the cutings. a fine day

Tuseday 2th ↜ a cloudey morning. Tom came & cut till Brackfast time. it came on to rain, in the after noon cleared away and Tom came to work, this after noon Hyram's mooved his chest away from my House to whare I dont know, in the evening it turned much colder then it was. I cover'd the peas

Wednesday 3th ↜ frose very hard last night and the wind Blow'd very hard. a clear cold windey morning. thare was Ice in the tub in the garden near 3/4 of an Inch thick. Tom has been cuting Box to day. a very cold windey day

1799 Thursday April 4th ↜ this morning Hyram came heare to bid the famely fare well. he's going to Baltimore. he bid his mother & sisters farewell, he came to me. I asked him if he was a going to leave me. he answer'd yes. I then till him

[170] Susannah Howard, daughter of Samuel Harvey Howard (see 31 October 1794), married John E. Edmondson of an old Talbot County family.

[171] Capt. Peter Gold lived at 44 Charles Street in Baltimore.

that he might go whare he pleased I had nothing to say to him, he went off — a cold windey day. Tom has finished cuting the Box. I finished planting a nursserey of Box by the Snow Ball Tree, Hyram did not go of to day. I suppose the wind Blow'd too hard

Fryday 5th ✐ a clear modarat day. I am informed that Hyram went off for Baltimore in som Boat to day.[172] he has not been near hear since yesterday morning

Saturday 6th ✐ a fine day. tom has finished the tabels round the grass walk. in the evening clouded up & looks like rain

Sunday 7th ✐ the peas that was sown the 26th of March in the Big Bed are just acuming up. a fine day

Munday 8th ✐ sow'd 36 drills of Parseley seed on the Border by the Bee house & I planted 200 roshemboles or Onions of Eagipt, Silve's putting dung on the bed for Parsneps. a very fine day. in the after noon, seems to cloud up & looks as if wee should have som rain. it is much wanted. Capt. Johns called hear this evening Bound out

1799 Tuseday April 9th ✐ a cold windey day Sylve's geting dung on the Bed for the Parsneps. I cover'd the peas on the Border for fear of a frost

Wednesday 10th ✐ Sylve's finished diging ye ground for the Parsneps. a windey cold day

Thursday 11th ✐ a fine modarate day to what wee have had, but still cold & windey

Fryday 12th ✐ a fine day. in the evening turned cloudey and looks like for rain

Saturday 13th ✐ a fine day

Sunday 14th ✐ a fine day

Munday 15th ✐ Abee[173] & Rebaca sow'd the parsnep & carrot seed, and Sylve's digging the other side of the lott for simlins & vines, I sow'd som Balsoms and aster seeds in a small bed in the yard. a fine day. I sow'd on the Border next to ye young onions of Eagypt 70 drills of spinige

1799 Tuseday April 16th ✐ Silve's finish'd digging the ground for the vines. I have planted 13 hills of simlins, 7 hills of cantilopes & 6 Hills of cucumbers. a fine day

172 Hyram's residence in Baltimore is not known. It is possible that he lived with his sister and brother-in-law, although there is no mention of him by his father in connection with the Pitts. The 1800 census listed thirteen people in William Pitt's household. In addition to family members, there were four slaves and five boys or young men, as well as one adult male between the ages of twenty-six and forty-five—this last individual might have been Hyram.

173 This is the first time that Abigail worked in the garden.

Wednesday 17th ✒ a fine day. in the evening clouded up & looks like for rain, its much wanted

Thursday 18th ✒ wee had a littel rain Last night. a fine day. cut assparagass for the first time this spring

Fryday 19th ✒ a coole windey day. I planted 5 Beens on the Border next the Lot, I got them from Sewell the painter[174]

Saturday 20th ✒ Last night was very cold & windey, a cold windey morning, I have planted the peas I got from Mr. Hopkins on the Border by the Bee house & I have taken up the Hedge of Time & replanted it and Silve's how'd the peas in the Big Bed — I planted sencitive plant seed in a pott, a fine evening but rather coole

Sunday 21th ✒ a fine day but too coole for the season. this evening Mr. Luke Barber was married to Miss Susana Rowles.[175] Mr. Hanson sent me a peace of the Chrysanthemum Indicum & I planted it in a pott

1799 Munday April 22th ✒ a cloudey morning. Silve's stiking the peas in the Big Bed, she has dug a littel peace of the end of the walnut tree Bed to plant the Tossminano corn sent me by Mr. Roger Lelson[176] and I sow'd the Large Imperial Hard Lettice No.1 & the large Yellow Holland loaf Lettice No. 2 betwen the goosberrey Bushes on the Big Bed, sow'd on the flower Beds by the grass walk No. 1 Red globe No.2 White globe seed and Silve's cleaning the walks. too cool a day for the season

Tuseday 23th ✒ a fine morning. sow'd some tricola seed. in the after noon clouded up & looks like for rain. wee had a clever littel rain this evening & looks like for more

Wednesday 24th ✒ wee had a fine rain last night, a dull coole windey day

Thursday 25th ✒ a fine day

Fryday 26th ✒ a fine day

1799 Saturday April 27th ✒ a rainey morning, left of raining about noon but continued cloudey and windey. I planted out about 40 plants & dugg up the rest & sow'd in the Box earley York, and cabage see[d] from W. Woodwards on the Border. in the evening rained very hard and thunder'd and Lightened a grate deel

[174] This could be John Sewell (b.1726), who is listed on the 1790 census, and who may have been, with his wife Martha, employed as St. Anne's sextons from 1769 to 1777. § Faris bought two lbs. of white lead from Sewell on 2 May of this year.

[175] Luke White Barber represented St. Mary's County in the General Assembly from 1798 to 1804 and again from 1810 to 1812. Susanna may have been related to Rezin Rowles, mentioned in the diary on 14 October 1798. It seems less likely that she would be the Susannah, daughter of Thomas and Sarah Rowles, who was born in October 1740.

[176] Roger Nelson (1759–1815) was a delegate from Frederick County in 1792 and 1793 and again from 1800 to 1802. He also served on the executive council, sat in the senate, and held a seat in Congress from 1804 to 1810. In 1788, he married Mary Brooke Sim (?–c.1794), the daughter of Maj. Joseph Sim (see 18 October 1793).

Sunday 28th ← a fine morning. Doctr Ghislin, wife & Famely all went of in Smith's stage for Baltimore and about 11 oclock Abee came home from Mr. William Whitcroft's Junr. its been a fine day, but in the evening clouded up and looks like for more rain

Munday 29th ← a fine day

Tuseday 30th ← a fine morning but a rainey after noon

Wednesday May 1th ← a coole raw dull cloudey day like for rain

Thursday 2th ← a clear cool day. so cold that wee had a Fire in the House

Fryday 3th ← a rainey morning. in the after noon clear & cool, the Chanceler & Mr. Stevens was heare this afternoon. Mr. Stevens asserted that it snow'd this fore noon. still a fire in the House

1799 Saturday May 4th ← a clear cold morning, thare was Ice in places. Jack Weelers[177] beens he tells me are Killed. I dont see that aney thing in my garden is hurt. I have planted 6 rows of the cherrey pepper on the Border joyning the parceley by the Bee house. a cold day — still a fire in the House

Sunday 5th ← a clear coole day, a fire in the House

Munday 6th ← a clear coole morning. Charles went of in the Packett at 9 oclock for Baltimore. in the evening it turned cloudey and looks like for rain

Tuseday 7th ← a fine clear day but too coole for the season

Wednesday 8th ← a clear cold morning and continued cold all the fore part of the day. Mr. Elijah Hopkins sent me 12 peas. I planted them on the Border by the Bee house. about 1 oclock, Charles & his sister Anne pitt and littel Marriah[178] came from Baltimore, Nancey brought me some rosemary from Mr. Hesler. I planted it by the grape vines

Thursday 9th ← a clear coole day

1799 Fryday May 10th ← a fine day

Saturday 11th ← a clear cool day

Sunday 12th ← a fine day but coole. Mr. Pitt has sent a Pilot Boat for Nancey, the peas in the Big Bed are in Blossom

[177] John Wheeler (d. 1804), a free black man, in 1798 rented a small frame house on a quarter-acre lot on Church Street from Ann Gaither (see 31 August 1793). In 1803 William Glover sold Wheeler part of the house formerly occupied by tavernkeeper James West (see 18 June 1792) for $1,100. Wheeler apparently continued to keep a tavern, for his estate—which totaled $1,314—included substantial amounts of rum, whiskey, and brandy. Wheeler left the property acquired from Glover to his widow, Sarah Cornish Wheeler, with the stipulation that his mother, Peggy Wheeler, continue to live there. His lot on the outskirts of town he ordered sold and the money used to free his sisters Sophia and Rachel, who were the slaves of Frederick Skinner in Calvert County. Wheeler also left forty dollars for the use of the African Church. In 1799, Wheeler, Smith Price (see 7 July 1802), and Thomas Folks had purchased a quarter-acre lot just outside the town gate on the northeast side of West Street; four months later they conveyed it to a small group of men, several of whom became the trustees in 1803 of the First African Methodist Episcopal Church of Annapolis.

[178] Although in his earliest references Faris called the child Rebecca, after this he always refers to Rebecca Maria as Marriah.

William Faris

Munday 13th 🙟 a fine morning. at 20 minits after 10 oclock the Boat turned of from the warf with Nancey & littel Marriah & her maid for Baltimore. in the after noon sow'd Brussel Cole seed on the Border nex the Bee House. a fine warm day

marked the Following flowers viz.

No. 1	Best	0	White Hyacinths	29 sticks
2	Dwarf tulips	11	Red	226
3	Red d^o	12	Blew	134
4	White	13	Winged	40
5	Black	14	Red Crown Imperial	6
6	Yallow	15	Yallow	9
7	Parrot tails	16	John Quills	
8	Doubel	17	White Narcess	
9	Red & white	18	Yallow	
10		19	Fross Nercess	
			from Mr. H. J. Stear	

sticks with a Hole in are not to be planted again

The Following Flowers whare named by Alexander C. Hanson Esqr 1798[179]

No.		No.	
1	Genl Washington	16	La Fayette
2	Lady Washington	17	Madame La Fayette
3	Genl Montgomery	18	Adams
4	d^o Warren	19	Jefferson
5	d^o Mercer	20	Hamilton
6	d^o Green	21	Madison
7	d^o Williams	22	Gallitin
8	d^o Wayne	23	Dr. Franklin
9	d^o Smallwood	24	Columbus
10	d^o Putnam	25	Harrison
11	d^o Harrey Lee	26	Merabeau
12	d^o Morgan	27	Rittenhouse
13	d^o Gates	28	Count Dillin
14	Colo. Howard	29	McPherson
15	Buonaparte	30	Trumbull

[179] Secondary sources credit Faris with naming these flowers, but the diary entry clearly indicates that they were named by Alexander Contee Hanson (see 17 July 1793).

No.		No.	
31	Hannebal	51	King Pryam
32	Aristides	52	Dr. Johnson
33	Fabius	53	Buffon
34	Scipeo	54	Goldsmith[180]
35	Pompey the Grate	55	Swift
36	Sir Isaac Newton	56	Pope
37	the Spectator	57	Chatham
38	Common Sense	58	Charles Fox
39	Junius	59	Butter Fly
40	The Farmer	60	the Brunette
41	Rights of Man	61	United States
42	Archimedes	62	The Aid du Camp
43	Indian Queen	63	Jack Custis
44	Indian King	64	Cincinnatus
45	America	65	the American Fair
46	the Grayhound	66	the President
47	Cato		1800 May 8th
48	Cicero	67	Genl Massena
49	Domostines	68	Doctr Priestly
50	Achillis	69	Hammelton Rowan

[180] Among the 135 volumes of books that Faris owned, he had seven volumes of *The Spectator* (#37), Cato's letters (#47), and the works of Goldsmith (#54). Unfortunately the inventory did not itemize his books; these few titles are known only from the list of sales, so that Faris likely owned works by other authors memorialized by Hanson's names.

1799 Tuseday May 14th ☞ Silve's dug the littel quarter by the old stabel & I sow'd it with algereen peas & she's diging the Border betwen the stabel & littel house. a Fine day

Wednesday 15th ☞ a fine morning. sow the nutmeg plant seed in drills on the Border betwen the stabel and littel house. this has been the finest & warmest day this spring. in the evening looks like rain

Thursday 16th ☞ a fine warm day. wee had 2 or 3 littel showers of rain in the course of the day. in the evening I planted out a few Balsoms that Mr. Hanson brought me. in the evening wee had a littel shower

Fryday 17th ☞ a fine day

Saturday 18th ☞ a fine rain last night & this morning. after Brackfast I Planted Plants betwen the peas. a fine day

Sunday 19th ☞ a fine day

1799 Munday May 20th ✍ a fine day but too coole for ye season

Tuseday 21th ✍ a fine day but very cold

Wednesday 22th ✍ a fine day, cut part of the sage, in the evening looks like for rain

Thursday 23th ✍ a fine warm day

Fryday 24th ✍ a fine day & in the evening wee had a fine rain. I broke of a good maney of the tops of the tulips

Saturday 25th ✍ a fine day. in the evening a fine shower

Sunday 26th ✍ a fine day. gatherard peas for the first time this spring

Munday 27th ✍ a fine day. finished brakeing off the tops of the tulips

Tuseday 28th ✍ a fine day

1799 Wednesday 29th ✍ plante[d] corn that Hiram got. thay on the Eastern Shore make use of the Husks to dye with. a fine day

Thursday 30th ✍ a fine day. in the evening wee had a fine rain

Fryday 31th ✍ a fine day

Saturday June 1th ✍ a fine day but in the after noon turn'd cold. this evening Charles had 2 piggs brought home & put in the pen

Sunday 2th ✍ a dull cold day

Munday 3th ✍ this after noon Sylve's weeding the pasnep bed, thare is so few of them that she is diging up the Bed & I intend to trans plant them

Tuseday 4th ✍ Silvee's digging the Bed in the lot. a fine day

Wednesday 5th ✍ a fine day. to day my son Charles left Boarding at Capt. Thomas's & came to live with me at home[181]

1799 Thursday June 6th ✍ a dull day. in the evening looks like for rain

Fryday 7th ✍ a dull cloudey coole day

Saturday 8th ✍ a dull drisley morning. planted out in the lott the Large Duch cabbage plants the seed from Mr. Hesler 3 rows & left room for Brussel

[181] Perhaps living at home held more appeal for Charles after Hyram's departure for Baltimore.

Cole betwen & the rest of the Bed with cabbace plants the seed from William Woodward & betwen brussel cole. about 10 oclock came on to rain, in the afternoon left of raining but continued cloudey. I filled up the betwens with Brussel Cole

Sunday 9th 🖝 this morning Abee & Mr. Rowles rode out to Mr. Whitcrofts and returned in the evening a fine day

Munday 10th 🖝 a fine warm day

Tuseday 11th 🖝 a fine day. Syras has finished the porch excepting the steps. I have no stuff for it at present.[182] I have sent to Baltimore for it

1799 Wednesday June 12th 🖝 gatherd Beens for the frist time this year. dug the Border ware the peas grew and planted Bunch Beans, a very Hot day to what wee have had

Thursday 13th 🖝 the Bees swarmed this morning and I hived. thay stay'd about 2 Hours and went off & I haved them again & thay stay'd about 2 or 3 Hours & went off. I hived them the third time in Jack Wheelers garden, & Brought them Home in the evening. a fine large swarm. a fine warm day. last night Mr. [blank] Welsh on the north side of Severon, had his House Burnt and Lost every thing he had but 2 beds, and two young men about 18 years of age whare Burnt in the House

Fryday 14th 🖝 a warm windey day

Saturday 15th 🖝 a fine day. in the evening put a Hive under the old Hive of Bees

Sunday 16th 🖝 a Hott day

1799 Munday June 17th 🖝 a very warm day

Tuseday 18th 🖝 verey warm day

Wednesday 19th 🖝 very Hott & dry

Thursday 20th 🖝 a fine day in the evening I made abegining to take up the flower roots

Fryday 21th 🖝 I finished takeing up the roots in the Bed next to ye grass on the right hand side. a very warm day. last night Mr. Charles Maccubin died, he was struck with the Palsey on Sunday evening last

Saturday 22th 🖝 Mr. Charles Maccubin was carried out of Town this fore noon to be Buried at Squerrel Neck.[183] I have finished another Bed to day. a very warm day

---

[182] Faris entered three payments in his account book to Syras for building the porch and steps, totaling £2.5.0, as well as paying "the carpenters" 5/7 on the 17th for "puting up a new post & makeing a new gate." A second payment to Syras in December covered "making the gate to the garden and fixing" it (i.e., installing the gate). Syras also covered the well in August 1800. As "Syras" is probably a given name, and Faris never indicates a surname, it is possible that Syras was a free black man, or at least a slave able to hire his own time.

[183] Maccubbin's plantation, which took its name from a 50-acre tract on the north side of Muddy Creek (at the head of the Rhode River in southern Anne Arundel County) patented in 1765 by Nicholas Maccubbin.

Sunday 23th ☞ a very Hott day

Munday 24th ☞ finis takeing up the roots of 1 Bed
& and a half to day. a very Hott day

1799 Tuesday June 25th ☞ finished the 2 long
beds on the right hand side of the grass walk. a very
hott day

Wednesday 26th ☞ this morning at 9 oclock
Charles went of for Baltimore in the Packett. a very
warm day. in the evening thare was an appearance of
rain but the cloud parted. wee had littel or none of
it. this cloude came round and wee had a cleaver
littel rain and wee plante the big bed with plants

Thursday 27th ☞ a fine day

Fryday 28th ☞ a fine day. in the evening it look'd
for a fine rain

Saturday 29th ☞ it rained, Tunder'd & lightened
very hard last night, a fine day. Charles has sent me
down a glass cillinder for my ellect'l masheen. in
the evening wee had a cleaver rain

Sunday 30th ☞ Abee has been very Iill to day,
call'd in the Doctr. he recomended Balm tea[184] &
Lemon Juce. in the after noon Charles returned
home from Baltimore & came with him my
daughter Nance pitt & her littel girl. the child is
but poorley. Nancy's very harty, a fine day

1799 Munday July 1th ☞ a warm day. in the
evening looks gustey like for rain

Tuseday 2th ☞ a fine day

Wednesday 3th ☞ a fine day

Thursday 4th ☞ a rainey morning. betwen 12 & 1
oclock clear'd away a fine after noon. in the evening,
Charles Nancey pitt & Beckey went to the play.
Abee was not well anuff

Fryday 5th ☞ about 9 oclock this morning Charles
& his sister Nancey pitt, child & servant sett of in
the packett for Baltimore. a very warm day. in the
evening looks like to be a gust

Saturday 6th ☞ a very warm day

Sunday 7th ☞ a very warm day in the evening
Charles returned from Baltimore. he left his sister &
famely all well

[184] Possibly tea made from
bee balm, or bergamot—
today's Earl Grey.

1799 Munday July 8th 🖝 I have been takeing up flower roots. I have don the first par of the garden. Sylve's digging the wallnutt tree Bed. I have sow'd lettis seed on one of the flower beds. a warm day

Tuseday 9th 🖝 a warm day. I have I have taken up all the roots except the nursserey Beds. I have made abegining, but it came on to rain in the after noon. it cleared up in the evening. I took up the 4 Fross nercess roots Mr. H. J. Stear gave me last year. Sylve's finished diging the wallnut tree Bed. a fine evening

Wednesday 10th 🖝 finishd one of the nurssery beds and took up the nercess roots from Mr. Steer. Sylve has taken up the seedling roots on the the Border next the Back street. a warm day

Thursday 11th 🖝 a fine day

Fryday 12th 🖝 a fine day. Simon Retalick[185] was Buried to day

Saturday 13th 🖝 a fine day

1799 Sunday July 14th 🖝 a very warm day

Munday 15th 🖝 ~~dunged and~~ dug up two of the nursserey Bed and on the firs I sow'd Large Imperial Dutch lettice and on the further end I sow'd Large Yallow Hollond Loaf Lettice, a fine day

Tuseday 16th 🖝 I finished takeing up the flower roots about a 11 oclock to day. Sylve's puting dung on the Beds & diging them up. a fine day, the schooner Hope sailed this evening for the West Indes[186]

Wednesday 17th 🖝 a fine day

Thursday 18th 🖝 a dull drisley day. in the after noon I planted out a few plants in the Wallnutt Tree Bed. in the evening it rained

Fryday 19th 🖝 it rain'd allmost all last night and all most all to day. I have fill the Wallnut Tree bed with Brussel Cole plants, and fill up the places wanting in the bed in the Lott

1799 Saturday July 20th 🖝 a coole cloudey day

Sunday 21th 🖝 a cloudey morning but turned out a fine day

Munday 22th 🖝 a fine day

[185] Simon Retallick married Elizabeth Miles (d.1808) in June 1782. A blacksmith and ironmonger, he lived in a one-story frame dwelling on Green Street, with a frame shop on the property. Retallick worked on a number of public buildings and town houses in Annapolis, including the State House, the Treasury building, and Edward Lloyd's house. When he died in 1799, Retallick left an estate, including mahogany furniture and a considerable amount of silver, that totaled £1,279. § Retallick bought steel in Baltimore for Faris in March 1792 and faced a hand hammer for him in April 1797. Faris also bought James River coal from John Retallick in November 1796 and had Simon Jr. repair two tablespoon punches in October 1798. Charles Faris's estate owed Retallick 3/9.

[186] This entry, and that for 3 August, are unusual—Faris does not usually record voyages in which he has no interest. It is possible that one of the vessels belonged to William Pitt and that Hyram sailed as a member of the crew of the other.

Tuseday 23th ✒ a fine day

Wednesday 24th ✒ a fine day

Thursday 25th ✒ a very Hott day

Fryday 26th ✒ about 9 oclock this morning Sirus finished the poarch and steps.[187] a very Hott day

Saturday 27th ✒ a very Hott day

Sunday 28th ✒ a very Hott day

1799 Munday July 29th ✒ a very warm day

Tuseday 30th ✒ a very Hott day

Wednesday 31th ✒ a very Hott day. I took up the onions of Egept

Augt 1th ✒ a fine morning. in the evening came on to rain. it looks as if wee should have a fine rain. its much wanted — Capt. Beriah Maberey[188] died last night

Fryday 2th ✒ a drisley morning. Betwen a 11 & 12 oclock Capt. Maburey was buried & I was informed that Mr. William Whitcroft was struck with a Parralicet last night. I went to see Mr. Whitcroft. he is entierley out of his senses, and if he dont get better verey shortley die he must. a fine after noon

Saturday 3th ✒ betwen 7 & 8 oclock, the scooner Aristides sailed for the West Indies. good Luck to her. and about 12 oclock Mr. William Whitcroft died

Sunday 4th ✒ a cloudey morning. in the afternoon wee had a fine rain. in the evening Mr. William Whitcroft was Buried

1799 Munday Augt 5th ✒ a fine day

Tuseday 6th ✒ Mr. Thomas Woodward call'd to see us and dined with us. a fine day but very warm

Wednesday 7th ✒ a fine day

Thursday 8th ✒ a fine day

Fryday 9th ✒ a fine day

Saturday 10th ✒ about 8 oclock, Charles, Abee & Rebaca went of in the stage for Baltimore. a fine day

Sunday 11th ✒ a fine day. this evening Doctr Allender[189] & Mr. Holley[190] call'd to se me

[187] With the job completed, Syras was paid £1.10.0 on the 26th for "Building the poarch and steps."

[188] Beriah Mayberry (c.1738–1799), a native of Cecil County, kept the Sign of the Golden Scales tavern in his house on Cornhill Street. Mayberry married Elizabeth Reynolds (b.1746), the daughter of John and Jane Reynolds, and the stepdaughter of silversmith John Inch (d.1763). In 1789, when St. John's College opened, Mayberry advertised that he could provide lodging for eight students. He served as a councilman from April 1781 until he resigned in February 1799. Mayberry was survived by his daughter Julia, who married John Barrett Onion (see 6 August 1792). § Mayberry served on the St. Anne's vestry with Faris in the 1770s and 1780s.

[189] Dr. Joseph Allender (c.1770–1834), a member of the Medical and Chirurgical Faculty of Maryland, who issued a public warning in the 1790s about the yellow fever epidemic at Fells Point. Allender, who lived at 27 Bond Street in Fells Point, married Mary Biays (see 16 August), daughter of Maj. Joseph Biays, in February 1800.

[190] Mr. Holley does not appear in the census records or in the Baltimore directories.

Munday 12th ✍ Doctr Allender & Mr. Holley Brackfasted with us, at 9 oclock sett of in the packet for Baltimore, in the evening Charles came home in the stage from Baltimore. he left his sisters all well

1799 Tuseday Augt 13th ✍ a fine day

Wednesday 14th ✍ a fine day. about a 1/4 after a 11 oclock at night Abee came home from Baltimore, left her sister Rebaca. she has been very unwell with a Bowel complaint but she is better and expects to come home on Fryday

Thursday 15th ✍ a fine day

Fryday 16th ✍ this morning ~~I enter'd into the 72 year of~~ I am 71 years of age, a fine day. in the evening my daughter Rebaca came Home in the stage from Baltimore and Miss polley Bias, she left Nancey pitt and the Fameley well

Saturday 17th ✍ thare was a preetey littel rain Last night — a fine day

Sunday 18th ✍ a drisley rainey morning in the afternoon. cleared away a fine evening

Munday 19th ✍ we ha[d] a fine rain this morning. Planted out Bussel Cale plants in the Lot and Sylve How'd the greens in the different Beds. a cloudey drisley day

1799 Tuseday Augt 20th ✍ a raney day

Wednesday 21th ✍ a cloudey morning, sow'd the following cabbage seed on the Border by the Balm

N.	1	next the Balm earley York	from
	2	Large Dutch	Hesler
	3	White Loaf	
	4	Seed from Mrs. Miller	
	5	d° from J. Cowman	
	6	Cabbage seed	

Thursday 22th ✍ a clear coole day

Fryday 23th ✍ a fine day

Saturday 24th ✍ a warm day

Sunday 25th ✍ a warm day

Munday 26th ☛ a warm day. in the evening turned cloudey as if wee should have rain

Tuseday 27th ☛ a fine day

1799 Wednesday 28th of Augt ☛ a fine day

Thursday 29th ☛ a fine morning. in the evening rain and looks as if wee should have a fine rain, Mrs. Leastrange[191] died last night and was Buried this after noon, she was the wife of one of the Players

Fryday 30th ☛ Mr. John Steel call'd to see us and told us that Nancy pitt & Fameley was weel. he did not stay in Town more than a Hour, a fine day. in the evening I had a letter from Nancey pitt

Saturday 31th ☛ a Charles & Samuel Green sett of on Hore back about 9 oclock for Baltimore. a fine day

Sunday Septr 1th ☛ a fine morning. in the after noon came on to rain

Munday 2th ☛ a fine morning. in the after noon cloudey & drisling, Charles & S. Green return'd from Baltimore this evening betwen 7 & 8 oclock

1799 Tuseday Septr 3th ☛ a fine morning. in the afternoon whe had a littel rain

Wednesday 4th ☛ a cloudey day. in the evening it came on to rain

Thursday 5th ☛ it rain'd the most of the last night. a cloudey day. I got some plums from Mrs. N[icholas] Carrol thay call them Magnum Bonum, others call them the egg plum. I have made some of them in wax. in the evening came on to rain and rained hard all the evening

Fryday 6th ☛ rained grate part of last night. a cloudey day — in the evening it rained

Saturday 7th ☛ rain the grater part of the night and raining this morning and looks like a setteld rain. a cloudey rainey day

Sunday 8th ☛ a dull cloudey day

Munday 9th ☛ rained hard Last night. a cloudey drisley day

1799 Tuseday Septr 10th ☛ a dull cloudey morning. about noon clear'd away a fine after noon & evening

[191] The wife of Joseph Lestrange. He died in Baltimore on 18 May 1805 at age 78 after a "lingering illness."

Wednesday 11th ☞ this morning I began to make a 6 light sash.[192] a fine clear day

Thursday 12th ☞ a very warm day

Fryday 13th ☞ a very warm day. I have finished the sash and prime'd it

Saturday 14th ☞ a very warm day. I paid Smiths twenty one shillings for Hawling 21 littel loads of dung from Mr. John Onions's. in the evening wee had a cleaver rain

Sunday 15th ☞ wee had a good deal of rain last night. a fine day. not so warm as it has been for some days past

Munday 16th ☞ a fine day. Mr. Whitcroft drove in in his chair and carried Abee home with him

Tuseday 17th ☞ I Planted about 200 Tulep root that the seed ware sow'd ware sowed in Augt 96 on the Border next to the Hors Radish. a fine day

1799 Wednesday Septr 18th ☞ a fine day. I have a dissagreeable Lax & straining for these 2 or 3 days past

Thursday 19th ☞ Last night was a very Blustering windey rainey night, and this morning, cleared away about noon but very coole. Abee came this evening with Mr. & Mrs. Whitcroft. thay are on thare way to the Eastern Shore

Fryday 20th ☞ a c[l]oudey morning. last night Walter Chandler was married to Miss Rodgers,[193] I have enoculated several Peach Trees, with the large clear stone Yellow Peach and & a very large fine sort both from Mr. Stevens. a cloudey drisley day

Saturday 21th ☞ it rained Last night & this morning. cept cloudey till about noon, then cleared away a fine after noon

Sunday 22th ☞ a clear cool day

Munday 23th ☞ a clear coole day. I have mad abegining to do up the Flower beds. I have dunged & dugg 5 beds to day

1799 Tuseday Septr 24th ☞ a fine day. I have been dunging and digging the flower Beds

Wednesday 25th ☞ a fine clear coole day. still digging ye flower Beds, in the evening Sylve finished digging ye flower beds

192 A window of six panes of glass, possibly three over three, or more likely three horizontal rows of two panes each.

193 Walter S. Chandler, who lived in Prince George's County, was adjutant of the 14th regiment of the county militia in 1794 and 1795. He and Margaret Rogers obtained their license on the 19th.

Thursday 26th ✒ I have finished Planting two of the nurrserey beds & thare's 250 mark'd Tuleps amongst the others that are Planted in them. a fine day

Fryday 27th ✒ Charles went of for Baltimore this morning in the packet, a fine day

Saturday 28th ✒ a fine day

Sunday 29th ✒ Charles returned home from Baltimore betwen 12 & 1 oclock. he left his sister & fameley well and thare negro girl Peg in prisson for an attempt to Poison her mistress, a fine day but coole

Munday 30th ✒ I have finished Planting the 4 nurrserey Beds. thay took 847 Tulip roots. in the afternoon Charles went over South River to Mr. John Gassaways wedden. He's to be married to morrow. a fine day

1799 Tuseday Octr 1th ✒ a fine day. Capt. John Gassaway is married to Miss Elizabeth Price over South River.[194] Capt. Gassaway is near 50 & Miss about 17 or 18

Wednesday 2th ✒ a fine day. in the evening Charles returned from the wedding

Thursday 3th ✒ I have Been aplanting Flower roots to day. a fine day

Fryday 4th ✒ a dull heavey morning. I planted the following stones

No. 1 Magnum Bonum, or egg plum

    2 a forward peach

    3 the Peckeling Peach very red at the stone will hang on the tree till Novr.

    4 a very large latter Peach in Octr

a dull cloudey day

Saturday 5th ✒ a cloudey drissley day. I have finished Planting the Beds round the grass. I have planted in them 7 bedes 718 Tulips besides other flowers

1799 Sunday Octr 6th ✒ about 8 oclock this morning Charles sett of on horse Back for Baltimore. a fine day

Munday 7th ✒ a fine day, Charles returned about 6 oclock from Baltimore

[194] Not the daughter of saddler Thomas Pryse and, as the wedding took place in All Hallow's Parish, probably not the daughter of bricklayer Thomas Price either. Both Thomas Price and Thomas Pryse (see 3 April 1792) patronized Faris's tavern in the 1770s. Faris distinguished between the two by putting "B" after Thomas Price's name and writing "saddler" after Thomas Pryse's name; Price was the more frequent customer.

129 ☛ William McParlin (c. 1780–1850)

William McParlin came to Annapolis in 1799 as an apprentice to Charles Faris.

195 William McParlin was born in Loughbrickland, Ireland and came to Annapolis at the age of 18 as an apprentice to Charles Faris. When Charles died in 1800, Faris assumed the apprenticeship. McParlin, who became a naturalized citizen in 1806, took over the Faris shop when William died and continued the business as jeweler, clockmaker, and silversmith. In January 1818, he also bought the lease to the Faris home, where Priscilla Woodward Faris had continued to live until her death on 14 March 1817. McParlin married Cassandra Woodward, of Prince George's County, on 15 December 1816; Cassandra was a great-niece of Priscilla Woodward Faris. McParlin served a number of terms in the 1820s as councilman, alderman, and commissioner.

196 Alexander Martin's *The American and Daily Advertiser*, established in May 1799; in November 1801, it was renamed *The American and Baltimore Daily Advertiser.*

197 Paca died at his home on Wye Island in Queen Anne's County, incorrectly reported in the paper as being in Talbot County. Although Paca had lived in Annapolis for nearly twenty years earlier in his life and still owned property in the city, as well as having been a three-term governor of the state, the *Maryland Gazette* did not report his death.

The Diary of

Tuseday 8th ☛ rain'd Last night & this morning. about 10 oclock clear'd away. I went to Planting & finished planting the flower Beds

in the Beds by the littel house	150 Tulips
nursserey Beds	847
the Beds round the grass walk & joyning	718
Besides other Flower	1715 Tulips

and turn'd out a fine day

Wednesday 9th ☛ Charles has got the young man from Baltimore. a dull cloudey day. the young man's Name is William Mc~~Glackland~~Farland[195]

Thursday 10th ☛ a dull rainey day

Fryday 11th ☛ a midling good day

Saturday 12th ☛ a fine day. I planted a Branch of the Chrysanthemum Indicum on the Border next the Burgamot Balm

Sunday 13th ☛ rained a good deal last night. fine morning. in the after noon & evening turned cloudey & looks like for more rain

1799 Munday Octr 14th ☛ last Night was a rainey Night and rains hard this morning and continued to rain all day

Tuseday 15th ☛ a fine day

Wednesday 16th ☛ a fine day

Thursday 17th ☛ rained Last night, a fine day but cold

Fryday 18th ☛ a clear cold day. Mrs. Faris is very unwell. she has cep her Bed allmost all day

Saturday 19th ☛ a fine clear coold morning, in Martin's paper[196] of the 17th I see an accot that Mr. William Paca died on the 13th at his seat in Talbot County[197] — a fine day. in the evening turned cloudey

Sunday 20th ☛ rained last night. a cloudey morning. about noon clear'd away.   in the evening cloudey. Mrs. Faris is very unwell

Munday 21th ☛ a fine day. Mrs. Faris is Better. she took a puke this morning

Tuseday 22th ☛ Mrs. Faris took 2 or 3 doses of Bark this morning but her feveour came on about noon & she has it smartley. I got 1 oz. of Bark from Doctr Ghislin & a littel salt of Tarter. a fine day

1799 Wednesday Octr 23th ✒ a fine day. Mrs. Faris has taken Bark to day

Thursday 24th ✒ a fine day. Mrs. Faris has miss'd her Fever to day

Fryday 25th ✒ Mrs. Faris is not so well this afternoon as yesterday. a Fine day

Saturday 26th ✒ Mrs. Faris is Better to day, a fine day

Sunday 27th ✒ Mrs. Faris is a good deal better. a cold, raw, dull, cloudey day

Munday 28th ✒ Last night was a very windey & rainey night. the wind Broke off one third of my Chrysanthemum Indicum. a dull cloudey day. I planted in two potts a sprig and one branch at the end of the new stabel of the Chrysanthemum Indicum

Tuesday 29th ✒ a fine morning. I planted on the Border at the Back of the garden 400 seedling Tuleps & 18 small Doubel Tulips, from Mr. Stevens. a fine day. Mr. Thomas Woodward dined with us to day. Mrs. Woodward is but Poorley

1799 Wednesday Octr 30th ✒ a fine day

Thursday 31th ✒ a fine day. Abee went down to her Brother Charles to tell him of me

Fryday Novr 1th ✒ Charles went of this morning in the Packett for Baltimore. a fine day. in the evening Mrs. Jane Waters, Jane Woodward[198] that was came heare

Saturday 2th ✒ Jane Waters sett of Home after diner. a fine day but in the evening looks cloudey like falling weather

Sunday 3th ✒ a cold cloudey dull morning, about 2 oclock Charles returned from Baltimore. a dull cold day

Munday 4th ✒ a clear cold morning, a smart white Frost. Old William Brought me a Holley Tree. I planted it directley after Brackfast By the littel House. a fine day

Tuseday 5th ✒ a fine day. in the evening looks like falling weather

[198] Jane Woodward Waters (b.1740) was the daughter of William and Alice Woodward (see 7 December 1792) and the niece of Priscilla Woodward Faris. She married William Waters in June 1785.

Wednesday 6th ✒ a fine day

1799 Thursday Novr 7th ✒ Mrs. Debero Sprigg came to Town to day. she stay'd about 2 or 3 Hours, and returned, a fine day

Fryday 8th ✒ a cloudey morning. about 10 oclock it sett in to rain & raind the rest of the day & looks like a setteld rain. I let Charles have 12 Hundred Shing[l]es towards covering his House

Saturday 9th ✒ a fine day. Charles had 1000 more shingels to day

Sunday 10th ✒ a fine day

Munday 11th ✒ a fine day. I had no Plate for my Broth at diner[199]

Tuseday 12th ✒ a rainey dull cloudey day

Wednesday 13th ✒ a clear cold day

Thursday 14th ✒ a dull heavy day

Fryday 15th ✒ a dull day

1799 Saturday Novr 16th ✒ a fine day

Sunday 17th ✒ a foggey day

Munday 18th ✒ a fine morning. in the after noon it clouded up turn'd cold & came on to rain. Sylve has Buried the cabbages in rows

Tuseday 19th ✒ a clear coole day

Wednesday 20th ✒ a fine day

Thursday 21th ✒ a fine day. the girles are pre-pairing for the Ball this evening. a littel before 7 oclock the girls went to the Ball in Mrs. Clemments carrage.   a fine night

Fryday 22th ✒ a fine day. in the evening Mr. Martin the Printer drank Tea with us

Saturday 23th ✒ a dull morning, continued to be a dull day

Sunday 24th ✒ a fine morning. in the afternoon turned cloudey & looks like bad weather cuming

1799 Munday 25th ✒ a fine morning. I planted out the onions of Egipt or roshembools for seed. a fine day

[199] Faris wrote this entry in a markedly agitated hand, but provided no details of the dispute that apparently left him at the table for dinner with no bowl from which to eat the broth being served.

Tuseday 26th ✒ a cold [day] to what it has been and a dull day. looks as if wee ware agoing to have bad weather

Wednesday 27th ✒ a cold dull day

Thursday 28th ✒ a dull morning. in the afternoon come on to rain

Fryday 29th ✒ a snowey morning. clear'd away about noon very cold. I moved the Potts into the seller for the winter

Saturday 30th ✒ a cold morning. Mrs. Faris went of in the stage for Baltimore Betwen 8 & 9 oclock in companey of Misses Byas, Lemon,[200] Doctr Ridgley & Joseph Evens[201]

Sunday Desr 1th ✒ a dull cloudey day

Munday 2th ✒ Last night was a very Blustering bad night. a fine day

1799 Tuseday Desr 3th ✒ a cloudey day

Wednesday 4th ✒ I bought 908# of Hogg meat at 5/ pr HH.[202] a fine day

Thursday 5th ✒ a dull rainey day

Fryday 6th ✒ Charles went in the packett for Baltimore this morning. a dull cloudey rainey day

Saturday 7th ✒ a rainey morning. clear'd away about noon a fine after noon

Sunday 8th ✒ a fine day

Munday 9th ✒ a fine day. this evening Charles returned in the stage from Baltimore. thay ware all well thare

Tuseday 10th ✒ a fine day

1799 Wednesday Desr 11th ✒ a rainey morning. its now a 11 oclock and Becke is not up. she has unweel all night. in the after [noon] she was better and came down stairs, a clear afternoon

Thursday 12th ✒ cloudey morning. looks like falling weather. this morning I Planted 3 Tulips in potts and put them in the seller. a rainey evening. Abee's gone to the Ball with Miss Onion & Miss Owens

[200] There were several Lemmon households in Baltimore to which Miss Lemon could have belonged, but given the wide circle of acquaintances that the Faris family had among the maritime community of Fells Point, the most likely would be that of Capt. John Lemmon, who lived at 27 Bond Street. Lemmon married Mrs. Esther Lawrence, also of Fells Point, in November 1799, and died in his 49th year in February 1805.

[201] Joseph Evans may have been the son of David and Elizabeth Evans, born 3 October 1762 in All Hallow's Parish. Evans was a merchant, frequently in partnership with Absalom Ridgely (see 3 November 1799), whose advertisements covered the years from 1785 to 1807. In 1799, the land stage to Baltimore left from his establishment. § In December 1800 Faris bought stockings from Evans for his granddaughter Marriah and in 1802 purchased eight pounds of rice, a half-gallon of "Mallago wine," and a pair of shoes for his wife Priscilla.

[202] Faris paid Henry Hammond £24.4.0 for 968 pounds of hog meat.

Fryday 13th ✐ a snowey morning, continued snowing all day till evening, the sun just appear'd clear an sett, its turned much colder then it was

Saturday 14th ✐ a fine day

Sunday 15th ✐ a fine day

Munday 16th ✐ a fine day but bad walking

Tuseday 17th ✐ a snowey morning. about noon cleard away a fine afternoon. thare came an accot To Town to day that Genl Washington died on Saturday night la[s]t[203]

1799 Wednesday Desr 18th ✐ a fine day

Thursday 19th ✐ snow'd last night, a dull cloudy day

Fryday 20th ✐ a fine day

Saturday 21th ✐ snow'd all the fore part of the day. in the after noon clear'd away. this evening Mr. Joseph Brewer was married to Miss Elizbeth Wilmott[204]

Sunday 22th ✐ a fine day

Munday 23th ✐ a fine day

Tuseday 24th ✐ a fine morning. about noon snow'd hard. clear'd away a fine after noon

Wednesday 25th ✐ a fine day[205]

Thursday 26th ✐ a fine day

Fryday 27th ✐ a fine day

Saturday 28th ✐ a dull cloudey day

1799 Sunday Desr 29th ✐ a dull cloudey day. in the evening came on to rain Hard

Munday 30th ✐ a fine day

Tuseday 31th ✐ a fine day

[203] George Washington died on the 14th. Faris makes no mention of the mourning that Washington's death occasioned, although the *Gazette* took note on 19 December of the resolutions passed by the General Assembly and devoted almost the entire 26 December issue to Washington's death and burial.

[204] Joseph Nathaniel Newton Brewer (d. 1803) was the son of John and Susannah Brewer (see 13 March 1792). Elizabeth Wilmot was the daughter of John and Ann McClellan Wilmot (see 27 June 1800) and the granddaughter of John and Dinah Brewer Wilmot (see 21 January 1793).

[205] On his first Christmas in the Faris household, William McParlin received a "Christmas box," or gift, of three shillings, nine pence, according to Faris's account book.

The Diary of William Faris

The Daily Life of an Annapolis Silversmith

PART FOUR
1800–1804

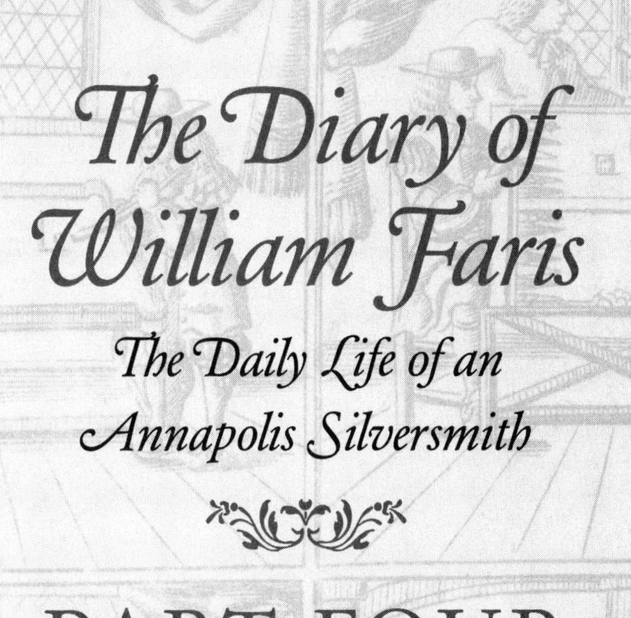

1797 Wednesday March 8th a Cloudey Morning Lawyer John Hall Died this more noon aged 69 years, Cleared away afore Day but the Wind Blowe very hard, Hiram made a beginning To Cart Dung Silue finished the Digging the [...] planted aline Radish Sed in the large Silue has dug up the line of Sage in the big bed & made good the Table & I Sow'd aline of Sage Seed Just with in the line of Sage on the little Quarter, made of Hill in the Lott for Vines

Thursday 9th a Cold windey Day could do nothing in the Garden in the afternoon I planted 10 hills of Simlins and 9 Hills of Cucumbers in the lott amongst the Sprouts, & in the outer lott I planted 4 Hills of water millions & 4 Hills of Cantilopes

Friday 10th Cold Day did little more than Plant the line of Sage on the big bed Mr John Hall was buried to Day, he was Carried to the vine yard

Wednesday January 1th 1800 ✍ a fine day

Thursday 2th ✍ a fine day

Fryday 3th ✍ a cold cloudey morning. looks like
for snow, but clear'd away in the afternoon, a fine
evening

Saturday 4th ✍ a clear cold day. in the evening it
came on to Blow Hard and turned very cold

Sunday 5th ✍ a clear fine cold day

Munday 6th ✍ a cloudey morning. about noon
began to snow a littel and continued at times to
snow a littel all the after noon. Charles has a 12th
cake and a large cumpaney at his house this evening[1]

1800 Tuseday Janry 7th ✍ clear cold day

Wednesday 8th ✍ a dull cloudey morning & snow'd
a littel and looked as if wee should have a good deal
of it but it cleared away a fine after noon but cold,
Charles was with a chill this after noon and went to
Bed in the evening very unwell

Thursday 9th ✍ a fine day. Charles is still unwell.
he ceps his Bed, in the evening about 8 o'clock he
took a pill which Doctr Ghislind sent

Fryday 10th ✍ the pill Charles took last night did
not opporate at all, I think he's Better. he has sett
up to day, about 8 o'clock this even the Doctr sent
him 6 pill. he took them, a fine day

Saturday 11th ✍ a cloudey dull morning, clear'd
away a fine day. Charles is still poorely but better
then he was I think

Sunday 12th ✍ Charles is Better — a fine day

1800 Munday January 13th ✍ Charles is much
Better. a fine day

Tuseday 14th ✍ Charles is bravely. only his mouth
is sore. a fine warm day

Wednesday 15th ✍ a fine day

Thursday 16th ✍ a fine day

Fryday 17th ✍ a dull cloudey day. in the evening
came on to rain hard

Saturday 18th ✍ Last night was a Terebel rainey
wi[n]dy night, a clear cold day but the wind has
Blow'd very Hard all day

[1] A Twelfth Night celebration,
to which—it appears—Faris has
not been invited.

130 ✍ FACING PAGE *On this
page, Faris recorded his gardening
successes and failures.*

131 ✒ *Ann Faris Pitt and her daughter, Hannah Williams Pitt. See also Figure 1A in color insert.*

2 The Pitts' third daughter, Hannah Williams Pitt, named after William Pitt's first wife, Hannah Williams, who died on 25 September 1795. She and Pitt had been married in Baltimore on 29 January of the same year. Hannah Pitt may have died in childbirth, but if so, the child also died.

3 The *Gazette* reported on 30 January that "Sunday last about 12 o'clock that large and commodious building, the poor house of Anne Arundel County, near this city, caught fire and the whole of the wood-work [was] consumed." All of the inhabitants were saved and housed temporarily in part of the new jail. In 1803 the Trustees of the Poor bought Richard Sprigg's Strawberry Hill estate from William Caton (see 29 April 1793) to serve as the new almshouse.

4 The 30 January issue also carried an account of the fire in the "work-shop and bark house occupied by Mr. Norman," which was put out without major damage.

5 Faris noted in his account book that he paid 2/6 to Len for hanging up the bacon.

The Diary of

Sunday 19th ✒ a clear cold, windey Blustering day

Munday 20th ✒ last Night was a very Blustering windey night. a dull cloudey cold day

Tuseday 21th ✒ a cold dull day

1800 Wednesday Janry 22th ✒ I received a letter from Mr. [Pitt] whare in he tells that Nancey pitt was Brought to Bed with a girl the 16th & that thay are all well.[2] a clear cold day

Thursday 23th ✒ Charles has come down stairs and got into the shop this morning. a clear cold day

Fryday 24th ✒ snow'd a littel last night — a fine cold day. Charles & sisters, are at a party at Capt. Thomas's

Saturday 25th ✒ a very cold, clear windey day

Sunday 26th ✒ Last night was a very windey Blustering night. a fine morning. betwen 11 & 12 o'clock the Poors House took Fire by some meens.[3] I could not learn how but it intirely burnt down. a fine day

Munday 27th ✒ a cloudey dull day. in the evening looks like for snow

Tuseday 28th ✒ a clear cold windey day

1800 Wednesday Janry 29th ✒ last night was a cold Blustering windey night. a clear cold day — we had another allarm of Fire to day. the Bark House at the Tan Yard took Fire[4]

Thursday 30th ✒ a fine morning but very cold

Fryday 31th ✒ in the night it came on to snow and has continued to snow hard all day and in the evening and in the night it Blowd excessively Hard and snow'd a near snow storm

Saturday Febuary 1th ✒ snowing a littel about 9 o'clock the sun came out a littel wile but soon shut up and continued a cold windey day

Sunday 2th ✒ a fine cold day

Munday 3th ✒ Hung up the meet in the Smoke House 9 goles 18 shoulders & midelings 19 Hamms besides Beef,[5] a dissagreeable day, snows rain & Hails and Blows Hard and continued the grater part of the night

1800 Tuseday Febry 4th ✒ a dull cloudey morning. in the afternoon clear'd away & the sun came oute Fine in the evening

Wednesday 5th ✒ a fine day. a grate deal of the snow is gone to day

Thursday 6th ✒ a clear cold day. I put the Ingreedients the Bottel, Flor. Dianna or the Philosophica Tree[6]

Fryday 7th ✒ a clear cold day

Saturday 8th ✒ a cold dull cloudey day, looks like more snow. came on to snow about 7 o'clock this evening

Sunday 9th ✒ snow'd all night. this morning snowing & continued a miseling snow till about 12 o'clock. stopt snowing but dull cold & windey. in the afternoon it commenc'd snowing again and looks likely to continue snowing

1800 Munday Febry 10th ✒ a clear cold day

Tuseday 11th ✒ this morning Charles went off in the stage for Baltimore. a fine day

Wednesday 12th ✒ a clear cold day

Thursday 13th ✒ a clear cold day

Fryday 14th ✒ snow'd a littel in the night. a cold rainey morning & continued till about noon then stopt raining but continued dull & cloudey. this evening Mrs. Faris & Charles came Home in the stage from Baltimore

Saturday 15th ✒ a clear cold day

Sunday 16th ✒ a clear cold day

Munday 17th ✒ clear & cold

Tuseday 18th ✒ clear & cold. very slipperey bad walking

Wednesday 19th ✒ I was taken with a violent agu this morning befor day & continued till about 10 o'clock. then came on a Feverour till late in the after noon. a clear cold day

1800 Thursday Febry 20th ✒ a clear cold day, sliperey bad walking

Fryday 21th ✒ a fine day

[6] *Arbor Dianae*, or philosopher's tree, is the treelike growth of silver amalgam that forms when mercury is placed in a silver nitrate solution.

Saturday 22th ✐ a fine day

Sunday 23th ✐ this morning the Boys were skeeting on the Ice in the street. a fine day. the snow and Ice has gone off a grate deal to day

Munday 24th ✐ a fine day. a grate deal of the Ice and snow is gone to day

Tuseday 25th ✐ a fine morning. I had dung putt on the Border next Iiam's. in the evening clouded up and looks as if we should have falling weather

Wednesday 26th ✐ dugg the Border next to Iiam's. a fine day but not so warm as yester day. in the evening sow'd earley York cabbage seed in a Box in the yard

Thursday 27th ✐ a dull cloudey day. in the evening snow'd & Hailed a littel

Fryday 28th ✐ this morning Haild & raind and continued raining all day & very raw & cold

1800 Saturday March 1th ✐ it Blow'd & snow'd hardar last night and continued snowing till noon then clear'd away a fine after noon but cold

Sunday 2th ✐ a clear day but cold

Munday 3th ✐ a clear cold day

Tuseday 4th ✐ a clear cold day

Wednesday 5th ✐ cloudey morning, clear'd away about 9 o'clock. still cold

Thursday 6th ✐ clear & very cold day

Fryday 7th ✐ clear & cold

Saturday 8th ✐ cold cloudey day. in the evening began to snow

Sunday 9th ✐ snow'd I belive all nigh & this morning it rian'd Haild, & Blow'd very hard. left of betwen 10 & 11 o'clock but cloudey and cold

Munday 10th ✐ a clear cold day

1800 Tuseday March 11th ✐ a fine clear day and not so cold as it has been

Wednesday 12th ✐ a fine day. this afternoon I sowed 17 rows of Peas on the Border and betwen the rows I sow'd white and red Lettis from Mr. Stevens and like wise I sow'd orris or French spinige

Thursday 13th ⚐ a fine day. I sow'd more early York cabbage seed in the Box from Mr. Stevens and cabbage seed betwen the peas

Fryday 14th ⚐ a fine day

Saturday 15th ⚐ a cloudey morning. this after noon I Planted a 11 of the Jacobin Lilley's. the other the ground was har frosen that I could not mak a hole in the ground to plant it

Sunday 16th ⚐ a fine day. in the evening cloudey like for rain

Munday 17th ⚐ a fine day. I planted a pear Tree in the midel of the scircel. I likewise planted 3 peach Trees one a forward peach, one a large fine pech and other a large peach with red meat. Sylve's been digging the Border nex to Mrs. Davidson & moovening the greens that ware Buried in the Bigg Bed & I have made abegining to cut Box. I have the Box on[e] Bed & made a begining on the second. in the evening wee have a fine rain

1800 Tuseday March 18th ⚐ wee had a fine rain last night with sharp Thunder & Lightening. a foggey morning. clear'd away fine, in the after noon wee had a shower of rain. clear'd away a fine evening. I am acutting of Box

Wednesday 19th ⚐ a fine day. I have been cutting Box

Thursday 20th ⚐ a fine day. I am still cutting Box. I have done at this Lower end expt a few Balls

Fryday 21th ⚐ a rainey day

Saturday 22th ⚐ a rainey morning. abut a 11 o'clock clear'd away. it soon came on cloudey and cold

Sunday 23th ⚐ a cold dull cloudey windey morning. I Planted 6 Tulips in the Box'd Bed on the Border by the grape vines. I took the Tulips out of the Buckett

Munday 24th ⚐ a fine day. I have been a Troweling some of the Flower Beds & Sylve's digging the Bigg Bed

Tuseday 25th ⚐ a fine day. Sylve's finished digging the Big Bed & I have sow'd it with 7 rows of Peas. I have been Troweling one or 2 Beds & I cutt a line or 2 of Box

1800 Wednesday March 26th ✍ a fine day. Sylve's done up the assparagrass Beds & I have been acutting of Box

Thursday 27th ✍ I have finished cuting the Box except the long line on the Border. I must leave that till I have don troweling the flower Beds. I am about them. I have sow'd 2 lines of spinige in the assparagass walks. a fine day

Fryday 28th ✍ a fine day. I have been Troweling the flower Beds. I have done these round the circel. in the evening cloudey, looks like for rain

Saturday 29th ✍ a rainey day. I planted the Bigg Bed with plants and planted a sweet sented plant in the yard by the window

Sunday 30th ✍ a fine day

Munday 31th ✍ Sylve's dug two littel Borders and moved the greens into the Walnut Tree Bed, and Rebacka has planted a parcel of onions and have Troweling the Flower beds. I have got into the nursserey beds. I have done one and a Half. a fine day but winedy

1800 Tuseday April 1th ✍ I Planted 6 Tulips with the others I planted the 23th of March. I sow'd the Ice plant seed & the sensetive plant seed, the nutmeg seed, Sylve's dug the littel quarter, and is wheeling dung on the lott and I have been troweling the flower Beds. a fine day

Wednesday 2th ✍ I sow'd the littel qurter by the new stabel with 7 rows of Bunch Beens. I finished troweling the Flower Beds & have made abegining to do up the tabel round the grass walk & have cut & planted the cutings of the roosmary and have got a man to dig the Parsnep Bed two spade dee[p]. a fine day

Thursday 3th ✍ planted Ocro on the Border at the end of the new stabel and planted the sweet sented pea. I have been troweling the Water Tabel round the grass wallk. a fine day. in the evening clouded up like for rain

Fryday 4th ✍ a dull cloudey drisley day

Saturday 5th ✍ a dull cloudey day. a neagro man Daniel dugg a square in the Lott for Parsneps. he trenched it two spade deep

1800 Sunday April 6th ☞ cloudey & rain at times through the day

Munday 7th ☞ a fine morning. I have planted 15 hills of simlins & 12 of cucumbers and the girls are planting the Parsnep Bed & Sylve's don up the Water Tabel round the grass walk and am acuting the long line of Box. a fine day

Tuseday 8th ☞ Charles sett of in the Packett for Baltimore this moring. I finished cutting Box, and sow'd the following flower seeds at the end of the new stabel, No. 1 white aster No. 2 Bonet aster 3 very doubel Blew d[o] 4 Blew d[o] 5 white Balsom 6 red d[o] 7 do 8 striped d[o] 9 white globe 10 red globe. a very fine warm day. in the evening looks like for rain

Wednesday 9th ☞ a fine day. I have been at Charles's shop all day.

Thursday 10th ☞ a dull glumey day. betwen 4 & 5 o'clock Charles return'd from Baltimore with his sister Pitt and the two children and a neagro girl. all well

1800 Fryday April 11th ☞ a fine day

Saturday 12th ☞ a dull drisley day

Sunday 13th ☞ a dull drisley day. in the evening Mrs. Ross[7] was buried. she died of a parrilicktec stroke, I cutt asspargrass to day for the first time this spring

Munday 14th ☞ a fine day but coole for the season

Tuseday 15th ☞ at 9 o'clock Nancey Pitt, her child & neagro girl & a littel girl that's Bound to her[8] and Abee & the two Miss Owens's went of in the packett for Baltimore. a fine day but cold for the season, Mr. Stevens told me that thare was a frost this morning but I saw nothing of it

Wednesday 16th ☞ had the carrot Beds dug and planted and planted cherry pepper seed on the Border by the Bee House. a fine day. in the evening I sow'd sencitive plant seed in a pott

Thursday 17th ☞ I sow'd radish seed that was saved in 1790. thay apear good. in the after noon Mr. Hanson gave the following seeds, thay ware given to him by Mr. Stear No. 1 Anemone in the littel Cherry Tree poot No. 2 Rununculas in the

7 Possibly the widow Ross who lived in Annapolis in 1783, who owned no land and no slaves, and had a household of three females. Or this may have been the widow of Nathaniel Ross, another 1783 resident, who married Anne Little in March 1784. Or perhaps the widow of William Ross, who married Rachel Allen in June 1783 (see 29 April 1793). The widow Ross rented a house from Charles Carroll of Carrollton on the north side of the second block of West Street in 1798.

8 In addition to a slave child, Nancy Pitt's household help included a young girl bound out to her by the orphans court or the trustees of the poor. The child would live with the Pitts until she reached the age of sixteen, and the Pitts would be expected to teach her to read and to learn domestic skills such as sewing, spinning, and knitting. She would also assist with childcare and other domestic chores.

Bigg Cherrey Tree pott, aster, Larkspur in the Bed
the right hand side of the grass walk. a fine day

1800 Fryday April 18th ☛ a fine day

Saturday 19th ☛ a warm Fine day

Sunday 20th ☛ a fine day. in the evening Mrs.
Stevens returned from Baltimore in the Packett.
thay had a rouf time of it

Munday 21th ☛ stuck the peas in the Bigg Bed.
a cloudey morning. about noon came on to rain &
rained the remainder of the day. the simlins that
ware planted the 7th are acuming up

Tuseday 22th ☛ Sylve's Hilled the Peas & dug the
ground betwen, & dug the littel Border betwen the
new stabel & littel House. this after noon she's
geting dung on the littel quarter by the old stabel.
its been a cold disagreeable day, a smart white frost
this morning and raind at times throught the day

Wednesday 23th ☛ a cold Night. a very smart
Frost. a grate maney of the Beens are Bitt Black
with the frost. a cold windey morning. Sylve's digging the littel quarter by the old stabel. I have sown
Lettis on the Border by the peppers. a very cold
windey day

1800 April 24th ☛ the wind Blow'd very Hard
Last night and cold — its not so cold this morning
as yesterday but the wind Blows hard, in the littel
quarter by the old stabel I sow'd all but 3 rows of
Dwarf or Bunch peas, the remainder of the rows I
planted with 38 Beens, three rows more which filled
the Bed I planted with Bunch Beans, and on the
Border by the littel house I planted 9 places with
cherrey pepper seed

Fryday 25th ☛ I sow'd a peac of a row of large peas
which was given me by Mrs. Randel. I sowd them
by the Iives. a windey day

Saturday 26th ☛ the Tuleps are just begining to
open, thare 10 or 12 open, a fine day but very
windey. in the evening William Brought me
another Holley, I planted it whare the other stood.
it looks as if wee should have rain to night

Sunday 27th ☛ a fine rain last night and this
morning clear'd away a fine day

Munday 28th ☛ a fine day

Tuseday 29th ⚓ a coole dull drisley day

Wednesday 30th ⚓ a cold dull day

1800 Thursday May 1th ⚓ a dull coole cloudey morning. about 12 oclock began to rain & continued till about 3 or 4 oclock & then cloudey the remainder of the day. I planted more cherrey pepper seed & planted out a few cabbage plants

Fryday 2th ⚓ finished planting the Big Bed with plants betwen the peas. a fine day

Saturday 3th ⚓ a coole morning. in the after noon wee had several showers of rain. in the evening the sun sett clear

Sunday 4th ⚓ a clear cold day for the season

Munday 5th ⚓ a clear cold day for the season

Tuseday 6th ⚓ a cold [day] for the season

Wednesday 7th ⚓ a dull cloudey drisley day. the peas on the Border are begining to podd. thare is some podds on them & the peas in the Bigg Bed are in Blossom

Thursday 8th ⚓ rain'd thunder'd & Lighten'd smartley in the night. a cold cloudey morning. clear'd away a fine day

1800 Fryday May 9th ⚓ a cloudey morning, sow'd Brussel Cole seed and lettis seed on the Border by the littel house — about 9 o'clock Charles & Marriah Pitt sett of in John Barbers packett for Baltimore. a cold cloudey day

Saturday 10th ⚓ very cold rainey morning, and continued very cold, cloudey, & drislin at times all day

Sunday 11th ⚓ betwen 2 & 3 oclock this afternoon Hyram came Home from Baltimore in the Packett. a fine day

Munday 12th ⚓ about 5 oclock in the afternoon Charles and Abee, Marriah & Miss Faney Jackson[9] came from Baltimore in a stage. a fine day

Tuseday 13th ⚓ a very warm day

Wednesday 14th ⚓ a warm day. planted out asters

Thursday 15th ⚓ a warm day

Fryday 16th ⚓ a fine warm day

[9] Possibly the daughter of John Jackson, a mariner who lived on Apple Alley in Fells Point in 1796. Sally Jackson, who may have been related to Fanny, married James Bias at Fells Point in June 1784; members of the Biays (Bias) family also visited the Farises in Annapolis.

Saturday 17th ~ a dull, cloudey drissley coole day

1800 Sunday May 18th ~ a rainey morning, a cloudey drisley day

Munday 19th ~ a fine day

Tuseday 20th ~ a dull cloudey day

Wednesday 21th ~ a fine day. gathered Peas for the first Time

Thursday 22th ~ a cold morning. about 9 oclock Abee, Miss Jackson & Charles sett of in a stage for Baltimore. continued a cool day

Fryday 23th ~ a fine day. in the evening Charles returned from Baltimore in the stage. left Left Nancy pitt and Fameley all well

Saturday 24th ~ a fine day. the old Bee hive swarmed to day

Sunday 25th ~ a fine day. in the evening I putt an emty Hive under the old Hive

Munday 26th ~ Hyram sett of this morning for Thomas Woodwards in prince george's. a fine day

1800 Tuseday May 27th ~ a fine day

Wednesday 28th ~ a fine day, the Bees in the second Hive came out 3 times to day and went Back again. in the evening I put an emty hive under, in the evening Hyram returned from Thomas Woodwards. a fine day

Thursday 29th ~ a fine day

Fryday 30th ~ a dull drisley day. I sow'd more senssitive plant seed

Saturday 31th ~ a warm Fine morning. about noon the Bees of second old Hive swarm'd the 8 time. 7 times thay swarmed and went back again but wee have hive'd them noow and put them in thare place if thay will but stay. in the evening looks like for rain. in the evening I Planted 4 Chrysanthemum Indicums in Flower beds

Sunday June 1th ~ a cloudey rainey day

Munday 2th ~ a fine day

Tuseday 3th ~ a fine day. about noon wee had a fine shower of rain. the Bees swarm'd. I hived them in a Flower Barrel

Wednesday 4th ✍ a fine day

1800 Thursday June 5th ✍ in the afternoon the Bees swarm'd. I hive'd them in a Flower Barrel. a fine day

Fryday 6th ✍ Betwen 8 & 9 oclock, my ungratefell son Hyram left me to go to Baltimore and I never expect to see him more,[10] a fine day, in the evening about 9 oclock Abee returned from Baltimore. she left her sister and Fameley all well

Saturday 7th ✍ this afternoon I had another swarm of Bees. this makes 5 swarms out of two Hives. a fine day

Sunday 8th ✍ a fine day

Munday 9th ✍ this morning betwen 7 & 8 oclock Charles Rebacca & littel Marriah sett of in Mr. Warfs Boat for Baltimore. a fine day but very littel wind

Tuseday 10th ✍ Mrs. Elizabeth Maccubin[11] died Last night or this morning. a fine day

1800 Wednesday June 11th ✍ betwen 10 & 11 oclock Mrs. Elizabeth Maccubin was Buried a warm day. in the evening it looks as if wee should have rain

Thursday 12th ✍ a warm day

Fryday 13th ✍ a very warm day. in the evening wee had a littel shower of rain

Saturday 14th ✍ a very warm day

Sunday 15th ✍ a fine morning. about noon clouded up and rain'd a littel. in the afternoon Charles and Marriah returned home from Baltimore. left his sisters and Mr. pitt and fameley all well. still cloudey and rains at times

Munday 16th ✍ a rainey night and morning, planted the Big Bed whare the peas grew with plants. a fine day

Tuseday 17th ✍ a dull cloudey day

Wednesday 18th ✍ this morning Miss Nancy Ashmead sett off in Barbers packett for Baltimore on her way to Philladelphia, a cloudey rainey morning and continued cloudey & raining at times all day

1800 Thursday June 19th ✍ a cloudey drisley day. in the evening the sun sett clear

[10] Faris will never see Hyram again.

[11] Elizabeth Creagh Maccubbin, the daughter of Patrick Creagh, widow of Richard Maccubbin (1716–1779), and mother of James (see 7 July 1793). She held two lots between King George and Prince George Streets inherited from her father. § Faris's second shop was on Prince George Street opposite Patrick Creagh's house.

[12] Nicholas Brewer (1771–1839) was the son of tavern keeper Joseph Brewer (1745–1790) and his wife Jane Brewer (b.1746) and the brother of John Brewer (see below). Sarah Allen Maccubbin (c.1774–1836), his second wife, was his cousin, the daughter of Dr. John and Eleanor Allen; she had married Charles Maccubbin (1756–1798) in 1793 (see 12 May). An attorney, Brewer served as a member of the executive council, delegate to the General Assembly, judge of the orphans court, registrar of the chancery court, and army paymaster during the War of 1812. § Brewer bought a pair of andirons and one book at the sale of Faris's property.

[13] Elizabeth McClellan, whose daughter Ann married John Wilmot (1752–1807). She owned a house and lot on School Street, purchased in 1774, where the Wilmots lived and which she willed to her grandson, John. Both Elizabeth and Ann signed the inventory of Capt. John Stewart (see 27 December 1792) as next of kin; Elizabeth may have been a sister of Stewart's or related to his wife Margaret.

[14] John Brewer (1778–1827) was the son of Joseph and Jane Brewer (see above). An attorney, he served as register of the Western Shore land office and as clerk of the house of delegates from 1805 to 1811 and from 1818 to 1826. Elizabeth Gaston (1784–1820) was the daughter of George and Ann Drane Gaston (see 15 July 1798). She inherited the lots near the corner of Cathedral and West Streets, down the block from Faris, that her father purchased in 1772. § At the sale of the Faris estate, Brewer bought two books.

[15] Probably Maj. Joseph Biays of Fells Point, whose daughter Mary visited the Faris family a number of times (see 18 August 1798). After his wife Elizabeth died in March 1800 at the age of forty-two, Biays married Mrs. Hannah Gantner in October 1801.

Fryday 20th ✒ a fine day

Saturday 21th ✒ a dull cloudey day

Sunday 22th ✒ a fine day. in the evening turn'd cloudey & Nicholas Brewer was married to Mrs. Sarah Maccubin the widdow of the late Mr. Charles Maccubin[12]

Munday 23th ✒ a fine day. I have been very unwell all day

Tuseday 24th ✒ a fine day

Wednesday 25th ✒ a fine day

Thursday 26th ✒ a fine day

Fryday 27th ✒ a very warm day, Mrs. McClening[13] died Last night and was Buried this evening

Saturday 28th ✒ a very Hott Night Last night and a very Hott morning and continued so all day

1800 Sunday June 29th ✒ a fine day. in the evening John Brewer was married to Miss Elizabeth Gastin[14]

Munday 30th ✒ a fine day. in the evening Mr. Josep Byas[15] drank Tea & spent the evening

Tuseday July 1th ✒ a fine Pleasant day. thare is a report about that Mr. Jefferson is dead but I don't beleve it's True

Wednesday 2th ✒ Charles sett off this after noon to see the Federal City. a fine day

Thursday 3th ✒ a fine day but coole for the season

Fryday 4th ✒ a dull morning. in the afternoon a fine rain

Saturday 5th ✒ a fine day

Sunday 6th ✒ a very warm day. in the afternoon Charles returned from the City of Washington

Munday 7th ✒ a warm day

[There were no entries for the 8th and 9th.]

Thursday 10th ✒ a very warm day. Mr & Mrs. pitt & Rebac Faris & the child came to see the Fameley. thay are all Harty. I had been very unwell since Sunday night and am very unwell still

1800 Fryday July 11th ☞ a very Hott day. I am still very unwell

Saturday 12th ☞ betwen 8 & 9 oclock Mr. & Mrs. Pitt, Rebaca & littel Hannah sett of for Baltimore, this after noon I took up the Tuleps that was sown the 16th of Augt 96. I am very unwell to day. a warm day

Sunday 13th ☞ I had a Feaveor to day. I have been wors to day then I have been since I have been unweel. a warm day. this afternoon I was ellectrefyd. I obtained 5 or 6 Loos stools by it

Munday 14th ☞ a cloudey morning. Charles cutt the Baulm. it looks very like for rain

Tuseday 15th ☞ a fine day

Wednesday 16th ☞ a cold dull cloudey morning and continued so all day

Thursday 17th ☞ a coole day

Fryday 18th ☞ a fine day but very warm

Saturday 19th ☞ a very warm day

1800 Sunday July 20th ☞ a very Hott day

Munday 21th ☞ wee had a cleaver rain Last night — I planted the big bed with plants and had the littel quarter dig up and Planted it with plants. Sylve's How'd the greens and is Howing the parsneps. a cloudey mistey day, took up the Leeks, came on to rain

Tuseday 22th ☞ a rainey morning. continued a rainey day

Wednesday 23th ☞ a cloudey drisley morning, planted the Leeks. dug up the littel quarter by the old stabel and planted it with Beens. a fine after noon

Thursday 24th ☞ a fine day

Fryday 25th ☞ took up the roshembole onions, and the common onions and the roshembole seed onions. a very warm day

Saturday 26th ☞ a very Hott day. in the afternoon looks like for rain, wee had a littel rain

Sunday 27th ☞ a very Hott day. Mr. Fredrick Gramer[16] informs me that in his countrey it is a rule to clean out the Bee hives on the 22th of February

[16] In subsequent years, Faris always cleaned out his bee hives on 22 February, weather permitting. Frederick Grammar (c.1751–1818), a native of Germany and a baker, was in Annapolis by 1783. Grammar lived on Southeast Street in a one-story frame dwelling with a brick bake house and frame kitchen and stable. Sometime shortly after 1790, he built the three-story brick building at the corner of Church and Green Streets, where Lewis Neth (see 15 May 1792) had his store. Grammar was one of the managers in 1790 for the lottery to raise funds to complete St. Anne's; filled the balance of Charles Faris's term as councilman after Charles's death and then served a second term; and was a city commissioner in 1806. Grammar announced in July 1807 that ill health forced him to retire, but that his son Henry would continue the business, selling spirits, groceries, etc. The *Gazette* reported on 29 October 1818 that Grammar died on the 15th at Pleasant Plains, his residence on the Severn River, in his 67th year. § Faris bought bread, tea, and brandy from Grammar between 1794 and 1801, and collected £0.16.10 from Grammar in February 1802 as administrator of Charles's estate.

[There were no entries from 28 July to 19 August.]

1800 Wednesday Augt 20th ✒ a fine day but no news from Baltimore

Thursday 21th ✒ Mr. Pitt & his Famely & Charles has come in Mr. Pitts Boate to the mouth of the Dock last night and was thare stapt by the gard and remaind thare all night. this morning the committe mett and thay all came on shore. thay left my Poor dear Rebaca Behind. she died on Tuseday last the 19th of a Billious Feveour.[17] I had forgot poor old Mrs. Pitt, she is with them. thay are all Bravely, better then I expected. a fine day

Fryday 22th ✒ littel hannah is rather Poorley to day. she has a littel Feveour, the rest are all braveley. a fine warm day

Saturday 23th ✒ Mr Pitt went of in his Boat this morning for the capes. a fine day. the fameley are all Bravely except Salley.[18] she still complains a littel

Sunday 24th ✒ I have had a bad lax and griping all night and this morning. I am very unwell. I am afraid Charles is going to be sick, he complains a grate deal I have given him 8 grains of callimell and [illegible]. he has gone to Bed, a dull rainey dissagreeable morning

1800 Munday Augt 25th ✒ Charles is very unwell. he has a smart Feveour, I am better to day. I took a dose of rubarb[19] this morning. it work'd me very littel. a cloudey day. in the after noon whee had a littel rain. it looks as if wee should have more before morning

Tuseday 26th ✒ Charles is better to day, my gripeing continues — a fine day

Wednesday 27th ✒ A Charles is still very poorley and I have Been a good deel griped to day. this morning I took castor oil. it did not woorke me. a very Hott day

Thursday 28th ✒ this morning Nancey receivd a letter from her Brother Hyram dated the 26th. he says that he shall go on Board in 4 or 5 Hour on board the ship Commerce Capt. Tompson[20] Bound to Amsterdam.[21] Charles is Bravely to day. my gripeing & lax still continues, Charles is very week and low. this after noon he gott up and walk'd 3 o[r] 4 steps to a chair and fainted through the exces-

---

[17] The Fells Point area was particularly hard hit by yellow fever in the epidemic of 1800, which began with an outbreak in mid-August. The *Federal Gazette* reported on 22 August that "On Fell's Point we find an inflammatory bilious fever now exists—it first made its appearance along the water next to the cove . . . and progressing gradually up Bond and Fleet Streets, and thence spread in various directions into other adjacent streets." By 20 August there had been 15 deaths, with another 112 persons ill. Fever deaths totaled 1,197 that year, nearly 5 percent of the city's population, and nearly half of those deaths (47 percent) occurred in Fells Point. The Pitt family must have remained in the city only as long as necessary to care for Rebecca, who would have been too ill to travel.

[18] Sally was not one of the Pitts' children; she may have been the girl who was bound out to them or she may have been a slave.

[19] The dried rhizome and root of *Rheum officinale*, used in a fluid extract or aromatic tincture as a purgative.

[20] Three (possibly four) Thompsons lived in Baltimore who might have been the captain of the *Commerce*: John, a mariner, who lived in Welcome Alley in 1800, and who may have been the Capt. John Thompson who married Mary Smith in May 1801; Capt. William, who married a Mrs. Anderson in August 1797; and Capt. Thomas, who married Mary Fomes in November 1801.

[21] Hyram will be the second of Faris's sons to die at sea, on 30 August aboard the *Commerce*, undoubtedly also a victim of the yellow fever epidemic that claimed his sister and brother. The *Federal Gazette* carried a notice on the 27th that the letter bag of the ship *Commerce*, for Amsterdam, to sail on the 30th, was up at the coffee house.

sive heat of the weather and his weakness to geather. it has been a very Hott day

Fryday 29th ✒ wee had a clever rain last night. Charles is better to day but he is extreem week & low. I think that I am better to day. a fine day

1800 Saturday Augt 30th ✒ Charles is clear of a Feveour but is very weeak and low all most in a stupid state. Charles is much worse to day, so much that the Doctr has no hopes of his recovery but while thare is life thar is hopes,

Munday Septr 1th ✒ about 2 oclock this morning my son Charles Faris died of the Yellow Fever in 36 year of his age.[22] a fine day

Tuseday 2th ✒ a fine day

Wednesday 3th ✒ a fine day. in the after noon I was taken with an ague

Thursday 4th ✒ after my Fever went of I had a prefuse swett the remainder of the night. I feel myself better this morning. I have taken a dose of castor oyl. I have sow'd early York & other cabbage seed on the Border next the Burgemot Balm, in the after noon I sow'd in a Box in the yard the Dutch Tulip seed I got from Doctr Scott. a dull coole day

[There were no entries from 5 September to 8 September. In this case, Faris himself was too ill to write.]

1800 Tuseday Septr 9th ✒ I missed my ague and Feveour last night, and am in hopes I sall soon get well and strong for I am at present very weeak. a fine day

Wednesday 10th ✒ I am very weeak and low yett. Billee has been cleaning out the shop,[23] a fine day but coole. in the evening looks like for rain

Thursday 11th ✒ a coole fine day

Fryday 12th ✒ a fine day

Saturday 13th ✒ a fine day. I have been mooveing the things from the lower shop

Sunday 14th ✒ Bille went out yesterday evening and I have seen nothing of him since.[24] a fine day

Munday 15th ✒ soon after diner Mr. & Mrs. Pitt sett of in thare Boat for the capes. a fine day

Tuseday 16th ✒ a fine day

[22] Charles's death ended his service as a councilman and as a militia company officer. His father placed a notice of administration of his estate in the *Gazette* on 15 October, and requested "those who have books belonging to the deceased, that they would immediately return them." The appraisers of Charles's estate, John Randall and Vachel Stevens, counted 86 volumes as well as three volumes of newspapers and a Bible when they recorded his possessions in the fall.

[23] William McParlin now became William Faris's apprentice.

[24] The first in a series of incidents of misbehavior on McParlin's part. Faris appears to have taken them with better grace than one might expect, given his quarrels with his own sons.

Wednesday 17th ✍ a fine day. Billee came home this morning

Thursday 18th ✍ a fine day

Fryday 19th ✍ a fine day but very dry

1800 Saturday Septr 20th ✍ a dull cloudey day. looks like for rain

Sunday 21th ✍ a cloudey drisley day. still looks like for rain

Munday 22th ✍ a dull cloudey day

Tuseday 23th ✍ a coole dull, cloudey day

Wednesday 24th ✍ still dull cloudey weather

Thursday 25th ✍ a Blustering rainey day

Fryday 26th ✍ a dull cloudey day

Saturday 27th ✍ a rainey day

Sunday 28th ✍ a cloudey day. I had a smart fitt of the ague & Fever

Munday 29th ✍ a fine day

Tuseday 30th ✍ a fine day. I had a fitt of ye ague and fever

Wednesday Octr 1th ✍ I Planted my seedling Tulips on the Border next to Mr. Ridgly's. a fine day

Thursday 2th ✍ Planted the Tulip & Hyacinth of setts from Doctr Scott. a fine day. in the evening wee had a littel rain

1800 Fryday Octr 3th ✍ a fine day

Saturday 4th ✍ this morning agot 120 Bushels of James River Coal at 1/10 pr Bushel.[25] a fine morning. in the after noon clouded up & looks like for rain

Sunday 5th ✍ a rainey night & rainey day & the wind Blows very Hard

Munday 6th ✍ this morning the ellection came on. the candidates whare John Johnson, Allen Quynn, P. B. Key. in the evening ye court adjurn'd the ellection untill to morrow 10 oclock. a very cold clear day

Tuseday 7th ✍ I putt up the grate in the stove to day, a clear cold day. Mr. Pitts Boate call'd here last

[25] Faris paid £11.5.0 for the coal plus the cost of carting it to his property.

night on Her way to the capes, she went off
directley. she did not stay an Hour

Wednesday 8th ✍ a fine clear day

Thursday 9th ✍ a fine day, in the evening the ellection was clos'd, when Mr. Quynn & Mr. Johnson
ware ellected, Mr. Key was left out, Mr. Delandel[26]
died last night and was Buried this evening

Fryday 10th ✍ a fine day

Saturday 11th ✍ a fine day

1800 Sunday Octr 12th ✍ a dull cloudey day

Munday 13th ✍ a dull drissley day

Tuseday 14th ✍ a coole clear day. William Maw[27]
died last night

Wednesday 15th ✍ a clear morning. in the after
noon clouded up and rain'd a littel. this evening
William Maw was Buried

Thursday 16th ✍ a rainey night & morning. cleard
away a fine after noon

Fryday 17th ✍ a fine day

Saturday 18th ✍ this morning earley Mr. & Mrs.
Pitt & child and Miss Williams[28] all came up from
the capes in his Boate. all right well and Harty. a
cloudey dissagreeable day

Sunday 19th ✍ last night it rained Blowd very hard
and continued so all the fore noon, in the after noon
cleared away but continued to Blow Hard, for the
first time this fall wee had a fire in the House

Munday 20th ✍ a fine day. this morning Mr. pitt
went of for Baltimore

Tuseday 21th ✍ a warm fine day. this after noon
Mr. Pitt returned from Baltimore

1800 Wednesday Octr 22th ✍ after Brackfast Mr.
pitt sett of for the capes. a fine warm day. in the
evening rain & thunder & lightening

Thursday 23th ✍ raind all night and a rainey
morning and continued a rayney day

Fryday 24th ✍ a fine day

Saturday 25th ✍ a fine day

Sunday 26th ✍ a fine day

[26] Francis Mary De la Landelle
advertised in the 10 May 1798
Maryland Gazette that he had purchased the store of William
Alexander and now offered groceries and two slaves for sale.
When he earlier wrote his will in
March, he was living in Allegany
County. De la Landelle was survived by his wife, Mary Emily
Sainte, and left an estate appraised
at $667. According to his tomb-
stone, De la Landelle was a native
of Brittany.

[27] William Maw was one of the
four sons of widow Elizabeth Maw,
who died in 1779. She named
William as her executor with her
"friend Allen Quynn" (see 9
September 1792). § Maw was a
shoemaker from whom Faris
bought five pairs of shoes in 1790
and 1791.

[28] Perhaps a friend of the Pitts
from Baltimore or possibly a sister
or cousin of Pitt's first wife,
Hannah Williams.

29 John Walraven (1771–1814) was a silver-smith in Baltimore, active from about 1792 until his death, and the maker of a creampot engraved "WAP," for William and Ann Faris Pitt. The exact nature of his business relationship with Charles is unknown. Faris's estate paid him £8.13.3 "as per judgment of a single magistrate."

132 ✒ *This fluted cream pot was made by Baltimore silversmith John Walraven ca. 1800. This cream pot could have been part of Charles's estate or perhaps was purchased by William and Ann Faris Pitt when they were living in Baltimore.*

30 Edward Holland (1763–1810) was the son of Edward Holland (1737–10795) and his wife Sarah, and the brother of Isaac Holland (see 15 May 1802). He married Mary Simson in December 1793. Holland held a number of city offices, including market clerk, constable, and chimney sweep. § Faris recorded payments in his daybook to Holland for carting 7 loads of dung in September 1800 and for a half bushel of mortar in November 1801.

Munday 27th ✒ this fore noon Mr. Walraven[29] call'd heare and I setteled with him what was betwen him & my son Charles. wee settel'd very smothly. he appears to be very cleaver. a fine day

Tuseday 28th ✒ a fine day

Wednesday 29th ✒ a fine day. in the evening clouded up and looks like for rain

Thursday 30th ✒ a coole dull day

Fryday 31th ✒ a dull cloudey day

1800 Novr 1th ✒ a dull cloudey day

Sunday 2th ✒ a fine day

Munday 3th ✒ a fine day. receiv'd a letter from my son William in Edenton North Carrolinga directet to Mr. William Pitt

Tuseday 4th ✒ a fine day

Wednesday 5th ✒ a fine day. in the evening clouded up like for rain

Thursday 6th ✒ a clear coole day

Fryday 7th ✒ a fine day

Saturday 8th ✒ a fine day

Sunday 9th ✒ a foggey cloudey day

Munday 10th ✒ a fine day

Tuseday 11th ✒ a fine day

Wednesday 12th ✒ a cloudey day. in the evening Mrs. Weeden was Buried

1800 Thursday Novr 13th ✒ this morning Mrs. Pitt sent Edward Hollond[30] exspess to Baltimore to enquire after Mr. Pitt. in the after noon Mr. Pitt arrived heare right well and harty. raind hard in the night. a cloudey morning but clear'd away a fine after noon

Fryday 14th ✒ a dull cloudey day

Saturday 15th ✒ I was taken an ague & a lax yesterday. I am very poorly to day with a lax & straining. a fine clear day

Sunday 16th ✒ I am bravely to day. a dull cloudey day. Billee gott Tipsey and in the evening he told Mrs. Faris that he wanted a candel to trascribe some musick[31] but instead of Transscribing musick he Bundeled up his cloaths and went of with him self. Mr. Pitt & my self went in search of him. wee met him in the street by the Ball house.[32] he was very saussey. wee brought him home & sent him to bed

Munday 17th ☛ Mr. & Mrs. pitt & Famely went off after Brackfast this morning for Baltimore. when thay ware gone I call on Billee to tell me whare he had left his clothes. he attended and told me he did not know whare thay ware. I took the cow skin down & declared I would give him a seaver whiping if he did not Immediatly tell me whare thay ware, he after a littel while thought better of it and told thay ware at McNemarrows (all the raskal Macnemarrow declard the evening before to Mr. Pitt & my self that he had not been thare ever since Mrs. Faris forbid him letting coming to his house). he and I went thare . Billee asked him for the things he left thare. at first he denied that thay ware thare but Billee insisted on it that he left them thare, thay then confissed that thay ware thare but would not give give them to me then but would bring to me in half an Houre. I & Bille came of and about half an Hour after Macnemarra Brought the things to my House to me. a fine day. Bille Promised to behave well for the futer and never to do the like again and so I Passed it over

Tuseday 18th ☛ a clear cold windey day

Wednesday 19th ☛ a clear cold day

Thursday 20th ☛ a dull cold cloudey day and in the evening snow'd

1800 Fryday Novr 21th ☛ snow'd all night and this morning a littel. clear'd away a clear cold day. in the evening I moved the Cryanthyeum Indicums into the seller & the Jeruselum Cherrey Trees

Saturday 22th ☛ a cold cloudey day

Sunday 23th ☛ a cloudey day. in the evening Mr. Lewes Duvall was married to Miss Sarah Harwood daugter of Mr. Nicholas Harwood[33]

Munday 24th ☛ a clear cold day

Tuseday 25th ☛ a clear cold day

Wednesday 26th ☛ a dull cloudey day look'd like for snow

Thursday 27th ☛ a dull day

31 The Faris Music Book Collection at the Maryland State Archives (MSA SC 2551) contains a photocopy of the "Musical Notebook of William Faris" (perhaps the music book listed in Faris's inventory). The book itself is inscribed as John Wade's book ("John Wade. Eius Liber") with the date 1764, and most of the music in the book consists of tunes popular in the 1760s. But the name "William," in a childish hand, appears on the front cover and the name "McParlin" elsewhere. Several pieces of music apparently date from a period later than the 1760s: "March of the College Infantry," "The College Artillery's Minuet," and "Annapolis March," as well as "The Dublin Minuet" (characterized as an "unusual" title, but the Irish-born William McParlin perhaps knew it well). The evidence suggests that McParlin used an older music book of John Wade's—who may have been a musician who performed in Faris's tavern—to transcribe a few tunes of his time. Kate Keller's analysis of the book notes that the "Annapolis March" may have been "an attempt to write down something heard." McParlin, like Faris, may have attended the militia exercises and parades that took place on the St. John's College campus, and transcribed the music that he heard played on those occasions. (Kate V. Keller, personal communication, 29 January and 5 February 2001.)

32 On Southeast Street, several blocks from Faris's home.

33 Lewis Duvall (1776–1829) was the son of Zachariah and Jemima Duvall. Sarah Ann Harwood was the daughter of Nicholas Harwood (see 29 April 1792). Duvall served four terms on the executive council, was an Annapolis delegate to the General Assembly from 1811 to 1816 and from 1819 to 1820, and was mayor of Annapolis from 1819 until his resignation in December 1823. He was a merchant, in partnership in the 1790s first with Robert Duvall and then with Zachariah Duvall. Duvall died in November 1829, leaving "a large family." § Charles Faris's estate paid Duvall £1.16.2. Duvall bought a quarter clock, a pair of files, and "sundry" swords at the sale of Faris's estate.

Fryday 28th ✒ this morning I took up the Jacobin Lilley roots, took up 6 radishes & Buryed them in sand in a Barrel in the seller. a fine day

Saturday 29th ✒ a fine day

1800 Novr 30th Sunday ✒ a cold cloudey dull day

Munday Desr 1th ✒ a fine day. in the evening covered the rosemarey

Tuseday 2th ✒ a fine clear cold day

Wednesday 3th ✒ a fine day

Thursday 4th ✒ a cloudey rainey day

Fryday 5th ✒ a Blustering rainey day

Saturday 6th ✒ a snowey night & continued snowing allmost all day. in the evening the sun fame out fine

Sunday 7th ✒ a fine morning. about 12 oclock clouded up and cloudey the remainder of the day

Munday 8th ✒ a cloudey morning & continued a cloudey day

Tuseday 9th ✒ a clear cold day

Wednesday 10th ✒ a fine day

Thursday 11th ✒ a drisley cloudey day

1800 Fryday Desr 12th ✒ last night it rain'd Hard and Blew a near storm, it has rain'd Hailed & snow'd at Intervells all day

Saturday 13th ✒ a Blustering windey night. a clear cold day

Sunday 14th ✒ a clear cold day

Munday 15th ✒ a clear cold day

Tuseday 16th ✒ a fine day

Wednesday 17th ✒ a fine day

Thursday 18th ✒ a fine day

Fryday 19th ✒ a dull cloudey day. this evening the Assembley Brok up

Saturday 20th ✒ rained Hard last night, a drisley cloudey morning. in the afternoon cleard away a fine afternoon

Sunday 21th ✒ a fine day

1800 Munday Desr 22th ✍ Mr. Pitt & Capt. Ginneo[34] came heare to day & dined with us. thay ware on thare way to the capes. thay went of in the after noon. a fine day

Tuseday 23th ✍ a fine day — Mr. pitt was heare this evening & drank Tea

Wednesday 24th ✍ I beleive Mr. pitt gone down the Bay this morning. the wind's got to the west ward. a fine day

Thursday 25th ✍ a cloudey dull day. Mr. Mynards wife[35] was Buried this evening

Fryday 26th ✍ a warm cloudey dull day

Saturday 27th ✍ a fine morning. in the afternoon clouded up & came on to rain. a wett afternoon and night but warm

Sunday 28th ✍ rain'd all last night & continued raining all day

Munday 29th ✍ Frose hard last night. a fine clear cold day

1800 Tuseday Desr 30th ✍ a cloudey day

Wednesday 31th ✍ a dull cloudey day

1801 Thursday January 1th ✍ a dull cloudey day

Fryday 2th ✍ a clear cold day

Saturday 3th ✍ last night very cold & to days the coldest day wee have had the winter. this morning a House by Severon Ferrey was Burnt[36]

Sunday 4th ✍ a very cold snowe night. this morning the ground was cover'd with snow, a snowe cold day

Munday 5th ✍ a clear cold day

Tuseday 6th ✍ a clear cold day

Wednesday 7th ✍ a dull cloudey day

Thursday 8th ✍ dull cloudey weather. in the afternoon clear and cold

Fryday 9th ✍ Mr. William Walker died to day. a fine day

1801 Saturday January 10th ✍ a fine day

34 Faris's entry appears to be either Ginneo or Ginnes, but no such individual appears in any record. Perhaps this visitor was the Samuel H. Ginnodo who married Eliza Skinner, both of Baltimore, in March 1809, or he may have been Capt. Nicholas Ginson, who lived in Baltimore in 1800.

35 Elizabeth Wilmot Maynard, the wife of James Pelham Maynard.

36 Daniel Fowler (c.1755–1819) was bound to John Howard in August 1772 at the age of 17 as an apprentice to learn the trade of a shoemaker. Of this fire, the *Gazette* reported: "On Sat morning last, the dwelling house of Mr. Daniel Fowler of this city took fire on the roof and was entirely consumed." The Annapolis end of the Severn ferry, where Fowler lived, was located near the end of Northeast Street. In 1801, Fowler bought a one-story frame house on East Street, between Prince George and King George Streets. Fowler married Mary Smith in August 1810. She survived him as did two of his three adult children. § Fowler bought one fishing line machine and a bench vise at the sale of Faris's property.

Sunday 11th ✒ a fine morning. about 11 oclock clouded up & continued a cloudey day

Munday 12th ✒ Billee went to wind the clocks too day as usual,[37] came home tipsey. betwen 12 & 1 oclock I went in the House, I returne'd into the shop some time after & I saw he had a watch to peaces. I asked him what watch that was. he told me it was one out of the window & that it wanted a new dovetail. I told him that he was very careless not to see that when he had her to peaces. I took the plate from him to look at it, I discover'd I did not recolect the makers name. I refer'd to the Book and could find no such name in the Book. he told me to let him look, at that time I was call'd to diner. when I returned after diner I did not see the watch. I asked him ware the watch was. he told me that he had thrown her away. I ask'd him whare, he said over the fence into Mrs. Davidson Lot. I asked him whose watch it was. he told me that Kerkwood[38] gave her to him and desired him to do her for him on his own accot. a fine day

1801 Tuseday Janry 13th ✒ this morning I talked to Billee about the watch, he saw fitt to tell me whare she was & went & got her. he had put her under my room in the lott. a fine day

Wednesday 14th ✒ a fine day

Thursday 15th ✒ a cloudey rainey day

Fryday 16th ✒ a fine day. trimed the Rose Bushes

Saturday 17th ✒ a fine day

Sunday 18th ✒ a fine day

Munday 19th ✒ a cloudey rainey day

Tuseday 20th ✒ a cloudey windey day

Wednesday 21th ✒ a fine clear day

Thursday 22th ✒ a fine day

Fryday 23th ✒ a fine day

1801 Saturday 24th ✒ a windey sleettey bad night and very disagreeable to day. the wind blows Hard & rain & sleets all day

Sunday 25th ✒ a cold snowey day. in the afternoon the sun came out

Munday 26th ✒ a cloudey day

[37] Faris was responsible for winding a number of clocks in town: those at the governor's residence and a dozen or so privately owned clocks.

[38] Peter Kirkwood (d.1801), a silversmith, worked from 1790 to c.1795 in Chestertown and from 1798 to 1801 in Annapolis. Faris's account book records payments to Kirkwood in 1799 and 1800 for work done for him. Kirkwood's tasks included making knee buckles, teaspoons, a pair of silver earrings, and new tops for a pair of spectacles as well as mending jewelry. In November 1801 Faris bought "chamber bellesses" [bellows?] at the sale of Kirkwood's estate.

Tuseday 27th ✍ this afternoon Mr. & Mrs. Pitt Miss Williams, my littel Hannah pitt & the littel girl to tend her came heare about 3 oclock from Baltimore. a fine day

Wednesday 28th ✍ a dull cloudey day

Thursday 29th ✍ a Blustering, rainey morning. in the after noon clear'd away fine, betwen 2 & 3 oclock Mr. & Mrs. Pitt & Famely sett of for Baltimore. all very Harty and well

Fryday 30th ✍ a fine day

Saturday 31th ✍ a fine day

1801 Sunday Febry 1th ✍ a fine day

Munday 2th ✍ a snowey Night & morning. a cloudey snowey, drisley day

Tuseday 3th ✍ a dull cloudey morning. about 12 oclock clear'd away a fine afternoon

Wednesday 4th ✍ a dull coudey day

Thursday 5th ✍ a fine day

Fryday 6th ✍ a fine day. last night Mrs. Randel wife of Mr. John Randel, was Brought to bed with a fine Boy

Saturday 7th ✍ a fine day

Sunday 8th ✍ a fine day. this evening Cornelious Mills's wife was Buried

Munday 9th ✍ dugg the Border next Mr. Ridgely's & dugg up the Althea & Laylack Bushes and planted two Laylack Bushes one in each corner of the Bed next the asparagrass Beds. a fine day

1801 Tuseday 10th ✍ this morning the ground was cover'd with snow & continued snowing all day

Wednesday 11th ✍ continued snowing all night and all day and it looks as likeley to continue as it did yesterday. this after noon a yung man by the name of Nathaniel Smith called heare to let us know that he was just from Edenton North Carrolina, that he was acquainted with my son William, thay Boarded in the same house together, and he tells me that my son has been in Edenton upwards of two years past & that he has 40 or 50 watches in his window[39]

39 Nevertheless, there are no known surviving pieces—clocks, watches, or silverware—made by William Faris Jr.

Thursday 12th ✍ a clear cold day

Fryday 13th ✍ a dull cloudey morning. about 12 oclock came on to snow & snow'd all the afternoon

Saturday 14th ✍ a clear cold day

Sunday 15th ✍ a clear cold day

Munday 16th ✍ a clear cold day

1801 Tuseday Febry 17th ✍ cloudey day. in the evening rain

Wednesday 18th ✍ rainey morning. wee have an accot that Mr. Jefferson is ellected president.[40] a rainey day

Thursday 19th ✍ a fine clear day. I walked by Mr. Hanson's garden this after noon. I saw his man adiging a Bed. he told me it was for peas

Fryday 20th ✍ a cloudey morning. about 12 cleared away a fine after noon

Saturday 21th ✍ a fine morning

Saturday 21th ✍ a fine day ✍ [double entry in original]

Sunday 22th ✍ this morning I cleaned the Bee Hives. a clear cold day

Munday 23th ✍ a clear coole day

1801 Tuseday Febry 24th ✍ this morning sow'd 16 rows of Peas on the Border next to Mr. Ridgly's and betwen the Peas I have sow'd spinige & some radish seed & at the end of the new stabel I have sowed cabbage seed, from D Wells Senr[41] & scatterd some lettice seed with it. a fine day

Wednesday 25th ✍ I trimed the goosberrey & curren Bushes & Sylve dug the Border next to Mrs. Davidsons. a fine day

Thursday 26th ✍ Planted a Pear Tree in the yard, from Mr. Stevens. a fine day

Fryday 27th ✍ Planted the roshembole onions on the Border nex to Mrs. Davidsons. a fine day

Saturday 28th ✍ a fine day

Sunday March 1th ✍ a fine morning. about noon turned cloudey & in the evening looks like for Bad weather comeing

40 The *Gazette* carried the news the following day, having learned of it from "a gentleman that arrived yesterday from the city of Washington." Jefferson and Burr had received the same number of votes when the electoral college met, requiring a vote by the House of Representatives (with each state's delegation casting a single vote) to choose between them. It required many ballots through the winter before Jefferson achieved the majority vote in his favor.

41 Daniel Wells Sr., an Annapolis butcher, was probably related to John and Richard Wells, who also appear in the diary. Wells and his wife Susannah (c.1745–1821) had nine children, three of whom—John, Frederick, and Richard—enrolled in the St. John's grammar school. The oldest son, William, married Susannah Gaston, widow of Thomas (see 23 February 1793) in 1794, and Wells's daughter Sarah Jane was the wife of John Hyde (see 15 November 1793). § As noted in the entry for John Wells, Faris made many purchases of beef, veal, lamb, and mutton from Daniel and his son Daniel Jr. Only with Daniel Sr. did he also exchange seeds or plants.

1801 Munday March 2th ✍ a dull drisley morning. I sent by John Barber 4 wascoats for Mr. Pitt, a pair stockings for Salley, & a gun — I have trimed the sage this morning & began Troweling the Tulep in ye nursserey Beds. we had a gust of rain this evening with sharp thunder & lightening

Tuseday 3th ✍ Billee has been troweling to day. he has finished the Nurssery Beds & has don them very well a fine day — Sylve has begun diging the big Bead this after noon

Wednesday 4th ✍ Sylve's diging the Big Bed but has not finished it. a clear cool day

Thursday 5th ✍ I got a man to cut the Willow Tree down. it fell the rong way and lodged against the play House. a cold cloudey drisley day. Sylve finished diging the Big Bed this morning before Brackfast. in the evening it snow'd a littel and turnd to rain

Fryday 6th ✍ rain'd all Night & continued raining all day & looks likely to continue

Saturday 7th ✍ a clear coole day, I gott the willow Tree down to day & cutt up without aney accident

1801 Sunday March 8th ✍ a cloudey morning cleard away a clear cold day

Munday 9th ✍ sowed 4 rows of Peas in the big Bed & Bille's a Troweling the circel Beds and Sylve's diging the Parsnep Bed in the Lott, a coole day. it frose Hard last night. this morning Daniel Well's Senr daughter Susan died

Tuseday 10th ✍ a fine morning. the peas on the Border are begining to marke thare appearance. Billee has troweled the Beds on the right hand side of the grass walk by diner time. in the after noon he went to Planting of Parsneps. Silve's still diging the Bed. a dull cloudey after noon. betwen 4 & 5 oclock Daniel Wells's daughter was Buried. in the evening it came on to rain

Wednesday 11th ✍ a fine morning. Sylve's don diging the parsnep & carrott Beds & Billee don Planting the carrotts & parsneps before diner. in the after noon he went in the garden to Troweling the flower Beds & Sylve to doing up the assparagrass Beds. she has finished them this evening, about noon it clouded up and wee had several showers of rain. I planted a row of Turnup radishes & a row of radishes on the end of the Big Bed & a row of radishes & a row of turnup radishes from Mr. Sewell on ye end of ye parsnep Bedd

1801 Thursday March 12th ✒ a dull cold windy morning. I planted the Parsnept 9 Inchs from line to line & 6 Inchs from seed to seed & the carrotts 7 Inchs from line to line & 4 Inchs from seed to seed — on the near assparagrass Beds on the end next to Mr. Ridgley's I sowed cabbage seed from D. Wells Senr & on the other end I sow'd the sugar loafed cabbag from Sewell. on the second Bed I sow'd 2 sorts of cabbag from Mrs. Randel & lettice on both Beds & a line of spinige in the walks Betwen the Beds, came on to rain a littel and cold & raw. in the evening the sun came out clear

Fryday 13th ✒ Bille has Finished Troweling the Flower Beds and I planted some Balsom appel seeds at the end of the new stabel, this has been a fine day

Saturday 14th ✒ a rainey day

Sunday 15th ✒ a windey rainey morning. about noon clear'd away

1801 Munday 16th ✒ a fine morning. Sylve's dug a peace on the Border by the Bee hives & I sow'd it with Parsley. Sylve's dug a line on the side of the littel quarter & I planted it with shallotts that Bare thare increes on the top & Sylve's clearing ye goosberrey Bushes of suckers & cleaning the walks. it has been a fine day but in the evening it clouded up & looks like for rain. I sent Nancey Pitts littel Trunk to her in the Packett

Tuseday 17th ✒ Silve's made Hills in the lott for vines. a dull cloudey day. in the evening looks like for rain

Wednesday 18th ✒ a rainey night and continues a rainey morning and continued raining & Blowing hard all day. in the afternoon Mrs. Fyers[42] was Buried, Smith Brought me betwen 30 & 40 cabbage plants & some lettice plants. in the evening I planted them & the sun came out fine a littel before setting

Thursday 19th ✒ a cloudey morning, clear'd away about 9 oclock. I troweled the seedling Tuleps on the Border by the Horse Radish & Billee's troweling The seedling Tuleps on the Border next the street & I planted 2 peas I gott from Mr. Stevens by a Rose

---

[42] Possibly the widow of Richard Tyers, a resident in 1783 who owned neither land nor slaves. His household contained two males (one child) and one female. Tyers appeared in court in March 1784 as a defendant.

Bush, this evening I planted the Jacobian Lilley. its turned cloudey and looks like for more rain

Fryday 20th ↞ a windey cloudey drisley day. in the evening I planted a peach Tree from Mr. Stevens. he says the peaches are ripe in June or begining of July

1801 Saturday March 21th ↞ I got som plants from Mr. Stevens to finis planting the Big Bed. a cloudey drisley windey day

Sunday 22th ↞ cloudey morning, Mr. Ridgely's man did not come yesterday as he promis'd, I thare fore this morning went about it my self. I grafted 5 or 6 Black Curran siances with the Rose grafts, this evening Mr. Samuel Howard's daughter Harvey's to be married to Doctr Tildon of the Eastern Shore[43] — a dull cloudey day

Munday 23th ↞ cloudey morning. made a begining to cut the Box & Silve to finishing the Hills in the lot. she finished them & I planted 12 Hills with simlins 4 with cantilope & 4 with cucumbers, then Silve dugg the littel quarter by the new stabel and Dick has been picking up the cutting of Box of the Beds. a dull cloudey day

Tuseday 24th ↞ cloudey morning, after diner wee finished the Box round the grass walk & Bille's began the Box by the littel house & Silve's Began doing up the Tabels round the grass walk. a dull day

Wednesday 25th ↞ a clear cold morning. Silve's doing the tabels. she has Finished the Tabels and Bille has Finished cuting the Box except the Long line, a cold cloudey day, Mr. John Barber tells me that old Mrs. Pitt is dead that she died on Munday last[44]

1801 Thursday March 26th ↞ a snowey drisley morning. continued a dull cloudey cold day

Fryday 27th ↞ a fine morning. Trimed the Holley Tree in the garden & putt Planks in the front of the Burgemot & Common Balms. about noon it clouded up & continued cloude the afternon

Saturday 28th ↞ a cold cloudey day. Mr. Jos[ep]h Brewer gave me 2 pink root. he says thay are fine. in the after noon Capt. Richard Pitt & Mr. Myers[45] came from Baltimore in a privet stage to take Abee to Baltimore. a drisley evening

43 William B. Tilden, of Kent County, in 1800 was the first physician to receive a certificate of membership in the newly formed Medical and Chirurgical Faculty of Maryland. Louisa Harvey Howard was the third daughter of Samuel Harvey Howard (see 31 October 1794). She died in Baltimore on 28 April 1805.

44 Ann Pitt, mother of William, died 24 March 1801.

45 Probably John McMyers, Pitt's brother-in-law.

Sunday 29th ✒ a rainey windey day

Munday 30th ✒ a cold windey morning, a littel after 9 oclock Mr. Myers, Capt. Pitt, my daughter Abee & a yung man by the name of Taylor sett off in the stage for Baltimore, a very windey cold day

Tuseday 31th ✒ a fine morning. planted 3 rows of Peas in the Big Bed, & planted 7 rows of Bunch Beens in the littel quarter by the new stabel, the first 2 rows & a peace, Beens from Mrs. Davidson, then 1 row & ½ of Sewell's, the rest my owne. sow'd a Bed in the garden with 37 drills of the nutmeg & a Bed in the lott with 7 drills of the nutmeg seed & sow'd the Ice Plant and the sencitive plant seeds. took the straw from the rosemary. a fine day

1801 Wednesday April 1th ✒ Planted ocoro in the Lott and on the end of the Border at the end of the stabel & planted Balsom seed on the same Border. cutt the long line of Box and planted the cuttings, dug up round the rosemarry and fill'd the line as far as the posts & Sylve's cleaning the garden. a fine day

Thursday 2th ✒ a dull cloudey day. this after noon Bille has been planting the cutings of Box

Fryday 3th ✒ finished Planting the Box cuttings. a fine day

Saturday 4th ✒ a dull cloudey day

Sunday 5th ✒ a dull cloudey morning. clear'd away a fine after noon & evening

Munday 6th ✒ stuck the Peas on the Border & How'd the peas & plants in the Big Bed. a dull cloudey day

Tuseday 7th ✒ a dull rainey morning, the Parsneps that ware planted the 11th of March are ~~making thare appearance~~ acuming up. a rainey day

Wednesday 8th ✒ a cloudey morning. the sensitive plant seed that was sown the 31th of March are acuming up

Thursday 9th ✒ a cold cloudey day

1801 Fryday Apl 10th ✒ last night was very cold & a cold cloudey morning. it snow'd a littel in the after [noon] clear'd away but very cold and windey

Saturday 11th ✍ a windey morning but clear and turned out a fine day

Sunday 12th ✍ a fine day

Munday 13th ✍ a coole cloudey morning, sow'd on the Border betwen the Bee House & the shed, on this end next the Parsily, Brussel Cale ~~sprout~~ seed next cabbage seed from Mr. John Cowman, and had the potts Brought out of the seller — I sow'd 13 flower seeds from Mrs. Majr Davidson in a pott. in the evening cloudey & looks like bad weather

Tuseday 14th ✍ sow'd radish seed on the Border betwen the new stabel & littel House, Sylve's stuck the 4 rows of Peas in the Bigg Bead & How'd them. a fine day

Wednesday 15th ✍ watered the garden this morning. a fine day

Thursday 16th ✍ a cloudey morning. planted the Tossminano corn & some of the corn thay dye with. Parted 1 of the Cryanthimum Indicum, in the even came on to rain

1801 Fryday April 17th ✍ about 2 oclock my daughter Abee came Home from Baltimore and Miss Allender with Her, Abee left Her sister and all well, and Capt. Richard Pitt was married on Tuseday evening to Miss Nancey Berrey,[46] a fine growing day rain & sunshine

Saturday 18th ✍ Mr. Hanson gave me some Narsstertion plants. I Planted them in the garden. a fine day

Sunday 19th ✍ a cloudey morning. about noone came on to rain and rain'd all day

Munday 20th ✍ a cloudey drisley day

Tuseday 21th ✍ a windey cloudey drisley day

Wednesday 22th ✍ very cold, windey & raine & snow at times all day

Thursday 23th ✍ a cold cloudey windey day

Fryday 24th ✍ a cold cloudey rainey day

1801 Saturday April 25th ✍ a dull cloudey day, in the evening Capt. Karr[47] came from Baltimore and call'd to see us and let us know that Nancey pitt and the Famely ware all well

[46] By the minister of Old St. Paul's (Episcopal) Church in Baltimore.

[47] The first appearance in the diary of Archibald Kerr, who married Abigail Faris (see 21 January 1802).

Sunday 26th ✍ a fine day. Capt. Kerr Brackfast'd dined & drank tea in the evening with us

Munday 27th ✍ Capt. Kerr Brackfasted with us and sett off for Baltimore betwen 8 & 9 oclock. Sylve's dug the littel quarter & I sow'd 4 rows of dwarf peas & 4 rows of Bunch Beans. a fine day

Tuseday 28th ✍ Sylve's stuck the 3 rows of Peas and How'd the Bed & I planted 4 Cryanthimums in potts. a fine day but the wind Blows hard

Wednesday 29th ✍ a dull day

Thursday 30th ✍ sow'd the sensitive plant seeds in a pott. a fine day

1801 Fryday May 1th ✍ a fine day but the wind Blows very Hard at S

Saturday 2th ✍ a dull day, looks like for rain

Sunday 3th ✍ the first crop of Peas are in Blossom, a fine day. in the evening turned cold

Munday 4th ✍ went to Doctr Scotts & got 25 aster plants and 4 Balsom plants. in the afternoon I went Mr. Hansons & got 26 Balsom Plants, I planted them all in potts. in the evening Sylve water'd part of the Tulip Beds. a fine day

Tuseday 5th ✍ a dull day. in the after noon Doctr Scott sent me 6 Jeraniums. in the evening looks like for rain

Wednesday 6th ✍ a rainey morning. planted betwen the peas & Beans in the littel quarter cabbage plants and filled up the spaces betwen the peas in the Big Bed with plants & Howed the peas. a drisley day

Thursday 7th ✍ Old William has brought me a parcel of dung from Mr. Ridgleys & I began to mark the Tulips. a fine day. this evening Miss Kittey Carrol was married to Mr. Harper[48]

1801 Fryday May 8th ✍ a rainey morning. about noon cleared away, I marked some more Tulips. a fine after noon

Saturday 9th ✍ betwen 8 & 9 oclock Miss Allnder sett off in the stage for Baltimore. an April morning. many showers of rain & sun shine. in the afternoon I marked more flowers. in the evening Mr. Perrey Fitzchew called to see me. he is just from the Gennessee countrey.[49] he is very harty

[48] Robert Goodloe Harper (c.1765–1825), a native of Virginia and a lawyer, represented South Carolina in four congressional sessions. He sat for less than a year in the 14th Congress as a Maryland representative and represented the western shore in the Maryland senate in 1820. Catherine Carroll (c.1778–1861) was a daughter of Charles Carroll of Carrollton (1737–1832), the only Catholic signer of the Declaration of Independence and the son of Charles Carroll of Annapolis and his wife Elizabeth Brooke. Carroll and his wife, Mary Darnall, had three daughters and one son. When Carroll, the last surviving signer, died in 1832, he was believed to be the wealthiest man in America. Although he was a customer of Faris's, he himself is never mentioned in the diary. Rosalie Calvert wrote of Catherine Harper in 1805 that "we had Mrs. Harper in Bladensburg for a fortnight; she came to drink the waters. . . . She is just the same as before her marriage. . . . Between Mrs. Harper and myself it was like a grand farce of politeness and nothing more. I know she likes me no better than she did in Annapolis." § Faris collected £3.16.1 from Carroll in December 1800 as administrator of Charles's estate.

[49] Fitzhugh's brother William Jr. settled in Genesee, Livingston County, New York, about 1800.

Sunday 10th ↝ a fine day. finished marking the Tulips

Munday 11th ↝ Old William's been weeling tan to day. a fine day,   ressow'd the carrott Bed

Tuseday 12th ↝ Old William has finish'd weeling Tan and has finished mixing the Tan and dung togeather for which I gave him 5/7 ½. a fine day

Wednesday 13th ↝ a fine day

Thursday 14th ↝ a fine day

Fryday 15th ↝ a rainey day

1801 Saturday May 16th ↝ a cloudey morning. cleared away a fine day. Billee is thining the Parsneps

Sunday 17th ↝ a fine day

Munday 18th ↝ a fine day but very coole for the season

Tuseday 19th ↝ a fine day but coole

Wednesday 20th ↝ a fine day

Thursday 21th ↝ a fine warm day

Fryday 22th ↝ a fine warm day

Saturday 23th ↝ a fine day

Sunday 24th ↝ a clear coole day cold for the season

Munday 25th ↝ a very windey day. in the evening looks like for rain

Tuseday 26th ↝ wee had a littel rain last night, a very windey coole day

1801 Wednesday May 27th ↝ a fine day. Broke of 3945 Tulip stalks in the diffent Beds in the garden

Thursday 28th ↝ a fine day

Fryday 29th ↝ a coole morning for the season, about 2 oclock Mr. & Mrs. Pitt, littel Hanna and the Fameley came heare from Baltimore. a fine day

Saturday 30th ↝ after diner Mr. Pitt went of in his Boat for Baltimore. a very warm day

Sunday 31th ↝ a warm day. in the after noon it looked as if wee should have some rain but it went by. rain is much wanted. the ground is very dry

Munday June 1th ⚘ there was a cleaver rain last night. a warm day. in the evening it looks likely for rain — Sylve's carried dung on the Walnut Tree Bed redy to begin diging to morrow

Tuseday 2th ⚘ Sylve's been diging the Walnutt Tree bed, and it has rained several times to day and has turned very cold

1801 Wednesday June 3th ⚘ Sylve's finished digging the Wallnut Tree Bed and I have planted one half of it with Brussel cale plants and had them watered in the evening — a fine day but in the evening turned very coole

Thursday 4th ⚘ I planted 3 Cryanthimum Indicums in the yard under the window. a fine day

Fryday 5th ⚘ wee had a fine rain last night. I finished planting ye Wallnutt Tree Bed this morning. in the afternoon wee had a fine shower of rain. a fine day

Saturday 6th ⚘ a fine day

Sunday 7th ⚘ a very cold dull cloudey day

Munday 8th ⚘ Sylve's Pulled up the peas in the Big Bed & digging the ground. a coole dull day. in the evening looks like for rain

Tuseday 9th ⚘ wee had a littel rain Last night, I planted the Bigg Bed with cabbage plants this morning. a fine day

Wednesday 10th ⚘ a cold dull drisley [day]. after diner Mr. Whitcroft called and took Abee with him to his House

1801 Thursday June 11th ⚘ a cold rainey day. wee have a Fire in the House to day

Fryday 12th ⚘ a rainey morning but cleared away a fine day. in the evening Abee returned home from Mr. Whitcrofts

Saturday 13th ⚘ a fine day but coole

Sunday 14th ⚘ a fine day

Munday 15th ⚘ to day the Pettey Jurey of the General Court was discharged. a fine day. in the evening clouded up & look as if wee shoul have rain

Tuseday 16th ⚘ a fine day. in the after noon wee had a clever rain, Mr. Pitt called hear this evening on his way to the capes

Wednesday 17th ✒ a fine day. wee had 2 or 3 fine showers of rain, in the evening Mr. Thomas Woodward came heare

Thursday 18th ✒ this morning earley Mr. Pitt left heare to go down the Bay & Mr. Thomas Woodward went of for Home this evening. a fine day

1801 Fryday June 19th ✒ a fine day

Saturday 20th ✒ a fine day

Sunday 21th ✒ just as wee ware going to diner Mr. Pitt came in from down the Bay. a fine warm day

Munday 22th ✒ after Brackfast Mr. & Mrs. pitt sett of in the Packett for Baltimore for a few days. Bille has taken up the seedling Tulips & the Dutch of setts, from Doctr Scotts, & a fine purpel Doubel Tulip a seedling, in the evening I took a Hive of Bees. a fine day

Tuseday 23th ✒ Bille's made abegining to take up the Tulip roots in the Beds by the grass walk. a fine warm day

Wednesday 24th ✒ Billee's taking up roots. a fine day. I sow'd som radish seed on one of Flower Beds. in the evening wee had a clever rain

Thursday 25th ✒ Billee's takeing up roots. Mr. Thomas Woodward called heare on his way to Baltimore. a fine day

1801 Fryday June 26th ✒ Billee's finished takeing up the roots at the grass walk & circel Beds. a fine day. in the evening looks like for rain

Saturday 27th ✒ Billee's finished the 2 Beds by the littel House. a fine day. the radishes that I sowed on Wednesday last are acomeing up

Sunday 28th ✒ a Hott day. betwen 9 & 10 oclock Mrs. Anne Pitt arrived heare from Baltimore in the Packett. Mr. Pitt is down the Bay

Munday 29th ✒ Billee has began to take the roots up in the nursserey Beds. a very Hott day

Tuseday 30th ✒ Bille's in the nursserey Beds. a very Hott day

Wednesday July 1th ✒ Bille's in the nursserey Beds. a very Hott day

Thursday 2th ✒ Bille finished takeing up the roots in the nursserey Beds at diner time & in the after noon he went about takeing up the roots on the Border next the street. a very Hott day

1801 Fryday July 3th ↳ Bille's Finished takeing up all the roots. a very Hott day, in the evening Mr. Kerr call'd hear from Baltimore

A List of Marked Tulips

No. 1	The President	36	Pompey the Grate
2	Genl Washington	37	Sir Isaac Newton
3	Ladey Washington	38	The Spectator
4	Genl Mongomery	39	Common Sence
5	Genl Warren	40	Junius
6	d^o Mercer	41	Rights of Man
7	d^o Green	42	The Farmer
8	d^o Williams	43	Archimedes
9	d^o Wayne	44	Indian Queen
10	d^o Smallwood	45	Indian King
11	d^o Putnam	46	America
12	d^o Harry Lee	47	The Grayhound
13	d^o Morgan	48	Cato
14	d^o Gates	49	Cicero
15	Coln. Howard	50	Domestines
16	Buonaparte	51	Achillis
17	La Fayatte	52	King Pryam
18	Madam La Fayatte	53	Doctr Johnson
19	Adams	54	Buffon
20	Jefferson	55	Goldsmith
21	Hamilton	56	Swift
22	Maddison	57	Pope
23	Gallitin	58	Chatham
24	Doctr Franklin	59	Charles Fox
25	Columbus	60	Butter Fly
26	Harrison	61	The Burnett
27	Marabeau	62	United States
28	Rittenhouse	63	The Aid du Camp
29	Cout. Dillon	64	Jack Custis
30	McPherson	65	Cincinnatus
31	Trumbull	66	The American Fair
32	Hannebal	67	Genl Messena
33	Aristides	68	Doctr Priestly
34	Fabius	69	Hammelton Rowan
35	Scipeo Scipeo	70	Thomas Pain

William Faris

A List of Flowers

No. 🠉 Tulips

1	Buff & Red	14	Black
2	Yallow & White	15	Red
3	purpel	16	White Hyacinths
4	Red & White	17	Red d^o
5	Red & purpel	18	Blew d^o
6	Red	19	Winged d^o
7	Yallow	20	Red Crown Imperial
8	Doubel	21	Yallow d^o
9	Parrot Tail	22	John Quills
o	seedlings	23	White Nercess
	Dwarf d^o	24	Yallow d^o
10	White	25	Troy d^o
11	White & Red	26	Blew Crocus
12	Red & White	27	Jacobin Lilley
13	Yallow		

1801 Saturday July 4th 🠉 a fine Pleasant day

Sunday 5th 🠉 a fine day. Capt. Kerr dined heare

Munday 6th 🠉 Capt. Kerr Brackfasted heare and went of in the Packett for Baltimore. a fine day. I took a Hive of Bees to day

Tuseday 7th 🠉 a fine day

Wednesday 8th 🠉 made a number of sticks (and Painted them) for the Tulips. a fine day

Thursday 9th 🠉 a fine day but very warm and every things suffering for want of rain

Fryday 10th 🠉 a fine day but in much want of rain

Saturday 11th 🠉 last night betwen a 11 & 12 oclock Mr. Pitt came heare from the capes — a fine day

1801 Sunday July 12th 🠉 last night Mr. James Brice died. a warm morning very Hott and dry

Munday 13th 🠉 very Hott & dry. Mr. Pitt went of for Baltimore this morning at 9 oclock and about a 11 oclock Mr. Mr. James Bryce was Buried. took up the garlick & pulled up the Been Vines

July, 1801

Tuseday 14th ✏ a fine day but very Hott & dry

Wednesday 15th ✏ a fine day but very Hott & dry

Thursday 16th ✏ a very Hott morning. in the afternoon wee had a clever littel rain but scarcely anuff to lay the dust, in the evening we had another cleaver rain

Fryday 17th ✏ wee had a littel rain in the night. a windey morning. I sow'd radish seed on the first nursserey Bed and Planted 6 rows of Beens on the littel quarter by the new stabel, Sylve's Howing the Plants in the Wallnutt Tree Bed and I Planted the garlick. in the evening Mr. Pitt came hear in his Boat from Baltimore & Sylve dug up betwen the greens in the littel quarter by the old stabel

1801 Saturday July 18th ✏ a fine morning. planted the next Nursserey bed with 6 rows of radsh seed. in the evening turned cloudey and look'd as if wee should have rain and turned cold

Sunday 19th ✏ no rain last night. a coole cloudey morning. in the evening still looks like for rain and is very coole

Munday 20th ✏ it rained a littel last night. a coole cloudey day

Tuseday 21th ✏ Betwen 8 & 9 oclock this morning Mr. & Mrs. Pitt sett of in thare Boat for Baltimore.* a drisley or fine rain at times all the morning. * and man Dick went with them. I Planted all the ground with plants. it continued drisling & raining at times all day

Wednesday 22th ✏ thare was a fine rain in the night. a cloudey morning. clear'd away about 10 oclock very warm. I sow'd some Lettice seed on the Border next to Ridgely's. a very warm after noon

Thursday 23th ✏ a clear warm morning, Bille's doing up the Tabels round the grass walk. in the after noon we had a fine rain

1801 Fryday July 24th ✏ a clear warm day

Saturday 25th ✏ a fine day. in the evening we had a fine rain

Sunday 26th ✏ thare was a cleaver rain last night. a fine clear coole day

Munday 27th ✏ very cold for the season. Old William has been weeling dung all day from Mr. Ridgely's

Tuseday 28th ~ a fine day. Old William finished his ding by diner Time. I have gatherd the roshembol seed onions and took up the onions for the House

Wednesday 29th ~ a fine day

Thursday 30th ~ a fine morning. in the afternoon wee had a fine rain

Fryday 31th ~ a fine day. in the evening Mrs. Pitt came heare in the Packett from Baltimore, Mr. Pitt is in a Brig on his way to the capes

1801 Saturday August 1th ~ a fine day. wee had a clever shower of rain

Sunday 2th ~ a fine morning. in the afternoon rain'd hard for a wile and continued cloudey and looks like for more rain and turned cold

Munday 3th ~ a very cold rainey night. a cold rainey morning, a cloudey rainey cold day

Tuseday 4th ~ a cold cloudey rainey day

Wednesday 5th ~ Sylve dug the Border and I planted the roshembole onions or the onions of Eygept that are for seed & sowed spinige on the rest of the Border. a dull cloudey day, Old Mrs. Dulaney the widdow of Walter Dulaney died to day[50]

Thursday 6th ~ a fine morning. continued a fine day but coole for the season

Fryday 7th ~ a fine day. in the evening Mrs. Dulaney was Buried

Saturday 8th ~ a fine day. in the evening turned cloudey looks like for rain

1801 Sunday Augt 9th ~ a cleaver rain this morning and in the afternoon wee had several showers of rain some Hail & several claps of Thunder one very sharp. I planted in the small Box some of the dark purpel Holleyhock got from Majr Davidson

Munday 10th ~ Sylve's taken up the flower roots & Balsoms that ware in the circul Beds & put on manure & dug them up & I Planted the Balsoms & roots again & I Planted the remander of the of the Holley Hock seed that came from Majr Davidsons at the end of the new stabel. a fine day. in the evening looks like for rain. I likewise planted the cutting aCryanthimum on one of the circul Beds

50 Mary Grafton Dulany (c.1727–1801) was the daughter of Richard Grafton, a wealthy Delaware landowner and merchant. She married Walter Dulany (d.1773), son of Daniel Dulany the Elder (1685–1753), about 1745. Walter held the offices of councilman, alderman, mayor, and delegate to the general assembly. Mary Dulany lived until her death in the family home located on land now part of the Naval Academy. Walter Jr. married Elizabeth Brice Dulany, the sister of James Brice (see 17 July 1793) and the widow of his half-uncle, Lloyd Dulany. § Faris added a silver spout to a china tea pot for Walter Dulany in April 1773.

Tuseday 11th 🙠 a fine morning. Sylve's finished the flower Beds by the littel House & is now about the Border next the street. betwen 11 & 12 oclock came on a shower of rain which stoped her. she was obliged to leeve of and I planted the following seeds in a Box in the garden, No. 1 Troy Nercess 2 Pershen Iris 3 Rush leeved Iris 4 Yallow Crown Imperial 5 Red Crown Inperial. it continued raining till after diner. in the after noon Sylve finished the Border & then went to cleaning & weeding the garden

1801 Wednesday Augt 12th 🙠 a rainey morning. a clear afternoon

Thursday 13th 🙠 a fine day

Fryday 14th 🙠 a fine day

Saturday 15th 🙠 a fine day

Sunday 16th 🙠 this morning I am 73 years old. a ~~fine morning~~ a fine day

Munday 17th 🙠 a fine day, Sylve's stired the ground betwen the greens, and has been cleaning the walks

Tuseday 18th 🙠 a fine day, Frederick Gramer lost a negro man to day with the Billious Feveour

Wednesday 19th 🙠 a fine day but very Hott

Thursday 20th 🙠 a Hott sultery morning. in the afternoon wee had a fine rain

Fryday 21th 🙠 a fine day but very Hott

Saturday 22th 🙠 very Hott

1800 [1801] Sunday Augt 23th 🙠 thare was some rain last night. a fine day

Munday 24th 🙠 Mr. Pitt came heare this morning betwen 4 & 5 oclock from down the Bay. in the evening I sow'd the following cabbage seed

No. 1 Sugar Loaf, from Mr. Sewels

  2 Cabbage seed from Mrs. Davidson

  3 d⁰ d⁰ d⁰ Mr. Cowman and at the near end I sow'd Red Crown Imperial and at the far end, Piney seed. a fine day

Tuseday 25th 🙠 a fine morning. after Brackfast Mr. Pitt and Mrs. Pitt and a Laydey he Brought from Virgina sett of in his Boat for Baltimore. thay left the two children and Salley with us. a fine day

Wednesday 26th ✍ a fine day

Thursday 27th ✍ a fine day but the morning & evening is coole. this morning Mrs. Sarah Duvall (Salley Harwood that was) was Brought to Bed of a daughter

Fryday 28th ✍ a fine day

Saturday 29th ✍ a fine day. the cabbage seed I sow'd the 24th are acomeing up

1801 Sunday Augt 30th ✍ a fine day. in the evening looks like for rain

Munday 31th ✍ wee had a cleaver rain last night. a fine day

Tuseday Septr 1 ✍ a warm day

Wednesday 2th ✍ a very warm day

Thursday 3th ✍ very warm day. in the after noon Mrs. Johnson and her sone came heare from Baltimore on thare way to the Eastern Shore

Fryday 4th ✍ this morning Mrs. Johnson & son sett off for over the Bay. a very warm day

Saturday 5th ✍ very warm

Sunday 6th ✍ a cloudey morning. a grate appearance of rain, it went of, we had no rain. a very Hott day

Munday 7th ✍ very warm

Tuseday 8th ✍ very warm

1801 Wednesday Septr 9th ✍ a very Hott day. in the evening wee had a littel rain and looked as if wee should have more

Thursday 10th ✍ a very Hott day

Fryday 11th ✍ a very grate change in the weather. a very cold clear day

Saturday 12th ✍ clear & coole

Sunday 13th ✍ a cold raw dull day

Munday 14th ✍ this morning I took up and Parted the roots and Planted the Polianthis's. in the after noon it clouded up & wee had a littel rain

Tuseday 15th ✍ a rainey night & morning. in the fore noon stop'd raining but continued cloudey. in the evening it came on to rain again & looks as if we should have a good deal of it

Wednesday 16th ✒ raind hard last night, a cloudey morning. at 9 oclock my daughter Abee, littel Hannah & her maid Salley sett of in G. Barber's Boat for Baltimore, the wind Blows fresh at N.E. a cloudey day

1801 Thursday Septr 17th ✒ a cloudey morning. clear'd away a fine after noon

Fryday 18th ✒ a fine day

Saturday 19th ✒ a fine day. in the after noon the sherrif called and served a writ on me as ~~the suit of James Thomas~~ edminis[tra]tor of of Charles Faris deceas'd at the sute of James Thomas[51]

Sunday 20th ✒ a fine day

Munday 21th ✒ the ellectors mett to day in the Councel Chamber in the State House.[52] a fine day. in the evening it looks like for rain. Doctr Ghislin brought his wife home from her mothers round by the Hed of Severon. she is very Iill

Tuseday 22th ✒ a fine morning. in the after noon clouded up like for rain. betwen 8 & 9 oclock in the evening the ellectors finish'd & ellected the following gentelmen as Senators Viz. for the Western Shore Walter Bowie pg & William Smith, city of B. J. Johnson Anna[poli]s. Doc John Tyler Fredk Town Samuel Ringold Washn County James G. McCulloch city of Bal[timor]e Richard Harwood[53] Ann Arundel County John T Worthington Balt County for the Eastern Shore William Polk of Somerset Coty James Brown of Queen Annes Coty William Hayward Talbt Coty William Whitely Caroline Coty Henry Hollingsworth Ceacil Coty Robert Wright Kent Coty

Wednesday Septr 23th ✒ a fine day

Thursday 24th ✒ a fine day

Fryday 25th ✒ a fine day

Saturday 26th ✒ a cloudey morning. this morning Capt James Thomas superseeded my warrant for 6 months, James Maynard & William Glover[54] securities. about 11 oclock began to rain, and had a rainey afternoon and turned very cold. in the evening wee had a fire in the House

---

51 The account of Charles Faris's estate shows a payment to James Thomas of £26.4.0, perhaps expenses related to the period when Charles boarded with Thomas.

52 Under the Constitution of 1776, senators were elected indirectly: voters chose a slate of electors who then met to choose the members of the senate.

53 Richard Harwood (1738–1826) was the eldest child of Capt. Richard Harwood (1707–1754) and his wife Ann Watkins (1719–1804). He married first Margaret Hall (1746–1795), the daughter of Henry Hall and the half-sister of John Hall (see 8 March 1797), and married second Lucinda Harwood Battee (1768–1835), the widow of John Battee (d.1803) and the daughter of his cousin Thomas Harwood. He had in all fourteen children, several of whom Faris mentions in the diary. Harwood sat as a justice of the peace from 1771 to 1782 and served as sheriff from 1782 to 1785 and from 1794 to 1797. He was a colonel in the militia, a member of the house of delegates from 1786 to 1793, and senator and president of that body from 1801 to 1805.

54 William Glover (d.1810) was soon to be a common councilman, elected in October 1801. Glover married Eleanor McKellen in September 1786. Glover was the owner of land near the city called the Newington Rope-Walk, which was sold by the sheriff in 1802, as it had been security for a debt owed to Jasper E. Tilly (see 28 November 1803). § Faris paid Glover in September 1798 for carting 9 loads of dung.

Sunday 27th ✐ a cold day for the season, in the evening Capt. James Thomas's daughter Mariah was married to Mr. Golsberrey of the Eastern Shore[55]

Munday 28th ✐ a cold morning. I took up the Horse Radish and planted it in the lott by the fence. Silves dunged & diging the Bed whare the Horse Radish grew. turned out a fine day

1801 Tuseday 29th ✐ a fine morning. Sylve's diging the Flower Beds & I have planted 115 Parrot tail Tulips that ware sown in 1798 on the Border next to the Snow Ball Bushes. next 94 Huanth off setts from Doctr Scott. next 83 Dutch Tulip off setts from Doctr Scoott — a fine day

Wednesday 30th ✐ a fine morning, Bille & my self have Planted 3 of the nursserey Beds with Tulips and Sylve has finished diging all the Beds. she has a littel peace to dig on the Border nex the street. in the evening turn'd coole & cloudey

Thursday Octr 1th ✐ finished Planting the four nursserey Beds. the first Bed 170. second 175 the 3 Beded 210 the 4th Bed 207. in the whole 762 Tulips besides Hyacinth, wing'd Hyacinths & John Quills. in the evening came on to rain

Fryday 2th ✐ a cloudey morning. finished planting two of the circel Beds and How'd the other. a fine day

Saturday 3th ✐ a rayney morning. clear'd away about noon. finished the circel Beds

1801 Sunday 4th ✐ a fine day

Munday 5th ✐ finished planting the Beds by the littel House. a fine day

Tuseday 6th ✐ a fine day. did nothing in the garden but Plant the Crown Imperial roots

Wednesday 7th ✐ a fine morning. planted the right hand Bed by the gate nex to Iiams's with seedling Tuleps that grew on the Border next to Ridgely's. the midel row some Reds & No. 1. Betwen 1 & 2 oclock Abee came home from Baltimore. she left her sister and Fameley awell. a fine day

Thursday 8th ✐ finished Planting the flower Beds. a fine day

55 Thomas Goldsborough, Esq. was the son of Thomas Goldsborough (c.1728–1793) and his wife Catherine Fauntleroy (c.1755–1825) of Virginia, a niece of George Washington. Thomas was a distant cousin of William and Richard Goldsborough, who appear earlier in the diary (see 8 November 1792 and 23 July 1793). Maria Thomas was daughter of Capt. James Thomas (see 25 May 1795); the Thomases were good friends of Faris and his family, and appear often in the diary. Maria gave Faris the gift of silk-worms (see 25 May 1795).

Fryday 9th ← Doctr Ghislin's wife died this morning betwen 5 & 6 oclock. Bille's planting the seedling Tuleps on the Borders. he has finished planting. a fine day

Saturday 10th ← between 9 & 10 oclock Mrs. Gislin was carried over Severon to be Buried in the famely Buring ground, a fine day

1801 Sunday Octr 11th ← a fine day

Munday 12th ← a fine day

Tuseday 13th ← a fine day but warm for the season

Wednesday 14th ← a warm day. in the afternoon wee had a cleaver rain

Thursday 15th ← Thomas McNear[56] Taylor came from Baltimore yesterday in Capt. Barbers packett. in the evening I am told that McNear suped at James West's and this morning he was found drownded at Carrols point.[57] he had pulled of his coat Hatt neckcloth & shews and left them on the shore side. a fine day

Fryday 16th ← a fine day

Saturday 17th ← a fine day

Sunday 18th ← a coole windey day

Munday 19th ← a clear coole day

1801 Tuseday Octr 20th ← a fine day

Wednesday 21th ← a fine day

Thursday 22th ← a fine day

Fryday 23th ← a fine day

Saturday 24th ← a fine day

Sunday 25th ← a fine day

Munday 26th ← a fine morning. this Fore noon Doctr Ghislin child died. a dull cloudey after noon looks like for rain

Tuseday 27th ← a fine day

Wednesday 28th ← a fine day

Thursday 29th ← a fine day

Fryday 30th ← a clear coole day

Saturday 31th ← a fine day, Trimed some of the Peach trees in the yard

1801 Sunday Novr 1th ← a coole dull day

[56] Thomas McNeir married Elizabeth Cobath in January 1788. Their son Thomas, born c. 1790, entered the St. John's grammar school in 1799. In 1794, McNeir advertised that George McNeir, an apprentice tailor, had run away, and in 1797 he appraised the estate of John Butcher (see 3 December 1796). After McNeir's death, Basil Sheppard announced in the 19 November 1801 issue of the *Gazette* that he had taken over McNeir's business on behalf of his widow. §The unrecoverable debts owed to McNeir's estate included £2.17.3 due from Charles Faris's estate.

[57] Probably a point along the northeast shore of Spa Creek on the property of Charles Carroll of Carrollton, most likely one end or the other of the cove in front of Carroll's house.

Munday 2th ↝ dull cloudey day

Tuseday 3th ↝ thay mad a House of Assembeley to day & chose ther speaker, Doctr Frazier[58] from the Eastern Shore. a fine day

Wednesday 4th ↝ a clear cold day

Thursday 5th ↝ a dull cloudey day

Fryday 6th ↝ rained and Blow'd very Hard last night, a clear cold day

Saturday 7th ↝ I have been directing Mr. Ridgely's man Nick to do up a Bed for Tulips. a clear cold day

Sunday 8th ↝ gathered the nesturtium Indicum seed. a clear cold day

Munday 9th ↝ this day Colln. Mercer[59] was chose govenor. a fine day

1801 Tuseday Novr 10th ↝ this fore noon the Assembley chose the Following gentelmen for the Govenor's Councel.[60] Francis Digges,[61] Allen B. Ducket[62] Edward Hall, Reverdey Ghislin, Davidson David[63] a dull cloudey day

Wednesday 11th ↝ a dull cloudy day

---

[58] Charles Frazier of Queen Anne's County, who was speaker in 1801, 1802, and 1804.

[59] John Francis Mercer (1759–1821) was born in Stafford County, Virginia, the son of Irish-born John Mercer, lawyer and secretary of the Ohio Land Company, and his wife Ann Roy. He served in the Revolutionary War as a major in a Virginia regiment. Mercer moved to Maryland after his marriage in February 1785 to Sophia Sprigg (d.1812), daughter of Richard and Margaret Caile Sprigg (see 13 May 1792). He was admitted to practice in the Anne Arundel County court in November 1787. Mercer was a delegate to the Constitutional Convention, represented Anne Arundel in the legislature, held a seat in congress for two terms, and served three terms as governor from 1801 to 1803. He died and was buried in Philadelphia, where he had gone for medical treatment. § Mercer patronized Faris's tavern in 1773, while still a Virginia resident. Faris collected £1.1.4 from Mercer in December 1801 as administrator of Charles's estate. On 12 December 1801, Faris recorded "cash of His Excellency," £7.2.9, in his daybook.

[60] This council contained a complete change of personnel from the previous council, which may be why Faris noted its composition in his diary—something he did not usually do.

[61] Francis Digges served five terms on the executive council from 1801 to 1805. He had previously represented Charles County in the general assembly from 1793 to 1796 and in 1799.

[62] Allen Bowie Duckett (1774–1809) was the son of Thomas Duckett (1744–1806) and his first wife, Priscilla Fraser Bowie (1750–1786), the daughter of Allen Bowie Sr., and was the stepbrother of Judson Magruder Clagett (see March 1795). Bowie married Margaret Howard in October 1799. In December 1795 he qualified as clerk of elections for Annapolis, but held no other city office. Duckett served five terms on the executive council from 1801 to 1805, and was associate judge of the circuit court of the District of Columbia. § Faris collected £0.13.1 1/2 from Duckett in January 1801 as administrator of Charles's estate.

[63] Davidson David, of Cecil County, served three terms from November 1801 until his death in Elkton in July 1804.

Thursday 12th ✒ a cloudey morning. it rained last night. cleard away about noon a fine afternoon. this evening a number of yung gentelmen are a going to Preform a play George Barnwell and the Farce Like Master Like Man[64]

Fryday 13th ✒ a fine day

Saturday 14th ✒ a fine day

Sunday 15th ✒ a cloudey fore noon. in the after noon rain'd

Munday 16th ✒ a cloudey drisley day. in the after noon, I Trimed the Peach Tree in the Big Bed by the circel

1801 Tuseday Novr 17th ✒ a dull day

Wednesday 18th ✒ a rainey morning. clear'd away in the after noon & I went to triming the Peach Trees

Thursday 19th ✒ a clear cold day

Fryday 20th ✒ a cold dull day

Saturday 21th ✒ dull & cloudey and in the course of the day it both rained and snow'd a littel. this evening betwen 6 & 7 oclock Mr. William Pitt came here on his way from the capes to Baltimore

Sunday 22th ✒ a snowey morning. a cold cloudey day

Munday 23th ✒ a clear cold morning. about 9 oclock Mr. Pitt, Mrs. Faris & littel Marriah went off in Mr. Pitts Boat for Baltimore. a cold day

Tuseday 24th ✒ a cold dull rainey day

Wednesday 25th ✒ a clear cold day. putt straw to my rosmary & mooved the potts with Chryanthimums & cherreys in to my green House

1801 Thursday Novr 26th ✒ a clear cold day

Fryday 27th ✒ a fine day

Saturday 28th ✒ a warm dull day. in the evening rain

Sunday 29th ✒ a fine day

Munday 30th ✒ a dull morning with snow. about noon clear'd away

Tuseday Desr 1th ✒ a clear cold day. this evening Abee's gone to Mr. N. Harwoods to dress & go to the Colts Ball with Nancey Harwood

[64] The 27 May 1802 issue of the *Gazette* announced a performance of "The Tragedy of George Barnwell," with the proceeds going to enclose the "Old Grave Yard." This may have been the burial ground around St. Anne's Church or the cemetery that had been in use since the 1780s.

Wednesday 2th ❧ a clear cold day

Thursday 3th ❧ a dull cloudey morning. in the afternoon rain

Fryday 4th ❧ this after noon Mr. Hanson brought me the following roots No. 1 15 anemones & No. 2 20 ranunculusses. I planted them on the border by the littel House. a dull cloudey day

1801 Saturday Desr 5th ❧ a dull cloudey day. Old William Finished digging up the Parsneps and covering them up in a Hill

Sunday 6th ❧ a cold windey day

Munday 7th ❧ clear & cold

Tuseday 8th ❧ a dull cold day. this after noon I had brought home 909lb. of Hogg meat[65]

Wednesday 9th ❧ a dull morning. in the afternoon rain

Thursday 10th ❧ a windey rainey night. a dull cloudey morning. about 12 oclock Mrs. Faris & Marriah came Home from Baltimore in the Packett. thay left Baltimore yesterday morning. Nancey not brought to Bed yet. she is as well as can be expected — a dull day

Fryday 11th ❧ a fine day

Saturday 12th ❧ a fine day

Sunday 13th ❧ a dull cloudey day. in the after noon I moved 6 or 7 poppey & emenoney roots. Mrs. Faris had a letter from Mr. pitt informing her that Nancey was brought to Bed on Fryday night last. she has got a son[66]

1801 Munday 14th ❧ this morning the d[r]um was aBeeting for the sale of Mrs. Clouds goods,[67] Charles Wallace was rideing up the street in his sulkey. the Horse took Fright at the drum, and run away and throughed him out just by Mr. Brices. he was a good deal Hurt, he was taken up and carried into Mrs. Clouds.[68] a dull cloudey morning. in the after noon it rained

Tuseday 15th ❧ a fine day

Wednesday 16th ❧ a dull cloudey day

Thursday 17th ❧ a fine day

Fryday 18th ❧ a fine day

[65] Faris paid £27.3.9 for the meat, but did not record to whom.

[66] William Faris Pitt, born 11 December 1801.

[67] Elizabeth Claude was holding a public sale of the personal property of her late husband. Smith Price (see 7 July 1802) carted the goods to the market house where they were sold. A slave boy belonging to Mary Boyle (see 20 June 1798) beat the drum.

[68] Wallace's right leg was crippled as a result of this accident, and he was advised to consult experts in Philadelphia about therapy for the injury.

Saturday 19th ✒ a clear cold day

Sunday 20th ✒ a clear cold day

1801 Munday Desr 21th ✒ a cold cloudey day and spits of snow at times

Tuseday 22th ✒ a fine day

Wednesday 23th ✒ a rainey morning, clear'd away about noon. a fine afternoon

Thursday 24th ✒ a fine day. in the evening took down the grate in the House

Fryday 25th ✒ a fine day

Saturday 26th ✒ a warm dull day

Sunday 27th ✒ a drisley rainey day

Munday 28th ✒ a snowey day

Tuseday 29th ✒ a fine day

Wednesday 30th ✒ a fine day

Thursday 31th ✒ a fine day. this evening the Assembeley Broke up

1802 Fryday January 1th ✒ a very fine warm day

Saturday 2th ✒ a fine day

Sunday 3th ✒ a dull cloudey day like for rain. in the evening Capt. Kerr & Capt. Robinson[69] came here from Baltimore. a wett evening

Munday 4th ✒ a cloudey drisley morning. Capt. Kerr & Capt. Robertson dined heare. a rainey day. in the evening clear'd away

Tuseday 5th ✒ a clear cold day. after Brackfast Capt. Robinson sett off for Baltimore

Wednesday 6th ✒ a dull cloudey day

Thursday 7th ✒ a fine day

Fryday 8th ✒ a dull drisley day

Saturday 9th ✒ a cloudey rainey day

Sunday 10th ✒ Blow'd very Hard last night. a clear coole windey day

1802 Munday Janry 11th ✒ a clear day

Tuseday 12th ✒ a clear cold day

69 William Robinson, gentleman and ship master, lived on Bank Street in Fells Point in the early 1800s. He married Deborah James, also of Baltimore, in February 1802.

Wednesday 13th ✒ a fine day

Thursday 14th ✒ a cloudey day

Fryday 15th ✒ a fine day

Saturday 16th ✒ a fine day

Sunday 17th ✒ about noon Capt. Kerr Miss Julian Owens & Abee rode out to Mr. William Witcrofts.[70] a fine day

Munday 18th ✒ a fine day

Tuseday 19th ✒ a fine day. to night Miss Polley Lloyd to be married Mr. F. Key[71]

Wednesday 20th ✒ a fine day

1802 Janry 21th Thursday ✒ a dull rainey day. in the evening my daughter Abigail was married Capt. Archibald Kerr by Mr. Ralph Higgenbothom[72] present Mr. Stevens & wife Miss Ranken[73] Mrs. Brice Mrs. Randel Nancey & Polly Harwood the 2 Miss Owens's Mr. Thomas Harwood & 3 gentelmen from Baltimore, Capt. Phillip Grabel,[74] Mr. Ruben Ettings[75] & Mr. Lemwell Taylor[76]

Fryday 22th ✒ a fine clear morning. a fine day

Saturday 23th ✒ a fine day

Sunday 24th ✒ a fine clear day

Munday 25th ✒ a snowey morning & at time all the fore noon. a fine after noon. in the evening Capt. Kerr, Abee & my self went to Mr. Randels

Tuseday 26th ✒ a fine day

Wednesday 27th ✒ a fine morning. in the afternoon clouded up like for Bad weather. in the evening Mrs. Faris, Capt. Kerr, Abee, Marriah & my self all went to Mr. Stevens's

1802 Thursday Janry 28th ✒ a very warm dull day. in the evening Mr. Kerr, Abee & my self went to Mr. Neth's

Fryday 29th ✒ a cloudey rainey day. in the evening Mr. Kerr, Abee & my self went to Mr. N. Harwoods

---

70 The eldest son of William Whetcroft, who was born on 17 April 1775. Living now in his own home in the country, he may have married by this time, but if so Faris never takes note of his wedding.

71 Francis Scott Key (1779–1843) was the son of John Ross Key (1754–1821) and his wife Ann Pheobe Penn Dagworthy Charlton (c.1756–1830). Elizabeth Ross Scott, the wife of Upton Scott (see 5 May 1792), was his great-aunt; Key lived with the Scotts while attending St. John's, receiving an A.B. degree in August 1796. Mary Tayloe Lloyd (1784–1859) was the daughter of Edward Lloyd IV (see 19 October 1792) and sister of future governor Edward Lloyd V (see 30 November 1797). Key practiced law in Georgetown with his uncle Philip Barton Key (see 29 May 1792) and was U.S. attorney for the District of Columbia from 1833 until 1841, as well as author of "The Defense of Fort M'Henry" ("The Star-Spangled Banner"). § Faris collected 5/7 1/2 from Key in December 1800 as administrator of Charles's estate.

72 Abigail and Archibald Kerr were also married by the rector of St. Anne's.

73 Probably Mary Ranken, the daughter of George and Mary Bull Ranken (see 26 April 1798). See 24 June 1804 for her marriage.

74 Philip Graybell was a ship captain who lived in Baltimore. In 1802, the Baltimore City directory identified him as a flour merchant, at 177 Baltimore Street.

75 Reuben Etting (1762–1848) was the son of German-born Elijah Etting and his wife, Shinah Solomon, daughter of a London merchant, who met and married in Pennsylvania in 1759. After Etting's death, the family moved in 1780 to Baltimore, where Reuben's brother Solomon established a hardware store that developed into a successful mercantile business. Etting's September 1794 marriage to Frances Gratz of Philadelphia united two prominent Jewish families. Etting served as an officer of the Independent Blues militia unit in 1798 and was appointed U.S. Marshall in 1801 by Thomas Jefferson.

76 Lemuel Taylor was a Baltimore merchant who lived at 66 Hanover Street and had a counting house at 11 Bowley's Wharf, Fells Point, in 1802.

Saturday 30th ✒ this morning about 8 oclock Capt. Kerr & wife went of in the stage for Baltimore[77]

Sunday 31th ✒ a fine day

Munday Febry 1th ✒ a cloudey morning. Sylve's diging the Border next to Mr. Ridgely's. in the afternoon it rained

Tuseday 2th ✒ a fine morning, I sow'd the Border that Sylve dug yesterday, with 16 rows of Peas. a dull cloudey after noon

Wednesday 3th ✒ rain'd hard in the night, a dull windey day

1802 Thursday Febry 4th ✒ a clear cold day

Fryday 5th ✒ a clear cold day

Saturday 6th ✒ a cold day

Sunday 7th ✒ a dull cloudey cold day

Munday 8th ✒ I have been very unwell all day. a fine day

Tuseday 9th ✒ a fine morning. I am Better this morning. Sylve's filled a Box with earth & I have sow'd No. 1 earley York No. 2 earley sugar loaf and I have fixed a new Barrel & have put erth in it for the Ice plant, Sylve's been wheeling dung on the Parsnep Bed. a fine day

Wednesday 10th ✒ Sylve's been digging in the Lott. a fine day

Thursday 11th ✒ a fine day. Sylve's finis'd digging the parsnep & carrot Beds in the lott. in the evening clouded up and looks like falling weather

1802 Fryday Febry 12th ✒ a dull cloudey day

Saturday 13th ✒ a dull cloudey day

Sunday 14th ✒ a fine day

Munday 15th ✒ a dull Foggey day

Tuseday 16th ✒ a fine day

Wednesday 17th ✒ a fine morning, about 1 oclock this morning Mrs. Elenor Harris, daughter of Mrs. Davidson died. sow'd betwen the peas on the Border radish, cabbage & letice seeds, a dull after noon

Thursday 18th ✒ a cold windey day

Fryday 19th ✒ a clear cold day

Saturday 20th ✒ a fine day

Sunday 21th ✒ a dull cloudey day. this evening Mr. Thomas Williams is to be married to Miss Elizabeth Thomas daughter of James Thomas[78]

1802 Munday Febry 22th ✒ rained and Blew very Hard last night, a snowey day and Blow'd very Hard all day

Tuseday 23th ✒ a very cold windey night. a fine sun shiney day but very cold. I cleaned the Bee Hives to day. I ought to have don it yisterday but could not the day was so bad

Wednesday 24th ✒ a dull cloudey day. this morning wee had letters from Abee. thay ware all well

Thursday 25th ✒ a rainey day

Fryday 26th ✒ a rainey morning. clear'd away in the after noon. I made abegining to plant onions of Eagipt, in the evening Mr. Pitt came heare. he had been down the Bay to gett a ship off that was aground, came with him Messrs Byas, & Jones & a yung gentelman who came Passenger in the ship from Ireland, Mr. Pitt tells us that Abee & Mr. Kerr is gone to House Keeping in a House that the seller's full of water[79] and that both Fameleys are all well

1802 Saturday Febry 27th ✒ a dull drisley rainey day. Mr. Pitt went off this morning before I was up

Sunday 28th ✒ a cold dull drissley day

Mund March 1th ✒ a dull drisley day. planted two Beds of the onions of Eagipt and began the 3d but it was two damp. wee left it

Tuseday 2th ✒ a cloudey drisley morning. in the after noon the sun came out, finished Planting the roshembole onions

Wednesday 3th ✒ made abegining to plant pasneps and I made good the long line of Box and it came on to rain and continued to rain all day

Thursday 4th ✒ Bille went to plant Parsneps but the wind Blew so hard he was oblig'd to leave off, I went to p[l]anting a line of Box on the Border nex to Mr. Stevens, but it was too cold. I left off. a cold raw windey day

[78] The 25 February 1802 issue of the *Maryland Gazette* reported that Mr. Thomas Williams Jr., of Alexandria, and Miss Eliza Thomas, eldest daughter of James Thomas, Esq., of Annapolis (see 25 May 1795), were married Sunday evening last, by the Rev. Mr. Higginbotham. Faris recorded her death on 2 January 1803. Thomas Williams may have been related to James Williams (see 19 June 1793); perhaps a cousin, the son of James's uncle Thomas, or a nephew, the son of James's brother Joseph.

[79] The Kerrs lived at 9 Alisanna (now Aliceanna) Street in Fells Point, a short distance away from the Pitts at 16 Alisanna.

Fryday 5th ✍ Bille's finish'd planting the Parsneps & carrots and Troweled some of the small Tulips on the border & I Planted a line of Box on the Border next the street. a fine day. in the evening about 9 oclock Mr. & Mrs. Kerr came hear from Baltimore, both well

1802 Saturday March 6th ✍ a fine morning. Sylve's diging the Big Bed. in the after noon came on to Blowd very Hard

Sunday 7th ✍ a clear cold windey day & Blowd very Hard all Last night

Munday 8th ✍ a fine day but cold

Tuseday 9th ✍ a fine day

Wednesday 10th ✍ a windey day

Thursday 11th ✍ this morning about 9 oclock Mr. & Mrs. Kerr sett off in the Packett for Baltimore. a fine morning. in the after noon I sow'd 4 rows of Peas in the Big Bed and Bille's made abegining to trowel the Flower Beds by the grass walk. in the evening it clouded up and look like for rain

Fryday 12th ✍ a drisley morning. continued to be a cloudey drisley day

Saturday 13th ✍ a fine day

Sunday 14th ✍ a fine clear cold day

1802 Munday March 15th ✍ last night was very cold. frose hard, a fine morning. the ground was so hard that wee could not trowel the flower Beds. I got the assparagrass Beds finished and sow'd on the near one, on the end next to Mr. Ridgleys early york, the other end, real cabbage seed both from Mrs. Neth's mother. on the end next to Mr. Ridgleys on the farther Bed, earley york from Mr. Stevens the other end sugar loaf cabbage from Mr. Sewell and Lettice on both and a line of spinige betwen the Beds, a cold windey day

Tuseday 16th ✍ Bille has finished troweling the nurssry Beds & Sylve's digging in the Lott nex the garden. a fine day

Wednesday 17th ✍ Bille has finished Troweling the Flower Beds & Sylve's diging the lott and I sow'd in potts No. 1 white Balsom No. 2 Red No. 3 Purpel No. 4 Striped Balsoms. a fine day. No. 5 a fine purpel Balsom

1802 Thursday 18th ✒ Sow'd 5 potts of asters

No ✒ 1 doubel white and purpel

2 doubel purpel asters

3 purpel

and Sylve's finished diging in the Lott, & I troweled the peas on the Border & planted the Jacobian Lilley. a fine day but very warm for the season

Fryday 19th ✒ a dull morning. cutt the long line of sage. finished cutting all the sage, & Bille has finished Troweling all the seedling tulips on the Borders. a fine day

Saturday 20th ✒ a cloudey morning. in the after noon came on to rain &c.

Sunday 21th ✒ a fine clear day but rather coole to what wee have had

Munday 22th ✒ a fine morning. Bille's made abegining to cutt Box and Sylve's stuck the Peas on the Border, and made Hills for simlins in the lott and I Hilled the Peas, last night Mr. William Davidson died

1802 Tuseday March 23th ✒ ~~a fine day Bille's cutting Box~~ and I Planted 12 Hills of simlins in the lott. did nothing in the garden. a dull rainey day

Wednesday 24th ✒ a raw dull morning. looks like for rain, not in the garden this morning, clear'd away, wee finished the Box round the circkel and the lower end of the garden & Bille has mad abegining to cutt the Box at the nursserey Beds. a fine day. in the evening looks like for rain

Thursday 25th ✒ finished cutting the Box & Sylve's cleaning the walks, a windey raw day, wee had a fine rain last night

Fryday 26th ✒ a cold snowey morning, & continued snowing all day and it dont look like leeveing off

Saturday 27th ✒ a cold Bad night. the Houses & ground was all covered with snow this morning. a cloudey morning, about 9 oclock the sun came out fine. a fine day but cold

Sunday 28th ✒ a clear cold windey day

1802 Munday March 29th ✒ a clear cold morning. in the afternoon clouded up like for rain

Tuseday 30th ☛ sow'd the stock July flower in a Box. a dull cloudey day

Wednesday 31th ☛ a dull drisley morning. I sow'd the Ice plant seed in the Barrel and the Sencitive Plant seed in a pott — a dull cloudey windey day

Thursday April 1th ☛ sow'd marygold seed on the Border by the seedling Tulips & sow'd radish seed in the lott. a dull day. in the evening came on to rain

Fryday 2th ☛ Sylve's dug the littel quarter and Bille's done up the Tabels round the grass walk. a fine day. I planted out 3 rows of early sugar loaf cabbage betwen the peas

Saturday 3th ☛ Sylve's finished the littel quarter and I planted it with 6 rows of Bunch Beens, & Sylve's dug a peace on the Border for the nutmeg seed. a warm fine day

1802 Sunday April 4th ☛ Planted reason stones in a pott. a dull cloudey coole day

Munday 5th ☛ a cold morning. sow'd 56 rows of the nutmeg seed & planted 62 Hills of Ocoro in the Lott, & Sylve's Howed the peas in the Big Bed. a fine day. not so cold as yesterday

Tuseday 6th ☛ dug the ground round the rosmary and planted out cutting to fill the line, and had dug the Border By the Bee House and planted 6 narssturtians seeds. a clear windey day

Wednesday 7th ☛ a dull cloudey morning. had the potts Brought out of the celler. putt fresh earth in them & replanted two Jerusalem Cherry Trees and four with Christanthimums. a fine afternoon

Thursday 8th ☛ a fine day

Fryday 9th ☛ a dull drisley day

Saturday 10th ☛ a fine clear windey day. the simlins I planted the 23th of March are acuming up

1802 Sunday April 11th ☛ a fine day

Munday 12th ☛ stuck the 4 rows of peas in the Bigg Bed. in the afternoon came on to rain

Tuseday 13th ☛ rained last night, a rainey morning. in the afternoon I Planted out a parcel of Plants in the Lott, and maded drills for 3 rows of Peas in the Bigg Bed, but it was so damp & cloudey I did not sow them. Mr. Ninnian Pinkeney is to be married to night to Miss Polley Gassaway.[80] a dull cloudey evening

Wednesday 14th ✒ a cloudey morning about 9 oclock clear'd away fine, the first 2 of the 3 rows I sow'd with Peas from Mrs. Cloud the other row next the curren Bushes with my own peas and Planted in the Bed full of plants 3 rows sugar loaf'd cabbage the other 3 with earley York cabbage

Thursday 15th ✒ Sylve's dug the littel quarter by the old stabel. a raw cold day

Fryday 16th ✒ very cold last night, this morning the Miss Owens's went in the Packett for Baltimore. a cold windey day

1802 Saturday April 17th ✒ a cold windey day

Sunday 18th ✒ rained a littel last night, a cold dull windey day. in the evening looks like for rain

Munday 19th ✒ a fine day

Tuseday 20th ✒ a fine day

Wednesday 21th ✒ a fine day, took up the stocks in Wallnutt Tree Bed & threw them away, thay ware so Lousey. the Peas that was sow'd the 2th of Febury are abegining to Blossom

Thursday 22th ✒ a fine day but coole for the season

Fryday 23th ✒ a fine day but coole

Saturday 24th ✒ a fine day but cold

Sunday 25th ✒ a fine warm day

Munday 26th ✒ a fine day. in the evening looks like for rain. this evening Mr. Owens & Miss Julian returned from Baltimore & left Miss polley thare

Tuseday 27th ✒ a fine day but very dry. rain is much wanted

Wednesday 28th ✒ a fine day. sent Nancey & Abee 130 stocks of assparagrass By G. Barber's Boat. this morning about 8 oclock Capt. Campbells[81] wife died at Charles Wallace's

1802 Thursday April 29th ✒ a rainey day

Fryday 30th ✒ a fine day. Mrs. Rebaca Campel was Buried this evening

80 Ninian Pinkney (1771–1824) was the son of Jonathan and Ann Rind Pinkney and the brother of William Pinkney (see 30 August 1793). Mary Gassaway was undoubtedly the daughter of Thomas and Elizabeth Gassaway (see 18 August 1792). Pinkney's second wife was Amelia Grason Hobbs (1779–1851), whom he married in May 1806. Pinkney, who attended St. John's grammar school briefly in 1790, was clerk of the executive council from about 1794 until 1824, and was the author of *Travels through the South of France*, published in 1809. § Pinkney's father patronized Faris's tavern in 1773 and 1774, and for 9 months in 1784 rented a small stable from Faris at 30 shillings per month.

81 Rebecca Burten, who married Capt. William Campbell in August 1777. Their son Charles, age fifteen, entered the St. John's grammar school in 1796. Campbell, one of the managers both of the lottery in 1790 to raise funds for completion of St. Anne's and for an orphans' school in 1791, was an associate justice of the peace in 1791. In 1792 he purchased the lot on which the present governor's residence stands, living in one of its houses and leasing the others. He sold his own residence in 1802, at which time he was living in Frederick County, to Faris's acquaintance Absalom Ridgely (see 30 November 1799). Rebecca Campbell's children shared the estate of Charles Wallace with the children of Rebecca Hanson and Catherine Latimer, the daughters of Wallace's sister Mary. It is likely that Rebecca Campbell was a sister or niece of Charles Wallace, in whose home she died.

Saturday May 1th ✍ a fine day but too cold for the season

Sunday 2th ✍ a fine day but still cold

Munday 3th ✍ stuck the peas that was sow'd the 14th of April. a fine day

Tuseday 4th ✍ a fine day. in the evening it looks like for rain

Wednesday 5th ✍ a coole morning, sow'd on the Border by the Bee House first Brussel Cole seed from Joseph Brewer. next Brussel sprout seed — a fine day

Thursday 6th ✍ a cold dull dissagreeable day. looks like for rain

Fryday 7th ✍ a fine day but cold. in the afternoon Mrs. Pitt and the children came hear from Baltimore. I had a letter from Abee. thay ware all well — I planted some small Indian corn, gave to me by Mr. Josep Harwood.[82] I planted it in the front of the Parsnep Bed

1802 Saturday May 8th ✍ a fine day. last night the Town was allarmed with a report that the Neagros ware armed & ware cuming into Town. the Citizens ware under arms till 12 oclock then disperced leaveing a gard of about 20 who continued all night

Sunday 9th ✍ a fine warm day but very dry

Munday 10th ✍ a fine morning. at 9 oclock Mrs. Pitt, Marriah & the two littel children & servents sett of in the Packett for Baltimore. in the evening looks like for rain. this after noon I Planted out som aster plants in the Bed round the grass walk

Tuseday 11th ✍ finished planting the asters and some Balsoms. a fine day. in the evening looks like for rain

Wednesday 12th ✍ whe had a fine rain last night and this morning I Planted 12 Red Beets from Mr. Joseph Brewer, & I planted out my Balsoms & asters and stock July flowers. a fine after noon

Thursday 13th ✍ a fine day

1802 Fryday May 14th ✍ a cold day. I think thare will be a frost to night

[82] Joseph Harwood (1775–1828) was the son of Capt. Richard Harwood (1707–1754) and his wife Ann Watkins (1719–1804). Several of his brothers and their children appear frequently in the diary.

Saturday 15th ✒ a cold morning. I planted 6 rows of Beens by the old stabel in the after noon. turn'd more warm, & I have got some Balsom appel seed. one seed from Mr. Isaac Hollond[83] I planted it at the root of the pride of Chiney. 8 seeds from Mr. Nicholas Maccubbin[84] I planted 6 seeds on the Border betwen the Bee House & stable & 2 on the Border by the nutmeg plants

Sunday 16th ✒ a rainey drisley day. in the evening Billee got Tipsey

Munday 17th ✒ a very cold cloudey morning. I sent Bille with some letters to the packett. he got tipsey. I did not discover it, he took a watch to alter her going, I then discovered it but too late. he broke the pivett of the verge — about 12 oclock the sun came out. a very cold & cloudey evening

Tuseday 18th ✒ a cold dissagreeable day but not so cold as yester day

Wednesday 19th ✒ a cold dissagreeable day. I expect'd Abee Kerr & Marria but thay did not come

1802 Thursday May 20th ✒ A cleard day but cold

Fryday 21th ✒ a drisley cold day

Saturday 22th ✒ a cloudey morning. sow'd Cherrey Pepper on the Border betwen the stabel and littel House. a rainey day

Sunday 23th ✒ a fine day. more moderate then it has been this some time past

Munday 24th ✒ a fine day. the Beens that ware sow'd the 15th are just acumeing up

Tuseday 25th ✒ a fine day

Wednesday 26th ✒ Capt. Kerr Mrs. Kerr and my littel Marriah came heare in the Packett from Baltimore. thay are all well but Marriah. she has a bad cold — thare was an extrodinary circel round the sun to day about a 11 oclock, such a one as I never saw before — a fine day

1802 Thursday May 27th ✒ a fine day

Fryday 28th ✒ a fine morning. in the after noon came on a fine rain

Saturday 29th ✒ wee had a fine rain last night. this is a fine morning. I got from Mrs. Viatt[85] the

[83] Isaac Holland (1766–1826) was son of Edward Holland (1737–1795) and his wife Sarah, and the brother of Edward Holland (see 13 November 1800). He married Jane Howard in April 1790 and Delilah Philips Sands, the widow of John, in 1811. When his son Joseph entered the St. John's grammar school in October 1803 at the age of ten, Isaac was identified as a carpenter. He lived between Church and Francis Streets in a two-story frame house with one-story frame shop. The 26 September 1826 issue of the *Federal Gazette* reported the death of former Annapolis resident Isaac Holland at the Halfway House between Annapolis and Baltimore, at age sixty-one. § Faris paid Holland 15s for carting Charles's possessions home after Charles died in September 1800.

[84] Possibly Nicholas Zachariah Maccubbin, the son of Nicholas Maccubbin (d.1786) and his wife Sarah Stevens, the daughter of John and Elizabeth Mercer Stevens. His father was a storekeeper, who had been apprenticed as a shoemaker, and who used the appellation "cordwainer" to distinguish himself from the other Nicholas Maccubbins. Nicholas Zachariah inherited the family home on Prince George Street, a two-story brick house with a frame smokehouse. At that time, the property ended at the waterfront.

[85] Margaret Peacock, or Peaco, who married Methodist minister Rev. Joseph Wyatt on 8 January 1795 in Annapolis. Margaret must have been his second wife, as Wyatt had two children who were born in the 1780s. She was most likely related to Samuel Peaco (see 22 February 1797), who named a son "John Wesley," indicating his Methodist beliefs. Wyatt lived in Fells Point in 1793 and 1796, but was in Annapolis in the intervening years, and in 1795 was chaplain of the legislature. In 1798, the Wyatts lived on Green Street in a home belonging to Francis Asbury, the itinerant Methodist preacher. Although Faris was a member of the St. Anne's vestry when younger, and presumably remained an Anglican, other members of his family were Methodists, including William and Ann Pitt, who had Wyatt baptize two of their children in August 1802.

Long and round Balsom appels, the Long ones I planted at the Pride of Chiney, the others on the Border next to Iiames's. a fine day

Sunday 30th ✒ a dull rainey day

Munday 31th ✒ a dull rainey day

Tuseday June 1th ✒ very cold this morning but turned more warm. a fine day

Wednesday 2th ✒ a cold windey day

Thursday 3th ✒ a cloudey rainey day

Fryday 4th ✒ the Bees swarmed this morning and I Put them in thare Place in the evening. a fine day

Saturday 5th ✒ this morning Capt. Kerr & Mrs. Kerr went of in the Packett for Baltimore. a fine day

1802 Sunday June 6th ✒ a fine day

Munday 7th ✒ this morning the Bees swarmed a gain. this is two swarms out of the same Hive. in the after noon a fine rain

Tuseday 8th ✒ a fine day. pulled up the Peas on the Border

Wednesday 9th ✒ sowed more Brussel Cole seed by the others. this afternoon I receved a Letter from Nancey Pitt. she & children are all well & she sent her mother a Chince gound. a fine warm day

Thursday 10th ✒ pulled up the 4 rows of Pea Vines and sticks and dugg the ground up. a fine day. Mrs. Ann Tootel died to day

Fryday 11th ✒ a fine day. this after noon Mrs. Tootel was Buried. in the evening look like for rain

Saturday 12th ✒ a warm day

Sunday 13th ✒ a warm day with severel gust of rain. I was very un well all day, I scarcely of the Bed all day

Munday 14th ✒ I had a letter to day from Abbe Kerr. a fine day. I am some thing better to day

1802 Tuseday June 15th ✒ a fine day

Wednesday 16th ✒ a fine day

Thursday 17th ✒ a fine day

Fryday 18th ✒ a fine rain. I planted out all the plants on the assparagrass Beds & that was on the Border and have not anuff. a fine day

Saturday 19th ✍ Planted more Plants to day. a fine day

Sunday 20th ✍ a fine warm day

Munday 21th ✍ a fine day. cutt part of the sage

Tuseday 22th ✍ a fine day

Wednesday 23th ✍ a fine warm day

Thursday 24th ✍ a warm day. in the evening looks like for rain

Fryday 25th ✍ I had a letter from Nancey Pitt. she tells me that Abbee's very Poorley. a fine day

Saturday 26th ✍ a fine day

1802 Sunday June 27th ✍ a fine day

Munday 28th ✍ about 9 oclock Mrs. Faris and Marriah sett of in the Packett for Baltimore. a warm day & very dry

Tuseday 29th ✍ sowed on the Border by the nutmegs cabbage seed from Mrs. Neth's mother — real cabbage — cabbage seed from Mrs. Davidson & Brussel Cole. a warm day

Wednesday 30th ✍ a fine day

Thursday July 1th ✍ this morning betwen 7 & 8 oclock Mr. William Pitt came to my house, and took Brackfast with me, he is very harty. the vessel arrived Last night about a 11 oclock from New Providence.[86] he sett of directley after Brackfast for Baltimore. I went with him on Board. he has a parcel of fine Turtel. a fine day

Fryday 2th ✍ a very warm day

Saturday 3th ✍ a Hott day. in the evening wee had a littel shower of rain

Sunday 4th ✍ Betwen 12 & 1 oclock Mrs. Faris & Marriah came from Baltimore. left them all well. a fine day. in the evening it rained a littel

1802 Munday July 5th ✍ a cloudey morning. I got my well cleaned out,[87] in the after noon wee had a fine rain

Tuseday 6th ✍ a dull dain. in the afternoon a fine rain. this morning Old Marriah the milk woman died[88]

[86] An island in the Bahamas, on which Nassau is located.

[87] Faris noted a cash payment of 11/3 for cleaning the well.

[88] Faris recorded regular payments in his cashbook for milk beginning on 21 April 1797. The first five entries, through 21 October, identify the recipient as "the milk woman"; after that date payments are always made to "Marriah." She may have been related to Henry Hicks, a free black man who owned a lot across West Street from Faris and who also supplied milk.

89 Smith Price (d.1807) was the son of Thomas Price, a free man, and Margaret Hall, a slave from St. Domingo who belonged to Daniel of St. Thomas Jenifer. Jenifer died in 1790; by the terms of his will, Price received his freedom in 1797. In addition to his involvement in the First A. M. E. Church (see 4 May 1799), Price owned the land on which a second meeting house may have been located. At his death, Price was survived by his widow Ann and six children: Henry, Ann, Betty, Smith, James, and Thomas. His will, witnessed by Nicholas and John Brewer, left his lots outside the town gate to his widow. His son Henry was one of the founders of Asbury Methodist Church in the early 1830s. § Faris's cashbook records payments to Smith Price from 1799 to 1802 for hauling dung, killing the hog, and cutting the grass, and for purchases of corn and simlins (squash).

Wednesday 7th ✒ a dull morning. Sylves finished digging the Wallnut Tree Bed & I planted 2 rows of Brussel Cale Plants, next to the shallots and 30 plants of Bore Cole from Mr. Joseph Brewer next to ye currun Bushes and in the Bigg Bed 2 rows of Plants from Smith Price.[89] thay look to be but very indifferent. this afternoon I took a Hive of Bees — I receiv'd By the Packett a pressent from Mr. Pitt of a parcel of Pine appels. a fine afternoon. I got some cabbage plants from Mr. Joseph Brewer and Planted them on the Border

Thursday 8th ✒ I got some more Plants from Mr. Brewer & I planted them with the others on the Border. a fine day

Fryday 9th ✒ a very warm day

Saturday 10th ✒ a cold morning, but turn'd out a fine day

1802 Sunday July 11th ✒ a fine day

Munday 12th ✒ a fine day

Tuseday 13th ✒ I distill'd 1 gallon of Balm Water, a fine day. Mr. Stevens's carpenters made a begining to frame his House

Wednesday 14th ✒ I have been a distilling Balm to day. a fine day

Thursday 15th ✒ I have been a distilling mint. a fine day

Fryday 16th ✒ a fine day. in the afternoon wee had a cleaver rain

Saturday 17th ✒ I have done distiling & I planted out 96 Brussel Cale plants. a showerrey day

Sunday 18th ✒ a fine day. in the evening wee had a littel shower of rain

Munday 19th ✒ Sylve's pull'd up the Beens in both Beds & dug the ground. a fine day

Tuseday 20th ✒ a very warm day

1802 Wednesday July 21th ✒ a very warm day. I sent 5 doz. of crabs to Baltimore

Thursday 22th ✒ a very morning. I sow'd some double pink alias carnation seed in a Box — 4 rows — this morning Mrs. Johnson & son called at the doore on thare way to Baltimore from the Eastern Shore. a very Hott day

Fryday 23th ✎ a very Hott day

Saturday 24th ✎ a very hott morning. in the after noon wee had a cleaver shower

Sunday 25th ✎ a Hoot cloudey day with thunder and in the afternoon wee had a clever rain

Munday 26th ✎ thare was a cleaver rain last night. a dull cloudey morning. I planted the littel qurter by the new stabel with 6 rows of Beens & Sylve's planted out a parcel of Plants & she is gathering the tops of the roshumbole onions and weeding the Bed. a rainey after noon

Tuseday 27th ✎ it rained hard last night. a cloudey morning, I have finished planting the Wallnutt Tree Bed. a fine day. ~~in the evening Bille went to see Woodberrey at the Play House and came home very drunk~~

1802 Wednesday July 28th ✎ a very Hott day

Thursday 29th ✎ a fine day. Mr. Willmore's white washing the Big Room

Fryday 30th ✎ a fine day. Willmore has finished white washing & Bille's apainting the roome. in the evening Bille went to see Woodberrey[90] at the Play house and came Home very drunk

Saturday 31th ✎ a very Hott day. bille's unabel to do aney thing to day

Sunday Augt 1th ✎ this afternoon Mr. Pitt, his wife & children came heare from Baltimore all well, thay tell me that Mrs. Kerr is well and that she has gone into the countrey to Govens Town[91] to a Mr. Woodelens. she went of this morning, a very Hott day. this afternoon old Mr. Lallee, the French Teacher in the college died[92]

Munday 2th ✎ this morning after Brackfast Mr. Pitt sett of in the Packett for Baltimore. in the after noon Mr. Lalle was Buried, a cloudey drisley day

1802 Tuseday Augt 3th ✎ a cloudey morning. in the after noon clear

Wednesday 4th ✎ a drisley morning. clear'd away a fine day

Thursday 5th ✎ Bille's been apainting the House. a fine day. I receiv'd a letter from Abee

Fryday 6th ✎ a fine day. in the evening it rained

90 Perhaps a performance by the John Woodberry who advertised on 22 March 1804 that he had opened a painting business (carriages gilded, rooms painted in imitation of wallpaper, and varnishing of all kinds) but "likewise attends to a few scholars in music, and sundry other branches of literature."

91 A settlement north of Baltimore along the road to York, Pennsylvania; now part of the City of Baltimore.

92 According to the 5 August 1802 issue of the *Maryland Gazette*, Mr. Nyol de l'Allie died Sunday last, August 1st, long a teacher of the French language at St. John's College, after a severe illness. He left an estate valued at $202, with 332 volumes of books appraised at $102; other property included a violin and music books, and a pistol and two swords. Elizabeth Claude, widow of Abraham (see 26 January 1796), served as the administrator of his estate; it is possible that de l'Allie boarded with her.

Saturday 7th ✎ last night Capt. pitt came hear about 12 oclock from Baltimore. a fine day

Sunday 8th ✎ a fine morning. in the after noon wee had a fine rain, in the evening Mr. Viatt christend Mr. & Mrs. Pitt's two children, a littel girl by the name of Hannah & the littel Boy by the name of William Faris, a fine evening

Munday 9th ✎ this morning at 9 oclock Mr. Pitt went of in the Packett for Baltimore. Sylve's Taken up the onions of Eagypt that grew in the Lott. thare was near 3 Bushels. a fine day

Tuseday 10th ✎ a fine day

1802 Wednesday Augt 11th ✎ a fine day

Thursday 12th ✎ a fine day, wee had a fine rain last night

Fryday 13th ✎ a clear cold day for the season

Saturday 14th ✎ a clear cold day

Sunday 15th ✎ this after noon Capt. pitt came here from Baltimore. he's right well, and informes me that on Thursday morning about 1 or 2 oclock Capt. Kerr asscaped a bad accident, his House was discoverd to be on Fire. it was Happyly putt out with out much damage. this has been a fine day not so cold as it has been for two or three days past

Munday 16th ✎ this morning I am 74 years old. a fine day

Tuseday 17th ✎ this morning about 8 oclock Mr. & Mrs. Pitt littel William & Salley went of in the stage for Baltimore. a fine morning. in the evening looks as if wee should have rain. it has been warm to day

Wednesday 18th ✎ a fine day

1802 Thursday Augt 19th ✎ a fine day

Fryday 20th ✎ a fine day

Saturday 21th ✎ a fine [day]. Capt. pitt sailed for Barbados

Sunday 22th ✎ a Hott day

Munday 23th ✎ this morning early my daughter pitt my littel William & Salley & the neagro woman came heare from Baltimore. thay had a long passage all night on the water. Capt. pitt sailed on Saturday last for Barbados. a fine day

Tuseday 24th ✒ this has been the Hottest day this sumer

Wednesday 25th ✒ very Hott. in the evening wee had a littel shower of rain

Thursday 26th ✒ a Hott day. in the evening looks as if wee should have a littel rain

Fryday 27th ✒ a Hott day

Saturday 28th ✒ a Hott day

Sunday 29th ✒ a Hott day

1802 Munday Augt 30th ✒ a fine day

Tuseday 31th ✒ a fine day

Wednesday September 1th ✒ Mr. Joseph Brewer gave me 2 roots of ginger, I Planted them in a pott. a dull cloudey morning. this evening Mrs. Pitt receivd a letter from Capt. pitt dated Augt. 26th from the capes. a dull day

Thursday 2th ✒ a dull coole day

Fryday 3th ✒ a coole clear morning. I have planted 4 almonds on the Border next to Mr. Ridgeleys with the yung Tulips. a fine day

Saturday 4th ✒ a clear cool day & very dry

Sunday 5th ✒ a very cold day for the season, clear & dry

Munday 6th ✒ a coole dull day. in the evening looks like for rain, it is very much wanted

Tuseday 7th ✒ rained a littel last night, and this evening. a dull cloudey cold day

Wednesday 8th ✒ a fine day but coole

1802 Thursday Septr 9th ✒ a fine day

Fryday 10th ✒ a fine day

Saturday 11th ✒ a fine day

Sunday 12th ✒ a fine day

Munday 13th ✒ last night betwen 10 & 11 oclock Capt. Kerr & Abee nock'd us up. thay came from Baltimore in the packett both well and Harty. a fine day

Tuseday 14th ✒ this morning about 8 oclock Capt. Kerr & his wife went of in the stage for Baltimore. a very Hott day. in the evening looks like for rain

Wednesday 15th ☞ a very hott day

Thursday 16th ☞ a Hott day

Fryday 17th ☞ a cloudey morning. a littel shower of rain and very littel. a pleasant day

Saturday 18th ☞ a fine day

Sunday 19th ☞ directley after diner wile at Tabel I was suddently struck as if a Ball had went through me with a violent ague which continued for a considerable time and a violent Feveour & sweet followed

1802 Munday Septr 20th ☞ I am very unwell to day. I have taken 12 gms of callomel, my physick worked me but very littel. I have been very unwell all day. in the evening it looks as if wee should have rain, its been a fine day

Tuseday 21th ☞ I had my ague. it came on about 12 oclock. a cloudey windey day

Wednesday 22th ☞ I have been taking the Bark to day. a dull cloude drisley day. in the evening came on to rain

Thursday 23th ☞ wee had a fine rain last night, a rainey morning & continued to rain all day. I missed my ague to day

Fryday 24th ☞ wee had more rain last night. a clear cold day. yesterday evening the following coupels ware married – Joseph Harwood to Miss Ann Chapman[93] – James Weems to Miss Elizabeth Ridgley[94] – Henrey Colter to Miss Ann Clark[95]

Saturday 25th ☞ a clear coole day

Sunday 26th ☞ a cloudey day

Munday 27th ☞ a clear cool day

1802 Tuseday Septr 28th ☞ I putt up the grate in the House to day. a fine day

Wednesday 29th ☞ a dull coole day

Thursday 30th ☞ a fine day

Fryday Octobr 1th ☞ a fine day

Saturday 2th ☞ a fine day. I planted the Buttons that grew on the top of the shallotts

Sunday 3th ☞ a fine day

Munday 4th ☞ a fine day

93 Anne Chapman was probably the daughter of William and Anne Sellman Chapman (see 2 April 1792), whose birth on 17 February 1783 was recorded in the All Hallow's Parish register. Joseph was the son of Col. Richard and Margaret Hall Harwood; Faris noted the marriage of his brother Richard on 23 October 1798.

94 James Nicholson Weems (1779–1823) was the son of Richard and Mary Ward Weems (see 15 October 1795) and the stepson of James Disney (see 4 May 1803). He died sometime prior to 1823, as the distribution of his mother's estate in May of that year included a one-fourth share for the heirs of James Weems. Elizabeth Ridgely (b.1777) was the daughter of Absalom and Anna Robinson Ridgely (see 30 November 1799). § James Weems was one of the major purchasers, aside from family members, at the sale of Faris's estate, buying sundry planes, a pair of pistols, a pair of hand vises, a bench vise, a large number of files, a pair of bullet molds, one box of "sundries," and a pair of scales.

95 Henry Coulter and Anne Clarke received a license on 23 September 1802. Their son, Henry Jr., was born about 1806.

Tuseday 5th ✒ a fine day

Wednesday 6th ✒ a fine day

Thursday 7th ✒ this evening the city ellection finished when Messrs Quynn & Ridgley[96] whare ellected, a fine day

Fryday 8th ✒ this morning earley Capt. Kerr & wife came heare from Baltimore. a fine day

Saturday 9th ✒ a very warm day, the ship Baltimore went by heare last nigh for Ireland

1802 Sunday Octr 10th ✒ a very warm day

Munday 11th ✒ a fine day

Tuseday 12th ✒ a fine day

Wednesday 13th ✒ a dull morning. about 9 oclock Capt. Kerr went of in the Packett for Baltimore. a fine day. in the evening Abee went to the Play. I got an excecusion for Cornelius Mills and put it in to the hands of Isaac Hollon to serve requesting him either to Bring me the money or put him to Prisson[97]

Thursday 14th ✒ a very warm day. wee had a littel sprinkel of rain this evening

Fryday 15th ✒ very warm day

Saturday 16th ✒ a warm day. Mrs. Pitt has been very poorley to day

Sunday 17th ✒ this after noon Capt. Kerr returned hear from Baltimore & Brings news that Capt. William Pitt has arrived at Baltimore. that he sold his vessel in the West Indies & has come in passenger. a dull cloudey day

1802 Munday Octr 18th ✒ a fine day

Tuseday 19th ✒ this morning Mrs. Pitt & sone William Faris & neagro girl went of in the Packett for Baltimore. in the evening I mooved the littel Barrel with Bees into the Bee House. a coole day

Wednesday 20th ✒ a cloudey day. John Rigel sexton of the church is ded. in the evening came on to rain. I mooved the pott with the gin[g]er in it into the shop

Thursday 21th ✒ a cloudey morning, in the after noon I receiv'd a letter from Capt. William Pitt. thay are all well & I expect them heare in a few days. a fine afternoon

96 City voters chose Allen Quynn and Richard Ridgely as their delegates to the lower house.

97 Faris had won a judgment against Mills for payment of a debt, but the judgment must also have gone unpaid. Faris's execution authorized the sheriff or his deputy (Holland) to collect the money for Faris.

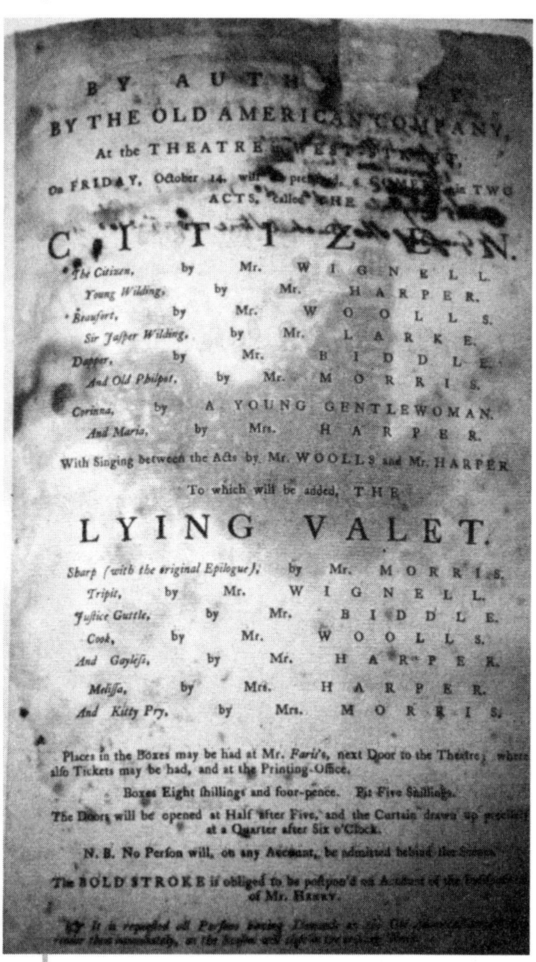

BY AUTH[...]
BY THE OLD AMERICAN COMPANY,
At the THEATRE [...]
On FRIDAY, October 14, will be presented, a COMEDY in TWO ACTS, called THE

CITIZEN.

Sbe Citizen,   by   Mr. WIGNELL.
Young Wilding,   by   Mr. HARPER.
Beaufort,   by   Mr. WOOLLS.
Sir Jasper Wilding, by   Mr. LARKE.
Dapper,   by   Mr. BIDDLE.
And Old Philpot,   by   Mr. MORRIS.
Corinna,   by   A YOUNG GENTLEWOMAN.
And Maria,   by   Mrs. HARPER.

With Singing between the Acts by Mr. WOOLLS and Mr. HARPER

To which will be added, THE

LYING VALET.

Sharp (with the original Epilogue), by   Mr. MORRIS.
Tripit,   by   Mr. WIGNELL.
Justice Guttle,   by   Mr. BIDDLE.
Cook,   by   Mr. WOOLLS.
And Gayless,   by   Mr. HARPER.
Melissa,   by   Mrs. HARPER.
And Kitty Pry,   by   Mrs. MORRIS.

Places in the Boxes may be had at Mr. Faris's, next Door to the Theatre; where also Tickets may be had, and at the Printing-Office.

Boxes Eight shillings and foor-pence. Pit Five Shillings.

The Doors will be opened at Half after Five, and the Curtain drawn up precisely at a Quarter after Six o'Clock.

N. B. No Person will, on any Account, be admitted behind the Scenes.

The BOLD STROKE is obliged to be postpon'd on Account of the Indisposition of Mr. Harry.

133 ✒ Playbill for *The Citizen* and *The Lying Valet*

Faris never missed an opportunity for free advertising, as shown in this playbill with its notice: "places in the Boxes may be had at Mr. Faris', *next Door to the Theatre."*

Fryday 22th ✍ a fine day

Saturday 23th ✍ a dull cloudey day

Sunday 24th ✍ a dull cloudey day. in the after noon Mr. & Mrs. Pitt & littel William came heare from Baltimore all well

1802 Munday Octr 25th ✍ a dull day. Mrs. pitt has been very unwell to day

Tuseday 26th ✍ a cloudey day

Wednesday 27th ✍ a fine rain last night. a cloudey morning. about 9 oclock Capt. Kerr & wife went of in the Packett for Baltimore. a dull day

Thursday 28th ✍ a fine morning. about 9 oclock Mr. & Mrs. pitt & children went of in the packett for Baltimore. I sent the 7 Tune Clock to Mr. Kerr. a fine day

Fryday 29th ✍ a clear cold day

Saturday 30th ✍ a fine morning. in after noon clouded up & looks like falling weather

Sunday 31th ✍ a rainey Night. a cloudey rainey morning. a dirtey cloudey day. in the evening Miss Hanson[98] was Buried

Munday Novr 1th ✍ a cloudey morning, it snow'd a littel. clear'd away a fine day but very cold, I receiv'd the candels by the Packett Mrs. Pitt sent me. I had a letter from her. thay are all well

1802 Tuseday Novr 2th ✍ a clear cold day. in the evening Mr. Allexander C. Hanson was heare and in conversation he said that this was his Birth Day and that he was 53 years old

Wednesday 3th ✍ a clear cold day

Thursday 4th ✍ dug up & prepair'd the littel square Bed at the end of the shed. in the after noon Planted 2 peach stones of very latter peaches in the yard By the fence & gather'd the Sencitive Plant seed. a fine day

Fryday 5th ✍ a fine day

Saturday 6th ✍ a fine morning. in the afternoon clouded up & looks like falling weather

Sunday 7th ✍ a fine morning. I planted a nercess I got from Mr. Stevens & 6 or 7 Hyacinths from Mr. Joseph Brewer at the end of the new stabel — in the

[98] Possibly Catherine Contee Hanson, sister of Alexander Contee Hanson. Hanson had four sisters, but the other three had died by this date.

after noon turned cloudey & cold. I receiv'd a letter
from Nancey & Abee to day. thay are both well

Munday 8th ✍ a fine day

Tuseday 9th ✍ a fine day. Old William Has finished weeling dung from Mr. Ridgeleys and is
amooveing the greens out of the Big Bed into the
littel Bed by the old stabel

1802 Wednesday Novr 10th ✍ a fine day. Old
William has been covering the flower Beds with
leaves & Tan

Thursday 11th ✍ Old William has finished covering the Flower Beds. a fine day

Fryday 12th ✍ a dull cloudey day

Saturday 13th ✍ a fine day

Sunday 14th ✍ a fine day

Munday 15th ✍ a fine day

Tuseday 16th ✍ a dull day. in the afternoon and
evening rained a littel

Wednesday 17th ✍ a raney night & morning.
cleard away about noon, a fine afternoon. I received
a letter from Nancey, she & Mr. pitt & the children
are all well

Thursday 18th ✍ a fine day

Fryday 19th ✍ a fine day

Saturday 20th ✍ a fine day. finished Triming the
peach Trees

1802 Sunday Novr 21th ✍ a fine day

Munday 22th ✍ a rainey day

Tuseday 23th ✍ a fine day. Old William dugg up
the Parsneps & cover'd them in a Hill

Wednesday 24th ✍ a fine day

Thursday 25th ✍ a fine day. in the evening
clouded up

Fryday 26th ✍ a dull cloudey day

Saturday 27th ✍ a clear coole day

Sunday 28th ✍ a clear cold day

Munday 29th ✍ I receiv'd a letter from Mrs. Pitt &
Mrs. Kerr. thay are both well. a fine day

Tuseday 30th 🖎 a cold raw day. in the evening came on to rain. cover'd the rosmary with straw

1802 Wednesday Desr 1th 🖎 last night was a very windey rayney night — a rainey morning. a dull drisley day

Thursday 2th 🖎 a fine day

Fryday 3th 🖎 a fine day

Saturday 4th 🖎 a fine day. in the evening clouded up

Sunday 5th 🖎 a rainey night last night. a rainey morning — a cloudey drisley day. this afternoon I mooved the potts with Cryanthymums and Cherrey Trees in to the seller

Munday 6th 🖎 a fine day

Tuseday 7th 🖎 a cold dull day

Wednesday 8th 🖎 a cloudey fore noon. look'd like for snow. in the after noon cleard away

Thursday 9th 🖎 a clear & very cold windey day

Fryday 10th 🖎 a cold day. in the evening clouded up

Saturday 11th 🖎 snow'd last night. a dull cloudey day

1802 Sunday Desr 12th 🖎 a dull cloudey day

Munday 13th 🖎 a fine day

Tuseday 14th 🖎 a dull cloudey drisley day

Wednesday 15th 🖎 a fine day

Thursday 16th 🖎 the wind Blew very hard last night, a very cold windey day

Fryday 17th 🖎 Last night was very cold, a very cold cloudey snowey day

Saturday 18th 🖎 a clear cold day

Sunday 19th 🖎 a fine morning. in the after noon clouded up & in the evening came on to rain

Munday 20th 🖎 a dull cloudey day. receiv'd a letter from my daughter Pitt whare in she tells me that her daughter Hannah is very ill with a feveour. ever since Saturday last was weak

Tuseday 21th 🖎 a dull drisley day

1802 Wednesday Desr 22th ✒ a dull cloudey day

Thursday 23th ✒ a dull cloudey day

Fryday 24th ✒ Betwen 1 & 2 oclock, Capt. Kerr and Abee came heare from Baltimore. a fine day

Saturday 25th ✒ an Asembleyman by the name of Crumwell[99] from [Washington] County died to day of a Plurisey. a fine day

Sunday 26th ✒ a cloudey drisley day

Munday 27th ✒ the masons went in Prossession to Church to day. a fine day

Tuseday 28th ✒ a very fine warm day. in the evening the masons gave a Ball

Wednesday 29th ✒ a rainey day

Thursday 30th ✒ a dull cloudey day

Fryday 31th ✒ a clear cool day. in the evening wee all went to Mr. Owens's & spent the evening

1803 Saturday January 1th ✒ a dull, cloudey day

Sunday 2th ✒ a fine morning, about noon Mrs. Elizabeth Williams daughter of James Thomas died. a cloudey after noon, looks like for falling weather. at night began to snow

Munday 3th ✒ a snowey morning. about noon it stop'd snowing

Tuseday 4th ✒ this morning about 8 oclock Mr. and Mrs. Kerr went of in the stage for Baltimore. about a 11 oclock Mrs. Elizabeth Williams was Buried. a fine day

Wednesday 5th ✒ a fine morning. in the afternoon cloudey

Thursday 6th ✒ a fine rain Last night. it has carried of all the snow, a cloudey day

Fryday 7th ✒ a clear cold day

Saturday 8th ✒ a fine day

Sunday 9th ✒ a clear cold day

Munday 10th ✒ a clear cold day. in the afternoon cloudey

1803 Tuseday 11th ✒ this afternoon the Assembley broke up. a fine day

99 The *Maryland Gazette* reported on 30 December that Richard Cromwell (1749–1802) died Saturday last, in Annapolis; a member of the house of delegates of this state, from Washington County. Cromwell sat in the house intermittently from 1792 to 1802.

Wednesday 12th ☞ a dull drisley cloudey day. I have had a dissagreebel Pain in my hed & a Feaveour all day

Thursday 13th ☞ rained a good deal last night. a dull cloudey morning. betwen 8 & 9 oclock Polley Ranken want of in the stage for Baltimore, a rainey day

Fryday 14th ☞ a cloudey dull rainey day

Saturday 15th ☞ a fine warm day

Sunday 16th ☞ a fine morning. in ye after noon cloudey

Munday 17th ☞ a cold day. in the afternoon cloudey

Tuseday 18th ☞ a clear cold day

Wednesday 19th ☞ a clear cold day

Thursday 20th ☞ a clear cold day

Fryday 21th ☞ a clear & very cold windey day

Saturday 22th ☞ a clear cold day

Sunday 23th ☞ a dull cloudey day like for snow

1803 Munday Janry 24th ☞ a fine day

Tuseday 25th ☞ a fine day

Wednesday 26th ☞ a cloudey day. Capt. John Gorden's[100] died

Thursday 27th ☞ a fine day. Capt. Gordon was Buried

Fryday 28th ☞ a clear cold day

Saturday 29th ☞ a clear & very cold day. Charrity went of in the stage for Baltimore this morning[101]

Sunday 30th ☞ snow'd a littel last night. a dull cloudey drisley cold windey day

Munday 31th ☞ a clear cold day

Tuseday Febuary 1th ☞ a fine day. I have been very un well all day

Wednesday 2th ☞ I am Better to day. a dull day

Thursday 3th ☞ a fine morning. trimed and nailed up the Rose Bushes and trimed the Goosberry Bushes. about 12 oclock it thunder'd & sprinkeld a littel rain. the wind shifted to the N.W{es}t & Blew hard and turned cooler then it was in the morning. I planted the seeds of reasons in a pott. the weather has turned cold

[100] John Gordon, a mariner, was the son of George Gordon, Esq. In 1783 he had owned five slaves but no land, and his household consisted only of himself and one woman. When he died, he left no widow and bequeathed legacies from his small estate to four members of the Sands family, naming John Sands as his executor. § Gordon's father patronized Faris's tavern in 1773.

[101] Lockwood Barr lists Charity as one of the children of Abigail and Archibald Kerr, but she is clearly a slave belonging either to Faris or to the Kerrs. Faris recorded the birth of Alexander, Abigail and Archibald's first child, on 16 November 1803.

1803 Fryday Febry 4th ✍ a clear cold day

Saturday 5th ✍ a dull morning. in the afternoon came on to snow and looks as if we should have a good deal of it

Sunday 6th ✍ snow'd, Hailed, & rained last night and this morning it rained till about noon. then a cloudey drisseley afternoon & evening

Munday 7th ✍ a very Foggey morning. in the evening turned to rain

Tuseday 8th ✍ a foggey morning. Sylve putt dung on the Border & dugg it up ready for Planting. a dull day

Wednesday 9th ✍ a fine morning. Planted 16 rows of Peas on the Border, & Old William has made good the fence Betwen the smoke house & stabel. I sow'd in a Box early York & sugar loafed cabbag from Smith Price & he is to have some of them. Old William is arepairing the fence betwen my Lott & Mrs. Mans garden

Thursday 10th ✍ a clear cold day

Fryday 11th ✍ a clear cold day

Saturday 12th ✍ a dull cloudey drisley day

1803 Sunday 13th ✍ a very windey rainey Night. continued a windey rainey day

Munday 14th ✍ Last night it Blow'd, Hailed rain'd & snow'd, a very cold dull windey day

Tuseday 15th ✍ clear & very cold morning. a clear cold day

Wednesday 16th ✍ a very cold windey night. a cold, cloudey windey morning. about 11 oclock it began to snow & continued snowing and Blowing very Hard all day

Thursday 17th ✍ a very Bad night last night, it snowed and Blew a near Harrican, I am afraid poor Collin is lost, he is not to be seen this morning. a cold dull morning about 10 oclock the sun came out fine. in the evening clouded up again, Poor Collin has got home again. I was afriad the poor dogg was ded

Fryday 18th ✍ a clear cold day

Saturday 19th ✍ a fine day

Sunday 20th ⚘ a fine day

1803 Munday Febuary 21th ⚘ a fine day

Tuseday 22th ⚘ this morning I cleaned the Bee
  Hives. a fine day

Wednesday 23th ⚘ a fine day

Thursday 24th ⚘ a dull cloudey drisley day

Fryday 25th ⚘ the ground was coverd with snow
  this morning. a snowey morning, about 9 oclock
  left of snowing. continued cloudey & the wind Blew
  hard and cold. about noon clear'd away a fine afternoon but cold and windey

Saturday 26th ⚘ Last night was a very cold night.
  a very cold morning. about 9 oclock it grew more
  modarate. a fine day but cold. in the evening Mr. &
  Mrs. Pitt, littel Hannah & littel William Faris Pitt
  & Salley came heare from Baltimore all well. a cold
  night

Sunday 27th ⚘ a cold morning but turned out a
  fine pleasant day

Munday 28th ⚘ a dull cloudey day. looks like for
  falling weather

1803 Tuseday March 1th ⚘ snow this morning.
  a very cold windey day

Wednesday 2th ⚘ a clear cold day

Thursday 3th ⚘ about 9 oclock Mr. & Mrs. pitt, &
  child; & girl & my self sett of in Capt. John Barbers
  packett for Baltimore. arrived and Landed at Fells
  point at ½ at 2 oclock. paid Capt. Barber 1 & ½
  dolors for my passage diner

[Faris made no entries in the diary while he was in
  Baltimore.]

Wednesday 9th ⚘ about ½ after 8 oclock, Capt.
  Kerr & my self sett of from Mr. pitts. left thare Mr.
  Pitt, Mrs. pitt & Mrs. Kerr all well. I sett of from
  Baltimore in Capt. George Barbers Packett a littel
  after 9 oclock & arrived in the dock in annapolis ½
  after 1 oclock. paid Capt. Barber 1 & ½ dollors for
  my passage and diner

Thursday 10th ⚘ a clear cold day. Sylve weeled
  dung on the Bigg Bed & I filled a new Barrel for my
  Ice plant

1803 Fryday March 11th ✍ Sylve's wheeled
dung on the lott for parsneps & carrots. a clear cool
day

Saturday 12th ✍ Sylve's digging in the lott (a fine
day) for Parsneps & carrotts

Sunday 13th ✍ a fine day

Munday 14th ✍ this morning I sow'd on the
Border betwen the peas No. 1 large white headed
cabbage No. 2 early sugar loaf d⁰, No. 3 earley
York. I like wise sowed Lettis & radish seed. Sylve's
geting ye ground ready for the onions in the Lott,
Sylve's spread the dung on the Big Bed in the
garden & Bille's sowing carrotts. a fine day, Bille
has finished sowing the carrotts

Tuseday 15th ✍ Bille has finished planting the
parsneps & Sylve's digging the Bigg Bed in the
garden. a fine day

Wednesday 16th ✍ Bille has finished planting the
onions of Eagipt or roshemboles & Sylve's digging
the Bigg Bed in the garden. Sylve's finished digging the Bigg Bed. a fine day. in the evening
turned cloudey. looks like for rain

1803 Thursday March 17th ✍ Sylve's done up
the asparragrass Beds & took up the seed onions of
Eagipt & dugg up the ground ready for planting. a
fine day. in the evening it came on to rain a littel &
looks as if wee should have a good deal of it. I sow'd
some stock July flower seed in a Box

Fryday 18th ✍ thare was a cleaver littel rain last
night. a fine morning, I sow'd a row of spinige
Betwen the assparagrass Beds and on the Beds I
sow'd No. 1 Large white headed cabbage No. 2
earley sugar Loaf No. 3 earley York begining next
to Mr. Ridgley's and Lettice on both Beds and sow'd
4 rows of Peas in the Bigg Bed, and Bille has made
abegining this after noon to Trowell the Flower Beds
round the grass walk, a fine day. & I sow'd the
white wall flower seed in a pott

1803 Saturday March 19th ✍ Bille's troweling
the flower Beds round the grass walk. a fine day

Sunday 20th ✍ it rained a littel this morning.
clear'd away a fine day. in the evening clouded up &
looks like for rain

Munday 21th ✒ a fine morning. I have sow'd a line of spinige the further side of the assparagrass Beds. Sylve's takeing the suckers from the Goosberrey Bushes & Bille is troweling the flower Beds. I sow'd the Ice plant seed in the Barrel & the Sentcitive Plant seed in a pott, and by the altheas I sow'd the Balsom appel & the Nersertion & Sylve's doing up the tabel round the Big Bed. Bille has finished Troweling the Beds round the grass walk & has got into the Beds leading to the Littel House, a fine day but the wind Blows Hard

Tuseday 22th ✒ Sylve has taken away the straw from the rosemarey & Planted out the carnations & Bille has got into the nurssery Beds & Sylve's moved the old Bricks out of the yard into the lott. a fine day but cold to what it has been

1803 Wednesday March 23th ✒ a cold, rainey and snowey morning. about 12 oclock left of raining. continued a cold cloudey day

Thursday 24th ✒ a cold windey day

Fryday 25th ✒ a clear cold windey day

Saturday 26th ✒ a cold windey morning. in the after noon turn'd cloudey & looks like for rain

Sunday 27th ✒ a clear cold day

Munday 28th ✒ I have planted the Jacobian Lilleys, Billee's doing the flower Beds & Sylve's made Hills in the Lott for simlins & dunging the ground for the Oakerea. a clear cold morning. finished digging the oacoro ground & Bille's finished troweling the Flower Beds, the two Borders of yung roots are to trowel & I have cutt one line of Box. a clear coole day

1803 Tuseday March 29th ✒ a clear day and not so cold as it has been, bille has finished Troweling all the Flowers, and has mad abegining to cut Box. this evening John Callahorn daughter, Salley is married to Majr Harwood's son Richard Harwood[102]

Wednesday 30th ✒ a fine day. Bille is cuting Box and Old William been awheeling dung from Mr. Richard Ridgley's

Thursday 31th ✒ a cloudey day. Bille has finished cutting Box all but the long line

Fryday April 1th ✒ a dull cloudey day

[102] Richard Harwood (1775–1835) was the son of Thomas and Margaret Harwood (see 8 May 1792). Sarah Callahan (c.1783–1833) was the daughter of John and Sarah Buckland Callahan (see 7 February 1793). Harwood, who graduated from St. John's with an A. B. degree in November 1794, held the offices of common councilman and commissioner, and served three terms as mayor from 1824 to 1826. The *Maryland Gazette* reported on 25 April 1833 that Mrs. Sally Harwood, wife of Richard Harwood, of Thomas, Adjutant-General of Maryland, and eldest daughter of the late John Callahan, died 22nd instant, in her 50th year, and on 9 April 1835, that Richard Harwood, son of Thomas, Adjutant-General of Maryland, died Saturday last in his sixty-first year.

Saturday 2th ✎ Bille has finished the Box and
Sylve's takeing up the cuttings. I planted 13 Hills
of simlins & sow in a small Box aster seed, Sylves
stuck the peas on the Border. a fine day

Sunday 3th ✎ a warm windey day. I toped the littel
peach tree in the Been Bed, it was in Blossom

1803 Munday April 4th ✎ Bille went about the
tabels round the grass walk & Sylve to digging the
Been Bed at the end of the new stabel. in the afternoon came on to rain, thay both came in and left it.
continued raining a moderate rain all the afternoon

Tuseday 5th ✎ Sylve dug the Border by the Bee
House. I sow'd Parceley on the end next the Bee
House. made 7 Hils in the Lott, sow'd 5 with the
Nutmegg Cantilope from Mr. Manedier & 2 with
cucumbers the seed saved in 1801. a fine day

Wednesday 6th ✎ Bille has finished the tabels
round the grass walk. a fine day but rather coole

Thursday 7th ✎ Planted 6 rows of Been 3 of yallow
& 3 of dark purpel, and on the side of the Bed I
planted the salmon, scarlet & short topd radis seed.
a clear cool day

Fryday 8th ✎ a clear coole day. in the afternoon
clouded up like for rain. in the afternoon Woodward
Evett[103] called hear. he & his daughter are going
over the Bay to see his Brothers

1803 Saturday April 9th ✎ a clear coole day

Sunday 10th ✎ a clear cold windey day

Munday 11th ✎ a fine morning, about 9 oclock
Mrs. Faris & Marriah pitt went of in the Packett for
Baltimore. this fore noon I sow'd the ocoro, or coffe,
Silve's watering the Flower Beds. I have put more
simlin seeds in the Hills. a fine day. in the evening
about sun sett John Wells's wife died

Tuseday 12th ✎ Sylve's swept the garden walks & I
planted a pott of sencitive plant seeds. a warm day
and very dry

Wednesday 13th ✎ Sylve's dug the Border for the
nuttmegs I sow'd 48 rows of seed, she then went to
sticking the 4 rows of Peas in the Bigg Bed. this
afternoon Mrs. John Wells was Buried, a dull
Heavey cloudey day

Thursday 14th ✎ a dull cloudey morning. I
receiv'd a letter from Mrs. pitt. Mrs. Faris got thare

[103] Woodward Evitt was the son of carpenter John Evitt, who died in 1774.
Evitt's will made no mention of a wife,
and named four sons, John Joseph,
Abraham, Woodward, and Seth Hill. At
the time the family lived on Prince
George Street, near the waterfront.
When he visited the Faris family,
Woodward lived in Frederick County
and his brothers in Caroline County. §
Priscilla Ruley Woodward left £10 current money when she died in 1773 to
her grandson, Woodward Evitt, but
without indicating which of her daughters (the sisters of Priscilla Woodward
Faris) was Evitt's mother. In 1765, John
Evitt was married to Mary, widow of
Thomas Pecker, but his first wife (certainly the mother of the three children
with Woodward family names) could
have been either Martha or Rebecca
Woodward. Evitt successfully sued Faris
in August 1783 for recovery of a debt.

thare about 6 oclock. thay are all well. a dull cloudey warm day, this afternoon Miss Harriot Quynn[104] died

1803 Fryday April 15th ✍ a cloudey morning. about 12 oclock at noon Miss Harriot Quynn was Buried. soon after came on to rain and Blow'd hard

Saturday 16th ✍ it Blow'd very Hard in the night. a cold cloudey windey morning, it snow'd a littel. I planted out one line of plants but it was so cold I left off — I went at again & finished the 3 lines of plants. Bille's makeing sticks to mark some of the flowers. very cold — it continued cold & cloudey & snow'd a littel at times through the afternoon

Sunday 17th ✍ snow'd in the night. the tops of the Houses were white with snow, a snowey morning, continued snowing till about 1 oclock then left of but continued very cold and cloudey all the after noon

Munday 18th ✍ sow'd 3 rows of Peas in the Big Bed & marked the Hyacinths, Crown Imperials Nercess's & Blew Crocus's, a fine day

1803 Tuseday April 19th ✍ a fine day but coole

Wednesday 20th ✍ a clear cool day. in the evening clouded up like for rain. I toped & shortened the limbs of the littel peach Tree By the well and made some of compossission and putt on the places whare I cutt of the limbs. betwen 9 & ten oclock at night Mrs. Faris, Capt. Kerr, Abee & Marriah came home from Baltimore

Thursday 21th ✍ a fine day

Fryday 22th ✍ a fine day

Saturday 23th ✍ a fine day. in the evening came on to rain

Sunday 24th ✍ a fine day, in the evening it rained

Munday 25th ✍ a rainey day

Tuseday 26th ✍ a rainey day and cold for the season

Wednesday 27th ✍ a clear day

1803 Thursday April 28th ✍ a clear day

Fryday 29th ✍ a dull morning, about 9 oclock Capt. Kerr & Abee sett of for Baltimore with Nat & Charrity. a fine day. in the evening it came on to rain

---

[104] A daughter of Allen Quynn.

Saturday 30th ✍ a cloudey mistey morning. clear'd away a fine day. I Topped the Peach Tree by Hogg pen & used the compossion

Sunday May 1th ✍ some body last night jumped the Fence at the Back of the garden & Broke of about a dozen Tulips. a fine day. in the afternoon wee had a littel shower of rain

Munday 2th ✍ rained last night. a fine day

Tuseday 3th ✍ a very cold clear day

Wednesday 4th ✍ last night Capt. James Disseney[105] died over South River, a clear cold day. this evening I Tarr'd round the Bottoms of the Peach Trees

1803 Thursday 5th ✍ a rainey morning. about noon cleard away a fine after noon. planted in the Lott the following cabbage plants Large White Headed cabbage earley Sugar Loaf d⁰ earley York d⁰

Fryday 6th ✍ a clear cold day

Saturday 7th ✍ a smart Frost last night and this morning the Beens & simlins ware bitt a good deal. a clear cold day

Sunday 8th ✍ rained Last night. a clear cold day

Munday 9th ✍ a clear cold morning. I finished marking the tulips, Sylve has howed the Beens & peas & are sticking the last 3 rows. finished sticking & Howing the Peas. a fine day

Tuseday 10th ✍ a fine morning. I sow'd on the Border by the Bee House the following seeds, first Large White Headed Cabbage, 2d two Kinds of d⁰ unknown from R. B. L.[106] Bore Cole from J. Brewer & Brussel Cole & salmon scarlet & short Top radish seed — a fine day

1803 Wednesday May 11th ✍ a fine day

Thursday 12th ✍ a fine day. in the evening looks like for rain

Thursday 12th ✍ a fine day [double entry in original.]

Fryday 13th ✍ a fine day. Old Terrey brought me some catnip & I planted it in the alley betwen the new stabel & the Fence

[105] James Disney (1751–1803) was the son of James (d. 1778) and Rachel Disney. In 1783, James married Mary Ward Weems, the widow of Richard Weems and mother of four. Disney had a tavern license in 1786 and was a justice of the peace in 1787. § Faris, with Richard Burgess, was surety for Rachel Disney's administration bond for her husband's estate in October 1779.

[106] Randolph Brant Latimer (see 2 March 1795).

Saturday 14th ✒ a fine warm day

Sunday 15th ✒ a fine day

Munday 16th ✒ a fine day. in the evening looks like for rain

Tuseday 17th ✒ a fine day

Wednesday 18th ✒ a fine day. in the evening looks like for rain

Thursday 19th ✒ a fine day. in the afternoon I began Brakeing of the stocks of the Tulips

1803 Fryday May 20th ✒ a cloudey morning. I finish'd brakeing off stoks of the Tulips round the grass walk. I Broke of 1520

Saturday 21th ✒ a fine morning. finish Brakeing of the Tulip stocks. some ware full 3 feet high. in the Beds round the grass walk thare was 1520 — By the littel house 150 on the Border next Mr. Ridgely's my Tulips 256 Dutch 37 — Parrot Tail seedlings 16 Nursery Beds 1276 on the Border by the street 161 — Totel 3566 — a fine day

Sunday 22th ✒ a dull cloudey day

Munday 23th ✒ a cloudey morning. last night Mr. John Wells (the Butcher died) and I sow'd a row of Peas in the lott this morning and Isac mow'd the grass in the garden, in the after noon Mr. John Wells was Buried. a cloudey drisley afternoon

1803 Tuesday May 24th ✒ a cold drisley morning. I Filled the Big Bed with Plants. in the afternoon wee had a fire made in the House. a cold wett day

Wednesday 25th ✒ a cold cloudey drisley day

Thursday 26th ✒ a dull coole day

Fryday 27th ✒ a coole day & cloudey at times

Saturday 28th ✒ a clear cold day. still a fire in the House

Sunday 29th ✒ a rainey fore noon & cloudey after-noon. a fire in the House

Munday 30th ✒ a dull cloudey drisley day. not so cold as it has been, betwen a 11 & 12 oclock Mr. Nicholas Brewer Senr[107] died

[107] Nicholas Brewer Sr. (1744–1803) was the son of John Brewer IV (1709–1754) and his wife Elizabeth Maccubbin (1708–1779). His twin sister Rachel was the first wife of artist Charles Willson Peale (1741–1827), whom she married on 30 May 1768. Brewer, a storekeeper, never married. Although he had 9 siblings, his will, written in 1786, mentions only his youngest sister Mary, the wife of James Boyle (see 20 June 1798).

Tuseday 31th ✍ a raney night & rainey morning
and continued raining till late in the afternoon.
cleared away fine. this evening Mr. Nicholas Brewer
was Buried

1803 Wednesday June 1th ✍ a fine clear warm
day

Thursday 2th ✍ a fine day. I have been adistilling
rose water

Fryday 3th ✍ a cloudey drisley morning. about
noon clear'd away a fine afternoon

Saturday 4th ✍ a fine day. in the evening wee had
a littel rain

Sunday 5th ✍ a cloudey rainey day

Munday 6th ✍ a clear day

Tuseday 7th ✍ a dull day, Sylve's dug the littel
qurter by the old stabel & I sow'd 8 rows of Beens 4
yallow next the Wallnutt Tree & 4 rows of Speckel'd
next to Ridgleys and Sylves taken up the sticks &
vines of the Peas on the Border. in the evening looks
as if wee should have rain

Wednesday 8th ✍ a rainey morning, clear'd away
about noon, a fine afternoon, I Planted out Plants in
the littel quarter betwen the beens, in the evening
it looks ass if wee should have more rain

1803 Thursday June 9th ✍ a fine day

Fryday 10th ✍ a fine day. Sylve's been cleaning the
garden

Saturday 11th ✍ a fine day

Sunday 12th ✍ a fine day

Munday 13th ✍ this morning Planted 8 or 10
Hills of cantilope seed from Mrs. Randel. a dull
morning. a warm dull day

Tuseday 14th ✍ a warm day

Wednesday 15th ✍ a dull cloudey day

Thursday 16th ✍ a dull cloudey day

Fryday 17th ✍ a warm day

Saturday 18th ✍ a warm day, Puled the Peas &
sticks up of the first 4 rows in ye Big Bed

134 ✍ Deborah Knapp Randall
(c.1763–1852)

*Deborah was the daughter of
watchmaker William Knapp
and wife of merchant John
Randall. Faris recorded the
births of two of her children.*

108 Aside from the one occasion when Priscilla Faris helped in the garden, this is the only domestic activity of hers that Faris recorded in the diary.

109 This may have been Richard Riston, who appears as a debtor to the estate of Jacob Hurst (see 7 October 1792) in 1792. Riston may have been the son of James Riston, who contracted in May 1766 to build a wharf at the end of Northeast Street.

110 It has not been possible to identify Maria Howard, although it is possible that Faris meant Mary Higginbotham Howard, the second wife of Samuel Harvey Howard.

Sunday 19th ☞ a Hott day

Munday 20th ☞ a coole clear day

Tuseday 21th ☞ a fine day. Mrs. Faris is abegining to make curran jelley108

[There are no entries from 22 June through 27 August but they may have been lost.]

1803 Sunday Augt 28th ☞ a very warm day. in the afternoon Mr. Ristans109 son was Buried, in the evening Capt. Kerr & Abee came heare from Baltimore Both well

Munday 29th ☞ this morning Capt. Kerr went of for Baltimore in the Packett. a very Hott day

Tuseday 30th ☞ a fine day

Wednesday 31th ☞ a fine day. in the evening it looks like for rain

Thursday Septr 1th ☞ a cloudey dull Blustering day

Fryday 2th ☞ a Hott day. in the evening turn'd cloudey

Saturday 3th ☞ a fine day

Sunday 4th ☞ a fine day. in the evening I was taken with a gripeing & lax

Munday 5th ☞ about 3 oclock Capt. Kerr came hear from Baltimore. about 9 oclock Capt. Kerr & Abee went of for Baltimore. my lax continued very bad all night and all day

Tuseday 6th ☞ the lax has left me, but I have a fever and am very weeak & poorley. I call'd in Doctr Ghislin & he gave me a dose of rubarb. a fine day

1803 Tuseday Septr 6th ☞ Miss Marriah Howard110 was Brought to Bed to day of a fine girl

Wednesday Septr 7th ☞ a very cold morning, I am still very poorley but better then I was yesterday. this afternoon Capt. Pitt came here from Baltimore right well. I had a letter from Abee. she & Capt. Kerr had a fine Passage to Baltimore. thay got thare before 2 oclock. thay are both well. a fine day but has turned coole

Thursday 8th ☞ I feel my self better to day. a fine coole day

406

Fryday 9th ✒ a fine morning. about 9 oclock Mr. Pitt. Mrs. Pitt. R. M. Pitt, Hanah pitt. William Faris pitt and Littel John Charles pitt[111] and the littel girl to attend them all sett of in the Packett for Baltimore. My poor littel Marriah cryed and was very unwiling to leave us.[112] a fine day. in the evening looks like for rain

Saturday 10th ✒ a fine day

Sunday 11th ✒ a fine day

Munday 12th ✒ a fine day. Sylve's getting ye weeds out of the garden

Tuseday 13th ✒ a fine day. Sylve's at work as yesterday

Wednesday 14th ✒ a fine day. Sylve's at work as yester day

1803 Thursday Septr 15th[113] ✒ a dull day. looks like for rain

Fryday 16th ✒ a fine day

Saturday 17th ✒ a fine day

Sunday 18th ✒ a fine clear day

Munday 19th ✒ Sylve's been digging the Borders. a fine day. I sow'd the following seeds in a Boxes No. 1 Troy Nercess 2 Rush leav'd Iris 3 Parrott Tail Tulip

Tuseday 20th ✒ a drisley rainey day. I planted about 30 Balsoms that grew on the Flower Beds

Wednesday 21th ✒ a fine day

Thursday 22th ✒ a fine day

Fryday 23th ✒ a fine day

Saturday 24th ✒ a fine day

Sunday 25th ✒ a dull cloudey day

1803 Munday Septr 26th ✒ a rainey morning, about noon clear'd away. I Planted out a number of Plants in the lott & garden. a fine afternoon

Tuseday 27th ✒ digging the Tulep Beds. a fine day

Wednesday 28th ✒ a fine day

Thursday 29th ✒ a fine day. this evening Miss Gastin was married to Mr. Henry Hall[114]

[111] John Charles Pitt was born on 2 August 1803. Faris made no diary entries at that time. His parents named the child for his paternal grandfather and his deceased uncle Charles Faris.

[112] For more than three years, it appears that Rebecca Maria lived mostly with her grandparents in Annapolis, although she made frequent short trips to Baltimore. This departure may have been planned as a more permanent move—hence her unwillingness to leave—but she was back in Annapolis in November and the following May started going to school in town.

[113] The entries from 15 September through 4 October are taken from William Faris Diary, Maryland State Archives, MSA SC 595, folder 7, 00/9/6/23.

[114] The 6 October *Maryland Gazette* reported that Mr. Henry Hall and Miss Ann Garsten, both of Annapolis, were married Thursday evening last by Rev. Mr. Higginbotham. Henry Sprigg Hall (d.1825) was the son of William Hall (1749–1815) and his wife Margaret Harwood (1755–1832). Ann Gaston (1787–1869) was the only daughter of Thomas and Susannah Gaston (see 23 February 1793).

[115] Richard Loockerman (1780–1834) was the son of Richard and Ann Wood Loockerman, of Caroline County. Frances Townley Chase (c.1780–1857) was the daughter of Jeremiah Townley and Hester Chase (see 4 April 1792). She and her husband lived in the house on Northeast Street built in the early 1770s by Mathias Hammond, but also owned property in Caroline County.

[116] This John Ross was probably not related to the John Ross who drowned in February 1793. He appears in the probate records around 1800 as the purchaser of a number of tools at the sale of Richard Wells's estate (see 14 October 1798). Ross was the executor of John Welch (d.<1805, see 10 November 1797), whose widow signed over Welch's estate to Ross as a trustee. Ross was eventually replaced after a petition by John Welch Jr. argued that Ross was not competent to hold the position. From 1804 to 1806, Ross owned a large part of the block bounded by State Circle and North and Tabernacle Streets. § Ross bought one fire screen from Faris's estate.

[117] Gottlieb Grammar (c.1766–1845), a nephew of Frederick Grammar (see 27 July 1800), married Kitty Countryman in November 1791. In 1799 he obtained a license to operate the Sign of the Pennsylvania Farmer in the house formerly run by Archibald Golder (see 7 April 1793). When Frederick died in 1818, he left to Gottlieb the use of a house and its two lots, which Gottlieb had been renting from him, as well as the stables, bake house, and other improvements.

[118] No surviving records provide any information about Charles Thompson. In 1801, a potter named Thompson rented a house and lot on Spa Creek, between Conduit and Charles Streets; it is possible that he was Charles Thompson.

Fryday 30th ✒ a fine day

Saturday Octr 1th ✒ a fine day. this evening Jeremiah Chace's daughter Miss Faney Chace is to be married to Mr. Richard Lockerman, of the Eastern Shore[115]

Sunday 2th ✒ a fine day

Munday 3th ✒ a rainey day & Blew very Har. it Blew so hard that the Packett turned Back

Tuseday 4th ✒ it rained hard last night and the wind Blew a near Harrican. a rainey windey morning. about a 11 oclock clear'd away a fine after noon

1803 Wednesday Octr 5th ✒ a fine day. in the evening I planted on the Border next to Mrs. Davidson's up by the callamus 4 peach stones. I next to the post is a very large peach gave me by Mr. John Ross[116] the other 3 from the Tree in the Bigg Bed

Thursday 6th ✒ this evening as thay ware raising G. Gramers[117] sign poss the sheers gave way & Brushed his shoulders Nocked him down & Hurt him a good deal. a fine day. Charles Thomson[118] died to day

Fryday 7th ✒ a fine day. in the evening Charles Tompson was Buried

Saturday 8th ✒ a fine day

Sunday 9th ✒ a fine day. in the evening clouded up looks like for Bad weather

Munday 10th ✒ a fine day

Tuseday 11th ✒ a fine day

Wednesday 12th ✒ I made abegining to Plant my Tulip roots, I planted one Bed with the marked Tulips. a dull cloudey day

1803 Thursday Octr 13th ✒ a fine day, I Planted another Bed of Tulips

Fryday 14th ✒ finished Planting the Nursserey Beds. a fine day

Saturday 15th ✒ a dull drisley morning, a fine afternoon. I made Holes in the Circle Beds for Tulips

Sunday 16th ✒ a fine day

Munday 17th 🖝 finished the Circel Beds next to the grass walk. a fine day but the wind Blows very Hard

Tuseday 18th 🖝 still at the Tulip Beds. a fine day

Wednesday 19th 🖝 Finished planting the Flower Beds. a clear cold day

Thursday 20th 🖝 a fine day

Fryday 21th 🖝 a fine day

Saturday 22th 🖝 whe had some rain last night. a cloudey morning. clear'd away about 11 or 12 oclock a fine after noon. this evening betwen 7 & 8 oclock John Callehorn died[119]

1803 Sunday 23th 🖝 a fine day

Munday 24th 🖝 a fine day. this evening John Callahorn was buried — Mr. Thomas Woodward brought me a root of the countrey, or wild Tulip. I Planted it on the Border next to Ridgleys at this near end of The seedling Parrott tail Tulips

Tuseday 25th 🖝 a fine day

Wednesday 26th 🖝 a fine day

Thursday 27th 🖝 Mr. Wilmore gave me 6 Polianthus's. I planted them the yard by the fence. a fine day

Fryday 28th 🖝 a fine day. Bille has finished planting Tulips on the Border next to the street and has finished planting

Saturday 29th 🖝 a fine day

Sunday 30th 🖝 a fine day

Munday 31th 🖝 a fine day

1803 Tuseday Novr 1th 🖝 a fine day

Wednesday 2th 🖝 a fine day

Thursday 3th 🖝 a fine day

Fryday 4th 🖝 a dull cloudey morning. about 9 oclock Mrs. Faris went of in the Packett for Baltimore. a dull cloudey day

Saturday 5th 🖝 a dull cloudey drisely day

[119] The 27 October 1803 *Maryland Gazette* reported that John Callahan died Saturday evening last, in his fiftieth year; Register of the Land Office for the Western Shore of Maryland. Although Faris does not mention it, Callahan's successor was Capt. John Kilty (see 27 October 1792).

120 The *Maryland Gazette* (10 November) noted the death as follows: Allen Quynn died Tuesday morning, in his seventy-seventh year; long a resident of Annapolis, and for twenty-five years a member of the house of delegates.

121 Tobias Emerson Stansbury (1757–1849) was the son of Tobias and Mary Hammond Stansbury. As a representative from Baltimore County, Stansbury served his first term as speaker of the lower house in 1803. He also held that post from 1805 to 1807, 1809 to 1812, 1819 to 1821, and in 1823. Stansbury was commissioned a brigadier general in 1809, commanding a Baltimore County brigade, which he led during the British invasion of Maryland in 1814.

135 ✍ Robert Bowie (1750–1818)

122 Robert Bowie was the son of Capt. William and Margaret Sprigg Bowie, and the husband of Priscilla Mackall. He served twice as governor, first with three consecutive terms from 1803 to 1806 and again in one term from 1811 to 1812. His daughter Mary was the second wife of Dr. Reverdy Ghiselin (see 13 April 1793). He died and was buried at his birthplace, Mattaponi, in Prince George's County.

123 Alexander, the Kerrs' first child.

Sunday 6th ✍ it rained all last night and all day till the evening. it stop'd raining but is cloudey and turns cold

Munday 7th ✍ a clear cold morning. in the afternoon turned cloudey

Tuseday 8th ✍ about 1 oclock this morning Mr. Allen Quynn died,120 this morning thare was members anuf to make a House. the members qullifyed and chose Mr. Stansburey121 Speaker. a clear cold day

Wednesday 9th ✍ a fine day. this evening Allen Quynn was Buried

Thursday 10th ✍ a fine day. Sylve has began to cover the Tulip beds. I had a letter from Mr. pitt, thay are bravely

1803 Fryday Novr 11th ✍ a clear cold day. moved the potts into the seller

Saturday 12th ✍ a clear coole day. moved the greens out of the Big Bed & littel Beds into the Bed by the old stabel

Sunday 13th ✍ a cloudey rainey day

Munday 14th ✍ mooved the littel Cherrey Tree from the side of the Fence & had the ground taken from the roots of the Peach Trees & left the roots Bare. a fine day

Tuseday 15th ✍ this day Genl. Bowe122 was quallifyed the govenor of the state, and the old councel was ree aellected, a dull cloudey day

Wednesday 16th ✍ a littel after one oclock Mrs. Faris and Marriah came home from Baltimore. a dull cloudey drisley day and left them all well. Abee is not Brought to Bed yet

Thursday 17th ✍ a fine day

Fryday 18th ✍ a clear coole day. in the evening received a letter from Nancey Pitt, she tells me that Abee was Brought to Bed on Wednesday night about 10 oclock with a fine Boy123 & that thay are all well & Harty

1803 Saturday Novr 19th ✍ a fine clear day

Sunday 20th ✍ a fine morning. a cloudey afternoon. looks like Falling Weather

Munday 21th ✒ a rainey morning. clear'd away about noon, a fine afternoon

Tuseday 22th ✒ a fine day

Wednesday 23th ✒ a fine day

Thursday 24th ✒ a fine day

Fryday 25th ✒ a fine day. I had a letter from Capt. Kerr. thay are all well

Saturday 26th ✒ a fine day

Sunday 27th ✒ a fine day

Munday 28th ✒ a fine day, the shirreff, Mr. Tille came with a Firefacious[124] to lay on my son Charls' property at the sute of Slater[125] in Baltimore

Tuseday 29th ✒ I heard no more of the shirreff to day. a dull day

Wednesday 30th ✒ a cloudey morning. in the afternoon came on to rain

1803 Thusday Decembr 1th ✒ rained hard last night and this morning it rain'd and Thunder'd & lighened. about 9 or 10 oclock it cleared away. a Fine warm day

Fryday 2th ✒ a right March day cloudey & sun shine. about 12 oclock it snow'd a littel

Saturday 3th ✒ a fine day

Sunday 4th ✒ a fine day

Munday 5th ✒ a fine day. this afternoon Mrs. Faris was taken with a Bad ague

Tuseday 6th ✒ a fine day. Mrs. Faris very unwell to day

Wednesday 7th ✒ a foggey morning. this morning Mr. Peter Wood one of the members of the House of Delagates for Prince Georges County died of a Perelitick stroke.[126] a dull day. Mrs. Faris ~~had a chill to day~~ in the afternoon I call'd in Doctr Ghislin. he gave her 8 grain of callomell

Thursday 8th ✒ Mrs. Faris had a chill to this fore noon but she is better this evening — Mr. Peter Wood was Buried this evening. a dull drisley day. had nothing from the doctr to day

Fryday 9th ✒ rain'd hard last night. a fine morning. Mrs. Faris' very unwell. the doctr sent

[124] A writ of *fieri facias*, ordering the sheriff to take sufficient property from the goods of a debtor to satisfy the amount of the debt, as determined by a court judgment.

[125] William Slater was an iron-monger located at 77 Baltimore Street, who advertised the sale of iron-mongery, cutlery, and hardware such as andirons, shovels, tongs, and other brass items. There is no evidence as to the nature of his suit, but Priscilla Faris's final account for the adminis-tration of Charles's estate included a payment of £93.01.08 as a judgment won by Slater. He married Polly Evans in April 1806 and died at the home of Col. John Cromwell, a Baltimore merchant, in July 1813, leaving a widow and children.

[126] Wood's death was reported more succinctly by the 8 December *Gazette*: Peter Wood died yesterday morning, one of the Delegates for P.G. County. Wood served from 1801 to 1803.

her a dose of rubarb. in the evening he sent her a composing draft, a fine day

1803 Saturday Desr 10th ✍ Mrs. Faris is still unwell. the doctr sent her 2 papers of antimonial Powder. a fine day

Sunday 11th ✍ a fine morning. Mrs. Faris is very unwell still. the doctr sent her some sineca snake root[127] to have a strong Tea made and to take a spoon full every Hour, about noon came on to rain & continued a raney afternoon and evening. Mrs. Faris continues still to be very unwell. at night the doctr sent Mrs. Faris a composing draft of Peregorick & wine drops, a very windey Blustering rainey night

Munday 12th ✍ Mrs. Faris is very unwell but I think she is something better then she has been. the doctr sent her som columbia root to take. this has been a very warm clear day

Tuseday 13th ✍ a cold cloudey morning. Mrs. Faris is better but not well anuff to leave her Bed. the doctr sent a dram more of the columbia root, a cold disagreeable day

Wednesday 14th ✍ Mrs. Faris is much Better to day. had nothing from the doctr to day. a fine day

Thursday 15th ✍ Mrs. Faris is Braveley. the doctr says she wants no more medicen — a fine day

1803 Fryday Desr 16th ✍ a dull cloudey day. Mrs. Faris is better. she has sett up a good deal to day

Saturday 17th ✍ Mrs. Faris is Braveley. a fine day

Sunday 18th ✍ Mrs. Faris still ceeps her room but she seems braveley now. a dull day. looks as if we should have snow or rain

Munday 19th ✍ Mrs. Faris is Braveley. she is down stairs all day. a fine day

Tuseday 20th ✍ Mrs. Faris is not so well to day as yesterd[ay]. a cloudey day. in the evening came on to snow

Wednesday 21th ✍ Mrs. Faris is Braveley. a fine day

Thursday 22th ✍ Mrs. Faris is v[ery?] un well this evening. a dull day

[127] The dried root of *Polygala senegal*, the main constituents of which are polygalic acid and senegenin. Used as an expectorant and emetic.

Fryday 23th ⚘ Mrs. Faris is still unwell. the doctr gave her a dose of rubarb & magneasa.[128] a rainey day

Saturday 24th ⚘ Mrs. Faris is Better. the doctr sent her a nother dram of the cullumba root. a fine day

1803 Sunday Desr 25th ⚘ Mrs. Faris is still complaining. a raney day

Munday 26th ⚘ Mrs. Faris is braveley. I finished shelling the ocro or coffee and I have 9 lb. & ½ of it. I had a letter from Nancey dated the 22th with some mince pies & a pott of mins meat & some confect-soneys such as redishes & shells for Marriah, a dull cloudey disagreeable day

Tuseday 27th ⚘ the masons walked in possession to church to day and Mr. Wiatt Preached a sermon to them. a dull cloudey day.

Wednesday 28th ⚘ a dull cloudey day

Thursday 29th ⚘ a fine day[129]

Fryday 30th ⚘ a dull dissagreeable day

Saturday 31th ⚘ a dull drisley morning. I receivd letters from Nancey, & Mr. & Mrs. Kerr and Capt. Kerr sailed on Tuseday last for Lisborn and the East Indies. the weather clear'd away. the sun came out in the afternoon

1804 Sunday January 1th ⚘ a rainey morning and rained all night, a dissagreeable rainey day

Munday 2th ⚘ a fine day

Tuseday 3th ⚘ a dull Heavey day

Wednesday 4th ⚘ a very windey cold day

Thursday 5th ⚘ this morning betwen 1 & 2 oclock wee ware allarmed with the cry of fire. the white House ware Gutlep Gramer lives was on fire & Burnt down.[130] luckeley no other House was burnt. several took fire but was put out — a fine day

Fryday 6th ⚘ a fine day

Saturday 7th ⚘ a fine day

Sunday 8th ⚘ last night was a rainey Night and is a raney morning. the two Houses of Asembley broke up Last night, Mrs. Faris was taken with a chill

[128] Magnesium oxide, used as a mild antacid laxative.

[129] The *Gazette* carried the news of the marriage of Betsy Patterson of Baltimore to Jerome Bonaparte, Napoleon's brother, but Faris did not make note of the event in his diary, neither of the parties being acquaintances of his.

[130] "This morning, about one o'clock, the house occupied by Mr. G. J. Grammar was discovered to be on fire, and the alarm bell sounded, but not withstanding the exertions of the citizens, and the members of the general assembly, the house was entirely consumed, with the kitchen and carriage-house. . . . By this unhappy accident, Mr. Grammar is a very considerable sufferer." (*Gazette*, 5 January)

about 10 oclock and continued the most of the afternoon, and a smart fevour followed it. a rainey day

Munday 9th ✍ Mrs. Faris is better to day. it rain'd a good deal Last night. a rainey morning, a dull drisley day

Tuseday 10th ✍ a clear cold day

1804 Wednesday January 11th ✍ a very cold windey day

Thursday 12th ✍ a clear cold day

Fryday 13th ✍ wee had a littel snow last night. a clear cold day

Saturday 14th ✍ a clear cold morning. in the afternoon came on to snow

Sunday 15th ✍ a fine clear cold day

Munday 16th ✍ a fine clear cold day

Tuseday 17th ✍ a rainey night & morning. a cold cloudey windey day

Wednesday 18th ✍ a clear cold windey day. I had a letter from Nancey & Abee to day. Abee is very Poorley, Nancey is well

Thursday 19th ✍ a cloudey cold morning. in the fore noon came on to snow and snow'd all day

Fryday 20th ✍ a clear cold day. Mrs. Faris had a chil this morning, was abed all day, and I had a chill

1804 Saturday 21th ✍ I have an ague to day [*in a very shaky hand*]

Sunday 22th ✍ a cold snowey day. I am very unwell

Munday 23th ✍ I am better to day, it snow'd all night and all day

Tuseday 24th ✍ a fine day & I am still but poorley

Wednesday 25th ✍ a fine clear cold day. I am much as I was yesterday

Thursday 26th ✍ I took a dose of castor oile this morning, it woorked 3 times. I think I am better. a fine clear cold day

Fryday 27th ✍ I wrought to the girls in Baltimore to day to go with Smith Price to morrow, I think I am better to day. a fine clear cold day

Saturday 28th 🖎 a snowey morning & fore noon, a fine sunshiney afternoon, in the evening clouded up. looks like for more bad weather, Smith Price did not go to day

Sunday 29th 🖎 a clear cold windey day

Munday 30th 🖎 a dull day

1804 January 31 Tuseday 🖎 snow'd last night. a dull cloudey day

Wednesday Febry 1th 🖎 a fine day. in the evening clouded up & looks like for more bad weather

Thursday 2th 🖎 a fine day

Fryday 3th 🖎 a fine day

Saturday 4th 🖎 a fine day

Sunday 5th 🖎 a fine day

Munday 6th 🖎 a fine day

Tuseday 7th 🖎 a fine day

Wednesday 8th 🖎 a dull day. Old William is ascraping the ruff Bark off the Peach Trees

Thursday 9th 🖎 rained last night and this morning. a dull cloudey day & the wind Blew Hard

Fryday 10th 🖎 a clear cold day. Old William has been a wheeling dung from Mr. Ridgeley's

Saturday 11th 🖎 a fine clear day. Old William is a wheeling dung

Sunday 12th 🖎 a fine day

1804 Munday Febry 13th 🖎 Old William is wheeling dung. he had dung'd the Border next Ridgleys & Sylve's made abegining to digg it. a fine day

Tuseday 14th 🖎 Sylve has finished the Border and I have sow'd 16 rows of peas on it, from Mr. Stevens's peas. Old William is wheeling dung, Old William has finished wheeling dung and has white washed the Peach Trees. a fine day

Wednesday 15th 🖎 cover'd the peas with dung, and trimed some of the Goosberrey & Currant Bushes. a fine day

Thursday 16th 🖎 a fine day

Fryday 17th 🖎 rained hard last night — a rainey drisley cloudey day

Saturday 18th ✒ a fine day

Sunday 19th ✒ a fine day

Munday 20th ✒ a cold dull windey morning. I sow'd in the Box No. 1 sugar loaf cabbage No. 2 earley dwarf cabbage No. 3 earley York cabbage. trimed Goosberrey & Curran Bushes. a clear afternoon

1804 Tuseday Febry 21th ✒ finish triming the curran and goosberrey Bushes. a fine day

Wednesday 22th ✒ cleaned the Bee hives, the Bees in one of the Hives are all ded, and thare was a good deal of Honey in it, in the after noon Mr. Hanson sent for the Peach Tree I gave him. it stood by the Layloc Hedge & Holley Tree. a fine day

Thursday 23th ✒ a very windey night. a cold snowey morning and continued snowing all day

Fryday 24th ✒ last night was a very cold windey night. a clear cold windey day

Saturday 25th ✒ a clear cold day but not so cold as yesterday

Sunday 26th ✒ Mrs. Faris has been very un well to day. she's abed the afternoon, a clear cold windey day

Munday 27th ✒ Mrs. Faris is better to day. a fine day. in the turned cloudey

Tuseday 28th ✒ snow'd in the night. a rainey morning. a dull cloudey day. in the evening the sun came out & sett clear

1804 Wednesday Febry 29th ✒ Fixed a new Box and sowed in it No. 1 earley York No. 2 sugar loaf cabbage seed from Mr. Joseph Brewer No. 3 earley York and some cabbage seed I had by me, redish seed amongst the wall and I fixed a new cask & filled it for the Ice Plant. a fine day. in the evening turned cloudey

Thursday March 1th ✒ a snowey Fore noon. in the after noon turnd to rain

Fryday 2th ✒ a clear cold day

Saturday 3th ✒ a cold windey day

Sunday 4th ✒ a verey cold, clear windey day. in the evening turned cloudey

Munday 5th ✍ a cloudey morning. in the afternoon clear and cold

Tuseday 6th ✍ a dull cloudey cold day

Wednesday 7th ✍ a dull cloudey cold day

Thursday 8th ✍ a clear cold windey day

Fryday 9th ✍ snow'd in the night. the grounds
covered with snow this morning and is now
asnowing & continued till 12 oclock & left off
snowing but continued cloudey all the rest of the
day

1804 Saturday March 10th ✍ a fine day

Sunday 11th ✍ cloudey & sun shine at times all day

Munday 12th ✍ Sylve's been wheeling dung on the
Bigg Bed and on the littel Bed at the end of the new
stabel. a fine day. in the evening turned cloudey

Tuseday 13th ✍ it snowed & rained in the night. a
cloudey drisley dull day. I filled the potts with erth
this afternoon

Wednesday 14th ✍ a clear cold windey day

Thursday 15th ✍ a cold raw dull day. Mr. Samuel
Howard gave me the following seeds, the Formoso a
flower from the Alleganey — simlin seed from
Malta, earley York cabbage seeds

Fryday 16th ✍ a fine clear coole day

Saturday 17th ✍ a clear cold windey day

Sunday 18th ✍ a clear cold windey day

Munday 19th ✍ about 9 oclock this morning I sett
off in Gorge Barbers Boat for Baltimore. got to the
point just at dark. found Nancey & Abbe & chilren
all well, Mr. Pitt came home from Philadelphia
about half an Hour after I got thare

[There are no entries during the time that Faris was in
Baltimore.]

1804 Thursday March 22th ✍ I returned home
in the evening from Baltimore. I left Mr. & Mrs.
Pitt & Abee and children all well

Fryday 23th ✍ a clear day. Sylve's digging in the
lott and Bille's made abegining to cutt Box by the
grass walk

Saturday 24th ✍ Bille's cuting Box and Sylve's digging in the lott. a fine day

Sunday 25th ✍ a fine day

Munday 26th ✍ Bille's cutting Box & Sylve's cleaning the Beds of the cuttings. a fine day

Tuseday 27th ✍ Bille has finished cutting the Box and Sylve's doing up the assparagrass Beds. a dull cloudey day

Wednesday 28th ✍ this afternoon Abee & child & nurs came here from Baltimore. a rainey day

Thursday 29th ✍ finished cutting the Box & trimed the althea, Bille's Troweling the flower Beds round the grass & Sylve's acleaning the garden. a fine day. in the evening looks like for rain

1804 Fryday March 30th ✍ it Thunder'd & lightened a good deal & rained all night. rained this morning and continued rainey & cloudey all day

Saturday 31th ✍ a clear cold day. this after noon Bille's Troweling ye flower Beds & sow'd spinige seed betwen the assparagass Beds & cabbage and lettice on them and I sow'd the Ice plant seed in the Barrel. a fine evening

Sunday April 1th ✍ it Blow'd Hard in the night and before day, a clear coole day. in the evening turned cloudey

Munday 2th ✍ a clear cool day. I sow'd 4 rows of Peas in the Bigg Bed 2 & ½ of Peas from Mr. Stepens and 1 & ½ of Peas from Mr. Rigeley Nick's. he say thay from Jack Wheeler. I took up the rushembole onions & planted them on the Border on the west side of the garden & Sylve's digging the Border whare thay grew, I sow'd Parsseley seed on the end next the littel House and spinige on the rest and sow'd radish seed on the Border betwen the Peas and Bille's Troweling the nursserey Beds. my radish and cabbage plants ware bitt with the frost last night in the new Box. a fine clear coole day

1804 Tuseday April 3th ✍ Bille's finished troweling the Flower Beds & Has sow'd 2 Bedes with carrotts and Old William has dugg the lott for ocro onions & simlins. a fine day

Wednesday 4th ✍ a fine morning. Billes finished planting The parsneps and is aplanting onions of Eagypt. in the afternoon came on to rain. it rained all the after noon & evening

Thursday 5th ~ a rainey night. a dull cloudey morning. I sow'd the ocro and Bille finished planting the onions, a dull cloudey day

Fryday 6th ~ a rainey morning. about noon clear'd away a fine after noon

Saturday 7th ~ Bille's finished doing up the Tabels round the grass walk & I have finished the wall by the garden gate. a fine day

Sunday 8th ~ a fine day

Munday 9th ~ I made 8 Hills in the lott & sow'd them with simlin seed. Sylvey's digging the littel quarter at the end of the new stabel & Bille's doing the littel garden by the gate. sow'd a pott with sencitive plant seed & the following Balsoms from Mr. Hanson

No. 1 Genl Washington white purple & crimson

   2 Franklin purpel

   3 Lady Washington flash mix'd

   4 The President crimson & pink

   5 Aristides white & purpel

   6 Genl Green

   7 Rebaca aButifull pink

   8 Mary Jane rose & white

   9 Mrs. Merrey scarlet & white

Sylve's finished digging the littel quarter and I Planted the Jacobian Lilleys and opened the Holes in Bee hives. a fine day

Tuseday 10th ~ planted the littel quarter with Beans & planted Beet seed by the leeks & planted the tops of the shallots & sow'd sage seed, and planted narsturcion seed round the althea Hedge and Planted the Balsom appel seed on the Borders. the Ice plants are up that ware sow'd the 31th of March & sow'd the evening primrose in 4 places on the Beds by the littel House. a fine day. in the after noon turnd coole

1804 Wednesday April 11th ~ a cloudey drissley morning. in the after noon I sow'd 3 papers of aster seed in a Box. a cloudey day

Thursday 12th ~ a clear windey morning. planted 2 rows of Beets in the front of the Parsnip Bed. a clear cold day

Fryday 13th ✍ a fine clear morning. about 9 oclock Abee & nurs & littel Allexander & Charrity went of in the Packet for Baltimore. in the afternoon I planted 3 sorts of Balsoms from doctr Ghislin No. 10 Rose. Rose. crimson & white in a pott — planted 1 pott of white glob & 1 pott with red globe. a fine day

Saturday 14th ✍ cutt the long line of sage. a fine day

Sunday 15th ✍ a fine day

Munday 16th ✍ a fine warm day. Sylve's digging The littel quarter

Tuseday 17th ✍ a fine morning. I planted two Hills in the lott with Punkin seed brought from China and two Hills of simlin seed from Malta, given me By S. H. Howard. a clear windey day

1804 Wednesday April 18th ✍ a coole morning. I sow'd the nutmeg seed on the Border by the Burgomot and on the Border by the Bee House I sow'd the Brussel Sprout Seed. a fine day

Thursday 19th ✍ last night Mr. William Brown marchunt's wife[131] died. a fine morning, Planted 3 hills of the nutmeg cantilope in the lott. a fine day

Fryday 20th ✍ water'd the flower Beds this morning. a dull cold windey day

Saturday 21th ✍ a rainey windey day

Sunday 22th ✍ a fine morning after the rain. in the afternoon wee had a fine warm rain

Munday 23th ✍ a fine morning. planted out 3 lines of cabbage plants & a pott with sencitive plant seed. in the afternoon I Planted 5 hills with cucumber seed, from Mr. Joseph Brewer who says thay are the early cucumber. in the afternoon cloudey and cold and the wind Blows Hard. Mrs. Brown was Buried this fore noon

Tuseday 24th ✍ took up the Burgomott and Common Baum & replanted them again. a fine day but coole for the season

1804 Wednesday April 25th ✍ Sylve's stuck the four rows of Peas in the big bed. a fine day. wee had some fine showers of rain to day

[131] Mary Brown, wife of William Brown (d.1808). Brown was born in England and came to Maryland shortly before the Revolution to safeguard the property of the firm Perkins, Buchanan, & Brown, of which he was a partner. His son William Henry, age eleven, entered St. John's grammar school in November 1789. The *Gazette,* in reporting Brown's death at the home of his son in St. Mary's County, described him as "for many years a respectable inhabitant of this city." § Faris collected £1.9.0 from Brown in January 1801 as administrator of Charles's estate. The account of Faris's estate included a debt to Brown of £1.10.0.

Thursday 26th ☞ a cold raw day

Fryday 27th ☞ a cold dull cloudey day

Saturday 28th ☞ a fine day

Sunday 29th ☞ a fine day

Munday 30th ☞ a fine morning, waterd the Border
that has the Peas and the Hills in the lott, and sowd
3 rows of Peas in the Bigg Bed. Brought the
Cherrey Trees and the other Potts out of the seller
and Place'd them in the yard, a fine day

Tuseday May 1th ☞ this morning R. M. Pitt began
going to school to Miss Juliott Owens. a fine day.
in the evening turn'd coole

Wednesday 2th ☞ a cold night, & a cold morning.
I pulld up the redishes in the Box & sow'd more
salmon radish seed in the Box, a fine day

Thursday 3th ☞ I have been very unwell to day. I
took a dose of castor oyl, it gave 3 passages. a fine
clear day

1804 Fryday May 4th ☞ a fine day

Saturday 5th ☞ a fine day. the Tulips in the Beds
round the grass are opened, but them in the nursery
Beds are not opened yet

Sunday 6th ☞ a fine morning. in the afternoon wee
had a fine rain

Munday 7th ☞ a cloudey morning. Planted the Big
Bed and the littel been bed with Plants, a fine day

Tuseday 8th ☞ a fine day

Wednesday 9th ☞ a dull drisley day

Thursday 10th ☞ rain'd hard all night. a rainey
morning. the streets like a river — continued
raining all day

Fryday 11th ☞ a dull cloudey morning. I sow'd
the following asters in a Box No. 1 white No. 2
striped No. 3 pail red No. 4 red No. 5 Purpel — a
dull drisley rainey day

Saturday 12th ☞ a drisley morning. sent to Mr.
Pitt 4 half Inch planks walnutt measure 53 feet 9
Inch & 9 Inch walnutt planks 81 feet 10 Inchs, in
all 135 feet 7. a cloudey day

1804 Sunday May 13th ✍ a fine day

Munday 14th ✍ a cloudey rainey day

Tuseday 15th ✍ a fine morning. half of one of the rows of Peas, of the last Planting rotted in the ground. I replanted them this morning, Sylve's Howing the Beens & plants. in the evening Bille's planted the chiney aster round the Circel Beds. a fine day. in the evening came on to rain and thunder & lighten

Wednesday 16th ✍ a grate deal of rain last night. a rainey morning. a cold dull drisley day

Thursday 17th ✍ a cloudey morning. a fine after noon

Fryday 18th ✍ a clear fine day but rather coole

Saturday 19th ✍ I planted in the end of the Box whare the asters are, 5 seed from John Brewer whiche he called the Ten Cummandements, a fine day

Sunday 20th ✍ last night & this morning I began to take the white Walnutt Bark pills. I got them from Mr. Benjamin Harwood[132]. he was cinde anuff to give me some and Mr. David West of Harford County the maker of them promisses to bring me some in June next, my Phissick has worked me very well to day, a fine day. in the evening turned cloudey

1804 Munday May 21th ✍ a fine warm day. in the evening look'd gustey

Tuseday 22th ✍ a fine warm day

Wednesday 23th ✍ a dull wett day

Thursday 24th ✍ I took last night & this morning more of the white Walnut Bark pills. thay worked me moderatly, a fine day

Fryday 25th ✍ a cold dull drisley day

Saturday 26th ✍ a cloudey drisley cold day

Sunday 27th ✍ a dull cloudey cold day

Munday 28th ✍ Broke the Tulip stalks of this morning

[132] Benjamin Harwood (1751–1826) was the son of Capt. Richard Harwood (1707–1754) and his wife Ann Watkins (1719–1804). Harwood operated an import business with his brother, Thomas Harwood Jr., in the 1770s and 1780s. He was also the treasurer of St. John's College in 1786 and in 1790 one of the managers of the lottery to raise funds to complete St. Anne's. Harwood never married, leaving his estate to his nieces and nephews and his last surviving sibling, his oldest brother Richard.

the Beds round the grass walk	1028
littel Huse Beds	134
nursserey d[o]	818
Border next the street	215
d[o] by Ridgeley	144
	2339 Total

a fine day

Tuseday 29th ✍ a cloudey day. in the evening looks like for rain

1804 Wednesday 30th of May ✍ this after noon Mrs. Pitt and the children and Salley & Mr. Joseph pitt[133] came here from Baltimore. a dull day

Thursday 31th ✍ a fine day. this morning Mr. Joseph Pitt went of to Baltimore

Fryday June 1th ✍ rain'd last night. a cloudey morning. I planted out Balsoms & white & red globe Amaranthus. a dull cloudey drisley day

Saturday 2th ✍ a fine day

Sunday 3th ✍ rain'd hard last night. a drisley morning. at times the sun comes out a littel and continued a right April day, showers & then sun shine all day. I took more of the white wallnutt pills. thay did not work me but a littel

Munday 4th ✍ Pulled up the Pea Vines & sticks on the Border & in the evening Bille thined the Parsneps and planted whare thay ware wanting. a fine day

Tuseday 5th ✍ a fine warm day

Wednesday 6th ✍ a fine warm day

Thursday 7th ✍ a fine morning. about noon clouded up and raind a littel. continued a cloudey after noon

1804 Fryday June 8th ✍ in the after noon I thined the Ocro and replanted whare missing. a dull cloudey day

Saturday 9th ✍ the Bees swarmed to day. a fine day

Sunday 10th ✍ a Hott day. in the evening wee had a fine rain

Munday 11th ✍ a clear warm day

[133] Joseph Pitt, a younger brother of William Pitt, was a pilot, living on Apple Alley in Fells Point in 1803. He married Elizabeth French on 7 January 1802 in a ceremony performed by Rev. Alexander McCaine of the Fells Point Methodist Church.

Tuseday 12th ✍ rained hard last night. a dull cloudey cold day. in the after noon & evening rain

Wednesday 13th ✍ a clear cold morning. turned out a fine day

Thursday 14th ✍ a cloudey dull drisley cold day

Fryday 15th ✍ a cloudey dull cold rainey day

Saturday 16th ✍ had picked 320 wallnuts of the Tree. a dull rainey day but not so cold as it has been

Sunday 17th ✍ a clear morning. in the afternoon clouded up & wee had several showers

1804 Munday June 18th ✍ fine morning. about 10 oclock Mr. Pitts Boat came to the dock for Mrs. Pitt, Mr. Pitt was on Board a ship going up. about a 11 oclock Mrs. pitt. littel Hannah and littel Faris & littel John & Salley went on board the Boat & sett of with a Fine Wind. in the after noon about 3 oclock it clouded up and came on to rain Thunder and lighten and continued the whole after noon, betwen 2 & 3 oclock one the Hives swarmed. I Hive'd them in a Flower Barrel

Tuseday 19th ✍ rained hard last night and is a rainey morning. in the afternoon the sun came out about 4 oclock. Marriah has been very unwell all day, she had a smart Feveour. Doctr Ghislin sent her a pill to take at bed time

Wednesday 20th ✍ raind a grate deal last night, a cold rainey morning, Sylve's planted the 4 rows of plants whare the peas ware, Marriah is braveley to day. this afternoon I receiv'd a letter from Nancey Pitt. thay had a fine Passage home and found every thing as thay left it. a cold raney day so cold that I have my flannel jacket and thick stockings on

1804 Thursday June 21th ✍ a cold cloudey rainey day. as Majr John Davidson & my self ware cuming from markett this morning he told me that this was his Birth Day and that he was fifty years old to day

Fryday 22th ✍ rained hard last night. a cold dull cloudey drisley morning. about 12 oclock clear'd away, the sun came out fine. in the evening clouded up and looks as if wee should have more rain

Saturday 23th ✍ rained this morning, about noon clear'd away a fine afternoon

Sunday 24th ✒ a fine morning. in the afternoon turned cloudey & in the evening rained a littel. this evening Mr. Lenard Selman is married to Miss Mary Rankin[134]

Munday 25th ✒ a dull cloudey morning. in the afternoon it rain'd

Tuseday 26th ✒ a fine warm day. in the evening turned cloudey

Wednesday 27th ✒ rained hard last night. a fine morning. this fore noone I trimed the Althea Hedge. turned Hott, about noon it turned cloudey, looks like for rain, about 4 oclock came on to rain & rained the rest of the afternoon

1804 Thursday June 28th ✒ a fine day

Fryday 29th ✒ a cloudey dull drisley rainey day

Saturday 30th ✒ the Cambrige Packett went from hear* with 18 or 20 passengers men women and children on Board on thare way to Cambridge and of Kent Point, she was over sett by a world wind.[135] thare happened to be a vessel not far from them which came to thare assistance and took them all on Board, and luckeley not one was Lost — a dull cloudey day

Sunday July 1th ✒ rained hard last night. a fine morning. in the afternoon it rain'd. clear'd away a fine evening

Munday 2th ✒ a fine morning, this morning Majr John Davidson mooved his Furniture into Quinns House.[136] in the afternoon I planted 2 Hills with simlin seed. a fine day. in the evening turned cloudey & looks like for rain

Tuseday 3th ✒ a fine day

Wednesday 4th ✒ Sylves weed the assparagrass Beds and dugg the ground Betwen the occro. a fine day

Thursday 5th ✒ Mr. William Harwood Late Clark to the House of Assembley died last nigh.[137] I got the grass walk mowed this morning & Bille's troweling the tabels round the grass walk. a Hott day. in the evening wee had a fine shower of rain

1804 Fryday July 6th ✒ Mr. William Harrod was carried out of Town in the Herse to be Buried over South River, Bille's finished the tabels round the grass and I sowed some curled savoy cabbage seed in the Big Box. a fine morning, a warm day

[134] The 28 June *Gazette* noted that Leonard Sellman and Miss Mary Ranken were married Sunday evening last, by the Rev. Mr. Higinbothom. Mary Walker Ranken was the daughter of George and Mary Bull Ranken (see 26 April 1798). Leonard Sellman (1757–1814) was the son of Jonathan Sellman (b.1724) and his wife Elizabeth Battee (b.1724).

[135] The 5 July *Gazette* reported that on Saturday last the Cambridge packet, under Capt. Mitchell, with several ladies and gentlemen as passengers, left Annapolis for Cambridge but was upset off Kent Point by a sudden gust of wind. The passengers were rescued by a nearby vessel from Port Tobacco; Capt. George Barber brought the boat back to Annapolis on Sunday.

[136] Quynn had no family members living with him when he died; the executors of his estate rented his house during the lengthy settlement of his affairs.

[137] The *Maryland Gazette* reported his death on 5 July: William Harwood, Esq., died yesterday afternoon, late clerk of the House of delegates of Maryland. He was in his fifty-sixth year. Harwood (c.1748–1804) was a son of Capt. Richard Harwood (1707–1754) and his wife Ann Watkins (1719–1804). Harwood served as clerk of the lower house from 1782 to 1803.

138 Possibly Robert Morris (1734–1806), who was the nephew of Robert Morris, agent in Oxford for Foster Cunliffe and Sons, a Liverpool tobacco firm, during the 1730s and 1740s. The younger Morris came to Maryland in 1747 and then was sent to Philadelphia where he eventually became a partner in the firm Willing and Morris. A signer of the Declaration of Independence, Morris was superintendent of finance from 1781 to 1784 and established the Bank of North America, which was chartered in 1781. He retired from public life after six years as a Pennsylvania senator to engage in trade with East India and China, but was bankrupt by 1798. Morris spent the years from 1798 to 1801 in prison for debt, and the remaining years of his life in relative obscurity. There are no likely local people to have been Faris's visitor and it is possible that he and Morris might have been acquainted through mutual friends or their Philadelphia connections.

139 Probably Henry Peck, proprietor of a hotel and coffee house at the corner of Bond and Fells Streets in Fells Point, formerly of the Columbian Inn.

140 The 26 July 1804 *Maryland Gazette* reported that George Bevans and Mary, daughter of Benjamin Ogle, Esq., "former Governor of this state" (see 14 November 1798), were married in Annapolis, on Sunday last, by the Rev. Mr. Duke, rector of St. Anne's Parish. The couple married at the home of Elizabeth Lloyd, widow of Edward Lloyd IV (see 19 October 1792). Bevans's death, at Talley's Point near Annapolis, was reported on 4 August 1814. Rosalie Calvert included news of this marriage in several of her letters. In 1804, she wrote to her father of "something that will really surprise you[,] . . . the marriage of Mary Ogle to Beavans whom you knew well in Annapolis. Mrs. Ogle must have lost her mind to have engaged her daughter— completely against [her husband's] will—to such a man. Because it is totally [Mrs. Ogle's] fault; she quarrelled with her son [Benjamin] and with Mrs. Tayloe [her daughter Ann, wife of John Tayloe] because they wanted to prevent it. Mrs. Lloyd was in on it, too—in short, it is an inconceivable affair. Yesterday my husband was with young Ben Ogle, who told him that his father was so grieved he feared he might die, being already in a very feeble state. He is going to take [his father] to Bath for

Saturday 7th ⚬ a warm day. the simlins I planted the 2d are up

Sunday 8th ⚬ about 3 oclock this afternoon Mrs. Kerr, littel Allexander & nurs & Charrity all came here from Baltimore all well. a very Hott day. in the evening looks as if we should have a gust

Munday 9th ⚬ Sylve's cutt up the stoks & weeds in the Wallnut Tree Bed. a very Hott day

Tuseday 10th ⚬ a very Hott day. in the evening wee had a fine rain

Wednesday 11th ⚬ a fine Pleassant day

Thursday 12th ⚬ this fore noon Mr. Morris138 called over to see me & in conversation I asked him his age. he told me that he was 69 the 10 day of May last, a Hott day. in the evening wee had a littel shower of rain

1804 Fryday July 13th ⚬ a fine day

Saturday 14th ⚬ a Hott day. betwen 5 & 6 oclock Mrs. and Mrs. Pitt & children & Salley came here from Baltimore all well and Mr. Peck139 came down with them. he is going to the capes for his helth

Sunday 15th ⚬ Mr. Pitt went of this morning earley. a Hott day. in the evening wee had a refreshing shower

Munday 16th ⚬ a Hott day

Tuseday 17th ⚬ Old William dugg the Wallnut Tree Bed. a fine day

Wednesday 18th ⚬ a fine day

Thursday 19th ⚬ a fine day. in the afternoon whe had a clever littel shower

Fryday 20th ⚬ a fine day

Saturday 21th ⚬ a fine day but rather coole for the season

Sunday 22th ⚬ a cloudey morning. in the afternoon wee had a fine rain. I have been very poorley to day. this day Mr. George Bevin was married to Miss Mary Ogel, at Mrs. Lloyds140

---

some time." She later described Bevans as "that uncouth Englishman you saw through so plainly." In 1816, shortly after the deaths of both Bevans and Henrietta Hill Ogle, Mary's mother, Rosalie wrote that Mary Ogle had "just married a common laborer," James Connor of Frederick County. § Faris collected £4.13.0 from Bevans in December 1800 as administrator of Charles's estate.

1804 Munday July 23th ✒ Sylve has planted the Wallnutt Tree Bed with Brussel Cale plants & filled some of the vacancey in the Bigg bed with cabbage plants & took up the Beens & dug the ground. a dull coole day

Tuseday 24th ✒ a dull coole day

Wednesday 25th ✒ a clear coole day

Thursday 26th ✒ a clear coole day. this afternoon in companey with Isaac Harris[141] I asked him how old he was. he told me that he should be sixty six in Desember next

Fryday 27th ✒ a clear fine day

Saturday 28th ✒ some of the Player and thare Baggage made thare appearance this morning.[142] a fine day

Sunday 29th ✒ a fine day

Munday 30th ✒ a fine day

Tuseday 31th ✒ a Hott day. in the evening wee had a shower of rain

1804 Wednesday August 1th ✒ a fine day

Thursday 2th ✒ a clear coole day

Fryday 3th ✒ a clear coole day

Saturday 4th ✒ a fine day

Sunday 5th ✒ a fine morning. in the afternoon wee had a fine rain

Munday 6th ✒ a rainey night last night, this morning Mr. Pitt came heare from the capes. a rainey day

Tuseday 7th ✒ a rainey night, & a rainey morning and continued raineing till about 3 oclock and stoped raining but continued cloudey and like for rain all the after noon

Wednesday 8th ✒ a coole dull day

Thursday 9th ✒ this morning after Brackfast, Mr. & Mrs. and the children & Salley & Miss Julia Owens went of in Mr. Pitts Boat for Baltimore. a fine day

End of Diary

[141] Isaac Harris (1738–1808) was a blacksmith, who married Ruth Shaw, the widow of Dr. John Shaw (d.1774). Ruth died in 1788, leaving Isaac the property—on East Street, near King George Street—from her first marriage, to be sold at his death. Shaw served several terms as a common councilman, in 1765, 1783, and 1790. He did smith's work for the Assembly Rooms during their construction and during the Revolutionary War advertised for workmen to make weapons. He was identified in an August 1786 court record as a "gentleman." § Harris patronized Faris's tavern in 1774 and 1775. Faris sued Harris in 1767 to recover a third-party debt, but defaulted by non-appearance. In August 1785, Harris and Faris were sureties for William Simpson's tavern license. Faris collected £0.11.3 from Harris in January 1802 as administrator of Charles's estate.

[142] The *Gazette* announced their first performance, on the following Friday, August 3rd. The bill consisted of a new tragedy in five acts, *Alfonso, King of Castile*, never before performed in Annapolis, and a three-act farce, *Love-a-la-Mode*, or *The Humours of the Turf*.

EPILOGUE

received there on the 10th of June, from the most respectable houses at Gibraltar, stating that admiral Nelson had sent into Toulon roads three sail of British ships of the line, who fired upon the town and shipping. The French sent out eight sail, to give them chace; when admiral Nelson, with four additional ships which were in the offing, gave chase to them and cut them off the land. The French commenced a running fight and bore away for Corsica, Nelson pursuing them. An American vessel arrived at Gibraltar from Marseilles, passed them when in chace.

Died—Yesterday morning, Mr. WILLIAM FARIS, an old inhabitant of this city.

136 ⚮ *Maryland Gazette*
16 August 1804

WILLIAM M'PARLIN,
CLOCK AND WATCH-MAKER,
RESPECTFULLY informs the citizens of Annapolis, and its vicinity, that he has commenced BUSINESS at the shop lately kept by WILLIAM FARIS, in West-street, where clocks and watches of every description may be repaired in the most approved manner, and on the most moderate terms, also gold and silver work made, sold, and repaired; engraving, such as cyphers, seals, &c. neatly executed, and he assures those who please to honour him with their commands, that the utmost of his abilities shall be exerted to give general satisfaction. N. B. Old gold and silver bought as usual.
August 22, 1804.

137 ⚮ *Maryland Gazette*
22 August 1804

THE 16 AUGUST 1804 *Maryland Gazette* reported the death yesterday morning of "Mr. William Faris, an old inhabitant of this city." The following week the newspaper carried an announcement that William McParlin was opening a clock and watch-making business at the shop lately kept by William Faris. The paper reported no details of Faris's funeral and burial, but the ceremony undoubtedly took place at St. Anne's and the burial in the church cemetery, where Faris joined Charles and his granddaughter Priscilla Ann. No stone marks the site of his grave, but it is perhaps near the marked graves of William and Cassandra McParlin. With no diarist like Faris to provide the details, we cannot know who served as pallbearers for his funeral. Perhaps some of the "long-livers" whose birth dates he noted so assiduously in the diary, or friends like Archibald Golder, Nicholas Harwood, and James Thomas.

Priscilla Faris assumed the administration of her husband's estate, a duty that also included completion of probate for Charles's estate. She placed an announcement in the 11 July 1805 *Gazette* of the sale "on Thursday the 8th day of August next, at the late dwelling of WILLIAM FARIS, deceased" of part of his personal property. The sale would encompass Faris's clock-maker's, watchmaker's, and silversmith's tools (some of them purchased by McParlin), carpenter's and cabinetmaker's tools, a variety of clocks, household and kitchen furniture, "one electrical machine, with apparatus complete," supplies of brass, copper, pewter, and lead, a "large collection of books, a large and very fine collection of tulip roots, and a great variety of other articles too tedious to mention." The goods mentioned in the sale encapsulate Faris as he revealed himself in the pages of the diary and in his work: a craftsman, a gardener, and a man with great curiosity about the world around him.

Shop Drawings
of William Faris

William Faris's shop designs provide the silver historian with a priceless record of a colonial American silversmith's shop. These drawings are the only working eighteenth-century American silver shop drawings known today. There has been some question as to whether these drawings were by Faris's hand or were imported from England. Although we can never be completely certain as to their origins, these drawings are original pen-and-ink bench drawings that were used in the actual making of silver products. Compass markings are evident in some of the drawings as well as additions in pencil made at a later date. Stylistic changes within the drawings themselves as well as from one image to another provide clear evidence that these drawings were not all acquired at one time. Some of these drawings are of styles that were popular in the 1760s and 1770s when Faris's shop was in its inception and others are of later examples, some even as late as the end of the eighteenth century.

The following figures illustrate all of the drawings in the Faris design book for silver (Maryland Historical Society, MS 348, Gift of Mrs. Howard Sill).

SD1 ✒ Shop Drawing for a **Teapot**, ca. 1760–1775, 6 ½" high, pen and ink with pencil. Rococo style with double-belly and scrolled handle.

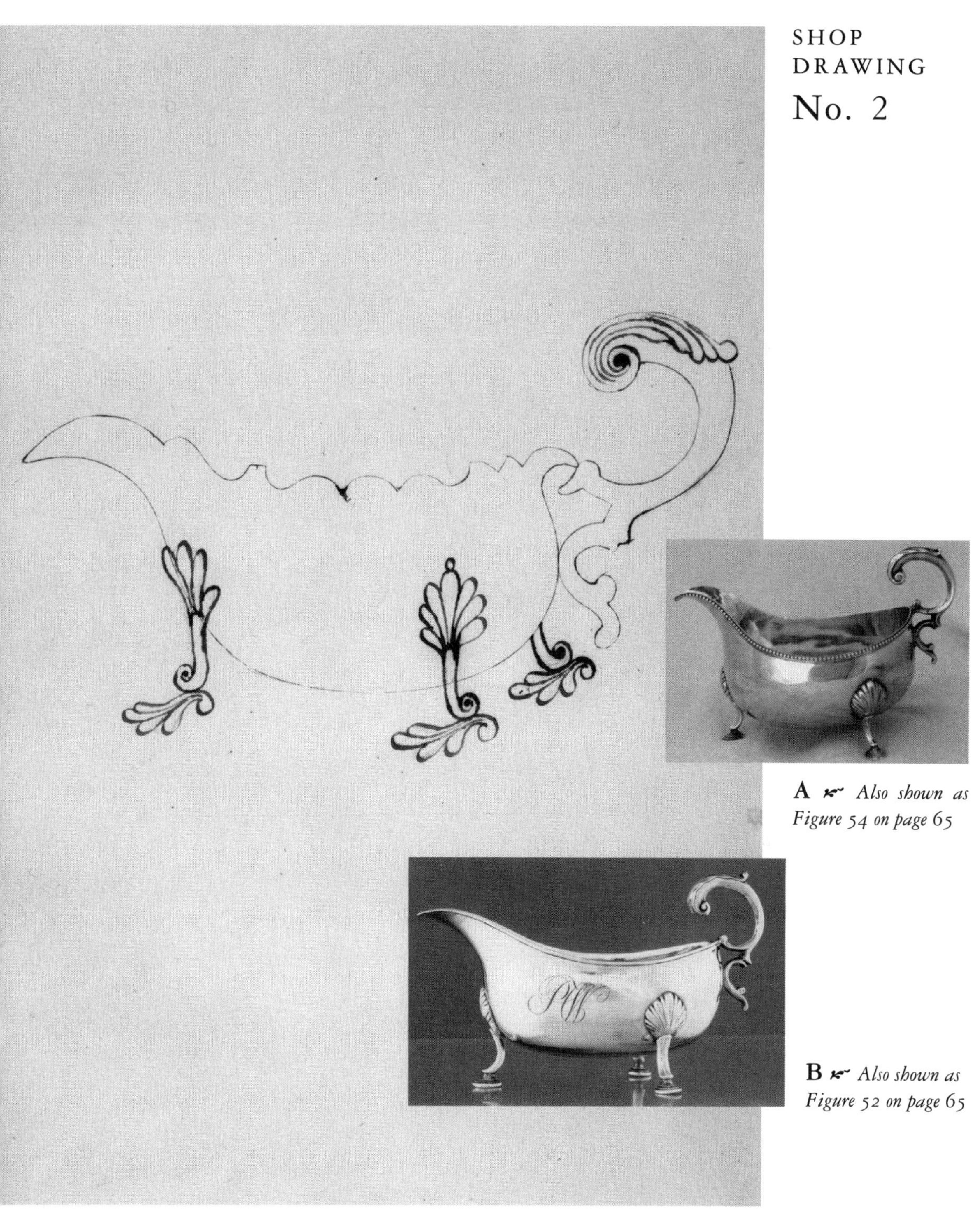

A ☛ *Also shown as
Figure 54 on page 65*

B ☛ *Also shown as
Figure 52 on page 65*

SD2 ☛ Shop Drawing for a **Sauceboat**, ca. 1760, 7½" long, pen and ink.
Full Rococo style with C- scroll handle, scalloped rim, and shell feet. See
Figures **A** and **B** for examples of sauceboats attributed to Faris's shop.

SD3 ✍ Shop Drawing for a **Tea Kettle**, ca. 1760–1770, 11½" high, pen and ink. Pencil lobing or fluting added later. This lobing was a post-1810 style.

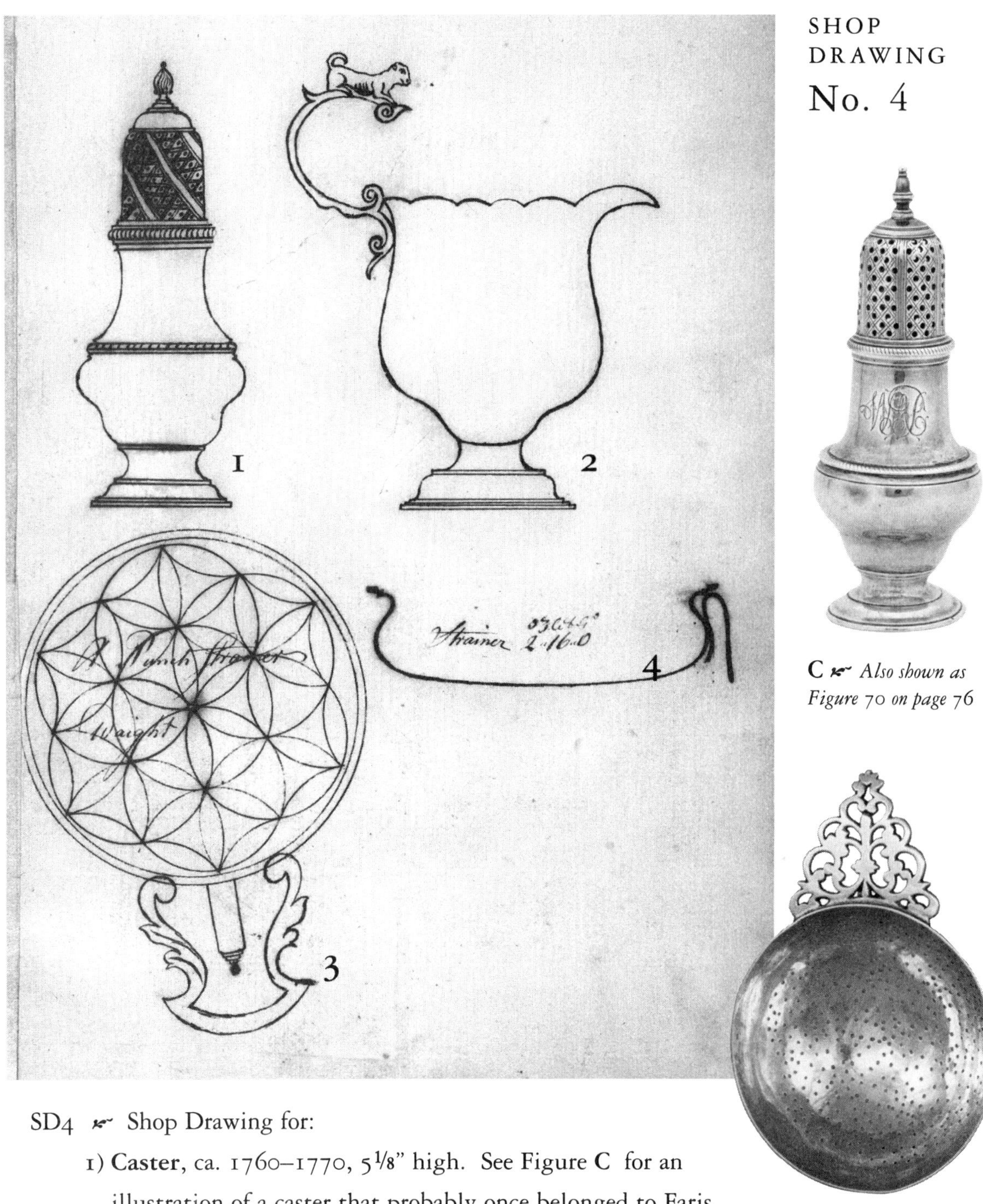

C ☞ *Also shown as Figure 70 on page 76*

D ☞ *Also shown as Figure 59 on page 68*

SD4 ☞ Shop Drawing for:

1) **Caster**, ca. 1760–1770, 5⅛" high. See Figure **C** for an illustration of a caster that probably once belonged to Faris.

2) **Cream pot**, ca. 1770, 5½" high.

3) **Strainer**, ca. 1760–1770, 5⅞" wide. See Figure **D** for an example of a very similar Faris strainer.

4) Section of **strainer**, ca. 1760–1770, 4⅛" diameter

433

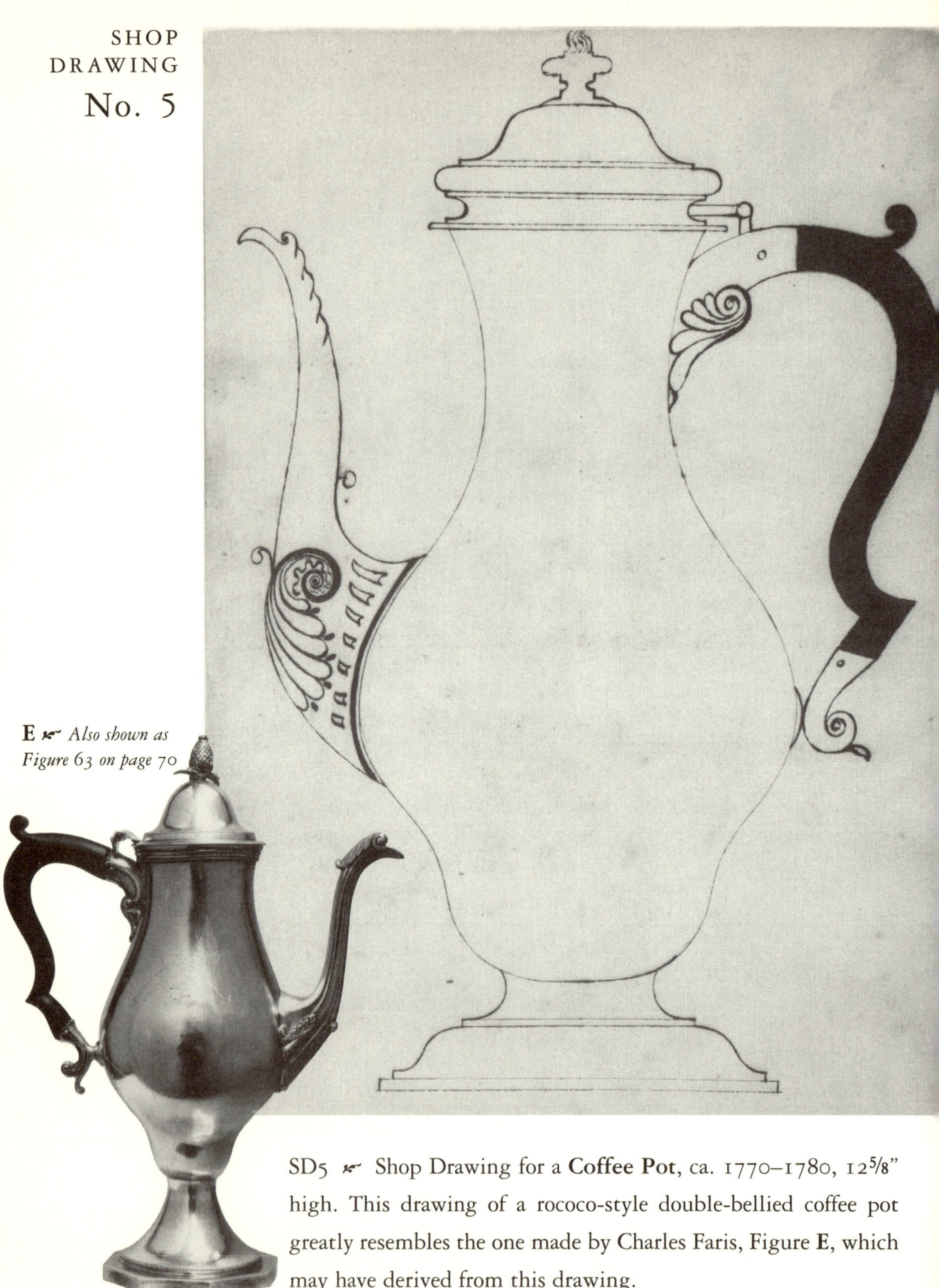

E ❧ *Also shown as*
Figure 63 on page 70

SD5 ❧ Shop Drawing for a **Coffee Pot**, ca. 1770–1780, 12⅝"
high. This drawing of a rococo-style double-bellied coffee pot
greatly resembles the one made by Charles Faris, Figure E, which
may have derived from this drawing.

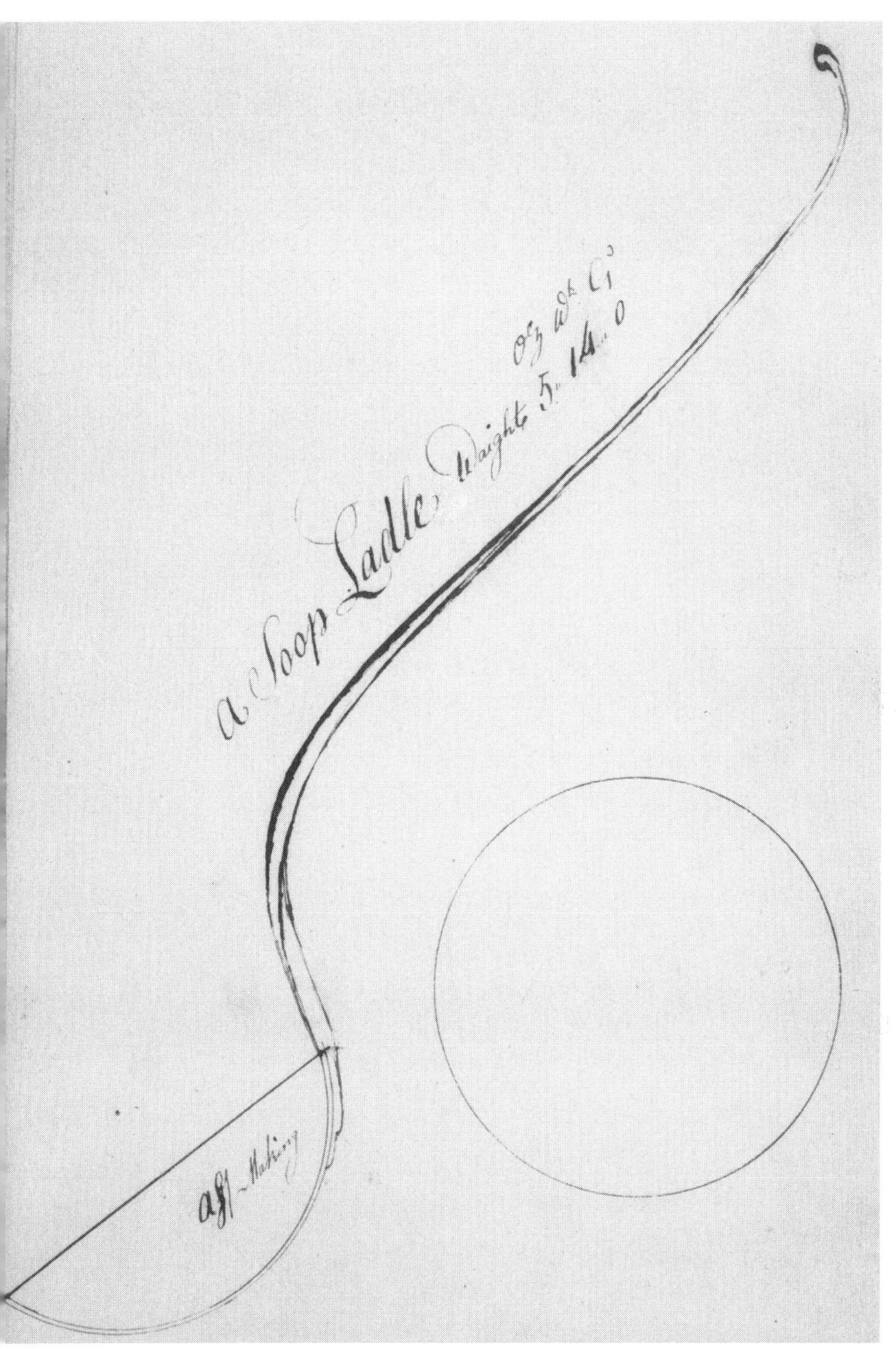

SD6 → Shop Drawing for a **Soup Ladle**, ca. 1770–1780, 14½" long.
Faris crafted "plain" ladles and "fluted" ladles in his shop, according to his
daybook.

SD7   Shop Drawing for a **Half-pint Cann**, ca. 1760–1770, 4½" high.
Canns were the most popular drinking vessel of the eighteenth century
and came in half-pint and pint sizes, as in the following drawing.

SHOP DRAWING
No. 8

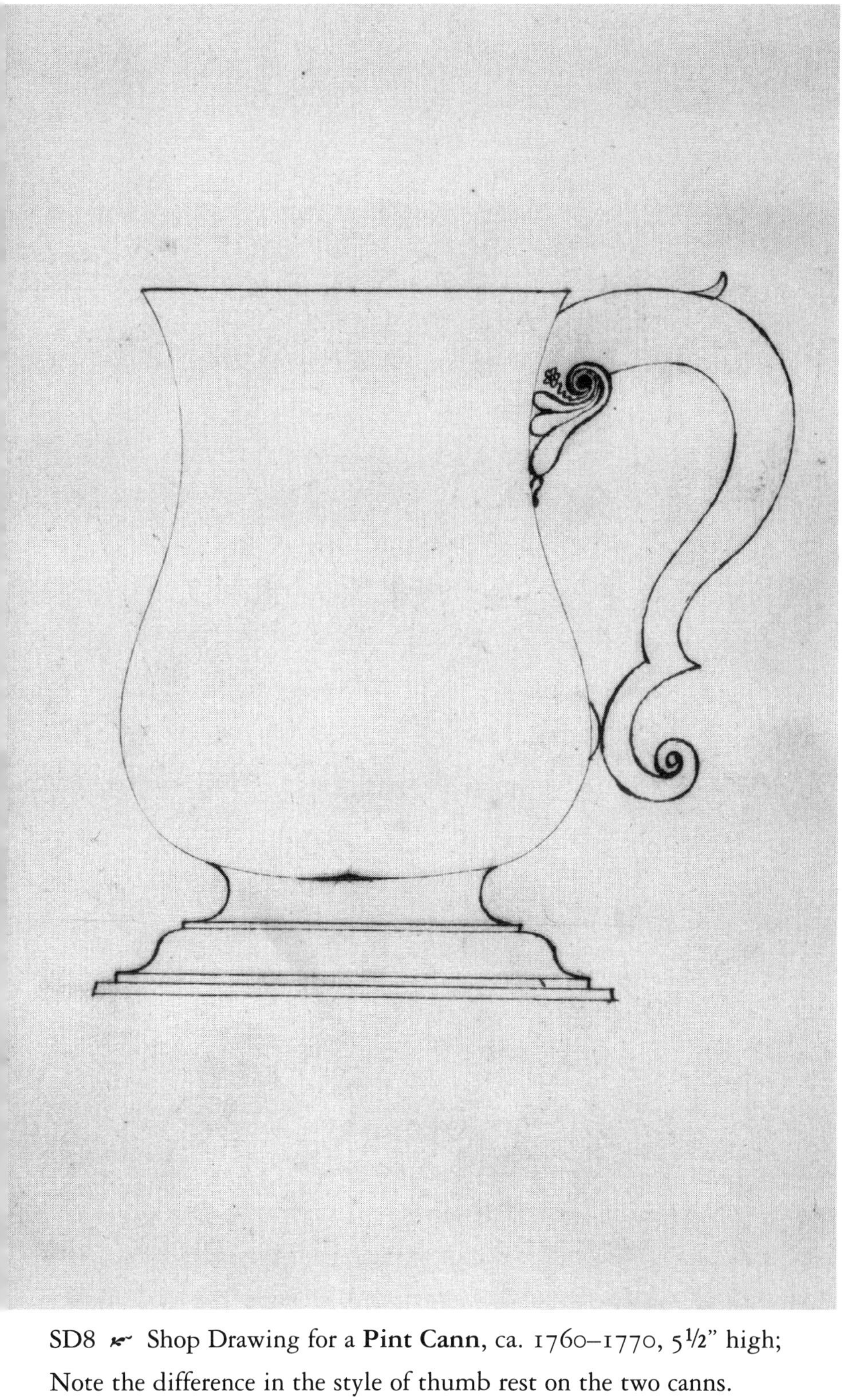

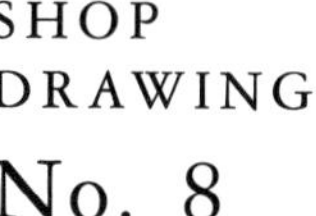

SD8 ☙ Shop Drawing for a **Pint Cann**, ca. 1760–1770, 5½" high; Note the difference in the style of thumb rest on the two canns.

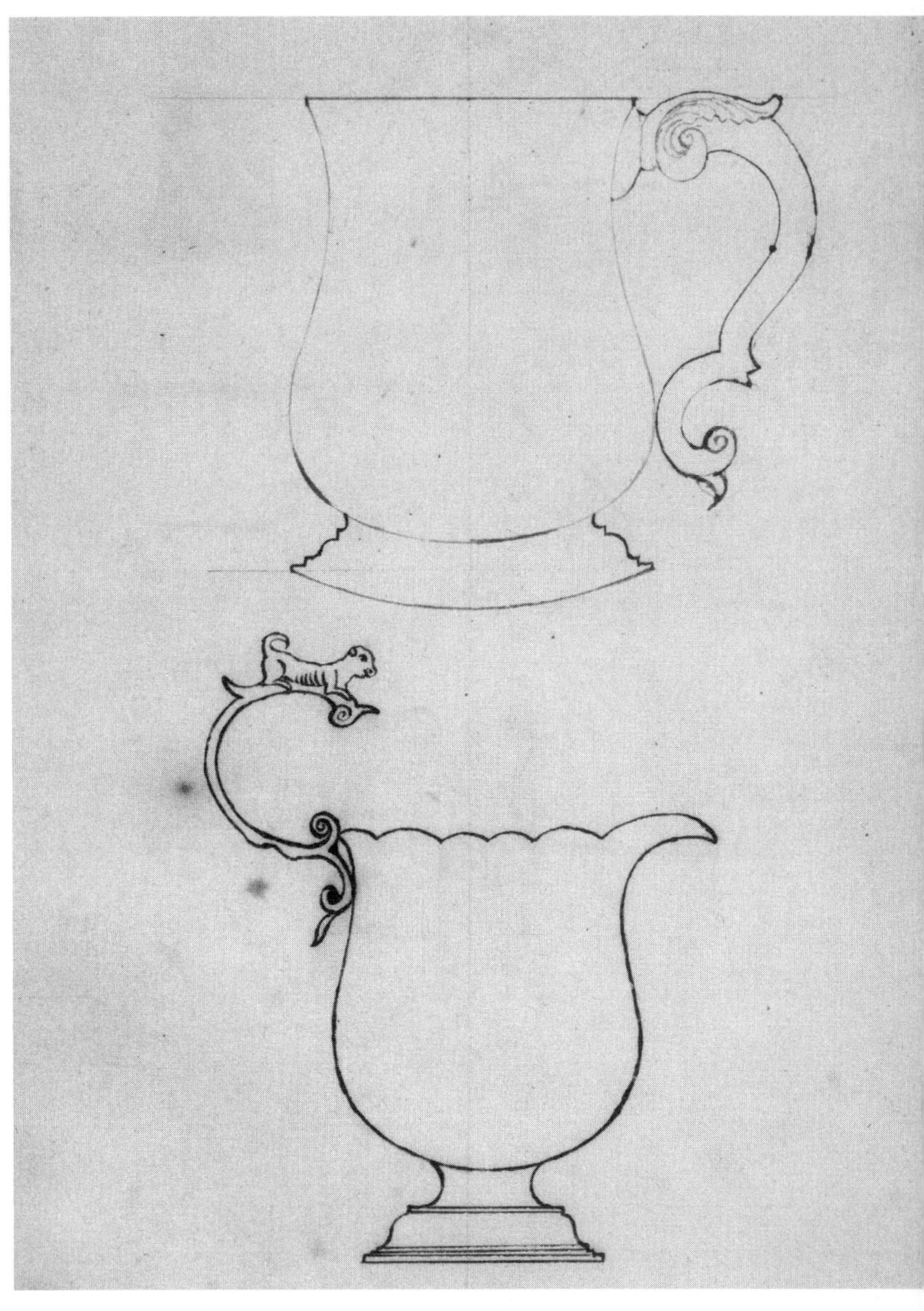

SD9 ✐ Shop Drawing: 1) **Half-pint Cann**, ca. 1760–1770, 4½" high.
Note the acanthus leaf on the handle of the cann, a typical rococo embel-
lishment. 2) **Cream pot**, ca. 1760–1770, 5½" high. The cast lamb or
dog on the handle of this drawing has not yet been found on an actual Faris
piece. This cast animal is more typical of late-seventeenth- and early-eigh-
teenth-century silver.

F ✒ *Also shown as Figure 22 on page 43*

SD10 ✒ Shop Drawing for a **Tankard**, ca. 1750, 9½" high. Tankards of this style were made in Philadelphia and England in the middle of the eighteenth century. See Figure **F** for an illustrated example of Faris's personal tankard. This drawing is slightly later in style than Faris's own tankard, due to its taller foot and more elongated proportions.

SD11 ☞ Shop Drawing for a **Wine Siphon**, ca. 1770, 20 inches total length. There is no evidence that Faris ever made a piece like this.

SHOP
DRAWING
No. 12

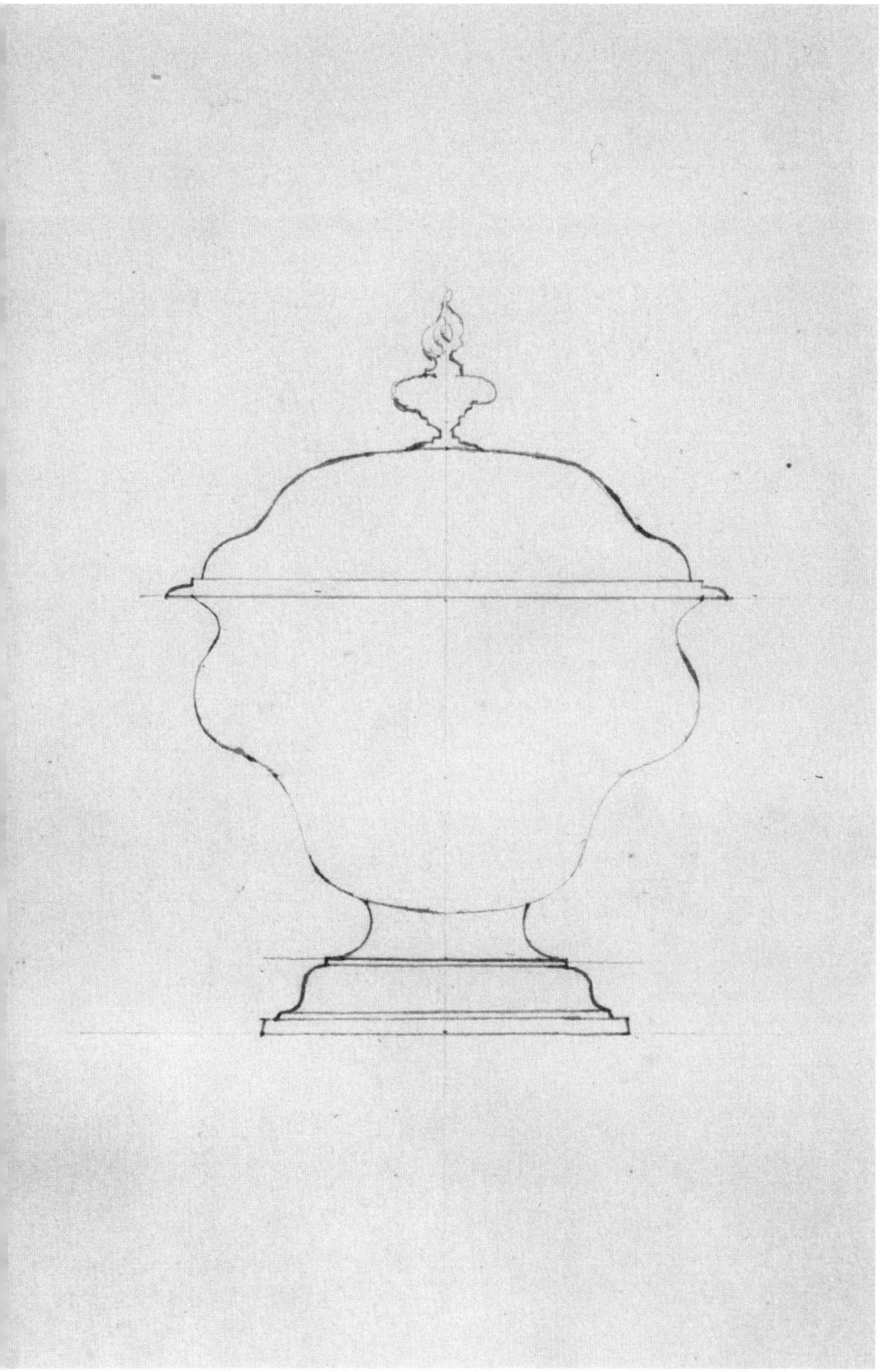

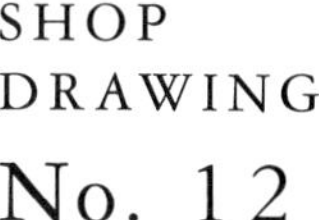

SD12 ☞ Shop Drawing for a **Covered Sugar Basin**, ca. 1760–1765, 5½" high. This was the standard form of English and American covered sugar basins of the mid-eighteenth century.

SD13 ✒ Shop Drawing for a **Skewer** and sectional view, ca. 1760–1780, 12 5/8" long. Skewers, made in great numbers in England, did not exhibit much stylistic change throughout the eighteenth century.

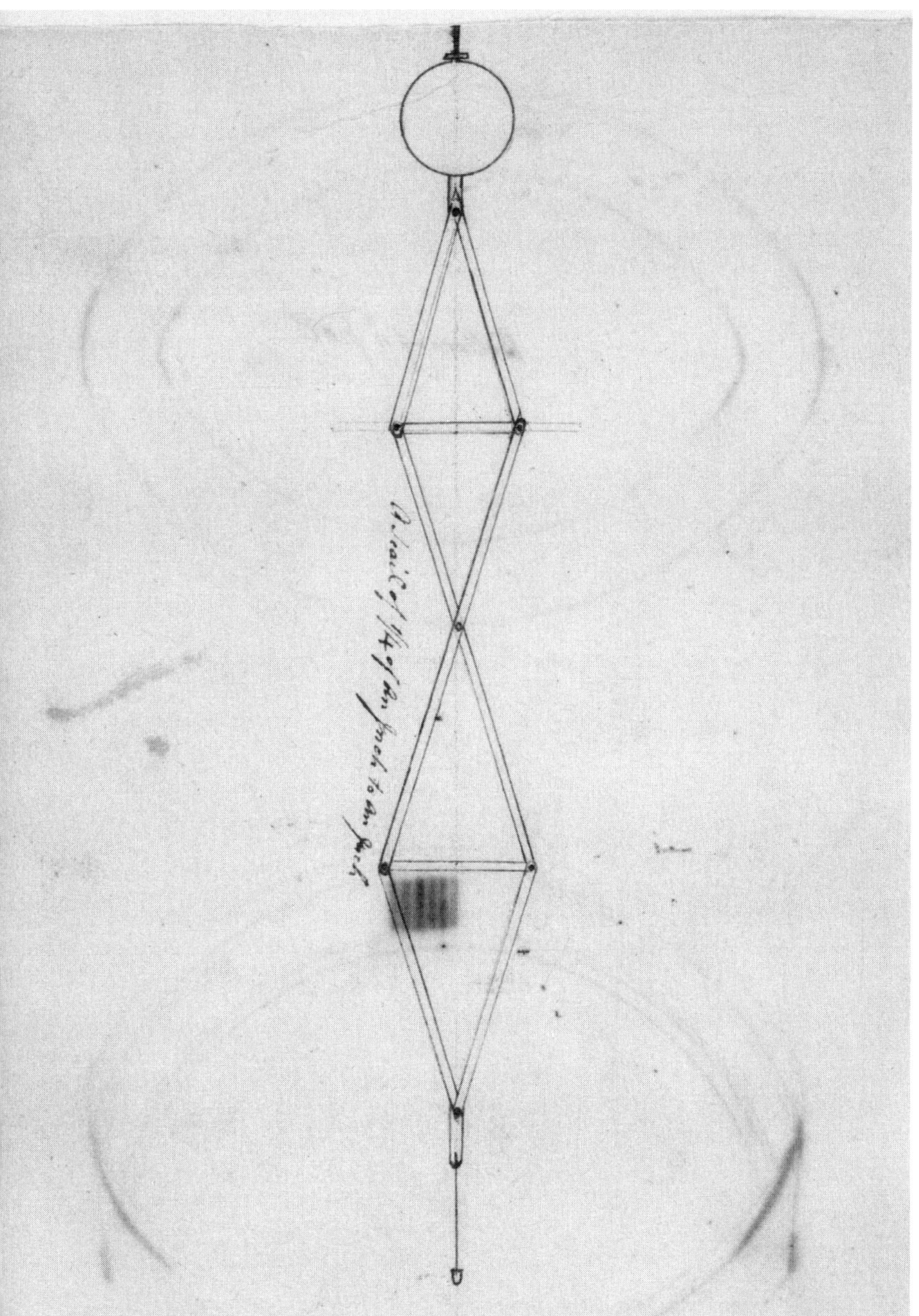

SD14 ✒ Shop Drawing for a **Spectacle Frame,** ca. 1770–1775, 10½"
long. This appears to be a sketch for an expandable kind of frame.
Although we know from Faris's daybook that he made silver spectacles, no
extant spectacles from this shop are known. Silversmiths often left delicate
items of this nature unmarked.

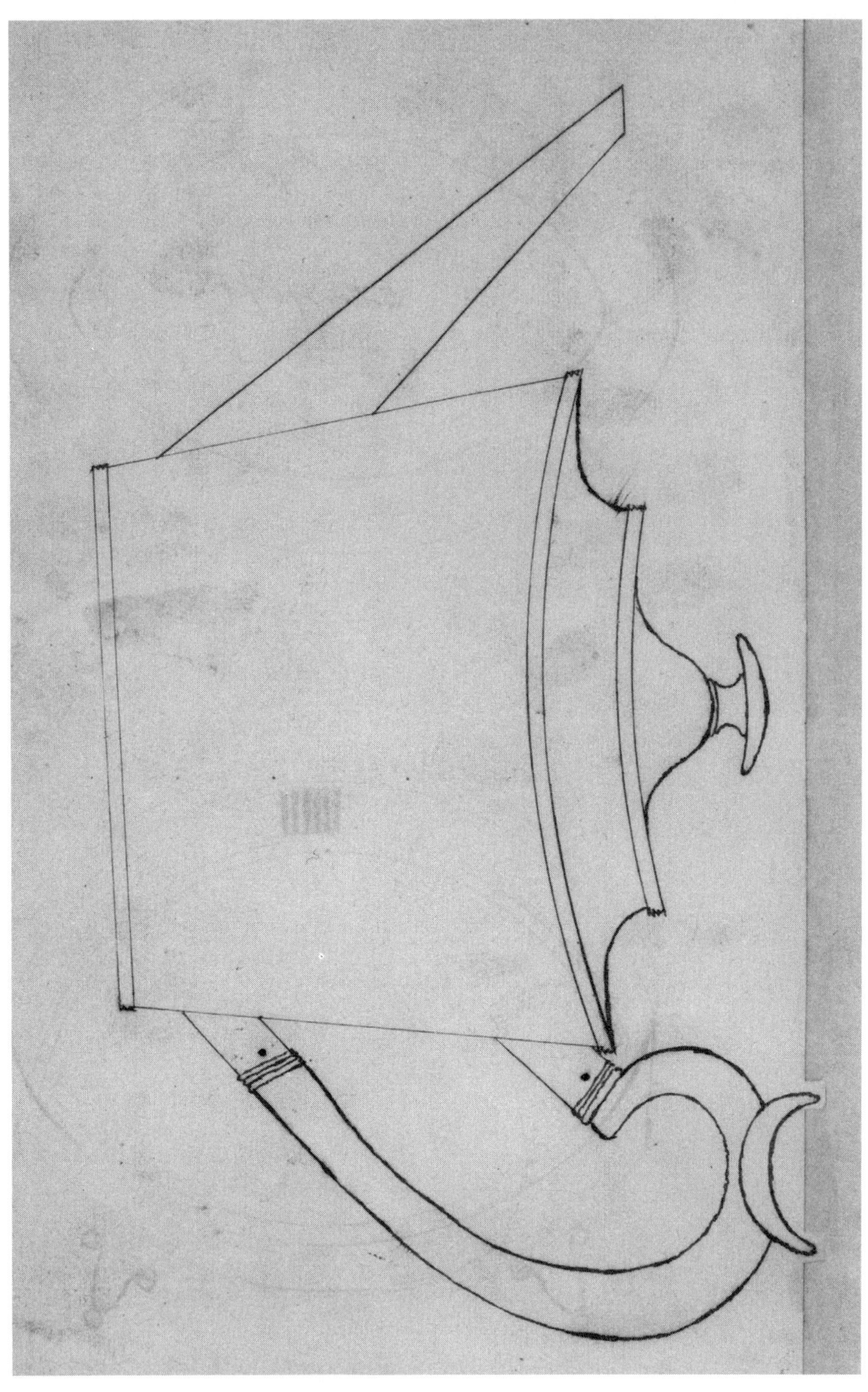

SD15 ☙ Shop Drawing for an oval drum **Teapot**, ca. 1790, 6⅛" high. This style of teapot became popular in the last decade of the eighteenth century. It is a type that could have been made in Faris's shop or very possibly one seen by him, perhaps when brought in for repair.

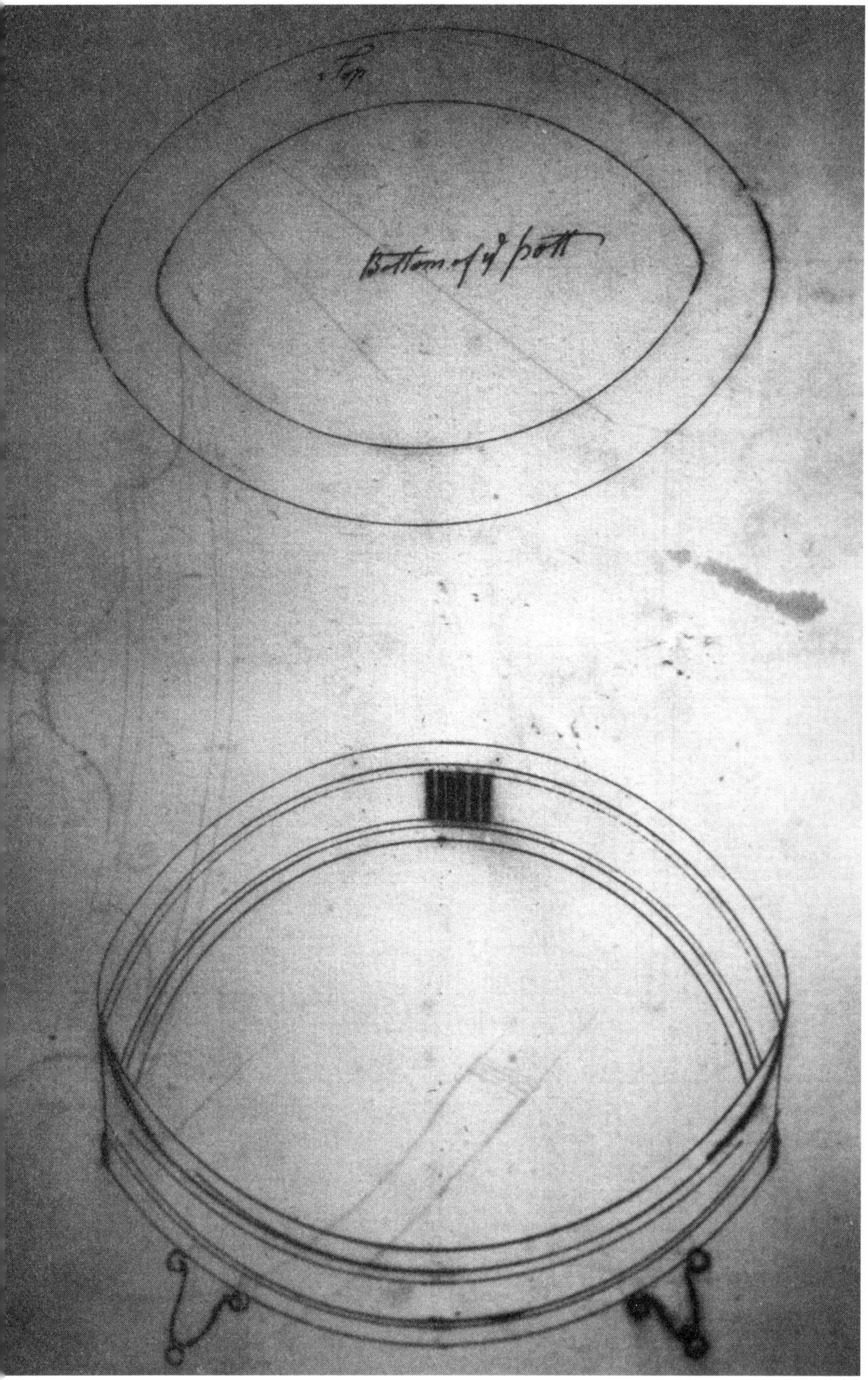

SD16 ☞ Shop Drawing of:

1a) **Bottom section of a Teapot**, ca. 1790, 5" long.

1b) **Top section of a Teapot**, ca. 1790, 6³⁄8" long.

2) **Teapot stand**, ca. 1790, 6¹⁄8" long. Teapots originally had a matching stand to protect tabletops from heat and moisture.

SHOP DRAWING No. 17

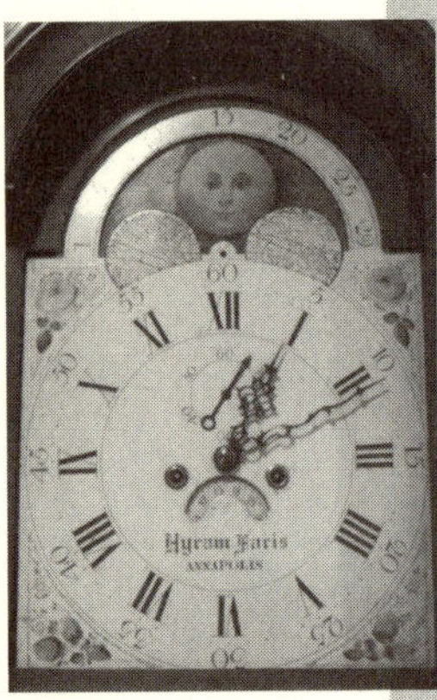

G ☛ *Also shown as Figure 39 on page 55*

H ☛ *Also shown as Figure 40 on page 56*

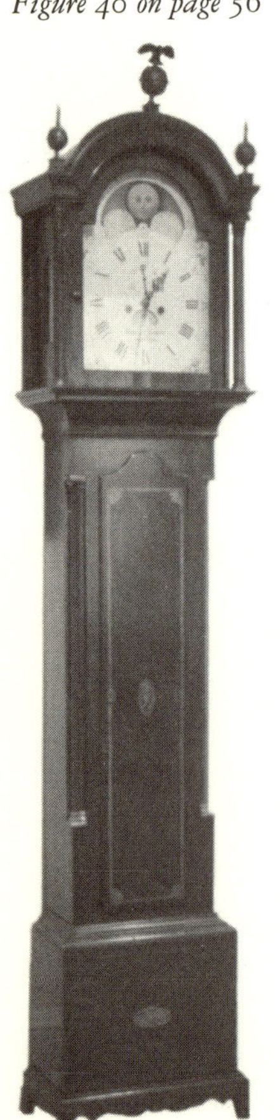

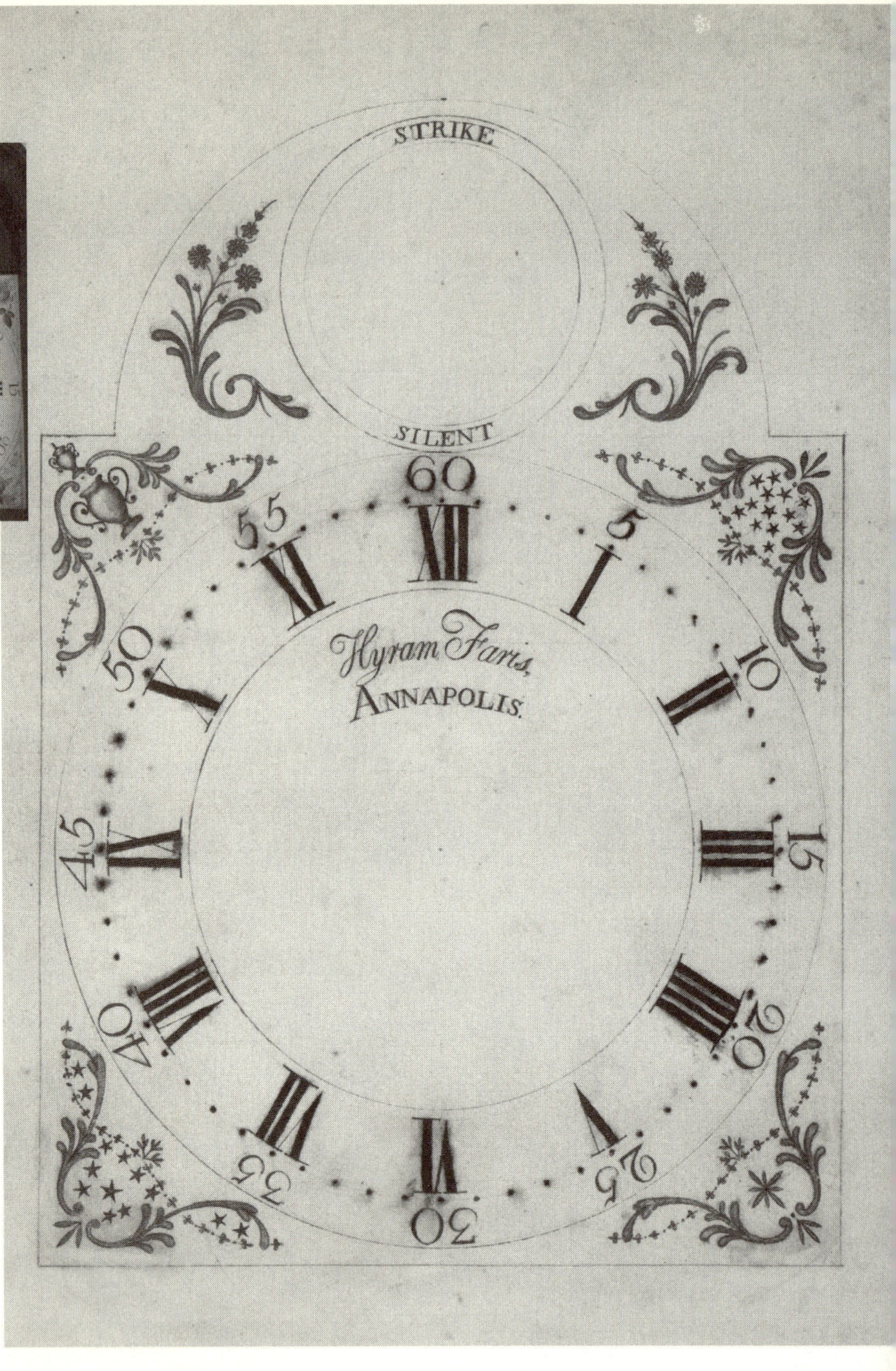

SD17 ☛ Shop Drawing of a **Clock Face**, ca. 1790–1800, 9½" high. Signed ***HYRAM FARIS*/ANNAPOLIS**. Hyram Faris, who made the clock in Figures **G** and **H**, may have made this drawing while working in his father's shop.

SD18 ✍ Shop Drawing of **Corner Decorations for Clock Face**, ca. 1790–1800, 8½" high. These patriotic decorations would have been applied to the corner of a white or painted dial.

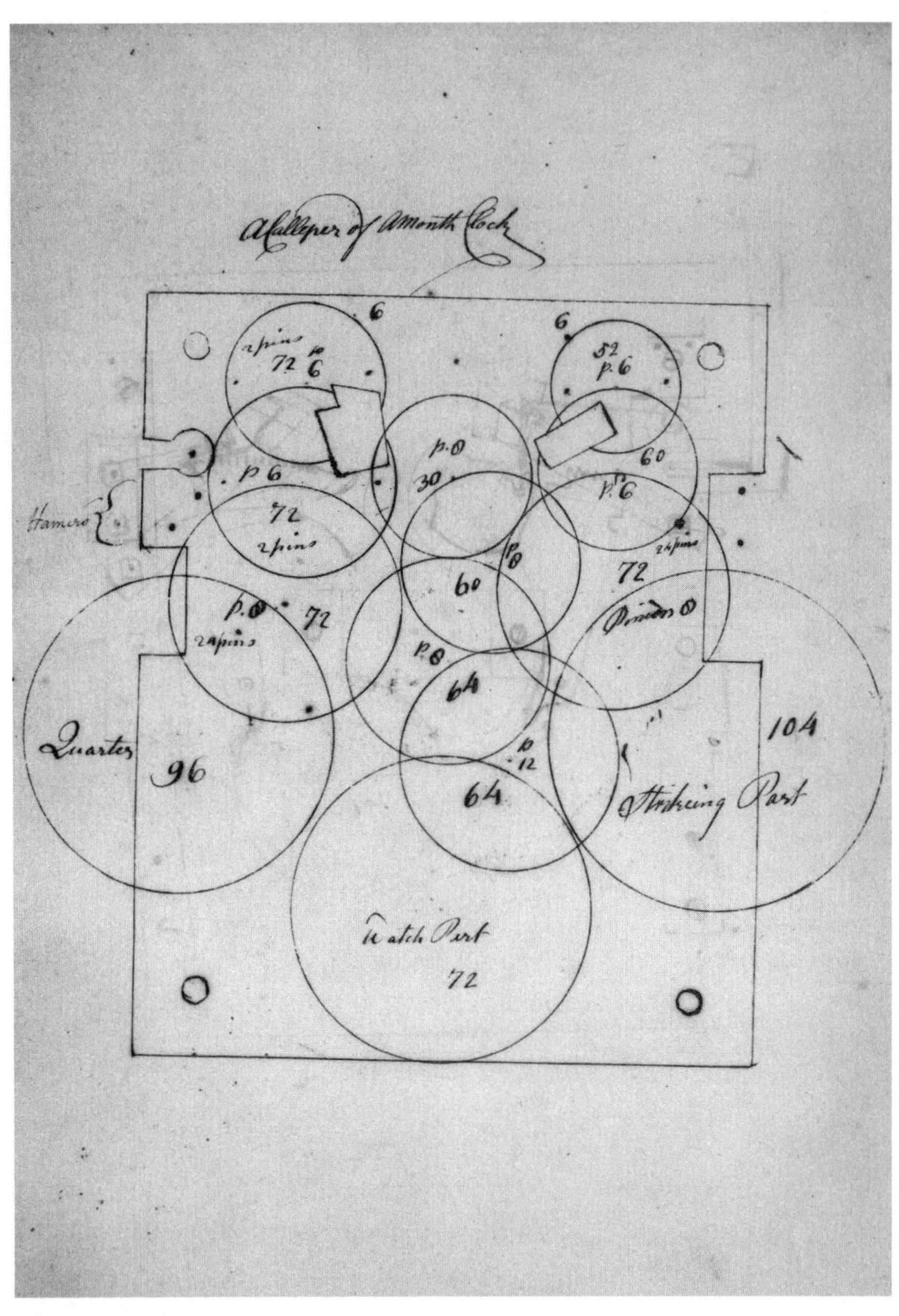

SD19 ✒ Shop drawing of a **Caliper for a Month Clock**, ca. 1760–1770.
Thirty-day clocks are very rare. Only one example of this movement from
Faris's shop is known to survive. It is a four-tune musical clock that
descended in the McParlin family of Annapolis. Faris did advertise clocks
to *"go either Eight days or Thirty, as the Purchaser shall fancy."*

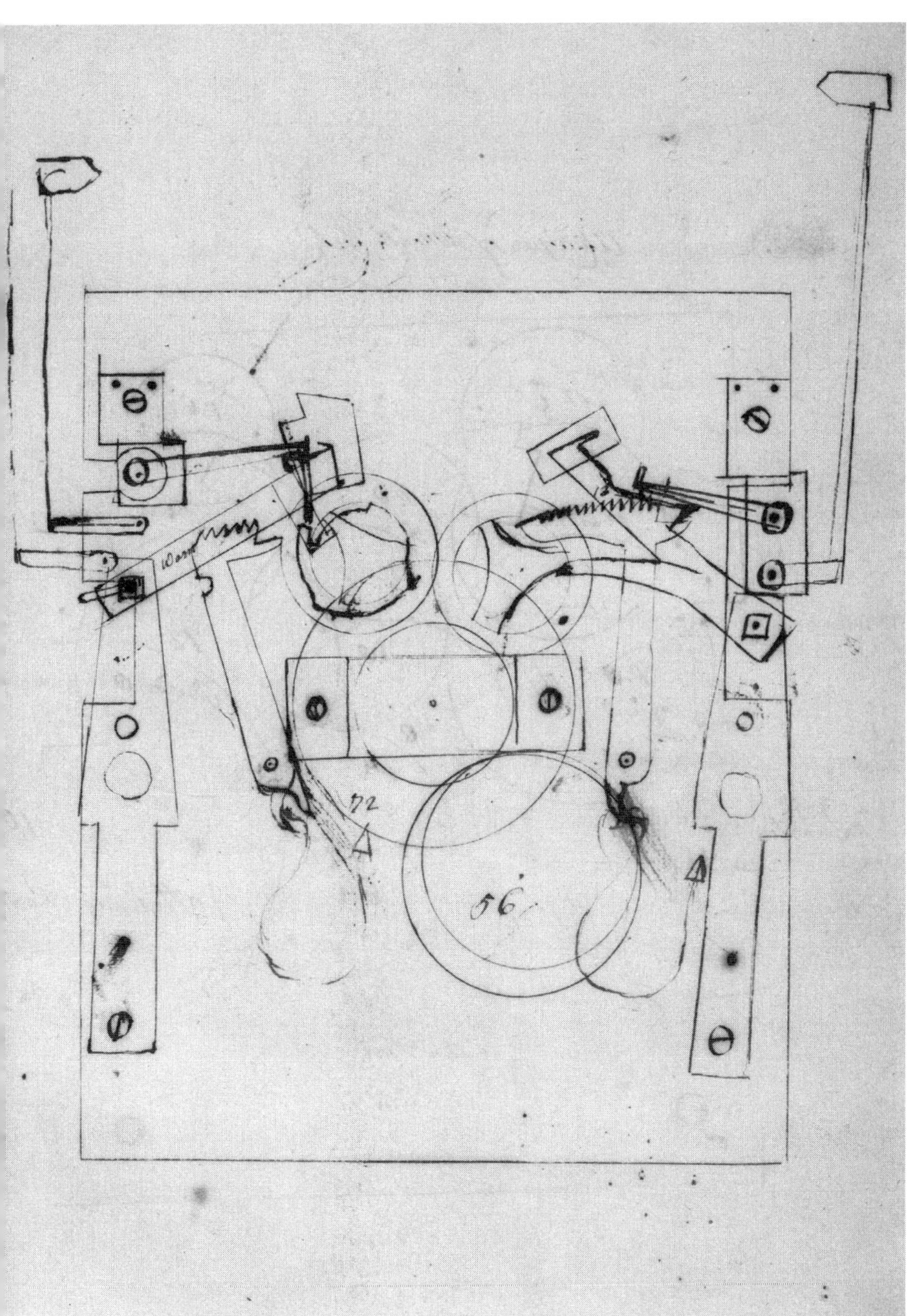

SD20 ☞ Shop drawing for a **Clock Mechanism**, ca. 1760–1770.
The motion and striking design for what appears to be a thirty-day clock
mechanism.

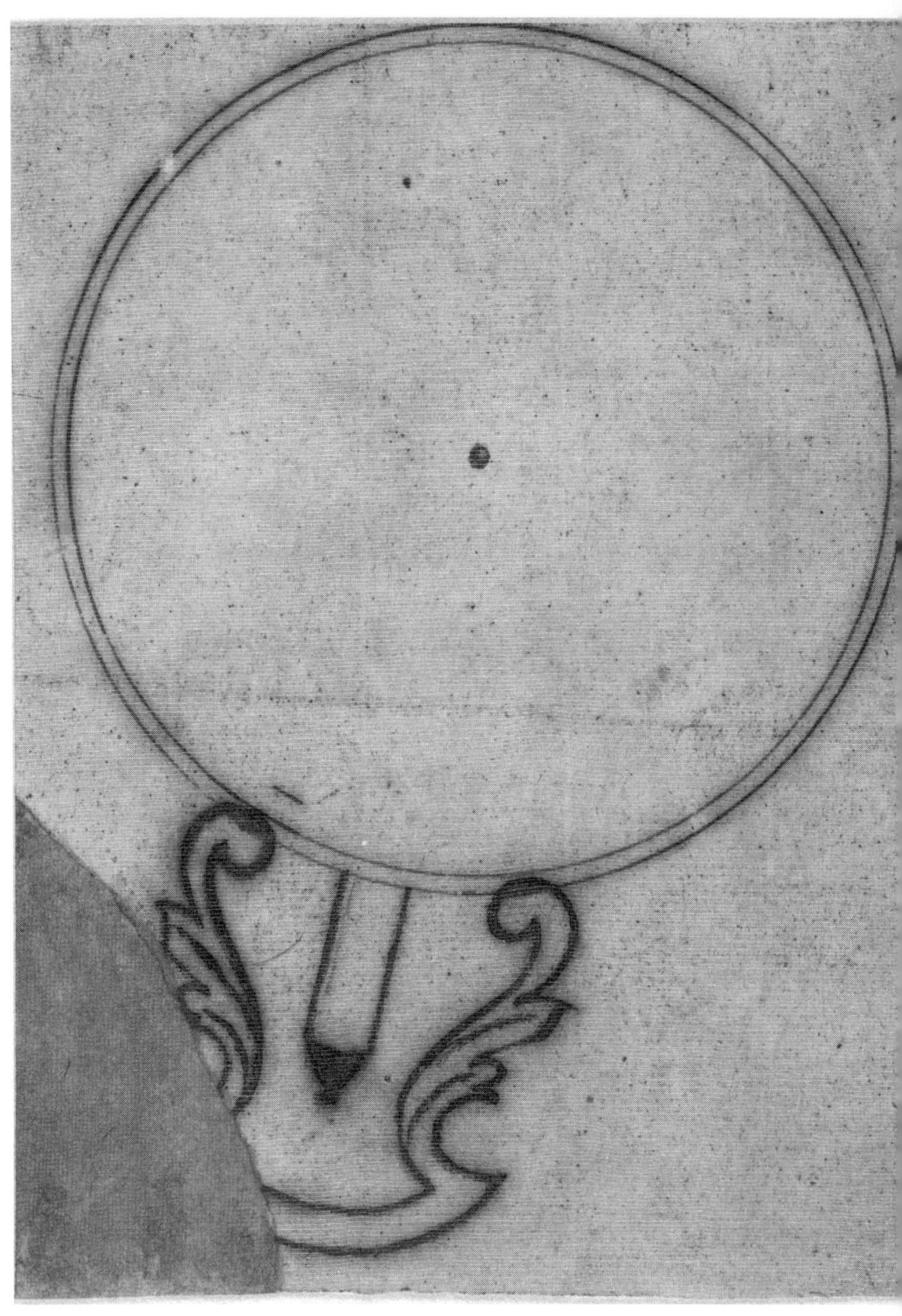

SD21 ✒ Shop drawing for a **Strainer**.

The last drawing in the shop book has a compass mark that has gone right through the paper. The strainer depicted in this drawing is the most typical form used in the eighteenth century on both sides of the Atlantic (see also Figure **SD4** on page 433).

APPENDICES

Plants Grown by William Faris[1]

THE PLANTS grown by William Faris were not particularly unique to the gardening milieu of the eighteenth-century Chesapeake. Many of these individual plants were widely cultivated throughout the colonies and even traded across the ocean with England. George Washington and Thomas Jefferson in Virginia and John Bartram in Philadelphia were growing and experimenting with these plants throughout the eighteenth century. Another Virginia gardener, John Custis IV of Williamsburg, corresponded with Londoner Peter Collinson and continually traded plants with him in the 1730s and 40s. Their correspondence is a telling reminder of the difficult and experimental times these were in the horticultural and botanical development of American gardening. The following list was compiled exclusively from William Faris's diary. All plants mentioned were grown or described by Faris.

African Marigold ✘ *Tagetes erecta*
Faris first planted this Mexican annual on 7 April 1792. Also known as Aztec marigold, this plant was a staple in gardens of the period.

Anemone ✘ *Anemone* Sp.[2]
A spring-blooming family grown from bulbs comprising several potential species that Faris may have grown. He first experimented with planting anemones on 14 May 1793.

Aster ✘ *Aster* Sp.
A myriad species candidates of this perennial genus were possible in Faris's garden. Faris raised over eight different varieties himself, recording them first in his diary on 7 April 1792.

Auricula ✘ *Primula auricula*
Faris obtained seeds of this type of primrose from Henri Stier on 26 April 1798. There were many colored varieties available in the eighteenth century. Thomas Jefferson raised auriculas as early as 1767.

Balsam Apple ✘ *Momordica balsamina*
Faris probably grew this annual plant, a relative of the cucumber also known as male balsam apple, for its ornamental red fruit. He first recorded it in his diary on 29 March 1793.

Bergamot Balm ✘ *Monarda fistulosa* or *M. didyma*
Bergamot, also known as bee balm, is a colorful perennial flower also used for medicinal purposes. Its blossoms are particularly attractive to hummingbirds. Faris distilled one gallon of balm water on 13 July 1802. Faris began recording this plant in his diary on 29 March 1793.

[1] The scientific names and other information included in this appendix are based on the following sources: Sarudy, "The Gardens and Grounds"; Sarudy, *Gardens and Gardening*; Brinkley and Chappell, *Gardens of Colonial Williamsburg*; Leighton, *American Gardens*; Griswold, *Washington's Gardens;* and E. G. Swem, *Brothers of the Spade.* Scientific names have been included only for the ornamental plants, shrubs, trees, and herbs but not for the vegetables, which are more generally known by their English names.

[2] Sp. follows the genus of a particular plant when the genus is known but not the exact species cultivated by Faris.

451

Bleeding Heart ⚘ *Dicentra spectabilis*
Faris received this perennial favorite on 13 August 1797, while it was still quite unknown in Europe, its introduction to England not being established until the nineteenth century. Faris planted bleeding hearts under the snowball tree, on the border by the walnut tree and in the lot.

Calamus ⚘ *Acorus Calamus*
Also known as Sweet Flag, this perennial native American plant was used as an herb. Faris planted four peach stones on the border next to the calamus on 5 October 1803.

Carnation ⚘ *Dianthus caryophylus*
Known as pinks or dianthus, these original carnations were also grown by Thomas Jefferson. They also belonged to a group known as gilliflowers and were widely grown in the period. Faris grew this common garden plant beginning on 5 May 1792.

Caterpillar ⚘ *Scorpiurus* Sp.
Faris planted caterpillars along with hedgehogs and snails on 1 April 1794.

Catnip ⚘ *Nepeta cataria*
Faris planted catnip in the alley between the new stable and the fence on 13 May 1803.

China Aster ⚘ *Callistephus chinensis*
Chinese asters were annuals commonly grown in American gardens throughout the eighteenth century. Faris planted several varieties in his garden beginning on 26 March 1795.

Chrysanthemum ⚘ *Chrysanthemum indicum*
Faris referred to his chrysanthemums by their species name, *indicum*. They were a feature of his garden and many others of the period. Modern hybrids are descended from this Chinese chrysanthemum. Faris recorded planting this species in his diary on 21 April 1799.

Columbine ⚘ *Aquilegia canadensis* or *A. vulgaris*
Columbines were native perennials commonly grown in Faris's day, and remain favorites with today's gardeners. Faris grew a double-flowered variety beginning on 7 April 1792, which could possibly have been the European columbine *A. vulgaris*, and not the American *canadensis*.

Cockscomb ⚘ *Celosia cristata*
Jefferson also grew this colorful annual at Monticello. Like the globe amaranth, this species is commonly used as a dried flower. This is one of the first plants Faris recorded in his diary on 7 April 1792.

Crocus ⚘ *Crocus vernus*
A perennial favorite, the crocus is one of the first flowers to bloom in the spring, at times, even while there is still snow on the ground. Faris mentioned the common blue variety on 18 April 1803.

Crown Imperial ⚘ *Fritillaria imperialis*
Native to Persia and cultivated since the sixteenth century, crown imperials were always considered among the greatest achievements to flower in the pleasure garden. Faris grew both red and yellow varieties of this spectacular spring bulb and first mentioned them on 1 May 1794. John Custis of Williamsburg received yellow varieties from Peter Collinson in the 1730s and wrote in 1739 "I had this spring a lemon colord crown imperiall you were kind to send me; which was lookd on as a great rarity; I have two roots of the orange colord."[3] Washington and Jefferson also cultivated this species.

3 E. G. Swem, *Brothers of the Spade: Correspondence of Peter Collinson, of London and of John Custis, of Williamsburg, Virginia 1734–1746* (Massachusetts: Barre Press, 1957), 63.

Daffodil 🖋 *Narcissus* Sp.

Known collectively as narcissus, jonquils and daffodils, this commonly grown group is difficult to differentiate and identify with certainty as to the exact cultivated species. Faris's reference to "Fross Narcess's roots" is an example of this type of confusion. Faris mentioned daffodils for the first time on 1 May 1794 in a list of bulbs he recorded planting.

Dwarf Morning Glory 🖋 *Convolvulus tricolor*

This is probably the plant that Faris was referring to when he wrote "Convolvalis Miner" on 3 April 1794. It was also known in the period as bindweed.

Evening Primrose 🖋 *Oenothera biennis*

Known also as the Virginia tree primrose, this American native biennial was requested from John Custis in Williamsburg by Peter Collinson of London in 1738. Faris first mentions this plant, long appreciated for fragrant blooms that open toward evening, early in the diary on 5 May 1792.

Female Balsam 🖋 *Impatiens balsamina*

Also known as garden balsam or impatiens, Faris labeled and exchanged many hybrids of this annual with his gardening colleagues. Many colorful varieties were available. Faris raised at least a dozen different kinds, beginning on 7 April 1792.

Flowering Pea 🖋 *Lathyrus latifolia*

Faris grew flowering or everlasting peas throughout the years of the diary, first mentioning them on 3 April 1794. They performed a dual function as an ornamental flower and a source of food.

Flower de Luce 🖋 *Iris pseudacorus*

Known also as fleur de lis, dwarf flower de luce and yellow flag, this iris species grows in moist areas and has long been a favorite in cultivation. First grown by Faris on 17 January 1793.

Formoso 🖋

Although unidentified, this plant was received by Faris from Samuel Howard on 15 March 1804, as a "flower from the Alleganey."

Garden Primrose 🖋 *Polyanthus* X4

Faris used the terms primrose and polianthus interchangeably. This plant is generally known as a hybrid of *Primula eliator*. It was one of the first plants Faris recorded in his diary on 7 April 1792.

Geranium 🖋 *Pelargonium* or *Geranium* Sp.

When Faris recorded receiving six geraniums from Dr. Upton Scott on 5 May 1801, he was probably referring to the South African species of *Pelargonium* commonly known today as geranium, and not to the perennial cranesbill of the genus *Geranium*.

Ginger 🖋 *Asarum canadense*

A versatile perennial herb, ginger was used in culinary preparations and for medicinal purposes. Faris recorded this plant late in his diary on 1 September 1802.

Globe Amaranth 🖋 *Gomphrena globosa*

This annual was very popular in old-fashioned gardens. Its flowers could also be dried and used in flower arrangements. Faris first wrote about this plant on 22 April 1799 and grew both red and white varieties. A tropical native, it has been widely grown on both sides of the Atlantic since colonial times and is still available today.

4 "X" denotes a cross or hybrid between two or more forms and not a true species.

Hedgehog ✍ *Medicago intertexta*
Faris planted this species also known as Medic on 1 April 1794.

Hollyhock ✍ *Alcea rosea*
A popular biennial still cultivated today. The tall spire of blooms is an ever-present character of old-fashioned gardens. Faris planted hollyhocks near his stable on 10 August 1801.

Horseradish ✍ *Armoracia lapathifolia*
A perennial herb long cultivated for its medicinal attributes as well as for its culinary uses. We learn from Faris that he grew this plant on 17 September 1799, when he planted "about 200 Tulep root. on the Border next to the Hors Radish."

Hyacinth ✍ *Hyacinthinus orientalis*
The common garden hyacinth was grown widely prior to the eighteenth century. Faris visited Henri Stier's garden in Annapolis on 27 April 1797 and exclaimed that "he has a fine collection of Hyacinths the Best I have seen." Faris grew four varieties of hyacinths, first mentioning them on 28 March 1794.

Iceplant ✍ *Mesembryanthenum aureum*
Known also as fig marigolds. Jefferson stated that "they should be raised in pots," which Faris annually did after he first recorded growing them on 6 March 1793.

Impatiens ✍ *Impatiens balsamina*
See Female/Garden Balsam.

India Pink ✍ *Dianthus chinensis/sinensis*
Colorful blanketing perennials. Pinks are a term used loosely for this genus, known also as dianthus. See Carnation. One of the first flowers recorded by Faris in his diary on 7 April 1792.

Iris ✍ *Iris* Sp.
We cannot always be sure to which of the several varieties of iris Faris was referring. Several of these rhizomatous species were common in cultivation at this time. Among those Faris grew were the Persian, *I. persica*, and a rush-leaved variety on 11 August 1801.

Jasmine ✍ *Gelsenium sempervirens* or *Jasminum officinale*
Known also as jessamine, this vine could have been the Indian jasmine or the Carolina yellow jessamine, *Gelsenium sempervirens*. Jasmines were favorites in the garden due to their intoxicating fragrance and graceful flowering habit. Faris recorded his "passhon Jessemon" on 17 January 1793.

Jerusalem Cherry Tree ✍ *Solanum pseudo-capsicum*
This decorative plant was grown for its red berries, which stay on the plant long after its small white flowers have faded. Faris planted this species in pots but occasionally also in his ornamental borders. Faris would take his potted Jerusalem cherry trees into the cellar for the winter and bring them out in the spring when danger of frost had passed. First mentioned on 3 February 1793, this was one of Faris's favorite ornamentals.

Job's Tears ✍ *Coix altissima*
A perennial grass that Faris used as a border plant on 2 April 1794.

Jonquil ✍ *Narcissus jonquilla*
See Daffodil. Mentioned by Faris in his long list of bulbs on 1 May 1794.

Joseph's Coat ✍ *Amaranthus tricolor*
Faris planted this annual on 19 April
1798. He referred to this plant not
by its common name but by its scientific one. This is undoubtedly the
same species Faris wrote about on 23
April 1799 and refers to as "tricola"
seed. Collinson sent Custis this
species in 1742.

Lady in Green ✍ *Cardamine pratensis*
or *Alchemilla vulgaris*
Faris sowed seeds of this perennial
flower, known also as lady's smock,
on the border at the end of the new
stable on 8 April 1793.

Larkspur ✍ *Delphinium exaltatum* or
D. carolinianum
Known also as delphiniums, the tall
flowered spires of these plants were
great ornamental features in the eighteenth-century garden. The larkspurs
grown by Faris were actually annuals
and not the fancy perennials we know
today. He first mentioned them on
17 April 1800.

Lily ✍ *Sprekelia* or *Lilium* Sp.
It is not always clear which lilies
Faris cultivated in the years of the
diary. He first mentioned growing
the Jacobean lily, *Sprekelia formosis-
sima,* on 26 May 1798, as well as the
Lily of St. Jaego.

Marigold ✍ *Calendula officinalis*
These plants were also known as pot
marigolds, a name that came into use
when the African marigold, *Tagetes
erecta,* was brought into cultivation in
the eighteenth century. Pot
marigolds were a common flowering
annual of the period. Faris planted
seeds of this plant on 25 March
1793.

Mignonette ✍ *Reseda odorata*
A popular annual, mignonettes produce clusters of fragrant flowers on a
long stalk. Jefferson also grew
mignonettes, which Faris called
"mininett." He recorded their cultivation quite early in his diary on 15
May 1792.

Mint ✍ *Mentha* Sp.
It is unclear which species of aromatic mint Faris used in his garden.
Faris distilled mint on 15 July 1802
for an unidentified drink. Long
favored as an herb for its culinary and
medicinal attributes.

Nasturtium ✍ *Tropaeolum majus*
Known also as Indian cress, this
native Mexican plant is used as an
herb and has long been a popular
ornamental flowering annual, with
its vine-like growing habit. It estab-
lishes quickly and blooms freely
throughout the spring and summer
months. Jefferson also grew nasturtiums at Monticello, as did
Washington at Mount Vernon.
Faris planted nasturtiums on 18
April 1801.

Nutmeg (Indian) ✍ *Nigella sativa**[5]
Known also as fennel flower. The
fragrant seeds of this plant, black
cumin, have long been used as a
food additive. Faris first planted the
indian nutmeg on 19 April 1798.
Jefferson called it the "nutmeg plant"
as did Faris later in his diary. It is
not always clear if Faris is referring
to this plant; he also wrote about
sowing "Nutmegg Cantilope" on
5 April 1803.

Parsley ✍ *Petroselinum crispum*
This biennial herb was used for its
medicinal as well as for its culinary
properties. Faris began planting it in
the utilitarian area of his garden on
27 March 1792.

[5] An asterisk denotes a
possible species candidate
but one not entirely con-
firmed.

Parson's Pride ✍
This plant remains unidentified. Faris first mentioned it on 19 April 1798.

Passion Flower ✍ *Passiflora incarnata*
Also known as May-pop, this southern American native was grown for its interesting flowers, the genus so named due to the flower's resemblance to some of the characteristics of Christ's crucifixion. The edible fruits are known as maracocks. Faris first recorded it on 17 January 1793.

Pickling Lime ✍ *Tilia caroliniana**
It is not clear if this is the exact species Faris was referring to but it is a possible candidate. This is one of the first plants recorded by Faris on 7 April 1792.

Polyanthus ✍ *Polyanthus X*
See Garden Primrose. This species is a hybrid between the cowslip *Primula veris* and the primrose *P. vulgaris*. In the first garden-related entry of the diary, Faris recorded receiving a root of polyanthus from George Mann on 6 March 1792.

Poppy ✍ *Papaver somniferum*
or *P. orientale*
The oriental opium poppy *P. somniferum* was popular due to its brightly colored blossoms. We cannot be sure which species Faris grew. The common poppy *P. orientale* was also grown widely in this period. This was one of the first plants recorded by Faris on 7 April 1792.

Primrose ✍ *Primula vulgaris*
Known also as common or English primrose. Faris began recording them in his diary in 7 April 1792.

Ranunculus ✍ *Ranunculus* or *Anemonella* Sp.
Ranunculus were popular perennials in the eighteenth century. They did not become part of Faris's garden until 17 April 1800.

Reason ✍
This plant remains unidentified, although Faris may have been referring to "raisins." Whatever it truly was, Faris planted the seeds and "stones" both in his flower beds and in pots. He wrote about these seeds on 3 February 1803.

Rose ✍ *Rosa rugosa* or *R. alba*
This widely known and cultivated genus should need no description. Although it is not always clear to which roses Faris was referring, these species are potential candidates. We first learn of these roses on 1 July 1793 when Faris "trimed the Rose Bushes the side next to Grayhams."

Rosemary ✍ *Rosmarinus officinalis*
Rosemary's varied uses in the kitchen as an herb did not eclipse its decorative effect in the garden. Faris edged his kitchen garden beds with trimmed rosemary but also planted them in pots. He covered his rosemary plants with straw to protect them through the winter months. They were first mentioned on 26 November 1793.

Saffron Crocus ✍ *Crocus sativus*
Faris probably used this plant, also known as saffron, only as an ornamental and not as a culinary herb. He first mentioned it on 22 September 1792 when he wrote that "the saffron croccus's is just making thare appearance acuming up."

Sage ✍ *Salvia officinalis*
Faris edged some of his vegetable beds with sage. We learn of this prac-

tice as early as 26 March 1792 and throughout the diary years.

Satin Flower 🖅 *Lunaria annua*
Also known as honesty. This perennial forms large clusters of flowers, which later become seed pods and can be used in dried flower arrangements. Faris first recorded this plant on 3 April 1794.

Sensitive Plant 🖅 *Mimosa pudica* or *Dionaea muscipula*
It is unclear which of these species Faris grew. It was probably *Mimosa pudica,* a plant whose leaves close up when touched, and less likely *Dionaea muscipula,* the widely known curiosity, Venus flytrap. Faris recorded growing these plants in pots as early as 7 April 1792.

Snails 🖅 *Medicago scutellata*
Faris planted snails, a relative of the hedgehog, along with caterpillars on 1 April 1794.

Snapdragon 🖅 *Antirrhinum majus*
A common border annual, snapdragons were available in a variety of colors. Blooming through the warmer months, it remains a favorite in today's gardens. Faris received his first cutting as a gift from Nelly Davidson on 2 May 1795.

Stock 🖅 *Mathiola incana*
Known collectively as July flowers or gilliflowers, stocks were common annuals grown in eighteenth-century gardens and were available in a wide range of colors. Faris recorded them on 30 March 1802.

Ten Commandments 🖅 *Maranta leuconeura*
Faris did not try his hand at this species, known as the prayer plant, until 19 May 1804, just three

months before his death. He planted the seeds in a flower box with the asters.

Thyme 🖅 *Thymus vulgaris*
A common perennial herb, thyme is native to the Mediterranean and has been used for centuries medicinally and as a culinary ingredient. Faris raised thyme in his vegetable beds as attested to by his entry of 14 April 1795.

Tobacco 🖅 *Nicotiana Sp.* *
Faris called this species tree or Persian tobacco on 16 March 1794 when Hyram sowed some of its seeds. This plant may have been *N. persica,* or the flowering tobacco *N. alata*, an annual species grown for its nocturnal fragrance and attractive tubular flowers.

Tuberose 🖅 *Polianthes tuberosa*
Faris grew single and double-flowered varieties of this perennial flower, unrelated to roses, from tubers. Tuberoses in a wide range of colors were popular perennials in colonial gardens. Faris first mentioned them on 7 April 1792, and recorded planting twenty double-flowered tuberoses on 20 March 1793.

Tulip 🖅 *Tulipa gesnerana*
Undoubtedly Faris's favorite flower and grown by him by the thousands. Faris's obsession with the cultivation of tulips, first recorded by him on 24 March 1792, was not a new phenomenon. Tulips had been responsible for a frenzy in the seventeenth century in Holland that came to be known as "Tulipomania." John Custis of Williamsburg was cultivating tulips in Virginia in the 1730s, and a great many varieties were known in Faris's time. Faris pressed several of his named varieties of tulips into the back of his design book in May 1799.

Variegated Palmach 🖌 *Ricinus communis**
Also known as Palma Christi or castor bean plant, this was possibly a variegated form of the species Faris referred to when he recorded it as one of the first plants in his diary on 7 April 1792. A tropical plant, castor bean has long been used medicinally to treat a variety of ailments.

Wallflower 🖌 *Cheiranthus cheiri*
Faris grew a double-flowered white variety of this old-time biennial favorite, first recording it on 8 March 1795. Many varieties were known in colonial gardens.

Trees, Shrubs, Vines, and Grasses

Almond 🖌 *Prunus glandulosa*
Also known as flowering almond, these medium-sized shrubs were grown for their lovely spring blooms, which cover the branches in clusters in the spring before the leaves emerge. Faris first wrote about them on 17 January 1793.

Althea 🖌 *Hibiscus syriacus*
Known commonly as Rose-of-Sharon, this relative of the mallow can get out of control in the garden as described by Faris when on 22 January 1798 he wrote that Sylve "thinned the Snow Ball Bush and althea that had growen into a wilderness."

Apple 🖌 *Malus pumila*
Faris first mentioned his apple trees on 4 June 1795 when the bees swarmed and settled on the "appel" tree. He wrote of them again on 4 March 1796 when he "cut down one Appel Tree by the little room & trimed the other."

Boxwood 🖌 *Buxus sempervirens 'suffruticosa'*
Faris and his garden helpers spent an enormous amount of time each spring trimming the boxwood, also known as box or edging box. Faris edged most of his ornamental beds with boxwood and kept a nursery bed where he rooted cuttings taken from the trimmings. He recorded them for the first time in his diary on 26 March 1792.

Cherry* 🖌 *Prunus* Sp.
Although Faris wrote that he planted cherry tree seeds on the border by the new stable on 25 March 1793, and again on 15 July 1793 that he "Planted two cherry trees in potts," it is not clear if he was planting actual fruit trees or merely more of his ornamental Jerusalem cherry trees.

Currant 🖌 *Ribes* Sp.
Faris cultivated currants in his kitchen garden and wrote about them on 2 March 1795. Priscilla Faris made currant jelly in the summer from the berries harvested in the garden, as Faris wrote on 21 June 1803.

Gooseberry 🖌 *Ribes* Sp.
Like their close relatives the currants, gooseberries are woody perennial

shrubs grown for their fruit, used in jams and jellies. Faris gathered and bottled his gooseberries in May and June in his Annapolis garden, first mentioning them on 18 March 1793.

Grapevines ✍ *Vitis rotundifolia*
Faris's grapes were either this species or *V. Labrusca*, the fox grape. Grapevines provided a ready source of fruit for the table. Faris routinely cleaned out the litter from the grapevines in the early spring, as he wrote on 7 March 1796. He did not indicate that he tried to make wine from his grapes, although because of his inquisitive nature it would be surprising had he not.

Holly ✍ *Ilex opaca*
Faris probably obtained his American hollies from the nearby woods where he would have his garden hand 'Old William' dig them and then plant them in the garden. One of the holly trees attributed to Faris's planting was taken down as recently as ca. 1985. Although Faris wrote about trimming his hollies, we do not know in what shape he cut them. He planted three separate trees during the years of the diary, the first apparently on 1 April 1797.

Horse Chestnut ✍ *Aesculus Hippocastanum*
Horse chestnuts have been cultivated in America since the eighteenth century. This tree produces beautiful clusters of white flowers in erect cone-like projections, which resemble candles. Mature specimens can attain great height. Faris planted horse chestnuts, which Hyram had brought over from South River, on 15 January 1793.

Ivy ✍ *Hedera helix*
This common vine is still grown widely today. Faris recorded planting his ivy on the border, where his boxwood nursery was located, on 26 March 1793.

Lilac ✍ *Syringa vulgaris* or *S. persica*
A long-time favorite in the garden, fragrant lilacs were often planted near a window where the aroma would be close to the house and enjoyed by all. John Custis was reputed to have the best collection of lilacs in the colonies. On 9 February 1801 Faris planted "two laylack Bushes one in each corner of the Bed next the asparagrass Beds."

Peach ✍ *Prunus persica*
Faris raised peaches in his garden as fruit for his family as well as for feeding to his pigs. He also experimented with grafting peaches in the utilitarian section of his garden and distilled brandy from them as well. He first recorded them in his diary on 17 March 1794.

Pear ✍ *Pyrus communis*
Faris planted pear trees in his garden on 17 March 1800 and on 26 February 1801, but never wrote of his success with their husbandry, perhaps because they had not matured sufficiently by the time of his death.

Plum ✍ *Prunus domestica*
Faris planted a variety of plum called "Magnum Bonum" received from Mrs. Nicholas Carroll on 5 September 1799 and even made some of them in wax. George Mason of Gunston Hall gave this same variety to George Washington in 1760.

Pride of China Tree ✒ *Melia Azedarach*
Known also as the Chinaberry or Pride of India, Faris planted this popular ornamental tree on 6 April 1796, a present from Mrs. Davidson. The following year Faris uprooted the tree and "planted it in the middle of the circkel in the garden."

Pride of the East ✒
Faris planted seeds of this unidentified species on 11 April 1794. It may be identical with the Pride of China tree or a totally unrelated plant.

Ribbon Grass ✒ *Phalaris* Sp.*
An unidentified form of ornamental grass, first mentioned by Faris on 31 March 1792.

Snowball ✒ *Viburnum opulus*
Known also as Geulder rose, this shrub produces large round clusters of white flowers in the spring. Faris planted bleeding hearts under his snowball tree on 13 August 1797. On 22 January 1798 Faris wrote that Sylve thinned his snow ball bush and the althea.

Strawberry Tree ✒ *Arbutus unedo*
A European native, strawberry trees have insignificant blooms in the summer but become covered with red berries throughout the winter. A beautiful large shrub or small tree, it was also cultivated by Jefferson and Custis. Faris first received it as several cuttings from Sarah Bordley's slave Jacob on 1 April 1794.

Sweet-scented Shrub ✒ *Calycanthus floridus*
Carolina allspice and sweet shrub are other names for this native American shrub. Faris received his first examples of this shrub on 18 March 1793 from John Leypold of Baltimore.

Sweet-scented shrubs produce red flowers in the spring and some individual plants can be intensely fragrant. A favorite with gardeners in colonial America, it was also used for its medicinal qualities. Faris planted one under a window on 29 March 1800, no doubt to take advantage of its aroma.

Tallow Tree ✒ *Myrica cerifera**
Wax myrtle is a possible candidate for this tree, which Faris planted "at the far end of the Border by the grapes with stick No. 12" on 7 April 1796.

Walnut ✒ *Juglan nigra* or *J. cinerea*
Black walnut or white walnut/butternut. We do not know which of these species of walnut Faris cultivated in his walnut tree bed. Whichever one it was, it was a great producer of nuts as testified by his diary entries, such as that of 6 September 1794.

White Mulberry ✒ *Morus alba*
Faris used white mulberry leaves to feed his silkworms. On 25 May 1795 he placed the leaves in a drawer and kept his silkworms on white paper. Faris also mounted dried mulberry leaves into the back of his book of shop drawings along with some of his named varieties of tulips.

Willow ✒ *Salix nigra**
Faris first mentioned a willow tree on his property when on 3 August 1795, a "Harrican Blow'd down the Willow Tree in the lot." Known also as black willow, this may have been the same type of tree which "fell the rong way and lodged against the play House" on 5 March 1801.

Golden Willow ✒ *Salix vitellina*
Known as the yellow willow, we do
not know if this was the only kind of
willow Faris grew, and if it was

indeed the same variety that fell
against the playhouse. He first
recorded planting cuttings of the
golding willow on 26 March 1793.

Vegetables[6]

[6] Many of these vegetables were not only grown by Faris but also purchased by him at market.

Asparagus	Corn	Parsnip
Beans	Cucumbers	Peas
Beets	Eggplant	Pepper
Broccoli	Garlic	Pumpkin
Brussel Sprouts	Kale	Radish
Cabbage	Leeks	Shallots
Cantaloupe	Lettuce	Squash (Simlins)
Carrot	Musk Mellons	Spinach
Cauliflower	Okra	Turnip
Cherry Peppers	Onion	Watermelon
Colewort or Kale	Orach	

An Inventory of the Goods and Chattels of William Faris Deceased —

$ 45.00	Nine silver watches @ $5
9.00	Three gilt watches @ 3
140.00	Two quarter clocks with cases @ 70
105.00	Three plain clocks without cases @ 35
20.00	One time piece
120.00	Two clocks with cases @ 60
20.00	One set of clock & watch makers tools
150.00	One case of jewellery
1.50	One nest of drawers for watch makers tools
1.50	One walnut essaying desk
1.50	One set of silversmiths cutting tools
4.00	One stand of scales weights &c.
3.00	One box with two beams & scales
5.00	One nest of drawers with patterns chapes &c.
2.00	One nest of drawers for
.25	Four stools
1.00	Six plated tea spoons
1.00	Sundry disorted work in the window
20.00	One watch engine
15.00	One drawer of watch glasses
3.00	One set of fire apparatus
.25	One table
4.00	Three boxes pipes
30.00	Sundry silver smiths tools in the forge
.25	Two clock makers brackets
2.00	One drawer with sundry clock makers tools
1.00	One oil & one paint stone
2.00	One large lathe

4.00	Four anvils with blocks
20.00	One mill for silver work
2.25	Eighteen silver smiths hammers
4.00	One pair bellows
12.00	One large brass morter & pestle
2.00	Sundry disorted iron work
1.00	Five ingot moulds
.25	One large oil jug lamp &c.
.25	Four pair forging tongs
3.00	One pair steelyards
1.50	One silver smiths anvil (large)
17.40	One ounce nine ctwt. go
18.00	Nine china bowls
5.00	Three china dishes
2.00	Twelve ditto plates
1.00	Eight ditto coffee cups & saucers
.25	Eighteen saucers
.25	Fourteen cups
1.50	Two china tea pots
.12½	Three queensware plates
.60	Two quart decanters
1.00	Sixteen wine glasses
.30	Five tumblers
.12½	One goblet
.06	One queensware coffee pot
.60	Ten jelly glasses
.15	Three beer glasses
1.00	One sett of castors
1.50	Three waiters & one bread basket
21.00	Twenty one walnut chairs
1.00	One easy ditto
6.00	One walnut desk
1.50	One mahogany tea table
4.00	Two walnut card tables
1.50	One ditto dressing ditto
.50	One walnut candle stand
20.00	Five ditto dining tables
1.00	One tea ditto
1.00	One mahogany corner cupboard
15.00	One liquor case
5.00	One case wax work
4.00	One carpet
9.00	Three looking glasses
1.25	Twenty framed prints
1.00	Two portraits
4.00	Two landskips
.25	One tea chest
.12½	One plate basket

40.00	One field bedstead with curtains bed and furniture compleat
4.00	Four low posted bedsteads
20.00	Two feather beds
7.00	Seven bed quilts
2.00	One cotton counterpin
4.00	One suit curtains
5.00	Five pair sheets
1.50	Six pillow cases
5.00	Five blankets
.50	One pair window curtains
1.50	Two table cloths
.75	Six towels
.50	Two pine writing desks
1.00	Four kitchen tables
4.00	Five large pewter dishes
2.00	Twelve pewter plates
1.00	Six ditto water ditto
1.00	Three ditto basons
.50	One ditto cullender
.50	One gallon pewter measure
.31	One quart ditto, one pint ditto
2.00	One copper fish kettle
1.00	One ditto stew pan
.50	One ditto sauce pan
1.00	One brass plate warmer
.12½	One ditto dripping pan
.25	One ditto warming ditto
.25	Three ditto chaffing ditto
.06	One ditto egg slice
.15	One ditto snuffer stand & snuffers
.12½	Two pair iron ditto
2.00	Eight brass candlesticks
.25	One ditto lamp
1.50	Two copper water kitchens
.30	Five tin dish covers
.20	Four ditto plate ditto
.25	Five tin panns
.01	One ditto cullender
.06	One ditto saucepan
.01	One ditto lantern
.06	One ditto coffee pot
.01	One ditto drudge box
.02	One ditto apple toaster
.12½	One pewter cheese stand
.12½	Fifteen tin patty pans
3.00	One brass jack with spits
.06	One iron ditto
.25	One Dutch oven
1.50	Four iron pots
1.00	Five iron kettles

.06	One frying pan
.25	Three pair pott hooks
.20	Three pott racks
2.00	One pair kitchen andirons shovel & tongs
.25	One pair flat irons
.09	One pair box irons
.25	One ladle one flesh fork & eight screws
.25	One wooden saw horse
.02	One iron triblet
.12½	One lignivite spice morter & pestle
.02	Two rooling pins
.50	One tub five piggins & three ½ bushels
.50	One walnut knife box
.03	One wooden bucket with top
.12½	Two ditto bread trays
.12½	One clothes horse
.01	One tin candle stand
.12½	Three pewter candle moulds
.06	Twelve tin ditto
.50	Ten case knives & forks
.50	Nine breakfast ditto & box
.25	Two meat tubs
.50	One vinegar cask
.12½	Three firkins & six barrels
2.50	Sixty quart bottles
1.50	Twelve jugs stone & earthen
.10	Ten fat pots - stone & earthen
1.00	One large spinning wheel
1.00	One small ditto
.12½	One clock reel
.10	One ladder
.12½	One cannon stove
1.00	One pair cast andirons
.50	Four empty flour barrels
1.00	One grind stone
30.00	One electrifying machine and apparatus compleat
3.00	One large bottle for inflammatory air
.25	One physiognatrace
3.00	Three fowling pieces
.06	One gun barrel
6.00	Three & ½ pair pistols
1.00	Two powder proofs
.25	One small brass cannon mounted
.50	Four pair bullet moulds
2.00	One pair shot moulds
3.00	Three swords & 3 files
.12½	one dirk
.06	One gun lock
.25	Seven pieces steel
.06	One musick pin
.06	One pair handcuffs
2.00	One box with glyster pipe compleat
2.00	Sundry articles for clock & watch makers
1.50	One hand organ
1.00	One flute and one cane
.25	One footman
7.00	One box with sundry carpenters tools
3.00	One clock graving tool
.50	One box with draw plates
.12½	One box paints
.01	Sundry old locks
.25	One old scale with silver smiths tools
1.00	One brass seeding machine
8.00	Three large rail vices
1.00	One large case with clock and watch makers tools
.50	One machine for twisting lines
.50	One pair large scales
2.00	One large laythe with wheel & apparatus
.02	One cow bell
2.00	One back gammon table
1.00	One bed pan
.12½	Two trowells
.50	Two bundles girt web
1.50	One pair and irons brass tips
.50	One cartridge box shot bag & powder horn
.75	One show case
.50	One large & one small organ
.50	One silk reel
.25	One tin box for baking clock faces
3½	Eleven bird cages
.25	One hackle
.02	One palate blower
3.00	Three pair bellows
.50	Three saddles
1.00	One bachus

.25 One basket with wax moulds
½ One crib
3.00 One copper still
.25 One copper plate mill
1.50 One laperdary mill
3.00 One cabinet makers screw (large)
.25 One cotton gin
1.00 One machine for polishing clock faces
.50 Two watering pots
2.00 One iron grate
2.00 Twenty four flower pots & pans
½ One cross cut saw
2.00 Sundry disorted articles over head
100.00 One hundred and thirty seven volumes of books
5.00 Sundry bottles of chymecall & physick
50.00 Sundry disorted clock & watch tools
5.00 Two pots with emery
4.00 Sundry disorted charts books &c.
.06 Two sifters
.06 One dark lantern
2.00 One glass funnel & two clock springs
.50 Two door locks & keys
.50 Six books silver leaf
.20 Two ditto gold ditto
.50 Sundry articles for clock work
.10 Five gimblets
20.00 Twenty pieces hair ribbon
.25 Sundry zink block tin &c.
4.00 Sundry blk lead pots crusibles &c.
6.00 One drawing swage with screws &c.
8.00 One chest with copper & brass
10.00 One lot of faill. & stones

.75 One dimijohn
2.00 One chest with pewter & lead
1.00 Two pair gardiners sheers
.25 One hand bell
4.00 Sundry brass & iron ware
1.00 One sett tooth instruments
2.00 Two egate morters
1.00 One stone morter & pestle
.50 Sundry tobacco
2.00 Two gaging rods
.50 One musick book
1.25 Seven jugs & potts
10.00 Sixty two pair cocks heels
4.00 One sett navagators instruments
1.00 One brass leavel
4.00 One watch makers
1.00 One box with scales chapes &c.
.50 One pair tobacco tonges
.75 One pair andirons
172.75 One hundred & fifty five ounces ten penny weight plate @ 8/4
6.00 Wareing apparel
60.00 One negro woman Silva
4.00 One sett hives with bees and empty ditto
100.00 One musickel clock with case
.50 One large chest
.75 One poker tonges & riddle
1.50 1 tea kettle (copper)
.50 1 large & 1 small tin tea cannister
1.00 One musket
.25 1 sett pockett steelyards
3.00 2 wheel barrows
.50 1 draw bench
1.50 Sundry garden tools
8.00 Quantity chalk
1.50 1 hand mill
2.00 Cart harness

$1786.12

Reverdy Ghiselin
CREDITOR

Joseph Sands
Vachel Stevens
APPRAISERS

Submitted 12th day of June 1805

LIST OF ILLUSTRATIONS

George Aiken, a Baltimore silversmith who repaired it. Height 4½" Length 7⅞"
Engraved *WAP* for William and Ann Faris Pitt on front cartouche.
On bottom of cup: *PW/1746*, for Priscilla Woodward; *AP/1804* for Ann Pitt;
*FCP/1876*for Faris Chappell Pitt and *NKP/1898* for Nettie Kurtz Pitt

Maryland Historical Society, 81.80.3
Gift of Mrs. C. Gordon Pitt

SHOP DRAWINGS

APPENDIX on page 429

BIBLIOGRAPHY

Papers of William Faris

Maryland Historical Society [MHS]:

MS 2160	William Faris Diary
MS 343	Faris Papers
MS 348	Faris Design Book of Silver
MS 353	Faris-McParlin Account Books
	volume 1: Daybook (section 2: William Faris, 1773–1784)
	volume 2: Memorandum Book, 1790–1800
MS 1104	William Faris Account Book and Diaries
	repairs of clocks at Government House, 11/1788–11/1791

Maryland State Archives [MSA]:

SC 595	Guy Weatherly Collection of McParlin Family Papers, 1763–1960
SC 2551	Faris Music Book Collection

Primary Sources

Annapolis Mayor, Aldermen, and Councilmen (Proceedings). MSA M 47.
Annapolis Mayor's Court (Minutes). MSA M 44.
Anne Arundel County Court (Accounts of Sales). MSA C 27.
Anne Arundel County Court (Inventories). MSA C 29.
Anne Arundel County Court (Inventories). MSA C 88.
Anne Arundel County Court (Land Records). MSA C 97.
Anne Arundel County Register of Wills (Wills). MSA C 153.
Appendix F: "Lot Histories and Maps." Final Report, NEH Grant #H69-0-178. MSA.
Baltimore City Directories.
General Assembly House of Delegates (Assessment Record), 1783, MSA S 1161-1.
General Court of the Western Shore (Judgment Record), JG 18:138, 1792, Oct.–1793, May, MSA S 497. (Kilty v. Gantt)
"Marbury-Brewer Bible Records." Filing Cabinet A. MHS.
Maryland Gazette. MSA.

Maryland State Papers (Federal Direct Tax), 1798. No. 7: Annapolis and Middle Neck
Hundreds. MSA S 37-2.
Matriculation Book, St. John's College, 1789–1860, SJ1. MSA SC 1181.
"Returns of taxes, levies, fees for St. Anne's Parish." Galloway, Maxcy, Markoe Papers. Vol.
1, 1764 and Vol. 2, 1765. MSA M1171.
Samuel Davidson, Ledger B, 1789–1810. #17848, MMC 2144. Library of Congress.

Secondary Sources

Arnett, Earl, Robert J. Brugger, and Edward C. Papenfuse. *Maryland: A New Guide to the
Old Line State.* 2d ed. Baltimore: Johns Hopkins University Press, 1999.

Arps, Walter E., Jr. *Heirs and Orphans: Anne Arundel County, Maryland,
Distributions, 1788–1838.* Westminster, Md.: Family Line Publications, 1985.

Arthur, Helen. "Thomas Sparrow, An Early Maryland Engraver." *The Magazine Antiques,*
LV (January 1949): 44–45.

Bailey, Chris. *Two Hundred Years of American Clocks & Watches.* Englewood Cliffs, N.J.:
Rutledge, 1975.

Barnes, Robert W. *British Roots of Maryland Families.* Baltimore: Genealogical
Publishing Co., 1999.

———. "Gleanings from Maryland Newspapers, 1776–1785." Lutherville, Md.:
Robert Barnes, 1975.

———. *Marriages and Deaths from Baltimore Newspapers, 1796–1816.* Baltimore:
Genealogical Publishing Co., 1978.

———. *Marriages and Deaths from the Maryland Gazette, 1727–1839.* Baltimore:
Genealogical Publishing Co., 1973.

Barr, Lockwood. "Family of William Faris (1728–1804)." *Maryland Historical Magazine,* 37
(December 1942): 423–32.

———. "William Faris, 1728–1804." *Maryland Historical Magazine,* 36 (December 1941):
420–39.

———. "William Faris, Annapolis Clockmaker." *The Magazine Antiques,* XXXVII (April
1940): 174–76.

Beal, Rebecca J. *Jacob Eichholtz 1776–1842, Portrait Painter of Pennsylvania.* Philadelphia:
The Historical Society of Pennsylvania, 1969.

Belden, Louise C. *Marks of Early American Silversmiths in the Ineson-Bissell Collection.* Henry
Francis du Pont Winterthur Museum. Charlottesville: University Press of Virginia,
1980.

Bierne, Rosamund Randall and John Henry Scarff. *William Buckland, 1773–1774, Architect
of Annapolis and Maryland.* Baltimore: Maryland Historical Society, 1958.

Boucher, Jonathan, ed. *Reminiscences of an American Loyalist, 1738–1789: Being the
Autobiography of the Reverend Jonathan Boucher.* N.Y.: Houghton-Mifflin, 1925.

Breig, James. "The Famously Obscure, Notoriously Infuriating Citizen Genet." *Colonial
Williamsburg* (October/November 1999), 45–52.

Brilliant, Richard. *Facing the New World, Jewish Portraits in Colonial and Federal America.*
New York: The Jewish Museum, 1997.

Brinkley, M. Kent, and Gordon W Chappell. *The Gardens of Colonial Williamsburg*. Williamsburg: The Colonial Williamsburg Foundation, 1996.

Brown, Joan Sayers. "William Faris, Sr. his sons, and journeymen — Annapolis Silversmiths." *The Magazine Antiques*, CXI (February 1977): 378–85.

Buhler, Kathryn C. and Graham Hood. *American Silver in the Yale University Art Gallery*. New Haven, Conn.: Yale University Press, 1970.

Callcott, Margaret Law, ed. *Mistress of Riversdale: The Plantation Letters of Rosalie Stier Calvert, 1795–1821*. Baltimore: Johns Hopkins University Press, 1991.

Christhilf, Stuart M. Jr. "Health Care." In James C. Bradford, ed. *Anne Arundel County, Maryland: A Bicentennial History, 1649–1777*. Annapolis, Md.: Anne Arundel County & Annapolis Bicentennial Committee, 1977, 229–60.

Clements, S. Eugene and F. Edward Wright. *Maryland Militia in the Revolutionary War*. Silver Spring, Md.: Family Line Publications, 1987.

Cordell, E. F. *The Medical Annals of Maryland, 1799–1899*. Baltimore: Williams & Wilkins Company, 1903.

Cressy, David. *Birth, Marriage & Death: Ritual, Religion, and the Life-Cycle in Tudor and Stuart England*. Oxford: Oxford University Press, 1997, 427–28.

Cunningham, Isabel Shipley. *Calvary United Methodist Church, Annapolis, Maryland: The First Two Centuries*. Edgewater, Md.: Lith-O-Press, 1984.

Dictionary of American History. Rev. ed. New York: Charles Scribner's Sons, 1976.

Dolmetsch, Jean D., ed. *Eighteenth Century Prints in Colonial America — To Educate and Decorate*. Charlottesville, Va.: Colonial Williamsburg Foundation, 1979. Pitt mezzotint, 127–28.

Dorland's Illustrated Medical Dictionary. 28th ed. Philadelphia: W. B. Saunders & Co., 1994.

Duffy, John. *Epidemics in Colonial America*. Baton Rouge: Louisiana State University Press, 1953, 1979.

———. *From Humors to Medical Science: A History of American Medicine*. 2d ed. Urbana: University of Illinois Press, 1993.

———. *The Healers, A History of American Medicine*. Urbana: University of Illinois Press, 1979.

Eisenberg, Gerson G. *Marylanders Who Served the Nation: A Biographical Dictionary of Federal Officials from Maryland*. Annapolis, Md.: Maryland State Archives, 1992.

Elder, William Voss, III and Lu Bartlett. *John Shaw, Cabinetmaker of Annapolis*. Baltimore: The Baltimore Museum of Art, 1983.

Estes, J. Worth. *Dictionary of Protopharmacology: Therapeutic Practices, 1700–1850*. Nantucket, Mass.: Science History Publications, 1990.

Favretti, Rudy J. and Joy P. Favretti. *For Every House a Garden: A Guide for Reproducing Period Gardens*. Hanover, N.H.: University Press of New England, 1990.

Fleischer, Roland E. *Gustavus Hesselius, Face Painter to the Middle Colonies*. Trenton, N.J.: New Jersey State Museum, 1988.

Forbes, Esther. *Paul Revere & The World He Lived In*. Cambridge, Mass.: Rutledge Press, 1942.

Ford, Thomas K. *The Silversmith in Eighteenth Century Williamsburg*. Williamsburg, Va.: Colonial Williamsburg Foundation, Williamsburg Craft Series, 1956, revised in 1972, reprinted in 1976,1980, 1989, 1990 and 1992.

Fuller, Thomas. *Pharmacopoeia Extemporanea*. London: B. Walford, 1710. Glyster pipe, 186–213, 219.

Gelles, Edith B. *Portia: The World of Abigail Adams*. Bloomington: Indiana University Press, 1992. Burney letter, 164–66.

Glanville, Philippa and Jennifer F. Goldsborough. *Women Silversmiths 1685–1845*. The National Museum of Women in the Arts. New York: Thames and Hudson, 1990.

Goldsborough, Jennifer F. *Eighteenth and Nineteenth Century Maryland Silver*. Baltimore: The Baltimore Museum of Art, 1975.

———. *Silver in Maryland*. Baltimore: The Maryland Historical Society, 1983.

Griswold, Mac. *Washington's Gardens at Mount Vernon*. Boston: Houghton Mifflin Co., 1999.

Haw, James F., Francis F. Beirne, Rosamond R. Beirne, and R. Samuel Jett. *Stormy Patriot: The Life of Samuel Chase*. Baltimore: Maryland Historical Society, 1980.

Heads of Families at the First Census of the United States Taken in the Year 1790. Baltimore: Genealogical Publishing Company, 1965.

Hoffman, Ronald. *Princes of Ireland, Planters of Maryland: A Carroll Saga, 1500–1782*. Chapel Hill: University of North Carolina Press for the Omohundro Institute of Early American History and Culture, 2000.

Honour, Hugh. *Goldsmiths & Silversmiths*. New York: G.P. Putnam's Sons, 1971.

Howard, George W. *The Monumental City: Its Past History and Present Resources*. Baltimore: M. Curlander, 1889.

Jackson, Ronald Vern and Gary Ronald Teeples. *Maryland 1800 Census Index*. Bountiful, Utah: Accelerated Indexing System, Inc., 1973, 1978.

Johnston, William R. *William and Henry Walters, The Reticent Collectors*. Baltimore: Johns Hopkins University Press, 1999.

Jourdan, Elise Greenup. *Early Families of Southern Maryland*. Vol.1. Westminster, Md.: Family Line Publications, 1992.

———. *Early Families of Southern Maryland*. Vol. 6. Westminster, Md.: Family Line Publications, 1998.

Kanely, Edna Agatha. *Directory of Ministers and the Maryland Churches They Served, 1634–1990*, 2 Vols. Westminster, Md.: Family Line Publications, 1991.

Kauffman, Henry J. *The Colonial Silversmith, His Techniques & His Products*. Camden, N.J.: Thomas Nelson, Inc., 1969.

Land, Aubrey C. *Colonial Maryland — A History*. Millwood, N.Y.: KTO Press, 1981.

Leighton, Ann. *American Gardens in the Eighteenth Century*. Boston: Houghton Mifflin Co., 1976.

Ludlum, David. *Early American Hurricanes: 1492–1870*. Boston: American Meteorological Society, 1963.

McIntire, Robert Harry. *Annapolis Maryland Families*. Vol. 1. Baltimore: Gateway Press, Inc., 1979.

McWilliams, Jane. *The Progress of Refinement: A History of Theatre in Annapolis*. Annapolis, Md.: The Colonial Players of Annapolis, 1976.

Martin, Peter. *The Pleasure Gardens of Virginia, From Jamestown to Jefferson*. Princeton, N.J.: Princeton University Press, 1991.

Masterpieces of American Silver. Richmond: The Virginia Museum of Fine Arts, 1960.

[Mayer, Francis B.] "Old Maryland Manners." *Scribner's Monthly*. XVII (January 1879): 316–18.

Middleton, Arthur Pierce. *Tercentenary Essays Commemorating Anglican Maryland, 1692–1792.* Virginia Beach, Va.: The Donning Company, 1992.

Miller, Lillian B., ed. *The Selected Papers of Charles Willson Peale and His Family.* Vol. 1: *Charles Willson Peale: Artist in Revolutionary America, 1735–1791.* New Haven: Yale University Press, 1983, 150.

Miller, Marcia M. and Orlando Ridout V, eds. *Architecture in Annapolis.* Crownsville, Md.: Maryland Historical Trust and Vernacular Art Forum, 1998.

Newman, Harry Wright. *Anne Arundel Gentry*. Vol. 2. Westminster, Md.: Family Line Publications, 1996.

Olmert, Michael. "The Dovecote: Remnant of the Middle Ages in Colonial Tidewater." *Colonial Williamsburg* (Autumn 2000), 78–87.

Owings, Donnell MacClure. *His Lordship's Patronage: Offices of Profit in Colonial Maryland.* Studies in Maryland History, No. 1. Baltimore: Maryland Historical Society, 1953.

Paltaits, Victor Hugo, ed. "A Journal of Benjamin Mifflin on a Tour from Philadelphia to Delaware and Maryland, July 26–August 14, 1762." *Bulletin of the New York Public Library* 39 (June 1935), 7–14.

Papenfuse, Edward C. *In Pursuit of Profit: The Annapolis Merchants in the Era of the American Revolution, 1763–1805.* Baltimore: Johns Hopkins University Press, 1975.

————. *An Historical List of Public Officials of Maryland: Governors, Legislators, and Other Principal Officers of Government, 1632–1990.* Vol. 1. *Archives of Maryland.* New Series. Annapolis, Md.: Maryland State Archives, 1990.

Papenfuse, Edward C., Alan F. Day, David W. Jordan, and Gregory A. Stiverson, eds. *A Biographical Dictionary of the Maryland Legislature, 1635–1789.* 2 vols. Baltimore: Johns Hopkins University Press, 1979, 1985.

Pavord, Anna. *The Tulip.* New York: Bloomsbury Publishing, 1999.

Peden, Henry C., Jr. *Revolutionary Patriots: Anne Arundel County.* Westminster, Md.: Family Line Publications, 1992.

————. *Revolutionary Patriots of Montgomery County, Maryland, 1776–1783.* Westminster, Md.: Family Line Publications, 1996.

Pleasants, J. Hall and Howard Sill. *Maryland Silversmiths, 1715-1830.* Baltimore: Privately Printed, 1930; Harrison, N.Y.: Robert Alan Green, 1972.

Powell, John W., comp. *Anne Arundel County, Maryland, Marriage Records, 1777–1877.* Pasadena, Md.: Anne Arundel Genealogical Society, 1991.

Quimby, Ian M. G. *American Silver at Winterthur.* Winterthur, Del.: The Henry Francis du Pont Winterthur Museum, Distributed by The University Press of Virginia, 1995.

Quynn, Dorothy Mackay and William Rogers Quynn. "Letters of a Maryland Medical Student in Philadelphia and Edinburgh (1782–1784)." *Maryland Historical Magazine,* 31 (September 1936): 181–215.

Radoff, Morris L. *Buildings of the State of Maryland at Annapolis.* Annapolis, Md.: Hall of Records Commission, 1954.

Rice, Kym S. *Early American Taverns, For the Entertainment of Friends and Strangers.* Chicago: Regnery Gateway, in association with Fraunces Tavern Museum, 1983.

Richardson, Edgar P., Brooke Hindle, and Lillian B. Miller. *Charles Willson Peale and his World.* New York: Harry N. Abrams, 1983.

Riley, Elihu S. *The Ancient City, A History of Annapolis, in Maryland, 1649–1887.*
Annapolis, Md.: Record Printing Office, 1887.

Sarudy, Barbara Wells. "A Chesapeake Craftsman's Eighteenth-Century Gardens." *Journal
of Garden History,* 9 (July–September 1989): 141–52.

———. *Gardens and Gardening in the Chesapeake 1700–1805.* Baltimore: Johns Hopkins
University Press, 1998.

———. **"The Gardens and Grounds of an Eighteenth Century Chesapeake
Craftsman." Master's thesis, University of Maryland, 1988.**

**Schulz, Constance B., ed. *The Maryland History Slide Collection: Master Guide.*
Annapolis, Md.: Instructional Resources Corporation, 1980. Reuben Etting.**

Sellers, Charles Coleman. *Portraits and Miniatures by Charles Willson Peale.* Vol. 42, Part 1.
Philadelphia: Transactions of the American Philosophical Society, 1952.

Shelley, Fred, ed. "Ebenezer Hazard's Travels Through Maryland in 1777." *Maryland
Historical Magazine,* XLVI (March 1951): 44–54.

Southern Silver: An Exhibition of Silver Made in the South prior to 1860. Houston: The
Museum of Fine Arts, 1968.

Stickle, Douglas F. "Death and Class in Baltimore: The Yellow Fever Epidemic of 1800."
Maryland Historical Magazine 74 (1979): 282–99.

Swem, E. G. *Brothers of the Spade: Correspondence of Peter Collinson, of London and John Custis,
of Williamsburg, Virginia, 1734–1746.* Barre, Mass.: Barre Press, 1957.

Trench, Lucy. ed. *Materials and Techniques in the Decorative Arts, An Illustrated Dictionary.*
Chicago: University of Chicago Press, 2000.

Trostel, Michael F. *Mount Clare, Being an Account of the Seat built by Charles Carroll,
Barrister, upon his Lands at Patapsco.* Baltimore: National Society of Colonial Dames of
America in the State of Maryland, 1981.

**Warfield, J. D. *The Founders of Anne Arundel and Howard Counties, Maryland.*
Baltimore: Regional Publishing Company, 1973.**

Weekley, Carolyn J. "Portrait Painting in eighteenth-century Annapolis." *The Magazine
Antiques,* CXI (February 1977): 344–53.

Weekley, Carolyn and Stiles Tuttle Colwill. *Joshua Johnson, Freeman and Early American
Portrait Painter.* Baltimore: The Abby Aldrich Rockefeller Folk Art Center and the
Maryland Historical Society, 1987.

Weidman, Gregory R. and Jennifer F. Goldsborough. *Classical Maryland, 1815–1845: Fine
and Decorative Arts from the Golden Age.* Baltimore: The Maryland Historical Society, 1993.

Whisker, James Biser. *Pennsylvania Clockmakers, Watchmakers and Allied Crafts, with Study of
Pennsylvania Clocks by S. Petrucelli and introduction by Stacy Wood.* Cranbury, N.J.: Adams
Brown Co., 1990.

Whisker, James Biser, Daniel David Hartzler, and Steven P. Petrucelli. *Maryland
Clockmakers.* Cranbury, N. J.: Adams Brown Co., 1996.

**White, Frank F., Jr. *The Governors of Maryland, 1777–1970.* Annapolis, Md.: Hall of
Records Commission, 1970.**

Wilbur, C. Keith. *Revolutionary Medicine, 1700–1800.* 2d. ed. Old Saybrook, Conn.: Globe
Pequot Press, 1997.

**Wright, F. Edward. *Anne Arundel County Church Records of the 17th and 18th
Centuries.* Westminster, Md.: Family Line Publications, 1989.**

INDEX

494

PLANT INDEX